INTIMATE VIOLENCE

—

INTIMATE VIOLENCE

—

A STUDY OF INJUSTICE

JULIE BLACKMAN

Columbia University Press ■ **New York**

Columbia University Press
New York   Oxford
Copyright © 1989 Columbia University Press

Library of Congress Cataloging-in-Publication Data

Blackman, Julie, 1953–
Intimate violence: a study of injustice / Julie Blackman.
p. cm.
Bibliography: p.
Includes index.
ISBN 0-231-05094-1 (alk. paper)
1. Family violence—United States.   2. Wife abuse—United States.
3. Victims of crimes surveys—United States.
I. Title.
HQ809.3.U5B57 1989   88-13898
362.8′2—dc19   CIP

Book design by Jennifer Dossin
Printed in the United States of America

Casebound editions of Columbia University Press books are Smyth-sewn
and printed on permanent and durable acid-free paper

In memory of my grandmother, Ida Blackman
For Mitch and Jed

CONTENTS

—

PREFACE

In November 1981, I testified at a trial of a battered woman who had killed her husband in self-defense. It was one of the early trials at which I testified as an expert on the psychological consequences of abuse in battered women. It just happened that this courtroom trial marked the beginning of a personal trial for me. During my testimony, I noticed that as I turned to face the jurors, who were seated to my right, my head would turn involuntarily to my left. At lunch, I noticed that my neck felt stiff and sore, but I attributed it to the tension of the trial process.

My symptoms continued. Soon, I was unable to move my head, and it was pulled sharply to my left. The pain was frightening and exhausting. I was forced to take a leave from my position as an Assistant Professor in the Psychology Department at Barnard College. In the spring of 1982, I went into the hospital. I took batteries of experimental drugs. Side effects from some of the medications af-

fected my short-term memory and increased my sense of impairment. Unfortunately, my neck was no better. After six weeks, I left
the hospital to begin the slow process of recuperation and adjustment.

I began to teach again in the fall of 1982, about nine months after
my attack of illness had begun. My health was still severely affected, but I was determined to get my life back. I was to be reviewed for tenure in 1984. I requested a delay in my tenure review,
because of my illness. The Dean of the Faculty explained that College policy mandated that single semesters of leave be "rounded
down." Only two consecutive terms would result in a delay prior
to tenure review. Since I had been away from teaching for only one
semester, my review could not be delayed. Further, I would certainly
be turned down for tenure since my research project on family violence was still in progress and had not resulted in a sufficient number of publications. This book, which I had begun in 1979, was only
half finished when my muscles went haywire. I tried to explain my
situation to the Dean, and although he seemed personally sympathetic, his commitment to College policy prevented him from doing
anything more than offering me one extra teaching year prior to ter-
mination. My department chairperson concurred with the Dean. She
sent me an "unofficial" letter which stated that while the Department was impressed by my courage, my illness had necessarily made
it impossible for me to do the scholarly work necessary for tenure.
I told her that if she sent me that letter "officially," I would sue the
College for discrimination on the basis of disability. She quickly took
the letter back and never sent me another letter explaining the Department's decision not to support me.

Perhaps, if I had been healthier then, I would have fought the
College's decision. As it was, I decided to accept it. However, I felt
deeply discouraged and found that the combination of physical pain
and disappointment impeded my research and my productivity. Also,
the effects of the drugs on my ability to feel and act like myself
made it more difficult for me to fight back, or to assert the worth
of my work.

In 1986, just before I was due to leave Barnard, I attended a faculty meeting at which a vote was to be taken that would provide
women with improved maternity benefits. In particular, extra time
was going to be given before tenure review for women who gave
birth or adopted babies. While I certainly supported that, I thought
provisions ought to be made for those whose productivity was in-

terrupted by illness. I spoke at that faculty meeting and to my great surprise and pleasure, Barnard enacted a new policy that advantaged new mothers and those with the misfortune of suffering "personal catastrophes."

I asked that the new policy be made applicable to me. My request was denied by the three senior faculty of my department. And the President of Barnard, whom I involved at the last, relied on my department's judgment and turned down my request for time to recover from the lost time caused by my illness.

I chose to relate these events, in some detail, because it helps me to explain the long time that passed from the conception of the idea to the birth of the book. Also, the feelings I experienced in the wake of a sudden assault on my body have deeply informed my thinking about the reactions of victims of intimate violence and about the sorts of shock waves that result from enduring injustices. The reactions of others, particularly the reactions of those to whom I appealed for special consideration, have also been instructive. And, I have a clearer, personal understanding of perceived and unperceived options and their relationship to the experience of injustice.

When I first thought about writing this book, I titled it (as it has remained) *Intimate Violence: A Study of Injustice*. As a result of my illness, my experience with injustice from personal and impersonal sources is intimate. Thus, the words of the title have taken on multiple meanings for me since the time when I first put them together.

My knowledge about vulnerability and injustice is both personal and professional. It is as subjective as my own victimization will ensure, and as objective as familiarity with the relevant literature, current research methods, and applicable statistical techniques will allow. In the chapters of this book, the social processes that have fostered attention to the problem of intimate violence—family violence and rape—are considered. Theoretical consideration is given to the nature of injustice, and the characteristics and experiences of victims and non-victims are explored in relation to specific research questions and topic areas. Talking to women and children who killed their abusers added depth to my understanding of the range of reactions to injustice and led to the inclusion of one chapter on the application of psychological theory and research to the case of battered women who kill their abusers.

ACKNOWLEDGMENTS

———

My first thanks go to the women and men who shared their stories with me. I hope that if they read the book they will feel that their experiences were represented with sensitivity and care.

Many people helped to make my work possible. Friends, family members, colleagues and students contributed their time to the project and provided me with consistent emotional support for finishing what I had begun.

I am especially grateful to my parents, Leonard and Frances Blackman, and to my brothers, Gary and Mark. They have always been supportive of me and their love helped me to get through my hard times. My parents became directly involved with this work. My father read and commented on the manuscript and talked to me about the work throughout; my mother attended interviewer training and conducted several of the interviews reported here.

David Doron, Michelle Fine, Jim Lyons, David Surrey, and Jane

Yip Chan helped me code the survey data. Frances Blackman, Sharon Fogge, Jane Irvine, Daphne Joslin, Miriam Lyons Kragen, Addy Levine, Diane McNeill, Serena Nanda, Sarah Onello, Harriet Ornone, Mary Rose, and Lynn Wohlers conducted the interviews along with me, as did Ellie Louis, who also coordinated their activities, with the help of Iris Alpert. Special thanks are due, as well, to Gayle Eisen, then Director of Alternatives to Domestic Violence in Hackensack, New Jersey and Diana Aviv, then Assistant Director of Alternatives to Domestic Violence, for making space available in their offices for the interviews. Many students from Barnard and Teachers College worked to code the interview data after the tapes were admirably transcribed by DeNice Jenssen. Elpida Athanasatos, Ellen Brickman, Ellen Cooper, Sandy Horowitz, Stuart Mattson, Leah Pappas, Lesley Pratt, Susanna Shields and Carolyn Springer pored diligently over thousands of pages of transcripts, coding for literally a thousand pieces of information. Ellen Brickman deserves special acknowledgment for sticking with the process into the data analysis phase. She also made innumerable valuable suggestions about the manuscript itself. Carl Brendan, then at Columbia's School of Social Work, contributed hours of his computer expertise and combined the survey and interview data sets. Jane Monroe of Teachers College provided statistical guidance. Megan Parke, my Research Assistant at Sarah Lawrence, helped to proofread the manuscript and checked references. Nadine Laguardia typed portions of the manuscript. Michelle Fine, who was there at the beginning coding data, was there at the end. Her comments on the final manuscript made this book better, and I thank her for her intellectual and emotional support of this work. I am grateful to all these people for their work on behalf of this project.

For financial support, I thank the Dorothy Spivack Fund administered through Barnard College, the Spencer Foundation, the Unified Faculty Grants Committee at Barnard for both financial and released-time support, the St. Luke's-Roosevelt Hospital Rape Intervention Program, Sarah Lawrence College and Columbia University Press. I am especially grateful to Columbia University Press for consistent support and interest through the long gestation period of this book. I also thank Sue Osthoff, formerly of Women Against Abuse in Philadelphia and currently the Director of the National Clearinghouse for Battered Women Defendants for making research funding available, for sending me many articles from the legal literature on the battered woman syndrome, and for her insight into the situation of battered women who kill. I would also like to acknowledge the inadvertent support of battered women who killed their abusers and at whose trials I testified. Several thousand dollars of my fees from such cases were used to pay project-related expenses.

Coincident with the last three years of work on this book, my own family came into being. Mitchell Dinnerstein, I thank you for the sweetness of our family life and for taking care of Jed almost every Saturday for a year so I could finish this book. Jed went to the American Museum of Natural History so often he started to call it "home."

INTIMATE VIOLENCE

—

1

THE EMERGENCE OF INTIMATE VIOLENCE AS A SOCIAL PROBLEM

——

Behind all women's movement struggles for temperance, married women's property rights, liberalized divorce, child custody and suffrage lay the grim fact that dependent women and children were subject to physical and sexual assault.

Ann Jones, *Women Who Kill*, 1980, p. 284.

In the last two decades, intimate violence has gone from the taboo to the talked about. Wife abuse, child abuse, and sexual assaults within and outside of families have become social problems. Historically, they were personal problems, and while they might have been the grim basis for the problems that were addressed by the women's movement of the mid-nineteenth and early twentieth centuries, they were not the explicit focus of efforts to effect social change. To explain why intimate violence is no longer neglected is the point of this chapter.

In the Declaration of Sentiments, issued in 1848 by those who convened in Seneca Falls on behalf of women's rights, wife abuse was mentioned as a part of a grievance about the marital contract: "In the covenant of marriage, she is compelled to promise obedience to her husband, he becoming to all intents and purposes, her master—the law giving him power to deprive her of her liberty, and to administer chastisement" (Women's Rights Convention, 1848/1969, p. 6). Unfortunately, the impact of this statement had no demonstrable effects on laws about the legality of wife abuse. For example, twenty-five years after the Declaration of Sentiments was issued, the state of North Carolina still permitted a husband to beat his wife with a stick provided it was no thicker than his finger, and until 1890 it permitted any sort of beating that did not result in permanent injury or was not malicious beyond all reasonable bounds (Martin 1976). Wife abuse did become illegal in most states at about the turn of the century, but even then was not seen as a "real crime." Changes in the law of New York State provide an example. The idea that rape within a marital relationship ought to be against the law did not receive legislative attention until the mid-1970s. And it was not until in 1977 that women could prosecute their abusive husbands in Criminal Court instead of Family Court, if they chose to do so.

Child abuse, incest, and stranger rape were not included in this 1848 mandate of the Women's Movement. In fact, not until 1874 was the Society for the Prevention of Cruelty to Children founded, *after* the founding of the Society for the Prevention of Cruelty to Animals. While stranger rape was illegal in 1848, concern with the victim's prior chastity was typically so great as to render any non-virgin suspect of complicity in her own victimization (Berger 1977).

In the early 1900s, when women united again as a force for social change, they secured the vote and voted in prohibition. As Jones' quote at the top of this chapter is meant to indicate, this *apparent* inattention to the problems of the "physical and sexual assault" of women and children may have been just that—apparent. The same reluctance that prevented a direct struggle against the perpetration of intimate violence kept those who suffered from realizing that their problem was much more than a personal one.

While prohibition proved short-lived, suffrage and the increased empowerment of women have endured. It is to the 1920s, then, that one can turn in order to look at the beginnings of legislative priorities that include the impact of voting women, and to illustrate emerging trends in attention to social problems. This historical review of emerging social problems in the half century that preceded direct attention to intimate violence is based upon these questions: Why did the problems of intimate violence emerge into general awareness in the 1970s? What aspects of the social climate distinguished the 1970s from the preceding decades and enabled activity in response to these problems that had previously been too personal, too private to deserve public attention? What explains the emergence of intimate violence as a social problem?

1920 AND BEYOND

As a consequence of the Great Depression, the federal government of the 1930s, through Roosevelt's New Deal Programs, engaged in social welfare activities for the first time, and broke previously inviolable boundaries between the individual and the government. The new attention to unemployment in the 1930s also marked the advent of applied social science in the development of solutions to social problems and the formulation of public policy (Rossi 1972). Social policy changed in relation to unemployed men (not women).[1] The appropriate role of the government in private affairs began an evolution that continued through the decades preceding the emergence of intimate violence as a social problem.

It is noteworthy that when President Roosevelt implemented his New Deal social welfare policies, very little was known about the actual extent or nature of unemployment. Since the government had never previously intervened on behalf of those out of work, unemployment and poverty were seen as problems of the individual, not as social problems. Men, not employed outside their homes, were ashamed and the burden of responsibility rested heavily with them for their families' hard times. Any research efforts conducted prior to the inception of the New Deal programs would have captured just the tip of the iceberg, with most men being unwilling to reveal their unemployed status to a data-gatherer, who could have offered nothing in return. Even the instigation of responsive governmental programs did little, at first, to facilitate data collection, and very little information was gathered systematically on either the incidence of unemployment or the effectiveness of New Deal programs. In fact, when the Kennedy administration's War on Poverty programs were designed in the early 1960s, a "fruitless search was made through the archives for studies that would provide some assessment of the effectiveness of such programs as the Civilian Conservation Corps."

---

1. Women were affected by the sudden change in employment availability which resulted from the Second World War. Public monies were allocated for daycare during the war. After the war, these programs ended. Although these changes affected women, it is hard to suggest that they were implemented to address women's concerns primarily. In this case, women's need for daycare was a derivative social problem that followed from the relative absence of men.

(Rossi 1972: 12) Unfortunately, almost nothing is known about the effectiveness of the New Deal Programs. Records were kept of only the grossest measures—numbers of projects funded, persons and families served, and funds expended. Nevertheless, some of the New Deal programs served as prototypes for the War on Poverty efforts.

By the 1940s, needs for information demonstrated during and after the Depression, were better met with the improved monitoring of the incidence of social problems and the effectiveness of governmental attempts at solution. About ten years after the New Deal programs were implemented, systematic measurement of the labor force was begun, with the establishment of the Current Population Survey (Rossi 1972). The mechanisms for measuring unemployment, once established, have remained and are reflected in our now commonplace national indicators of unemployment and the impact of social-welfare policies.

In many respects, the course of the evolution of social problems was halted by the national absorption with World War II. However, the nature of this war—the deaths of six million Jews in concentration camps, the incarceration of Japanese-Americans in inland camps in the United States, the atomic bomb explosions in Hiroshima and Nagasaki—had a direct impact upon the next major social problem to emerge and meet with governmental responsiveness. This issue was civil rights and the Bill of Rights' promise of equality of opportunity to all regardless of "race, color, creed or national origin."

The effectiveness of the civil rights activities of the 1950s was highlighted by the 1954 Supreme Court decision (*Brown v. the Board of Education*) that "separate educational facilities are inherently unequal." The decision, written for a unanimous Supreme Court by Chief Justice Warren was noteworthy for its far reaching implications, its reliance on the research of psychologists and sociologists, and its foray into what had formerly been the nonregulated, private domain of parents making personal educational decisions for their children. Little was known about any actual differences in quality that existed between schools for white children and schools for black children. Based on research by social scientists, however, the Warren Court concluded that the segregation of white and black children was detrimental to the black children and that it particularly affected the motivation of these children to learn (Bramfeld 1949; Chein 1949; Clark 1950; Deutscher and Chein 1949; Frazier 1949; Myrdal 1944; Witmer and Kotinsky, 1952).

In this Supreme Court decision, as with the New Deal programs of the 1930s, the government advocated a moral position. The New Deal programs designed to ameliorate poverty proved easier for middle class white Americans to swallow than the decision to desegregate public schools, and thereby to afford equal educational opportunities to all children. More than 30 years after the Supreme Court decision, our metropolitan areas are still marred by de facto, if not de jure segregation. In fact, the same Brown whose case went before the Supreme Court in 1954 is part of a pending legal action against Topeka. Sadly, the issue is the same as it was then.

The social problem of inequality of educational opportunity has received judicial and governmental attention. The information gathered since 1954 by Coleman (1966) and by governmental agencies has supported the Supreme Court's assumption that separate was inherently unequal. Yet, this move by government into the domain of the private citizen has been strongly resisted. Anti-integration demonstrations and school sit-ins have persisted during the years since governmental action was first taken on behalf of the educationally deprived. In 1981, for example, the California Supreme Court granted the Board of Education of Los Angeles the right not to bus children involuntarily, for the purpose of desegregation.

Nevertheless, the 1960s reflected a broadening, in all senses, of the mandate that had coalesced in the 1950s. More issues and more people came to be included in the problems of inequality of opportunity. Emerging social problems reflected concerns over the injustices of discrimination because of race, class and later gender (Blackman-Doron 1979; Fine 1986; Kidder & Fine 1986). Within the United States, the new major social welfare programs of the 1960s dealt with class-based inequities and their effects on pre-school children. The establishment of nationwide Head Start programs in 1964 signalled an offer to a new population—the very young and the very disadvantaged. And, as with the major social problems of the preceding decades, action had preceded research. But this time, a new cloud appeared on the horizon. Late in 1965, the Planning, Programming, Budgeting System was initiated. A conflict with profound implications for the future of efforts to solve social problems developed. Williams and Evans (1972) described it this way:

> What we are seeing is a head-on collision between two sets of ideas developed in the mid-1960s. On the one hand, there was the implicit promise of the early years of the War on Poverty, that

effective programs could be launched full-scale, and could yield significant improvements in the lives of the poor. Head Start was the archetype of this hope. Born in late 1964, the program was serving a half-million children by the end of the following summer. On the other hand, the federal government, during roughly the same period, implemented the Planning, Programming, Budgeting System (PPBS), founded on the premise that rigorous analysis could produce a flow of information that would greatly improve the basis for decision-making. (p. 248)

This change marked the beginning of a new era in the large-scale treatment of social problems. It was no longer sufficient to implement improvement programs and to assume that they would work. People with new ideas about solutions for the problems of the 1960s were on the line to prove that their solutions had achieved pre-established goals, that their programs had not only worked, but could actually produce impressive cost-benefit indices. Head Start, it seemed, had not worked within this frame of reference. In his Economic Opportunity message to the Congress in February 1969, President Nixon mentioned that the results of the Westinghouse Learning Corporation—Ohio University evaluation indicated that the "long-term effect of Head Start appears to be extremely weak" (in Williams and Evans 1972: 247). Although Head Start programs were severely cut back, the late 1960s and the early 1970s continued to be characterized by deepening concerns over equality of opportunity and social justice.[2]

The Vietnam War stole the lives and diminished the opportunities of thousands of young men, who were too likely to be poor and members of minority groups for justice to have prevailed in the draft that fed that war (Surrey 1982). Inner-city riots in Detroit, Watts, and elsewhere provided dramatic evidence that equality of opportunity represented a vision that many had seen, but few had realized. The traumatic consequences of these inequities were reinforced with the intensity of the violence that daily news broadcasts of battlefields and body counts brought into our homes.

Historical records suggest that times of high levels of societal violence coincide with increases in family violence (Pleck 1981). Per-

2. For the purposes of this historical review of attention to social problems, it seemed appropriate to consider the impact of Head Start programs, as they were assessed through the early 1970s. However, it should be noted that evaluations of the impact of Head Start continued long after this time. See Saxe & Fine (1981) for a review of the studies done to evaluate the short- and long-term impacts of Head Start programs.

haps, some real increase in the incidence of family violence, together with the impact of a televised war, provided the impetus for the developing awareness of family violence and rape that characterized the 1970s. The growing realization that the consequences of societal violence take their toll on family life contributed to the new attention to problems that previously had been seen as deeply rooted in domains of familial and personal privacy. The sorts of social problems that had emerged during the preceding fifty years and had met with governmental responsiveness—poverty, discrimination based on race and class—also influenced society's readiness to see yet another problem that had always been there: violence against women.

An active women's movement took shape again in the wake of the Vietnam War. Firestone (1971) suggested that women's limited opportunities to play significant roles in the civil rights movement provided an important impetus for the establishment of a separate women's movement. Similarly, societal violence, epitomized by the war in Vietnam, was perpetrated and orchestrated by men. Again, women were excluded from significant decision-making positions, although they regularly suffered and continue to suffer the consequences of these events (Surrey 1982). The women's movement of the 1970s emerged as a multi-issue movement as political skills developed in the civil rights and anti-war movements were applied to the problems faced by women in a sexist society. Violence against women and children, which had probably increased during the preceding violence-ridden years, received focused attention within this burgeoning women's movement. As attention to violence against women and within families increased under the active press of the women's movement of the 1970s, the concerns and needs of battered women and rape survivors emerged as social problems.

PUTTING THE PROBLEMS IN PERSPECTIVE

[We] have seen how scholarly works have been used to launch major new government policies or programs over recent years. It was a study on the learning abilities of school children that launched the nightmare of busing. . . . To avoid the risk of the government inadvertently aiding one side of an argument, many people, myself included, consider the best policy is for the government not to involve itself at all.

Representative Ashbrook (R-Ohio) in the 1979 and 1980 *Congressional Record*, in *Advance*, Association for the Advancement of Psychology, August, 1981, p. 3.

In considering the nature of the social problems described here, there is evidence for the growing involvement of the government in life events that had previously been seen as private concerns. From concerns over employment and schooling to the workings of intimate relationships, the government demonstrated an expanding willingness to become involved. Public attention was drawn to problems that had formerly been considered matters of personal conscience and within the bounds of individual domain. Although the recent emergence of the problems of marital rape (Blackman-Doron 1979, 1980a, 1981a; Frieze 1979a,b; Russell 1982a, 1984) and the sexual abuse of children (Finkelhor 1979, 1981, 1984, 1985; Russell 1983, 1984) would suggest that the pattern of intensifying public awareness and involvement has continued, the 1980s have brought new directions to the flow of social problems. Representative Ashbrook's statement, above, reflects a resistance to the trend of the preceding fifty years.

This advocacy for government nonintervention counters the mandate of the preceding decades. In addition, in considering the issues that have been the focus of social activism in the 1980s, it seems that the flow of things has changed. Those active in the anti-abortion movement provide us, sadly, with an example of advocacy for governmental intervention on private matters that would enforce conformity with specific moral positions. This represents a change from the earlier advocacy for governmental interventions designed to promote equality of opportunity and individual fulfillment. The extent to which this change will undo the results of the post-New Deal era remains to be seen. Certainly, such social indicators as the composition of the Supreme Court do not bode well for the longevity of the post-New Deal trend.

In an effort to be thoughtful about the ebb and flow of social problems into general awareness, a model is proposed here—one intended to be both descriptive and predictive, to provide a template for understanding the changes of the past and to aid in contemplating the future. Thus, I am proposing that problems that affect individuals emerge into general social awareness, become perceived as social problems, and receive governmental attention in characteristic ways. It should be noted that, as in the rest of this chapter, attention is given only to social problems that are experienced first by individuals and then brought to the attention of the state, and not vice versa. State-initiated social problems, like McCarthyism, reactions to the use of nuclear power plants, or the public debate over the merits of a nuclear freeze, are not the focus of this discussion.

STAGES IN THE EMERGENCE OF
A SOCIAL PROBLEM

Stage 1: From the "taboo" to the "talked about": Altered Views of Who Suffers and Why

Those who have felt embarrassed after having had a personal problem revealed to them have an intuitive understanding of what it means for a problem to be "taboo." When a listener becomes embarrassed upon hearing intimate revelations, her embarrassment typically is the result of her perception that this problem should not be discussed in "polite company."

A sense of discomfort may pervade the conversation without affecting the way in which listeners perceive sufferers. However, it is more likely that sufferers who make us feel uncomfortable will be negatively affected by our efforts to make sense of their pain. That is, the sufferers will be seen as responsible for their own problem. Problems that affect the lives of individuals (particularly those that cannot easily be fixed) are most often seen as explicable in terms of the individual's character or actions (e.g., Janoff-Bulman 1979; Petersen, et al. 1981, Ryan 1971). This conclusion is reflected not only in feelings of personal embarrassment but also in social policy doctrines that suggest, by acts of omission or commission, that the problem is a personal one, for which the involvement of the state would be inappropriate (Elazar 1966; Kalmuss & Straus 1981). As the previous section indicates, such problems as unemployment, the segregation of public schools, and the education-related disadvantages that result from poverty emerged as social problems following times when they were considered beyond the scope of proper governmental intervention. Importantly, the unavailability of opportunities for self-improvement created by public inattention functions to impede the sense of injustice that might promote action by the sufferers. If no alternatives exist to one's current situation, a kind of de facto justice may be experienced—whatever is must be fair. Only the perception of viable alternatives can render the status quo unjust (Blackman 1986; Deutsch 1985, 1986; Fine 1980). (See chapter 4 for a detailed consideration of the impact of alternatives on perceptions of injustice.)

While the government is the most powerful source of increased opportunities, people, through organized activism or sheer numbers, can create alternative perceptions of "embarrassing" problems. In the case of intimate violence, increasing amounts of grass-roots activities and the accelerating involvement of concerned interest groups (e.g., NOW) have fostered a new societal awareness of the extent and nature of family violence and rape. Although knowledge about the actual prevalence of these problems was scarce, and controversy existed among interest groups that differed in their formulations of "the problem," publicity nevertheless began to spread about particular instances, judged by the activists and the media to demonstrate that only the surfaces of the problems had been scratched (Schechter 1983). This publicity enhanced the perception that the problems were widespread, and increased the belief that this concern had societal implications.

More specifically, the early 1970s saw a great deal of publicity in the general media, first on the experience of rape victims, and then on battered women. Articles on rape appeared in such popular newspapers and magazines as the *Washington Post*, the *New York Times*, *Ms.*, *Reader's Digest*, *Time*, and *Rolling Stone*. In June of 1974, *Ms.* magazine featured an article on England's Women's Aid—the first shelter for battered women. By 1976, *Ladies' Home Journal*, *Newsweek*, *McCall's*, the New York *Daily News*, *Woman's Day*, *People*, *Good Housekeeping*, and other wide-reaching publications had printed articles on wife abuse.

In 1975, Brownmiller's *Against Our Will: Men, Women and Rape* was published. It was the first major book on the history of rape. In 1976, Martin's *Battered Wives* appeared, the first book to deal with the situation of the battered woman in American society. This publicity worked to redefine the characteristics of the victims by leaving no doubt that they were undeserving of the violence inflicted on them. Feminism provided the impetus and the philosophical base for the naming of these injustices that accrue disproportionately to women and children within sexist societies. As feminist activists moved the problem from the "taboo" to the "talked about," new notions of justice were advocated, and the inalienable rights of women and children were emphasized.

It is the media-supported attempt to change prevailing conceptions of justice and entitlement that seems best to characterize the emergence of social problems through Stage 1.[3] During this stage, efforts are underway to redefine the victims as those who suffer unjustly for reasons that are beyond their control. It is important to note that the increased awareness that follows these efforts may not be accompanied by immediate, measurable attitudinal changes. For example, two nationwide surveys of attitudes toward violence in families were conducted during this time, the first in 1968 by the United States Violence Commission (reported by Stark and McEvoy 1970) and the second in 1976 by Straus et al. (1980). Of the 1176 randomly sampled respondents in 1968, about one-fourth thought that it would be all right for a husband to hit his wife or a wife to hit her husband. In the Straus et al. study of 2143 randomly sampled Americans, slightly fewer than one out of four wives, and one out of three husbands, saw slapping between spouses as at least somewhat necessary, normal and good. Even though the eight years that passed between these two collections of data coincided with greatly increased media attention to family violence, the resulting heightened awareness occurred without a rapid or measurable decrease in the view that it was acceptable for a husband to use physical violence against his wife. By 1976, it seems likely that most Americans knew that many women were being physically abused by their husbands. Perhaps people were reluctant to believe that this problem was sufficiently widespread or severe to merit a change in traditional attitudes. Or perhaps these findings reflect the high degree of violence tolerated in family life and the extent to which socialization about the acceptability of such violence persists even in the face of information that demonstrates its dramatic, negative consequences. In large part, the studies on the incidence and the specific forms of violence that characterize a later stage in the emergence of social problems are conducted to change attitudes and to affect the general public, as well as social policy makers and resource allocators.

---

3. Of course, the media do not present a singular or one-sided view of the problem. The notion here is that a preponderance of the media coverage is sufficiently positive to mark emergence through Stage 1.

Stage 2: Political Action and
Governmental Responsiveness

Even without measurable changes in general, societal attitudes, problems which receive sufficient exposure, about which the public becomes aware, come to be seen by legislators as ones which justifiably deserve governmental attention, and which are within the proper sphere of the government. Political impact sought through demonstrations, interest groups, lobbyists, and conferences like the International Tribunal on Crimes Against Women (1975) becomes a goal of those seeking solutions to the social problem (Kalmuss & Straus 1981). Legislative and judicial action is sought. A change in attitudes would be expected to follow from what is newly made legal or illegal, but at a slower pace than the rate at which knowledge about the problem's presence is acquired.

Legislative changes regarding the problems of family violence and rape have occurred. By 1968, every state had laws mandating the reporting of child abuse to state authorities (Libbey & Bybee 1979). Indeed, the specific problem of child abuse has received the most concerted positive governmental attention within established agency-based structures (Finkelhor 1981; MacFarlane 1981a, 1981b). By 1980, 45 states and the District of Columbia had passed some form of legislation to deal with domestic violence; 21 states had laws which included appropriations for services and five imposed surcharges on marriage licenses to fund domestic violence programs (Kalmuss & Straus 1981). As of September 1986, 38 states allowed women to prosecute their live-in husbands for rape. These laws, designed to protect the rights of victims of family violence, have provided new and potent alternatives to those who previously had been powerless under the law. The existence of good laws, however, does not guarantee enforcement or serious consideration within a judicial system unfamiliar with the nature and consequences of family violence. In December 1976, for example, 12 battered women in New York City instituted a class action suit against the police for having "engaged in a pervasive pattern and practice of denying to abused wives the legal protection and assistance to which they were entitled under state law" (Woods 1978: 7). On June 26, 1978, this case, *Bruno v. Codd*, was settled when the police department defendants agreed to meet the plaintiff's conditions and entered into a consent judgment with them. The police department agreed that its employees had a duty to honor and would respond to "every request for assistance or protection from or on behalf of a woman based on an allegation that a violation or crime . . . has been committed against her by . . . her husband" (Woods 1978: 32). This was an important victory for battered women, who historically have been denied adequate protection from the police and the legal system (Schechter 1983; Woods 1978). It was not a cure. The need for adequate police involvement continues to be a prime concern for battered women. Now, at least, policy is on their side.

One might conclude that a discussion of centuries-old rape laws should not be combined with this consideration of new family violence laws. Unfortunately, though, they do belong together. The laws on rape questioned the credibility and innocence of the survivor/victim and thereby linked her with victims of family violence who, like her, suffered without effective legal recourse. Berger (1977), in setting forth the "peculiarities" of the rape laws, noted their difference from those dealing with nonsexual assault: (1) they often required evidence of the victim's forcible resistance; (2) the penalty structure was harsh (e.g., as of 1977, more than thirty states permitted the sentence of life imprisonment for rape, death was the maximum penalty or rape in at least ten states, Rose 1977); (3) husbands could not then be charged with raping their wives in most states; (4) they often required corroboration of material aspects of the crime (i.e., force, penetration and the attacker's identity); (5) the victim's chastity was at issue and was used as a measure of her credibility (i.e., unchaste women lie); and (6) cautionary jury charges were frequently offered, warning the jurors that women can cry "rape!" falsely.

Thus, in spite of the longevity of rape statutes, rape survivors, like battered women, who have pressed charges against their attackers have encountered weighty resistance from the judicial system. This resistance seems likely to result from slow-to-change attitudes, which lag behind the pace of new or reformulated legislation. Since Stage 2-type systematic changes are often accomplished without concomitant attitudinal changes, policy implementation and enforcement require special attention.

Stage 3: Implementing Policy: The Advent
of Action Programs

The social service orientation to "personal problems," begun in the
New Deal era, is epitomized during Stage 3 by the establishment of
action programs designed to repair and remedy the problem. With
regard to battered women and rape survivors, the early action programs were community-based, volunteer programs. The women who
ran these programs were represented among the activists who lob-
bied for the establishment of government-funded programs.[4] While
these lobbying efforts met with short-term success, it is important
to note the central and continuing role played by privately funded
and volunteer organizations.

Early funded programs on intimate violence, like the government
sponsored action programs on other issues that preceded them, were
begun before data had been collected on the nature and incidence of
the problem and without concomitant program evaluations. This
pattern of action-before-research has typified responses to social
problems both before and after the creation of the Office of Management and Budget. Providing services to those in need should certainly be a high priority. However, the ethic that demands measurable signs that a goal is being attained jeopardizes the long-term
funding of these programs. In the case of intimate violence, the establishment of such federal programs as the Family Violence Program at the Law Enforcement Assistance Administration (LEAA) in
1976, and the National Center for the Prevention and Control of
Rape (NCPCR) within the National Institute of Mental Health
(NIMH) in 1977, signalled the advent of Stage 3 and led to the support of social services that offered new alternatives to victims of
intimate violence. While governmental support was quite limited,
the attention paid to this problem by federal agencies added weight
to the work of grass roots activists and to the sponsorship of private
foundations. The number of social services established and designed
specifically for victims of intimate violence grew dramatically in the
1970s, especially during the latter half of that decade. The first shelters for battered women and crisis intervention programs for rape

---

4. While many community-based activists sought governmental support, others believed
that government involvement would mean cooptation and a loss in grass roots control. Thus,
while governmental resources make the large scale introduction of social programs possible,
controversy does and did exist as to the costs that follow from such support.

survivors were established in the United States in 1972; by 1978, the United States Department of Justice listed 310 shelters and/or services for battered women. Five years later, there were about 700 shelters listed in national directories (Back et al. 1980; Warrior 1982). According to the NCPCR, as of March of 1981, there were approximately 600 crisis intervention programs for survivors of sexual assaults in this country. Without exception, these agencies did not replace any sort of existing treatment facility. They offered a new service.

It is intrinsic to this model that the attainment of a particular stage is not enduring. With regard to family violence, the societal tendency to "move on" came fast. In 1978, the Domestic Violence Act, sponsored by Representatives Mikulski, Boggs, and Steers was defeated in the House. In 1979, LEAA changed its funding priorities and encouraged programs for battering men, rather than for battered women. Then, in 1981, the Family Violence program at LEAA was ended, less than five years after it had begun. The political climate of the Reagan era saw a sharp decline in available funds for services to victims of family violence. The political New Right, with its opposition to abortion and its emphasis on "the family," named domestic violence counseling services as "anti-family" (Joffee 1986; Petchesky 1980, 1984). Reagan's persistent popularity and his allegiance to the New Right also contributed to the shift away from services for women and toward activities that would aid men and preserve families with a history of violence.

Thus, in part, attitudinal changes about the proper role of government in the personal affairs of citizens contributed to this shift away from programs for victims of intimate violence. In addition, recent changes in public policy are due to some of the same difficulties that plagued the Head Start programs. Action programs are judged unsuccessful because they did not achieve some goals that were not clearly defined at the outset. With regard to shelters for battered women, for example, one could judge the high proportion of women who returned home after their first time in a shelter as an indication that the program was a failure. One can assert, however, that shelters are intended to provide only short-term aid, so they cannot be expected to solve the problem completely.

The implicit promise of a cure for our social ills, like the campaign promises of charismatic politicians, compels our interest and raises our hopes. In spite of the tendency for major social change to happen slowly, immediate change is regularly anticipated by program planners, recipients, and interested observers. Disenchantment results from the certain disparities that emerge between program goals, like the reduction of family violence, and measurable achievements. The belief that action programs will produce rapid, measurable changes is deeply rooted, still, in the unrealistic construction of family violence as a personal problem that will be solved primarily on an individual level.

Attitude changes lag far behind societal willingness to act. It is as if the action program is a bet, behind which we are willing to place some of our national resources. When the bet does not pay off quickly, we resume our former way of looking at things—which was suspended only for the purposes of the bet, anyway—and move on. The capacity to redefine problems as truly societal in origin is difficult for those of us raised in individualistic cultures. Horatio Alger's characters may be mythic, but he sets the pattern for those who really believe that the individual *can* triumph over a culture that affords limited opportunities if one just tries hard enough.

The unrealistic belief that action programs will produce rapid, measurable change provides an impetus for Stage 4, as the expectation that social change will happen quickly goes unfulfilled, and researchers set about the task of finding out what went wrong. I am suggesting here that most often what went wrong is that social change is best measured in terms of generations, not decades. Nonetheless, even the brief presence of interventions provides direction in the flow of social change. The existence, albeit short-lived, of government-supported action programs reflects a recognized injustice and shapes evolving cultural norms. Problems countered by action programs draw high levels of societal attention and provide some treatment to literally millions of people. Thus, they exert substantial influence on the development of cultural priorities, whether or not the solutions are quick to occur.

Stage 4: Responsive Research

The post-1965 addition to the emergence of social problems is characterized by empirical studies designed to address the questions raised by the activities of the preceding stages. At this point, one can assert that the issue is an acknowledged social problem. Stage 4 activities occur contemporaneously with activities that typify each of the preceding stages. In fact, the three goals of responsive research correspond with the emphasis of each of the three preceding stages, respectively: (1) quantification, to document the problem's sizable presence, (2) qualification, to shape policy recommendations, and (3) program evaluation, to determine the effectiveness of funded programs.

Quantification. Inevitably, this goal is difficult to achieve, since newly emerged problems retain old "attitudinal baggage," and may continue to be seen as outside the public domain. Nevertheless, with equal inevitability, the quantity of the problem is always a primary concern for those public representatives who would act on behalf of those suffering from the deprivations embodied in the social problem. Specifically, three characteristics of emergent social problems account for the impossibility of conducting reliable and representative studies. The private nature of these events historically, the likelihood that revealing one's victimization will diminish the sufferer's worth in the eyes of the community, and the belief that reporting one's experiences will serve no useful purpose (e.g., the rapist will not be prosecuted), have all inhibited the reporting of these events to the police, social service agencies, or researchers.

Although some sampling strategies are specifically designed to deal with these problems (e.g., multiplicity or "snowball" sampling), research on intimate concerns exists as a kind of "lamppost" research, since only those who are willing to stand exposed in the "light" of a researcher's survey are counted among the victims. Although the scope of the "beam" varies, ultimately, all research on intimate violence is "lamppost" research, in which we investigate and build upon the experiences of those who are willing to come into the light. How many victims remain in the dark, and their reasons for not reporting their experiences (e.g., their distress was too great to allow reporting, or their distress was too small to motivate action), are questions whose answers can only be estimated.

These realities notwithstanding, major efforts to collect data have been undertaken; their primary purpose is to determine the frequency of rape and family violence, and the characteristics of the victims. For example, in 1974 and 1975, the U.S. Department of Justice, through LEAA, conducted a study, "Rape Victimization in 26 American Cities," in which interviews were conducted with representative samples of approximately 22,000 individuals from 10,000 households in each of the 26 cities. McDermott (1979), the author of the report on this study, acknowledged that this large-scale study, like others in this area, was affected by the "general problem faced in all victimization survey interviews, of victims being unable or unwilling to report the incident to the survey interviewer" (p. 2). The refusal rate for this study was not reported, so it is impossible to estimate the representativeness of the samples from the cities. Nevertheless, these data were used to suggest that young women, black and other minority women, women who were single, divorced or separated, women whose major activities took them out of the home, and women with low family incomes were more likely to be raped (or nearly raped) than their respective counterparts. Further, McDermott (1979) reported a total of 39,310 victimizations (i.e., rape by strangers and non-strangers) in the population of 12,658,176. Assuming that each individual is victimized only once (an unlikely event), this yields an incidence estimate of .31 percent.

The large sample size is deceiving because we still do not know who did not answer. The characteristics of the women who reported rape may not reflect the characteristics of those actually raped. Further, such research may serve to perpetuate stereotypes about who gets raped, causing women to feel that they are responsible for their own victimization, if they are divorced, or black, or if they spend time outside their homes.

Five years later, Russell (1982a) undertook a smaller scale incidence study, in which she surveyed a probability sample of 930 women over the age of 18 from San Francisco. Russell believed that this city's female residents would be more willing to talk about their rape experience than women from other parts of the country. Of the 930 women, 24 percent reported at least one completed rape. Only 9 percent of the total number of rape and attempted rape incidents in this study were ever reported to the police.

At about the same time as Russell's survey was conducted, the FBI Uniform Crime report (1979) indicted that 76,000 women had been raped. The vast disparity between Russell's 24 percent statistic and the figures generated by the LEAA and the FBI surely reflects the impact of underreporting on national indicators of the incidence of rape. Russell's 24 percent figure may be an overestimate, caused perhaps by a selection bias which led rape survivors to over-participate relative to their actual numbers in the population, or by a form of sensitization that leads cooperative participants to redefine unpleasant sexual experiences as rape for the purposes of the study. Whatever the cause for the disparity, these studies are reviewed here as evidence for the diverse efforts exerted to gather quantitative incidence data, as well as for their debatable worth due to representativeness-of-sample problems.

Not surprisingly, research on the incidence of violence in families shares the problem of underreporting with research on rape. Nevertheless, in response to Stage 4 (and Stage 1) concerns over quantification, Straus et al. (1980) —endeavored to discover the incidence of family violence using traditional random sampling procedures. They selected a population of adults from intact families only, with no children under the age of three. Thirty-five percent of those sampled refused to be interviewed or could not be reached. Again, concerns with representativeness, based on both the criteria for inclusion and the return rate are key, but cannot be easily resolved. From their data, Straus et al. (1980) concluded, for example, that approximately 28 percent of American husbands and/or wives had committed at least one violent act against his or her spouse. However, as a result of their sample's nonrepresentativeness, they concluded: "It is very likely a substantial underestimate" (p. 33).[5]

Alternative, nontraditional research strategies have been used in efforts to reach those who typically have not reported their experiences. Studies that employ surveys printed in newspapers or magazines afford participants the opportunity to respond and report their involvement with intimate violence without sacrificing their desire for privacy (Bart, 1975; Blackman-Doron, 1980a, 1980b). The findings from such research can then be contrasted with the results of prior research and explanations can be generated which may help to illuminate the relationship between reporting behavior and the nature of one's experiences with intimate violence.

In 1979, I attempted to conduct such an "alternative, incidence" study. A newspaper survey was printed in *The Record*, a suburban (Bergen County area) New Jersey newspaper. This survey, was entitled "You and Violence," and was adorned with a grotesque drawing of a person with blood dripping from facial scratches (provided by the newspaper artist). Statistically, I made efforts to "reclaim" representativeness by comparing the demographic characteristics of the survey respondents with the characteristics of the newspaper

---

5. Interestingly, Straus and Gelles' (1986) incidence study was conducted for the explicit purpose of drawing comparisons in rates of wife and child abuse between 1975 and 1985. Thus, while concerns over *how many* people are affected may be complemented by attention to *how* they are affected, incidence studies retain perceived importance that legitimizes such research. Their 1986 study attained an 84% response rate for telephone interviews and reported that the "very severe" child abuse rate was 47% lower in 1985 than in 1975, and that the wife abuse rate was 27% lower.

readers in general. The sample of 612 respondents approximated the population of 250,000 newspaper readers of which they were a part, with the strong exception of the number of women in the sample— 83 pércent of the newspaper survey respondents were women, as compared with 54 percent in the population of county residents who read the newspaper. In my sample, approximately 28 percent had been victims of current and/or past spousal abuse, 24 percent had been victims of child abuse, 7 percent had been raped by their husbands, and 14 percent had been raped by men besides their husbands.

The statistics from my research, which are reported in more detail later in this book, are not unlike the numbers reported by other researchers in the field (Finkelhor 1979, 1984, 1985; Russell 1980, 1982b, 1983; Straus and Gelles 1986; Straus, et al. 1980). They are very different from the numbers provided by the Department of Justice and the FBI. We can only speculate on the reasons for these sizable and significant differences. Politics, and one's sense of the importance of making these problems salient, may play a role in the ways in which crimes of intimate violence are defined, the vigor with which research participants are pursued, and the sorts of analyses conducted. Attention to the "lamppost" phenomenon must bring humility to all would-be incidence researchers. There are no simple solutions to this problem. Only a demonstrable and lasting change in societal attitudes toward victims of intimate violence can bring these people out of the shadows. Presumably, attitudinal changes made manifest in an altered responsiveness on the parts of significant others, police officers, juries, judges, and legislators would facilitate reporting behavior and improve incidence studies.[6]

I think it is worthwhile to challenge the need for this "Quantification" stage. It reflects a presumed need to know "how much," when "how much" is not really the problem. Research designed in response to such concerns is expensive in terms of both time and money, and often leaves us unable to speak to the nature of the problem. While the magnitude of a problem is typically taken to be symptomatic of how much energy we should put into solving it, it seems a pernicious, secondary consequence that the energy ex-

6. The 84% participation rate in Straus & Gelles' (1986) more recent incidence study— a 19% increase over their earlier study—may be seen as an indicator of improved attitudes and a reduced embarrassment at the discussion of violence in one's family. However, one is also obliged to note that in 1975 the interviews were longer than in 1985 and were conducted in person. The use of telephone interviews instead of face-to-face contacts for the 1985 study may be the best explanation for the increased willingness to participate.

pended in the process of counting victims serves to slow down the remediaiton process. Especially because action programs appear to have such short half-lives, it may be crucial for researchers to assert that "enough" of a problem exists for efforts at social change to proceed, even if the exact numbers are never known. Instead, then, researchers can focus on qualifying the experiences of the victims in their societal context. This comment does not reflect the way things are. It is quite clear that, as a society, we still require the "proof" that numbers provide to be convinced that a problem deserves attention. Incidence concerns remain central and receive federal funding even as other research agendas are explored (Straus and Gelles 1986).

Qualification: The Experiences of Victims. Research attention was first directed toward the experience of victims of child abuse (e.g., Bakan 1971; Brown & Daniels 1968; De Francis 1963; Elmer 1960, 1961; Elmer & Gregg 1967; Galdston 1965; Gelles 1973; Gil 1970; Helfer & Kempe 1968/1974; Johnson & Morse 1968; Kempe et al. 1962; Kempe & Kempe 1978; Melnick and Hurley 1969; Silverman 1953, 1974; Young 1964). Later, the growth of the women's movement fostered societal awareness of violence against women in their homes (e.g., Carlson 1977; Dobash and Dobash 1980; Eldow 1972; Frieze 1979a, b; Gelles 1972; Pizzey 1974; Roy 1977; Straus 1978; Straus et al. 1980; United States Commission on Civil Rights 1978; Walker 1979), and on the street (e.g., Bard 1976; Brodyaga et al. 1975; Brownmiller 1975; Burgess and Holmstrom 1973, 1974a, 1974b, 1974c, 1976, 1978, 1979a, 1979b; Evans and Sperekas 1976; Gager & Schurr 1976; Griffin 1971; Hayman & Lanza 1972; Hilberman, 1976; Katz & Mazur 1979; Medea & Thompson 1974).

These publications served the essential function of presenting the perspectives of professionals in relation to descriptive data offered by self identified, reporting victims. The data came from many sources, but all involved those who had come forward and related their experiences in some nonanonymous way in academic publications: (1) first-person accounts (Davidson 1978; Gingold, 1976; Hake 1977; Langley & Levy 1977; Martin 1976; Metzger 1976; Remsburg & Remsburg 1979; Renvoize 1978; Russell 1975; Warrior 1976; (2) clinicians' files (Fassberg 1977; Fox & Scherl 1972; Hilberman & Muson 1978; Nadelson & Notman 1979; Notman & Nadelson 1976; Sutherland & Scherl 1979); (3) police and/or legal system records (Amir 1971; Gil 1973; Pittman & Handy 1964; Wilt 1977); (4) social service agencies (Burgess & Conger 1979; Carlson 1977; Flynn 1977; Pfouts 1978; Young 1964); (5) hospital emergency room contacts (Burgess & Holmstrom 1973, 1974a, 1974b, 1974c; Burgess & Johnson 1976; Miller et al. 1978; Rounsaville & Weissman 1978; Williams & Williams 1973); and (6) shelters for battered women (Community Planning Organization, Battered Women Study Committee 1976; Frieze 1979a, b; Gayford 1975; Pizzey 1974; Roy 1977; Walker 1979).

As the lengthy list of preceding citations demonstrates, the move into Stage 4 qualification efforts was expansive. A statistical overview of the numbers of publications appearing over time supports the notion that there was indeed a publication "boom." Katz and Mazur (1979), for example, reported that the first empirical study of the rape victim was conducted in 1962 in Denmark (Svalastoga 1962). The "avalanche" of publications on rape began in 1971; of the 262 publications listed in Katz and Mazur's bibliography, 75 percent were published after 1965; 59 percent after 1971. Lystad's (1974) annotated bibliography on violence in the home demonstrated a similar pattern, listing 190 publications, of which 88 percent were published after 1965, 43 percent after 1971. As of 1987, the Family Violence Program at the University of Texas which functions as a national clearinghouse listed 1500 articles in its directory.

As a result of these publications, we know a great deal about the dimensions and the nature of the experiences of victims of intimate violence—at least of those who have come forward to participate in these studies. We know less about how victims of different forms of intimate violence compare with each other in terms of such issues as coping, recovery, and sense of injustice. Similarly, there is little work done comparing such victims to meaningful comparison groups (See Browne 1985; Frieze 1979a, 1979b; Walker 1984 for some notable exceptions.) In an expansion of the newspaper survey research described earlier, I conducted intensive interviews with a subset of 113 respondents. The results of those interviews, with victims and nonvictims, are reported in detail in later chapters of this book.

Program Evaluation. The establishment of action programs during Stage 3 and subsequent concerns over programmatic effectiveness contribute directly to this next part of Stage 4 in the emergence of social problems. Experimental or quasi-experimental evaluation research provides the basic structure for Stage 4 empirical efforts. Examples of such efforts are provided by Kilpatrick et al.'s

(1979) longitudinal assessments of a program which applied behavioral desensitization techniques to the reduction of fear and anxiety in rape survivors, and by Becker and Abel's (1981) investigation of their treatment program for sexual dysfunction in rape survivors. Similarly, a large-scale study on the relationship between the criminal justice system and domestic violence programs has been conducted (Fagan & Lewis 1981).

In general, evaluation studies on family violence programs are newer and less likely to pertain to the effectiveness of specific treatment modalities (e.g., desensitization) than studies on rape intervention programs. These differences are due to the shorter-lived existence of federal programs in the area of family violence, relative to programs for rape survivors and to the differential emphases of the agencies that sponsored the programs. (LEAA earmarked funds for family violence programs, while the NCPCR allocated funds for Research & Demonstration projects in the area of rape.) Given our action-before-research model, time and targeted attention are required for the program evaluation stage even to be reached. If funds are withdrawn too soon, program evaluations will not be conducted, and if the need for an evaluation goes unmet, the opportunity to derive meaningful, data-based summaries of past activity or policy recommendations for future action will be lost. Support for program evaluations, like the backing provided the programs themselves, must be sustained and emphatic to ensure the attainment of this stage. Even ideal financial and ideological conditions will not guarantee that program evaluation efforts will be successful. Like all such research, the evaluation of treatment programs for survivors of rape and family violence arouses a certain defensiveness among those who planned and implemented the program under evaluation. Since the survival of any program may actually depend upon positive evaluations, efforts by outside evaluators to conduct objective assessment acquire complex, politicized implications, even if both research and program person agree that the program should exist.

By their nature, intimate violence victimizations create special difficulties for evaluation researchers. For example, rape survivors often change their places of residence as a way of coping with the trauma, which imposes special hardships on longitudinal studies (Burgess & Holmstrom 1978, 1979b). Finally, as noted earlier, short-term interventions may not put much of a dent in long-term problems. While studies designed to assess program effectiveness are important, they should be designed as longitudinal studies in which recipients of treatment are assessed several times over periods of up to ten years. This long-term time frame would also serve to reduce the concern that an evaluation can bring about the death of a program, since the evaluation itself would continue. The rate of social change must be acknowledged so that those who conduct evaluations, those who are evaluated, and those who make decisions about a program's longevity understand that immediate changes in a treatment recipient's condition are not required.

Longitudinal studies, with six week or six month reassessment periods (e.g., Kilpatrick et al. 1979), must be expanded so that gradual changes that emerge over more extended periods of time can be documented. Burgess and Holmstrom's (1979a) five-year followup study with rape survivors is an excellent example of this sort of evaluation research. Commitments to social problems that reach Stage 4 are required in order to learn from the experiences of the activism instituted during the preceding stages. Sadly, if commitment fades before this stage is reached, efforts at social change may go largely undocumented.

Stage 5: Experts Come Forward to Tell What They Have Learned

If the 1970s proved to be the decade of first data-gathering on the problems of intimate violence, the 1980s were the years of dissemination. The "Battered Woman Syndrome," the "Rape Trauma Syndrome," and the "Child Sexual Abuse Syndrome" provide important examples of conditions that were named and acquired substance during the 1970s. In particular, the works of Walker on battered women, (1979, 1984), Burgess and Holmstrom on rape survivors (1973, 1974a, 1974b, 1974c, 1978, 1979), and Finkelhor (1979, 1984, 1985) on victims of child sexual abuse have been remarkable for their breadth of impact.

While there are many examples of public reliance on expert opinion (e.g., testimony before Congressional committees, consultation on the design of a new elementary school curriculum to warn children of the risks of sexual assault), the one I have chosen to focus on here is the involvement of experts in trials involving rape survivors, and battered women and children. (See chapter 11 for extended attention to Stage 5 issues.) I have selected this example of "experts telling what they have learned" because, in many ways, societal policies are most clearly set, modified and re-set in the courtroom. Precedents are noted and inconsistencies must be resolved in order to do justice. Further, cases are presented—most often on an individual basis—so that, once again, we are dealing with a social problem as it was originally perceived—as residing within a single individual. Now, however, the expert can report data that indicate the extent to which individuals operate within social circumstances that limit their apparent personal control. The dearth of real alternatives available to battered women, for example, can now be documented. Thus, the implications of the lack of freedom to choose freedom from abuse can be taken into account. If a woman is being judged for the killing of her husband, knowledge about her inability to escape him can prove crucial to the jury's deliberation.

Social scientists have become a frequent part of the trial process, as the judicial system has acknowledged the body of relevant information that exists and is "beyond the ken of the average layperson." (The quoted phrase is a part of the standard set of criteria for the admissibility of expert testimony.) In the years since 1979, I have testified frequently as an expert witness at the trials of battered women who killed their husbands, abused children who killed family members, and accused rapists. Informed by the knowledge gained as the problems of intimate violence passed through the stages described here, I am able to educate jurors and judges about the range of circumstances that deserve consideration in judging the justice or injustice of the act that brings about a trial. If such testimony is effective, then the individual is seen in context, and the complexities of the individual trapped in negative life circumstances can be contemplated.

SUMMARY

Social problems reflect injustices, individually and then collectively experienced and publicly acknowledged. The interpersonal injustice of physical and sexual violence against women and children emerged as social problems during the 1970s, when a multi-issue women's movement focused attention on these crimes. This movement was successful in that it brought about legislative and judicial changes that made new opportunities for action and treatment available to survivors of intimate violence.

Intimate violence emerged as a social problem within the context provided by a pattern of increasing governmental support for access to equality of opportunity and self-fulfillment. Like other social problems, intimate violence emerged through a stage which altered prevailing, cultural conceptions of the "taboo," and of who suffers and why. This initial emergence was followed by governmental action on behalf of those who experienced intimate violence, the establishment of action programs, the conduct of responsive research studies, and the dissemination of new knowledge by social scientists.

Currently, federal attention to the problems of intimate violence is much diminished relative to its presence in the late 1970s. Yet, violence in our homes and on our streets continues to undo idealized views of human interaction and to threaten individual safety and liberty. Cutbacks in funds for remedial activity in the area of intimate violence are particularly troubling, because if there is anything that the flurry of work in the 1970s demonstrated, it is that interpersonal violence is learned, can be passed from one generation to the next, and is regularly expressed in power-related ways, by men against women, and by adults against children. The acquired knowledge, though, is not lost, even if the burst of activity that accompanies the emergence of a social problem fades. As the final stage in the emergence of a social problem is reached, the knowledge assumes a place in the culture, affecting the individuals who inhabit it and who pass on an altered, enhanced vision of they way things ought to be in and out of families, between women and men, between parents and children.

That vision is informed by books like this one, I hope. The remaining chapters of this book include a three chapter sequence on the nature of injustice. Chapter 2 provides a general framework for explanations of injustice, as they are perceived by those who witness others' suffering. Chapter 3 focuses on the self-perceptions of battered women, abused children and rape survivors. Chapter 4 discusses the impact of alternatives on the sense of injustice and details the paradoxes inherent in any person-based attention to social injustice. Chapter 5 reviews the method of the study I conducted, Chapter 6 summarizes the findings from the newspaper-survey portion of that study, Chapters 7 through 9 present the results of the interview part. Chapter 10 is a summary of the study's findings. Chapter 11, the final chapter, represents a move beyond the study and presents a consideration of the dissemination of research findings within the judicial system. Battered women who kill are its focus. In this final chapter, the process of taking the results of research into real world settings is exemplified and illuminated. Since that process represents a major goal of this book, such a chapter seemed a fitting conclusion.

2

PERCEPTIONS OF INJUSTICE

—

In Herman Wouk's (1978) *War and Remembrance*, a speech is made by a Jewish author to his fellow prisoners at Theresienstadt, a concentration camp in Czechoslovakia. The topic is the parable of Job, a story set in the context of a religious tradition which allows for no accidents, only the intentional acts of an all-powerful God. In the story of Job, retold by the author, Satan taunts God, and says:

> "Naturally Job is upright. Seven sons, three daughters, the wealthiest man in Uz . . . But just take away his rewards and see how upright he will remain!"
>
> "All right, take them away," God says. And in one day marauders carry off Job's wealth, and a hurricane kills all his ten children. . . . A horrible sickness strikes Job. Too loathsome an object to stay under his own roof, he crawls out and sits on an ash heap, scraping his sores with a shard. . . . Three of his pious friends

come to comfort him. A debate follows. . . . His comforters
maintain that since one Almighty God rules the universe, it must
make sense. Therefore, Job must have sinned. Let him search his
deeds, confess and repent. The missing piece is only what his offense was.

And in round after round of soaring arguments, Job fights
back. . . . He knows that the Almighty exists, that the universe
must make sense. But, he . . . knows now that it does not in fact
always make sense; that there is no guarantee of good fortune for
good behavior; that crazy injustice is part of the visible world and
of this life (Wouk 1978: 1063–1064).

Job calls upon God for an answer. God responds that the reason
is beyond Job's comprehension; that Job is unable to understand the
reasons why God acts as he does. Job accepts this explanation of
why the injustices were done to him and humbles himself. Then,

God rebukes the comforters for speaking falsely of Him, and praises
Job for holding to the truth. He restores Job's wealth. Job has seven
more sons and three more daughters. He lives a hundred and forty
more years, sees grandchildren and great grandchildren and dies
old, prosperous and revered (Wouk 1978: 1065).

In this retelling of the story of Job, Wouk raised the central social
psychological concerns that accompany injustice: (1) the search for
the reasons why, (2) the reactions and perceptions of others, (3) the
self-perceptions and coping activities of the victim, (4) the victim's
ability to see alternatives to prevailing explanations for and responses to injustice, and (5) the paradoxical nature of prevailing explanations for injustice, with their focus on the victim's culpability.
Each of these concerns will be examined, first in terms of research
on injustice in general, and then in relation to the problems of intimate violence as injustices. The first two of these issues are discussed in this chapter, the third in the next, and the remaining two
in chapter 4. The primary purpose of these chapters is to illuminate
the psychological properties of injustice and to provide a context for
the study reported in chapters 5 through 10.

THE SEARCH FOR THE REASONS WHY

A continuum of reasons for victimization can be constructed. At one end is the belief that luck or chance is the sole cause, at the other end, is the belief that the victim is in some meaningful way responsible for or deserving of the harm experienced. Explanations for victimization that fall in the middle range of this continuum would combine the two. For example, consider the rape survivor who says of her victimization, "I guess I was just in the wrong place at the wrong time; but, in retrospect, I feel that I was foolish to have walked alone at two in the morning." Here, notions of chance and of the victim's responsibility or deservingness are both raised as explanations.

Why then do people seek explanations for human suffering? And, under what circumstances will victimization be attributed to chance and when to the sufferer's deservingness?

Theorists from Freud (1922, 1935) to Festinger (1957) and beyond (e.g., Abelson et al. 1968; Heider 1958; Lerner 1975, 1977, 1980; Lerner & Miller 1978; Walster 1966; Wortman 1976; Wortman & Brehm 1975) have emphasized the human need for homeostasis or psychological calm, and the attendant drive to reachieve this state after it has been disrupted by tension. Within social psychology, cognitive consistency theorists have advanced the view that the arousal caused by the experiencing or awareness of a victimization is distressing, and that this distress motivates the individual to seek a reduction of tension (Abelson et al. 1968; Janoff-Bulman & Frieze 1983; Lerner 1980; Walster 1966; Wortman 1976). In theory, tension can be reduced by "good" explanations about why a distressing event has occurred; understanding will restore psychological harmony. (Miller & Porter 1983; Silver et al. 1983).

Chance as an Explanation

Chance is a word devoid of sense. Nothing can exist without a cause.

Voltaire, *Philosophical Dictionary*

One might expect that "good" explanations would distribute themselves evenly across the hypothetical range, from chance to deservingness, in correspondence with the actual causes of an event—at least in those cases where the "actual" causes can be known. However, to explain psychologically involving events as the product of chance has been shown to be remarkably unsatisfactory. Research (Langer 1975, Langer & Roth 1976), in which a variety of chance tasks (e.g., gambling) was employed, demonstrated that people prefer to believe in an illusion of control, rather than to attribute their outcomes to chance—even if it is the true, immediate cause. Further, the research showed that the stronger the subject's sense of involvement (e.g., an opportunity for choice, familiarity with the stimulus or responses, active physical involvement, or a competitive known. However, to explain psychologically involving events as the product of chance has been shown to be remarkably unsatisfactory. Research (Langer 1975; Langer & Roth 1976), in which a variety of chance tasks (e.g., gambling) was employed demonstrated that people prefer to believe in an illusion of control, rather than to attribute their outcomes to chance—even if it is the true, immediate cause. Further, the research showed that the stronger the subject's sense of involvement (e.g., an opportunity for choice, familiarity with the stimulus or responses, active physical involvement, or a competitive atmosphere), the more unwilling the subject was to attribute the outcome to chance or to behave as if it were randomly determined.

A study by Anderson et al. (1980) presented subjects with information about a strong positive or negative correlation between risk-taking and fire-fighting ability. After writing essays about why such relationships might exist, subjects were debriefed and told that the actual relationship between these two variables was unknown. They were then resurveyed about their opinions. Again, chance proved to be an unsatisfactory explanation and subjects continued to advocate the positions they had been assigned at the beginning of the experiment—even though they had been told that these views were fabricated. This study and Langer's research are presented here as illustrations of the idea that even in situations where the stakes are quite low—no one is severely victimized—accurate attributions to chance are avoided. Incorrect, but more elaborate, conceptually developed explanations are preferred.

When the stakes are higher and the impact of the events greater, this tendency to avoid chance explanations apppears to be even greater. Bulman and Wortman (1977) conducted a study with 29 people who had suffered traumatic events that left them paralyzed. The researchers asked these subjects if they had ever asked themselves the question, "Why me?" All 29 respondents affirmed that they had done so, and offered their answers. Answers were grouped into six categories, four of which rendered the suffering meaningful and indicated that the individual had become paralyzed for some "good" reason: God had a reason, predetermination, reevaluation of the victimization as positive or as deserved (e.g., you reap what you sow). The two remaining categories attributed the paralysis to chance alone or to a probabilistic notion of chance (e.g., it was bound to happen eventually). Only one person attributed her/his accident to chance alone, without also invoking some other meaningful explanation.

These results support the idea that explanations which do not depend on chance are preferred. In addition, Bulman and Wortman (1977) asked hospital staff members about the effectiveness of coping in these individuals, who had suffered highly traumatic, self-involving victimizations. Presumably, good coping is an indication of effective tension reduction. Victims who blamed themselves and believed there was nothing they could have done to avoid it coped better than those who blamed bad luck or chance and believed they could have done something to avoid their victimization.

Research with other sorts of victims—parents of children stricken with cancer (e.g., Chodoff et al. 1964; Hamburg and Adams 1967), concentration camp survivors (e.g., Cohen 1953), survivors of technological disasters (e.g., Baum et al. 1983), rape survivors (e.g., Burgess & Holmstrom 1978, 1979a, 1979b) and battered women (e.g., Frieze 1979a, 1979b)—has supported this reluctance to attribute one's victimization solely or primarily to chance and has indicated that those who blame behavioral (i.e., changeable) aspects of themselves cope best, although they may get less social support than those who do not blame themselves (Bulman & Wortman 1977; Coates et al. 1979; Janoff-Bulman 1979; Peterson et al. 1981).

It is essential to note that those who attribute their misfortunes to chance "sidestep" the issues of justice and injustice. Bad luck is not unfair; it is simply bad luck. However, it is quite clear that chance is, in general, not a satisfactory explanation for events that are psychologically arousing or distressing, and that the greater the upset, the stronger the press to generate meaningful explanations (Lerner 1980; Miller & Porter 1983; Walster 1966; Wortman 1976).

A number of reasons are proposed for this avoidance of chance explanations. First, such attributions render suffering meaningless, and rather than leading to a reduction in psychological tension, as explanations should, may instead cause the individual to experience a heightened sense of injustice and frustration, as a result of suffering for no reason. Second, the Judeo-Christian tradition symbolized in the story of Job discounts the possibility of chance and would label as irreligious and sinful anyone who favored chance over the powers of an all mighty deity and predestination. Third, beginning in childhood, people are positively reinforced for explanations that are characterized by cognitive complexity and reflect the thinker's ability to put events together in a logical, causal sequence. Simply to respond with "luck" when asked "why?" is not enough. Fourth, chance attributions may create a psychological state of vulnerability in which the victim or observers may fear that similar randon misfortunes will recur at any moment. Finally, the Freudian psychoanalytic tradition has influenced societal attitudes and contributed to the tendency to believe that nothing is an accident. Even slips of the tongue are meaningful. Thus, chance is greatly underutilized as the explanation for suffering. Most misfortunes, for most people, are explained in terms of the sufferer's characteristics and deservingness, and are therefore experienced as injustices.

Deservingness and the Nature of Injustice

The concept of deservingness provides the structure for most definitions of justice and injustice (Deutsch 1975, 1985; Lerner 1975, 1977, 1980; Sampson 1975; Walster et al. 1973). Justice may be said to obtain whenever individuals receive the valued resources (e.g., food, shelter) and/or positive treatment (e.g., kindness, respect) they deserve, or to which they are entitled in terms of some resource distribution scheme. (See Deutsch's 1975 discussion of equality, equity, and need as bases for the potentially just distribution of resources.) Injustice occurs whenever there is a mismatch between what the individual deserves and what she/he gets. (This definition of injustice allows for the injustice of getting more than one deserves. However, the focus of the discussion here is on the injustice of people getting less than they deserve.)

While such a definition can be stated quite simply, concepts like deservingness and entitlement are not objective and are heavily shaped by moral values. When discussing such concepts, we have in Kohlberg's (1969) language, moved from "is" to "ought." The moral quality of justice and conceptions of "ought" raises the paradox of efforts to define injustice in any absolute or objective sense. Moral values

vary among individuals and across groups of people. Social units—
families as well as ethnic and religious groups—often develop shared
conceptions of justice. One is tempted to argue, then, that justice
is an "eye of the beholder" phenomenon—it has to be seen to be
there. Thus, an event would constitute an injustice if and only if it
were experienced as such by the victims. However, as Kohlberg's
(1969) highest-level moral processors would point out, an event can
be unjust even if none of those directly involved experiences it that
way. For example, even if a husband was himself a victim of family
violence and believes that it is a husband's right and entitlement to
hit his wife, and even if a wife was abused as a child and has no
personal basis for expecting better treatment, the physical violence
enacted by this husband against this wife is still unjust. (See the
discussion in chapter 4 on true and false connections in explanations of injustice.)

And, yet, psychologically speaking, without at least an initial, even
fleeting, awareness of the painful withholding of what one is entitled to , there is no psychological experiencing of injustice. Injustice
is, at once, the tree that falls in the forest, is silent if no one hears
it, and yet makes a sound. The impossible perspective of an all-
knowing, objective observer would have to be adopted in order to
determine the real reasons why victimization occurs, or to conceptualize "true injustice." Without the vision this perspective would
afford, psychological reality prevails and concepts of deservingness
are freely, if inaccurately, applied in response to events that bring
about suffering.

Many different sorts of events may bring about suffering and be
experienced as injustices: natural disasters, disease, societal preju-
dices, intentional bad acts by others (e.g., rape, murder), unintentional acts by others with bad consequences (e.g., some car accidents), intentional bad acts by oneself (e.g., suicide attempts), and
unintentional acts by oneself with bad consequences (e.g., diving accidents). Combinations of these events may also create distress.

While these events share the capacity to produce distress and to
be perceived as injustices, it is certain that reactions and attributions vary in relation to the "objective" cause. Specifically, the role
of human intention is key. For example, research by Hornstein and
his colleagues (Blackman & Hornstein, 1977; Holloway et al. 1977;
Hornstein 1975, 1976; Hornstein et al. 1976; LaKind 1974) has demonstrated that people who heard about disastrous events reacted with
an increased psychological vigilance (e.g., they behaved more com-

petitively, judged human nature more harshly, and were more restrictive about whom they perceived as being similar to them), when the disaster was caused by the intentional act of another human being. This increased vigilance did not occur as a result of disasters caused by natural forces. Indeed, the role of human intention in bringing about an injustice seems crucial to the nature of the psychological reactions experienced by both observers and victims. The assumption that the victimizer is or should be capable of understanding the suffering of others, should intensify the outrage that results from the awareness that someone has been hurt.

In fact, though, the sense of injustice can be lessened if the role of intention is misperceived. On September 20, 1986, I heard a radio interview on National Public Radio, with an American woman living in Beirut. Jean Sutherland, whose husband had been kidnapped in 1985 by terrorists, was asked by the interviewer if she was angry; she responded that she was not. She reported that she thought of her husband's kidnapping as a catastrophe, like a hurricane or a flood. In this way, she redefined the injustice as a nonintentional act and stemmed the flow of her own anger, and her own psychological sense of injustice.

An objective appraisal of acts of intimate violence would indicate that these events all result from the intentional action of one human being against another. Yet, as in the case of the woman in Beirut, subjectivity plays an important role in determining the perception of intentionality. For example, in an interview I conducted with a woman on trial for the stabbing death of husband, we discussed the reasons for his violence. I asked, "Why did he beat you?" She responded, "He didn't mean to do it. You know how sometimes you drum your fingernails on the table, and one of them breaks? Well that's how it was when he hit me." This woman, who had been badly beaten for over three years, seemed to have absolved her husband of any blame or responsibility simply by seeing his intentional act as unintentional. She used a similar process of denial to absolve herself, and told the jury that she could not have been the one to stab her husband, although she admitted to being alone with him at the time of the stabbing. She thought he might have stabbed himself, but could not cast herself as the intentional actor. The jury did not believe her denial, but did believe that her act was just, in the context of the violence of her marital relationship. They acquitted her.

These examples are intended to illustrate the idea that the apparent causes for suffering embodied in the events listed above need not correspond with the ways in which they are perceived. The apparent causes may be distorted in terms of concepts of intentionality (e.g., "The fire that burned my house down was an expression of God's will.") to fit with the perceivers' sense of deservingness and with their need to give their victimization meaning, without invoking chance. The focus of this work, though, is on the forms of injustice that most would agree are the results of intentional, interpersonal bad acts. Therefore, from here on, this category alone will be considered. However, the context from which it is drawn and the potential for seeing the intentional as unintentional (and vice versa) should be kept in mind.

THE REACTIONS AND PERCEPTIONS OF OBSERVERS OF INJUSTICE

Observers will not always respond to injustice. Certain psychological events must take place in order for the observer to realize that an injustics has occurred. A model of the necessary psychological processes is presented below, and provides the framework for a discussion of current theoretical and empirical research on observers' reactions to victimization in general, and intimate violence in particular.

Noticing

The event that is the injustice must be perceived. Simply, it must be noticed. The observer must become aware of the suffering of another.

Perceived Relevance and Concomitant Arousal

The event must be seen as relevant to the observer's environment, and the noticing of the event must produce an arousal in the observer that is greater than he or she can explain simply in terms of "paying attention" to the event. Certainly, awareness may occur without a sense of arousal or upset that exceeds the amount of energy spent in noticing. For example, suffering that occurs in a geographic location far removed from the observer may be viewed dispassionately. Lerner and Miller (1978) commented:

> People of course, do not believe, nor do they have a need to believe that everything that happens in the world is just. . . . people will be concerned primarily with their own world, the environment in which they must live and function. (p. 1031)

Vulnerability and Identification

The observer must become aware (even briefly), that the source of his or her arousal is the event that produced another's suffering, and this arousal must be experienced (again, even briefly), in terms of the observer's own vulnerability to such an event. If the observer would at that moment, acknowledge, "What happened to someone else could have happened to me and would have been an injustice," then one can say that an injustice has been noted.

In addition, in the case of interpersonal injustice, the observer must be able to identify both a victim(s) and a perpetrator(s), and must experience some degree of identification with the victim, and perhaps with the perpetrator as well. Identification with or empathy for the victim is generally recognized as the psychological base upon which a sense of injustice is built. Identification with the perpetrator as a route to the realization that an injustice has occurred represents an idea that has not received much attention in theoretical or empirical considerations of the ways in which nonvictims perceive injustice. This idea suggests that one can experience a sense of injustice through identification with a perpetrator who violates the values of the observer. For example, while women seem certain to identify with the victim of a sexual assault, a man may experience the injustice of rape through his identification with the perpetrator and his awareness that the rapist's outrageous injustice was an act he himself would never commit.

Scroggs' (1976) research may be interpreted as providing an example of the consequences of such sex differences in identification. In this study, male and female subjects read descriptions of a rape in which the victim either offered physical resistance or did not. Women saw the rape as more severe when the victims described did not resist physically, since in their identification with the victim, they understood that no resistance meant no chance of escape, and was not a sign of compliance. Men, in their identification with the perpetrator, read "no physical resistance" as compliance and judged the rape to be less severe and assigned these rapists a lesser penalty than did the women.

It also seems probable that the more similar the observer is to the victim, or the more experiences of victimization the observer has had, the more likely that person will be to identify with the victim. The exception to this rule may be provided by those who are or have been victims themselves and who have endured severe and lasting victimizations. Such experiences have been shown to result in identification with the perpetrator or aggressor (Bettleheim 1943). In general, Lerner (1980) has suggested that the extent to which the sufferer shares the observer's societal role, status, we-group membership (e.g., ethnic group, family system), and politico-religious ideology may determine the observer's capacity to identify with the victim (or the perpetrator).[1]

Explaining the Injustice and Reducing the Arousal

Observers will seek to explain the injustice and to reduce the arousal (i.e., distress, upset, dissonance) that has accompanied the perception of injustice. They will seek explanations that are least disruptive of their view of how justice works, enable them to construct meaningful (non-chance) reasons for the victim's suffering, and meet their own psychological needs for a sense of personal safety and self-esteem (Coates et al 1979; Lerner 1980; Wortman 1976; Wortman & Brehm 1975). This explanation-seeking step in the psychological process of responding to injustice has received the most concerted attention by researchers, since it is during the final, arousal-reduction phase that evidence appears for the psychological activities of the preceding stages. The issue of compelling and continuing interest in this area is the tendency of observers to make sense of injustice by derogating the victim (Coates et al. 1979; Lerner 1977, 1980; Lerner & Matthews 1967; Lerner & Miller 1978; Lerner & Simmons 1966; Shaver 1970, 1975; Walster 1966). Theoretical and empirical work on observers' reactions to victims has led to the delineation

---

1. These concerns about identification are of great importance to attorneys, who wish to select jurors likely to share their view of where the injustice lies. Asking the right questions and knowing what answers to listen for during the jury selection process (voire dire) has led to an active collaboration between lawyers and psychologists (see chapter 11).

of two points of view. The more broadly constructed view notes that observers derogate victims in order to perceive the world as just. The victim may be blamed by virtue of his or her character, or in terms of transient, behavioral qualities (Janoff-Bulman 1978; Janoff-Bulman and Frieze 1983; Wortman 1976). Others have stated that this position is too sweeping—That if one identifies strongly with a victim, then derogation will not occur, since it would be tantamount to self-derogation (Aderman et al. 1974; Shaver, 1970, 1975).

The Role of Identification in Explanation: Two Hypotheses. Researchers acknowledge that the extent of an observer's vicarious involvement or identification with another's suffering is the essential component in the creation of the observer's need to seek a reduction in tension through explanation and in the form this explanation will take (Lerner 1977, 1980; Shaver 1970; 1975; Wortman 1976). Lerner's Just World hypothesis states that the victim is selected—and therefore derogated—in order to explain the injustice. The observers' identifications with the victim is presumably moderate: while they can imagine themselves in the victim's position, they can nevertheless make easy distinctions between the victim and themselves, for either behavioral or characterological reasons (Janoff-Bulman 1979). Shaver (1970, 1975) proposed however, in his Defensive Attribution theory, that the victim will not be used as the basis for arousal reduction and will not be derogated when the observer's identification with the victim is high. Such as explanation would be akin to a self-derogation. (If identification is very low, then no sense of aroused injustice is created; there is no need for an explanation.) Let us now examine these hypotheses more closely.

The Just World. Lerner and other researchers whose work has supported the Just World Hypothesis have argued that observers do identify with victims (although they do not say how much), and that through this identification, they confront their own vulnerability to such victimization. (See for example Janoff-Bulman & Frieze 1983; Lerner 1980; Lerner & Matthews 1967; Lerner & Simmons 1966; Rubin & Peplau 1975.) Presumably, this sense of personal vulnerability frightens the observers and accounts for a large portion of the injustice-related distress they experience. This fear motivates a detailed examination of the circumstances of the injustice, and in particular, causes observers to search for and to create evidence for dif-

ferences between the victims and themselves. These differences are
then applied to the process of explaining why the victim is suffering
when the observer is not. This explanatory process also serves to
reduce the observer's sense of identification with the victim. A belief in the Just World exists as an outgrowth of what Heider (1958)
described as a "pervasive cognitive tendency stemming from the
general principle of cognitive balance." In this view, people who act
as if the world were just are expressing their motivated urge to
maintain cognitive balance or psychological homeostasis. The distress which results from an experienced sense of injustice must be
reduced and leads the observer to restore balance by creating a match
between the "bad" event and the "bad" victim, thereby derogating
the victim.

This reaction to victimization counters idealistic expectations
about the sort of response victims should evoke from others and
indicates that victims of injustice may be met with rejection, instead of compassion. This tendency is especially potent if the observer is unable to help or compensate the victim, another factor
which points out the role of the observer's ego in determining reactions to victims (Lerner & Matthews 1967; Walster et al, 1973).
Clearly, the belief in a Just World and the conclusions about the
victim that follow from it function to "protect" the observer. As
Coates et al. (1979) noted: "the judgments and evaluations that people make about unfortunate others are primarily determined by their
own needs for security or self-esteem rather than the reaction or
behaviors of the victim" (p. 25).

In some sense, the ultimate "proof" of this process resides with
the fact that the victim may be derogated even in the face of events
that are clearly the results of chance or bad luck. Studies have demonstrated that observers derogated victims of low numbers in the
draft lottery (Rubin & Peplau 1975), and people whose parked cars
became involved in an accident (Walster 1966).

In studies where the consequences of the chance victimizations
were most severe, and the victims suffered the effects of physical
disability, violent crimes, and sickness or death, the tendency of nonvictims to avoid, reject, blame, and denigrate victims of these injustices was exacerbated (Kleck 1968; Kleck et al. 1966; Symonds
1975; Wortman & Dunkell-Schetter 1979). Two interdependent psychological processes appear to be operating in these observers of terrible misfortune. First, the observers, through their moderate identification with the victim, fear that the suffering they witness might

also befall them. This fear gets resolved as they call upon the second psychological process—the motivated urge to believe that events in their lives are meaningful, the world is just, and only those who deserve to suffer do so. Thus, the fear of one's victimization, together with the reluctance to attribute suffering to bad luck (which would heighten the observer's fear of victimization) bring about derogation of the victim.

It seems likely that the apparent absence of meaning and the role of chance in noninterpersonal victimizations is especially threatening. Then, there is no intentional perpetrator to blame; the only other person in the situation is the victim, who becomes the center of attention for the observer, and therefore, the center of causal thinking about why the victimization occurred (Jones & Davis 1965; Nisbett & Valins 1972; Ross & Ditecco 1975). One might believe, then, that when an intentional perpetrator is involved, that this perpetrator will be assigned responsibility for bringing about the suffering, and that the victim would be offered the observer's support. Paradoxically, this is not the case. Interpersonal victimizations, which implicate an intentional perpetrator, have also been shown to result in negative evaluations of the victim and an unduly heavy assignment of blame to the victim for her or his own victimization (Coates et al 1979; Lerner & Matthews 1967; Lerner & Simmons 1966). Perhaps an explanation for injustice in terms of the perpetrator's intentions, much like an attribution to chance, is too threatening. If the perpetrator is to blame, he or she could strike again and hurt the observer.

Defensive Attribution Theory. Shaver (1970, 1975) stated that high identification does not facilitate high perceived vulnerability. The results of a Lerner-style study by Aderman et al. (1974), in which subjects were instructed to observe others receive electric shocks, included this modification: Subjects were asked to imagine that they were in the victim's place. Results supported Shaver's contention. Empathic observers did not derogate the victim.

Attribution theory has also been applied in elaboration of this finding. A basic tenet of attribution theory notes that actors attend to the situational constraints and influences on their behaviors when explaining why they acted as they did. Observers attend to the actors, and their causal attributions tend to focus on characteristics and propensities of the actor, not on the surrounding environment. Ross and Ditecco's (1975) research has supported the finding that when observers assume the role of the victim or actor, their focus of attention shifts and the situational factors come into focus as the important causal factors. Thus, the tendency to derogate the victim is diminished.

In Sum. The Defensive Attribution view should hold when the observer's identification with the victim is so high that it is as if the observer were the victim. Then ego defensive motives should combine with an altered attributional perspective and promote the elaboration of explanations for injustice that do not derogate the victim. Otherwise, when observers can avoid intense identification with victims, they should do so, and Lerner's Just World Hypothesis should predict the behavior of observers of injustice. Note that identification with the aggressor may create an incapacity to identify with the victim and may eliminate the sense of injustice. This inability to see injustice functions as a derogation of the victim and his or her plight.

IMPLICATIONS FOR INTIMATE VIOLENCE VICTIMS

When considering the reactions of others to victims of intimate violence, the model outlined here and the theoretical perspectives reviewed above help to shape an understanding of why victims of rape and family violence have often experienced nonsupportive, victim-blaming responses from others. Historically, myths about rape victims cast these women as seductresses, or at least as willing participants in their own abuse (Berger 1977; Brownmiller 1975; Griffin 1975; Russell 1975). Similar stereotypes have existed for battered women, who were further victimized by the prevailing view that, "If she stays, she must like it. She must do something to provoke it."

The condemnatory attitudes of police, family court workers and social service personnel toward battered women have been well documented (e.g., Schechter, 1983, Woods, 1978). Even family members may be unsympathetic. Consider this comment by a woman in a shelter who was asked why she did not turn to her mother for help. She replied, "I did ask her for help. She said, 'You made your bed. Now lie in it.'"

Intimate violence assaults are severe and traumatic for victims and seem likely to elicit high levels of distress in those who learn about such victimizations. The history of these events as personal and taboo, which were supposed to evoke feelings of shame in the victims, continues to shape the reactions of others. Simply by applying these traditional, victim-blaming attitudes to the situation of rape survivors or battered women, uncomfortably high levels of distress may be reduced and observers may feel protected from the fear that such victimizations could befall them. Understandably, confronting such attitudes in others is disastrous for the victim, who, like the vicariously involved observer, experiences a high level of upset that requires resolution. In the next chapter, the self-perceptions of victims of intimate violence and their coping activities are explored.

3

SELF-PERCEPTIONS OF BATTERED WOMEN, ABUSED CHILDREN, AND RAPE SURVIVORS

———

A former abused child talked about abuse by her husband:

I didn't know anything else. I didn't really think I had a choice. I know it sounds strange, but it was like I had only one path all my life . . . and I just didn't have anything to really guide myself by.

A woman who left an abusive relationship said:

I felt very cheated and sometimes I still do. I'm getting over it, but I feel I did everything right. I tried very hard, I was a good girl. I raised my kids right, I behaved right as a wife and mother and I did everything I could do and everything came out wrong anyway. And now I realize that it's because the whole thing was a naive dream, even if it was culture-wide, it was stupid.

Another woman who left an abusive relationship commented:

I came to feel like I was no good . . . he was constantly repeating . . . 'you're no good,' or 'you should feel guilty.' And, after a while . . . I was accepting the punishment, along with being afraid to fight back . . . What he said were the only words I heard. And there were no good ones. He became my conscience in a way. When I was away from him, I would almost hear his voice and feel guilty.

A survivor of rape by casual acquaintances offered this self-perception:

The rape itself, I actually have to blame . . . part of it on myself, and a good majority of it on the guys, because . . . they . . . actually instigated the whole thing. But, . . . I think that my overfriendliness may have given them the wrong idea, too. . . . I think if I had been more to myself and . . . not so enjoying of people's company, and just stayed back a little bit, maybe that would not have happened.

These quotes, from four different women, show how they attempt to explain their perceptions of themselves in the contexts of their violent relationships or—in the case of the last individual—to explain her rape, itself. They are taken from the interview data my research assistants and I gathered from newspaper readers in northern New Jersey in 1980.

These statements also illustrate, by example, the nature of much psychological research on victims. This body of research is based on reports from victims *themselves*. Thus, research with victims of rape and family violence differs markedly from the laboratory-type research done with observers of victimization.

The research strategy of choice is the intensive interview, in which victim-subjects are asked to talk at some length about their experiences with and reactions to violence (Becker and Abel 1981; Blackman-Doron 1980b, Blackman 1987a, 1987b; Browne 1987; Burgess & Holmstrom 1974a, 1974b, 1974c, 1978, 1979a, 1979b; Dobash & Dobash 1980; Frieze 1979a, 1979b; Pagelow 1981, 1984; Walker 1979, 1984). An exception to that choice is exemplified in the literature on child abuse. Child victims are typically not interviewed. The parent-perpetrator is seen as a victim of his or her life circumstances. In this way, adults may be studied for retrospective accounts of their victimization as children, and if they are child abusers, they may be asked about this.

The intensive interview method is quite effective at revealing reactions to victimization, although the specific characteristics of the abuse may vary greatly from one subject to another (even within a single "category" of abuse). The control typical of a laboratory experiment simply cannot be attained. This reality has limited researchers' abilities to make causal or explanatory statements about self-perceptions or coping in victims of intimate violence.

In addition, concerns over representativeness affect the potential generalizability of research findings. (See chapter 1, for a detailed discussion of this problem.) Interviews can be conducted only with those willing to be interviewed; underreporting places limits the implications to be drawn from research with victims.

Nevertheless, a number of large-scale, interview studies have been conducted with victims of family violence and rape. Researchers have contacted and interviewed women in shelters and hospital emergency rooms, women and men who have responded to newspaper and magazine advertisements, signs in laundromats, and "word of mouth" communications about the location of an interested psychologist. The collective, qualitative data base now reflects the experiences of thousands of people. Nontraditional sampling procedures notwithstanding, the detailed reality of subjects' elicited experiences has illuminated an area of former darkness—the psychological reactions of victims/survivors, themselves.

Early publications on the nature of victims' experiences relied primarily on first-person accounts (Davidson 1978; Gingold 1976; Hake 1977; Langley & Levy 1977; Martin 1976; Metzger 1976; Remsburg & Remsburg 1979; Renvoize 1978; Russell 1975; Warrior 1976) and clinicians' files (Fassberg 1977; Fox & Scherl 1972; Hilberman & Muson 1978; Nadelson & Notman 1979; Notman & Nadelson 1976; Ottenberg 1978; Sutherland & Scherl 1970). These studies involved small numbers of subjects and presented the experiences of victims of rape and family violence in terms of illustrative case study examples. Interpretations by the authors of these articles underlined the severe psychological consequences of acts of intimate violence. Fear, anxiety, loss of one's sense of safety, varying crisis-time reactions (ranging from pseudo-calm to severe upset), and self-implicating attributions of blame are among the consequences noted in these early publications as sequelae to family violence and rape (Burgess & Holmstrom 1974a, 1974b, 1974c; Fox & Scherl 1972; Ottenberg 1978; Sutherland & Scherl 1970). Later, larger-scale research efforts elaborated these findings and contributed to current descriptions of battered women and victims of child abuse and rape.

RISKY RESEARCH ON THE PSYCHOLOGICAL CHARACTERISTICS OF BATTERED WOMEN

Psychological research on the victims of a social problem is always risky in conceptualization and in the tension between intended and actual impact. As Wardell et al. (1983) aptly pointed out, research which focuses on the characteristics of victims inherently assigns blame to them. Even if the traits identified as characteristic of battered women are viewed as reactions to the abuse and not as predisposing conditions for abuse, the emphasis still remains, perniciously, on the victim. Simple inattention to the batterer lessens the sense of his culpability. Perhaps this result of victim-focused research explains the relative shortage of such work by psychologists. Sociologists, whose training leads to an emphasis on the social structure rather than the individual, are better represented than psychologists on the list of the most active researchers on the problems of intimate violence.

In spite of the risks, I believe that research that emphasizes the individual's psychology and life circumstances can be of significant value. (See Kidder & Fine 1986 for a discussion of the effects of defining problems at different "levels," i.e., individual, societal.) The people who are the victims of social problems live their lives as individuals, not as social issues. They do not conceptualize themselves as social scientists might conceptualize them, and we would do them a disservice to insist that they represent their problems only in terms of the social order and its inherent injustices. It is not simply unlikely but actually insufficient for a battered woman to say to herself, "I am a victim of the patriarchy, of the unequal distribution of power in this society." That level of explanation provides little in the way of direct coping with day-to-day life. Further, many battered women do not consider themselves to be feminists and do not see themselves as activists in the Women's Movement. As a result, the advantages they may gain from our work are derivative—if indeed our work succeeds at decreasing such violence— and are more likely to be reflected in the lives of their daughters or granddaughters than in their own lives.

Another reason why work on the psychology of victims of intimate violence is important is reflected in the plight of a battered woman who has killed her abuser and pleads not guilty by reason of self-defense. When she does so it is her psychology that actually goes on trial. While the severity of the violence that she has endured will certainly be presented to the jury, they will be instructed to acquit or convict on the basis of their assessment of the reasonableness of her act. The jury's deliberations will center around the victim's mental state and the correctness of her perception that her life was at stake.

Thus, while a feminist perspective has been rightly influential in drawing attention away from blaming the victim, our scholarship can best be of use at such trials of battered women who kill if we are prepared to address their psychological state. Social scientists can provide material aid only if they are able to respond with relevant theory and data. And attention to the individual should be a scientific, not an intuitive, enterprise (Blackman 1987c; Blackman & Brickman 1984).

This advocacy for the development of theory and research which attends to the victim's psychological state is not an advocacy for changing the prevailing definition of the problem as a *social* problem. In fact, the individual should be clearly placed in her social context. Work on the psychology of victims of abuse should stand together with the more broadly conceived work of which it is a part.

To the extent that the work of psychologists provides insight for therapeutic interventions or shapes the legal decisions and precedents that moderate individuals' fates, psychology's contribution to the growing body of research is justified. With attendant risks acknowledged here and throughout, the results of psychological research are presented. When the research reviewed here provided bases for the questions investigated in my study, those connections are stated here. What follows is not intended as an exhaustive review of the literature, but instead is a presentation of several "highlighted" studies, the theory and results of which had an impact on my own research.

ON THE PSYCHOLOGY OF BATTERED WOMEN

Only three years after the first book was published on battered women (Martin 1976), the first book based on a large-scale psychology study of battered women appeared. Walker's *The Battered Woman*, (1979), was based upon detailed interviews with a self-volunteered, self-identified sample of about 120 battered women. Walker, a clinical psychologist, summarized the characteristics of these women who had endured chronic abuse at the hands of their husbands, and offered a theory to explain why these victims remained in abusive relationships. She listed nine characteristics of battered women, including low self-esteem, traditional attitudes about family life, feelings of responsibility and guilt in relation to the batterer's actions, and severe stress reactions. In addition, Walker offered an advance over previous work in this area by applying Seligman's (1975; Abramson et al 1978) theory of learned helplessness to the situation of battered women. The relevance of this theory was deduced by listening to the tapes of the interviews.

Thus, Walker suggested that battered women remained in abusive relationships because they learned to be "helpless"—learned that they were unable to control or prevent their husbands' violent outbursts. In spite of this belief, these women still maintained a sense of responsibility for provoking the assaults against them. Thus, they would appear to be trapped in a situation of inherent inconsistency. They may believe that they cause the abuse, but cannot cause it to stop. They are simultaneously in control and out of control. While Walker does not develop this point, the fundamental inconsistency that must exist in such an individual's mental life seems staggering and may be immobilizing. This idea became one of the topics for investigation in my own research. (See the findings and the discussion relevant to the notion of "tolerating cognitive inconsistency in chapters 9 and 10.)

In Walker's (1984) subsequent research, she continued her investigation of learned helplessness as an explanation for why women stay with men who abuse them. While her theory "held" in some respects, its limitations also became clear. Walker suggested that women who volunteer to participate in studies may suffer less from this state of mind than those battered women who remain at home. Still, in some cases, her subjects were active and effective and saw themselves as such. Further, Walker has acknowledged that any women available for interviewing had obviously been active enough to keep themselves alive, even in the face of serious physical attacks. Finally, by 1984, Walker had testified in numerous trials for battered women who had killed their husbands and was led to conclude that, at least under some circumstances, battered women were capable of perceiving the need for their own effective action. Even a woman who has been abused for a long time may finally retain the ability to defend herself.

Walker did point out that these women were unlikely to consider

escape as a viable option and that this was consistent with the idea
that learned helplessness narrows perceived options. Again, while
she did not explore the diminution in perceived options, she created
a basis for such a consideration. That idea, too, is explored in chapters 9 and 10.

In addition to its remarkable sample size of 403, Walker's (1984)
study was important to psychology for its attention to personality
traits and lifestyle factors (e.g., prior abuse, short courtship, early
pregnancy), as they related to victimization. Also, in an effort to
create a comparison group, Walker gathered data on 203 of her subjects about times of abuse and times of nonabuse in their intimate
relationships and used them as their own controls. She concluded
that battered women displayed behaviors that were fundamentally
reactive to the beatings. The major source of power was seen to reside in the batterer. While no overall victim-prone personality ty-
pology could be created, there did seem to be a abuser-prone personality which began in childhood and worsened as the men aged.

With regard to specific personality traits, one surprising finding
showed that battered women rated themselves high on a self-esteem
measure. Not surprisingly, they reported themselves high on depression indices. However, this finding is muddled by the observation
that they do not report feeling depressed. And contrary to expectation, Walker found, "Women out of the battering relationship for
the longest time seen to have a higher risk of depression than those
women still in the relationship" (p. 151).

By any account, these findings are difficult to make sense of and
may be best understood as indications that more research is needed.
One of the dangers of a large sample size and many questions is that
statistical significance may be found more readily for small, psychologically trivial relationships and differences. Efforts to establish
the meaningfulness of these relationships and differences may be an
exercise in conceptual futility. Whether or not this has happened in
the case of some of Walker's conclusions (see Walker 1984: 148–
151), requires further investigation.

At about the same time that Walker (1979) was conducting her
first major research project on battered women, Frieze (1979a), a social psychologist, undertook an empirical study of 74 battered women
living in the Pittsburgh area. Frieze's work followed in the tradition
of attribution theory researchers. The focus of her work was on the
battered women's explanations for their husbands' and their own
behaviors. With regard to the first violent episode, she asked, "Did

you understand at the time why he was violent?" Responses were coded in terms of the two major dimensions of attributional processes—the locus of causality (internal or external to the respondent), and the stability of the causal factor (a stable characteristic of the individual or situation or an unstable, changeable characteristic).

With regard to the first violent incident, the most frequently offered locus of causality was no explanation at all. Approximately 37 percent of the 68 battered women responded with "don't knows." This finding is interesting in itself when we consider the general reluctance to avoid chance explanations for events that affect us strongly. However, it should be remembered that subjects were describing the first incident only.

For those who offered some explanation, wives (selves) were 1.3 times as likely as husbands to be blamed; 32 percent blamed themselves while 25 percent blamed their husbands, and 6 percent explained the violence in terms of joint blame. This result must be contrasted with Frieze's finding that for a *hypothetical* battering situation, 82 percent blamed the husband and less than 10 percent blamed the wife. The issue of perceived blame is important for the psychological functioning of the individuals involved and for the way they are perceived by others. (Especially in the courtroom, one's depictions of who was to blame plays a crucial role in determining trial outcomes.) Questions of blame are addressed in my study as well, and explorations into patterns of blame and related perceptions of the marital relationship (e.g., as good or bad) are detailed in chapter 7.

With regard to the stability of the explanations in Frieze's study, 56 percent were unstable, and 54 percent were "don't knows" or uncertain. Only 6 percent were stable attributions to invariant aspects of the husband or the situation. Frieze (1979a) concluded that battered women were quite high in self-blame but that, at least at the time of the first incident, they did not consider the reasons for the violence to be stable. While this is an interesting finding, the use of first-time data only may be misleading. Further analysis of the data revealed tendencies for women who had been more seriously hurt to see their husbands as the cause and to see the cause as more stable.

Frieze (1979a) also gathered data about coping. She reported that "Attempting to change their behavior was a typical response . . . regardless of whether they blamed themselves or not" (p. 103). Further, she discovered that self-blaming women, who saw the cause for the abuse as stable, were twice as likely to have sought psychotherapy for marital problems as women who blamed their husbands. This latter group of husband-blamers was more likely to want to leave the relationship and so were women who made stable attributions for the violence. However, wanting to leave was not the same as actually trying to leave, and these significant relationships did not occur for women who actually tried to leave.

Efforts to regain control seem to underlie the trends reported by Frieze. Changing one's behavior may be a way of controlling the occurrence of violence. Seeking psychotherapy provides a new perspective and new insight on viable options. Such activity may function to promote a sense of injustice in the victim and lead to psychological activity designed to reduce that press. Wanting to leave also expresses a wish for control over one's life and safety.

The pursuit of control delineated here is inconsistent with Walker's finding that battered women suffer from learned helplessness. Instead, Frieze's findings seem more consistent with the theory of psychological reactance, a process through which victims assert their own strength and seek to regain control over their outcomes. The theory of psychological reactance predicts that victims will protect and defend their egos and good self-concepts. They will not become passive or self-derogating in response to adversity but instead will fight back.

Obviously, with regard to battered women, psychological reactance and learned helplessness make opposite predictions. Fortunately, in 1975, Wortman and Brehm collaborated on an article which integrated these two perspectives, and while their work did not deal specifically with battered women they did suggest which theory should work best in which general case. They stated that reactance should occur only if control is expected and outcomes are important. They suggested that reactance will precede helplessness for those who originally expected control but that when people become convinced that they cannot control their outcomes, they will stop trying. In addition, they noted that helplessness or passivity may not be all bad:

> If an organism finds itself in a less stressful state as a result of becoming passive, it is likely to be motivated to remain in a passive state, and to resist attempts by outsiders to provoke active responses. (Wortman & Brehm, 1975: 328)

The "adaptive value" of helplessness and reactance may vary over time. Presumably, if Wortman and Brehm (1975) are correct, reactance will rise in value if one expects to be in control and feels the issue at contest is important. Expectations about real control are shaped not only by factors in the lives of individuals but also by social factors, like the inequitable distribution of power by class, race and gender. Thus, in considering the psychological "choice" of adaptive strategy, constraints on the realities of women's lives must be acknowledged. I investigated the presence of "adaptive" strategies under the title of "Coping Activities," and the results of this portion of the study appear in chapter 8. Also, real world constraints figure directly in the perception of alternatives, a topic considered from a theoretical perspective in chapter 4. Data on this issue appear in chapter 9.

ON ABUSED CHILDREN

Unlike research on wife abuse and rape, research on child abuse typically has focused not on the victims but on the perpetrators and on explanations for the victimization that rest with the social forces (e.g., poverty, discrimination) that create stress in the abuser's life and render the abuser a victim. This difference in focus is an interesting phenomenon, given the tendency to emphasize the victim rather than the perpetrator or environmental factors in efforts to explain most sorts of interpersonal injustice.

Perhaps, our shared belief that small children are innocent and entitled to good treatment has led to this attention to the perpetrators of child abuse. If attention to the victim is too close to blaming the victim, then the relative absence of children from the literature on child abuse suggests that children will not be blamed for their own abuse. That is, we will not risk derogating children by a search for the causes for abuse in them. Explanations *must* lie elsewhere.

However, this view would suggest that victims of child abuse should receive concerted positive attention from our social institutions. This has not been the case (Nelson 1983). In the extreme case of children who kill abusive parents, the state seems to deal with them more harshly than with women who kill abusive husbands. Based on the cases of which I am aware, children were more likely than women to be convicted and to go to jail (Blackman 1986; Morris 1984).

A better explanation for the relative inattention to child victims, seems to rest with the view that the adult abuser is not a true perpetrator but, as Zigler (1979) suggested, "another victim of social forces beyond his or her control" (p. 37). This position dominates research on the abuse of children within families, a factor which has not only supported the special tendency not to blame the victim, but has also fostered an empirical inattention to the consequences of such violence for the victims themselves—the children. As Elmer and Gregg (1979) noted, "Although abuse has been widely assumed to be harmful beyond the immediate physical effects, to date there has been a paucity of definitive studies to document this belief . . . This (theirs) is the only known study of abuse which was based on examination of the children as well as interviews with the caretakers; the study was retrospective in nature" (p. 295).

More recent research on child abuse has touched on the nature of children's experiences in violent families (Newberger & Bourne 1985; Snyder & Newberger 1986). However, research on child abuse has a strong policy emphasis—something which is less true for research on battered women. Thus, children's experiences are detailed with a view toward improving the identification of abused children in hospital settings, toward enhancing decisions about where abused children should live, and so on (Hampton & Newberger 1985; Newberger & Snyder 1986). Less attention has been paid to the nature of children's psychologies, to the impact of their parents' violence on their beliefs about justice, blame, or the nature of intimacy.

With regard to the nature of intimacy, research with maltreated and neglected children has focused on a construct called "security of attachment" which speaks to the psychological consequences of parental mistreatment (Ainsworth 1978, Stern 1985). The experiences of maltreated or neglected children are described in terms of a poor or insecure attachment to the parent. Their resulting tendency to avoid parental contact, not to seek parental comfort even when in a strange situation, has been documented as one of the earliest signs of negative parent-child interactions (Kagan 1984).

However, analogous attention has not occurred in specific connection to abuse and its psychological impacts on the child. As Elmer and Gregg (1979) noted, the harm is assumed. Perhaps the reasons for this greater emphasis on policy, and lesser emphasis on the psychological consequences for the child, are obvious after all. Researchers can not ethically study that relationship, which once discovered *must* be changed. Treatment takes strong precedence over any academic interest in in-vivo observation.

Elmer and Gregg (1979) did study 20 children, drawn primarily from a group of 50 abused children admitted to Children's Hospital in Pittsburgh between 1949 and 1962. They reported that only two of the 20 children were normal in all the areas considered (e.g., physical growth and size, intelligence, emotional stability), "thus confirming the speculation that severe physical abuse is predictive of unusual difficulties in development" (p. 305).

Additional developmental difficulties seem certain to exist in the area of moral development, as these children struggle to resolve the essential dilemma of their lives: a loving parent who inflicts severe injury. One resolution is reflected in our knowledge that many abusing parents were themselves abused children (Gil 1979; Kempe et al. 1962; Steele & Pollack 1968, Zigler 1979).

With regard to conceptions of justice, per se, it is certain that ideas about fairness are strongly influenced by the way parents treat their children. If, from the time of earliest memory, those who provide love are also those who inflict suffering, then it seems likely that children will acquire distorted perceptions of their entitlement to good treatment at the hands of their caretakers. Further, early victimization by an all-powerful parent seems likely to leave lasting scars on the individual's psychological understanding of justice. High levels of interpersonal violence will be more easily tolerated.

Research on the authoritarian personality demonstrated a clear connection between a child's experiences with harsh parental discipline and such subsequent psychological limitations as rigidity, intolerance of weakness, and suspiciousness (Adorno et al. 1950). This line of thinking also revealed that child victims might resolve their upset at being abused by identifying with the abuser (Bettleheim 1943). Such an identification yields an obvious explanation for why abused children grow up to be abusing parents.

The focus on authority embodied in Adorno et al.'s (1950) and Bettleheim's (1943) work, coincides with the central concerns of Piaget's (1928) first, heteronomous, stage of moral development. At this point, children see outside sources of authority as all-important in determining right and wrong, justice and injustice. Young children are said to have moved beyond this authority-based conception of justice when they become more flexible and relativistic (as opposed to absolute) in their thinking. Consider, however, what happens to abused children who may be desperately engaged in psychological efforts to identify with the abusing parent. Will they be able to risk a change in their perceptual schema for understanding unfairness? Or, is the stress of their environment too great to permit such developmental growth? It seems likely that abused children fixate at this early stage in their moral development and that this fixity characterizes and influences their own adulthood and child-raising practices. (This suggestion is investigated in chapter 4, on the perception of alternatives, since the move from the early, heteronomous stage of development to the later, autonomous stage depends on the acquired knowledge that any formulation of what is just is only one among several. No single authority can provide all justice. Data on this topic are presented in chapters 7 and 9.)

While the results of intensive interviews with individuals who were abused as children appear in chapters 7 through 10, an anecdote from this study is useful here. A woman responded to the newspaper survey (described in chapter 5), and volunteered to be interviewed by writing her name and telephone number at the bottom of the page. She was called by one of the project research assistants, and she set up an appointment to be interviewed in person. All potential interviewees were given my name and telephone number and were told they could call me if they had any questions about the study. The day after she had agreed to be interviewed, this woman called me. She was quite upset and said that she could not participate in the study. She could hardly believe that she had volunteered to be interviewed. She then proceeded to explain that as a child she had been abused by her mother. She was currently married and had three children. She reported that she had never told anyone, including her husband, about her mother's abuse of her. She continued, "I could never come in and be interviewed. My mother is still alive and it would hurt my mother too much if she knew that I talked about anything. I could never hurt my mother that way. I love my mother, I could never hurt her that way."

I explained that, of course, she did not have to participate, but that she should know that anything she said would be kept in strict confidence and her mother need never find out. The woman seemed surprised by that, and replied that, of course, her mother would know—she would find out. The woman refused to reconsider although she was 37 years old at the time of our conversation. She had retained a child's sense of imminent justice, of the omniscience of an all-powerful authority figure who always knows when wrongdoing has occurred.

ON RAPE SURVIVORS

When I began this project, I was involved with research on both family violence and rape and I believed that, with enough elaboration, a conceptual link could be made between them, under the single heading, "Intimate Violence." However, the double meaning inherent in the word "intimate" has troubled me. Simply, it means different things when it is being applied to family violence than when it is being applied to rape. Family violence is intimate emotionally. Rape acquires properties of intimacy only in the physical intimacy of the invasion. Thus, intimate violence, in this work, simply has two meanings. In this section, I deal with the second meaning: when violence is physically intimate, but the perpetrator is a stranger. (The real differences between the sorts of suffering that attend family violence and those that result from rape made it impossible to include rape survivors among the "victims of intimate violence" whose interview responses are considered in chapters 7 through 10. However, survey data from the rape survivors are presented in chapter 6.)

While I am on the issue of language, I would like to explain my use of "rape survivor" instead of "rape victim" (Blackman 1985a). Because of the acute nature of the assault, it seems right and empowering to characterize rape as a victimization and the individual as a survivor. Rape most often involves a single, acute assault, although some substantial number of survivors of rape are raped more than once (Miller et al. 1978). (It should be noted that marital rape is considered here within the context of spousal abuse.)

Here, in an effort to maintain general comparability with the preceding attention to different sorts of family violence, the literature on reactions to rape is reviewed. However, the themes explored in this section are not re-raised in the presentation of my findings. They are taken into account, though, in the summary chapters of this book, where reflections are offered on the nature of reactions to the bodily victimization of the less powerful by the more powerful.

Thus, while attention to rape is a part of this study in some ways it can provide only a comparison group for victims of family violence rather than a "kindred" group. Ultimately, there are three conceptual groups represented here: victims of ongoing abuse in intimate relationships, nonvictims of such treatment, and survivors of a single interpersonal assault where the nature of the assault cruelly mimics and violates intimacy. The forms of victimization share something in that they reflect a more powerful person preying on a characteristically weaker one. Husbands hurting their wives, parents hurting their children, and males hurting females all exist within the significant context of power differences. This commonality, notwithstanding, I acknowledge that the consideration of rape survivors in this study is, in some respects, ancillary. They are here because I believe that their reactions add to the completeness of the images I am trying to put forth about injustice, intimacy and power inequity.

In general, studies on self-perceptions and coping in survivors of rape can be categorized in terms of the survivor's temporal distance from the rape. Studies have been published describing the immediate, short-term, and long-term consequences of rape (e.g., Burgess & Holmstrom, 1974a, 1974b, 1976, 1978, 1979a, 1979b; Ellis et al. 1981; Fox & Scherl 1972; Hardgrove 1976; Kilpatrick et al. 1979, 1981; McCombie 1976; Nadelson & Notman, 1979; Notman & Nadelson, 1976; Sutherland & Scherl, 1970; Symonds, 1975, 1976). Researchers have described two or three phases in recovery: (a) an acute phase which includes both immediate (within 24 hours) and short-term reactions (generally defined as occurring between 24 and 72 hours, although they may last as long as several weeks), and (b) a long-term or reorganization phase (which may begin as soon as two or three weeks after the rape and last for years). Since this research deals only with retrospective accounts of past rape experiences, and since long-term psychological consequences are my primary concern in this study of reactions to injustice, the research on immediate and short-term effects of rape is not reviewed here.

There are studies that document the long-term consequences of rape, although for the most part, the term "long-term" refers to a relatively short time in the course of one's life—sometimes as little as six months (Kilpatrick et al. 1979). In other studies, the time following the rape may have been a year (Ellis et al. 1981; Kilpatrick et al. 1981), or as long as four to six years (Burgess & Holmstrom 1978, 1979a, 1979b). In retrospective studies, the time frame may be longer and sometimes involve recollections and reports of recovery from rapes that are more than ten years old (Bart 1975; Becker 1981; Queen's Bench Foundation 1975).

Anecdotal data from my study demonstated that rape can be perceived as having dramatic long-term effects. A 48-year-old woman who responded to my newspaper survey on intimate violence attached this letter to her survey.

I think the age of the victim is an important factor; it bears heavily on one's sex knowledge, whether or not there is previous experiences, and an awareness of the possibility of the occurrence. In my case, I had no preparation, no warnings, no instruction on what to do. My age was 12, a very sensitive and impressionable time of life. . . . The experience was devastating to me, I was frightened to the point of being *petrified*. . . . The results were a drop from grades A and B to D at school, a distrust of all males, withdrawal from all social activities, rarely dating while growing up. I married late in life (35) and not until I was asked by a man who said he understood that I didn't want children and that it was all right with him. To me, this meant no sex, but afterwards, he changed his mind and pressured me to have the marriage consummated or get a divorce, this was 10 years after the wedding.

The studies cited above are quite diverse in terms of their theoretical orientations, the variables emphasized, the sampling methods, and the research instruments applied to the task of assessing survivors' psychological recovery from rape. Because of this study's focus on psychological reactions to injustice, three published studies which focus almost exclusively on behavioral consequences of the rape (e.g., sexual dysfunction, anxiety on dimly lit streets), are simply mentioned (Becker 1981; Kilpatrick et al. 1979, 1981).

The work on the psychology of rape survivors has paid little attention to the woman's efforts to reduce her upset by explaining the injustice done to her. Instead, the major emphases shared by the studies considered here have been on the nature of the survivor's distress (e.g., fear, depression) and on non-explanation-based forms of recovery from the assault (e.g., changing residences, decreasing fear through desensitization, reducing sexual dysfunction).

Perhaps the fact that rape is an acute assault rather than on ongoing form of abuse fosters this inattention to elaborate explanations as tension-reducers. Or, the perceived and/or real disappearance or inaccessibility of most rapists, coupled with the extreme upset that accompanies thinking about them, functions to draw attention away from the intentional actions of the rapist as an explanation for the injustice. The survivor is then left as the "only" participant, a factor which creates an automatic kind of victim-blaming in its inattention to the perpetrator. The consequences for the survivor's coping may be damaging. However, researchers have avoided making the problem of victim-blaming worse by not addressing the

"Why me?" question. Instead, the central question has been, "How bad does she feel after being raped and how long do these feelings last?"

This more descriptive approach has yielded results which demonstrate clearly that rape is an event with profound psychological consequences. For example, the studies conducted by the Queen's Bench Foundation (1975), Bart (1975) and Burgess & Holmstrom (1978, 1979a, 1979b) each included some measure of self-reported impact of the rape. The Queen's Bench Foundation study reported that 47 of the 55 respondents "Felt that they had suffered long-term psychological effects as a result of the rape; 89 percent felt the rape had affected their lives in a major way" (p. 24). According to Bart (1975) 98 percent of the 1070 subjects reported that the rape had an effect on their lives; 74 percent of the victims followed for four to six years by Burgess and Holmstrom (1978, 1979a, 1979b) had been affected by the rape, but felt recovered by the time of the long-term followup study—half of these within months, half within years. The remaining 26 percent remained affected by the rape and still did not feel recovered by the time of the followup study.

Burgess and Holmstrom (1978) reported that economic stress, chronic personal problems, alcohol or drug abuse, psychological disorders, prior victimization, and the absence of supportive responses from significant others tended to slow recovery (see also Miller and Porter 1983; Scheppele & Bart, 1983; *Journal of Social Issues* [1983] 39 [2]: entire issue). In contrast, women who had previously (at least two years prior to the rape) experienced a severe trauma (e.g., loss of parent or child), recovered sooner, presumably because they had developed greater inner resources for dealing with stressful life experiences. In their 1979 study, Burgess and Holmstrom reported that survivors recovered faster if they demonstrated positive feelings of self-esteem, generated cognitive explanations or attributions of blame, minimized or suppressed what had happened, dramatized their experience, and increased their level of activity. In a finding reported in the popular literature, they noted that women who were able to name a specific cause for the rape recovered more quickly than those who were faced with an entirely random, meaningless event (reported in the *New York Times*, April 14, 1978). Maladaptive responses, such as suicide attempts or serious abuse of drugs or alcohol, tended to slow recovery.

SUMMARY

Intensive interview studies have yielded much information about the self perceptions of battered women, abused children, and rape survivors. The interview as a strategy of choice was advocated and the results of significant studies were summarized with an explicit focus on their contributions to this study. In particular, the psychology of battered women was constructed around her tolerance of cognitive inconsistency, her perception of alternatives, the way she blames, her perceptions of her relationship as generally good or bad, and the nature of adaptive coping. While these concerns are generally relevant for abused children, too, the special additional concern created by attention to children focused on their concept of justice and the damage to their sense of justice that results from family violence. Information on the reactions of rape survivors is presented, although it does not lay the groundwork for predictions in this study (since rape survivors are not included in the interview data base). Instead, this review of "highlighted" studies in the area of rape research was intended to make elaborate the comparison group of rape survivors. The emphases and suggestions culled here from the literature on victims of marital battering and child abuse were used to provide the context and basis for my investigation of differences between the self perceptions of victims and nonvictims of family violence.

4

RECOGNIZING ALTERNATIVES AND SEEING PARADOXES

A man left his home and walked down the block to the bus stop. He got into an argument with a stranger and proceeded to hit him several times. When told of this encounter we ask, "Why was he so violent?" The man then returned home and got into an argument with his wife. He hit her several times. We ask, "Why did she stay?"

—from Fagan and Wexler (1987): 5

This example of two different explanations for one man's resort to interpersonal violence illustrates not only the role of bias in such attributions but also the clear potential for different solutions to the same problem—the reasons for the man's violence. "Real" reasons are unknowable at worst and elusive at best. Yet, the search for explanations for human behavior can be rivaled in enormity and complexity only by the range of human behavior itself.

THE JIGSAW PUZZLE ANALOGY

Psychologists who seek to explain behavior, especially those who study justice, do something that may be analogized to working a jigsaw puzzle. Pieces of a certain shape belong in certain spaces in the puzzle. A good fitting piece may be analogized to a just resolution of a problem. The piece has been properly fitted, based on its characteristics, which in this case involve only its shape.

Efforts to impose an incorrect solution on a jigsaw puzzle piece may be analogized to unjust resolutions of a problem. A piece may be forced to fit, in which case the piece's shape is distorted. Here, the fit is incorrect and the puzzle-worker would be expected to feel the constraints of the improper resolution. Or, the puzzle-worker might cut the piece to fit an available spot, thereby altering the very composition of the piece itself. While some initial discomfort might occur in the puzzle-worker, this re-formulated piece would ultimately achieve a snug, but an incorrect fit.

Note that this analogy is different from what one might expect of a thinker about justice. One might imagine that a seesaw or a balance would provide a better image. Our justice system lends weight to such a concept. Lady Justice carries scales that represent justice as a balance between what one deserves and what one gets.

There is a quantitative aspect to the scales image that works well for the weighing of evidence and the naming of outcomes, but does not capture the qualitative nature of individuals' efforts to make sense of their own experiences. Further, the scales image provides us with visual space for only two linked events. Injustices which occur in ongoing, interpersonal relationships may be understood in terms of many different formulations, some of which fit the problem better than others.

The jigsaw puzzle analogy also provides another useful image. There are right and wrong answers. And, at least theoretically, it should be possible for an observer to say when a piece was not properly a good fit, but was subject to distortions or dismemberment. It is also possible for us to imagine that several pieces—of different colors, say—might properly fit into the same size space. Thus, we are not obliged to see one resolution, or one even balance of the scales as the correct image for justice.

It might seem that puzzle workers would be motivated to get things right and find the correct niche for each piece. However, for any number of reasons, including the urge to make an individualized contribution to the puzzle process, one might derive a sense of satisfaction from fitting a piece incorrectly. Further, such misfits may call for continuing attention and involvement in a way that is unnecessary for a proper resolution, which brings an end to a problem-solving process.

Finally, in this analogy, it is possible for individuals to take puzzle pieces and put them in their pockets, and not work the puzzle at all. That is, the effort to make a match between some problem and its solution can simply be avoided.

While I do not invoke this analogy again until the end of this chapter, I hope that the reader will keep it in mind. It makes explicit some of my values, most particularly that there can be "right" answers, even in complex interpersonal relationships. Conversely, I think some solutions to problems are just wrong, even if the puzzle-worker has forgotten the original shape of the piece and sees only a part of the puzzle.

MAKING THE RIGHT CONNECTIONS

I was in the women's prison on Riker's Island in New York, speaking to Lurleen (not her real name), a battered woman who had killed her abusive common-law husband. She spoke about the violence she had committed against her 12-year-old daughter: "It's automatic," she said angrily. She meant that welts followed automatically from her use of an extension cord to beat her daughter. She was angry at me for reminding her that it was against the law for her to beat her child, to cover her body with welts. I had raised this issue with her because I was concerned that jurors would react negatively toward her if they learned that she was both a victim of abuse and an abuser of her children. She didn't see the connection and railed at me about the injustice being done her. "I didn't do anything wrong," she said, referring to wresting a knife out of her common-law husband's hand and stabbing him to death.[1]

Making the "right" connections, finding the "right" fit, is essential for understanding what is injustice. Connecting one's past to one's present, connecting one's personal experiences to the conditions of society, connecting the way things are to a way they could be, connecting injustices endured with injustices inflicted, create the bases for seeing alternatives to injustice and for acknowledging paradoxes that follow from false connections.

---

1. In this case, the jurors never learned of her abuse of her daughter. Her actions in the context of her common-law husband's attack against her constituted legal self-defense. She was acquitted of all charges, as she should have been. The law is crime-specific—her history of prior violence against a child was not relevant to her need to defend herself against her husband's abuse. Still, her lawyer took the proper precautions against prejudice in excluding her background from the jurors' consideration.

Lurleen, who "justified" her abuse of her daughter by invoking automatic properties of an extension cord striking flesh missed properties of her action that allowed her to avoid seeing herself as a "bad mother." She missed the "obvious" connection between her own intentions and her actions. She also missed the connection forged by the abuse she had experienced as a child at the hands of an aunt with an extension cord. And, she "failed" to attend to the way in which society had shaped her, what it meant to be a black female raised with six other children by an aunt in the South while your mother is in New York, to become pregnant at 15 and a mother of a son at 16. She did not consider the lasting consequences of slavery on American blacks, nor the effects of having spent all of her adult life on welfare, raising three children without the benefit of an earned source of income. The culture of violence and poverty in which she was raised, and which she was passing on to her children, allowed for little reflective thought about her life and the connections that preceded, shaped, and followed it.

The false connection she saw between the extension cord and the welts, the connections she failed to see between so many of the facts of her existence and her involvement in her child's suffering or her partner's death gave her a distorted sense of injustice. I would not want to rely on her sense of injustice as a guide to the rightness or wrongness of anyone's actions, including her own.

My judgmental feeling, my rejection of her standards for determining what was right, suggest that I know more about what is just than she does, that I make more "right" connections, and that my judgment is therefore better. The assertion about the rightness of connections is subjective. Perhaps I have selected her as an example because she provides such an easy contrast to prevailing, conventional standards for judging the rightness of such acts as the beating of one's child. Few of us defer to the "will" of the whip. Thus, she provides an easy illustration of making false connections and failing to make true ones.

Words like "false" and "true" suggest the existence of some absolute body of reference knowledge. As is the case for most of what interests psychologists, the referent in efforts to name what is unjust resides only in ourselves and others. The truth about injustice is not self-evident. The capacity to imagine, name, and prove connections determines one's sensitivity to injustice. That capacity is not innate, and is most seriously limited by those experiences that batter the individual. The earlier the violence against the person begins the greater the propensity to make false connections and never to see true ones.

For example, consider the missed connections in Lurleen's case between herself as a victim of racism, classism, and sexism and her current status as a battered woman and an abusive parent. For a specific injury by one person against another to feel like an instance of social injustice, alternatives to explanations that implicate people must be seen and connected to one's own circumstance (Crosby 1982; Crosby and Clayton 1986).

Thus, even if a battered woman saw that women, in general, were outpowered by men, it would not be enough to ensure that she would see herself as a victim of sexism. If she does not personally see the influence of men's advantage in her own life, then the effects of this social injustice would go unperceived and unexperienced. To refer briefly to the opening puzzle analogy, she would be keeping the problem-piece in her pocket.

Consider this quote from one of the women interviewed for this study. She was working to explain her rape by a stranger:

> I think our society is very violent. And that's going to show every-where. We condone it. We applaud it. We yell, "yea!" when the hero socks the villain or kills him or something like that, so I think that's going to raise the level of it, but I think a certain level of it is going to appear, no matter what. It is in the biology, it's in the uneven strength between the two sexes and the fact that women can be overpowered. (Was there anything you could have done to prevent what happened to you?) Yes, I could have not gotten into the car.

While she initially emphasized our society and its support of violence, in the end she held herself individually responsible for her own victimization. She exemplified a connection nearly forged between the personal and the political. Lurleen provided an extreme example of missed connections. More generally, it seems that most individuals engage in disconnections between social problems and their own lives (Crosby 1982; Crosby and Clayton 1986). Importantly, it is quite clear that personal suffering will not necessarily lead to an awareness of social injustice. Lane (1962) noted that the "common man" views his life in "morsels;" Abelson (1968) wrote about "opinion molecules." Experiences with personal injustice do not reliably lead to the forging of connections between one's own experiences and those of similar others. Indeed, our prevailing cultural tendency to blame the individual for his or her misfortune would seem to work directly to reduce the possibility of seeing interpersonal similarities. Thus, more often, it seems that an awareness of how one's personal victimization can be attributed to broader social factors will come first from relatively advantaged individuals who empathize with the greater suffering of others and set about to redefine its cause. Those blacks who came to redefine the causes for their suffering as a result of the actions and words of Martin Luther King provide an example of what seems likely to be the typical flow of injustice-awareness. That is, a leader inspires followers by naming a situation as unjust and proposing actions designed to make things better.

BECOMING AWARE OF INJUSTICE

Even in the presence of charismatic leaders, general awareness of the impacts of such social problems as sexism and racism makes halting progress into the personal awareness of individuals seeking solutions to their own life problems. However, such change *does* occur, as collective action by large numbers of people indicates. When some collective of people acknowledge together that things should be better, a sense of injustice can be said to be "mobilized," as action follows the shared belief that change is necessary. Such action may be effective or it may not, but is in either case based on a revised view of true connections and achievable alternatives. In large part, the process of making new alternatives felt is the basis for naming injustices and crafting reactions (Deutsch 1974, 1985, 1986; Fine 1980).

Failed attempts at change may produce decreases in the perception of alternatives as viable, and ultimately may lead to an incapacity to see future alternatives at all. However, a sense of resignation or despair, rather than a sense of injustice, would be expected to characterize those who had tried, but failed, and now, again, saw no alternatives as viable (Fine 1980; Steil 1980, 1983; Steil et al. 1978).

It is the first awareness of injury as injustice that I am concerned with here. Deutsch (1974) called it an "awakening," suggesting that it reflects an acknowledgement of a situation that was there, but was not seen. The injustice is not new: only the individual's awareness of it is.

Ways of Experiencing Injustice: Awareness and Action as Separate Dimensions

I propose here that there are five kinds of individual responses to injustices that can be attributed, in a larger analysis of personal problems, to the nature of society:

1. The injustice is not experienced because one neither sees nor connects to oneself any alternatives to the current situation.

2. An injustice comes to be experienced as one sees and "connects" with alternatives and thus cultivates a sense of hope for better times.

3. An injustice has been experienced for some time (or sometimes) when alternatives are seen and tried, but is replaced by a sense of resignation or despair when attempts to redefine and right the wrong fail.

4. An injustice comes to be experienced as alternatives are seen and "connected," and it motivates one toward effective action that reduces or eliminates the injustice and results in a sense of justice achieved.

5. An injustice is experienced as alternatives are seen, "connected," and continually recognized, but never attained. In this case, one would expect the presence of a strong and enduring sense of injustice and an accompanying willingness to engage in violent, reckless, or vengeful action that may not redress the existing injustice, per se, but will change the nature of the victims' suffering or cause others' suffering.

The scheme for ways of experiencing injustice is presented here as a context for the responses about injustice elicited by my study. The options available in this scheme are intended to address both the fundamental awareness that an injustice exists and the implications for action of an achieved awareness. While one could use this scheme of possible responses to injustice to categorize individuals, the categorizing would make these options appear prescriptive of an individual's state, or static, when I intend them actually to reflect potentially different aspects of the same individuals at different times. That is, the model names points in a dynamic flow from unseen to seen injustice, unanswered to answered injustice. It is not intended to provide lasting "diagnostic" category placements for single individuals and is not used in that way in my research. Instead, these options provide a context for the ebb and flow of awareness of injustice and action in the lives of victims and non-victims of family violence. One particularly important aspect of awareness is reflected in the ability to see alternatives to what exists.

Alternatives

One cannot mobilize a sense of injustice about one's own life if one is unaware of the alternatives. That this realization is acutely personal, far from objective, and not necessarily expressed in action is illustrated by the question in my experience most frequently asked about battered women:

"Why don't they leave?" This is a question about their apparent failure to recognize alternatives and then to take relationship-ending action, and is frequently, perniciously constructed as evidence for their sense that no injustice exists (Blackman 1987b). That battered women do not leave their men easily speaks to the difficulty of formulating, accepting, and acting on alternatives that would end the relationship. Because the relationship-ending alternative may be unavailable, avoided, or acknowledged only sporadically, one would expect battered women variously to experience resignation, despair, a sense of hope for the future, and a sense of injustice. (The ultimate relationship-ending alternative, the killing of the batterer, is discussed in detail in chapter 11 and is therefore not elaborated here.) It is important to acknowledge that battered women may be consistently adept at thinking about many "alternative" things to say or do within the relationship, in the hopes of stopping the violence and preserving the relationship.

Another class of alternatives exists that are especially unlikely to be seen when violence has long prevailed in family relationships. Here, I am raising the alternatives that would end violent relationships and that would repudiate the use of violence. That is, I am naming as "extra-relationship alternatives" those options based on an ethic of nonviolence, not on the importance of preserving the relationship.

These alternatives too often reside outside the imagination of the individual whose own life experiences are filled with violence. The nonviolent alternatives are, then, a kind of meta-alternative that may need to be advocated and explicitly taught in order to be understood as viable, especially by long-term victims of violence. Thus, the rationale for this sort of attention to alternatives derives from the emphasis on "connecting" societal injustice to one's personal situation, but is also influenced by my values. I believe that intimate relationships ought never to include violence, and that it is important to put forth this view. I am advocating for the view that, as a society, our most valued response to violence ought to follow from a belief in the worth of individual safety and integrity and not from beliefs in the primacy of marital bonds or biological kinship relations. I believe that much social injustice and personal pain follow from the worth attached to values that do not put the individual's entitlement to good treatment first.

Even if the process of "connecting" the value of individual entitlement to one's own life were easy—and we have good reason to believe it is not (Crosby 1982; Crosby & Clayton 1986)—it is still not surprising that this value does not seem to promote the perception of alternatives in victims of ongoing, interpersonal violence. Such an anti-violence value has little place in our culture. The value that would forbid intimate violence is a radical alternative to prevailing values about the importance of marriage (in spite of our very high divorce statistics), the general right of biological parents to raise their children (even if abuse or neglect is suspected), and the effectiveness of violence or the threat of violence to get other people to do what we want.[2]

For Women and Children. Cultural norms and values may profoundly limit individuals' perceptions of alternatives. The pathetic nature and inadequacy of our foster care system can be seen only as a reflection of our ambivalence about protecting children, when this protection would disrupt their being raised by their biological kin. For adult women who would leave abusive men, the way in which society limits their options may be more subtle—since society does not even pretend to find new homes for women endangered by their

2. Please note that it is my intention for this never-use-violence ethic to apply to all thinking, feeling beings. I am aware that anti-abortionists would apply a similar ethic to fetuses. However, the violence that some of these individuals enact against medical facilities that offer abotions speaks to an essential inconsistency in their view. They are advocates not for the life of one "individual," but against the freedom of another—the pregnant girl or woman. The uses of violence and techniques of harassment are consistent with the anti-freedom ethic, not with an unqualified respect for life.

husbands' violence—but certainly has no less of an impact. The inadequacy of shelters for battered women makes them no real option in and of themselves, although the shelter may give some women the physical and psychological respite from fear that will enable them to find a more lasting, viable alternative.

More importantly, though, socialization limits women's options. For girls and women, general social values about the importance of marriage may be buttressed by religious values that forbid divorce and abortion (in the case of Catholicism), or allow only the husband to initiate divorce and allow abortion only under specific conditions (in the case of orthodox Judaism). Further, the relative economic deprivation of women, may make options based on financial independence simply unattainable, even if they are imaginable and "connectable." As of 1985, women earned only 64 cents for every dollar earned by men (Hewlett 1986).

Dobash and Dobash (1980) detailed the scope of the situation for women, historically:

> The legal, political and economic institutions were committed to, benefitted from, and reinforced the patriarchal structure and ideology. It would have been inconceivable for them to have supported any other form of family relations (i.e., no alternatives). All institutions were organized along these lines and all people were socialized into the supporting ideology, which emphasized authority, obedience, service and hard work and rested firmly on the ideals of love, dedication and loyalty. These ideals and their accompanying practices formed the foundations of the subordination and control of women (p. 74).

What contributes most to an individual's initial inability to see alternatives must rest with what is there to be seen in the culture. The constraints placed on married women within nuclear families in patriarchal societies are many and illustrate the ways in which culturally mediated injustice can be effectively perpetuated. (See for example, Chodorow 1978; deBeauvoir 1953; Dinnerstein 1976.) Importantly, our social structure reifies the isolation of women in the home, away from other adults besides their husbands.

Only a few individuals in a society seem to engage consistently in a political analysis of their personal situation. While it has been one of the central missions of the Women's Movement to make the "personal political," most people nevertheless continue to experience their own problems as personal rather than as manifestations of the patriarchy—even if the latter alternative is objectively more correct.

Further, with problems still tainted by their historical taboo-ness, the activity that would best facilitate the perception of alternatives is all but prohibited by cultural constraints. Other people may see alternatives that would benefit victims of abuse at the hands of their husbands or parents, or by rapists, but victims of these forms of interpersonal violence share a compendium of problems. As a result of the structural isolation of women and children in nuclear families, the feeling that problems that affect one personally are personal in origin and in solution, and the anticipated negative consequences of revealing "taboo" information, victims are culturally deprived of that resource most likely to facilitate their experiencing of injustice and effective action: other people's alternatives and an experience of collectivity.

Seeing Alternatives: Isolation, Inconsistency, and Individual Experience

In the domain of "seeing alternatives," isolation is a potent deterrent. Isolation diminishes the perception of alternatives. Victims of violence, situated in families or attempting to escape from them, have few spontaneous opportunities for meaningful contact with others. And, they are likely to avoid such contact for fear of reprisals from the abusers, harm to others in their families, or degradation from the listeners.

Within these boundaries, individuals live intense, emotion-filled lives. They work to understand what they are experiencing, in whatever terms make sense to them. They live with the inconsistencies contained in the knowledge that someone who is supposed to love them also hurts them. They live with the knowledge that family life does not go as smoothly as TV shows from *Father Knows Best* to *The Cosby Show* promise. Their sense of personal inconsistency may be compounded by the contrast between the fair, reasonable fathers of TV-land and the movie-romanticized male vigilantes, who are lurking, waiting for someone to "make their day." These macho men are waiting for the slightest provocation to release their righteous violence. If Clint Eastwood is so popular, how can a woman expect her husband to act like Bill Cosby?

An example of the publicity given to battered women is provided by a made-for-TV movie, *The Burning Bed*. To its credit, it did address directly the plight of a battered woman, Francine Hughes. However, she ended her abusive relationship by killing her husband and was then acquitted on the grounds of temporary insanity. What messages of hope are there here for women suffering at home as Farrah Fawcett (the actress who played Hughes) suffered on the screen? What models of strength and control over one's life are offered? Perhaps, the strongest positive message of this movie is its acknowledgement that such abuse is serious and can be made known.

Individually, in private, women and children are too often obliged to apply their personal resources to the act of staying alive. Their perceptions of alternatives also reflect the pressure of this survival orientation. It may be hard to think expansively—to review available alternatives—when fear is high. However, it is hard to stop thinking even for a moment if you believe that you may be able to come up with the solution, to make the violence stop.

The painful paradox contained in dedicated thinking about a problem that almost certainly will not be solved in this manner is a part of the victim's psychological character and burden. The commitment to finding the way to make violence stop within a personal context—without the help of outside resources or the dissolution of the violent relationship—is almost certain to fail. In my study, only one woman (of the 55 female victims interviewed) reported that she was able, by herself, to get her husband never to beat her again after the first time. She told him that if he ever did it again, she would leave him. She meant it and he knew it. Yet, it is hard to believe that this would be a generally successful strategy or that women do not say this all the time, to no avail.

In 1986, an attorney referred a client of hers to me for consultation. Her characteristics are altered here to eliminate the possibility that she or others might recognize her description. She was a physician and had endured ten years of abuse at the hands of her husband who was the owner of his own business. She and her husband had separated, but he was eager to reconcile and she was seeking my advice. She brought a beautiful leather briefcase with her and during our conversation she pulled out a yellow pad, upon which she had written rules for his conduct, if he were to return. I asked if he had ever lived by such rules before and she admitted he had not. However, she was filled with an urgency to believe that this time he would keep his promise never to hit her again. She explained that she was 35 years old, and that she was familiar with "those statistics that say that a woman my age is more likely to get blown up by a terrorist than to marry." She believed, in a way that accounted for no alternatives, that if this marriage ended, she would never again be involved in an intimate relationship with a man. Finally, she asked me what was the central question in her decision-making: Could I promise her that her husband would beat her again? If I could not make that promise then there was a chance that he would not. I tried to make the likelihood of his future abuse seem a virtual certainty. However, as she pointed out, I had never even met her husband. I could not make the alternative of continued abuse real for her, even though she had been enduring his abuse for a decade. A week after I spoke to her, she and her husband resumed living together.

This woman was more afraid of being alone than of being with an abuser. Other women may make similar choices between what is known and a seemingly worse unknown. A question to raise, though, is what makes the unknown seem so bad when the circumstances under which they are living are acknowledged as bad? What leads to their inability to engage an alternative that may provide a way out of a life filled with upset and threat?

One answer rests with low self-esteem, which seems certain to affect creativity or expansiveness in the perception of alternatives. Walker (1979), Frieze (1979a) and Dobash and Dobash (1980) all named lowered self-esteem as characteristic of battered women. (Walker's 1984 work is somewhat equivocal on the issue of self-esteem in the contrast between currently and formerly battered women.) Nonetheless, it seems likely that a diminished self-image is a direct consequence of abuse. Lowered self-esteem seems likely to impair a woman's perceptions of the way others see her and to distort her own potential for effective thought or action.

While it may seem counterintuitive at first, it is probably easier for a woman in a reasonably good relationship to decide she wants something better and to leave, than it would be for a woman in a bad relationship. The former woman seems more likely to be higher in self-esteem and to feel that her life is within her control. The latter woman, involved in a bad relationship, is likely to feel dismayed at having decided to get involved in such a relationship to begin with, depressed at the state of her relationship, and doubtful of her ability to make a decision that would improve her life. Lowered self-esteem sets in motion a cycle that deprives its victims of the ability to believe in their capacity to help themselves. Yet, the isolation characteristic of most victims mandates that they should help themselves. The causes for the isolation and the low self-esteem may be steeped in the patriarchy, but the consequences are distinctly personal and psychological, and may keep these women from making the "reconnection" to the bigger picture.

Further, it seems likely that battered women "think hard" about how to prevent and avoid future violence and that the activity of "thinking hard" stymies them. There is an immediate paradox inherent in this suggestion, since surely some thinking is good and should provide insight and potential solutions to problems. Also, in general, one might think that if some thinking is good, more is better. However, in the case of battered women, over-thinking about a solution within the relationship may make it impossible for them to leave. Further, if they have formed the habit of thinking all the time about the violence and ways to prevent it, leaving the relationship may create a feeling of psychological emptiness. For a woman who spends a large portion of her personal time thinking about ways to respond to violence and to prevent future violence, leaving the abusive relationship may make life feel meaningless, as what have been her central psychological concerns become irrelevant. Further, it may be especially difficult to find an alternative experience to efforts to fix a violent relationship that will match its intensity or cause the same degree of psychological involvement.

It is essential to note that this idea is not intended to imply that the victim enjoys her/his mistreatment. Intensity is not a replacement for enjoyment. High involvement may be destructive to the individual's well being and peace of mind and yet may include patterns that are difficult to break. The dearth of real alternatives and the nonresponsiveness of social institutions are centrally implicated in the creation of this problem.

There is yet another factor which may diminish the victim of violence's ability to generate complex alternatives to her/his current life situation. Severe, recurrent, life-threatening violence seems likely to put victims in a state of perceptual alert, in which their abilities to think beyond the immediate situation may be sharply curtailed by the ever-present danger around them. This sort of survival thinking is likely to be highly focused on the specific situation in which the individual is involved. High levels of fear do not promote complex cognitive activity. The comments of battered women who have killed their husbands in self-defense have often reflected this narrowed perspective on available alternatives: "It was him or me," or "I thought, it's now or never." Elaborate alternatives are not generated by those under extreme stress, by people backed against the wall.

The issues raised here—the societally based limitations of a patriarchy, the psychological decrements in self-esteem, the high intensity of violent interactions and the fear-induced restrictions on an individual's ability to think in complex terms—contribute to the dearth of real and perceived alternatives available to chronic victims of wife abuse.

Abused children suffer some of these same deprivations and are in many respects even more powerless than adult women confronted with a violent family environment. Obviously, the experiences of rape survivors differ from victims of family violence, in terms of the ideas raised here. However, rape survivors are also likely to suffer from the inaccessibility of good alternatives. The rapist may never be captured, and even if he is, many survivors find the prosecution process unmanageable. While some women are pressing civil charges for damages against rapists or other responsible parties (e.g., the landlord who does not provide adequate window gates may be held responsible if one of his tenants is raped by someone who breaks through the window), this is a relatively new alternative. More generally, rape survivors share in the feeling that there are few good alternatives available to them.

As a result of these real, perceptual limits placed on the individual and as a result of people's tendency to see events as specific to them and not global in implication, many psychological strategies have evolved to enable coping. They inhibit the ability to see alternatives premised on the ethic of nonviolence. Further, these coping strategies cannot provide the solution, since the problems do not lie in the individual, but in the culture that unfairly obliges the individual to engage in "bootstrap" activities that can have only limited success.

Psychology is itself limited by such parameters, especially as it struggles to generate encompassing models that focus on the individual. However, just like the individuals who are obliged by the nature of our culture and their commitment to the meaningfulness of their own lives to talk in personal terms, psychologists have something to say. It is one of the complicating paradoxes of this area of study that to focus on something may be to strip it of its right context. However, not to focus on the individual because of the attendant political problems would silence that voice entirely and create a new basis for isolation. In this hopeful time of transition away from injustice, these private voices should be our guide, as public statements are made.

As alternatives are made less remote and more imaginable, so the sense of injustice becomes attainable (Deutsch 1975; Fine 1980). Alternatives are too often beyond the real and perceived reach of victims of intimate violence. A full realization of the injustice is thereby kept from them. Alternatives made real can make the awareness of injustice emerge and may mark the path to freedom from violence.

Focus on a Theoretical Alternative: When the Piece Never Fits

The research reviewed in chapters 2 and 3 of this book on observers' and victims' perceptions of injustice suggests that the arousal or upset that accompanies an awareness of suffering promotes distress and creates a press for tension reduction that would restore homeostasis. Just World and Defensive Attribution theorists alike would support this view. They disagree only about the psychological route taken to restore homeostasis. However, these points of view overlook a possibility raised by the awareness that ongoing violence in an intimate relationship may be upsetting in a way that defies resolution.

It seems reasonable to assert that people do not always seek homeostasis. We are not always distressed by a sense of psychological tension. In fact, one would expect battered women and abused children who live with family members who treat them in ways that are both loving and hateful to experience and to tolerate rather high levels of non-homeostasis or cognitive inconsistency (Blackman-Doron 1980b; Fine 1986; Horowitz 1981). If it is true that violence in ongoing relationships regularly undoes calm, but that the relationships continue anyway, then it would seem that the concept of homeostasis is of limited explanatory value.

This hypothetical, heightened tolerance for cognitive inconsistency is reflected in remarks made by some of the victims interviewed for this study. All victims (and nonvictims) were asked the following questions: "Did you see any alternatives to this situation? Was there anything you could have done to prevent these events?" The tolerance of inconsistency is reflected in these subjects' tendencies to say first that there were no alternatives, and then to describe available alternatives. Examples are provided here. A detailed analysis of these findings appears in chapter 9.

One battered woman responded, "No, there was nothing. But I could have had him arrested, you know. I knew a guy who was a cop."

Another said, "No. No. No. Nothing in my power. I called the police on one or two occasions."

A former abused child reported, "Not really. I never went to anyone. If I did it was only on the surface. . . . I would say things to my aunts and I would look at their faces."

A rape survivor said, "No. I could have made decisions not to go into the woods. Looking back, I think he probably would have stopped if I had really fought."

These verbal responses illustrate the concept of cognitive inconsistency. After all, these individuals did not simply say "no," and stop there. They continued to respond in ways that elaborated an affirmative response to the question. That is, they did detail alternatives.

The presence of such cognitive inconsistency counters homeostatic views of personality, and counters the idea that individuals in high stress situations will feel psychologically obliged to reach a cognitively consistent state of equilibrium. These respondents evidenced no upset at their inconsistency. Indeed, they seemed not to notice it. Further, they tolerated inconsistencies on issues that were important and vital to their well-being. Theoretically, inconsistencies on issues of importance should be most likely to evoke the press for tension reduction (Deutsch et al. 1962). The questions, then, are why do these individuals tolerate the presence of important, inconsistent cognitions and what are the consequences of this heightened tolerance for inconsistency?

The answers may lie not only with cognition, but also in the affective domain. The role of affect—how one feels (rather than how one thinks)—is underemphasized in theories built upon the premise that all individuals strive to be cognitive, logical, and singular in their response to a problem. One might even note that the orientation of these theoretical positions is more consistent with the socialization of males than of females. Women, more than men, have been socialized to nurture, to empathize, to act with affect, to make decisions in relational contexts (Gilligan 1977).

The excerpts from the interview data presented above suggest that not everyone strives to be cognitively consistent, and that some people, perhaps especially those who live in inherently inconsistent situations (i.e., where those who love you also hurt you), may tolerate inconsistency on issues of importance over extended periods of time. Further, the incomplete quality of such inconsistent ideas coexisting in the same individual may promote a continuing experience of psychological intensity that functions to keep involvement in the violent relationship high. (These ideas are explored further in chapter 9, where interview data on the perception of alternatives and the tolerance of cognitive inconsistency are presented.)

RECOGNIZING PARADOXES

Whether it is fully perceived or not, the broader society provides a potent context for our personal activities. The very real but often unacknowledged role of the culture shapes the paradoxes in thinking that characterize explanations for injustice that overimplicate the sufferer. In the last section of this chapter, these underutilized connections are made.

Remember the parable that appeared at the beginning of Chapter 2?

The universe . . . must make sense. Therefore, Job must have sinned" (Wouk 1978: 1063). So spoke Job's friends, his "comforters." Confronted with another's victimization, they advanced the view that the sufferer must be at fault. In the Bible, Job is described as pernicious; he would not accept the idea that he was responsible for his own victimization. Still his friends persisted. Job must be to blame for his own suffering. At the end of the parable of Job, as God restores Job's wealth and allows him to have a new family, He also rebukes those who would have held Job responsible for his own suffering. He says that they have spoken falsely of Him. Presumably, God knows that the universe does not always make sense, that suffering does not always occur in direct relation to the actions of the sufferer. As we know, in the case of Job, God Himself was responsible for Job's suffering.

This parable, with its clear exculpation of Job, should have provided a framework for explanations of injustice that do not implicate victims in their own suffering. After all, if there is anything that this parable proves it is that Job is not to blame. Nonetheless, attention to alternatives to blaming the victim is terribly underdeveloped.

Paradoxically, a substantial body of research has supported and elaborated the nature of explanations for injustice that focus on the victim and lead to the derogation of an already-suffering victim. While some writers have been explicitly critical of this tendency (Ryan's 1971 *Blaming the Victim* is perhaps the best example of naming and railing against holding victims responsible for their own suffering), work in social psychology has tended to explore it as an interesting phenomenon. The resulting inattention to the perpetrators, society-based deprivations, or simply bad luck as the primary causal factors has led to a reification of victim-blaming.

When it comes to blaming the victim, it seems that everyone does it. There is little work to suggest that people do anything else. Unfortunately, there is little work that allows people to do anything else. Lerner (1980) called the belief in a just world, with its attendant derogation of the victim, a fundamental delusion. However, his research is focused entirely on the victim, to the exclusion of the one who is, in fact, directly responsible for the injustice—the perpetrator. How can subjects help but appear deluded if they are not afforded the opportunity to chastise the source of the suffering? Of course, in experimental examples, like those provided by Lerner's research, the perpetrator is the experimenter. Thus, we see a motive based in the researcher's self-interest for not drawing the subjects' attention to the "perpetrator." It is possible that enlightened subjects provided with an opportunity to blame the perpetrator would want to withdraw from the study or worse.

In addition, there is something intriguing about blaming the victim. Since the beginnings of experimental social psychology in the 1930s, social psychologists have been intrigued by findings that did not quite make sense. For example, it was very interesting to discover that people would come to like doing such unpleasant things as eating grasshoppers *more* the *less* they were paid (Festinger 1957; Festinger and Carlsmith 1959). Similarly, it has been provocative to demonstrate that the more actively someone suffers, the less compassion and the more derogation she or he can expect from others (Coates et al. 1979).

Certainly, the tendency of research subjects to attribute undeserved responsibility to hapless victims has been compelling. However, this has occurred, at least in part, because of the relative lack of attention to other areas in which blame can be assigned. Scenario studies on rape, for example, have typically varied characteristics of the victim, not of the perpetrator (e.g. Feldman-Summers and Lindner 1976; Jones & Aronson 1973; Smith et al. 1976; Stokols & Schopler 1973). Laboratory studies of observers' perceptions of another's suffering, in which a victim is seen to endure electric shocks, are devoid of an apparent perpetrator (Lerner & Matthews 1967; Lerner & Simmons 1966).

The subject's attention is focused on the victim and outcome measures delve into the subject's perception of the victim and explore the subject's tendency to judge the victim harshly. Nevertheless, the reality of the situation would indicate that observers must notice the impact of the experimental scene and might make attributions in these terms if such outcome measures were included in the studies.

One interesting study conducted by Shotland and Straw (1976) showed that aspects of the perpetrator can be significant. In their study a man and a woman enacted an argument within earshot of the experimental subjects. The man was heard to attack the woman, and the woman, depending on the experimental condition, shouted either, "Stop it. I don't even know you," or "Stop it. I don't know why I married you." Subjects were more likely to help if the "attacker" was a "stranger." While the nature of social values about the privacy of marital fights makes this finding expected, it is nonetheless interesting to note that some knowledge about the perpetrator may affect an observer's willingness to act on his victim's behalf. Even in this study, which emphasizes the perpetrator, it is the victim who reveals the perpetrator's identity. Further, what is varied is not some characteristic uniquely the perpetrator's (his age or tone of voice), but the perpetrator's relationship to the victim.

Perhaps, ultimately, the presence of a prior relationship between the victim and her attacker is seen to reflect on the victim. Subjects who hear a woman being attacked by her husband may be less likely to go to her aid because they hold her responsible for her own victimization. After all, she married him. The woman assaulted by a stranger is less likely to be seen as responsible for her own victimization, less likely to be derogated and more likely to be helped. Thus, even when some trait of the perpetrator is highlighted, the victim's implied role is still crucial to determining who gets blamed.

Not "Why?" But "Why Her?"

It may be that interpersonal injustice can be conceptualized only in relation to the victim. Victims and those who notice the suffering of others may be obliged to ask themselves not simply "Why?" but

"Why her?" That is, the injustice must be connected to its victim in order for conceptions of justice to be applied. (Bulman and Wortman 1977)

The acknowledgement that searches for explanations for interpersonal injustice must necessarily include the victim leads to the likely, if inaccurate, application of conceptions of deservingness, rather than to chance explanations. Thus, paradoxically, meaningful explanations which emphasize the victim's deservingness may be preferred. This situation prevails even when any sort of objective appraisal implicates particular perpetrators, and even when the historic, ingrained social forces that promote the victimization of some people more than others can be named.

The paradox of victim blaming lies with its twin traits: inaccuracy and popularity. In a social world where some ideas are righter and truer than others, explanations for injustice that make the victim the key piece of the puzzle are destined for circularity and distortion. It is essential to reconstruct our prevailing attitudes so that the causal role of social institutions and the perpetrators they breed are judged responsible for the fate of victims.

SUMMARY

Thus, some of the difficulties of the individual puzzle-worker are considered. And, reality notwithstanding, it seems most likely that those who set about to fit their pieces into the jigsaw puzzle do so with little awareness of how their puzzle fits into the larger puzzle of society. Instead, they are constrained by the absence of real and perceived alternatives, damages that result from the violence they endure, and coping activities that keep their focus on themselves as individuals. In that context, they tolerate non-fitting ideas and experience what may be a heightened sense of involvement in the more difficult aspects of their lives.

We need to stop blaming victims and we need to get to know them. The study described in the following chapters is intended to make a contribution to that effort.

5

METHODOLOGICAL ISSUES
AND HOW THIS STUDY
WAS DONE

———

After arson, there are tell tale ashes; after murder, a body. Not so with intimate violence—these crimes and the experiences of the victims are often made invisible. Bruises are hidden or explanations for them are fabricated. Negative societal attitudes toward victims of family violence and rape are reflected in widely believed, but inaccurate, myths about the victim's culpability or willingness. Police officers are typically perceived as nonresponsive (Athanasatos 1981; Berger 1977; Schwartz & Clear 1978; Shields 1981; Woods 1978). Abusers' threats of retribution and the sense of humiliation that still attend family violence and rape also reduce the likelihood that victims will report their experiences in any public way.

Therefore, victims of intimate violence are hard to count. Nonetheless, anyone concerned about these problems wants to know how many people are affected. In a way that is consistent with the model for the emergence of social problems described in chapter 1, incidence estimates come to be seen as necessary. It is as if without them it would be impossible to justify serious public attention or to request deserved portions of public and private resources. Incidence estimates are so concrete, so easy to remember, and so difficult to refute without some statistical expertise, that they provide powerful, front-line ammunition in the fight to bring continuing attention to victims of family violence and rape.

Incidence studies are of some importance, and yet, without exception, such research efforts in the area of intimate violence are foiled by victims' understandable reluctance to come forward and be counted. Data bases suffer from nonrepresentativeness and limited generalizability, since information can be gathered only from those who are willing and/or able to relate their experiences to the police, social scientists, or health care personnel. In addition, incidence studies require the participation of nonvictims who, like the victims, are apt to participate in studies on such topics because of their greater interest or concern. Thus, they do not represent the general population exactly.

This situation is complicated by researchers' acknowledgement of the public's felt need for numbers. While numbers take on the form of objectivity, those who would provide them are human and are influenced by their ideologies in their efforts to attain incidence estimates. And researchers, like most Americans, share an awareness of the political impact of precise national indices. A prevailing view suggests that unless you know how much of a problem exists, you cannot formulate an adequate and an appropriate response to it.

Many incidence estimates have been offered by researchers within the area of intimate violence. Two early examples are provided here to illustrate some of the difficulties inherent in this endeavor. The first major effort by social scientists was carried out by Straus et al. (1980), in their survey of 2143 randomly sampled individuals. However, this sample represented only about 65 percent of those initially selected for the survey; the remaining 35 percent refused. The proportion of these refusers who were victims of family violence remains unknown. An additional limit on generalizability was created by the nature of the targeted population from which the sample was drawn—only husbands or wives from intact families with children between the ages of 3 and 17 were eligible. As Straus et al. (1980) acknowledged, this definition of the relevant population almost certainly led to an underestimation of the numbers of families engaged in some form of violence. For example, if the use of violence is related to stress, as many researchers have claimed, then the exclusion of non-intact families and families with children under the age of 3 would tend systematically to distort and lower incidence estimates (Elmer 1979; Gil 1973; Johnson & Morse 1968; Libbey & Bybee 1979; Parke 1977; Parke & Colmer 1975).

At the time that Straus et al. (1980) were conducting this study, the United States Department of Commerce Bureau of Census (1977) reported that only 34 percent of all American households were two-parent families with at least one child living at home. These limitations were acknowledged and an incidence estimate was offered. Straus et al. (1980) wrote, "every other home in America is the scene of family violence at least once a year" (p. 3). It is worth noting that, ultimately, the language of this statement is unqualified by the many restrictions on its accuracy.

In her first book, Walker (1979) also offered an incidence statistic on battered women. Although her own data included only self-identified and self-selected battered women, Walker (1979) wrote: "Who are the battered women? If you are a woman, there is a 50 percent chance it could be you!" (p. 19). Obviously, Walker intends the impact of her statistic to be taken personally. However, it is more a reflection of what she believes than of what she could know from her research. Here, the impact of ideology on science becomes overt, and thus, our own efforts at substantiation and legitimization through numbers are undermined.

Intimate violence has emerged as a social problem, and yet victims of these crimes are not routinely accorded the sympathy offered to victims of other forms of interpersonal violence. Victims of robberies or of physical assaults by strangers can reasonably expect positive, concerned attention from those they tell (e.g., the police). Victims of rape and family violence often do not expect or receive the same sort of attention from those they would tell. (See the report of the New York State Committee on Domestic Violence and Incarcerated Women, "Battered Women and Criminal Justice," issued 6/87.) They may remain silent or report their experiences only to family members or friends. In either case, they remain unrepresented in incidence estimates generated not by social scientists, but by public agencies.

For the reasons discussed above, it seems to me that the situation remains as Martin described it in 1976: "Accurately determining the incidence of wife-beating (or other sorts of intimate violence), per se, is impossible at this time" (p. 11). However, the role of accurate incidence studies in the area of intimate violence has been over-rated. The conditioned American need to know precisely "how much" of a problem exists has overshadowed the larger importance of the need to understand the causes, correlates, and consequences of family violence and rape. It is clear that millions of Americans are affected by these problems. The effort to discover the exact number of millions functions to sidetrack more important efforts to find out how best to help. Valuable resources lost in incidence efforts cannot be reclaimed. Political and financial realities dictate priorities that seem unlikely ever to equate the need for social services with the "need" for the "Star Wars" missile defense system.

In 1980, I wrote, "It seems certain that the low level of government funding available to programs for victims of intimate violence in the late 1970's, will be virtually absent in the 1980's. Resources will never be allocated in relation to the demonstrated prevalence or severity of intimate violence. Even the knowledge that most of those who commit violent crimes at home and on the street experienced violence at home is insufficient to motivate concerted or enduring preventive action" (Blackman-Doron, 1980c:12). By 1987, the proof was in; the resources were gone.

As researchers, we must be the first to say that incidence statistics do not represent our most important contribution to the remediation of violence in families and rape. We must know our strengths and must not allow our substantial wealth of qualitative knowledge to be co-opted by the too simple question, "How much?" Instead, we should move on and address the questions that we are best able to address, with our commitment to the scientific method firmly intact: "What is the nature of these experiences for these victims? And, then, how can these findings be applied on behalf of victims of family violence and rape"

I will shortly discuss how I attempted to answer these questions, but it is important to note first that social scientists devote a great deal of attention to another question that also needs answering. This question is deceptively simple to raise, and infinitely more difficult to answer: "Why?" It is in the nature of the scientific enterprise to undertake to explain the events of interest. The social scientific community, in deference to the rigors of the methods in which we were trained, regularly employ the tools of analysis to prove causality. However, the robustness of our results, the certainty with which we can assert knowledge, regularly pale beside the standard of the natural sciences.

In addition to being "resistant" to experimental control, our phenomena are overdetermined—the results of many, interacting causes, all of which are important some of the time. Thus, the answers to the "why?" question are complex and must be qualified by the many factors that singly and together contribute to the nature of intimate violence. Interpersonal violence and aggression are as characteristic of humankind as any other social behavior, and are as complexly determined. A myriad of factors impinge upon individuals and families within social systems, and lead to the acceptance and use of violence.

The search for these "impinging factors," the putative causes for violence, has been extensive. Some are listed here: traumatic socialization experiences in those who resort to violence, as well as poor control of impulses, sadistic urges, unrealistic expectations about the feelings and capabilities of others, unemployment and employment-related stresses, poverty, too-large families, racism, sexism, classism, alcoholism. Those reasons that implicate societal-level factors probably provide us with the most accurate insight into the causes and, sadly, the most limited opportunities to make change happen. If poverty offers the best "explanation" for why violence occurs, then the elimination of poverty is required to prevent violence. Macro-level approaches yield macro-level solutions, the very size of which deter action (Walster et al. 1973).

So, in choosing to focus on the nature of victims' reactions to violence, I am choosing away from the emphases of research methods that might enable assertions about the causes of violence or its incidence. I have selected a quasi-experimental method, making comparisons between victims and nonvictims and among victims of different forms of violence. The purpose of this study, generally stated, is to describe the nature and consequences of intimate violence in terms of a context shared by nonvictims, who detailed their experiences with conflict in a relationship. Thus, this study is primarily descriptive rather than explanatory. However, like the individual who cannot accept chance as a sufficient explanation for misfortune, I find it hard to think about my own results without considering their possible explanatory import. My resolution of this dilemma of interpretation has been to connect my descriptive findings not to the potentially causal, past events (in this case, the acts of violence), but to the future. In this way, I am able to use the implications of the findings reported in chapters 6 through 10 in applied settings. In my case, the primary setting for these applications has been the courtroom. (See chapter 11 for a discussion of the usefulness of psychological research within the justice system. See the remainder of this chapter for a report on the methods used to accomplish this study.)

OBJECTIVES AND HYPOTHESES

The Method

"You and Violence" was the title of a 44-item survey that appeared, in 1979, on the front page of the "Lifestyle" section of *The Record*, a Hackensack, New Jersey metropolitan-area newspaper, then with a circulation of approximately 250,000. The full-page questionnaire was eye-catching—it was bordered in bright orange, and a newspaper artist added a grotesque drawing of two blood-streaked people clawing at each other's faces. (See Appendix A for a copy of the research instrument.) The instructions which appeared together with the survey are presented below:

A questionnaire on your experiences
One of the most pressing problems in American society is violence. We read about it in the newspapers and see it on TV and in the movies. Many of us confront it personally in our lives. Some crimes of violence are easy to detect, as in the cases of murder or arson. The damage is immediate and obvious. However, other acts of violence are more difficult to detect, and so to solve. Victims of rape may choose not to report the harm done to them because they fear reprisals from the rapist or because they feel too embarrassed to discuss such intimate matters. People also experience violence in their homes. Parents may abuse their children, spouses hurt each other. The victims of family violence may also be reluctant to report their troubles. They may believe that their problems with violence are unusual and that no resources are available to help them anyway.

Resources are available to help, although we know very little about the numbers of people who could make use of such resources. These questions ask you for information about your experiences with violence that is not immediately obvious, about intimate violence. Intimate violence is something to be concerned about, and something to study. Who has experienced the effects of intimate violence? What do people do when confronted with such situations? What can people do when they confront violence?

Only a large and varied group of people, such as the readers of *The Record* can answer such questions. Your participation will be anonymous and you can participate in this study whether or not you have ever been involved with intimate violence.

Here is what you do:

- Read the questions carefully and write or circle your answers on this page.
  Before Sunday, mail your answers to: *The Record*

- If you have any comment on any questions, write it on a separate piece of paper (be sure to include the question numbers) and mail it in with your answers.

- Your answers will be kept confidential. Indeed, you need not give your name at all. A few people, though, will be interviewed at length. If you are willing to be interviewed, write your name and phone number at the bottom of this page.

- Remember, you are qualified to answer these questions even if you have never been involved with intimate violence. In fact, the results won't be meaningful unless all kinds of people respond.

- Please be honest. Only honest answers can be used to help increase our understanding of intimate violence.

Six hundred and twelve people filled out the questionnaire and sent it in; 180 volunteered to be interviewed and provided their names and telephone numbers.

Respondents included victims of child abuse, spousal abuse and stranger rape. Respondents were also asked if they ever abused their children. Thus, a small group of self-identified perpetrators of child abuse ($n = 20$) exists in the survey (not the interview) data base. (Those who experienced stranger rape only were also dropped from the interview data base.)

The prevailing wisdom on perpetrators of child abuse casts them as victims of their own backgrounds (see chapter 3), and for the purposes of the survey portion of this study they are considered, together with the direct victims, as "experiencers of intimate violence." Nonetheless, this may cause some conceptual confusion in what would otherwise simply be the "victims" group. However, even if some confusion is created, the inclusion of these parents could only weaken, not strengthen, between-group differences. Since between group-differences are the focus of the portion of the data analysis that includes this group, it seemed methodologically acceptable (and substantively justifiable) to construct the comparison groups in this way.

A second contrast to much of the prior research on violence in families and rape involves the respondents. My study participants were predominantly white (93 percent), and middle class. The median income was $25,000 per year, in 1979. Reaching this group of people represents an alternative to those who typically have been studied. Further, the presence of high levels of violence in this sample—49 percent of the respondents had experienced at least one sort of intimate violence—refutes the myth that it happens *only* in lower class families (although, of course, no generalizable incidence statistics can be drawn from this self-selected sample).

Third, the survey highlighted areas that were implicated by previous research and by attention to the nature of victimization in this society. Data were gathered in the following areas:

1. Demographic characteristics (e.g., sex, age, income, education, ethnicity);

2. Intimate violence experiences (their number, frequency, severity and duration); and

3. "Reporting" behavior—to whom people reported their experiences with violence, if they reported them at all (e.g., friends, police, clergy).

This last concern with reporting behavior, and the respondents' opportunity to report their experiences anonymously through the newspaper survey, enabled data to be gathered from victims who might not have been able or willing to report their experiences in a more public way. Approximately 24 percent of the victims surveyed indicated that they had *never* reported their experiences to anyone before responding to the newspaper questionnaire.

Fourth, data were gathered from both victims and nonvictims. Approximately 51 percent of the survey respondents were nonvictims. And all respondents were requested to volunteer for in-person interviews. Approximately 29 percent did so, of whom 63 percent (n = 113) were successfully interviewed; 42 percent of the interviewees were nonvictims or controls; the remaining 58 percent were victims of at least one sort of intimate violence. The possibility of comparisons between victims and nonvictims is unusual for research in this area, and I hope that the perspective provided by the framework of theorizing on injustice will foster insight in these contrasts. Specifically, the questions asked during the interviews enabled comparisons to be drawn between victims and nonvictims in the following areas. (The question numbers which appear in parentheses after each area refer to questions on the Interview Schedule in Appendix B.):

■ Perceptions of early times in the relationship (#2);

■ The nature of "hard times" in the relationship (#3 for those who had not experienced intimate violence, #5 for those who had);

■ The way conflict was perceived (#6);

■ Actions before, during, and after difficult or violent episodes (#7);

■ Attributions of blame (#8);

■ Descriptions of coping behavior (#9);

■ Satisfaction with the relationship (#10);

■ Intensity of the relationship (#11)

■ Effects on other aspects of life, e.g., sexual relationships, family life (#12);

■ Perceptions of what others thought about them (#13); and

■ Perceptions of alternatives to the situation (#14).

Predictions were offered and questions were raised in relation to both the survey and interview results. (These predictions and questions are presented together with the findings in chapters 6 through 9.)

Once the Surveys Were Mailed Back and the Interviews Were Conducted

The survey data, the responses of the 612 subjects, were analyzed, and on July 1, 1979, I wrote an article for *The Record* that detailed the results of the survey. (See Appendix C for a copy of this article.) Thus, feedback was provided to all participants, something that can not be accomplished with anonymous respondents without the use of a dissemination "vehicle" like a newspaper.

Efforts were made to contact each of the 180 interview volunteers. After three months of repeated telephone calls, we had contacted 172 of these people. Of this number, 24 had changed their minds and refused to be interviewed, 26 scheduled interview appointments but did not keep them. We interviewed 120 subjects in person, and two over the telephone. Machine malfunctions with the tape recorders led to a loss of nine of the tapes, yielding a total of 113 interviews, which were transcribed in their entirety and content analyzed.

Content Analyzing the Interview Data

Once all the interview transcripts were typed, my research assistants and I pulled ten at random and read subjects' responses in an effort to formulate categories of responses. Several thousand statements or themes were listed on index cards. We included anything that was relevant and clearly stated. Then, the cards were sorted into categories for each question in the interview. In the final version of the list of categories, there were nearly one thousand separate bits of information that could be coded as present or absent. The codebook which listed all the categories, was 45 pages long, and consisted of 20 sections. The list of the 20 areas for coding appears here, in an order which parallels the order of questions in the interview schedule:

1. Specific Data (e.g., responses to such specific questions as "Were you ever raped?")

2. Factual Descriptions of the Relationship

3. Descriptions of the Early Relationship

4. Descriptions of the General Relationship between the Subject and the Partner (i.e., the individual with whom the subject shared an intimate relationship and/or was the perpetrator of intimate violence against the subject)

5. Descriptions of Specific Incidents of Conflict/Violence

6. Descriptions of the Nature of the Conflict/Violence (e.g., what caused it)

7. Demographic Descriptions of the Subject and His/Her Family of Origin

8. Feelings Expressed by Subject and Partner (e.g., anger, annoyance, comfort)

9. Personality Characteristics of Subject and Partner

10. Actions of Subject and Partner

11. Thoughts of Subject and Partner

12. Any Physical Consequences of Violence

13. Attributions of Blame

14. Feelings of Responsibility

15. Descriptions of Roles and Role Expectations

16. Descriptions of Coping Strategies

17. Descriptions of Effects on Other Aspects of the Subject's Life

18. Reactions of Others

19. Perceptions of Alternatives

20. Values of the Subject and Partner

This elaborate and detailed system was created in an effort to preserve as much of the richness of the data as possible and still be able to use quantitative methods of data analysis.

For example, for "Personality Characteristics," there were 92 separate personality descriptions coded in the original pass through the interview data. Such traits as "active, affectionate, aggressive, ambitious, bad, cold, cowardly, crazy, dependent, dishonest . . . pleasant, trusting, unable to cope, and warm" appeared as possible responses. Later, after all the interviews were coded, the popularity of these items was checked by computer, and the list of "personality characteristics" was reduced to the 20 which were most frequently mentioned. (Ultimately, the complete list of more than 1000 possible responses was reduced to the approximately 400 which were mentioned often enough to be included in further analyses.)

The coding itself proceeded on a question-by-question basis. Each response to each question was read by two coders. Disagreements in the assignment of a response to a category were adjudicated by a third judge-coder who would ask for the reasons for the disagreement and then effect a resolution. All coders, including the judge-coder were blind to the hypotheses of the study, although of course, not blind to the condition of the respondent (i.e., whether she was a victim or a nonvictim). The same list of categories was used for all respondents, except for those responses unique to the victim's circumstances. For the most part, such responses were factual, rather than interpretive in nature (e.g., Subject reports a rape occurred.)

While this description of the coding process is relatively brief, the enormity of this coding task should not be minimized. The transcribed interviews averaged 30 single spaced pages and it took a group of eight coders about 18 months to content analyze the data contained in the interviews.

In addition, while computers are useful for numerical comparisons between groups of subjects, the precise nature of what was said is lost. We did use a computer, though, to facilitate a search through the qualitative data for illustrative, verbatim quotes. For example, the computer identified those subjects who blamed themselves for episodes of conflict or violence. We then returned to the appropriate transcripts and picked up precisely what had been said. (These "verbatim data" are presented along with the numerical comparison results in chapters 7 through 9.)

A SUMMARY STATEMENT ON THE METHOD

This study on the differences and similarities between victims and nonvictims of intimate violence was designed to maximize the amount that could be learned from the respondents. Pre-structured response choices were largely absent from the interview portion of the study. Instead, what subjects actually said provided the basis for analyzing their responses. Ideally, social science research reflects a collaboration between the researcher and the participants. Here, by allowing the subjects to frame the categories of response, I have tried to give their words power. What appears in the following chapters are their ideas, their frames of reference, applied to a series of questions they were asked. Their responses to the structured, survey questions (chapter 6) are intended to provide a context for the more detailed insight they provide into their psychological reactions to violence and conflict in the remaining results chapters (7–10).

6

THE SURVEY RESULTS

The quantitative data provide a context of demographic and experiential descriptions for the individuals who responded to the newspaper survey. Four sorts of descriptive images of these respondents are offered here. First, the demographic characteristics of the sample of people who filled out the newspaper survey is compared to the population of the general readership of that newspaper. Second, the sample of newspaper respondents is divided into victim and nonvictim categories and demographic comparisons are made between different victim groups and the nonvictim controls. Third, the violence-related experiences of the victims are explored in terms of their survey data, especially with regard to the nature, severity, and frequency of the violence they experienced and whom they told about it. Fourth, demographic and violence-related information is provided on those who participated in the interview portion of the study. Thus, in this last section, the sample of interviewees is introduced. Their substantive responses provide the data bases for chapters 7 through 9.

DEMOGRAPHIC CHARACTERISTICS AND THE
LARGER POPULATION

One of the advantages of surveys conducted through newspapers is the opportunity to compare the demographic characteristics of the respondents with those of the general newspaper readership. Marketing surveys provide newspaper managers with information about the demographic characteristics of their readers. By comparing my 612 survey respondents with the general newspaper readership (of about 250,000) I was able to determine the extent to which the sample differed from or resembled the population of which it was a part. Six variables—age, sex, income, education, marital status, and employment status—provided the bases for statistical comparisons between the sample of newspaper respondents and the population of newspaper readers. Three of these variables distinguished survey respondents from the general Sunday newspaper readership. Survey respondents were younger—their median age was 35, as compared with 45 in the general population $(p < .001)$. They were more likely to be female—82.8% as compared with 54.1% $(p < .001)$. They were better educated—44.9% held at least a bachelor's degree as compared with 21.8% in the general population $(p < .001)$. Differences in income, marital, and employment statuses were statistically nonsignificant. The median income of the sample was $25,000 (in 1979); 63.6% of the respondents were then married, 20.2% were single and 16.0% were divorced, separated, or widowed; 65.1% were employed out of the home on a part- or full-time basis (see table 6.1).

While this survey is not intended to be an incidence study, dealing with percentages is certain to draw some of this sort of consideration. With regard to the central concern of incidence studies—representativeness—I have two general comments to make on the differences and nondifferences between the survey sample and the newspaper readership.

First, to the extent that the survey respondents did differ from the general readership, these differences were consistent with research on the ways in which volunteers tend to differ from nonvolunteers in any sort of psychological research (Rosenthal and Rosnow 1969). That is, relative to nonvolunteers, volunteers for studies on a range of topics tend to be female, younger, and better educated. Therefore, the overrepresentation of these groups on this survey may not simply follow from their being overinvolved with violence, but may be due in part to the tendency of these individuals to overvolunteer relative to others.

Second, violence has been theorized to go together with circumstances of low power. While this explains the overinvolvement of women, it does not provide insight into the overrepresentation of somewhat younger, better educated individuals. If one assumes that

TABLE 6.1

Demographic Comparisons between the Newspaper Survey Respondents and the General Newspaper Readership

	"You and Violence" Survey Respondents (n = 612)	General Newspaper Readership (n = 684,700)
Age: Chi-Square = 15.50 with 3 df, p = .001		
14–28	24.5	24.8
29–35	26.0	13.0
36–45	24.1	12.8
46–77	25.4	49.4
Sex: Chi-Square = 19.07, with 1 df, p = .001		
Male	17.2	45.9
Female	82.8	54.1
Household Income: Chi-Square = 2.93 with 2 df, p = .231		
Up to $14,999	19.9	29.5
$15,000–$24,999	30.0	30.2
$25,000–$39,999	32.2	40.3
$40,000 or more	17.9	—
Education: Chi-Square = 16.30 with 3 df, p = .001		
Not H.S. Graduate	9.6	15.9
H.S. Graduate	22.9	43.5
Some College	22.6	18.8
College Graduate	16.2	21.8
College Graduate +	28.7	—
Marital Status: Chi-Square = 1.06, with 2 df, p = .589		
Single	20.2	20.6
Married	63.6	68.3
Separated/Divorced/ Widowed	16.0	11.1
Employment: Chi-Square = 2.04 with 1 df, p = .153		
Employed	65.1	55.2
Not employed	34.9	44.8

experiences with violence increased the willingness to respond to the survey and that violence occurs more often in individuals with less power, then the direction of the differences between the survey respondents and the general newspaper readers should have been reversed with regard to educational status. That the comparisons went as they did may suggest that well educated people do experience intimate violence in substantial numbers, though they may be less likely to report it in non-anonymous ways. Alternatively, these results may indicate that this survey did quite a good job of eliciting nonvictims and victims—which was an objective of this study. (As part of a later analysis will show, those involved with intimate violence were not quite so well educated as those who were not involved. However, they were still far better educated than the general readership: 40.5% of those who reported experiences with intimate violence held college degrees or more, compared with 21.8% of the general readership. The percentage for the control group of survey respondents was 49.2%.)

An additional piece of information relevant to the usefulness of these numerical data comes from comparing the percentages reporting violence with the percentages drawn from the Straus et al. (1980) nationwide survey. The percentages in general approximate one another. For example, in my newspaper survey, approximately 28 percent (159 out of the 568 respondents) said "yes" when asked if they had been abused by a spouse currently, in the past, or both. (When asked about the nature of this abuse, 181 respondents or 32% provided information on their experiences. While this discrepancy suggests that some confusion existed in the respondents about just how to fill out the questionnaire, the discrepancy is not too large.) The numbers from my survey are certainly consistent with Straus et al.'s (1980) report that a physical assault occurred in 28 percent of all American homes during 1976.[1]

The investigation of the incidence of intimate violence is not an objective of this study. However, it is important that this group appear to be reasonably representative of the population from which it was drawn and also be comparable to other research groups. These criteria have been met, rendering this sample one worth pursuing.

In addition, this sample is remarkable for a way in which it is *not* representative of the population of all Americans. It is distinctly middle class—the social class rarely studied by researchers on this

---

1. The more recent Straus and Gelles (1986) incidence study showed a 27% drop in the wife abuse rate relative to their 1975–1976 study. However, their earlier study provides a better basis for comparison for my study since it occurred closer in time to my research.

subject. Data gathered from people who seek attention from shelters, hospital emergency rooms, police departments, and the criminal justice system are likely to exclude systematically those who can afford to seek private aid for their problems. Too often, the role of poverty in enhancing the likelihood that public agencies will become aware of an individual's involvement with violence is overlooked. Incidence estimates from such sources are created anyway, contributing to popular beliefs that overassociate family violence and rape with lower class status.

In part, then, my research with this select sample should dispel the myth that violence is a lower class phenomenon. The debunking has already begun and is highlighted by the recent attention devoted to the death of Lisa Steinberg, the six-year-old adopted daughter of an attorney and his college-educated girlfriend. Children die of abuse with horrifying frequency and rarely receive the sort of attention that this case did. The greater measure of attention and concern that Lisa's death engendered can be understood only as a consequence of the public shock that came from having to acknowledge that such lethal violence happens here, too. While the participants in my study were not involved with lethal violence, their involvement with violence at all counters the stereotype that violence, while a part of lower class life, is not a part of middle class life. Therefore, these individuals not only add to the body of knowledge about the nature and impacts of intimate violence, but also do so in a way that directly confronts the inaccurate but prevailing view that "this does not happen to people like us." It does. The remaining pages of this chapter present my contribution to the fund of quantitative knowledge on family violence and rape, drawn from the reports of middle class, predominantly white suburbanites.

INTIMATE VIOLENCE: YES OR NO

Approximately 49% (48.6%, $n = 297$) of my respondents were victims or perpetrators ($n = 20$) of at least one sort of intimate violence; 51.4% ($n = 315$) had no experiences with intimate violence. Unlike those who experienced intimate violence, this nonvictim control group circled "No," or did not respond when asked all of the following violence-specific questions:

■ As a child were you ever physically abused (punched, kicked, bruised) by your parents?

- As a parent, have you ever physically abused any of your children?

- Have you ever been physically abused by your current spouse or lover?

- In any past relationships, were you ever physically abused by your spouse or lover?

- Has your spouse or lover ever used violence or the threat of violence to force you to have sexual intercourse?

- Were you ever raped?

Among the 297 respondents who said "Yes" to at least one of these questions, 40.1% (n = 119) had had only one kind of experience with intimate violence. (Victims of current and past spousal abuse were both considered victims of the same kind of abuse, while each of the others—abused children, abusing parents, victims of marital rape and victims of nonmarital rape—represent distinct conditions.) Approximately 18 percent (18.2%, n = 54) of these respondents had experienced two forms of abuse (e.g., victims and perpetrators of child abuse, victims of spousal abuse and perpetrators of child abuse), 24.9% (n = 74) had experienced three kinds of intimate violence (the most frequently occurring combination of three experiences involved victims of child abuse and spousal abuse, who were also perpetrators of child abuse [n = 60/74 cases]; 16.8% (n = 50) had experienced four kinds of intimate violence.

TESTING THE SURVEY HYPOTHESES AND ANSWERING THE RESEARCH QUESTIONS

Comparisons between those involved with violence and the controls were computed in two ways. For comparisons involving demographic variables for which predictions could be generated from the pre-existing literature on family violence, seven categories of experience with intimate violence were named:

1. Abused children (n = 48)

2. Abusing parents (n = 20)

3. Battered spouses (n = 30)

4. Rape survivors $(n = 21)$

5. Those with two experiences with intimate violence $(n = 54)$

6. Those with three experiences with intimate violence $(n = 74)$

7. Those with four experiences with intimate violence $(n = 50)$

Predictions involving (1) gender, (2) household income, (3) educational attainment, (4) marital status and longevity, (5) employment status, and (6) family size were tested, first by contrasting each of the above-named groups with each other and with the controls. Then, the seven categories of experience with intimate violence were combined into one and comparisons were drawn between this combined group and the controls. This two-step comparison procedure was designed to test the extent to which victims and perpetrators of different sorts of intimate violence shared characteristics and experiences and to examine differences and similarities between those who had experienced any sort of intimate violence and the controls in areas where previous statistical analyses have revealed trends.

For two additional variables—religion and birth order—the sample was divided differently. The sample was constructed in terms of three groups: those with one experience, those with two or more, and the controls. This less refined analysis seemed better suited to these newer areas of inquiry. Predictions were not offered; research questions about among-group differences were raised.

The hypotheses presented below are based on the current state of knowledge and theorizing about victims of family violence. If there is one organizing principle for the hypotheses, it is that victims will be lower in power or have less in the way of valued resources (e.g., income, education) than nonvictims. Note that such predictions are offered even in this sample, which is quite "rich" in access to valued resources overall. And, they are offered in the context of my previous statements about the importance of acknowledging the place of violence in the middle class. However, the fundamental notion here is not that access to fewer resources (or poverty) causes violence, but that violence, experienced in any social class, inhibits more constructive life activity, leading to a lesser ability to accumulate valued resources.

Hypothesis 1. Females will be overrepresented among the intimate violence groups, relative to the control group.

As noted earlier, females were overrepresented in this sample, overall. Further, in six of the seven intimate violence groups, the proportion of women exceeded their 83% representation in the sample. Only among the abused children were women underrepresented relative to their numbers in the sample. Even so, their rate of abuse was still nearly twice that of the male respondents. Approximately 63% of those who had been abused as children were female, as compared with 97% of the abused spouses, 95% of the rape victims, 93% of those with two experiences, 89% of those with three experiences, and 96% of those with four experiences. Of those who

TABLE 6.2

A Chi-Square Analysis of Sex Differences among the Seven
Violence Conditions and the Control Condition

	SEX		
CONDITION	Male % (n)	Female % (n)	TOTAL
Abused Children	37.5 (18)	62.5 (30)	7.9 (48)
Abusing Parents	15.0 (3)	85.0 (17)	3.3 (20)
Abused Spouses	3.3 (1)	96.7 (29)	4.9 (30)
Rape Survivors	4.8 (1)	95.2 (2)	3.4 (21)
Two Experiences	7.4 (4)	92.6 (50)	8.9 (54)
Three Experiences	11.0 (8)	89.0 (65)	12.0 (73)
Four Experiences	4.0 (2)	96.0 (48)	8.2 (50)
Control	21.7 (68)	78.3 (245)	51.4 (313)
Total	17.2 (105)	82.8 (504)	100.0 (609)

Chi-Square = 36.469 with 7 df, $p < .001$

TABLE 6.3

A Chi-Square Comparison of Sex Differences between the
Intimate Violence and Control Conditions

	SEX		
CONDITION	Male	Female	TOTAL
Intimate Violence	12.5 (37)	87.5 (259)	48.6 (296)
Control	21.7 (68)	78.3 (245)	51.4 (313)
Total	17.2 (105)	82.8 (504)	100.0 (609)

Chi-Square = 8.439 with 1 df, $p = .004$

reported they had abused their children, 85% were female. Approximately 78% of the controls were women. When all of the intimate violence experiences were combined, about 88% were females—which exceeded the percentage for controls by about 9%. Thus, even in this predominantly female sample, these findings support the obvious hypothesis that victims of violence (including child abusers) are too likely to be females (see tables 6.2 and 6.3).

Hypothesis 2. Those with experiences with intimate violence will have lower household incomes than the controls.

In general, the more experiences with intimate violence an individual had, the more likely she or he was to report a household income under $25,000 per year (the sample's median) and the more they differed from the controls ($p = .07$). Those who were victims of three forms of intimate violence were the most likely to earn below the median—about 65% earned less than $25,000 with approximately half of this group earning less than $15,000 per year. They were followed by those who reported four kinds of violence—60% earned less than $25,000 with about half this group earning less than $15,000. Approximately 53% of those with two experiences earned less than $25,000 as did about 52% of the rape survivors. Those who had endured spousal abuse followed in this sequence with about 48% earning less than the median income. About 46% of the controls earned below the median. Those who reported involvement with child abuse—as victims or perpetrators—were least likely to be in the lower income group, about 41% and 43%, respectively (see tables 6.4 and 6.5).

When all those with experiences with intimate violence were considered together, the trend toward lower income among the violence groups achieved statistical significance ($p = .004$). About 54% of the intimate violence group earned below the median, nearly 8% more than the controls. Income analyses that considered those with incomes under $15,000 per year showed that about 26% of the violence group was in this lowest income category, as compared with about 15% of the controls. These findings are consistent with the hypothesis presented above. Thus, even in this relatively high income sample, victims tended to have lower household incomes than nonvictims.

Hypothesis 3. Those who have experienced intimate violence will be less likely to be well-educated than those who report no experience with such violence.

TABLE 6.4
A Chi-Square Analysis of Differences in Household Income among
the Seven Violence Conditions and the Control Condition

	INCOME				
CONDITION	<14,999	15,000–24,999	25,000–39,999	40,000 and up	TOTAL
Abused Children	23.9	17.4	43.5	15.2	7.8
	(11)	(8)	(20)	(7)	(46)
Abusing Parents	5.0	35.0	35.0	25.0	3.4
	(1)	(7)	(7)	(5)	(20)
Abused Spouses	24.1	24.1	34.5	17.2	4.9
	(7)	(7)	(10)	(5)	(29)
Rape Survivors	19.0	33.3	42.9	4.8	3.6
	(4)	(7)	(9)	(1)	(21)
Two Experiences	24.5	28.3	32.1	15.1	9.0
	(13)	(15)	(17)	(8)	(53)
Three Experiences	33.3	31.9	22.2	12.5	12.3
	(24)	(23)	(16)	(9)	(72)
Four Experiences	28.9	31.1	26.7	13.3	7.7
	(13)	(14)	(12)	(6)	(45)
Control	14.7	31.3	32.7	21.3	51.2
	(44)	(94)	(98)	(64)	(300)
Total	20.0	29.9	32.3	17.9	100.0
	(117)	(175)	(189)	(105)	(586)

Chi-Square = 31.236 with 21 df, p = .070

TABLE 6.5
A Chi-Square Analysis of the Difference in Household Income
between the Intimate Violence and Control Conditions

	INCOME				
CONDITION	<14,999	15,000–24,999	25,000–39,999	40,000 and up	TOTAL
Intimate Violence	25.5	28.3	31.8	14.3	48.8
	(73)	(81)	(91)	(41)	(286)
Control	14.7	31.3	32.7	21.3	51.2
	(44)	(94)	(98)	(64)	(300)
Total	20.0	29.9	32.3	17.9	100.0
	(117)	(175)	(189)	(105)	(586)

Chi-Square = 13.124 with 3 df, p = .004

TABLE 6.6
A Chi-Square Analysis of the Educational Attainment Difference
Between the Intimate Violence and Control Conditions

	EDUCATION		
	Less than College	College or More	TOTAL
CONDITION			
Intimate Violence	59.5 (175)	40.5 (119)	48.6 (294)
Control	50.8 (158)	49.2 (153)	51.4 (311)
Total	55.0 (333)	45.0 (272)	100.0 (605)

Chi-Square = 4.298 with 1 df, p = .038

As noted earlier, this sample, overall, was quite well educated—
approximately 45% held college degrees or more. Controls exceeded
this percentage slightly—about 49 percent of them held college degrees or more. None of the intimate violence groups exceeded this
percentage, although victims and perpetrators of child abuse approached it closely, with about 48% and 45% respectively. The percentage of those with at least college diplomas among victims of
spousal abuse, rape, and multiple intimate violence experiences approximated 39%. These differences did not achieve statistical significance. When the intimate violence groups were combined, a statistically significant difference did emerge, with the controls being
significantly more likely than the intimate violence groups to hold
at least a college degree. There was about a nine percentage point
difference. Thus, only in its more general form did this hypothesis
receive support (see table 6.6).

Hypothesis 4. Those who have experienced intimate violence will
be less likely to be currently married than controls, and more likely
to have been married previously or to have never married. Those
with intimate violence experiences who are married will be married
for fewer years than the controls.

With 90% of them reporting they were currently married, abusing
parents were the group most likely to be currently married, followed
by about 77% of the abused spouses and 72% of the controls. Rape
survivors, abused children, and those with two experiences with intimate violence occupied a middle range in terms of the numbers
who were currently married: 67% of the rape survivors, 65% of the

abused children, and 61% of those with two experiences reported that they were currently married. Victims of three or four experiences with intimate violence were least likely to be currently married. Only about 38% of those with three experiences and 32% of those with four experiences were currently married.

Victims of three or four experiences were most likely to have been previously married—about 40% of those who had experienced three sorts of intimate violence were previously married, as were 38% of those who had experienced four types. In none of the other groups, including controls, did this proportion exceed 15%.

Thirty percent of those with four experiences were single, making them the group most likely to have never married. They were followed by abused children and rape survivors at 29%, and those with two experiences with intimate violence at 24%. Approximately 22% of those who had three experiences with intimate violence were single, as were 21% of the controls, and 10% of the victims of spousal abuse (i.e., abuse by a lover) (see table 6.7).

When the intimate violence groups were considered as one group and contrasted with the controls, the two groups were about equally likely to be single; victims were less likely to be currently married and more likely to be previously married—55% of the victims were currently married, as were 72% of the controls. About 22% of the

TABLE 6.7
A Chi-Square Analysis of Living Situations Among the Seven
Violence Conditions and the Control Condition

	MARITAL STATUS			
CONDITION	Single	Currently Married	Previously Married	TOTAL
Abused Children	29.2 (14)	64.6 (31)	6.3 (3)	7.9 (48)
Abusing Parents	—	90.0 (18)	10.0 (2)	3.3 (20)
Abused Spouses	10.0 (3)	76.7 (23)	13.3 (4)	5.0 (30)
Rape Survivors	28.6 (6)	66.7 (14)	4.8 (1)	3.5 (21)
Two Experiences	24.1 (13)	61.1 (33)	14.8 (8)	8.9 (54)
Three Experiences	21.9 (16)	38.4 (28)	39.7 (29)	12.0 (73)
Four Experiences	30.0 (15)	32.0 (16)	38.0 (19)	8.3 (50)
Control	21.3 (66)	71.6 (222)	7.1 (22)	51.2 (310)
Total	21.9 (133)	63.5 (385)	14.5 (88)	100.0 (606)

Chi-Square = 97.591 with 14 df, $p = <.001$

TABLE 6.8

A Chi-Square Analysis of Living Situations Between the Intimate Violence and Control Conditions

| | | MARITAL STATUS | | |
CONDITION	Single	Currently Married	Previously Married	TOTAL
Intimate Violence	22.6 (67)	55.1 (163)	22.3 (66)	48.8 (296)
Control	21.3 (66)	71.6 (222)	7.1 (22)	51.2 (310)
Total	21.9 (133)	63.5 (385)	14.5 (88)	100.0 (606)

Chi-Square = 30.742 with 2 df, <.001

victims were previously married, as were about 7% of the controls (see table 6.8).

With regard to the length of current marriages, those with two experiences with intimate violence reported the greatest marital longevity—over 70% had been married for more than ten years. This group was followed by abusing parents, of whom 65% had been married for more than a decade. Controls were third, with about 64% married for over ten years; rape survivors were next at about 53%. In none of the remaining groups of those with intimate violence experiences were more than 50% married for more than ten years. When all the intimate violence groups were considered as one, about 53% had been married for more than ten years, about 10% fewer than the controls. While these trends only approached statistical significance ($p = .058$ and $p = .075$, respectively), they are consistent with the direction of predicted differences between those who experienced violence and those who did not (see tables 6.9 and 6.10).

Hypothesis 5. Those who have experienced intimate violence will be less likely than controls to be employed outside the home.

This hypothesis was not supported. Those with experiences with intimate violence, considered in terms of the seven groups and as one combined group, were as likely as controls to work outside the home. Approximately 65 percent of the respondents in both conditions were so employed.

Hypothesis 6. Those who have experienced intimate violence will be members of larger families than will controls.

TABLE 6.9
A Chi-Square Analysis of Years of Marriage Among the Seven
Violence Conditions and the Control Condition

| | YEARS OF MARRIAGE | | | |
CONDITION	1–10	11–20	21+	TOTAL
Abused Children	50.0 (16)	15.6 (5)	34.4 (11)	7.5 (32)
Abusing Parents	35.0 (7)	35.0 (7)	30.0 (6)	4.7 (20)
Abused Spouses	55.6 (15)	22.2 (6)	22.2 (6)	6.3 (27)
Rape Survivors	46.7 (7)	26.7 (4)	26.7 (4)	3.5 (15)
Two Experiences	29.3 (12)	36.6 (15)	34.1 (14)	9.6 (41)
Three Experiences	59.5 (22)	24.3 (9)	16.2 (6)	8.6 (37)
Four Experiences	52.2 (12)	43.5 (10)	4.3 (1)	5.4 (23)
Control	36.5 (85)	30.9 (72)	32.6 (76)	54.4 (233)
Total	41.1 (176)	29.9 (128)	29.0 (124)	100.0 (428)

Chi-Square = 23.160 with 14 df, p = .577

TABLE 6.10
A Chi-Square Analysis of Years of Marriage between the Intimate
Violence and Control Conditions

| | YEARS OF MARRIAGE | | | |
CONDITION	1–10	11–20	21+	TOTAL
Intimate Violence	46.7 (91)	28.7 (56)	24.6 (48)	45.6 (195)
Control	36.5 (85)	30.9 (72)	32.6 (76)	54.4 (233)
Total	41.1 (176)	29.9 (128)	29.0 (124)	100.0 (428)

Chi-Square = 5.194 with 2 df, p = .075

No support was found for this hypothesis, in terms of the number
of children the respondent had, the number of children living in the
respondent's home, or the number of children in the respondent's
family of origin.

Research Question 1. Does one's religion relate to the likelihood that one will have experiences with violence?

Jews were most likely to report they had no experiences with intimate violence, followed by Catholics, Protestants, and Others

TABLE 6.11

A Chi-Square Analysis of the Relationship Between Religion and
Extent of Violence Experiences

	EXTENT OF EXPERIENCES			
RELIGION	Two or More	One	None (Control)	TOTAL
Catholic	26.0 (66)	22.4 (57)	51.6 (131)	42.0 (254)
Jewish	12.9 (13)	22.8 (23)	64.4 (101)	16.7 (101)
Protestant	27.7 (49)	24.3 (43)	48.0 (85)	29.3 (177)
Other	26.0 (19)	32.9 (24)	41.1 (30)	12.1 (73)
Total	24.3 (147)	24.3 (147)	51.4 (311)	100.0 (605)

Chi-Square = 14.518 with 6 df, p = .024

(Buddhists, Moslems, and Agnostics/Atheists), in that order. More
than 64% of the Jews were in the control group, as were about 52%
of the Catholics, 48% of the Protestants, and 41% of the Others.
Protestants, Catholics, and Others were about equally likely to have
had two or more experiences with violence. Their percentages of
involvement ranged between 26 and 28 percent. For Jews, only 13%
reported two or more experiences with intimate violence. These differences achieved significance at p = .024 (see table 6.11).

Research Question 2. Does one's birth order influence the
likelihood that one will have experiences with violence?

The answer to this question only approached statistical significance at p = .093. The trend indicated by the analysis was that being
a youngest child meant that one was least likely to experience violence. Sixty percent of the youngest children in this sample were
controls, as were 50% of the oldest children, 48% of the middle
children, and 43% of the only children. Only children were most
likely to have one experience with violence, followed by middle,
oldest, and youngest borns. More than 32 percent of the only children had one experience with violence, as did 30% of the middle
children, 24% of the oldest and 18% of the youngest children. The
percentages for involvement with two forms of violence were about
equal for all birth order groups and ranged between 22 and 26 percent (see table 6.12).

TABLE 6.12
A Chi-Square Analysis of the Relationship between Birth Order
and Extent of Violence Experiences

	EXTENT OF EXPERIENCES			
BIRTH ORDER	Two or More	One	None (Control)	TOTAL
Only	24.6 (15)	32.8 (20)	42.6 (26)	10.0 (61)
Oldest	25.8 (64)	23.8 (59)	50.4 (125)	40.7 (248)
Middle	22.7 (32)	29.8 (42)	47.5 (67)	23.1 (141)
Youngest	22.5 (36)	17.5 (28)	60.0 (96)	26.2 (160)
Total	24.1 (141)	24.4 (149)	51.5 (314)	100.0 (610)

Chi-Square = 10.851 with 6 df, p = .093

THOSE WHO EXPERIENCED INTIMATE VIOLENCE: WHAT HAPPENED TO THEM AND WHOM THEY TOLD

There were 297 individuals who reported on their experiences with child abuse, spousal abuse, marital rape, and rape by someone other than the spouse. In this section, each of these types of intimate violence will be considered. No tables are included. The data are reported in the narrative. Numbers of subjects are reported without percentages when the categories of response were not mutually exclusive.

Child Abuse: The Victims

Nearly one-fourth of the respondents (23.2%, n = 142) reported that they had been abused as children: 26.5% (n = 39) by their mothers, 42.9% (n = 63) by their fathers, and 21.1% (n = 31) by both. (About 9% were abused by others as children.) About one-third of these respondents (34.0%, n = 49) said that the abuse happened "regularly" (defined for them as "between 7 and 12 times a year"), or "often" (defined as "more than 13 times a year"). Nearly one-fifth (17.4%, n = 25) said they were abused only once or twice. The remaining half (48.7%, n = 68) checked "rarely" ("less than twice a year") or "occasionally" ("between 2 and 6 times a year"). For 15 of these people, the abuse began when they were less than three years old, with abuse being most likely to occur between the ages of 10 and 15 ($n = 102$) and 6 and 9 ($n = 88$). Forty-six reported that they had been abused between the ages of 3 and 5. Forty-seven respondents reported that they were still being abused after the age of 16.

Fifteen people sought care from a doctor, six went to a hospital, ten called the police. When asked whom they had told, 61 of the 142, or about 43%, said they had told no one. Smaller numbers told family members ($n = 49$) and/or friends ($n = 53$). Much smaller numbers told teachers ($n = 6$), social workers ($n = 6$), or family doctors ($n = 6$).

Child Abuse: The Perpetrators

About one-sixth of the 496 respondents with children reported that they had abused their children (15.7%, $n = 78$). Nearly half of these parents (48.7%, $n = 38$) said it happened only once or twice, with only 7.7% ($n = 6$) indicating that they were abusive "regularly" or "often." Less than half characterized their own abusiveness as happening "rarely" or "occasionally" (43.6%, $n = 34$).

Two sought a doctor's care; in one case there was police involvement. Twenty-seven told no one, 33 told a family member and 25 told a friend. Eleven went to a counselor, ten saw a psychiatrist or psychologist, six told a social worker and five a family doctor. Only one respondent participated in a self-help group.

Three-children families were more likely to be the scenes of abuse according to these parents, than smaller or larger families. In 30.9% ($n = 21$) of three-children families, parents reported abuse, compared with 10.3% ($n = 12$) of one-child families, 19.4% ($n = 27$) of two child families, and 14.3% ($n = 4$) of 4 or more child families (Chi-Square $= 12.74$, $p = .005$).

Spousal Abuse

Ninety-nine people reported that they were currently being abused by their spouse or lover, 100 reported that they had been so abused in a past relationship. A total of 159 (25.9%) individuals said yes to one or both of these questions, although an additional 22 responded to the more detailed questions on the nature of this abuse. For about

40% of these individuals, the violence occurred only once or twice (40.3%, $n = 73$), for 17.1% ($n = 31$) it happened rarely, for 28.7% ($n = 52$) the violence was occasional. For 13.8% ($n = 25$) it was regular or often.

Twenty-five of these individuals (14.2%) married after the first episode of abuse had already happened. An additional 34.7% ($n = 61$) became victims of their spouse's violence before they celebrated their first wedding anniversary. Another 29.5% ($n = 52$) experienced their first marital violence between years one and five. For the remaining 21.6% ($n = 38$) violence began after the fifth year of marriage. Help was sought from doctors by 48 of these respondents, 20 went to hospitals and 42 called the police.

Thirty-three of these abused spouses told no one, 83 told family members, and 105 told friends. Police ($n = 38$), psychiatrists, or psychologists ($n = 31$) and counselors ($n = 32$) were told with substantially less frequency. Only eight individuals had sought shelter from a residence for battered women. Only two had called a hot line.

Unwanted, Pressured and Forced Sex

Just over two-thirds (67.1%, $n = 390$) of the respondents reported that they had sex with a spouse or lover when they did not want to. Approximately half (51.4%, $n = 301$) said they were pressured into having sex. These experiences were nonviolent and are offered here as background to the focus on sex obtained by violence or its threat. Seven percent ($n = 41$) reported themselves to be the victims of forced sex by a spouse or lover. That is, they were victims of marital rape. For 34.8% ($n = 16$) it happened only once or twice, for 19.6% ($n = 9$) it happened rarely, for 26.1% ($n = 12$) it happened occasionally, and for 19.6% ($n = 9$), it happened regularly.

Rape by Someone Other Than a Spouse

With regard to rape by a non-spouse, 14.0% ($n = 81$) answered yes, and 1.4% ($n = 8$) reported an attempted rape. The rapists were predominantly casual acquaintances ($n = 29$) and strangers ($n = 22$). Family members were responsible for 17 of the rapes, friends for 10, and neighbors for 7. Sixteen of these rape victims told no one, 42 told friends, and 24 told family members. Sixteen told psychologists or psychiatrists, ten told the police, and nine told counselors. Only one called a hot line.

IDENTIFYING THE INTERVIEWEES

A total of 113 women and men were interviewed. While the qualitative analyses presented in chapters 7 through 9 deal with seven fewer individuals, the entire group of interviewees is described here. (Three interviewees who were child abusers only, and four who were survivors of rape by nonfamily members, were not included in the analyses of the qualitative data because their experiences were different from those of victims of family violence.) Of the 106 individuals whose responses were analyzed for the interview portion of this study, 56.6% ($n = 60$) were victims and 43.4% ($n = 46$) were not.

The total sample of interviewees was 75.2% ($n = 85$) female, and 24.8% ($n = 28$) male. Among the victims, 82.1% ($n = 55$) of the 67 interviewees were females, as were 56.5% ($n = 26$) of the 46 non-victim controls. Thus, the victim group is highly female, while the nonvictim control group is more evenly divided between females and males. In terms of specific experiences with intimate violence, 86.7% ($n = 13$) of the 15 participants who had been abused by a spouse in the past were female, as were 64.3% ($n = 9$) of the 14 abused children, all three of the abusive parents, all four of the rape survivors, 95.0% ($n = 19$), of the 20 individuals who had had two experiences, and all ($n = 10$) of those who had had three or four experiences with violence.

Data on educational attainment showed that 5.3% ($n = 6$) had high school diplomas, 16.8% ($n = 19$) had completed some college, 45.1% ($n = 51$) held bachelors degrees, and 32.7% ($n = 37$) had graduate degrees. About a quarter (24.8%, $n = 27$) earned less than $15,000 per year in 1979, 26.6% ($n = 29$) earned between $15,000 and $24,999, 32.1% ($n = 35$) earned between $25,000 and $39,999, and 16.5% ($n = 18$) earned over $40,000 a year. Over two-thirds were employed outside the home (67.3%, $n = 76$). Nearly two-thirds were currently married (62.8%, $n = 71$), 22.1% ($n = 25$) were previously married and 15.0% ($n = 17$) were single. One-third of the interviewees were Catholic (33.0%, $n = 37$), one-third were Protestant (33.0%, $n = 37$), and the remaining third were Jewish (21.4%, $n = 24$) or Other (12.5%, $n = 14$).

It is especially significant that among those who had been abused as children, 43.6% ($n = 17$) reported that prior to their participation in the study they had told no one. Neither had 17.1% ($n = 6$) of the abused spouses and 18.5% ($n = 5$) of the survivors of rape.[2] The

process of being interviewed however, required a move from anonymity to confidentiality for these participants. While great care was
taken to reassure study participants that their confidentiality would
be protected, they still had to come face to face with an interviewer
who knew their names. That they did so is to their great credit and
their willingness to participate is gratefully acknowledged.

A CONCLUDING COMMENT

The major findings presented in each of the chapters are summarized in chapter 10. The point I want to emphasize here, though, is
that the survey data from over 600 individuals are an addition to
the large and growing literature on quantitative aspects of violence
in families and rape. In particular, the individuals' middle-class
standing, the inclusion of men and women, nonvictims and victims
of different sorts of intimate violence, and the use of a followup
intensive interview with over 100 of the survey respondents represent the significant features of this study.

2. These n's include individuals who were victims of multiple experiences. That is, while
14 respondents were abused children only, others who were victims of multiple forms of
intimate violence also were abused as children and their responses are included here.

7

ON THINKING ABOUT
JUSTICE, VIOLENCE AND
CONFLICT

—

In 1933, Kurt Lewin wrote to Wolfgang Kohler, the director of the Psychological Institute at the University of Berlin, where Lewin taught. The letter was never mailed, but was found in Lewin's files and was published in the *Journal of Social Issues* (1986). While Lewin was writing about the abuse of Jewish children by Anti-Semitic Germans, his statement is applicable to the damage suffered by the victims of abuse that occurs in families.

> There have probably been very few Jewish children of any generation who have not been singled out from the natural group of their peers between their 6th and 13th year. Quite suddenly and without any kind of predictable cause, they have been beaten up and treated with contempt. Whether instigated by teachers, by students or simply by people on the street, these recurring experiences pull the ground out from under the feet of the young children and cut off all possibility of objective discussion or unbiased

evaluation. They throw the child totally back upon its own resources. They make all natural supports appear entirely deceptive
and force the young person to exist in a conflicting world of appearance and reality right from the start. Very few children are
capable of surviving such disrupting experiences without suffering
serious damage to their natural growth. After all, these experiences are not just casual irritations, but instead involve the very
foundations of life itself on which all important decisions are based.
Thus the effects are ever present.

Shortly after the letter was written, Lewin left Germany and came
to the United States.

In describing the plight of Jewish children abused by Anti-Semitic
Germans, Lewin makes a number of points about the damage abuse
causes to "natural growth." In particular, his point about existing
in a "conflicting world of appearance and reality" speaks to the concerns of those abused by intimates, too. Mothers, fathers, husbands,
wives are supposed to be loving. When reality betrays this image,
the victim is forced to live in a world beset by fundamental conflict.
Certainly, Lewin's unspoken hope that the Germans would accept
and love the Jews as their own lends this passage its strong applicability to those abused by family members.

The fundamental premise of this chapter is that intimate violence does harm to victims' concepts of justice. Abuse, especially
that which occurs early in one's life, creates a distorted sense of the
way things are supposed to be. What "is" takes on properties of
"ought" as a consequence of the development of the capacity for
moral thinking, whether or not true justice is present (Kohlberg 1969).
Even pain deliberately caused is no sure guide to the absence of justice. It requires an interpretation and there it acquires second order
properties of meaning. That is, violence is *assigned* its lasting meaning. It has no cognitive or moral meaning of its own, in spite of its
high-impact nature. Thus, enduring violence may be connected by
the sufferer to valued ends, such as teaching discipline, asserting
one's rightful authority, or even showing love. The extent of support
for such values is reflected in the general, ready knowledge about
the utility and the worth of violence. Beatings can be easily justified
in phrases that flow from our tongues. Surely most readers can complete these phrases with scarcely a moment's hesitation:

Spare the rod and _____ .
I'm only doing this for _____ .

This will teach you ————————————————————— .
You always hurt ————————————————————— .

The justification of violence, the attention to its potential for educating, socializing, and controlling another human being, seems likely to be present in the reasoning of its victims. Then, if violence is seen as enhancing the likelihood that something good will result, the violence itself may take on positive properties. Those who are the victims of violence are moved by its power and are compelled to make sense of their experiences.

To add to the complexity of deciphering the message of violence, everyone knows that some acts of violence earn the actor high praise. Acts of heroism are too often acts of violence enacted on behalf of one side in a violent conflict. Thus, we are obliged to acknowledge what our world history too amply demonstrates: violence makes change happen. Because some of these changes may be positive, may lead to the protection of valued ideals, property or people, violence can not be simply constructed as injustice.

How then can one be really sure that abuse by someone close is not designed to do some good? To acknowledge that no good can come from family violence seems likely to result in the derogation of the abuser. Such a cognitive choice may be too painful to be tolerated. Such distress may far outstrip the physical pain caused by intimate violence.

Victims of violence in intimate relationships know personally about the multiple ways to "read" and make sense of pain and violence. They know that some interpretations are more tolerable than others and that some thoughts are all but unthinkable. In large part, I undertook to write this book in order to make this point about the profound fragility of knowing what is just in an interpersonal relationship. Being exposed to violence in intimate relationships damages and distorts the "justice concept." (I believe it also narrows the vision of the victim, diminishing the ability to perceive alternatives and leads to an unusual level of acceptance of cognitive inconsistency as a way of coping—subjects addressed in chapter 9).

An undistorted concept of justice is consistent with and a product of Lewin's "natural growth." When natural growth is disrupted, so is the justice concept. Intimate relationships between adults can also suffer from disruptions in natural growth and resulting distortions in the justice concept. The construct holds true for any relationship where persistent injustice does not signal a dissolution of the relationship, but instead is integrated into the very fabric of the relationship.

I present next my interviewees' beliefs about who is to blame, and their descriptions of their relationships as good or bad, fair or unfair, and of their partner's behavior as deserved or undeserved, typical or atypical. Finally, their overall assessments of the extent to which their expectations for intimacy were met are related. Throughout, responses from victims and nonvictims are presented together.

In each section, the concepts are introduced and a prediction is offered. Then, the results of the statistical analyses are presented. The trends revealed by these analyses are then elaborated in respondents' verbatim quotes that reflect and illustrate the major findings.

WHO'S TO BLAME?

It is more than an abstract construct to say that concepts of justice are subjective, influenced by context (Fine 1986). Evidence for distortions that are attributed here to violence in families must be present in what victims of violence actually say about their experiences. The distortions must be observable. Further, they should, in theory, be more blatant and occur more often in the statements of victims than of nonvictims.

Here, the search for distortions in the justice concept took place within the context of issues of blame for episodes of violence (for victims) or conflict (for nonvictims). In some objective sense, the perpetrator or the instigator would seem to be the most blameworthy party, although, of course, other choices for the allocation of blame may be right some of the time. Self-blame for one's own suffering seems likely to result more from distortion (and efforts to cope) than from objectivity.

Victims should tend toward distortion, so it was predicted that they would be most likely to attribute blame to themselves rather than to other factors, and that they would do this more often than nonvictims. Sixty percent ($n = 36$) of the victims implicated themselves in their explanations of the violence.[1] The next most popular

1. The variables used to investigate issues of blame were, in four cases the computed sums of themes and in two cases were single themes that occurred with sufficient frequency to enable analyses to be conducted. Those who were coded as self-blamers said at least one

choice was to say "it was not my fault." Here, participants talked about blame *not* resting with themselves. This response was made by 46.7% ($n = 28$) of the victims. Twenty-five percent ($n = 15$) blamed outsiders, 21.7% blamed the partner, 18.3% ($n = 11$) thought both were at fault and 13.3% ($n = 8$) thought no one was at fault, that it had just happened.

Self-blame was also the most popular choice for the control group, although it occurred somewhat less frequently than it did among victims: 45.7% ($n = 21$) made such remarks. Their second most frequent response allocated blame to both. Nearly a third (30.4%, $n = 14$) thought it was both their faults. About a quarter (26.1%, $n = 12$) thought it was no one's fault, that it just happened; 23.9% ($n = 11$) said it was not their fault, 17.4% ($n = 8$) blamed their partner and 13.6% ($n = 6$) blamed outsiders.

While most of the differences between the victim and nonvictim groups appear substantial, the only one to achieve statistical significance was the tendency to say "it was not my fault." Victims were about twice as likely as non-victims to say episodes of violence were *not* their fault (46.7% vs. 23.9% $p = .028$).[2]

It is interesting that this response choice, with its egodefensive tone, is the one that best distinguishes victims from nonvictims. Further, the content of the remark "it is not my fault" can be understood as a defense against the feeling that it *is* one's fault. That a within-group consideration of responses showed that victims were more likely to blame themselves than to mention any other factor suggests that the nagging thought of self-blame may be lurking be-

---

and as many as five of these themes: it was my fault, I placed myself in a compromising position, I provoked my partner, I feel responsible, I feel partly responsible, I feel responsible at an unconscious level, I blamed myself.

Those who were coded as blaming their partners stated at least one and as many as three of these themes: it was my partner's fault, my partner provoked me, my partner felt responsible, my partner instigated the incident, my partner tricked me.

Those who were coded as saying "it was not my fault" stated at least one and as many as three of these themes: it was not my fault, I did not blame myself, I did not feel responsible.

Those who were coded as saying that outsiders were to blame stated at least one and as many as four of these themes: it was an outsider's fault, it was beyond human control, an outsider did not intervene or try to stop the abuse, an outsider did not want to get involved.

Two remaining analyses of blame involved the choice to blame both oneself and one's partner and the choice to blame no one, to think that it just happened. These analyses were based on participants who said precisely that; they are not computed variables.

2. Small sample sizes mediated against statistical significance in the other analyses where the trends indicated that victims were more likely than nonvictims to blame themselves ($p = .20$), and to blame outsiders ($p = .20$), and were less likely to blame both themselves and their partners ($p = .22$) or to say it was no one's fault, it just happened ($p = .16$). The tendency to blame the partner was equal for victims and nonvictims ($p = .76$).

hind this assertion that it was not their fault. Finally, the apparent contradiction between implicating and not implicating oneself can be understood, I think, in terms of a tension about one's own culpability that, in either case, excludes the perpetrator. It seems likely that the feelings and conflicts that underlie either the attribution or the denial of self-blame are not so very different.

Consider these examples of distortions in the justice concept. These excerpts were selected because they reflect the nature of what the analyses showed to be a central issue for victims in their efforts to allocate blame for episodes of violence: their own contributions. These excerpts from the interview data support the notion that intimate violence can be seen by the victims in terms that implicate themselves more strongly than the perpetrators of the violence. These responses were elicited by question 8 on the interview schedule: "How do you explain the violence (conflict)? Who was to blame?"

A female victim of child abuse said:

> Parents have the right to punish their children. . . . If I got found out or stuck with the blame, I was willing to take it because I knew I had been somewhat guilty. . . . Most of the things that initiated this response [violence] had been something I'd done wrong. I was far from the blameless child.

A female victim of child abuse said:

> When you're that young . . . I had all this love and a wonderful relationship with my father and when things started going wrong, I thought maybe I did something wrong. . . . And for a while . . . I felt responsible for this. I can't distinguish when I became aware it wasn't me, it was him, but I knew there was a time I knew it wasn't me, it was him.

A female victim of her husband's violence said:

> I think it's mostly my fault because I put up with it. . . . I should have just done something definite. Either gotten divorced or really improved it, if I cared enough about him which I did, to go to somebody and really try to improve the relationship. . . . I think he's wrong in being abusive toward me, but there again, it's like, which came first, the chicken or the egg? . . . because of his upbringing, I can see . . . why his reactions are . . . like they are. And mine too. So it was his fault for doing it, and my fault for taking it.

A male victim of spousal abuse said:

Of course, I feel responsible. . . . I was the cause of it because there was something that I did that provoked her.

A male victim of child abuse said:

I really thought it was normal. I thought that was what I deserved because my cousins weren't exactly handled with kid gloves either. . . . I just thought that was the normal course of events—when I think back, that was the only time there was any type of closeness.

Thus, the tendency of victims of violence to see themselves as central to their explanations for the violence they endure—either in part or wholly, either temporarily or in a more lasting way—is exemplified.

EVALUATING THE RELATIONSHIP: GOOD OR BAD?

While pain may provide no innate guide to injustice, it still hurts. Violence does damage the way relationships are evaluated. Unlike attributions of blame, which seem more vulnerable to the urge not to derogate or blame the abuser, words like "good" and "bad" seem likely to be more resistant to modifications in meaning. It may be understandable or justifiable to be hurt, but that does not make it "good." In the simple construction of violence as "bad" and nonviolence as "good," I predicted that victims would be less likely than nonvictims to describe their relationships in good or positive terms, and that victims would be more likely than nonvictims to describe their relationships in bad or negative terms. Further, I predicted this would be true from the beginning or earliest recalled phase of the relationship as well. That is, victims would say things were bad right from the start, while nonvictims would say things were good right from the start. These predictions were supported without exception. Again, quotes that illuminate the statistical trends follow the analyses.

In discussing their relationships, the violence had a direct effect on whether the respondents thought their relationships were "good" or "bad." (Here, in coding the interview data, we looked simply for descriptions of the relationship that were positive or negative.) More than three-quarters (76.1%, $n = 35$) of the nonvictims described their relationships in positive terms. No more than 25% of any of the four victim groups (victims of past spousal abuse, child abuse, two experiences, or three–four experiences) offered such positive descriptions. The fewest positive descriptions came from those with three–four experiences with violent intimate relationships. Only one of these ten individuals described her selected relationship positively.[3] (Chi-Square = 36.102 with 4 df, $p < .001$). Overall, 18.3% of the victims offered positive descriptions of their relationships.

Conversely, describing the relationship as generally bad or negative occurred infrequently among nonvictims: only 10.9% ($n = 5$) offered a generally negative view of their relationship, while 90.0% ($n = 9$) of the victims of three–four experiences, 86.7% ($n = 13$) of the victims of past spousal abuse, and 57.1% of the victims of child abuse ($n = 8$) and two experiences ($n = 12$) described their relationships negatively. (Chi-Square = 42.542 with 4 df, $p < .001$). Overall, 70.0% of the victims described their relationships negatively. In illustration of this finding, these remarks were made by victims as they characterized their relationships negatively:

A woman who had been abused by her father said:

> I don't remember anything affectionate. . . . there wasn't a relationship. . . . I was just trying to survive long enough to get out of there, that's all. It was a combat situation.

A woman who had been abused by her mother described her relationship with her mother with these words:

> Cold, indifferent. We do not have a mother–daughter relationship. . . . It doesn't compare at all with any intimate relationship. . . . there's just no relationship.

Another female victim of abuse by her mother said:

> It was a very hostile, volatile relationship. It was not a good one. It was a love-hate relationship. . . . She never listened. . . . We never sat down and talked. . . . I can never remember any tenderness, any demonstrative kind of love.

A woman who was a victim of past spousal abuse described her marriage this way:

---

3. Note: Respondents talked primarily about one selected relationship, even if they had multiple violence experiences, and this one experience was used in the analyses.

It was a very strained relationship. . . . I think there was always a lack of communication. . . . I had become very indifferent and he was . . . nonexistent to me.

Another woman who had experienced past spousal abuse talked about herself in the relationship:

I tried desperately for years to like him. I will not use the word love. It's impossible to love a man of his character. . . . I was very uncomfortable as his wife. . . . Very ill at ease, not knowing what would trigger off an explosion.

One woman who was a victim of both child and past spousal abuse commented:

Both bad. . . . but one as a child and one when I was a woman . . . they're both very demeaning and mentally exhausting.

Nonvictims' remarks that reflected their tendency to offer generally positive descriptions of their relationships are illustrated by the following:

A woman spoke about her relationship with her spouse:

I was 14 when I met him and was really—he's really been the only man in my life. And it's been a good relationship. We've been happy, and I think we're best friends, we get along. We really don't fight—like when everybody talks about working on a marriage, we don't. It just kind of comes naturally.

Another woman said this about her relationship with her husband:

It was one of those things, that neither of us ever had second thoughts, ever—we weren't even nervous at the wedding. But it was just a very lovely thing. And, fortunately it has remained so.

A man said this about his wife:

I'm in love with my wife. She's in love with me, and I don't know why. It just happens to be that way. And, I think that's great. . . . We're close.

The difference between victims' and nonvictims' comments here is vast. Nonvictims represented themselves as happily involved in good intimate relationships, while victims characterized their relationships with words that reflected the hostility that violence causes.

Although it is not related to prediction, it is interesting to note that these nonvictims made it a point to disclaim insight into the reasons for their positive relationships, describing them as "natural," "fortunate," something that happened even though they "don't know why." Perhaps knowing that they were participants in a study on violence and conflict made these nonvictims hesitate to over-explain the good times. Victims, in the context of these remarks, offered no such disclaimers for their negative relationships.

The Early Relationship

Violent relationships were troubled right from the start. Forty-five percent $(n = 27)$ of the victims mentioned between two and four descriptions of negative aspects of their early relationships.[4] Only 13% $(n = 6)$ of the nonvictims offered an equal number of negative descriptions of early times. Over half of the nonvictims (52.2%, $n = 24$) mentioned *no negative* characterizations of their early relationships, 21.7% $(n = 13)$ of the victims said nothing bad. About one-third of the respondents in the victim and nonvictim groups had one bad thing to say about early times (33.3%, $n = 20$ for victims, 34.8%, $n = 16$ for nonvictims). (Chi-Square = 15.500 with 2 df, $p = .0004$).

The results for good descriptions of early times in the relationship showed the expected pattern. One-third of the victims $(n = 20)$ had nothing good to say, only 6.5% $(n = 3)$ of the nonvictims said nothing good. The highest category of good responses included those who mentioned between three and seven positive aspects of their early relationship. Nearly half (45.7%, $n = 21$) of the nonvictims were in this highest praise group, as were only 13.3% $(n = 8)$ of the victims. One or two good words were offered by 53.3% $(n = 32)$ of

4. Responses to the questions on the early part of the relationship were coded as follows: There were many possible ways that a relationship could be positively or negatively characterized at its beginning. A list of specific, possible responses was generated. These responses were then searched for in the interview transcripts and counted. So, the variable called "EARLYBAD" was the computed sum of the number of times respondents mentioned the following themes in response to the prompt, "TELL ME ABOUT YOUR *EARLIEST RECOLLECTIONS* OF THIS RELATIONSHIP: We argued, things were bad, difficult/strange/weird/peculiar, not fun, there were problems from the beginning, we had nothing in common, violence was present, communication was closed. Similarly, "EARLYGOOD" was the computed sum of these themes: We did things together, things were exciting, fun, good, we had good sex, there was an immediate positive feeling, communication was open, we saw each other a lot, things were wonderful.

the victims and 47.9% (n = 22) of the nonvictims. (Chi-Square = 19.488 with 3 df, p = .0002.)

The sense that things were not good is illustrated by these excerpts from victims.

A woman who was a victim of past spousal abuse made this remark:

I was desperate because I had two kids and no family to help me out and I didn't use my head as far as getting married. . . . I realized I had made a mistake and I just really wanted to get out of it, but I didn't know where to go. . . . I didn't stop to think because there were already signs that he didn't want my children and I was just so afraid of being alone. . . . a voice said it shouldn't be, but I was trying to overlook it.

Another woman who was a victim of past spousal abuse said:

The day I got married I knew I had made a mistake. . . . It was just like . . . getting caught in a trap. . . . I really thought things would change and it just got steadily worse. . . . every day it got worse. . . . I couldn't believe the change.

A woman whose husband abused her after their marriage offered this view:

He was kind of messed up and I should have recognized it then. I remember him getting frustrated and frightening me. I was going to fix him up. I was into rescuing him then. I also wanted to get out of the house and getting married was an honorable way of doing it.

Nonvictims' remarks were generally positive and are illustrated by these examples:

A man who was in the nonvictim group said:

She was completely different than anyone else I had dated. I found her refreshing. She was easy to talk to and when I speak to her I feel like I'm being understood, not just listened to.

A woman from the nonvictim group said:

It was a good relationship. . . . even at first we would talk things out. . . . it was a magnetic thing. . . . we just got along really well. . . . I really liked him a lot.

A man from the nonvictim group described his early relationship:

Our relationship developed immediately. . . . we fell in love right away. . . . we had the same views about life. . . . we couldn't be apart and more than anything we were friends, good friends. I think that's the most important thing.

Thus, these data strongly support the view that notions of "good" and "bad" seem to retain intrinsic meaning and that victims of violence see their relationships as less good and more bad than do nonvictims. In addition, there appears to be no "honeymoon" period for violent relationships. Even then, they are characterized as bad more often and as good less often than are nonviolent relationships.

FAIRNESS, AND THE RELATED CONCEPTS OF DESERVEDNESS, TYPICALITY, AND EXPECTEDNESS

Asking about fairness directly is a somewhat complicated process. I predicted that victims would be more likely than nonvictims to say "No" when asked if what they had experienced was "fair." However, social psychological definitions of fairness usually include aspects of deservingness, and I wondered if victims might see violence as unfair, but deserved in some way. In any case I thought it important to explore what respondents would say when asked if they got what they deserved. I also wondered how the perceived typicality of the partner's actions would differ from their perceived fairness. Perhaps, actions are seen as unfair, but typical, and therefore tolerable. Respondents' expectations for their partners were investigated, too, on the theory that the expectations of victims may be undeveloped or met even if violence is present, leading to a heightened tolerance for violence. While such expectations cannot be taken to suggest that "violence is fair as long as it is expected," still, knowledge about expectations can be useful for understanding how people think about episodes of violence, in terms of some construct of what is to be expected, and perhaps what is therefore tolerable.

Thus, overall the only prediction I offer here is that victims will be more likely than nonvictims to say their treatment was not fair. The other concepts named here are the subjects of victim–nonvictim comparisons, but were not the bases for prediction.

Questions 8A and 8B were worded as follows: "DOES/DID IT SEEM FAIR? LIKE DESERVED TREATMENT? WERE YOUR EXPECTATIONS FOR THE WAY PEOPLE IN THE ROLE OF (PARTNER) BEHAVE FULFILLED? DID YOU FEEL

THAT YOUR (PARTNER) HAD SIMPLY BEHAVED AS HUSBANDS/LOVERS/
PARENTS/MEN SHOULD SIMPLY BE EXPECTED TO BEHAVE? As part of
Question 10, they were also asked WERE YOUR EXPECTATIONS MET?
Because not all interviewees addressed all of these concepts in their
answers on the general issue of fairness, the available sample sizes
for each analysis fell below 80.

Fairness

Consistent with prediction, almost all the victims said the violence
was not fair: 92.9% ($n = 39$) said "no" when asked if it was fair, as
did 72.4% ($n = 21$) of the nonvictims. It is interesting to note that
of the three victims who thought the violence was "fair," two were
victims of child abuse. (Chi-Square $= 4.026$ with 1 df, $p = .045$).

Consider these excerpts from interviews with victims:
A victim of abuse by her former husband reported:

It was never fair . . . the physical part. Sometimes the only way
I'm going to realize how strongly he feels about something is for
him to get downright angry and yell and scream. . . . I take great
offense to the physical part, it's unfair and undeserved. . . . I'm
just doing the best darn job that I can and it's not appreciated.

A woman who had been abused as a child commented:

It wasn't fair. I never understood it. It was like I didn't know what
was going on . . . like playing Monopoly and not knowing the
rules. I was the first born. . . . maybe my parents were still trying
to establish their own rules about bringing up kids.

A female victim of past spousal abuse said:

It never seemed fair because I don't believe in any kind of violence. . . . but I felt I was trapped in the situation and I would
try to rationalize it all . . . but it always seemed unfair.

Deservedness

When the word in question was "deserved," no significant difference
emerged between victims and nonvictims. More than three-quarters
(76.5%, $n = 26$) of the victims said "no," as did 83.3% ($n = 10$) of

the nonvictims.[5] Even the content of victims' and nonvictims' remarks were similar in this area. Consider these responses to the question on the deservedness of their experiences.

A female victim of past spousal abuse reported:

> I often asked myself what I had done to ever deserve something like this. . . . but he couldn't help it . . . and I got into it on my own and there wasn't anyone to help me. It was my own problem and I had to live with it.

Another woman whose husband had abused her said:

> Nobody has the right to make someone else that miserable. . . . I didn't deserve it. . . . I just blame myself for ever getting involved with him.

A man who had been abused as a child said:

> I don't think I was responsible, other than being born at the wrong time. . . . that is the only mistake I made.

A female victim of past spousal abuse said:

> I really didn't think the response I got was warranted . . . part of me felt responsible and part of me felt that it was totally unfair. . . . I mean you are responsible for everything you say and do, but that doesn't mean that you deserve a beating.

Here are illustrative remarks from nonvictims which speak to the same concerns as remarks from victims. Here, both women were talking about conflict in their marital relationships:

> I felt wronged . . . even if I brought it on or could have avoided it, it shouldn't have happened.

> I don't think it's fair, not fair to me or fair to him. . . . there were fleeting moments when I felt responsible, but no, I didn't deserve it.

---

5. When the victim groups are looked at individually, victims of 2 or 3–4 sorts of intimate violence appeared to be more likely than victims of single forms of violence to feel that the violence had been deserved. Numbers of cases were few, though. Two of the five victims of 3–4 types of violence said "yes," as did 4 of the 13 (30.8%) victims of 2 types.

Typicality

The question which referred to the typicality of the partner's behavior elicited the largest difference between victims and nonvictims. Over five out of six (85.6%, $n = 42$) of the victims saw their partner's behavior as atypical for those in the partner's role. Nearly half (46.7%, $n = 14$) of the controls saw their partner's behaviors during conflict situations as atypical. (Chi-Square = 11.920 with 1 df, $p = .0006$.)[6]

Here are examples of victims' disavowals of their abusers' typicality.

A woman who had been abused by her father said:

It must have been when I started school that I realized not all daddies act like my daddy does. . . . all dads don't have to be like mine. . . . some love and play with their kids.

A woman whose former husband had abused her reported:

He's more selfish than the average husband. . . . other husbands are willing to share and take responsibility. . . . I don't think he acts as an average husband would act.

Another victim of past spousal abuse by her husband said:

I thought there has got to be something better than this. He thought I deserved it, but no one deserves being hit and kicked. This wasn't like a marriage. We weren't even friends. I couldn't believe all marriages were like this.

Thus perceived typicality would appear to provide no justification for violent acts. The great majority of victims see violence as plainly atypical, as far from a legitimate part of being a husband or father. Justifications for violence may rest with the individuals involved, but little credence is accorded the view that their problems are attributable to the nature of the roles being filled.

---

6. Victims of child abuse were less likely than the other victim groups to see their partner's behavior as atypical. Seventy-five percent ($n = 9$) of these interviewees believed that their parents' abusive behavior was atypical of parents; 83.3% ($n = 10$) of victims of past spousal abuse saw the behavior as atypical as did 88.2% ($n = 15$) of the victims of 2 experiences with intimate violence. All of the eight respondents who were victims of three or four sorts of intimate violence saw the behavior as atypical.

Expectations

Four response categories were created: Respondents could indicate that their expectations were (1) high and met completely, (2) high and met partially, (3) high and not met or (4) they had no expectations. Among the victims, the most popular response choice was "no expectations," which was mentioned by 34.9% (n = 15) of them. Their second most frequent choice was "high and not met," a feeling expressed by 32.6% (n = 14) of them. Only about one-sixth (16.3%, n = 7) of them reported that their high expectations were met completely or partially. Among the nonvictims, 52.8% (n = 19) reported that their high expectations were completely met; 27.8% (n = 10) reported that they had no expectations, 13.9% (n = 5) said their high expectations were partially met and 5.6% (n = 2) said that their high expectations were not met. The differences between victims and nonvictims achieved statistical significance (Chi-Square = 15.372 with 3 df, p = .0015).[7]

Examples of respondents' remarks are provided for the following three categories: (1) victims who reported that they had no expectations, (2) victims whose high expectations were not met, and (3) nonvictims whose high expectations were met. Sample comments from victims with no expectations are here:

A woman whose former husband had abused her said:

I didn't have expectations. No one is perfect. I don't care about how the rest of the world thinks a husband should behave. He didn't drink often or run around with other women.

Another woman who had been a victim of child abuse said this about her abusive husband:

I didn't know what a husband was supposed to do . . . I have no expectations.

A female respondent whose mother had abused her reported:

I didn't have any expectations. She didn't act like a mother, so I didn't expect anything. I don't think she was a mother person. She

7. Looking at the victim groups individually revealed that those with three or four experiences with intimate violence were very likely to report that they had no expectations (80%, n = 4), as were victims of two experiences (43.8%, n = 7). Victims of past spousal abuse were most likely to say that they had high expectations which were not met (53.8%, n = 7). The nine victims of child abuse in this analysis distributed themselves quite evenly across the four choices, with one-third saying that their expectations were high but not met, and one-third saying that they had no expectations.

didn't care one way or another. I mean some women are meant to be mothers, mine wasn't. She had her own problems to deal with.

Victims who had high expectations that were not met elaborated this feeling with statements like these:
A woman whose former husband had abused her remarked:

I expect a relationship to be somewhat free. I expect people to understand each other and mostly be each other's friend. None of these expectations were met because the person who pretended to be my friend one minute was my absolute enemy the next.

Another female victim of past spousal abuse said:

I really wanted to have a good, sound marriage. . . . I wanted to be the couple next door, a nice family, a nice house. . . . this was the opposite.

In contrast, the modal response for nonvictims indicated that their high expectations were "completely met," as their remarks indicate:
A woman described her expectations for her husband this way:

We talk to each other about everything, anything. He even talks to me about his job, which is apparently strange, because the other guys he works with—I've talked to their wives and they have no idea what's going on at work. I couldn't expect more. We talk, he includes the children and we get time alone. I can't think of anything else I'd need.

Two husbands offered these favorable descriptions of their fulfilled expectations:

My expectations were met in every way. . . . I'm sure if something were to happen to me she would go right to the bitter end. . . . Love, care, consideration, kindness . . . you couldn't ask for more.

She was very supportive and I anticipated her acting exactly the way she did. . . . spouses, in general, should behave that way. . . . part of being married. . . . you know, you're not two anymore, you're one.

So, expectations do distinguish between victims and nonvictims. There is a particular poignancy associated with the finding that "no expectations" was the most popular response for victims. In the absence of expectations, it seems that it would be difficult to maintain

a high standard for acceptable treatment. Further, this view seems
certain to be the sad result of a fundamental distortion in the justice
concept. If one cannot expect anything from those with whom one
is most intimate, how can just or unjust treatment be recognized?

With regard to concepts of justice or fairness, the results in this
section, overall, indicate that the overwhelming majority of victims
(nearly 93%) saw their violent mistreatment as unfair. In support of
this view, large majorities saw this mistreatment as undeserved (77%),
atypical (86%), and as inconsistent with expectations or as occurring
in the absence of expectations (68%).

Interestingly, the majority of nonvictims (72%) also saw the course
of their conflicts as unfair. Further, 83% of those who mentioned
deservedness saw their treatment by their partner during the conflict as undeserved. However, less than half of the nonvictims judged
their partners' behavior as atypical (47%) and more than half reported their high expectations for the relationship were met (53%).

The differences between victims and nonvictims were statistically significant with regard to three of these four concepts, the exception being deservedness. It seems then that victims suffer from
a strong sense of the unfairness of their experiences with violence,
although the key to understanding this sense or the difference between victims and nonvictims does not appear to lie with the notion
of deservedness. Instead, our efforts to construct victims' experiences of injustice might better focus on their beliefs about the atyp-
icality of violence for spouses or parents, about why one too often
may not have expectations for an intimate relationship, and about
what it means to endure in a relationship when expectations are not
being met.

A CONCLUDING COMMENT

The results reported in this chapter provide strong support for the
notion that violence is related to the perception of one's intimate
relationship in negative terms. However, the connection between
these negative descriptions and the clear and consistent recognition
of violence as an injustice, of the perpetrator as blameworthy is far
from established. The nature of such nonconnections and the implications of inconsistency in the thinking of victims are considered
more fully in chapter 10, and the reader is referred there for an interpretive discussion of these findings.

8

COPING: FEELINGS, PERSONALITY CHARACTERISTICS, THOUGHTS AND ACTIONS

———

Throughout the interviews, respondents talked about their feelings, their thoughts, their actions. They described their partners and attempted to characterize their personalities, their styles. They were asked how they felt before, during, and after episodes of violence or conflict and what they said to themselves as they tried to cope with what had happened.

My efforts to quantify these data were extensive. While the richness of comments-in-context is necessarily lost in factor analyses and t-tests, the ideas we counted in the interview transcripts were carefully specified—and there were many. Here, as in the preceding chapter, quantitative data analyses are presented together with illustrative verbatim material from the interview participants. Again, quotes are consistent with the direction of measured differences between victims of violence and those who had experienced conflict in intimate relationships.

GENERAL RESPONSE CLASSES

In order to deal with individuals' responses holistically, general response classes were created: feelings, personality characteristics, thoughts, and actions. Within each class of response, many possible specific ideas were accounted for. Figure 8.1 lists the feelings that were included in the final analyses of these data and shows how

FIGURE 8.1
Counts of Feelings

	Self	Partner
Anger	81	65
Annoyed/Frustration	61	31
Anxiety/Tense/Nervous/Nearing breakdown	61	21
Broken/Depressed/Hopeless/Failure/Unworthy of Success	40	7
Certain/Sure/Secure/Comfortable/Relaxed/ Calm	24	11
Continuing love for other	59	47
Disbelief/Shock	38	14
Disappointment/Disillusionment	17	9
Dislike for self	13	9
Dislike for other	29	15
Embarrassed	43	4
Fear/Panic	70	21
Good/Positive/Enthusiastic/Pleased	65	26
Guilty	35	11
Hatred	30	10
Hurt	50	13
Jealous	7	25
Lonely/Alone/Isolated	24	3
Manipulated	46	11
Regret/Sorry	11	12
Rejecting/Frigid	10	6
Resentment	25	9
Respect/Admiration	11	5
Sympathy for Other	18	4
Sympathy for Self	8	2
Terrible/Bad/Upset/Distressed	92	40
Thrill at leaving	13	1
Tired	40	11
Insecure	16	10

many individuals offered these descriptions of themselves and of their partners. Figure 8.2 shows such an accounting of personality characteristics for self and other. Frequently appearing thoughts appear

FIGURE 8.2
Counts for Personality Characteristics

	Self	Partner
Active	55	43
Affectionate	50	53
Aggressive	19	36
Bad	18	37
Cold	17	36
Cowardly	44	33
Crazy/Disturbed	4	23
Easy-going/Relaxed	17	20
Forgiving	5	21
Good/Nice	16	33
Honest	13	21
Illogical/Irrational	4	19
Intellectual	18	24
"Martyr"	8	3
Naive	22	3
Non-assaultive/Non-violent	21	8
Physically strong	4	20
Suppressed	6	8
Traditional	10	17

FIGURE 8.3
Counts for Thoughts

Bad vibes	14
Behavioral change is coming	11
It'll be over at one point until next time	14
I have to do something about this now	24
Is there something wrong with me?	22
Wishes/Needs	
Live peaceably without pressure	37
Wanted to call police	28
Memory	
Blocked memory	27
Blurred/Fuzzy memory	11
Didn't remember anything	48
Remembered clearly	13

in figure 8.3. Figure 8.4 provides a look at responses which pertain to verbal and physical actions by oneself and by the partner.

While simply looking at these numbers (which represent the sums of responses for victims and nonvictims) provides some insight into the feelings, personality characteristics, thoughts and actions that characterize those who experience violence and conflict in intimate relationships, these numbers are like the pieces of a puzzle that have not yet been fit together.

The great advantage of quantitative data analysis is that it allows

FIGURE 8.4
Counts for Verbal and Physical Actions

	Self	Partner
Verbal Actions		
Accused Other	14	22
Apologized	14	30
Argued with other	49	44
Belittled	31	42
Complained	7	10
Cursed	13	13
Didn't yell/Scream	26	19
Forgave other	13	3
Gave silent treatment	23	28
Lied	12	4
Lost temper/Went crazy	14	37
Pleaded with other to stop/Take self home	14	0
Screamed/Yelled	61	37
Talked calmly/Discussed	37	34
Threatened—		
to abuse other	3	9
to kill other	5	12
to kill self	4	3
to leave	15	7
Physical Actions		
Abused other—		
by hitting/slapping/scratching	16	41
by throwing objects	15	29
by shaking/grabbing	5	20
by pushing/shoving	5	30
by pulling hair	3	21
by choking	1	17
by kicking	5	14

a picture to be assembled. It enables patterns of response to be documented and allows comparisons to be drawn between groups. To these ends, the many variables represented in figures 8.1 through 8.4 were divided into groups of approximately 16 (so that there were about seven times as many subjects as there were variables in each analysis) and were used as the bases for a series of factor analyses. Variables were grouped by area (e.g., feelings) and by actor (whether the self or the partner was being described). The number of factors that could be derived was limited to three for each analysis. See

---

FIGURE 8.4 (continued)
Counts for Verbal and Physical Actions

	Self	Partner
by punching/beating	8	53
by burning	3	6
by stabbing/shooting	1	3
Broke things	12	18
Chased other	3	10
Cried	50	19
Did not do what other wanted	15	5
Extramarital affairs	7	7
Fainted/Blanked out	4	0
Got weapon	5	8
Hugged/Kissed	5	1
Initiated abuse/Conflict	10	26
Protected self	26	2
Provoked other with acts	19	7
Reasoned with other	45	16
Received psychological abuse	10	3
Stopped other from leaving	1	5
Tried to do whatever other wanted	43	12
On Fighting		
Attacked other	30	6
Didn't fight back	38	4
Unable to do anything	17	0
On Flight		
Hid in house	14	4
Left for good	22	7
Left temporarily (out of house)	29	12
Ran away in house	14	1
Walked away	22	12

tables 8.1 through 8.7 (on the following pages) for the presentation of the factor analysis results.

Weighted and standardized factor scales were created from the results of these factor analyses. That is, for any variable which loaded

---

FIGURE 8.5

Ten Weighted Factor Score Scales Used in T-Tests as the Dependent Variables where Condition was the Independent Variable

---

SELF REACTS WITH NEGATIVE FEELINGS = .14223 * (EMBARRASSMENT − 1.0354)/1.8561 + .16098 * (HATRED − .8673)/ 1.9296 + .43007 * (REJECTING − .4779)/3.0122 + .38115 * (BAD − 3.8319)/1.7923

PARTNER WAS DIFFICULT = .35631 * (AGGRESSIVE − .8230)/1.6703 + .31875 * (ILLOGICAL − .3097)/.9362 + .2344 * (PHYSICALLY STRONG − .3717)/.9277

PARTNER WAS ACTIVE = .39321 * (ACTIVE − .7876)/1.3980 + .29970 * (NON-VIOLENT − .0796)/.3030

BAD ANTICIPATIONS = .90499 * (BAD VIBES − .1770)/.5860 + .0309 * (BEHAVIOR CHANGE − .1416)/.5152

WANTING CHANGE = .51504 * (OVER TIL NEXT TIME − .1416)/ .4976 + .20397 * (WANTS TO CALL POLICE − .4690)/.9643

SELF ENGAGES IN DEFENSIVE MANEUVERS = .36500 * (ACCUSED OTHERS − .2212)/.7408 + .38180 * (PROTECTED SELF − .4602)/ 1.2395 + .16814 * (RAN AWAY − .2743)/.9566

SELF REACTS TO VIOLENCE/CONFLICT WITH STRATEGIES = .22641 * (PLEADED WITH OTHER TO STOP − .2124)/.6742 + .22812 * (ATTACKED OTHERS − .6018)/1.2855 + .22244 * (HID IN HOUSE − .2389)/.7353

SELF REACTS TO VIOLENCE/CONFLICT WITH EMOTIONAL INTENSITY = .14476 * (BELITTLED SELF − .61951)/1.3384 + .19338 * (COMPLAINED − .0796)/.3312 + .37957 * (WENT CRAZY − .1947)/.6248 + .2414 * (SCREAMED − 1.1858)/1.8398 + .12605 * (THREATENED − .0708)/.3463 + .14759 * (THREATENED TO KILL SELF − .0442)/.2066

PARTNER CONCILIATORY = .10587 * (PARTNER DIDN'T YELL − .3717)/1.0539 + .39048 * (DISCUSSED − .6903)/1.4885 + .42128 * (TRIED TO DO WHATEVER OTHER WANTED − .1416)/.4793 + .26404 * (LEFT HOUSE TEMPORARILY − .2655)/1.0179

PARTNER THREATENS SUBJECT = .46576 * (PARTNER ACCUSED − .3097)/.8027 + .16344 * (THREATENED TO KILL − .2743)/.9088 + .36432 * (GOT WEAPON − .1416)/.5488

---

on a particular factor, the mean for that variable was subtracted from the value, the resulting difference was divided by the standard deviation for that variable, and the quotient was multiplied by the weighted factor score coefficient. Then, once these computations were complete, the results for the variables which loaded on the same factor were added together, yielding the total score for that factor scale. See figure 8.5 for the specific computed scales.

T-tests were computed using 20 scale scores as dependent variables, and one's status as a victim or a nonvictim as the independent variable. (Here, there were no separate considerations of the four victim groups.) Thus, in all, 20 t-tests were computed, of which 10 achieved statistical significance at p < .05. See table 8.8 for the statistically significant t-test results for all the computed variables.

TABLE 8.1
Factor Analysis of Total Counts of Subjects' Feelings

	VARIMAX ROTATED FACTOR MATRIX		
	Factor 1	Factor 2	Factor 3
ANXTYTOT	0.32864	−0.09292	0.31526
BROKETOT	0.90411	0.25051	0.09222
SHOCKTOT	0.89822	−0.09662	0.18576
OTHRDTOT	−0.00005	−0.05490	0.28934
EMBARTOT	−0.02982	0.57699	0.20078
FEARTOT	0.40998	0.35736	0.47633
GOODTOT	0.09871	0.37798	−0.03496
HATETOT	−0.02898	0.58023	0.00536
HURTTOT	0.82354	0.18729	−0.02696
JEALSTOT	0.03022	0.33008	−0.06000
RJCTGTOT	0.37843	0.80524	−0.10335
RSENTTOT	0.70257	−0.00926	−0.02444
SYMPOTOT	−0.00992	0.02948	0.62590
SYMPSTOT	0.00769	0.01438	0.61706
BADTOT	0.75042	0.57152	−0.04922
TIREDTOT	0.54441	0.44261	−0.05512
Factor	Eigenvalue	Pct of Var	Cum Pct
1	4.89895	63.5	63.5
2	1.59849	20.7	84.2
3	1.21817	15.8	100.0

Feelings

In the area of one's own feelings, three comparisons between victims and nonvictims yielded only one statistically significant difference: The scale was termed "Self Reacts with Negative Feelings," and it was a composite of embarrassment, hate, rejection, and feeling bad. Here, victims were more likely than nonvictims to report that they experienced these negative feelings as a result of violence/conflict with their partners. Two feelings scales that did not distinguish between victims and nonvictims reflected depression and sympathy (for oneself and others). Three comparisons involving the partner's feelings did not achieve statistical significance. Here, the issues involved the partner's depression, feeling bad about oneself, and anger.

TABLE 8.2

Factor Analysis of Total Counts of Subjects' Descriptions of Partners' Feelings

	VARIMAX ROTATED FACTOR MATRIX		
	Factor 1	Factor 2	Factor 3
ANGERPTT	0.07523	−0.05684	0.71254
ANNOYPTT	0.18117	−0.01377	0.80924
ANXTYPTT	0.53159	0.08013	0.02061
BROKEPTT	0.80683	0.03274	−0.13001
DISAPPTT	0.59907	0.00792	0.08517
OTHRDPTT	0.63211	−0.00648	0.08312
FEARPTT	0.42132	0.02611	0.05628
GOODPTT	−0.00097	0.32053	0.45840
ALONEPTT	0.65288	−0.00623	0.07844
MANIPPTT	0.23761	0.53280	0.03040
SYMPSPTT	−0.06052	0.70334	−0.00602
BADPTT	0.61195	0.00815	0.27553
THRLVPTT	−0.05791	0.99545	0.05069
Factor	Eigenvalue	Pct of Var	Cum Pct
1	2.93900	47.8	47.8
2	1.89025	30.7	78.5
3	1.32000	21.5	100.0

Here are quotes from victims that illustrate the presence and nature of negative feelings in themselves. Such feelings were the only ones of those tested to distinguish victims from nonvictims:

Two women whose ex-husbands had abused them said:

> I felt contempt for him and for myself shame and disgust because I was part of the situation. I felt bad about myself because if I was all right than I wouldn't be treated like this. I was ashamed of myself for staying in the situation and for the situation itself. I was ashamed that any of it was happening.

> I was afraid. I wanted to get away from him. But, if I did anything it was worse. I felt like a little kid, a fool. I would wonder what people would think if they were to know. I'd be so embarrassed. I'd look like such a fool.

A man whose mother had abused him said:

> When I got in trouble for playing with fire my mother locked me in my room. I began burning my baseball cards. I was holding the cards and burning my fingers. I was so overwhelmed I didn't re-

TABLE 8.3
Factor Analysis of Total Counts of Subjects' Personality Traits

	VARIMAX ROTATED FACTOR MATRIX		
	Factor 1	Factor 2	Factor 3
ACTVTOT	−0.04144	0.31865	0.01108
AFFECTOT	0.01452	0.19965	0.54041
AGRESTOT	0.00956	0.34893	0.04054
GNICETOT	0.15029	0.46962	−0.16950
INTLTTOT	−0.07446	0.57825	0.08950
NAIVETOT	0.37236	0.00733	0.15869
NONVITOT	0.03072	−0.06183	0.32937
STRNGTOT	0.69776	−0.06511	0.01991
TRADTOT	0.70077	0.04130	−0.17058
CRAZYTOT	−0.01262	−0.00623	0.50805
Factor	Eigenvalue	Pct of Var	Cum Pct
1	1.15907	42.5	42.5
2	0.86411	31.7	74.2
3	0.70443	25.8	100.0

TABLE 8.4
Factor Analysis of Total Counts of Subjects' Descriptions of Partners' Personality Traits

| | VARIMAX ROTATED FACTOR MATRIX | | |
	Factor 1	Factor 2	Factor 3
ACTVPT	0.15213	0.55850	0.08424
AGRESPT	0.63317	−0.08575	0.13002
COLDPT	0.35589	0.20461	0.05049
CWRDPT	−0.13453	0.35312	−0.02144
GNICEPT	−0.01875	−0.02869	0.34825
ILGICPT	0.60828	0.02965	−0.08949
NAIVEPT	0.35263	0.00936	−0.12506
NONVIPT	−0.11900	0.48216	0.03269
STRNGPT	0.51071	−0.10599	−0.05071
RELAXPT	−0.05209	0.07848	0.68808
CRAZYPT	0.20058	0.33814	−0.08653
Factor	Eigenvalue	Pct of Var	Cum Pct
1	1.38955	48.1	48.1
2	0.87467	30.3	78.4
3	0.62558	21.6	100.0

TABLE 8.5
Factor Analysis of Total Counts of Subjects' Thoughts about Episodes of Violence/Conflict

| | VARIMAX ROTATED FACTOR MATRIX | | |
	Factor 1	Factor 2	Factor 3
BADVITOT	0.92731	0.03969	0.13075
BECHATOT	0.42939	0.20230	0.21851
TILNXTOT	−0.00731	−0.03054	0.60257
DONOWTOT	0.03169	−0.11399	0.26672
WRNGMTOT	0.37941	−0.18101	−0.03118
WRENDTOT	0.14245	0.11936	0.34062
FUZMMTOT	−0.02586	0.43061	−0.08707
NOMEMTOT	0.02428	0.76135	0.05188
Factor	Eigenvalue	Pct of Var	Cum Pct
1	1.32637	49.0	49.0
2	0.85251	31.5	80.5
3	0.52682	19.5	100.0

alize I was burning my fingers. The burning hurt but it wasn't as painful as the fear of my mother beating me. My mother, my whole foundation was doing this to me and that was more than I could take.

As noted above, such negative feelings as those expressed by these individuals occurred significantly more often in victims than in non-victims.

Personality Characteristics

In the area of personality characteristics, three comparisons involving the respondents' own characteristics yielded no significant differences. The areas tapped by these scales pertained to the interviewees' traditionality, positive qualities (intelligence and being good or nice) and the tendency to show emotion. However, both of the two comparisons involving characteristics of the partner achieved statistical significance. One scale, termed "Partner Was Difficult," was a composite of responses that characterized the partner as aggressive, illogical, irrational, and physically strong in the context of violence/conflict. Victims were significantly more likely than non-victims to describe their partners as difficult.

Consider these examples. Three female victims of past spousal abuse described their partners with these remarks:

He was insulting, calling me names. . . . after awhile I didn't even know what was going on. . . . He's really strong. I already knew how strong he was. . . . to fight back would be like punching a wall. . . . he's always had manual labor jobs so he's pretty muscular. It would be ridiculous for me to offer resistance to a person like that.

He knew verbally he could never win an argument. He wanted to use his strength over me and his power to prevent me from getting out in the world. He wanted to protect me and his relationship with me. He didn't want me to change because that might change something with us. He'd get mad and take over.

He was kind of like a volcano. He had a lot of pent up violence. He would get frustrated and bang the top of the car to frighten me.

The second scale about partners' personality was termed "Partner Was Active" and was a combination of the responses that described the partner as active or assertive and as nonviolent. Nonvictims were more likely than victims to describe their partners as active.

Two women who were not victims of their husbands' violence characterized their partners in ways that emphasized their nonviolent qualities and their more positive styles of conflict resolution:

> He's a very gentle man. He has a lot of self control. People with self control have different ways to channel frustration. He doesn't have to be violent.

TABLE 8.6

Factor Analysis of Total Counts of Subjects' Actions in Relation to Episodes of Violence/Conflict

	VARIMAX ROTATED FACTOR MATRIX		
	Factor 1	Factor 2	Factor 3
ACCUSTOT	0.70456	−0.04261	−0.04178
BELITTOT	0.33513	0.04585	0.36937
CMPLNTOT	−0.03548	−0.09692	0.47410
SILTXTOT	0.36797	−0.02387	0.00768
LIEDTOT	0.38731	0.04225	−0.04908
WCRAZTOT	−0.04310	−0.03548	0.63900
OSTOPTOT	0.12551	0.54456	0.03779
SCRMDTOT	0.25237	−0.16612	0.48813
DISCSTOT	−0.00624	−0.31479	−0.14401
THRETTOT	−0.04899	0.13543	0.36287
TKILOTOT	−0.10244	0.17302	0.34505
PRSLFTOT	0.69729	0.22468	0.05640
PSYABTOT	−0.01889	0.39261	0.01242
DOFOTTOT	0.03323	0.34461	−0.13318
ATCKOTOT	0.06409	0.53601	0.13876
NOFTBTOT	0.25951	0.37374	−0.06610
HIDTOT	0.06702	0.53891	−0.01985
LEFTGTOT	−0.02422	0.36963	−0.00103
LEFTTTOT	0.21654	0.32157	0.30049
RANAWTOT	0.52938	0.13615	0.02265
Factor	Eigenvalue	Pct of Var	Cum Pact
1	2.36993	46.6	46.6
2	1.39038	27.3	73.9
3	1.32936	26.1	100.0

There was never any violence. Some people are more prone to be violent. A man that is assured of himself, has a good job is more likely to be a man who helps with the dishes and isn't violent. We never needed to resort to violence.

Thoughts

In the area of thoughts, three t-test comparisons were computed, of which two achieved statistical significance. The first, termed a "Bad Anticipations Scale," was a composite of responses in which respondents reported having "bad vibes" and thinking that a behavior

TABLE 8.7

Factor Analysis of Subjects' Descriptions of Partner's Actions in Relation to Episodes of Violence/Conflict

	VARIMAX ROTATED FACTOR MATRIX		
	Factor 1	Factor 2	Factor 3
ACCUSPT	−0.02442	0.02936	0.73402
APOLGPT	−0.00968	0.36259	0.02798
CURSEPT	0.01778	0.58013	0.12922
NOYLLPT	0.37760	0.01081	−0.11824
LIEDPT	−0.00259	−0.02457	0.16557
WCRAZPT	0.01517	0.56034	−0.07643
SCRMDPT	−0.06433	0.24837	0.14953
DISCSPT	0.67907	−0.10534	−0.08335
TKILOPT	−0.02167	0.02407	0.48716
NOTDOPT	−0.02835	0.35653	−0.13212
WEAPNPT	0.01612	0.00252	0.67231
INITAPT	−0.04525	0.02079	0.10473
RESNDPT	0.29980	0.03416	0.01567
DOFOTPT	0.58356	0.61674	−0.01673
LEFTTPT	0.65779	−0.07611	0.01769
Factor	Eigenvalue	Pct of Var	Cum Pct
1	1.67995	40.0	40.0
2	1.40740	33.5	73.5
3	1.11170	26.5	100.0

change was coming. Victims did this more often than nonvictims.
Three women who were the victims of past spousal abuse and

TABLE 8.8

T-Test Comparisons between Victims and Nonvictims on Ten
Aspects of Feelings, Personality Characteristics, Thoughts
and Actions

Group	n	Mean	SD	t-value	two-tailed p
Self Reacts with Negative Feelings					
Victims	64	−0.1758	0.629	2.13	.036
Nonvictims	46	−0.3697	0.311		
Partner Was Difficult					
Victims	64	0.1994	0.571	3.66	.000
Nonvictims	46	−0.0860	0.211		
Partner Was Active					
Victims	64	0.1657	0.351	−2.47	.016
Nonvictims	46	0.3822	0.515		
Bad Anticipations					
Victims	64	0.1647	1.168	2.44	.017
Nonvictims	46	−0.2108	0.324		
Wanting Change					
Victims	64	0.1261	0.728	3.19	.002
Nonvictims	46	−0.1824	0.222		
Self Engages in Denfensive Maneuvers					
Victims	64	0.1606	0.916	3.10	.003
Nonvictims	46	−0.2106	0.236		
Self Reacts to Violence/Conflict with Strategies					
Victims	64	0.1778	0.620	5.34	.000
Nonvictims	46	−0.2388	0.058		
Self Reacts to Violence/Conflict with Emotional Intensity					
Victims	64	0.2530	0.755	2.03	.045
Nonvictims	46	0.0339	0.355		
Partner Conciliatory					
Victims	64	0.0284	0.329	−3.10	.003
Nonvictims	46	0.4720	0.931		
Partner Threatens Subject					
Victims	64	0.1452	0.989	2.63	.010
Nonvictims	46	−0.2097	0.365		

one woman who had been abused as a child offered insight into the experience of having "bad anticipations."

> It was a split second change. I just knew that the look on his face was different. . . . I was too afraid to look in his eyes and see what was happening. . . . [He was] like a rabid animal. . . . it would be a very even keeled plane and all of a sudden he'd just have this look in his eye and I knew I had better get out of there quick.

> When I started to say something that might get him inside I caught it—an instinct not an actual acknowledgement. . . . I couldn't quite put my finger on it, but I had bad vibes. . . . I thought, this person has violence inside him or a lot of anger or something. I knew it was time to be scared.

> I was folding laundry and he came in and told me he was sick of not getting the rights he expected as a husband. I just continued to fold the laundry and I heard him in another room in the basement. I suddenly got a feeling that all was not well and I headed for the stairs. He turned the corner and held up a shot gun and said if I took another step I was dead. I was really scared and I believed him. I knew then I had to get out.

> I could hear the train and I knew my father would be on it. Two blocks of walking and I would hear the door slam. Then I'd be scared. I knew then if it was going to happen or not. I knew what I was in for. I could tell and expect it.

The second area involved the wish for change and was called the "Wanting Change" scale. The thoughts included here were, "It'll be over until next time," and "I want to call the police." Victims were more likely to have such thoughts than nonvictims.

A woman describing her reactions to her husband's violence described the feeling of "wanting change" this way:

> I wanted to call the police and have him locked up but I was feeling too much of his emotions and not enough of my feeling of survival. It was hard for me to separate my problems from his. I know I could have had him locked up. I even wanted to, but I just couldn't bring myself to do it.

The "thought" which did not distinguish victims from nonvictims involved reported memory disruption or loss.

Actions

Five actions scales were computed, three which involved actions by the interviewees and two which involved actions by their partners. All achieved statistical significance in the comparisons between victims and nonvictims. The "Self Engages in Defensive Maneuvers" scale was a composite of responses which indicated that the respondent accused the other, protected her/himself and ran away. Victims were more likely than nonvictims to engage in these defensive maneuvers.

Here are two examples, the first from a woman who was abused as a child and the second from a woman whose husband had abused her:

> I would defend my face or my head or whatever he was trying to hit . . . just trying to block it. Afterwards I would go through a depression stage. I would just cry and cry and fantasize about getting away. I would fantasize about a different kind of family. It was an escape. It would help me get over that period of being depressed and feeling rejected.

> I tried to calm him down, it didn't do any good. I pleaded with him to stop . . . at least to let me go or just to get him out of the house, but he wouldn't go along with that. I tried to get out of the room, but he slammed me into the dresser. . . . I was trying to be rational it just didn't do any good.

The second area involved the "Self Reacts to Violence/Conflict with Strategies." The summed responses were these: the respondent pleaded with the partner to stop, she/he attacked the partner, and she/he hid in the house. Victims were more likely than nonvictims to react with these strategies.

A woman who was abused as a child described her reactive strategies:

> I would run away, mentally that is. I would imagine things and fantasize. I would imagine I had different parents, happy, loving, together. I would just run away into my fantasy world. It helped. I saved me from being crazy.

A woman who had experienced past spousal abuse reacted this way:

I would try to calm him down, mollify him, sort of play for time because I knew eventually he would fall asleep . . . I'd say, I'll go make you a cup of coffee and I'd spend half an hour in the kitchen making coffee, things like that. . . . one time I said the dogs were out and I had to get them inside and I went to a neighbor's house for two hours. I knew he'd be asleep when I came back.

The third scale, "Self Reacts to Violence/Conflict with Emotional Intensity" included those who reported that they belittled, complained, went crazy, screamed, made threats (in general) and threatened to kill themselves. Victims were significantly more likely than nonvictims to report these reactions of emotional intensity.

A woman whose husband abused her offered this description of her emotional response:

I would scream and yell—tell him I'd fix him, or something stupid like that. After it was over I would want to hurt myself, thinking it would hurt him. I figured if I was dead I couldn't get hurt anymore. I would do horrible things to myself. I didn't really want to kill myself. I just wanted to scare him into realizing what he'd done. I'd take pills and hurt myself and think that my kids would be better off without me. All I would do is make a mess of things.

Another woman victim of spousal abuse said this:

I would say things that I knew would really hurt him and then I would run and hide and cry by myself, hoping that I would die because I couldn't take anymore. I remember sitting in the bathroom with the door locked, trying to cry quietly so he wouldn't hear me. I thought I was going crazy.

With regard to the partner actions scales, one was termed the "Partner Conciliatory" scale. It included descriptions of partners who did not yell, who talked calmly, discussed, tried to do whatever the other wanted and left the house temporarily. The nonvictims were more likely to report that their partners were conciliatory than were the victims.

Nonvictims, first a husband, then a wife, exemplified their perceptions of their partners as conciliatory as follows:

I don't like to go to sleep without things solved. I knew that before the night was over, if she didn't say anything about what had happened, I would. I always try to figure out what she's saying and try to figure out if I'm out of line. I think she does that too. I mean, besides my wife, she is my best friend.

When we are angry we let it go for a while and then talk it out. I want to work out the problem and so does he. He gets angry and I try to understand his anger. That's part of the commitment I made when I married him.

The second scale was called the "Partner Threatens Self" scale and included accusations, threats to kill, and getting a weapon. Victims were significantly more likely than nonvictims to report that their partners threatened them in these ways. Here are two comments from female victims of their husbands' violence:

He said, "I'm getting my razor, I can do a better job than this." . . . he said over and over. "I'm going to kill you." . . . this was the first time he said it and I really believed it. Other times I didn't feel like he meant it. . . . other times it was just a threat.

I was really scared for my life sometimes. One time he held a pillow over my face and I couldn't breathe. He told me he was going to kill me. He enjoyed scaring me, it made him feel very in control.

In ways that were consistent with what one would expect, actions that involved the initiation of intense activity or reactions to it were more characteristic of victims than of nonvictims. Actions that reflected lower intensity conflicts were more characteristic of nonvictims than of victims.

AN INTEGRATIVE CONSIDERATION OF THE FINDINGS ON FEELINGS, PERSONALITY CHARACTERISTICS, THOUGHTS, AND ACTIONS

It was not equally easy to find differences in all of these areas of comparison. In particular, no differences emerged in characterizations of the partners' feelings or in descriptions of one's own personality traits, even though two personality scales and two actions scales distinguished abusers from nonabusers and three actions scales distinguished victims from nonvictims. One feeling scale of three tested distinguished victims from nonvictims, as did two thoughts scales of three tested.

The interpretation of nonsignificant differences and the consideration of how significant and nonsignificant differences together form a coherent whole are complicated processes at best. Still, a major purpose of these global, holistic assessments was to capture the "bigger picture"—to allow life's complexities to be reflected comprehensively with attention to detail, rather than to represent them only in terms of specific, illustrative examples of violent or conflictful times.

From the nondifferences between victims and nonvictims, and between their descriptions of abusers and nonabusers, we can learn not only about how they are not different, but also about the real gap that can exist between actions and what we might assume to be their antecedents. For example, it seems from the pattern of findings discovered here that violence is not a consequence of extraordinary feelings in the partner. Victims did not generate a separate vocabulary, unfamiliar to nonvictims, to characterize their partners' feelings during violent times. Instead, the feelings that were said to accompany conflict were apparently the same as those that accompanied violence. (As general constructs, these similar feelings were reflected in scales that tapped the interviewees' depression, the partners' depression, the interviewees' sense of sympathy for themselves and their partners, and descriptions of the partners' feeling bad for themselves.)

Nor did victims see their characters in ways that were distinct from the ways nonvictims saw themselves. They used the same kinds of words to describe their personalities whether they resolved conflict with or without violence. (At issue in these three comparisons were the interviewees' traditionality, positive qualities, and tendency to show emotion.) Partners were seen as characterologically different. Both of two comparisons which touched on the partner's personality achieved statistical significance ("Partner Was Difficult," "Partner Was Active"). Victims were more likely to see their partners as difficult; nonvictims were more likely to see them as active.

In the areas of one's own feelings and thoughts, victims expressed themselves differently from nonvictims in areas that reflected reactions to violence. All three differences (out of six tested) were reactive: "Self Reacts with Negative Feelings," "Bad Anticipations," and "Wanting Change." Yet, as noted above, in terms of basic personality characteristics, victims did not describe themselves any differently from nonvictims. All three comparisons in this area proved nonsignificant.

In fact, it was only in relation to actions, per se, that victims and nonvictims differed from each other in five out of five comparisons. Victims were more likely than nonvictims to engage in defensive maneuvers, to employ strategies in their efforts to stop the violence, and to react with great emotional intensity. (This last category is not included in the category of "feelings" because the emotional intensity had to be reflected in behaviors like screaming or yelling or making threats in order to be counted.) Abusers were characterized as making threats more often, nonabusers as being more conciliatory.

Overall, then, these findings suggest that victims are not very different from nonvictims. Five of the six comparisons that involved feelings and personality traits of the interviewees were statistically nonsignificant. Only "Reacting with Negative Feelings," certainly a variable that suggests a response to the violence, distinguished victims from nonvictims. Thus, these data support the assertion that victims are not characterologically different from those who do not experience violence. Instead, the differences are reflected in their reactions to the violence itself, in their coping responses to the acts perpetrated against them. And, then the victims appear to be often resourceful and reactive in ways that do distinguish them from nonvictims, whose experiences with conflict present them with challenges of apparently lesser intensity.

A fuller consideration of the implications of these differences and nondifferences between victims and nonvictims appears in chapter 10.

9

THE PERCEPTION
OF ALTERNATIVES

The perception of alternatives to violence is basic to the developed awareness of violence as an injustice and is fully as subjective as the nature of injustice, itself. Complexities abound in efforts to say what is an alternative and what is not, and what might be an alternative for someone else but not for oneself. Violence is a stressor which seems certain to inhibit the sorts of creative, expansive thinking that would enable the perception of many, varied alternatives. Further, violence in intimate relationships is fundamentally confusing, as one who is supposed to be an ally acts like an enemy.

Having already explored differences between victims and nonvictims with regard to conceptions of justice (in chapter 7) and their general reactions to violence or conflict (in chapter 8), we now turn our focus to the respondents' views of their problems set within the context of "other considerations." These "other considerations" reflect my efforts, as expressed in the interview questsions, to get the interviewees to take the long view, to see their difficulties in alternative ways, with alternative solutions, and to be detailed in their explanations for what they had experienced and for how it might have been different.

Thus, this chapter deals with (1) the alternatives the respondents saw, did not see, and nearly saw to their situations, (2) the sorts of explanations they generated for the problems in their relationships, and (3) the extent to which they saw their experiences as frequent, or not, in the general population. Again, comparisons between victims and nonvictims are emphasized throughout, and illustrative quotes from the respondents accompany the statistical analyses.

SEEING ALTERNATIVES AND THE TOLERANCE OF COGNITIVE INCONSISTENCY

Question 14, the last on the interview schedule, asked: DID YOU SEE ANY ALTERNATIVES TO THIS SITUATION? WAS THERE ANYTHING YOU COULD HAVE DONE TO PREVENT THESE EVENTS? In reading through transcripts early on during the data gathering, I noticed an unusual pattern among the responses. Many participants, particularly those who had experienced violence, gave answers that were internally inconsistent. For example, one man who answered this question about his father's abuse of him said this:

No. There were no alternatives. As I said, I took the blame upon myself. [The Interviewer asked, "Was there anything you could have done to prevent these events?"] Yes. I could have been totally passive, totally compliant, and totally responsive to everything he wanted. I could have avoided it, yes.

A woman who was talking about her husband's violence said this about the availability of alternatives:

No. None whatsoever. The police were my only alternative. [The Interviewer asked if she ever called the police.] Yes. And I will again. All he has to do is lift a hand or attack my children or me.

As I read these responses, my first thought was that they did not make sense. If the woman quoted above knew that the police afforded her an alternative to her husband's violence, why did she begin her answer by saying, "No. None whatsoever?" It seemed to me that a consistent response from this woman would have read more like this:

"I had an alternative. I called the police and I would do so again."

Responses like those cited above caught my interest and I made a detailed study of the responses by victims and nonvictims to the "alternatives" question. Even the presence of a few such responses confirmed my belief that the psychological press to restore and maintain consistency that has been advanced by dissonance theorists may not hold under complex, real-life circumstances. (See Fine 1986 for an excellent discussion of the reality and importance of what she terms "contradictory consciousness.") However, I wanted to document the extent to which such inconsistencies occurred, to go beyond these anecdotal observations.

Because this analysis depended upon the consideration of ideas in the context of other related, but often contradictory, ideas, this analysis was conducted not by computer but by hand. Each response to Question 14 was read and coded as either internally "consistent" or "inconsistent." In total, 95 subjects responded to this question. (For a number of reasons including tape failures, interviewers who skipped question 14, interviewers who suggested to the respondents what their alternatives might have been, the number of cases is somewhat reduced.) Of the 95, 54 were victims of violence, 41 were not. In both conditions, the majority of the respondents gave responses that were internally consistent: 63% ($n = 34$) of the victims and 81% ($n = 33$) of the nonvictims gave responses that were consistent from beginning to end. However, 37% ($n = 20$) of the victims and 19% ($n = 8$) of the nonvictims gave responses that were internally inconsistent. This difference between victims and nonvictims approached statistical significance (Chi-Square = 3.30 with 1 df, $p = .07$). Examples of inconsistent responses by victims and consistent responses by nonvictims are provided here.

A woman whose husband had abused her offered this response:

> At the time, no. [I could have] called the police and had him locked up, but . . . I was feeling too much of his emotions and not enough of my feeling of survival. . . . I felt the police betrayed me. They didn't really.

A woman whose husband had abused her offered this insight into the inconsistency experience:

> When my kids were little I didn't. I couldn't have left. . . . There was no serious alternative. [Interviewer said, "Later on . . .] I consciously made a choice to do two things. I was going to take my punishment and stick with this thing and try to make it work

and I was also going to go and get a way to make a living, in case it didn't.

Here is an example of what happened when the interviewer pointed out the respondent's inconsistency. The respondent was a victim of her husband's violence.

The only alternative that I could think of was just to leave. And take the children with me and try to fend, one way or another. And that seemed like an impossible situation with no money, no job, no car, no place to go. . . . [Interviewer reminds her that she had left once] . . . that was only for a couple of days and I'd have to say that was the only time I really left. I guess it was just one of those times when I felt I was at the end of my rope and I was going to get out of that house come hell or high water, and out I went. [She then goes on to recall other times she left and times she called the police.]

One woman, who had been abused by her father when she was a child, reported that she had had four years of intensive psychotherapy. Her insight into the inconsistency issue was compelling:

Finally, I said, "You know I hate you—you're a creep, you're a bastard, but I love you. I'm not going to hold that back anymore," I said, "but, you're really a bastard." And I went on and on like this and he was just flabbergasted. . . . I felt so good after saying that. Of course, he didn't know how to take it. I didn't care how he took it. That's about it.

Nonvictims were more likely than victims to offer internally consistent descriptions of their alternatives, as is exemplified in these quotes:

A man described alternatives to his marital breakup this way:

The alternative would have been to throw in the towel earlier. . . . I don't think I could have done anything to avoid the eventuality (of breaking up).

Another man said this about his relationship with his wife:

We could move to neutral ground (geographically). That's one alternative. The other alternative—probably a more realistic one would be to talk it out and get it out more in the open.

A woman offered this response about her husband:

No. No. I don't think so. I don't believe in trying to change somebody.

There are several significant points to highlight about the general presence of inconsistency in these responses and about the somewhat greater likelihood that inconsistencies were present in the responses of victims than nonvictims. First, there is support in these findings for the idea that the press for cognitive consistency or psychological equilibrium is not universal and cannot be assumed to be a motivating force in the psychologies of all people. Further, inconsistency seemed not only tolerable, contrary to what has been theorized, but also, at least sometimes, barely noticed. And, in those instances when it was pointed out, it seemed to cause little or no disruption to the individual's sense of self.

Second, to the extent that the awareness of alternatives really is basic to the awareness of injustice itself, the fleeting and sporadic knowledge of alternatives captured in the responses to this question support the notion that knowing injustice is no simple process. While one might imagine that a victim would build a case for injustice in a linear, cumulative way, mentally stacking one injury upon another, these data suggest that the building process occurs simultaneously with a dismantling process. It is as if knowledge is at once acquired and forgotten. Exposure to an idea—even an idea expressed by oneself—is not enough to insure that another idea, inconsistent with the first, will be rejected. Seemingly, ideas that do not go together logically may go together psychologically. Knowing that a tolerance for inconsistency may be characteristic of as many as 35 to 40 percent of victims of family violence fosters new insight into the psychological processes that inhibit the development of a consistent, cumulative sense of injustice in the face of violence.

Third, it seems likely that this tolerance for inconsistency reflects a general defense strategy of denying—at least sometimes—the pain that would come from confronting fully the implications of a loved one's violence. Denial is a classic defense mechanism when it operates completely, and when it does, it is an aspect of neurotic functioning. Here, though, we are seeing the incomplete, only partially effective operation of such an ego-protective strategy. Thus, while defense mechanisms can be expected to reduce the amount of energy available for conscious processing, the tolerance of inconsistency would be expected to keep the level of one's psychological energy high. Inconsistency should hold some tension around it, and that tension may be absorbing in a way that its resolution in consistency would not be. Victims of violence seemed to divide their energies between knowing the violence, which is important for their physical safety, and not knowing the violence, which is important for their psychological safety. As their own words indicate, they are thinking two things at once. Under these circumstances, thinking a third thing—developing alternatives premised in nonviolence—may be psychologically impossible. Thinking only one thing (i.e., that violence is intolerable) and continuing to live in a violent intimate relationship may also be impossible.

PERCEPTIONS OF THE CAUSES OF PROBLEMS IN THE RELATIONSHIP

With regard to the perception of the causes of problems in the relationship, an a priori prediction had been made. I hypothesized that victims would have a narrowed view of the causes of problems in their relationships and that they would tend to focus on their partners as the cause. Nonvictims were hypothesized to be more expansive in their consideration of the reasons for problems. Other factors, external to their partners, were hypothesized to receive causal attention when the problems did not include violence. Four categories of causes were generated, based on the most frequently occurring responses to QUESTION 6: WHAT DO YOU THINK CAUSED THIS (THESE) INCIDENT(S)?

The response categories were: (1) general, enduring times of stress (e.g., the loss of a job); (2) specific external pressures (e.g., the death of a parent); (3) children, and (4) personality problems in the partner. Before considering the actual patterns of response, it is worth invoking the tenets of attribution theory, a theory in social psychology which advances the idea that most people tend to attribute their own problems to external, situational factors (e.g., *I* failed the test because it was a hard one), but tend to attribute the problems of others to internal, personality factors (e.g., *you* failed the test because you did not study hard enough). (See for example, Jones and Davis 1965; Kelley 1972; MacArthur 1972). To the extent that my interviewees saw the problems in their relationships as their *own* problems, the more likely they should have been to make *external* causal attributions (e.g. to general, enduring times of stress). Alternatively, if they did not see their relationship problems as their own, they should have been more likely to attribute the problems to personality issues in the other person—in this case, their partner in an intimate relationship. Thus, in part, a finding that interviewees attributed responsibility for problems in the relationship to the partner's personality, would support the idea that they did not see the relationship's problems as *their* problems, that they had some psychological distance from the troubles in their relationship. Attribution theory would lead to these predictions and would also purport that a bias is revealed in the perceiver when such a pattern of causal thinking is present. To the extent that this attributional bias protects the self, the function of the bias is clear. For this reason, under the stress to oneself imposed by violence, the biased tendency to make external attributions for oneself, but internal attributions for others, may be further exaggerated. In addition, as a matter of reality, victims may see themselves as powerless to prevent the other's actions, and therefore may find it simply incredible that they must bear the responsibility for their problems in the relationship.

In the statistical comparisons between victims' and nonvictims' attributions, three of the four comparisons—specific external pressures, children, and personality problems in the partner—achieved statistical significance at $p < .05$, and the fourth—general times of stress—approached significance at $p = .087$. See table 9.1 for these findings.

TABLE 9.1
A Comparison of Perceptions of Causes of Problems in Relationships between Victims and Nonvictims:[*]

	No Violence	Violence	
General times of stress	50.0 (23)	31.7 (19)	$p = .087$
Specific external pressures	41.3 (19)	21.7 (13)	$p = .049$
Children	28.3 (13)	6.7 (4)	$p = .006$
Personality problems in the partner	13.0 (6)	58.3 (35)	$p < .001$

[*]This table presents the cells from 4 Chi-Square analyses, each with 1 df, where the presence of each response was noted, for victims and non-victims. The p values reported are the significance levels of the Chi-Square values.

Personality Problems in the Partner

As predicted, victims were significantly more likely than nonvictims to attribute their relationship problems to personality problems in the partner. Fifty-eight percent of the victims offered this
explanation, as compared with only 13 percent of the nonvictims.
This category, among the four, was the most popular for the victims,
but the least popular for the nonvictims. Here are two examples from
women describing problems in their relationships in terms of their
husbands' personalities:

> It was never related to any concrete conflict. . . . I mean, I'm
> sure there were inner conflicts but it never related to any tangible
> conflict. There was just part of him that was like an ani-
> mal. . . . in a split second, for no real reason, he would start going
> crazy and getting angrier . . . that was just part of the way he
> was.

> It's his personality. He's a bigot. If you know something, he knows
> more than you do, no matter what. He was in the war, and I think
> that did something to him, I couldn't hate him even though he
> was like that. I just hated my life.

For victims, the next most popular attribution was to general times
of stress (32%), followed by specific external pressures (22%), and
children (7%). In all of these cases, nonvictims were more likely to
make these sorts of attributions, though the statistical difference for
general times of stress only approached significance. Fifty percent
of the nonvictims attributed their problems to a situational factor,
general times of stress, making this the most frequently occurring
attribution among the nonvictims; 41% attributed their problems
to specific external pressures, and 28% named children as the cause.
    Examples from nonvictims are provided for these three response
categories:

General Times of Stress

These three examples came from interviews with women who talked
about their relationships with their husbands:

> I really hated the job I had and so he said, well, then just quit if
> you hate it so much. I did, but then there wasn't much money.

That's when our hard time started. There was little money around and we were both stressed. It would cause dumb arguments. What do we really need? Why did you buy that? I blame that hard time on finances.

There was a time that he was having problems at work. Then he lost his job. This really hurt his ego. He would just blow up . . . this was a hard time for both of us. He wasn't telling me exactly what he was going through because being out of a job made him feel bad and since we weren't communicating I couldn't understand why he was being so difficult.

There was no sudden incident. I got bored and tired of just taking care of the kids and doing housework. I felt like I needed something more in my life. I was feeling insecure about our relationship. It was just a bad time for us. Once my feelings were out in the open things got better. I have more friends and I do more than I used to.

Specific External Pressures

Two women describing their marital relationships provided these instances of specific external pressures:

Our biggest problems were all within the year after his mother died. I knew what he was going through but we were both going to school and trying to work on the side and we'd come home exhausted and moody. When things got more secure so did our relationship.

I got upset because his family and friends were around and we had planned to spend some time alone. He kept putting our time together off and I ended up feeling hurt. Our conflicts are always about instances like that . . . little misunderstandings.

Children as the Cause of Relationship Problems

A husband and two wives commented on problems caused by their children:

With her [my wife] in school, I definitely have to spend more time babysitting than I'm used to. Sometimes how I regulate the kids differs and so I will allow the kids to do things that she doesn't allow them to do and then when we are together and I allow the kids to do this or that there is a conflict. This kind of thing has put a lot of strain on our relationship.

Any time there's a second marriage, if there are children it is difficult. I mean you never know if you are going to get along with their children or not. You have to adjust to not one person but sometimes three or four. This has always been a conflict for us. I'll bet this change is hard for most people.

It was hard when the kids were younger. We had no time alone. The kids always came to our house. There was always kids' friends over for dinner. Now that they are older and doing their own thing there is more time for us.

Thus, victims illustrated a narrowed focus on the partner's personality as the source of their troubles, while nonvictims seemed to adopt a more expansive view of the causes for their problems. The idea that victims suffer from a narrowed focus which is evidenced in their overreliance on the partner's personality for explaining the violence is based on an implicit premise that I would like to make explicit: The characterization of their thinking in terms of a "narrowed focus" implies that they are deficient in their thinking about the causes of their problems. Implied here is the idea that the more expansive explanations that attend to situational concerns, and that are more characteristic of nonvictims, reflect a more fully developed consideration of alternatives. This premise derives first from the knowledge that the "attributional bias" (i.e., the tendency to attribute the problems of others to their personality traits) names a cognitive short-cut—the too speedy tendency to see the individual as central (or figure) and the situation as background (or ground). It reflects the reliance upon a cognitive schema, the function of which is to streamline perception (Taylor and Fiske 1984). It does not result from a thorough perusal of possibilities. Second, attributions to the person's characteristics decontextualize the individual to a great extent. It seems likely that such person attributions must be missing some aspect of the environment's impact on the person. Third, there is a concomitant narrowing in problem-solving opportunities, since nothing short of intensive psychotherapy seems likely to instigate personality change. Thus, alternative avenues to the resolution of problems are rendered invisible.

With that said, it must be noted that it may be hard for anyone to make expansive attributions about an individual's use of violence. As a society, we encourage a focus on the individual and an inattention to background, external circumstances that may be potent contributors to that individual's actions. A person brought to trial on a charge of violence is unlikely to be excused because he or she acted in response to major life stressors—general or specific. Only disturbances of that individual's personal, emotional state may provide a mitigating excuse, though not a full justification of that action, unless the individual is judged not just upset but insane.

So, in some sense, the same sorts of attributions or explanations that society allows for violent behavior are mirrored in the thinking of the victims of violence. And yet, it can be argued that at both levels—the individual and the societal—it is a limiting perspective that affords little opportunity for change in the larger systems being affected—either the family system or society.

THE PERCEIVED FREQUENCY OF CONFLICT AND VIOLENCE IN INTIMATE RELATIONSHIPS

Interviewees were asked these questions on the issue of frequency: QUESTION 13: DID THE SAME OR SIMILAR THINGS HAPPEN TO OTHERS IN YOUR FAMILY/CLOSE FRIENDS? IN GENERAL, DO YOU THINK THESE THINGS HAPPEN TO OTHER PEOPLE? OUT OF 100 PEOPLE/WOMEN/FAMILIES, HOW MANY WOULD YOU SAY EXPERIENCE VIOLENCE/HARD TIMES?

Responses were coded in a way that reflected the perceived frequency of one's own experience (whatever it was) and the perceived frequency of violence (whether or not the interviewee was a victim of violence). In both cases, comparisons between victims and nonvictims approached statistical significance. With regard to their own experiences, nonvictims thought their experiences happened to more people. About 68% ($n = 26$) of the nonvictims thought their experiences happened to most people (defined as a frequency estimate of 50% or higher), as compared with about 46% ($n = 22$) of the victims who saw their experiences as happening to most people ($p = .058$).

Three quotes from nonvictims and two from victims illustrate the sorts of thinking that accompanied their percentage estimates.

A woman and two men offered these assessments of their marital relationships:

> I would imagine that most couples, I mean things can't always go smoothly, there are hard times. Life goes up and down, it's not even. I'm sure that relationships go up and down too.

I think lots of people have conflict like ours. All the role changing
and expectations for men and women are unclear and this causes
conflict. I'll bet a lot of people are going through the kinds of problems we are.

You've got to have times that are bad. I mean the job, or you have
to move or a child is sick . . . there are bound to be stressful
times. I don't think our situation was unusual.

Two women victimized by their husbands' violence had this to
say:

I think a lot of people experience this, but they don't say anything
about it. I think there is a lot of violence that goes on that nobody
knows about. Some are embarrassed or scared to tell people because who knows what they might think. A lot of times I was
embarrassed or worried that people would wonder what I did to
cause it. He seems fine around them. Unless you've been in the
situation yourself it is very hard to understand.

Lots of people are going through this. . . . Actually I have a special knack for zeroing in on people going through it too. I can just
tell . . . I think it happens all the time . . . I know some women
who get abused. I can relate to their problems. . . . I want to help
them and get them to leave the situation but I know it's not that
easy.

Both victims and nonvictims were asked to estimate the frequency with which violence in families occurs, although in many
cases this question either was not asked or was not answered in a
codable way. Victims were somewhat more likely than nonvictims
to believe that violence is highly prevalent. About 74% ($n = 14$) of
the victims who were asked this question believed that 50% or more
of the general population had experienced intimate violence. Only
about 41% ($n = 9$) of the nonvictims believed violence occurred to
at least 50% of the general population. The number of interviewees
asked this question was quite small, causing this difference only to
approach statistical significance ($p = .105$).[1] In spite of the reduced
sample size for this question, the trend is consistent with what one
would expect—victims believed that there were lots of other victims out there; nonvictims' estimates were more moderate. Even so,

1. All interviewees should have been asked this question but it appeared near the end
of the Interview Schedule and often got skipped after the preceding question about the frequency of one's own experience was asked.

individuals in both groups believed rates of violence were quite high. Surely, these high estimates are explained in part by these people's involvement in a study on family violence. Research in cognitive psychology shows that the process of thinking about something, an idea's accessibility, enhances its perceived importance (Taylor and Fiske 1984). In this case, it seems likely that perceived importance is reflected in these overestimates of the size of the problem—an effect that is especially pronounced in victims of violence.

These findings are relevant to the consideration of perceived alternatives, since it seems likely that alternatives to violence will be harder to see if one believes that violence is happening almost everywhere. These findings also revealed an interesting characteristic of victims' perceptions. Victims reported that their own experiences with violence were relatively infrequent when compared with the frequency of violence in general. They thought violence was widespread, but that their experiences had occurred with less than normal frequency. This finding suggests that these individuals experience a sense of difference and of isolation from what most people are like, even when the domain of comparison is family violence and they are its victims.

Thus, these victims are stymied in their search for alternatives in two ways. First, they believe that violence is epidemic. If violence were as widespread as these victims indicated, then, indeed, where could one go to escape it? Second, in this world where violence is almost everywhere, they saw their experiences as relatively unusual. Therefore, they could not count on support from a world of people unlikely to have experienced what they have endured. These findings bespeak a real "Catch-22" in the victims' belief system. They would seem to think, "Safety from violence is elusive; almost everybody is enduring episodes of violence. Even so, only a minority of these many victims have had experiences like mine and could understand me." It is hard to imagine a set of beliefs that could more effectively block action to prevent or escape violence than these. Ideas such as these are roadblocks on the path to the perception of alternatives.

SUMMARY

The findings reviewed in this chapter underline the complexity of characterizing alternatives seen, nearly seen, and not seen. The tolerance of cognitive inconsistency displayed by a substantial minority of victims (37%) was interpreted as support for the view that victims exist in a context of fundamental inconsistency. Their loved ones are sometimes their enemies. Those who are supposed to love them also hurt them. Efforts to resolve inconsistency would seem to be doomed in a social environment where intimacy and violence coexist. Further, there is little sign from the individuals in this study that the inconsistency is, in and of itself, disquieting. Contrary to popular theorizing on the impact of inconsistency, even drawing respondents' attention to inconsistencies provoked little apparent disruption or signs of efforts to restore homeostasis or to achieve consistency.

In theory, the psychological energy that resides in enduring inconsistency is not readily available for the other mental tasks that rely on our energy resources. In particular, efforts to explain problems in one's relationship require complex consideration and intensive thought. For those whose energies were too likely to be consumed elsewhere, a narrowed perspective about the causes of problems occurred. Victims were more likely than nonvictims to attribute their problems to personality problems in the abuser and to give short shrift to alternative explanations that placed more emphasis on environmental contributors to stress and times of difficulty. This limits not only the ways in which problems can be perceived, but also the ways in which problems might be solved. Society colludes in this heavy attention to the decontextualized individual and suffers, as does the individual, from the presence of perceptual blinders with regard to problem definition and resolution.

With regard to their views about others, victims saw violence as widespread, but their own experiences as less typical than that. By seeing violence as a part of the vast majority of families and by seeing their own experiences as relatively unusual, potential courses of action away from violence were blocked. Thus, here in these beliefs, the content of some of the ideas that would prevent action was revealed.

These findings, taken as a whole, lend support to the view that one's sense of injustice is likely to be fluid and that the process of experiencing alternatives is likely to be fraught with inconsistency. Under these psychological circumstances, one would expect leaving violent relationships to be very difficult, and of course, we know that it is. Only as insight becomes firm, as alternatives emerge from their initial context of inconsistency, can the discussion of alternatives mobilize an awareness of injustice or motivate restorative action.

10

A COMPLEX CHORUS: SUMMARIZING THE FINDINGS

Social psychologists' search for meaning should produce a complex chorus, a textured story, a thick description, not a single truth.

—Michelle Fine (1986) in "Contextualizing the Study of Injustice," in *Advances in Applied Social Psychology*, p. 106.

The study of injustice reported in this book reflects a search for meaning, an effort to put experiences of violence and conflict in context, to know and to understand what the participants know about themselves and their intimate relationships. While the framework and the choice to focus on reactions to injustice were mine, the substance of the stories that rests on that framework and that makes it elaborate is theirs. This is not a study about episodes of violence or conflict themselves, but a study of how people explain those episodes to themselves, how they react to them, how they construct alternatives to them.

The review of the relevant literatures presented in chapters 2 through 4 focused on three primary aspects of victims' thinking: the search for the reasons why, self-perceptions and coping activities, and the ability to see alternatives to prevailing explanations for and responses to injustice.[1] Each of these areas was considered in chap-

1. Two other substantive areas, (1) reactions and perceptions of others and (2) the paradoxical nature of prevailing explanations for injustice with their focus on the victim's culpability were also reviewed in those early chapters. However, they are not primary aspects of victims' thinking, but issues for context and interpretation. Thus, these concerns are raised here to add those qualities to victims' and nonvictims' remarks, but were not treated as areas for primary data collection.

ters 7, 8, and 9 respectively. In chapter 6, the demographic characteristics and quantitative violence experiences of the respondents were detailed. The special mission of chapter 10 is to present these findings in one place, to consider the results holistically, to allow the complex chorus of real human experience to sound.

Women and men, victims of intimate violence and nonvictims, participated in this research project. In all, 612 people were surveyed; 106 of them also provided usable information about their thoughts, feelings, and experiences in intensive, in-person interviews. Of those surveyed, 49 percent had experienced intimate violence; among those whose interview responses were reported here, 57 percent had experienced intimate violence. Thus, while no selection procedures were used to generate these samples, in both cases, natural, nearly equal comparison groups of victims and nonvictims emerged. The representation of women and men was not as even. Over 82 percent of those who responded to the survey were women, as were over 75 percent of those interviewed. Even among the nonvictim interviewees, where males were better represented than in any other group, a majority of 57 percent was female. Thus, while this study reflects the views of both men and women, it is certain that women's voices ring louder than those of the men, especially among the victims.

Demographically speaking, the participants in this study were predominantly white, well-educated, Christian, and middle class. That is, they were mainstream Americans. Indeed, the character of this sample marks one of its contributions to the research literature on family violence. The myth that violence is a lower-class phenomenon that does not affect the middle class is debunked here. However, it must be clearly acknowledged and realized that these respondents can represent only their socioeconomic class and no other. In particular, the results reported here are unlikely to generalize to the very poor. The availability of resources is an issue of great significance when violence is present. For most of the individuals in my study, those resources that represent advantage in our society were objectively present or at least were present to a greater extent than they would be in a sample of very poor people. This is so even among the victims in this sample, who were in general not quite as well off or quite as well educated as the nonvictims.

Because the socioeconomic status of these victims of violence afforded them apparent opportunities, their personal psychologies seem likely to be affected in ways that reflect a diminished ability to see existing options. For very poor victims of violence, a different sort of psychology would be expected. In their case, there is no need to invoke a diminished ability to perceive options. The options do not exist.

With these caveats about social class noted, I believe the individuals who participated in this study have a great deal to teach us about the psychology of injustice as it emerges in relation to episodes of violence and conflict in middle class family settings. In some ways, their knowledge is especially instructive, because theirs are the families our society idealizes. We imagine families like theirs to be free of violence. These participants are the nonreporters, the people who seek care from private physicians not hospital emergency rooms, the people who rarely come to the attention of the police or other data-gathering agencies. And yet, for many of these research participants, violence is a significant part of their family lives.

AN INTERPRETIVE SUMMARY OF THE FINDINGS

The remainder of this chapter is devoted to summarizing and interpreting the survey and interview findings. No new data are presented here, although the opportunity to consider all the results together in one chapter provides a new connectedness among the findings that enhances insight into the trends discovered. Also, this is primarily a chapter about the victims' perceptions, in which the comparison group plays a more secondary role. The comparisons between the victims and the nonvictims are significant, of course, but in an ultimate sense, this book was written to explore the psychology of victims and their views are highlighted in this summary. The survey results are considered on their own; the results of chapters 7, 8 and 9 are considered in concert.

CHAPTER 6: WHAT THE SURVEY DATA SHOWED

Chapter 6 presented the results of demographic comparisons between victims—considered in terms of seven specific groups and as one general group—and nonvictims. Six predictions involving gender, household income, educational attainment, marital status and longevity, employment status, and family size were tested. The results showed that females were more likely than males to be over-represented among the intimate violence groups. Even in this predominantly female sample, too many victims of violence were female. The second contrast showed that the more experiences with intimate violence an individual had, the more likely she or he was to report a household income under the sample's median and the more they differed from the nonvictims. Even in this relatively high-income sample, victims tended to have lower incomes than nonvictims. When it came to education, a similar trend emerged. Victims were significantly less likely than the nonvictims to hold a college degree. With regard to both of these markers of social class—income and education—violence should not be seen as the result of low income or education. Instead, experiences with violence can be better seen as impediments to achievement, as destructive disruptions in the formation of one's sense of self that result in lowered life productivity.

With regard to marriage and marital longevity, it was apparent that violence was hard on the tenure of relationships. Victims were less likely to be currently married and more likely to be previously married than the nonvictims. While the longevity effect only approached significance, it was consistent with prediction and suggested that nonvictims stayed married longer than victims did. Predictions that involved employment status and family size differences between victims and nonvictims were not supported. That is, there were no statistically significant differences between victims and nonvictims on these variables.

Investigations into the impact of religion and birth order on the occurrence of violence showed, first, that Jews were least likely to report experiences with violence, followed by Catholics and Protestants. With regard to birth order, a trend which approached significance showed that youngest borns were least likely to experience family violence.

Survey data on the different sorts of intimate violence experiences revealed that about 23 percent of the respondents had been abused as children, and that for about 34 percent of them, the abuse happened regularly or often (that is, at least seven times a year). The most frequent age for the onset of child abuse was between 10 and 15 years of age ($n = 102$), although 15 of the 142 child abuse respondents indicated that the abuse had begun before they turned three, and 46 reported themselves to have been abused between the ages of three and five. Forty-three percent of these victims had told no one about their suffering.

Only one sort of abuser was elicited by the survey questions: parents who abused their children. About 16 percent of the respondents who were parents reported that they had abused their children. Here, the largest number—49 percent—said that it only happened once or twice. Three-children families were more likely to be the scenes of abuse than were smaller or larger families. About 35 percent of these parents said that they had told no one about their abusiveness.

About 28 percent of the married respondents reported themselves to have been victimized by a spouse either currently or in the past. For about 40 percent of these individuals, the abuse was reported to have occurred only once or twice. Only for about 14 percent of these individuals was the violence characterized as regular or often. By the first year of the marriage about 49 percent of these abused spouses had experienced violence. Eighteen percent had never told anyone, making spousal abuse the most likely sort of family violence to be revealed.

Seven percent of the respondents reported that their spouse or lover forced them to have sex. For about 35 percent of these individuals, such rape episodes occurred only once or twice; for about 20 percent they happened regularly.

Fourteen percent affirmed that they had been raped by someone besides their spouse. The rapists were predominantly casual acquaintances and strangers, although family members were also among the rapists. About 20 percent of these survivors of rape had never told anyone.

Implications of the Survey Data

In part, the results of the survey illustrated that those surveyed, although subjected to violence under varying conditions, had much in common. Merged analyses—in which the seven violence conditions were considered as one—tended only to provide consistent clarifications of what the more specific analyses showed. Further, the quantitative statistics on each of the intimate violence groups considered separately suggested that they were more similar than different in the frequency with which violence occurred and the likelihood that they had reported it. In general, it seemed that violence was, for most respondents, something that happened occasionally, rather than something that happened regularly or often. They were more likely to report their experiences with violence than not, although substantial minorities in each case reported that they had not told anyone about their experiences with violence.

As a group, the victims among the survey respondents appear to be in the middle of some hypothetical continuum of the severity and the frequency of violence. Their experiences are typically moderate rather than severe or mild, occasional, rather than often or rare. The severity and the frequency of the violence endured seems likely to be of significant value for gauging the extent of the psychological damage suffered. For those who endured the most severe and frequent violence, one would expect to see the most profound and lasting damage to their concepts of what is just. For those who endured moderate amounts of violence, who are in the majority here, one would expect to see signs of a higher level of inner conflict and turmoil as they explore, reject, and/or accept options that are *not* made entirely inaccessible or unimaginable by extraordinarily high levels of violence.

My interest in documenting and understanding such inner turmoil in response to injustice was a central purpose of this work, and the statistical portrait of the survey respondents made it seem likely that I had identified a good group of people for such explorations. Thus, the basic statistical information reported here provided a context and a rationale for the next step of this study, the analysis of the interview data. Of the 106 individuals whose responses are reported here, 15 had been abused by a spouse in the past, 15 had been abused as children, 20 individuals had had two experiences with violence and 10 had had three or four experiences. Analyses were conducted in which these four groups—victims of spousal abuse, child abuse, two sorts of intimate violence, and three or four sorts of intimate violence—were considered separately. In addition, these groups were merged and considered as one. Increasing the victim group size to 60 created a viable comparisosn group for statistical tests with the 46 individuals who reported no experiences with family violence.

A Few Words about the Interviewees

As a whole, the interviewees were highly educated: 78 percent held college degrees or more; their median incomes were like those in the sample of respondents, overall—$25,000. More than 67 percent were employed outside the home, 63 percent were currently married, 22 percent were previously married and 15 percent were single. One third were Catholics, one third were Protestants, and about 21 percent were Jews. Fifty-seven percent were female. With these background data drawn from the survey responses, the sample of interviewees whose responses are reflected in chapters 7 through 9 is described.

CHAPTERS 7–9: INJUSTICE: UNDERSTANDING IT, COPING WITH IT, AND SEEING ALTERNATIVES TO IT

Organized around a search for distortions in the justice concept, much of what appears in these chapters is founded on exploring the nature of victims' and nonvictims' explanations for times of violence or conflict. Throughout, there is attention to the idea that violence does far more than harm one's physical self and that, in particular, violence damages one's ability to construct what is just. Society is implicated in defective reasoning about what is just. Too often, as a society, we reward and encourage violence, especially violence which is purported to serve some valued end. It is too easy for individuals to ascribe valued ends to the use of violence and thereby to justify it, to make violence just. As individuals, we all reflect the influences of our culture and prevailing wisdom about such things as the nature of family life. Thus, though this study deals with the perceptions of individuals, it is also a study about the American, middle class culture in which those individuals live—a culture that fosters certain explanations for violence and that is reflected in their thinking.

What follows is an interpretive summary. Findings are considered in conceptual categories that occasionally transcend chapter divisions. All major findings are included.

The Search for the Reasons Why: The Role of Inconsistency

Attention to attributions of blame opened the discussion in chapter 7 on the thinking of victims and nonvictims. Answers to the first question considered—on "Who's to blame?"—presaged much about what a further consideration of responses would reveal. A majority of victims—60 percent—blamed themselves for the violence that occurred in their relationships. The next most popular category, which was mentioned by almost 47 percent of the victims, was the seeming opposite of this response: "It was not my fault." I say that this second response is the "seeming opposite," because the true opposite in an interpersonal dyad would be to blame the other person. (That choice, of blaming the partner, was made by only about 22 percent of the victims.) So, victims said, "It was my fault," and/or "It was not my fault." (It is possible, given the way these data were coded, that the same person said both things, although the number of people who did so is not specified in these analyses.) What is striking about these twin responses is the narrowness of range, the impossibility of seeing all the way to the influence of social conditions when even the partner has little centrality in the attributional thinking of the victims.

For the nonvictims, self-blame was also the most popular attribution about hard times in the relationship and was mentioned by about 46 percent of them. However, their second most frequent response allocated blame to both. Here, only about 24 percent of them said it was not their fault. Tests of statistical significance computed between-group differences for each of six responses. The only one to achieve significance was the one that did seem particularly to characterize victims' cognitive style: "it was not my fault." Victims were about twice as likely as nonvictims explicitly to disavow responsibility for the episodes they described.

This response pattern is noteworthy, especially when it is considered in the context of other, related responses. In chapter 7, the partner or perpetrator was not a focus of attention in victims' responses to a question that used the word "blame." However, results reported in chapter 9 showed that another question which asked for the "causes" of the problems in the relationship led to a much greater likelihood of a focus on the partner. In fact, that question led 58 percent of the victims to name the partner as the cause for the problems. No more than 32 percent of them implicated larger issues that might have caused problems. (And, no response category was even created for attributing the cause of problems in the relationship to oneself. It simply did not occur often enough.) This heavy attention to the partner's personality was interpreted as evidence for an overly narrow perspective on causes of the relationship's problems. Nonvictims, in this case, were more expansive in their thinking and were more likely to name general times of stress, specific external pressures, and children as the causes of problems in the relationship.

In the difference between the words "blame" and "causes," and in the difference between talking about the blameworthiness of the people in the relationship, as opposed to talking about problems with the relationship, different explanations for violence emerged. When the word had negative overtones, the victims tended not to mention their partners. They could shoulder the blame. When the words were connotatively neutral, ("causes for problems"), the partner's influence was described as being more significant. Thus, language appears to be an important consideration in the pursuit of knowledge from victims of violence. Words make a real difference and evoke different ideas.

And yet, while the explanations presented in chapters 7 and 9 can be said to be different in content, they are not different in kind. In both cases, victims evidenced a focus on persons that nonvictims were more likely to avoid. Nonvictims seemed to be better able to generate broader explanations with regard to "blame" or "cause" and did not seem as drawn to the idea that the individuals involved were central. Even in the inconsistent attention to the role of the partner, there is some consistency in a perceptual focus on characters rather than context.

Another example of inconsistency in the thinking of victims was reported in chapter 9. It pertained not to the precursors of violence, but to perceived alternatives to the violence once it had begun to occur. In a trend that approached statistical significance, victims were more likely than nonvictims to evidence logical inconsistencies in their responses. Most often, the nature of the inconsistency was characterized by an initial "No" response to this question: "WAS THERE ANYTHING YOU COULD HAVE DONE TO PREVENT THESE EVENTS?" Then, after this initial "No," elaboration was provided that explained things they *had* done, in spite of the apparent inconsistency of this elaboration, given their initial negative response. Thirty-seven percent of the victims and 19 percent of the nonvictims offered responses that were inconsistent in this way. Unlike the analyses which investigated issues of "blame" and "causes of problems," this analysis was conducted on responses considered in context. Thus, the suggestion of the earlier analyses—that single individuals evidenced internal inconsistencies—is here explicitly supported.

The fundamental inconsistency of victims' lives lies with the reality of living with people who both love them and hurt them. Their abusers are people they love and hate, adore and fear. Efforts to make sense of this most basic inconsistency seem all but doomed to failure, and perhaps, it is most simply the failure to achieve resolution or "sense" that is tapped in the inconsistency findings. Indeed, I think it likely that in any attempt by victims to understand the use of violence by a loved one, logical inconsistencies will occur. In some basic sense, the willingness to hurt someone you love defies logic. At least in some temporary sense, the willingness to use violence bespeaks the suppression of loving feelings and the emergence of bad feelings that overwhelm or obliterate the good ones. In intimate relationships, where love is idealized as "forever," lapses into violence seem likely to be paralleled by inconsistencies in understanding.

Knowing Injustice: "Good" and "Bad" as Undistortable Concepts

The idea that the meaning of words like "good" and "bad" is resistant to distortion was borne out in this study. It was clear that violence led to more frequent descriptions of the relationship as "bad," while nonviolence was related to seeing the relationship as "good." This pattern appeared with the earliest recollections of the relationships and continued for the duration. For example, about 70 percent of the victims offered negative assessments of their relationships, as compared with only about 11 percent of the nonvictims.

While these findings about the goodness or badness of the relationships were expected, it is important to realize that these negative assessments did not necessarily or immediately signal the relationship's dissolution. Therefore, information about the badness of a relationship coexisted with knowledge of its continuing. Because such a conflict would seem to undermine perceptions of injustice, in spite of the apparent accuracy of the "good" or "bad" assessments, related investigations were conducted into the extent to which the episodes of violence or conflict which occurred were seen as fair, deserved, typical, and expected.

While fair and good may be near synonyms in certain contexts, the concepts of deservedness, typicality, and expectedness are different from goodness, though related to it. Uncertainty about how these latter concepts differed from goodness in individuals' belief systems led me to offer a prediction only with regard to fairness: that violent relationships would be seen as less fair than nonviolent ones. Consistent with prediction, 93 percent of the victims classified violence as "not fair." About 72 percent of the nonvictims also felt that their experiences with conflict were not fair. Thus, the word "fairness," like "good" and "bad," seemed to retain meaning. Violence was rarely perceived as fair. It is interesting to note that most of the time conflict was not seen as fair, either. Even though the difference between groups was statistically significant, the actual difference is smaller than one might expect. One wonders what does constitute a fair argument and if it is simply unlikely that disagreements will give rise to a sense of fairness.

Although most victims saw violence as undeserved (77%), they were not significantly more likely to classify it as undeserved than were nonvictims (83%). Also, an apparent difference emerged here with regard to the difference between fairness and deservedness. Fewer than 8 percent of the interviewees saw violence as fair, and yet 23 percent described violence as deserved. In theory, fairness and deservedness should elicit more similar patterns of response. Instead, we learn that even violence acknowledged as unfair can be seen, at least by some, as deserved. In part, this speaks to the complexity of the inner experience that violence causes. The finding also indicates that an explanation for violence which suggests that it was deserved, does not necessarily mean that it was experienced as fair or just treatment. In educating us about the complexity of their thinking, victims also educate us about the importance of language that reflects highly specific, defined constructs.

The findings on typicality and expectedness support the position that the concept of "deservedness" is the most vulnerable to distortion. Significant differences did occur between victims and nonvictims with regard to both typicality and expectedness. In fact, the question on typicality elicited a large difference between victims and nonvictims. Nearly 86 percent of the victims saw violent behavior as atypical, while only about 47 percent of the nonvictims saw conflict-related behavior as atypical.

With regard to expectations, the most popular response choice for victims was "no expectations." Endorsed by about 35 percent of the victims, this response spoke directly to the idea that repeated experiences with violence inhibit the development of a concept of justice. One woman said simply, "I didn't know what a husband was supposed to do. . . . I have no expectations." Like the Jewish children Lewin described in the excerpt from his letter which appears at the beginning of chapter 7, victims of violence perpetrated by intimates were too likely to indicate that their sense of what would be just, in terms of what can be expected, was damaged.

Interestingly, the second most popular category of response for victims indicated that they had high expectations that were not being met. Nearly 33 percent of them expressed this feeling. Thus, while, for some, violence undid their capacity to define what was just or expectable, for others, a sense of injustice persisted strongly and they were able to name expectations and feel the discrepancy between what they wanted and what they were getting.[2] A question that is left unanswered by this finding involves those qualities that distinguish between the sorts of experiences with violence that lead the victim to have no expectations and those that lead the victim to express more clearly a sense of injustice, to say that high expectations for good treatment were not met. Given that intimate violence is an injustice, the search for differences between these two reactions to violence is really a search for those factors that damage most completely one's sense of what is just and what is not. In theory, very early experiences with violence would be expected to do more damage to developing concepts of justice. At any age, severe and lasting violence might be predicted to produce more of this inability to formulate what is just than less severe or less enduring violence. These issues are not resolved by the findings reported here, though I think they are central to a discussion, in future research, of precisely what damages the justice concept in what ways.

Coping with Violence or Conflict: Actions Speak Louder than Anything Else

Historically, psychology's efforts to understand differences between victims and nonvictims looked for personality-based differences. However, much of the work of the last ten years on battered women can be understood as a reaction to the earlier work that had focused on personality issues and had cast battered women as masochists. The psychoanalytic tradition, especially, with its underlying philosophical commitment to the idea that nothing is an accident, that everything has meaning, explained violence in women's lives in terms that implicated defects in those women's psychological conditions.

---

2. Non-victims evidenced a very different pattern of response, with about 53 percent of them indicating that their high expectations were completely met. Here, about 28 percent reported that they felt themselves to have no expectations.

From this perspective, the most significant contribution of Walker's (1979) book, *The Battered Woman,* can be said to be her explicit denunciation of the Masochism Myth and her work's alternative to that view.

The findings reported in chapter 8 of this book and summarized here continue in the new tradition created by Walker's work and add empirical weight to it. Three attempts to find personality differences between victims and nonvictims in the areas of traditionality, positive qualities (intelligence and being good or nice), and the tendency to show emotion failed. Three comparisons which dealt with feelings experienced during the relationship with special emphasis on hard times or times of violence yielded only one difference between victims and nonvictims. In this one case, victims were more likely than nonvictims to portray their emotional states negatively. They described themselves as embarrassed, feeling hatred, feeling rejecting, and feeling bad more often than did nonvictims. (The two areas where differences did not occur involved the extent to which the interviewees represented themselves as depressed or as sympathetic.)

Nor were efforts to distinguish between victims and nonvictims on the basis of their partners' feelings successful. In terms of three comparisons—depression, feeling bad about oneself, and anger— victims' partners did not differ from nonvictims partners. This finding was surprising, since one would expect that victims of violence would see the emotional states of their partners differently from the way nonvictims would see them. Further, we know from other analyses that victims see personality problems in the partner as causally responsible for the problems in their relationship. And, indeed, there were differences in personality descriptions of abusers and nonabusers. These differences, however, did not extend to their feeling states. To the extent that feelings can be said to be, at least in part, transient reflections of underlying personality traits, it is surprising that feelings did not provide a basis for perceived differences.

With regard to the partners' personalities, abusers were more often seen as difficult—aggressive, illogical and strong—and nonabusers were more often characterized as "active" (that is, assertive without being violent). These differences are highly specific and bear directly on the acts that distinguish violent from nonviolent activity. Thus, while these traits were characterized as aspects of personality, it is reasonable to see them as inferred extensions of the partners' actions.

And, it is in the area of actions that differences between victims and non-victims occurred consistently. Five t-tests were computed in this area and all five achieved statistical significance. Three of these pertained to the interviewees' actions. Interviewees who were victims described themselves as more likely to engage in defensive maneuvers (accusing, protecting oneself, running away), more likely to employ strategies (trying to get the partner to stop, attacking the partner and hiding), and more likely to have reacted with emotional intensity (belittled, complained, went crazy, screamed, threatened). Two scales described the partners' actions and showed that victims' partners were more likely to threaten them with serious harm. Non-victims were more likely to describe their partners' actions as conciliatory.

Three comparisons computed in the area of interviewees' thoughts also yielded two statistically significant comparisons. Victims were more likely to have bad anticipations about what was about to happen and were more likely to want things to change. No difference emerged with regard to memory disruption or loss. It is significant that these thoughts were related not to personality dispositions or feeling states, but to actions. Thus, this finding serves to underline the sorts of differences noted above.

Thus, the major differences between victims and nonvictims lay in the realm of actions. It seems that violence speaks for itself and drowns out the competing, but softer voices of feelings and personality traits. When individuals described their experiences and a detailed accounting was made of how they did so, the primacy of violent acts in their thinking was revealed. One can only wonder whether the perceptual focus that violence draws to itself masks real differences in these other areas, or if indeed violence is the major distinguishing feature between violent relationships and nonviolent ones. Future research is needed in this area to separate the impact of violence from its likely antecedents and to seek further insight into the underlying person factors, particularly in the abuser, that violence, at once, reflects and conceals.

Experiencing Violence and Estimating Violence's Frequency

Victims and nonvictims offered estimates of the frequency with which their own experiences occurred and the frequency with which violence occurred in the general population. In the case of both esti-mates, statistical significance was approached and suggested that nonvictims saw their experiences as more typical than did victims. Sixty-eight percent of the nonvictims thought that what happened to them happened to most people. Only 46 percent of the victims thought that what happened to them happened to most people. When the question asked about "violence in general," though, victims re-vealed a greater readiness to believe in the high incidence of vio-lence. About 74 percent of the victims thought that 50 percent or more of the general population was affected by violence. By com-parison, about 41 percent of the nonvictims concurred in this esti-mate.[3] Thus, while victims saw their own experiences as somewhat atypical, they believed that the general prevalence of violence in in-timate relationships was quite high.

Of course, the right answers to these estimate questions are un-known. Yet, the perceived right answers give us quite a bit of in-formation in their own right. Neither victims nor nonvictims saw violence as rare or unusual. The incidence estimates offered here are high in both cases, and suggest, as a general conclusion, that most people interviewed thought most people in the general population are the victims of intimate violence. This is a sobering finding whether they are right or wrong, because in part it is the perception of high levels of violence that functions as a kind of justification for it, and as a defense against taking action to stop it. Problems that are per-ceived as enormous inhibit effective activity to solve them (Walster et al. 1973). Particularly in the case of family matters where the right to privacy is breached only under extreme circumstances, the idea that half of all families might require "supervision" is daunting and would be expected to discourage the development of interven-tionist programs. Thus, this finding speaks not only to the perceived extent of violence in families, but also to a high level of likely re-sistance to intervention among those who think it especially prev-alent. In some respects, this finding illuminates a Catch-22 in the perceived seriousness of family violence. Thinking that violence is too prevalent supports the seriousness of the problem at the same time that it is likely to inhibit effective problem solving activities. Like other findings reported here, there is, in this finding, the sug-gestion of a potential inconsistency. To the extent that it is correct

3. While the response trend is interesting here, it should be noted that the sample sizes for both victims and nonvictims were quite small, as not all respondents answered this question.

to say that seeing a problem as too big inhibits effective problem solving, this finding can be understood to illustrate the "location" of yet another inconsistency in the ideas of victims of violence. They seem, by implication, too likely to believe that violence is prevalent and that little or nothing can be done.

SUMMARIZING THE SUMMARY

If there is one major theme to emerge from the presentation of these findings in concert, I believe it is the role of inconsistency in the thinking of victims. In the language of the dissonance theorists, they express nonfitting cognitions, ideas that would appear not to belong together. Contrary to what dissonance theorists would suggest, though, there is little evidence here of interviewees' efforts to resolve these inconsistencies or to bring their psychological lives into balance. Thus, the presence of inconsistency bespeaks the presence of an inner imbalance, and seems likely to be the observable sign of the inner experience of an ongoing sense of injustice.

This central inconsistency theme is embellished by knowledge of a kind of perceptual narrowing that makes victims more likely than nonvictims to focus on the individuals to explain their problems and to miss the contributing properties of more generally constructed problems or situational concerns. Further depth is provided on the inconsistency theme by noting the greater place of actions, relative to feelings or personality traits (and, to a lesser extent, thoughts), in distinguishing between the reactions of victims and nonvictims. It is as if the added energy required for insight into the concerns that underlie actions is unavailable and actions attain a primacy in the thinking of victims. Thus, feelings or personality traits that would appear not to correspond with actions may go unnoticed or may be dismissed as not illuminating. Such a tendency would be expected to foster the tolerance of inconsistency. And yet, this overattention to actions that accompany violence can be easily understood as a survival skill. Violent actions demand attention and there may be real adaptive value to attending to actions above any other concerns.

As a final coda in the inconsistency concerto, victims of violence showed signs of expectations for their partners that were underdeveloped or unfulfilled. Expectations reflect directly one's sense of what is just treatment, and their acknowledged absence by a substantial group of victims serves to underline the damage that violence causes to the justice concept.

There is a contrapuntal message in the results of this study as well. The importance of language, of specificity of word choice, is revealed throughout this study as conceptually related, but differently worded questions reveal distinct patterns of response. Sensitivity to such concerns is crucial to a full understanding of what people mean to say and issues of definition deserve direct attention in interview studies on topics where words are fraught with meaning, embedded in the richness and history of interpersonal experiences.

11

APPLYING RESEARCH ON INTIMATE VIOLENCE: EXPERT TESTIMONY IN CASES OF BATTERED WOMEN WHO KILL[1]

In 1985, in New York, Madelyn Diaz was tried for the shooting death of her sleeping husband. Nearly ten years had passed since Francine Hughes of Michigan was acquitted for having set fire to her husband while he slept. Francine Hughes pleaded temporary insanity and the jurors' belief that she was insane at the time of the killing led them to acquit her. Madelyn Diaz offered a different plea at the time of her trial. She claimed justification and testified that when she killed her husband she had been acting in self defense.

Her testimony revealed many episodes of physical and sexual violence perpetrated against her by her husband, who happened to be a police officer. He had broken her nose on one occasion. On an-

1. Much of what appears in the first half of this chapter is based on or drawn directly from a paper I wrote, "Potential Uses for Expert Testimony: Ideas toward the Representation of Battered Women Who Kill," which appeared in the *Women's Rights Law Reporter* (1986) 9(3/4):227–238.

other, he had taken her out in his car, in the winter time, forced her to undress, and then invited a stranger, a passerby, to have sex with her. While Madelyn was raped in the back seat by this stranger, her husband sat in the front seat of the car and watched.

On the day before he died, Madelyn's husband threatened their six month old daughter—something he had never done before. He was very drunk. He told Madelyn that if she did not start to "come across" in bed, he would kill their child. He held his service revolver to the baby's head and clicked the trigger. He said that he would "splatter the baby's brains all over the place." Then, he put down the gun and went to sleep. Madelyn also slept that night.

When she awakened, she dressed her three children and put them in the car. She planned to go grocery shopping. As she was about to leave, she realized she had forgotten her money. She went back upstairs to get it. The drawer where they kept their money was the same drawer where her husband kept his gun. When she opened the drawer, she saw the gun and experienced a sudden flashback to the moment when he held the gun to her baby's head. She heard him threaten her as if he were speaking at that moment. She picked up the gun and fired twice into his sleeping body. Then, as if nothing had happened, she went shopping for groceries with her children. She bought things he would have liked, as if he were still alive.

She returned home about three hours later, found her apartment door ajar and "discovered" her husband's body. Her niece called the police. Madelyn said that the apartment had been burglarized and that her husband had been shot by the intruder. Later, she said that that was what she had believed at the time. Three days after her husband's death, a fellow police officer came to give Madelyn the first of the checks to which she was entitled as the widow of a police officer. As the officer handed her the check, she said, "I can't take this. I killed him." It was her first moment of memory. She was arrested and subsequently indicted for Murder in the Second Degree, the highest murder charge in New York State.

Madelyn was acquitted of all charges by a jury that deliberated only a few hours. Unlike Francine Hughes, she walked out of the courtroom a free woman. (Hughes spent about six weeks in a mental institution before she was judged sane and released.) Importantly, Madelyn had affirmed the rightness, the saneness of her act and the jury had agreed. They extended the definition of self defense to include the circumstances Madelyn described. She knew that if her husband were awake, she would not be able to stop him as he prepared to kill her baby. While his threat was not imminent in an ordinary sense, the jury believed that it was psychologically imminent and that she had acted within the bounds of what the law allowed.

I testified as an expert witness at Madelyn's case, and in large part the substance of this chapter is devoted to the kinds of issues raised during such testimony. The opportunity to do expert testimony and the content of that testimony are direct results of the research that has been conducted on the psychological consequences of violence in families. Thus, the research reviewed and reported in this book reflects a body of social scientific knowledge that can be and is being imparted in applied settings.

MAKING THIS CHAPTER'S CONNECTION TO THE REST OF THIS BOOK EXPLICIT

This chapter epitomizes a kind of work described in chapter 1 of this book, where stages in the emergence of social problems were reviewed. During the 1970s, intimate violence effected a real emergence through stages of awareness and activism, to stages during the 1980s that reflect the acquisition and then the dissemination of knowledge. This book, overall, is the result of the emergence of intimate violence as a social problem. This chapter can be written because Stage 5 in the emergence of a social problem, when "experts come forward to tell what they have learned," has been reached. Thus, while this chapter diverges from the focus on theorizing and research that characterizes most of this book, it is a part of the whole. This chapter shows the results of the progression through the stages in the emergence of the social problem of intimate violence, from knowledge acquired to knowledge applied.

ON TO THE COURTROOM

Indeed, research on the psychological consequences of violence in families is highly relevant in legal cases where the nature and consequences of such violence are at issue. Throughout the country, psychologists are going into courtrooms to describe the results of this research and to offer a context for the consideration of victims and perpetrators of violence in families (see, for example, Blackman

1986, 1987c; Browne 1987; Ewing 1987; Walker and Browne 1985).

Since 1979, I have testified as an expert witness at approximately 20 trials of battered women who killed or injured their abusers in self defense.[2] I have participated in the defense of approximately 20 more such individuals, who did not go to trial but who pled guilty to reduced charges, or in three cases did not stand trial because the grand jury did not indict them, or because a judge dismissed the indictment in the interests of justice. Two recent books in this area by Browne (1987) and by Ewing (1987), both psychologists, reflect the acknowledgment and synthesis of the new application of psychological research in cases of battered women who kill.

This chapter reflects my wish to exemplify the immediate and significant usefulness of research on intimate violence to the criminal justice system. Of course, the research has other important applications, (e.g., counselling programs, educational curricula), but the one with which I am most involved is the presentation of the results of psychological research in legal settings and the case of battered women who kill.

Before proceeding into a consideration of the aspects of the research that are highlighted in courtroom settings, I want to consider the problem of homicide as it pertains to battered women who kill— that is, when is it justifiable to kill under the law and when is it not? While there is much research on violence, there is little on homicides in families, so the direct applicability of research on violence "breaks off" just before the lethal act. There simply has not been enough research into the psychological events that precede justifiable or nonjustifiable killings. For example, there has been no research done contrasting the experiences or psychologies of battered women defendants who get acquitted at trial as compared with those who get convicted.[3]

Thus, ideas about what constitutes a justifiable killing come only from legal opinions. The complementary work that would come from psychology remains to be done. In general, the idea that a killing may not be a crime is one for which there is little general support

2. Conceptually similar expert testimony is also being offered on behalf of abused children who kill their abusers, and I have testified in three such cases. However, the focus here is on cases of women who killed their spouse or lover.

3. A new organization, the National Clearinghouse for Battered Women Defendants, is seeking to conduct such a research project. I am on the Board of this organization and am contributing the results of trials with which I have been involved to the data base. I am also analyzing these data, together with Sue Osthoff, the coordinator of the National Clearinghouse. Still, this project is in its infancy, and there is no other, comparable study completed in this area.

outside the realm of wartime activity, in classic self-defense situations, or among the supporters of capital punishment or euthanasia. Only considerations about appropriate self-defensive action are relevant to battered women who kill, since one would not want to find reason for her action in a portrayal of the family home as a battleground. Nor would one want to suggest that the killing of an abusive spouse is morally justified, as proponents of capital punishment or euthanasia might contend about those sorts of deaths.

Unfortunately for battered women, "classic" self-defensive action is embodied in male, stranger-to-stranger assault. The victim uses only the amount of force necessary to resist the assault and the attacker is killed. The emotions that may understandably cloud the victim's judgment about the necessary amount of force derive from the victim's fear of the attacker's violence and of his unknown potential for presenting a life-threatening risk to the victim. The victim of the assault must be reasonable in his belief that the danger of death is imminent.

For battered women who act in self-defense, the context for their action is distinct from stereotypic, stranger-to-stranger assaults. They know their abuser; specifically, they know his potential for causing them physical injury. Thus, they may strike back at times that sound less dangerous than previous episodes of abuse, or that may not sound life-threatening at all. Nonetheless, they may reasonably believe that their lives are at risk because of the changes in the abuser's routine style of assault, or because the abuser says or does something that, in the past, has signalled great danger. If information supporting such notions are supplied by the battered woman in response to questions about why she acted when she did, then a self-defense scenario can be reported.

Crocker (1985), in her article, "The Meaning of Equality for Battered Women Who Kill Men in Self Defense," wrote:

> Battered women in particular may perceive danger and imminence differently from men. Because they become attuned to stages of violence from their husbands, they may interpret certain conduct to indicate an imminent attack or a more severe attack. A subtle gesture or a new method of abuse, insignificant to another person may create a reasonable fear in a battered woman (p. 127).

A recent New York State Supreme Court decision, *People v. Torres*, reported in the *New York Law Journal* (April 26, 1985) also addressed the issue of the reasonableness of a battered woman's perceptions. Specifically, Judge Bernstein wrote:

The Standard for the evaluation of the reasonableness of the defendant's belief and conduct is not what the ordinary prudent man would have believed or done under the same circumstances. The test is, rather whether the defendant's subjective belief as to the imminence and seriousness of the danger was reasonable [*People v. Desmond*, 93 AD 2d 822]. It is the defendant's state of mind and sense of fear which is critical to a justification defense [see *People v. Miller*, 39 NY 2d 543].

In this regard, proof of violent acts previously committed by the victim against the defendant as well as any evidence that the defendant was aware of specific prior violent acts by the victim upon third parties is admissible as bearing upon the reasonableness of the defendant's apprehension of danger at the time of the encounter [*People v. Miller, supra*, 39 NY 2d 543].

It is important to note that both Crocker and Judge Bernstein explain the reasonableness of a battered women's perception of danger as an alternative form of reasonableness. That is, battered women are constructed as reasonable in a relational framework and with a sense of history that is quite explicitly different from the traditional, legal standard of reasonableness. This redefinition might be interpreted as the introduction of an added layer of subjectivity, or even a separate standard, to the standard used to determine whether or not an aggressive act is justifiable. However, this would be a misinterpretation. Careful attention to the battered woman's past experience with her husband's violence enhances one's capacity to understand her attack against him as reasonable or not. A true standard of reason is best approximated when all relevant factors that bear on good judgment are considered (see also Schneider 1986 and Schneider & Jordan 1978).

Thus, information provided by a psychologist about the psychology of battered women at the trial of a battered woman who has killed her abuser enhances insight into her reasonableness. Such testimony develops the context in which this central concern about the reasonableness of an attack can be best considered. In particular, claims of self-defense made when no assault is going on or imminent may require expert testimony by a psychologist to illuminate the psychological bases for a sense of immediacy and life-threatening risk, even under such conditions. This aspect of expert testimony is described by Crocker (1985):

The battered woman perceived an imminent danger of physical injury even though there was no overt act of violence. Defendants offer battered woman syndrome expert testimony to explain why their perception of danger was reasonable—why they acted in self defense after a "reasonable man" would have cooled off or before he would have acted. The testimony may demonstrate how repeated physical abuse can so heighten a battered woman's fear and her awareness of her husband's physical capabilities that she considers him as dangerous asleep as awake, as dangerous before an attack as during one (p. 141).

The idea that a "reasonable man" would have acted differently supports the position that "common sense" alone could not provide an adequate basis for evaluating the evidence and reaching a verdict. And, due to prevailing common sense notions about "fair" fights between physically equal men, the very idea of killing when an assault is not occurring defies traditional definitions of self-defense. When conventional common sense can not provide a reasonable basis for understanding the justification for a battered woman's actions, expert testimony on her psychology may be critical.[4]

EXPERT TESTIMONY ON THE PSYCHOLOGY OF THE BATTERED WOMAN

Typically referred to as testimony on the "battered woman syndrome," expert testimony about the psychology of battered women details those psychological traits that typify battered women and their perceptions of the potential dangerousness of the abuser's violence. The nature of expert testimony begins with a description of what studies have shown to be characteristic of battered women and research by Walker (1979, 1984) is without question the most influential and popularly cited work in courtroom settings. In addition,

---

4. Note also that expert testimony is permitted by judges only when they are persuaded that the content of that testimony "goes beyond the ken of the average layperson," or is not contained within the province of common sense. The other two criteria employed to determine whether or not expert testimony may be admissible are first, whether there is indeed a body of scientifically valid and reliable knowledge to report, and second, whether the individual who purports to be an "expert" really is one. The inclusion of expert testimony is always discretionary, and judges may do as they choose, and exclude expert testimony on the bases of these criteria or because it is deemed irrelevant. In general, across the country, the trend favors the admission of expert testimony in cases of battered women who kill. However, in some states, it has been excluded and not seen as a basis for reversible error by an appellate court. See Blackman (1986) for a review of the states which have allowed expert testimony at trial, and for the range of uses for expert involvement within the criminal justice system.

other empirical studies in which battered women were the subjects are cited and their results summarized. An important aspect of this portion of the testimony comes from the fact that research findings often go against prevailing misconceptions about battered women. Thus, misconceptions can be corrected. The concluding portion of expert testimony involves the presentation of information about the defendant herself and the extent to which her experiences and reactions are consistent with what one would expect of a woman whose spouse or lover abused her.

A sample of the sort of summary of the research findings that I present during expert testimony follows. In the review of psychological concerns that follows, I have included comments about the process of expert testimony. I hope that this presentation of content and commentary will interest all readers, and will particularly serve the interests of those psychologists who are providing expert testimony or would like to do so. I have also tried here to illuminate some of the complexities of this work with a view toward the special concerns of attorneys who represent or who prosecute battered women who kill.

The results of data-based studies in psychology and sociology show that battered women may find it nearly impossible to leave abusive relationships because of the psychological changes that follow from remaining in an abusive relationship after a second episode of abuse. (A battered woman is defined as a woman who is abused by her spouse or lover on more than one occasion.) Research by Walker (1979, 1984) and Dobash and Dobash (1980) supports this definition. In addition, at this point in the testimony, the real constraints that prevent battered women from leaving abusive relationships—no money, no job skills, no one to care for small children, no where to go—are acknowledged. For those jurors who may have believed that battered women remained with abusive men because they derived some pleasure from the abuse, this new knowledge may be enlightening.

It is also important for the jurors to understand that the psychological changes that result from intimate violence are "normal." That is, it is never suggested that these women are insane or mentally diseased or defective (the legal language for insanity). Instead, I make efforts to ensure that the jurors will know that any individual subjected to the sort of abuse endured by a battered woman would be changed and damaged psychologically. Physical bruises may be easier to see but certainly fade more quickly than the psychological bruises and scars that are also the results of violence inflicted by one's intimate.

Following this general introduction about psychological changes, I specify the nature of these changes. I describe four sorts of changes that occur. Three of these changes are related to remaining in abusive relationships. A fourth characteristic pertains to battered women's elaborate knowledge of their abuser's style of violence. It is important to note that not all women display all these characteristics. Sometimes, one sort of damage is more prevalent than others. However, if I am to feel that my expertise is relevant and agree to testify in such a case, I must feel persuaded that at least three of the four characteristics described below are present.

"Learned Helplessness" and What It Means

First, many battered women experience psychological changes that cause them to believe that they are unable to control what happens to them, and especially that they are unable to stop the violence. Walker (1979) termed this feeling a condition of "learned helplessness." I find this terminology difficult and think that the choice of language is a poor one in this case. The suggestion that battered women are "helpless" is really a misnomer. Battered women are often resourceful and active in their efforts to avoid violence within the context of the relationship. They simply tend not to act in ways that would enable them to leave the relationship. Further, especially for battered women who kill, the suggestion in Walker's language that they must be "helpless" if they have been battered can function to predispose the jurors against them. The jurors may believe that a helpless woman could never pull a trigger, that a helpless woman could only endure the abuse, but could not respond in kind.[5]

5. It is not only jurors who draw such inferences from this language. In 1984, I testified at the trial of Doris Ciervo, a woman indicted for shooting her husband as he paused in his violence against their five-year-old son. Another psychologist testified for the prosecution. She did not know much about the research literature on battered woman, but she had read Walker's (1979) *The Battered Woman*. She misunderstood the meaning of "learned helplessness" and testified that Doris could not have been a "true battered woman," in spite of multiple serious injuries inflicted by her husband during their fifteen-year marriage. This psychologist testified that a "helpless" woman could not have fired the gun. Doris was convicted at trial of Manslaughter in the First Degree—a conviction reversed on appeal for reasons unrelated to the admission of expert testimony. In preparation for her new trial, a motion was filed to exclude that psychologist from offering her opinion again during the retrial. Walker submitted an affidavit declaring that the prosecutor's psychologist had misunderstood and misinterpreted her work. However, a decision was never made on the motion, because Doris was offered a plea to a reduced charge of Manslaughter in the Second Degree. Her sentence would include no jail time, so Doris chose not to stand trial again.

Therefore, instead of talking in detail about "learned helplessness," I describe the feelings that are contained within the "learned helplessness" construct. When I do use Walker's language explicitly, I quickly define what it really means. Battered women are often depressed and may feel convinced that attempts to leave their violent, intimate relationship would be futile. This sense that control is impossible may be exacerbated by their tendency to endure these relationships in isolation. Often, they do not report the source of their injuries to medical personnel, out of a fear of reprisal and a sense of shame.

As the pattern of violent events is repeated again and again (and of course most battered women are battered far more often than twice), this portion of the resulting psychological changes or syndrome becomes more pronounced. This psychological state keeps women from leaving violent relationships. It may or may not co-occur with economic hardship, the need to care for young children, and/or the genuine absence of a place to go.[6] (See the section of this chapter entitled "The Social Class Bias in Expert Testimony" for attention to the importance of social class issues.)

Tolerating Cognitive Inconsistency

In chapters 9 and 10, interview data are presented and summarized that bear on this idea of "cognitive inconsistency." Fine (1984, 1986) has also advanced this concept, in the form of "contradictory consciousness," in her work. Because the treatment of this construct is thoroughly elaborated elsewhere, my treatment of it here will be brief. In displaying a high tolerance for cognitive inconsistency, bat-

6. While research remains to be done elaborating the relationship between social class and the experiences represented in the "learned helplessness" construct, it seems to me from my contacts with very poor women, and with women who are not very poor, that social class makes a difference. In particular, the genuine absence and unavailability of another place to go, exists for very poor women as an unalterable fact, in a way that might not be true for women of some means.

Further, for poor women, their sense of noncontrol comes not only from their inability to stop their abuser's violence, but also from their inability to make other significant, negative aspects of their lives better. For women who have greater access to valued resources, the sense of noncontrol may be more limited and specific to their experiences with their abuser's violence. Thus, for women who can change very little of what goes on around them, in spite of their wishes, one would expect different psychological reactions to the abuser's violence. For example, the violence may not be experienced as unusual or intolerable if there is no comparison experience that is more positive and controllable. Instead, the abuser's violence may be seen as "of a piece" with the rest of their negative life experiences and may be accepted as such. Police nonresponsiveness to their requests for aid may evoke resignation rather than outrage. One's sense of injustice is muted by enduring unfairness in access to what is good.

tered women express two (or more) ideas that would appear to be logically inconsistent. For example, during an initial interview with a battered woman who had killed her husband, I asked if he drank or took drugs and if such alcohol or drug use was associated with his violence. She said, "No, he did not drink or take drugs." Then, just a moment later she said, "He was drunk the night I killed him." When I asked her about this inconsistency, she said that he did not always drink but he did drink and he did take drugs. Responses that would appear not to make sense together followed one another in short order. I have also heard women say, "He only hit me when he was drunk." And, then, later on they describe an episode during which he was abusive and *not* drunk.

I believe that this tolerance of inconsistency is a reflection of the fundamental inconsistency of their lives: that the man who supposedly loves them also hurts them. This characteristic of battered women is particularly important for jurors to understand, since it may cause her to describe the events of her life in ways that are seemingly contradictory and may be misinterpreted as signs of a generally poor memory or of bungled attempts to be deceptive. Typically, though, these inconsistencies in no way serve the defendant's legal interests, and are best understood as the results of her efforts to make sense out of an inherently unsensible situation. One's lover is not supposed to be one's enemy.

The Diminished Perception of Alternatives

Battered women often experience a sense that alternatives are not available to them. They feel unable to stop the violence, as noted earlier, and believe that there is no escape from the relationship (Blackman 1987b; Browne 1985, 1987; Walker 1979, 1984). They focus their energies on their survival within the relationship, which further limits their capacity to perceive options that might exist outside the relationship. Especially for those women who have remained in an abusive relationship for an extended period of time, alternative life choices may seem entirely unattainable. Thus, when their lives are threatened, an escape route that might have been seen by someone not victimized by years of abuse, may not be seen by a battered woman as viable or may not be seen at all.

The reduced ability to perceive alternatives is not meant to suggest that they would take life-threatening action more easily. Indeed, it would seem that women survive in and cope with abusive relationships by minimizing the severity of the violence they endure and of the need to respond. Further, while their knowledge of alternatives to the relationship may be limited their knowledge of their husband's violence is detailed.

Consider as an example of the reduced ability to see alternatives the case of Dorothy Rapp, a woman who went to trial in 1981 for the shooting death of her husband. Dorothy and her husband had been married for close to 30 years. They had two children in their twenties. While they were both originally from the West, they had lived for most of their marriage in a suburban community outside of New York City. Dorothy had not worked outside the home during this time, except for one occasion when she made afghans and sold them. She stopped this practice however, when her husband beat her severely for using her earnings to purchase their son a bed.

It was Dorothy's practice to put her husband's dinner on a TV table at about 4:30 P.M., to eat her dinner, and to go to bed. This way, she minimized contact with him. He would come home, eat his dinner while watching television, get drunk and, if Dorothy was lucky, he would fall asleep without abusing her. Every morning he would vomit on the front porch. Every morning, Dorothy would hurry to clean it up before the mailman arrived. Drinking was a chronic problem for Dorothy's husband. Once, prior to the episode that ended in his death, Dorothy had stabbed her husband in the back during a fight. He had been hospitalized for a couple of weeks, during which time he could not get drunk. Dorothy remembered that time as one of the best times of their relationship.

On the night that he died, Dorothy followed her usual routine. It was wintertime, so she also filled the fireplace with wood before she went to bed. She was awakened by her husband's violence. He was drunk and he hit and kicked her, as he accused her of putting too much wood in the fire. He said that the fire was burning too hot. As he struck her, she did what she always did. She tried to "talk him down." She said, "You don't want to kill me. If you kill me, the police will come and put you in jail." Usually, that line worked for her and he would calm down. This night, uncharacteristically, his rage heightened. He pulled a Winchester rifle out from under their bed and loaded it while Dorothy watched. He placed the loaded gun on the bed and told Dorothy that he was going to go into the backyard for a few minutes and that when he returned he was going to kill her. He told her not to move. "Just lie there."

Dorothy did lie there for a few minutes. She was not sure for how long. She could hear her husband yelling and talking to himself in the backyard. Finally, she picked up the rifle and walked toward the back door. Her husband approached the house, and when he was about six feet away from her she fired once. He was shot through the heart and died instantly.

At her trial, on cross examination, the prosecutor asked her one question repeatedly. It was also the keystone of his summation, "Why didn't Dorothy Rapp walk out the front door in her suburban neighborhood and get away without inflicting harm on her husband?" Her husband had given her time while he went to the backyard. Why didn't she use that time to get away? Dorothy answered simply as she affirmed that she had acted in self-defense. She said, "I never thought of it." The jury accepted her explanation and her assertion of self-defense and acquitted her of all charges.

When I testified at Dorothy's trial I explained to the jury that a reduced ability to see alternatives is a normal consequence of extreme fear and repeated experiences with violence. Dorothy's "failure" to think of the front door reflected her level of fear and the damage done to her by years of abuse. However, in the jury's acquittal there is affirmation of Dorothy's right to defend herself under these circumstances. Dorothy did not plead temporary insanity. She declared that her act was reasonable and spoke of her belief that when her husband returned to the house he would kill her. The psychological damage she endured as a result of her husband's abuse made the front door vanish from her view. The perceptual narrowing she evidenced, the over-focus on her husband's impending return, were present in her as the normal consequences of intimate violence. While there is a weakness present in this sort of thinking, the perceptual narrowing lays the cognitive groundwork for an aspect of battered women that reflects acuity of perception.

The Continuum of Tolerability and Knowing What Is Off the Continuum

While the preceding attention to a diminished awareness of alternatives suggests battered women may be limited in their thinking, the constructs which foster the creation of the "continuum of tolerability" bespeak insight and acumen. Repeated instances of violence enable and cause battered women to develop a continuum along which they can "rate" the tolerability or survivability of episodes of their husband's violence (Browne 1985, 1987). Thus, signs of unusual violence are detected. For battered women, this response to the ongoing violence of their situations is a survival skill. Research shows that battered women who kill experience especially severe and frequent violence, relative to battered women who do not kill (Blackman 1987c; Browne 1985; Walker 1984). They know which sorts of danger are familiar and which are novel. They have had myriad opportunities to develop and hone their perceptions of their husbands' violence. And, importantly, they can say what made the final episode of violence different from the others. They can name the features of the last time that enabled them to know that this episode would result in life-threatening action by the abuser.

Jane Melandovich went to trial for the ax-killing of her father. He had been struck over a dozen times with an ax, as he lay on their living room couch, half-unconscious from drinking. Jane and her family were recent immigrants from the Soviet Union. There, Jane's father had served time in prison for rape. Jane herself was conceived as the result of her father's rape of her mother. Her father abused her mother often and severely. Once, Jane's mother was hospitalized for a month because of injuries he inflicted on her.

Only a few years after the Melandovich family arrived in this country, Jane's father decided he wanted to emigrate to Israel. He received money from a Jewish agency for his trip and moved his wife and three children to a settlement apartment in the Negev Desert. He was in Israel only a month when he realized he did not want to stay. Since the Jewish agency would not pay for him to return to the United States, he could not afford to take the whole family back with him. He took only Jane who was 18 years old. Jane's mother and two brothers remained behind in Israel.

The first night they were back in Brooklyn, the sexual abuse began. Jane's father explained to her that he had promised her mother that he would not have extramarital sex, but that Jane was the "seed of his own apple," and therefore, it was all right. He did not penetrate Jane, but rubbed his penis against her and ejaculated on her. The next morning, Jane called her mother in Israel and told her what had happened. Jane's mother told her that there was nothing she could do and that Jane should just tolerate her father's mistreatment. Jane's mother said that if she did not take it, her father would never bring the rest of the family back from Israel.

Jane tolerated her father's sexual abuse for about a year. She told

him she wanted to be a virgin when she got married and he agreed
not to break her hymen. However, he continued to have sexual contact with her. Finally, he went to Israel and brought the rest of the
family home. Jane had hoped that the sexual abuse would stop once
her mother was there, but her mother was powerless to stop it. Then,
on the day he died, Jane's father told Jane that he was going to take
her to Atlantic City and "break her virginity." Then, he said he was
going to kill Jane's mother and marry Jane, so that she would love
him as he loved her. Then, he passed out.

Jane left the apartment and went to find her mother who was
working in the family business, a shoe repair shop. They closed the
store and Jane and her mother went home. They believed that they
could not prevent him from carrying out his threat. Jane said that
he had never before made this threat against her. They took an ax
from the closet. Jane struck the first blow. The ax stuck in his head
and she could not continue. Jane's mother pulled the ax from his
head and continued to strike him.[7]

Jane waived a jury and was tried by Judge Anne Feldman. I testified at Jane's trial about the "continuum of tolerability" notion
and about Jane's ability to detect behavior by her father that "fell
off" the continuum. In general, the continuum must be flexible, expansive. New episodes of violence that are tolerated cause the continuum to grow longer and more refined. However, some episodes
of actual or threatened violence are so extraordinary that they can
not act to extend the continuum. Instead, they stand out in the mind
of the victim in contrast to all that has come before.

For Jane, with her extensive knowledge of her father's potential
for physical violence against her mother, and for sexual violence
against her, the father's novel threat was terrifying. She and her
mother believed they could do nothing to stop him, that there was
nowhere to go. The fact that they were recent arrivals in this country (Jane's mother did not even speak English) heightened their sense
of isolation and their feeling that there was nowhere to turn.

Judge Feldman found the continuum of tolerability construct and
the ideas about the diminished perception of alternatives to provide
a useful context for considering Jane's action against her father. She
was persuaded that Jane had acted out of a reasonable fear for her

---

7. Jane Melandovich's mother's involvement in her husband's death was not made known
until the trial, when, during her testimony, she inculpated herself. Judge Feldman stopped
the proceedings and a Legal Aid lawyer was secured for Irina Melandovich. The Brooklyn
District Attorney's Office chose not to indict Irina.

mother's life and for her own bodily integrity and that her action was consistent with what the right to self-defense allowed. Judge Feldman acquitted Jane of all charges.

A Summary on the Psychology of Battered Women (Who Kill)

Thus, while three of the four psychological changes presented above suggest impairment—"learned helplessness," tolerating cognitive inconsistency, and a diminished perception of alternatives—this last characteristic of battered women—knowing what is off the continuum of "routine" violence—reflects an enhanced capacity, an affirmation of the reasonableness of the need to act (Schneider 1986). The general consequences of remaining in an abusive relationship create negative states in battered women, while the particular perceptual changes related to moments of abuse are adaptive. The context for considering the battered woman's mental states is different. For the first three characteristics, she is placed within the framework of an intimate relationship, where her functioning is diminished in direct relation to the extent to which her relationship deviates from what is considered normal, or even ideal. For the fourth trait, though, her mental activity is considered only within the context of the violent act and her perception of its survivability, based on her exposure to prior violent acts by the same individual. Here, her functioning can be ideal. Ultimately, it is within this latter context that her life-taking act is judged.

Making the Link Between General Constructs and Specific Defendants

With regard to the application of these general constructs to particular individuals, the self-descriptions of the defendant determine which aspects of the general model may be emphasized. As noted earlier, women must display signs of three of these four characteristics. Even with that said, it is worth noting that no woman should be expected to possess every trait that has been shown to be present in groups of battered women. The empirical descriptions of battered women that are currently available are not intended to be wholly applied in each case. That is, a "diagnosis" of abuse may be concluded if most, but not all, of the traits shown to result from abuse are present in some individual. For example, it is entirely possible for a battered woman to have a constructive, effective work style outside the home—for her to show no signs of "learned helplessness." This should not be taken to mean that her marital relationship is untroubled or that she recognizes an escape from the violence in her capacity to be financially self-sufficient. While economic dependence may explain why some women remain in abusive relationships, it is not the only reason. Psychological factors, like the hope that the abuse will stop or the belief that relationships should be preserved at almost any cost, may also prevent women from leaving. The psychology of battered women is complex and the traits associated with it may vary somewhat as the severity and frequency of the violence rises and falls. Expert testimony should clarify this complexity by emphasizing those characteristics that a particular defendant exhibits.

PERSONAL REFLECTIONS ON EXPERT TESTIMONY: DILEMMAS OF OBJECTIVITY AND BIAS[8]

This section of the chapter is constructed around four examples that I hope will illustrate different aspects of dilemmas of objectivity and bias in trials involving violence between intimates. The heart of the dilemmas in all four cases rests with the tension between the researcher's commitment to objectivity (and even truth) within the adversarial, nonobjective context of the courtroom.

The first dilemma has to do with the urge to be correct, clever, and consistent, the second with the tension between being an advocate and being an educator in the adversarial environment of the courtroom, the third with the influence of experts' life experiences and presumed values on the content and the reception of their testimony, and the fourth with the bias that has resulted from family violence researchers' neglect of social class as a significant contributor to the experiences of battered women. With regard to this last concern, data are presented on the relationship between social class, expert testimony, and outcome for 31 battered women who killed their abusers.

8. Much of what appears in this section was based on a presentation that I gave at the 1987 meeting of the American Psychological Association, entitled "Expert Testimony for Battered Women Who Kill: Dilemmas of Objectivity and Bias."

The first example comes from a case in which a young woman was seriously injured as a result of her boyfriend's action. The other three involve cases of battered women who killed their abusers.

Ego and the Willingness to Change One's Opinion

Recently, an attorney was preparing me to testify at a deposition. I was going to be asked questions by the attorneys representing the other side in a civil suit. The basis for the suit involved an episode of alleged abuse in a dating relationship that occurred in a college dormitory. The girl had complained to the dormitory authorities, but they did not act to remove the boy from the dormitory or even from her floor. About two months after the complaint, the boy attempted to prevent the girl from getting away from him. He tackled her around the knees. She pitched forward and cracked her head on the floor. Three months later, she awakened from a coma with lasting neurological damage.

I was to testify about the nature of abuse in dating relationships and to offer the opinion that the dormitory had not acted with sufficient regard for the girl's well being. The boy was denying that he was responsible for the girl's fall. The lawyer for the girl asked me this, "If the boy's lawyer asks you if you would change your opinion of the situation if you discovered that the boy had not ever abused this girl, what would you say?" I hesitated for a moment. He continued, "You would say, of course, that it would change your opinion." He wanted to be sure that I did not become so ego-involved in holding one view that I would fail to admit that a total change in what I believed to be the facts would change my opinion. While I might want to be outraged at this suggestion that my opinion had a life of its own, and would not be changed by new and contradictory facts, I have at times found myself thinking about ways of holding only my original opinion, even as I was being presented with facts that would make my opinion untenable. I believe I have so far resisted that urge to reconstruct reality so as to hold onto my opinion, but I have felt it as I sat in the witness box. I am certain that some of the prosecutors who cross examine me would disagree with my belief that I resisted that urge. And, arguably, I am not the best judge of my own objectivity, in spite of my great wish to be objective.

When I admit to a change in my position, I must also admit to a certain inner reluctance to have done so. That reluctance is not based in science, which is intensely self-critical by nature. Instead, it is my human nature, my wish to be clever, correct, and consistent that is at the heart of this dilemma.

Scientist vs. Advocate

Once, at the end of my expert testimony in the case of a battered woman who killed her husband, the defense attorney asked, "Was she justified in killing him?" The prosecutor objected, but was over-ruled by the judge, who turned to me and said, "Doctor, I am in-terested in hearing the answer. Was this killing justified?"

During the suspended moment between that question and my an-swer, I felt my life, my politics, my feminism, my personal com-mitment to nonviolence in families flash by. My knowledge of the social scientific literature on family violence, my own research in this area, had not adequately prepared me for this question. My knowledge of the law had led me to believe that I could not ever be asked this crucial question—that the answer fell within the juror's province. However, the judge more than allowed the question to be asked and answered; he encouraged it.

So, I answered by outlining what the law says constitutes justi-fication—the reasonable belief in imminent life-threatening in-jury—and then spoke in the defendant's voice, with a qualification, "She would have believed her action was justified at the time, if she was indeed suffering from the effects of having been physically beaten in her own home over an extended period of time. I think she was a battered woman with the psychological characteristics I outlined earlier." While I made reference to the scientific literature, I have come to think that at that moment, I was an advocate offering an opinion with very little of the mantle of science left. The respon-sibility of being an expert witness in cases of battered women who kill their abusers felt especially heavy at that moment.

More generally, the distinction between advocate and educator becomes fine whenever a social scientist steps into the adversarial environment of the courtroom. It is not enough to describe a phe-nomenon. Experts' opinions and interpretations of the events are of greatest interest. That different experts may see the same events very differently leads to trials that come down to battles between experts.

The emphasis on interpretation and advocacy fosters the "hired gun" problem. This label is applied to those experts who seem always to testify for a particular position, regardless of the facts in any particular case. The presumption that this attribution about the expert will be believed by the jurors is reflected in the routine cross examination-question, "So, Doctor, how much are you being paid for your testimony?" The right answer is that one is not paid anything for one's testimony, only for one's time. Even so, it always seems that jurors are disturbed to learn that "the truth" costs money. And, the more one is paid, the larger it seems is the damage to credibility. Being paid by only one side in a dispute, as is always the case, further heightens issues of bias and advocacy and undermines the perception of the expert as objective educator.

The problem with trying to be an educator and not an advocate in an adversarial context is largely structural, derived from the nature of the judicial system. However, a part of the problem must reside in the expert, who shows a willingness by her or his presence in a courtroom to shape opinions that go beyond science. There are researchers who avoid courtrooms for this very reason. There are some who believe that neither aggregate data analyses nor clinical experiences with other people lend themselves to explaining the behaviors of singular individuals. Thus, in a construction of the problem that is all dilemma and no resolution, the very choice to testify marks the beginning of advocacy.

The Importance of Values and Life Experiences

Being an expert on intimate violence means being an expert on something that everyone knows something about. Therefore, the credentials of the expert witness go beyond educational background, publications, and professional memberships. I have been asked "Are you a battered woman?" In a West Virginia case, the defense attorney asked me to review the history of where I had grown up. Luckily, I had been born in Illinois and raised for a little while in Tennessee. Importantly, I had not lived all of my life in New York. I have been asked if I am married, if I have children, how old I am.

One prosecutor quoted from the introduction to Lenore Walker's *The Battered Woman*, to discover if I was a feminist and/or a revolutionary. In Queens County, New York, where Archie Bunker provides the model for the prototypic juror, a prosecutor asked if I saw "sexism as the underbelly of all human suffering." She asked if I

saw the problems of battered women in terms of a feminist vision
and if I was working to overthrow the existing social order.

While I do not like to answer such questions and feel somewhat
offended and personally invaded by lawyers and judges (and presumably jurors) who seem to think they provide a relevant context for
my opinions, my feeling is best understood, I think, as defensiveness. I do not want my testimony to be discounted because of the
presumed influence of my own life experiences and values. However, I do want to acknowledge the importance of making known
potentially relevant life experiences, values, and ideology in cases
that involve violence between intimates. Certainly, when intense
conflict and strong feelings toward intimates are at issue, the pure
influence of "science" may be blunted by the relevant personal experiences of the expert. Further, the relevant personal experiences
of everyone else will influence the process and will have particular
impact on the reception of the expert's testimony. Living through
conflict and violence in an intimate relationship shapes one's sense
of how such things happen "normally." However, these intuitive
ideas about normal family relations are not always right. Indeed,
they are often wrong. In fact, one of the three major bases for ad-
mitting expert, data-based testimony on the battered woman syndrome is that the opinion of the expert goes beyond the ken of the
average layperson. Thus, it is the presence of relevant, but not necessarily representative life experiences that argues for the inclusion
of expert testimony at trial time. Presumably, accurate information
can mitigate the impact of unrepresentative life experiences. However, no one would argue that values and beliefs held for a lifetime
will be completely undone by expert testimony. Life experiences remain relevant and are still taken into consideration by the defense
and prosecution. Logically, then, even experts who learn much from
the data they study must still show some effects of their life experiences, values, and beliefs in their understandings of what they
study.

The Social Class Bias in Expert Testimony

The fourth concern pertains directly to the impact of class on the
experiences of battered women. Early in the ten-year history of expert testimony on the battered woman syndrome, the women who
received expert attention were not impoverished. The first case of

a homicidal battered woman to receive a great deal of general publicity was Francine Hughes'—the woman mentioned at the beginning of this chapter. She is a white, working class woman, who set
fire to her sleeping husband after he had set fire to her college text-
books. Farrah Fawcett played her in the TV movie *The Burning Bed*.
While her defense was insanity, the immediate shift away from that
defense to legal choices that emphasized the reasonableness of the
woman's act caused her case to acquire special significance. It marked
the end of an era.

Since 1978, and the beginning of the use of testimony on the battered woman syndrome, I have seen a "filtering down" effect in terms
of the social class of the women whose lawyers have sought expert
testimony. Still, there is an awareness on the part of these attorneys
seeking expert testimony in cases of very poor women that their
clients present problems for experts on women who are not poor.
Much of the psychology of the battered woman that is reflected in
our existing literature is about women for whom violence is confined to their marital relationship. Even if their life histories include
other violent relationships, such violence is depicted serially. The
image of multiple, simultaneous violent relationships or experiences is largely absent from the work on battered women.

When I hear an attorney say, "My client is not a typical battered
woman, but I wonder if you can help her anyway," I understand this
to mean that the woman is very poor and is part of a lifestyle in
which violence is rampant. In contrast to the battered women whose
experiences psychologists made "typical" through their work, very
poor, atypical battered women are often the victims and sometimes
the perpetrators of violence from many sources. They may be abused
not only by husbands, but also by their mothers, siblings, neighbors,
and friends—to say nothing of their real and reasonable expectation
that the police afford them little reliable protection.

Further, unlike the "typical" battered woman, these women do
not endure their abuse in isolation; nor do they retreat into mo-
nogamy, passivity, or a class-based notion of traditionality. In stark
contrast to the depiction of battered women in much of the early
work, I have come to know that some battered women are prosti-
tutes. Some battered women abuse their children and some are involved in near lethal acts of violence against their abusers prior to
the moment at which they do the thing that results in his death.

To date, the work of experts in this area—my own included—
has been classist and, as a result, not comprehensive or objective

beyond its boundaries. The definition of battered women who killed has been too narrow, and has been narrow in a way that directly reflected the class perspective of the researchers. For poor women who were fighting to stay alive in many ways and who also had to fight off abusive men, our work has not been as illuminating as it ought to be. To acknowledge this weakness is a beginning. Still, much work remains to be done with regard to very poor battered women, an undertaking that requires the most astute collaboration with the women themselves, in order to understand how chronic violence has affected their psychologies. Certainly future research must be designed with a view toward understanding the impact of social class on the psychology of battered women.

Illustrative data on the relationships among my expert testimony, the defendant's social class, and the outcome are presented here as a part of the beginning effort on behalf of very poor battered women. The 31 homicide cases that are my data base involve battered women who killed their abusers between 1978 and 1987. Sixteen of these women were welfare class, 15 lived on earned incomes. I testified at the trials of 14 of the 31, and was involved in the disposition of the case but did not testify 17 times. See table 11.1 for a breakdown of the specific outcomes of these cases.

These data indicate an effect on outcome attributable to a combination of expert testimony and the defendant's social class. The impact of expert testimony, considered alone, significantly increased the acquittal rate. The defendant's social class, considered alone, did not significantly relate to outcome, although expert testimony was offered significantly more often when the defendant was not welfare class. See tables 11.2 through 11.4 for the data on these relationships.

Finally, taken together, women who were not poor and who offered expert testimony were most likely to be acquitted (or not indicated)—90% (or 9 out of 10) achieved this result. Women who were poor and offered expert testimony were acquitted in 75% (or 3 out of 4) of the cases; women who were poor and did not offer expert testimony were acquitted in 42% (or 5 out of 12) of the cases. Interestingly, those who were *not poor* and did *not offer expert testimony* fared worst, with a 20% (or 1 out of 5) acquittal rate. See table 11.5 for these results.

Thus, it seems that for women who would appear to have options based on their socioeconomic status, the defense's failure to provide insight into their psychologies through expert testimony left their situations hardest for the jurors to understand. Then, the jurors were most likely to convict. The situation of poor women provides an informative contrast. Apparently, to a greater extent, the situation of very poor women spoke for itself; 75% were acquitted without expert testimony (although the number of cases here was particularly small). Nonetheless, the even higher acquittal rate achieved for non-poor women who offered expert testimony (90%) would suggest that there is still reason to believe that the absence of expert testimony disadvantaged poor women.

TABLE 11.1

The Impacts of Social Class and Expert Testimony on the Specific Outcomes of Homicide Cases Involving Battered Women Defendants

	Welfare Class		Not Welfare Class	
Expert Testimony	Yes	No	Yes	No
Outcome				
Acquittal	3	5	8	1
Conviction	1			1
Conviction-reversal			1	
Pled-Probation		2		1
Pled-Jail time		5		2
No Indictment			1	
Total	4	12	10	5

TABLE 11.2

The Relationship between the Inclusion of Expert Testimony and Outcome

	OUTCOME		
	Acquittal	Conviction	TOTAL
Expert Testimony			
Yes	85.6 (12)	14.4 (2)	45.2 (14)
No	35.3 (6)	64.7 (11)	54.8 (17)
Total	58.1 (18)	41.9 (13)	100.0 (31)

Chi-Square = 7.87 with 1 df, p = .04

The import of these preliminary data comes from the justification they provide for attention to issues of social class, expert testimony, and outcome. To the extent that the limitations of current research and its inattention to poor women cause the situation of poor battered women to fall outside the established model, our research has been remiss; and to the extent that informed expert testimony would provide a right and illuminating context for the consideration of the lethal acts of poor battered women, we are doing poor women who kill in self-defense a particular disservice.

So far, we know too little about the differences in the psychologies of poor and non-poor battered women to characterize them with confidence. It seems certain that they exist. Perhaps, very poor

TABLE 11.3

The Relationship between the Defendant's Social Class
and Outcome

| | OUTCOME | | |
	Acquittal	Conviction	TOTAL
Social Class			
Welfare Class	50.0 (8)	50.0 (8)	51.6 (16)
Not Welfare Class	66.7 (10)	33.3 (5)	48.4 (15)
Total	58.1 (18)	41.9 (13)	100.0 (31)

Chi-Square = .87 with 1 df, p = .30

TABLE 11.4

The Relationship between Expert Testimony and the Defendant's
Social Class

| | EXPERT TESTIMONY | | |
	Yes	No	TOTAL
Social Class			
Welfare Class	25.0 (4)	75.0 (12)	51.6 (16)
Not Welfare Class	66.7 (10)	33.3 (5)	48.4 (15)
Total	45.2 (14)	54.8 (17)	100.0 (31)

Chi-Square = 5.34 with 1 df, p = .06

battered women do not experience a diminution in their ability to see alternatives as a consequence of marital violence. It may be that poverty renders so many options so truly unattainable that the options stolen by violence are scarcely distinguishable from the options stolen by poverty. Or, the direct, personal knowledge of many individuals who die as the result of another's intentional act may make the "continuum of tolerability" for violent acts a less relevant construct. Maybe, in the real absence of alternatives, anything that can be survived can be tolerated.

In particular, especially for those women who use violence to stay alive on more than one occasion, we must work toward a conception of women as agents. Such women are agents of their own survival even in oppressive relationships and are at least nominally agentic in their life-taking acts. Much of the existing construction of battered women has been all but tailor-made to fit with the view that battered women are reactive, but not active, and so could not be dangerous again to anyone else.

Issues of future dangerousness of course deserve a place in this work and require our careful and dedicated consideration. Ultimately, we must be prepared to know that some women are dan-

TABLE 11.5
The Combined Impacts of Expert Testimony and Social Class
On Outcome

	OUTCOME		
	Acquittal	Conviction	TOTAL
Expert Testimony and Social Class			
Expert Testimony + Not Welfare Class	90.0 (9)	10.0 (1)	32.3 (10)
Expert Testimony + Welfare Class	75.0 (3)	25.0 (1)	12.9 (4)
No Expert Testimony + Welfare Class	41.7 (5)	58.3 (7)	38.7 (12)
No Expert Testimony + Not Welfare Class	20.0 (1)	80.0 (4)	16.1 (5)
Total	58.1 (18)	41.9 (13)	100.0 (31)
Chi-Square = 9.36 with 3 df, p = .002			

gerous and that some are not. Unfortunately, up until now, poverty has too often been taken to be a sign of dangerousness.

Summary. The differences that must exist between the psychological reactions of poor and non-poor battered women reveal the overly narrow construction of the psychology of battered women. As a result, the application of research in courtroom settings has too often been impossible in the cases of poor, "atypical" battered women. Thus, they have been deprived of the illumination that social scientists could provide. It is difficult to transcend class issues and to achieve a real understanding of the impact of battering by an intimate in the lives of women of different backgrounds. Learning to separate social class issues from dangerousness concerns should provide direction to all those who would serve justice in cases of battered women who kill their abusers in self-defense. As our images of battered women grow broader and more complex, our theories grow in practical value, enhancing the usefulness of psychology within the criminal justice system.

CONCLUSION

Descriptions of cases of battered women are used to illustrate, first, the content and process of expert testimony, and then the dilemmas inherent in the transition from researcher to expert witness—an example of Stage 5 activity in the emergence of this social problem. Following a discussion of the "reasonable man" standard as it applies to battered women, this chapter includes description of four aspects of battered women's psychology. First, battered women experience a feeling of "learned helplessness," which means feeling unable to control what happens to them especially with regard to their wish to stop the violence. Second, battered women evidence a tolerance for cognitive inconsistency that reflects the fundamental inconsistency of enduring abuse in an intimate relationship. Third, battered women show a diminished ability to perceive alternatives that would move them out of the relationship. Instead, their focus appears to rest primarily with the relationship and with efforts to survive within it. Fourth, battered women, in part because of their narrowed focus on the relationship and the abuser's violence, generate a continuum of tolerability, which enables them to know when a violent episode is distinct from other, previous episodes and when their lives are at risk. This four-part model is described to juries during the course of my expert testimony and the characteristics of individual battered women defendants are "fit" to this model in an effort to illuminate their psychological state during the relationship and at the time of the killing.

However, expert testimony can only be as good as the expert, and that "goodness" rests with her or his ability to retain a commitment to objectivity and the pursuit of real understanding. This process is fraught with dilemmas that come from the expert's ego, values, and life experiences, from the adversarial nature of the courtroom process, and from limitations inherent in the research itself. In particular, a significant social-class bias has shaped research on battered women; and to date we do not know enough about the psychology of very poor battered women.

Understanding reactions to injustice in intimate relationships is what this work is all about. Taking the results of research on battered women into the courtroom is intended to help jurors and judges discern what is unjust, so that they can further the interests of justice. Knowing what is just and what is not is complicated at best, but is more likely to happen under conditions of information and insight than under conditions of ignorance. We know far more about victims of intimate violence today than we did even ten years ago. There is more to learn. In particular, it is time for us to increase our understanding of the nature of violence in very poor families, where alternatives are absent objectively and subjectively. If we know more, we can do more to help.

Ultimately, it is the goal of this work to turn the title of my book into words that can not be deciphered, to foster a world where "intimate" and "violence" make no sense together.

APPENDIX A: THE
NEWSPAPER SURVEY

The survey is discussed in chapters 5, 6, and 10.

A QUESTIONNAIRE ON YOUR EXPERIENCES

One of the most pressing problems in American society is violence. We read about it in newspapers and see it on TV and in the movies. Many of us confront it personally in our lives.

Some crimes of violence are easy to detect, as in the cases of murder or arson. The damage is immediate and obvious. However, other acts of violence are more difficult to detect, and so to solve. Victims of rape may choose not to report the harm done to them because they fear reprisals from the rapist or because they feel too embarrassed to discuss such intimate matters. People also experience violence in their homes. Parents may abuse their children, spouses

hurt each other. The victims of family violence may also be reluctant to report their troubles. They may believe that their problems
with violence are unusual and that no resources are available to help
them, anyway.

Resources are available to help, although we know very little about
the numbers of people who could make use of such resources. This
questionnaire asks you for information about your experiences with
violence that is not immediately obvious, about intimate violence.
Intimate violence is something to be concerned about, and something to study. Who has experienced the effects of intimate violence? What do people do when confronted with such situations?
What can people do when they confront intimate violence?

Only a large and varied group of people, such as the readers of
The Record, can answer such questions. Your participation will be
anonymous and you can participate in this study whether or not you
have ever been involved with intimate violence.

Here is what you do:

- Read the questions carefully and write or circle your answers
  on this page.

- Before Sunday, mail your answers to:
  The Record
  Lifestyle 79
  Dept. L
  150 River St.
  Hackensack, N.J. 07602

- If you have a comment on any questions, write it on a separate
  piece of paper (be sure to include the question number) and
  mail it in with your answers.

- Your answers will be kept confidential. Indeed you need not
  give your name at all. A few people, though, will be interviewed at length. If you are willing to be interviewed, write
  your name and phone number at the bottom of this page.

- Remember, you are qualified to answer these questions even if
  you have never been involved with intimate violence. In fact,
  the results won't be meaningful unless all kinds of people respond.

- Please be honest. Only honest answers can be used to help increase our understanding of intimate violence.

Dr. Julie Blackman-Doron of Barnard College will use a high-speed computer to analyze your answers at Columbia University. She will report the results in The Record in about two months.

(6–7)   1. What is your age? _____ years old

(8)   2. What is your sex?
    1. Male
    2. Female

(9–10)   3. In which town do you live?
    (specify)

(11–12)   4. How long have you been living in your present community? _____ years

(13)   5. What is the total income of your family?
    1. Less than $5,000
    2. $5,000 to $9,999
    3. $10,000 to $14,999
    4. $15,000 to $19,999
    5. $20,000 to $24,999
    6. $25,000 to $29,999
    7. $30,000 to $39,999
    8. $40,000 to $49,000
    9. $50,000 or more

(14)   6. What is the highest level of education you have completed?
    1. Grade school or less
    2. Some high school
    3. Graduated high school
    4. Some college
    5. Graduated college
    6. Some graduate or professional school
    7. Received a graduate or professional degree

(15)   7. Are you currently employed outside the home?
    1. Yes
    2. No

(16–17)   8. What is your living situation? Please pick the one category which best represents your current living situation.
    1. Single, living alone
    2. Single, living with a roommate

     3. Living with an opposite-sex lover
     4. Living with a same-sex lover
     5. Married, for the first time with no children
     6. Married, for the first time with children
     7. Remarried, once with no children
     8. Remarried, once with children
     9. Remarried, more than once with no children
   10. Remarried, more than once with children
   11. Separated, with no children
   12. Separated, with children
   13. Divorced, with no children
   14. Divorced, with children
   15. Widowed, with no children
   16. Widowed, with children
   17. Other (specify: _____)

(18–19) 9. How many children (of your own) do you have? _____ children

(20–21) 10. How many children are living in your home now? _____ children

(22–23) 11. If you are married, for how many years have you been married? __years

(24) 12. Are you or is the woman of your household currently pregnant?
     1. Yes
     2. No

(25) 13. What is your religion?
     1. Buddhist
     2. Catholic
     3. Jewish
     4. Moslem
     5. Protestant
     6. Agnostic/Atheist
     7. Other (specify: _____)

(26–27) 14. With what racial/ethnic group (for example: Black, Chinese, Italian, Irish, Jewish, Puerto Rican, etc.) do you identify most?
(Specify: _____)

(28–29) 15. How many children were in your family when you were growing up? _____children

(30) 16. Which of the following describes your birth order? Were you the oldest, one of the middle children or the youngest in your family?
1. Only child
2. Oldest
3. Middle born
4. Youngest

(31) 17. As a child, were you ever physically abused (punched, kicked, bruised) by your parents?
1. Yes
2. No

If you answered "Yes" to question 17, continue on and answer questions 18 through 22. If you answered "No" to question 17, skip to question 23.

(32) 18. I was abused by:
1. My mother only
2. My father only
3. Both parents
4. Other (specify _____)

(33) 19. How often would you say you were abused?
1. Only once or twice
2. Rarely (less than twice a year)
3. Occasionally (between two and six times a year)
4. Regularly (between seven and twelve times a year)
5. Often (more than thirteen times a year)

(34–38) 20. How old were you when you were abused? Check as many as apply.
1. Less than three years old
2. Three to five years old
3. Six to nine years old
4. Ten to fifteen years old
5. Sixteen to twenty years old

(39–42) 21. Was the abuse ever severe enough to require any of the following?

1. A doctor's care
2. Hospitalization
3. Police involvement
4. Other (specify _____)

(43–50) 22. Did you ever tell anyone about having been abused? Whom did you tell? Check as many as apply.
1. No one
2. Family member(s)
3. Friend(s)
4. Teacher(s)
5. Hospital staff
6. Social worker(s)
7. Family physician
8. Other (specify _____)

(51) 23. As a parent, have you ever physically abused any of your children?
1. Yes
2. No

If you answered "Yes" to question 23, continue on and answer questions 24 through 27. If you answered "No" to question 23, skip to question 28.

(52–57) 24. If yes, which of your children have you abused? Check as many as apply and specify son or daughter.
1. First born child _____(son or daughter)
2. Middle born child (ren) _____

_____

_____

3. Last born child _____

(58) 25. How often would you say you have abused your children?
1. Only once or twice
2. Rarely (less than twice a year)
3. Occasionally (between 2 and 6 times a year)
4. Regularly (between 7 and 12 times a year)
5. Often (more than 13 times a year)

(59–62) 26. Was the abuse ever severe enough to require any of the following?

    1. A doctor's care
    2. Hospitalization
    3. Police involvement
    4. Other (specify _____)

(63–73) 27. Have you ever talked with anyone about this abuse? With whom did you talk? Check as many as apply.
    1. No one
    2. Family member(s)
    3. Friend(s)
    4. Hospital staff
    5. Social worker(s)
    6. Family physician
    7. Police
    8. Self-help group for parents who want to stop abusing their children
    9. Counselor or psychotherapist
    10. Psychiatrist or clinical psychologist
    11. Other (specify _____)

(6) 28. Have you ever been physically abused by your current spouse or lover?
    1. Yes
    2. No

(7) 29. In any past relationships, were you ever physically abused by your spouse or lover?
    1. Yes
    2. No

If you answered "Yes" to questions 28 and/or 29, continue on and answer questions 30 through 34. If you answered "No" to both questions 28 and 29, skip to question 35. Please answer these questions about your most recent relationship which included physical abuse:

(8) 30. How often would you say you are/were abused by your spouse or lover?
    1. Only once or twice
    2. Rarely (less than twice a year)
    3. Occasionally (between 2 and 6 times a year)
    4. Regularly (between 7 and 12 times a year)
    5. Often (more than 13 times a year)

(9) 31. How long had you been married or living together when
    the abuse began?
    1. The abuse began before the marriage or living together
    2. Less than 1 year
    3. Between 1 and 5 years
    4. Between 6 and 10 years
    5. Between 11 and 20 years
    6. More than 20 years

32. What is/was the nature of physical abuse in your rela-
    tionship?
(10)   1. It only happened once or twice and then stopped
(11–12)   2. It stopped after __years (specify)
(13–14)   3. The relationship ended after __years (specify)
(15)   4. My spouse/lover still abuses me

(16–19) 33. Was the abuse ever severe enough to require any of the
    following?
    1. A doctor's care
    2. Hospitalization
    3. Police involvement
    4. Other (specify _____)

(20–31) 34. Have you ever told anyone? Whom did you tell? Check
    as many as apply.
    1. No one
    2. Family member(s)
    3. Friend(s)
    4. Hospital staff
    5. Social worker(s)
    6. Family physician
    7. Police
    8. Crisis hot line
    9. Staff of a shelter for battered women
    10. Counselor or psychotherapist
    11. Psychiatrist or clinical psychologist
    12. Other (specify _____)

(32) 35. Have you ever had sex with your spouse or lover when
    you did not really want to?
    1. Yes
    2. No

(33) 36. If yes, how often?
    1. Only once or twice
    2. Rarely
    3. Occasionally
    4. Regularly
    5. Often
    6. Always

(34) 37. Have you ever felt pressured to have sex with your spouse or lover?
    1. Yes
    2. No

(35) 38. If yes, how often?
    1. Only once or twice
    2. Rarely
    3. Occasionally
    4. Regularly
    5. Often
    6. Always

(38) 39. Has your spouse or lover ever used violence or the threat of violence to force you to have sexual intercourse?
    1. Yes
    2. No

(37) 40. If yes, how often?
    1. Only once or twice
    2. Rarely
    3. Occasionally
    4. Regularly
    5. Often
    6. Always

(38) 41. Were you ever raped?
    1. Yes
    2. No

If you answered "Yes" to question 41, continue on and answer questions 42 and 43. If you answered "No" to question 41, go to question 44.

(39–43) 42. I was raped by:

    1. A stranger
    2. A casual acquaintance
    3. A neighbor
    4. A friend
    5. A family member other than spouse (for example, brother, stepfather, uncle)

(44–54) 43. Did you ever tell anyone about having been raped? Whom did you tell?
    1. No one
    2. Family member(s)
    3. Friend(s)
    4. Hospital staff
    5. Social worker(s)
    6. Family physician
    7. Police
    8. Crisis hot line
    9. Counselor or psychotherapist
    10. Psychiatrist or clinical psychologist
    11. Other (specify _____)

  (55) 44. If you are willing to volunteer for a personal interview, please print your name and phone number in the space provided below.

Name _____

Phone No. _____

APPENDIX B: THE INTERVIEW SCHEDULE

This material is discussed in chapters 5, 7–10.

INTERVIEW SCHEDULE

Instructions to Interviewers: Before you begin each interview, please look over the interview schedule in order to re-familiarize yourself with the issues to be discussed. Begin each interview by giving the interviewee the *Consent Statement* to read and sign. Explain to all interviewees that we need their permission in order to interview them and to tape record the interviews. Be sure the interviewees are aware that you are obliged to report any cases of current child abuse they describe to you. Finally, reassure them that the information gathered will be kept confidential. Their names will not be attached to the tapes.

Key for interviewee's condition:

  C victim of child abuse or victim of incest
  P parent who abuses child
 CS victim of current spousal abuse
 PS victim of past spousal abuse
KR victim of known rapist
SR victim of stranger rapist
  X control condition or an abusing spouse or someone who does
     not fit into any of the other conditions

Administer these *Instructions to Interviewees:*

> In order to do these interviews in as scientific and as objective a way as possible, I have not seen your responses to the questionnaires that appeared in The Record. So, if I ask you questions that you think I should already know the answers to, please understand that I am uninformed for a reason—so that I can be free of any preconceptions as I listen to what you have to say.
>
> I wonder if, before we begin, you could give me some idea of what you think we're going to talk about today.

Who to ask	*Section*	*Suggested Text and Questions*
All	Intro-duction	1. Have you had any direct, personal experiences with any sort of intimate violence?

(Do not offer the interviewee a list of alternatives, just wait. If interviewee hesitates a long time or seems uncertain about what you meant, then continue and ask)

Note to Interviewers:

After interviewee has responded to this question (1), read through the list of alternatives, anyway, so that we can be sure that we have covered all possibilities with all interviewees.

Have you ever been abused by your spouse or lover, either currently or in the past?

As a parent, have you ever abused your children?

As a child, were you ever abused by your parents or other close family relatives?

Were you ever raped by a stranger, or by someone you knew?

(After interviewee has responded to this question—with or without prompts—note her/his response on an index card which has only the interviewee's ID number on

Who to ask	*Section*	*Suggested Text and Questions*

<table>
<tr><td></td><td></td><td>it. You can refer to it later as a reminder if you need to.)

One of the things we are hoping to accomplish through these interviews is to get a sense of people's intimate or close, important relationships; and the role of conflict and violence in these relationships.</td></tr>
<tr><td>X only</td><td></td><td>Since you have not experienced any sort of intimate violence directly, I would like you to select the intimate relationship that you consider to be your strongest or closest relationship.</td></tr>
<tr><td>C, P, CS, PS</td><td></td><td>Since you have experienced intimate violence in an on-going relationship, I would like you to begin by describing your relationship with your _____ (parent, child, spouse, ex-spouse) to me. (If interviewee named several experiences with intimate violence, ask her/him which one was most recent and discuss that one.)</td></tr>
<tr><td>SR, KR</td><td></td><td>Since you have experienced sexual assault, I would like you to begin by describing your experiences and your feelings about them.</td></tr>
<tr><td>X, C, P,
CS, PS</td><td>Early
relation-
ship</td><td>2. Tell me about your earliest recollections of this relationship.

Areas to be covered:
  a) How many years ago did the relationship begin?
  b) What was the relationship like for you at the beginning?
  c) What did your partner do/feel/say to you about the relationship?
  d) What did you do/feel/say about the relationship?
  e) What do you think were your expectations for this relationship at the beginning?
  f) During the early phase of your relationship, were your expectations met?</td></tr>
</table>

Who to ask	*Section*	*Suggested Text and Questions*
X only	Hard times	3. Just briefly, what would you say was the **most difficult experience** in your relationship with *partner*? Think carefully, because this is the incident we will discuss in more detail today. What event or time stands out in your mind when you think about **hard times** in the relationship? This difficult experience may be one particular event or a series of events that you see as related.

Note to Interviewers:

The criteria for the selection of "good" incidents are:
difficulty, significance and representativeness.

(*To interviewer: In text from here on, the named event is referred to as "hard times." This term should be replaced with an appropriate phrase. The word "violence" should be similarly replaced.*)

X, C, P, CS, PS	When	4. When did the violence/hard times begin/occur in the relationship?
KR, SR		or When did the rape occur?
		Areas to be covered:
All		a) How many years ago?
C, KR, SR		b) How old were you? For victims of continuing abuse: How old were you when the abuse began? ended?
(X), C, P, CS, PS, KR, SR		c) How often did/does it occur?
X, CS, PS		d) After how many years of the relationship?
P		e) How old was your child when you first abused him/her?
All	What happened	5. Describe exactly what happened. Give the details of particular incidents.
		Areas to be covered:
(X), C, P, CS, PS, KR, SR		a) Extent of physical damage to you and to property.
X, C, P, CS, PS		b) Who initiated the violence/hard times? Did you fight back? (if you were not the initiator)
All		c) Were others present? Witnesses?
All		d) What were the intentions of the abuser/initiator and of the abusee/responder?

Who to ask	Section	Suggested Text and Questions
All		e) Describe verbal exchanges/physical exchanges in detail
All		f) Where did incident occur? Time of day? Other relevant details?
All	Conflict as the cause	6. What do you think caused the incident(s)? A. Was the violence/hard times related to some conflict/disagreement or efforts to resolve conflict? Or was the violence/hard times "random" or "spontaneous?"
C, P, CS, PS, (KR)		B. (*If the violence was seen as conflict-related*) When conflicts/disagreements did occur in the relationship, were they sometimes resolved without violence? What were the differences between conflicts that led to violence and those that did not?
X		C. (*If the hard times were seen as conflict-related*) When hard times like the one you are describing occurred in the relationship, how did you resolve them? What did you and your partner do to end the hard times? Did you or your partner ever consider using violence to resolve a conflict? Do you think people in intimate relationships use violence to settle conflicts? What do you think are likely to be the differences between conflicts that lead to violence and those that do not?
All	Before, during & after	7. What did you do just before, during and after the violent episode/hard time? How did you feel during each of these times?
All	Attributions of blame	8. How do you explain the violence? Who is to blame? or whose fault was it? Were drugs or alcohol involved?
All		A. Does/did it seem fair? Like deserved treatment? Did you ever feel responsible?

Who to ask	*Section*	*Suggested Text and Questions*
All		B. Were your expectations for the way people in the role of *partner* behave fulfilled? Did you feel that your *partner* had simply behaved as husbands/lovers/parents/men should simply be expected to behave?
All	Coping	9. How did you cope/deal with these incidents? What did you do? A. What did you say to yourself? B. What did you tell others? Who did you tell? C. How did you feel as you tried to cope?

| X, C, P, CS, PS | Satisfaction | 10. Overall, how satisfied were/are you with your relationship with your *partner*? On a scale from 1 to 10, where 10 is completely satisfied, and 1 is completely dissatisfied, what rating would you give your relationship? |

Note to Interviewers:

Use: "Why did you select your partner?" as a prompt if the interviewee has trouble thinking of good points.

What were your expectations for your relationship with your *partner*?

Were your expectations met?

What would you say were/are the strengths and good points of your relationship with your *partner* who abused you/who went through hard times with you/who you abused (*for P only*)?

| X, C, P, CS, PS | Intensity | 11. In terms of intensity or excitement, how intense was/is this relationship? On a scale from 1 to 10, where 1 is not intense at all and 10 is very intense, what rating would you give this relationship? |

How would you say that this compares with your other intimate relationships? (*Explain that comparisons need not be with romantic love relationships only—can be made with relationships with parents/children/friends.*)

| KR, SR | | In terms of intensity, how intense is the memory of the rape? On a scale from 1 to 10, where 1 is not intense at all and 10 is very intense, how would you rate your memory? |

Who to ask	Section	Suggested Text and Questions
		How would you say that this compares with other memories of bad times?
All	Effects on other aspects of life	12. Do you think this violence/hard time had an effect on other aspects of your life (KR, SR)/your family life (X, C, P, CS, PS)?
		Areas to cover:
		a) Sexual relationships
CS, PS		1. Was violence or the threat of violence ever used to obtain sex?
KR, SR		2. Have you been able to establish or to resume satisfying sexual relationships?
C		3. Have you been able to establish satisfying sexual relationships?
		b) Relationships with other family members/friends at or near the time of the incident
All		1. Did family members/friends know? Did you tell them? Did they find out some other way (how)?
		2. What were their reactions (supportive or not)?
X, C, P, CS, PS		3. Effects on children: Did children witness/experience violence/hard time?
		c) If the time of the incident has passed, ask about current relationships with family/friends (see b above).
All	What others think	13. What do you think other people thought about you and your situation?
		Did the same or similar things happen to others in your family/close friends?
		In general, do you think these things happen to other people? Out of 100 people/women/families, how many would you say experience violence/hard times?
All	Alternatives	14. Did you see any alternatives to this situation?
		A. Was there anything you could have done to prevent these events?
		B. If you did act on alternatives (e.g., run-

Who to ask	Section	Suggested Text and Questions

ning away), how was it that you came to see alternatives to your situation?

CS, PS, KR, SR

C. Have you considered or acted on pressing charges against the abuser?

All   Conclusion

15. Are there any other things you would like to tell me about you or your experiences?

Thank you.

APPENDIX C: THE NEWSPAPER ARTICLE REPORTING THE RESULTS OF THE SURVEY

The survey is discussed in chapters 5, 6, and 10.

MORE THAN 600 PARTICIPATE IN RECORD SURVEY
By Dr. Julie Blackman Doron

If he didn't feel that I did right he would hit me. He held a knife to me once; he had been drinking. On one occasion he broke my nose, but I was too upset to do anything about it.

A woman is terrified of a husband who beats her; another woman is still filled with remorse because 14 years ago she pulled her 10-year-old daughter's hair in a fit of anger; another has memories of being sexually abused by her grandfather.

They are among the 612 people who answered a survey on intimate violence—sexual abuse or violence between family members or friends—that appeared in The Sunday Record this spring. Almost 83 percent of those returning the questionnaires were women.

About 24 percent of those responding said they had been abused as children, 16 percent abused or had abused their own children, 17 percent were abused by a current spouse or lover, and 17 percent had been abused by a former spouse or lover.

Sixty-eight percent said they had had sex when they did not really want to, 52 percent said they felt pressured to have sex, and 7 percent reported their spouses or lovers had used violence or the threat of violence to force them to have sex. Fourteen percent said they had been raped.

> I think the age of the victim is an important factor. It bears heavily on one's sex knowledge, whether or not there is previous experience and an awareness of the possibility of the occurrence. In my case, I had no preparation, no warning, no instruction on what to do. My age was 12. I had been protected from the world, and still had the impression that the world was a good place, and that adults were all decent people. The experience was devastating to me; I was frightened to the point of being petrified, had absolutely no idea how to defend or protect myself or what to do afterwards.
>
> —Woman respondent

Broken Arms, Broken Hearts

Intimate violence is not new. Broken arms appear to be as much a part of intimate relationships as broken hearts. But the problem has become more visible recently, thanks largely to the efforts of the women's movement.

The difficulties that victims of intimate violence face are complex and in many ways apply equally to victims of family violence and rape. The finger of blame often points at the victim, with the stereotype of the nagging wife and the seductive woman often used to explain physical and sexual abuse.

> When I was 11 or 12 I was attacked on a lonely country road. I was grabbed and fondled by two teen-age boys. I fought them off. I kicked, screamed, and cursed. I blamed myself for allowing my-

self to get into that situation, and told no one for fear of being
hollered at.

—Woman respondent

Psychologists say that it's comforting to blame the victim; it sat-
isfies our need to believe that we live in a world where people get
what they deserve. Even victims have this need, and they may therefore blame themselves. People who are continually abused are especially likely to see themselves as at fault.

This belief accounts, at least in part, for the fact that many victims continue to live with a spouse or lover who abuses them. It is
also a reason why many rape victims never report their attacks or
seek help in coping with the trauma they suffer.

Abuse from Husbands

Only recently has the dimension of intimate violence in this country begun to emerge. A survey in 1978 indicated that 1.8 million
women in the United States are beaten by their husbands. New Jersey's Division of Youth and Family Services estimates that 100,000
couples in the state have had moments of serious violence.

My husband only used two versions of abuse: One, punching
in the face, and two, (the one I feared most by far) tightening his
hands around my throat and forcefully shaking me by the neck. I
was well aware of the reason why after 19 years of marriage this
suddenly started. He suffered a very bad heart attack. He loves life,
and by expressing his rage this way at the fear of dying I suffered
untold heartbreak. I remember so clearly the last time the abuse
took place. My mind will never erase it, although I knew he didn't
ever realize how serious his attack was.

—Woman respondent

A look at the responses to The Record survey gives some idea of
the problem, and its causes, in North Jersey.

One conclusion is that the willingness to use and to tolerate
physical violence is learned. People who said they were abused as
children were more than four times as likely to abuse their own
children as parents who had not been abused when they were
youngsters.

Abused children were more than twice as likely to become involved in a relationship with a spouse or lover that included violence. People who left one relationship because of violence were quite likely to enter into another which became violent. Contrary to the idea that violence is largely a lower-class phenomenon, the level of a person's education and income, and the type of job held, were not good indicators of likely violence.

Intelligent, Well-off

The people who answered the survey were, for the most part, young, affluent, and well-educated. Most were female and many were divorced or separated.

> My parents felt they had the duty to discipline me in order for me to be good. They did not beat me as a cruelty, but because they felt this is what parents did. I still feel bitterness and shame for the times I was beaten so severely and loudly that neighbors had to come in to stop my mother or father.
>
> —Woman respondent

The survey indicated:

- Women were twice as likely as men to be abusing parents and three times as likely to be abused spouses.

- Women—with children—who were formerly married were the most likely victims of abuse. Child abuse was also highest among the formerly married.

- Jews were less likely than Catholics or Protestants to be abused children or to be abused by spouses or lovers.

> I have had many experiences in child abuse, which includes three parents (one a stepfather). I am very concerned about what has happened in the past; I really don't have any showing of violence right now, but in the future who knows. If I am going to have any effects later on with my children I want it taken care of. There is one member of my family who shows [the effects of violence] very much, my younger brother.
>
> —Woman respondent

Rape differs from family violence because its intimacy comes from the nature of the assault, and not necessarily from the relationship between attacker and victim.

Unreported Rapes

More than half of those raped said the attack was by a stranger or a casual acquaintance. Twenty-one percent of those who were raped had been victims of a family member other than the spouse.

The survey suggests that most statistics on intimate violence are almost certainly grossly underestimated, since they are taken from records of police, hospitals, and other agencies. No more than 25 percent of those abused by a spouse or lover said they reported the incident to police, a social worker, or a family physician.

> I have never badly hurt either of my children, but there are times when I have lost control to the point where I have screamed mean things at them or slapped them on the face rather than the bottom or pulled them along roughly. I think even on these occasions that I would have not seriously injured them, but there is a fine line.
>
> —Woman respondent

With intimate violence's greater visibility, the efforts to combat it have increased. In 1976, Congress established the National Center for the Prevention and Control of Rape; in 1977, the National Law Enforcement Assistance Administration began a family violence program. The Center for Constitutional Rights and the National Jury Project joined last year to establish the Women's Self Defense Law Project, which works with battered women.

In Bergen and Passaic counties, emergency shelter for battered women and their children is available through Shelter Our Sisters, Women's Haven, and the Community Action Program (CAP).

> My husband's abuse was isolated to one period in our marriage—he was suffering guilt from having an affair. I was 7-1/2 months pregnant; he was drinking. It had never happened before and, aside from those few times in a span of six months, hasn't happened since.
>
> —Woman respondent

Help for Victims

The Hackensack CAP program, says clinical director Diana Aviv, "is a comprehensive service with a shelter, hot line, individual and group counseling, legal department, housing, job training, and placement services. We provide a warm, supportive milieu in which women can explore alternatives available to them in light of their circumstances and needs."

Gayle Eisen, CAP administrative director, said: "We must talk about the prevention and elimination of family violence. I am committed to trying to work with the male batterer and with children from these families."

"We encourage women in violent situations to bring their husbands in," said Ella Wilson, director of Women's Haven in Paterson. "We do in-depth work with wives and husbands."

Sandy Ramos, director of Shelter Our Sisters in Fort Lee, said: "People are finally becoming aware that violence has unfortunately become a substantial part of American society. We need shelters in every town."

> I was raped. However, I never admitted rape in the emergency room because I was quite upset. It seems I made the correct decision because of my husband's attitude. I listened in horror as he told the police he was relieved actual rape hadn't happened or he'd never touch me again. The police said that that was a normal reaction and divorce often happened even though the wife was a victim.
>
> —Woman respondent

St. Luke's Hospital, on 114th Street and Amsterdam Avenue in Manhattan, has a Rape Intervention Program which operates out of its emergency room. When a rape victim seeks care there, a trained volunteer advocate is called. The advocate stays with the victim in the emergency room, informs her of hospital procedures, and discusses her likely reactions to the rape.

■ As a child, were you ever physically abused (punched, kicked, bruised) by your parents?

Yes	23.5	(142)
No	76.5	(461)
		603

I was abused by:		
My mother only:	26.5	(39)
My father only:	42.9	(63)

Both parents:	21.1	(31)
Other:	9.5	(14)
		147

How old were you when you were abused? Check as many as apply:

Less than 3 years old:	10.5[a]	(15)
3 to 5 years old:	32.4	(46)
6 to 9 years old:	62.0	(88)
10 to 15 years old:	71.8	(102)
16 to 20 years old:	33.1	(47)

How often would you say you were abused?

Only once or twice	17.4	(25)
Rarely (less than twice a year)	18.8	(27)
Occasionally (between 2 and 6 times a year)	29.9	(43)
Regularly (between 7 and 12 times a year)	13.2	(19)
Often (more than 13 times a year)	20.8	(30)
		144

■ As a parent have you ever physically abused any of your children?

Yes	15.7	(78)
No	84.3	(418)
		496

If yes, which of your children have you abused? Check as many as apply.

	Sons	Daughters	Unspecified Sex	Total
First-borns	38	19	7	64[b]
Middle-borns	13	9	7	29
Last-borns	8	7	9	24

How often would you say you have abused your children?

Only once or twice	48.7	(38)
Rarely (less than twice a year)	20.5	(16)
Occasionally (between 2 and 6 times a year)	23.1	(18)
Regularly (between 7 and 12 times a year)	5.1	(4)
Often (more than 13 times a year)	2.6	(2)
		78

[a]Percentages for this question are based on an assumed total of 142 and do not add to 100 percent since respondents could check more than one age category.
[b]Numbers reported without percentages since a total figure could not be determined.

■ Have you ever been physically abused by your current spouse or lover?

Yes	17.0	(99)
No	83.0	(483)
		582

How often would you say you are/were abused by your spouse or lover?

Only once or twice	40.3	(73)
Rarely (less than twice a year)	17.1	(31)
Occasionally (between 2 and 6 times a year)	28.7	(52)
Regularly (between 7 and 12 times a year)	6.1	(11)
Often (more than 13 times a year)	7.7	(14)
		181

How long had you been married or living together when the abuse began?

The abuse began before the marriage or living together	14.2	(25)
Less than 1 year	34.7	(61)
Between 1 and 5 years	29.5	(52)
Between 6 and 10 years	12.5	(22)
Between 11 and 20 years	5.1	(9)
More than 20 years	3.4	(6)
		175

What is/was the nature of physical abuse in your relationship?

It only happened once or twice and then stopped	31.2	(59)
It stopped after: less than 8 years	7.4	(14)
8 to 22 years	5.8	(11)
The relationship ended after:		
1 to 4 years	15.3	(29)
5 to 10 years	14.8	(28)
more than 11 years	12.7	(24)
My spouse/lover still abuses me	12.7	(24)
		189

■ Have you ever had sex with your spouse or lover when you did not really want to?

Yes	67.5	(390)
No	32.5	(188)
		578

If yes, how often?

Only once or twice	12.9	(51)
Rarely	28.3	(112)
Occasionally	43.2	(171)
Regularly or more[c]	15.7	(62)
		396

■ Have you ever felt pressured to have sex with your spouse or lover?

Yes	51.6	(301)
No	48.4	(282)
		583

If yes, how often?

Only once or twice	11.1	(34)
Rarely	27.4	(84)
Occasionally	43.0	(132)
Regularly or more[c]	18.6	(57)
		307

■ Has your spouse or lover ever used violence or the threat of violence to force you to have sexual intercourse?

Yes	7.0	(41)
No	93.0	(544)
		585

If yes, how often?

Only once or twice	34.8	(16)
Rarely	19.6	(9)
Occasionally	26.1	(12)
Regularly or more[c]	19.6	(9)
		46

■ Were you ever raped?

Yes	14.0	(81)
No	84.7	(491)
Attempted	1.4	(8)
		580

I was raped by

[c]Regularly or more refers to these responses, grouped together: regularly, often and always.

A stranger	27.2	(22)
A casual acquaintance	35.8	(29)
A neighbor	8.6	(7)
A friend	12.3	(10)
A family member other than spouse	21.0	(17)
An ex spouse	7.4	(6)
		81

■ As a parent have you ever physically abused any of your children?

Sex of Respondent	Yes	No
Female	17.1 (71)	82.9 (343)
Male	7.5 (6)	92.5 (74)
Total		494

■ Have you ever been physically abused by your current spouse or lover?

In any relationships, were you ever physically abused by your spouse or lover?

	Current Spousal Abuse	
	Yes	No
Female	19.1 (93)	80.9 (393)
Male	6.4 (6)	93.6 (88)
Total		580

	Past Spousal Abuse	
	Yes	No
Female	19.1 (91)	80.9 (386)
Male	9.3 (9)	90.7 (88)
Total		574

■ As a child were you ever physically abused by your parents?

Religion of Respondent	Yes	No
Catholic	24.9 (62)	75.1 (187)
Jewish	13.1 (13)	86.9 (86)
Protestant	24.4 (43)	75.6 (133)
Other	32.9 (24)	67.1 (49)
Total		597

REFERENCES

Abelson, R. P. 1968. "Computers, Polls, and Public Opinion—Some Puzzles and Problems." *Transaction* 5: 20–27.

Abelson, R. P., E. Aronson, W. McGuire, T. M. Newcomb, M. J. Rosenberg, and P. H. Tannenbaum, eds. 1968. *Theories of Cognitive Consistency: A Sourcebook.* Chicago: Rand McNally and Company.

Abramson, L. Y., M. E. P. Seligman, and J. D. Teasdale. 1978. "Learned Helplessness in Humans: Critique and Reformulation." *Journal of Abnormal Psychology,* 87: 49–74.

Aderman, D., S. S. Brehm, L. B. Katz. 1974. "Empathetic Observation of an Innocent Victim: The Just World Revisited." *Journal of Personality and Social Psychology* 29: 342–347.

Adorno, T. W., E. Frenkel-Brunswick, D. J. Levinson, and R. N. Sanford. 1950. *The Authoritarian Personality.* New York: Harper.

Advance 1981. Association for the Advancement of Psychology, August.

Ainsworth, M. D. S. 1978. *Patterns of Attachment.* Hillsdale, NJ: Lawrence Erlbaum.

Amir, M. 1971. *Patterns in Forcible Rape.* Chicago: University of Chicago Press.

Anderson, C., M. R. Lepper, and L. Ross. 1980. "Perseverance of Social Theories: The Role of Explanation in the Persistence of Discredited Information." *Journal of Personality and Social Psychology,* 39(6): 1037–1049.

Athanasatos, E. 1981. "The Legal Aspects of Spousal Abuse." Paper presented at the Association for Women in Psychology Meeting, Boston, March.

Back, S. M., J. Blum, E. Nakhnikian, and S. Stark. 1980. *Spouse Abuse Yellow Pages.* Denver, CO: Denver Research Institute, University of Denver.

Bakan, D. 1971. *Slaughter of the Innocents: A Study of the Battered Child Phenomenon.* Boston: Beacon Press.

Bard, M. 1976. "The Rape Victim: Challenge to the Helping Systems." *Victimology: An International Journal.* New York: Research Utilization Unit of the Community Council.

Bart, P. 1975. "Rape Doesn't End with a Kiss." *VIVA.*

Baum, A., R. Fleming, and J. E. Singer. 1983. "Coping with Victimization by Technological Disaster." *Journal of Social Issues,* 39(2): 117–138.

Becker, J. 1982. "The Effects of Sexual Assault on Rape and Attempted Rape Victims." *Victimology* 7 (1–4): 106–113.

Becker, J. and G. Abel. 1977. "The Treatment of Victims of Sexual Assault." *Quarterly Journal of Corrections.* (Spring) 1(2): 38–42.

Berger, V. 1977. "Man's Trial, Woman's Tribulation: Rape Cases in the Courtroom." *Columbia Law Review* 77(1): 1–103.

Bettleheim, B. 1943. "Individual and Mass Behavior in Extreme Situations." *Journal of Abnormal Psychology,* 38: 417–452.

Blackman, J. 1978. *Arousal as a Function of Cognitive and Moral Problem Solving Situations,* Teachers College, Columbia University. Doctoral dissertation.

Blackman-Doron, J. 1979. "The Emergence of Social Problems and Responsive Research." American Psychological Association Annual Convention, September.

—— 1980a. "Conflict and Violence in Intimate Relationships: Focus on Marital Rape." American Sociological Association Annual Convention, New York, August.

—— 1980b. "Quantitative and Qualitative Perspectives on Violent and Nonviolent Intimate Relationships." American Psychological Association Annual Convention, Montreal, September.

—— 1980c. Working version of chapter 5. Unpublished manuscript.

—— 1981a. "Multiple Victimizations: Those Who Suffer More Than Once." National Family Violence Researcher's Conference, University of New Hampshire, Durham, N.H., July.

—— 1981b. "Battered Women and Rape Victims: The Social Psychological Nature of the Experiences of These Victims of Injustice." Paper presented at the International Interdisciplinary Congress on Women, Haifa, Israel, December.

Blackman, J. 1984. "Battered Women Who Kill: New Perspectives on the Concept of Self Defense." American Psychological Association Meeting, Toronto, August.

—— 1985a. "The Language of Sexual Violence: More Than a Matter of Semantics." In S. R. Sunday and E. Tobach, eds., *Violence Against Women: A Critique of the Sociobiology of Rape.* The Genes and Gender Monograph Series, Vol. 1, New York: Gordian Press.

—— 1985b. "Conceptions of Justice and the Use of Expert Testimony on the Battered Woman's Syndrome." Fourth Annual Adelphi University Applied Experimental Psychology Conference, October.

—— 1986. "Potential Uses for Expert Testimony: Ideas Toward the Representation of Battered Women Who Kill." *Women's Rights Law Reporter* 9(3/4): 227–238.

—— 1987a. "Battered Women Who Kill and the Passover Question: Why Is This Night Different From All Other Nights? Or Is It?" Association for Women in Psychology, Denver, March.

—— 1987b. "A Narrowed Vision: Clarity and Clouds in Victims of Family Violence." Presented at the University of New Hampshire Family Violence Researchers' Conference, Durham, N.H., July.

—— 1987c. "Expert Testimony for Battered Women Who Kill: Dilemmas of Objectivity and Bias." Presented at the American Psychological Association Meeting, New York, August.

Blackman, J. and E. Brickman. 1984. "The Impact of Expert Testimony on Trials of Battered Women Who Kill Their Husbands." *Behavioral Sciences and the Law* (Fall) 2(4): 413–422.

Blackman, J. and H. Hornstein, with C. Divine, M. O'Neill, J. Steil, and L. Tucker. 1977. "Newscasts and the Social Actuary." *Public Opinion Quarterly* (Fall) 41(3).

Braunfeld, M. 1949. "Education Costs." *Discrimination and National Welfare.* New York: Harper.

Brodyaga, L., M. Gates, S. Singer, M. Tucker, and R. White, eds. 1975. *Rape and Its Victims: A Report for Citizens, Health Facilities and Criminal Justice.* Washington D.C.: U.S. Government Printing Office.

Brown v. Board of Education of Topeka. 1954. Case #347US483.

Brown, J. A., and R. Daniels. 1968. "Some Observations on Abusive Parents." *Child Welfare* 47: 89–94.

Browne, A. 1985. "Assault and Homicide at Home: When Battered Women Kill." In Saks, M. J., and L. Saxe, eds. *Advances in Applied Social Psychology,* 3. Hillsdale, New Jersey: Lawrence Erlbaum Associates, Inc.

Browne, A. 1987. *When Battered Women Kill.* New York: Free Press.

Brownmiller, S. 1975. *Against Our Will: Men, Women and Rape.* New York: Bantam Books.

Bruno v. Codd 90 Misc. 2d 1047, 396 N.Y.S. 2d 974 (Sup Ct. 1977), rev'd in part, appeal dismissed in part, 407 N.Y.S. 2d 165 (App Div. 1978).

Bulman, R. J., and C. B. Wortman. 1977. "Attributions of Blame and Coping in the 'Real World': Severe Accident Victims React to Their Lot." *Journal of Personality and Social Psychology* 35(5): 351–363.

Burgess, A. W., and R. D. Conger. 1979. "Family Interaction Patterns Related to Child Abuse and Neglect: Some Preliminary Findings." *International Journal of Child Abuse:* 269–278.

Burgess, A. W., and L. L. Holmstrom, 1983. "The Rape Victim in the Emergency Ward." *American Journal of Nursing* 73(10): 1740–1745.

—— 1974a. "Rape Trauma Syndrome." *American Journal of Psychiatry* 131(9): 981–986.

—— 1974b. *Rape: Victims of Crisis.* Bowie, Md.: Robert J. Brady, Co.

—— 1974c. "Crisis and Counseling Requests of Rape Victims." *Nursing Research,* 23(3): 196–202.

—— 1976. "Coping Behavior of the Rape Victim." *American Journal of Psychiatry* 113(4): 413–418.

—— 1978. *The Victim of Rape: Institutional Reaction.* New York: Wiley.

—— 1979a. "Adaptive Strategies and Recovery from Rape." *American Journal of Psychiatry* 136(10): 1278–1282.

—— 1979b. *Rape: Crisis and Recovery.* Bowie, Md: Robert J. Brady Company.

Burgess, A. W., and P. M. Johnson. 1976. "Assault: Patterns of Emergency Visits." *Journal of Psychiatric Nurses and Mental Health Sources* 11(14): 32–36.

Carlson, B. E. 1977. "Battered Women and Their Assailants." *Social Work:* 455–460.

Chein, I. 1949. "What Are the Psychological Effects of Segregation Under Conditions of Equal Facilities?" *International Journal of Opinion and Attitude Research* 3: 229.

Chodoff, P., S. B., Friedman, and D. A. Hamburg. 1964. "Stress, Defenses and Coping Behavior: Observed in Parents of Children with Malignant Diseases." *American Journal of Psychiatry* 120: 743–749.

Chodorow, N. 1978. *The Reproduction of Mothering: Psychoanalysis and the Sociology of Gender.* Berkeley: University of California Press.

Clark, K. B. 1950. "Effects of Prejudice and Discrimination on Personality Development." Paper presented at the midcentury White House Conference on Children and Youth, Washington.

Coates, D., B. Wortman, and A. Abbey. 1979. "Reactions to Victimization: A Social Psychological Analysis." In I. Frieze, D. Bar-Tal and J. Carroll, eds. *New Approaches to Social Problems.* N.Y.: Jossey Bass.

Cohen, E. A. 1953. *Human Behavior in the Concentration Camp.* New York: Grosset and Dunlap.

Coleman, J. S. 1966. *Equality of Educational Opportunity.* Washington, D.C.: United States Printing Office.

Community Planning Organization, Battered Women Study Committee. 1976. *Battered Women: The Hidden Problem.* St. Paul, Minnesota: The Organization.

Crocker, P. 1985. "The Meaning of Equality for Battered Women Who Kill Men in Self Defense." *Harvard Women's Law Journal* (Spring)8:127.

Crosby, F. 1982. *Relative Deprivation and Working Women.* New York: Oxford University Press.

Crosby, F., and S. Clayton. 1986. "Introduction: The Search for Connections." *Journal of Social Issues* 42(1): 1–9.

Davidson, T. 1978. *Conjugal Crime.* New York: Hawthorne.

deBeauvoir, S. 1953. *The Second Sex.* New York: Bantam Books.

De Francis, V. 1963. *Child Abuse: Preview of a Nationwide Survey.* Denver, Colorado: American Humane Association.

Deutsch, M. 1974. "Awakening the Sense of Injustice." In M. Ross and M. Lerner, eds. *The Quest for Justice,* pp. 19–42. Toronto: Holt, Rinehart and Winston.

—— 1975. "Equity, Equality and Need: What Determines Which Value Will Be Used as the Basis of Distributive Justice?" *Journal of Social Issues* 31(3): 137–150.

—— 1985. *Distributive Justice: A Social Psychological Perspective.* New Haven: Connecticut: Yale University Press.

—— 1986. "Conflicts, Cooperation and Justice." In H. W. Bierhoff, R. L. Cohen, and J. Greenberg, eds. *Justice in Social Relations.* New York: Plenum Press.

Deutsch, M., R. M., Krauss, and N. Rosenau, 1962. "Dissonance or Defensiveness?" *Journal of Personality,* 30, 16–28.

Deutscher, M. and I. Chein. 1948. "The Psychological Effects of Forced Segregation: A Survey of Social Science Opinion." *Journal of Psychology* 26: 259.

Dinnerstein, D. 1976. *The Mermaid and the Minotaur.* New York: Harper Colophon Books.

Dobash, R. P. and R. E. Dobash. 1980. *Violence Against Wives.* New York: Free Press.

Elazar, D. 1966. *American Federalism: A View from the States.* New York: Thomas Y. Crowell.

Eldow, M. 1972. "Theoretical Considerations of Violent Marriages." *Social Casework* 58: 515–526.

Ellis, E. M., B. M. Atkeson, and K. S. Calhoun. 1981. "An Assessment of Long-Term Reaction to Rape." *Journal of Abnormal Psychology* 90(3): 263–266.

Elmer, E. 1960. "Abused Young Children Seen in Hospitals." *Social Work* 5: 98–102.

—— 1961. *Children in Jeopardy: A Study of Abused Minors and Their Families.* Pittsburgh: University of Pittsburgh Press.

—— 1979. "Child Abuse and Family Stress." *Journal of Social Issues* 35(2): 60–71.

Elmer, E., and B. Gregg, 1967. "Developmental Characteristics of Abused Children." *Pediatrics* 40: 596–602.

—— 1979. "Developmental Characteristics of Abused Children." In D. G. Gil, ed. *Child Abuse and Violence*. New York: AMS Press, 295–309.

Evans, H. I., and N. B. Sperakas, 1976. "Community Assistance for Rape Victims." *Journal of Community Psychology* 4: 378–381.

Ewing, C. P. 1987. *Battered Women Who Kill*. Lexington, Mass: D.C. Health.

Fagan, J. and E. Lewis 1981. "Evaluating Criminal Justice Impacts on Domestic Violence." Paper presented at the National Conference of Family Violence Researchers at the University of New Hampshire, Durham, July.

Fagan, J. and S. Wexler. 1987. "Crime at Home and in the Streets: The Relationship Between Family and Stranger Violence." *Violence and Victims* 2(1): 5–23.

Fassberg, E. 1977. *Crimes of Violence Against Women: Rape and Battered Women*. Hackensack, New Jersey: Bergen County Commission on the Status of Women.

Feldman-Summers, S., and K. Lindner. 1976. "Perceptions of Victims and Defendants in Criminal Assault Cases." *Criminal Justice and Behavior* 3: 135–149.

Festinger, L. 1957. *A Theory of Cognitive Dissonance*. Evanston, Ill: Row, Peterson.

Festinger, L. and J. M. Carlsmith. 1959. "Cognitive Consequences of Forced Compliance." *Journal of Abnormal and Social Psychology* 58: 203–211.

Fine, M. 1980. "Options to Injustice: Seeing Other Lights." Doctoral Dissertation. Teachers College, Columbia University.

—— 1983. "The Social Context and a Sense of Injustice." *Representative Research in Social Psychology* 13(1): 15–33.

—— 1984. "Coping with Rape: Critical Perspectives on Consciousness." *Imagination, Cognition and Personality: The Scientific Study of Consciousness* 3: 249–267.

—— 1986. "Contextualizing the Study of Social Injustice." In M. Saks and L. Saxe, eds. *Advances in Applied Social Psychology*, III. N.J.: L. Erlbaum, 103–126.

Finkelhor, D. 1979. *Sexually Victimized Children*. New York: Free Press.

—— 1981. "Four Preconditions of Sexual Abuse: A Model." Paper presented at the Family Violence Researchers' Conference, Durham, New Hampshire, June.

—— 1984. *Child Sexual Abuse: New Theory and Research*. New York: Free Press.

—— 1985. *Child Sexual Abuse*. New York: Free Press.

Firestone, S. 1971. "On American Feminism." In V. Gornick and B. K. Moran, eds. *Woman in Sexist Society*. New York: Basic Books.

Flynn, J. P. 1977. "Recent Findings Related to Child Abuse." *Social Casework*, 13–20.

Fox, S. S., and D. Scherl. 1972. "Crisis Intervention with Rape Victims." *Social Work* 17: 34–43.

Frazier, E. F. 1949. *The Negro in the United States*. New York: McMillan.

Freud, S. 1922. *Group Psychology and the Analysis of the Ego.* New York: W. W. Norton.

—— 1935. *Introductory Lectures on Psychoanalysis.* New York: W. W. Norton.

Frieze, I. H. 1979a. "Perceptions of Battered Wives." In I. H. Frieze, D. Bar-Tal, and J. Carroll, eds. *New Approaches to Social Problems.* New York: Jossey-Bass.

—— 1979b. "Power and Influence in Violent and Nonviolent Marriages." Paper presented at the annual meeting of the Eastern Psychological Association, Philadelphia, April.

Frieze, I. H., J. Knoble, G. Zomnir, and C. Washburn. 1980. "Types of Battered Women." Paper presented at the meeting of the Association for Women in Psychology, Santa Monica, California, March.

Gager, N., and L. Schurr. 1976. *Sexual Assault: Confronting Rape in America.* New York: Grosset Dunlap.

Galdston, R. 1965. "Observations of Children Who Have Been Physically Abused by Their Parents." *American Journal of Psychiatry* 122(4): 440–443.

Gayford, J. J. 1975. "Wife Battering: A Preliminary Survey of 100 Cases." *British Medical Journal* 1: 194–197.

Gelles, R. J. 1972. *The Violent Home: A Study of Physical Aggression Between Husbands and Wives.* Beverly Hills, California: Sage Publications.

—— 1973. "Child Abuse as Psychopathology: A Sociological Critique and Reformulation." *American Journal of Orthopsychiatry* 43(4): 611–621.

Gil, D. G. 1973. *Violence Against Children: Physical Child Abuse in the United States.* Cambridge: Harvard University Press.

—— 1979. *Child Abuse and Violence.* New York: AMS Press.

Gilligan, C. 1977. "In a Different Voice: Women's Conception of Self and Morality." *Harvard Educational Review* 47(4): 481–517.

Gingold, J. 1976. "One of These Days . . . Pow! Right in the Kisser: The Truth About Battered Wives." *Ms.* (August)5: 51–54, 94–98.

Griffin, S. 1975. "Rape: The All-American Crime." In L. Schultz, ed. *Rape Victimology.* Chicago: Charles C. Thomas.

Hake, L. M. 1977. *Diary of a Battered Housewife.* Independence, Kentucky: Feminist Publications

Hamburg, D., and J. Adams. 1967. "A Perspective on Coping Behavior." *Archives of General Psychiatry* 17: 277–284.

Hampton, R. L. and E. J. Newberger. 1985. "Child Abuse Incidence and Reporting by Hospitals: Significance of Severity, Class, and Race." *American Journal of Public Health* 75: 56–60.

Hardgrove, G. 1976. "An Interagency Service Network To Meet the Needs of Rape Victims." *Social Casework* 57(4): 245–253.

Hayman, C. R., and C. Lanza. 1972. "Rape in the District of Columbia." *American Journal of Obstetrics and Gynecology,* 113(1): 91–97.

Heider, F. 1958. *The Psychology of Interpersonal Relations.* New York: Wiley.

Helfer, R. E., and C. H. Kempe. 1968/1974. *The Battered Child.* Chicago: University of Chicago Press.

Hewlett, S. A. 1986. *A Lesser Life: The Myth of Women's Liberation in America.* New York: Morrow.

Hilberman, E. 1976. *The Rape Victim.* New York: Basic Books.

Hilberman, E., and K. Muson. 1978. "Sixty Battered Women." *Victimology: An International Journal* 2(3–4): 460–471.

Holloway, S., L. Tucker, and H. Hornstein. 1977. "The Effects of Social and Nonsocial Information on Interpersonal Behavior of Males: The News Makes News." *Journal of Personality and Social Psychology* 35(7): 514–522.

Hornstein, H. 1975. "Promotive Relationships, Tensions and Prosocial Behavior." Paper presented at Eastern Psychological Association, New York.

—— 1976. *Cruelty and Kindness: A New Look at Aggression and Altruism.* Englewood Cliffs, N.J.: Prentice Hall.

Hornstein, H., E. LaKind, G. Frankel, and S. Manne. 1976. "Effects of Knowledge About Remote Social Events on Prosocial Behavior, Social Conception and Mood." *Journal of Personality and Social Psychology* 32(6): 1038–1046.

Horowitz, S. 1981. "The Tolerance of Cognitive Inconsistency." Paper presented at the meeting of the Association for Women in Psychology, Boston.

International Tribunal on Crimes against Women 1975. ISIS International Bulletin Newsletter, Brussels. Women's International Information and Communication Service, March.

Janoff-Bulman, R. 1979. "The Two Sides of Self Blame: Inquiries Into Depression and Rape." *Journal of Personality and Social Psychology* 37(10): 1798–1809.

Janoff-Bulman, R., and I. H. Frieze. 1983. "A Theoretical Perspective for Understanding Reactions to Victimizations." *Journal of Social Issues* 39(2): 1–17.

Joffee, C. 1986. *The Regulation of Sexuality: Experiences of Family Planning Workers.* Philadelphia: Temple University Press.

Johnson and H. A. Morse. 1968. "Injured Children and Their Parents." *Children* 15: 147–152.

Jones, A. 1980. *Women Who Kill.* New York: Holt.

Jones, C., and E. Aronson. 1973. "Attribution of Fault to a Rape Victim as a Function of Respectability of the Victim." *Journal of Personality and Social Psychology* 26: 415–419.

Jones, E. E., and K. E. Davis. 1965. From acts to dispositions. In L Berkowitz, ed. *Advances in Experimental Psychology* 2. New York: Academic Press.

Kagan, J. 1984. *The Nature of the Child.* New York: Basic Books.

Kalmuss, D. S., and M. A. Straus 1981. "Feminist, Political, and Economical Determinants of Wife Abuse Services in American States." Paper presented at the National Conference of Family Violence Researchers, University of New Hampshire, Durham, July.

Katz, S., and M. Mazur. 1979. *Understanding the Rape Victim: A Synthesis of Research Findings.* New York: Wiley.

Kelley, H. H. 1972. "Attribution in Social Interaction." In E. E. Jones, D. E. Kanouse, H. H. Kelley, R. E. Nisbett, S. Valins, and B. Weiner, eds. *Attribution: Perceiving the Causes of Behavior.* Morristown, N.J.: General Learning Press.

Kempe, C. H., F. N. Silverman, B. F. Stiele, W. Dioegmueller, and H. K. Silver. 1962. "The Battered Child Syndrome." *Journal of the American Medical Association* 181: 17–24.

Kempe, R. S., and C. H. Kempe. 1978. *Child Abuse.* Cambridge: Harvard University Press.

Kidder, L., and M. Fine. 1986. "Making Sense of Injustice: Social Explanations, Social Action and the Role of Social Scientists." In J. Rappaport and E. Seidman, eds. *Redefining Social Problems.* New York: Plenum Press.

Kilpatrick, D. G. 1979a. "The Rape Victim: Issues in Treatment Failure." Paper presented at the 87th Annual American Psychological Association Convention, New York, September.

—— 1979b. "The Scientific Study of Rape: A Clinical Research Perspective." In C. Gren and J. Wiener, eds. *Methodology and Sex Research.* Washington, D.C.: U.S. Government Printing Office.

Kilpatrick, D. G., P. A. Resick, and L. J. Veronen. 1981. "Effects of a Rape Experience: A Longitudinal Study." *Journal of Social Issues* 37(4): 105–122.

Kilpatrick, D. G., L. J. Veronen, and P. A. Resick. 1979. "Assessment of the Aftermath of Rape: Changing Patterns of Fear." *Journal of Behavioral Assessment* 1: 133–148.

Kleck, R. 1968. "Self-Disclosure Patterns of the Non-Obviously Stigmatized." *Psychological Reports* 23(3): 1239–1248.

Kleck, R., M. Ono, and A. M. Hastorf. 1966. "The Effects of Physical Deviance Upon Face to Face Interaction." *Human Relations,* 19: 425–436.

Kohlberg, L. 1969. "Stage and Sequence: The Cognitive-Developmental Approach to Socialization." In D. A. Goslin, *Handbook of Socialization Theory and Research.* Chicago: Rand McNally, 347 480.

LaKind, E. 1974. "Expanding and Contracting We-Group Boundaries: The Effects of News Broadcasts on Philosophy of Human Nature and Juridic Decisions." Doctoral dissertation. Teachers College, Columbia University.

Lane, R. E. 1962. *Political Ideology: Why the American Common Man Believes What He Does.* New York: The Free Press.

Langer, E. J. 1975. "The Illusion of Control." *Journal of Personality and Social Psychology,* 32: 311–328.

Langer, E. J., and J. Roth. 1976. "Heads I Win, Tails It's Chance: The Illusion of Control as a Function of the Sequence of Outcomes in a Purely Chance Task." *Journal of Personality and Social Psychology* 33: 951–955.

Langley, R., and R. C. Levy. 1977. *Wifebeating: The Silent Crisis.* New York: Dutton.

Lerner, M. J. 1975. "The Justice Motive in Social Behavior: Introduction." *Journal of Social Issues* 31(3): 1–19.

—— 1977. "The Justice Motive in Social Behavior: Some Hypotheses as to Its Origin and Forms." *Journal of Personality* 45: 1–52.

—— 1980. *The Belief in a Just World.* New York: Plenum.

Lerner, M. J., and G. Matthews. 1967. "Reactions to Suffering of Others Under Conditions of Indirect Responsibility." *Journal of Personality and Social Psychology* 5: 319–325.

Lerner, M. J., and D. T. Miller. 1978. "Just World Research and the Attribution Process: Looking Back and Ahead." *Psychological Bulletin* 85, 1030–1057.

Lerner, M. J., and C. H. Simmons. 1966. "The Observer's Reaction to the 'Innocent Victim': Compassion or Rejection." *Journal of Personality and Social Psychology* 4: 203–210.

Lewin, K. 1986. " 'Everything Within Me Rebels:' A Letter from Kurt Lewin to Wolfgang Kohler, 1933." *Journal of Social Issues,* 42(4): 39–48.

Libbey, P., and R. Bybee. 1979. "The Physical Abuse of Adolescents." *Journal of Social Issues.* 35(2): 101–126.

Lystad, M. 1974. "Annotated Bibliography: Violence at Home." On microfiche. Available from the Law Enforcement Assistance Administration.

—— 1975. "Violence at Home: A Review of the Literature." *American Journal of Orthopsychiatry.* 3(45): 328–329.

MacFarlane, K. 1981a. "Common Features of Family Abuse and Social Policy Implications." Paper presented at the National Conference of Family Violence Researchers, University of New Hampshire, Durham, July.

—— 1981b. "Factors in Institutional and Social Response to Problems of Sexual Abuse." Paper presented at the National Conference of Family Violence Researchers, University of New Hampshire, Durham, July.

McArthur, L. A. 1972. "The How and What of Why: Some Determinants and Consequences of Causal Attribution." *Journal of Personality and Social Psychology* 22(2): 171–193.

McCombie, S. L. 1976. "Characteristics of Rape Victims Seen in Crisis Intervention." *Studies in Social Work* 46(2): 137–158.

McDermott, J. 1979. *Rape victimization in 26 American cities.* A publication of the United States Department of Justice.

Martin, D. 1976. *Battered Wives.* San Francisco: Glide Publications.

Medea, A., and K. Thompson. 1974. *Against Rape.* New York: Farrar, Straus & Giroux.

Melnick, B., and J. D. Hurley. 1969. "Distinctive Personality Attributes of Child Abusing Mothers." *Journal of Clinical and Counseling Psychology* 33: 746–749.

Metzger, D. 1976. "It Is Always the Woman Who Is Raped." *American Journal of Psychiatry* 133(4).

Miller, D. T. and C. A. Porter. 1983. "Self-Blame in Victims of Violence." *Journal of Social Issues,* 39(2), 139–152.

Miller, J., D. Moeller, A. Kaufman, P. Divasto, D. Pathak, and J. Christy. 1978. "Recidivism Among Sex Assault Victims." *American Journal of Psychiatry* 135(9): 1103–1104.

Morris, G. W. 1984. *The Kids Next Door.* New York: William Morrow.

Myrdal, G. 1944. *An American Dilemma: The Negro Problem and Modern Deemocracy.* New York: Harper and Row.

Nadelson, C. C., and M. T. Notman. 1979. "Psychoanalytic Considerations of the Response to Rape." *International Review of Psychoanalysis* 6: 97–103.

Nelson, B. J. 1983. *The Politics of Child Abuse and Neglect: A Study of Issue Creation and Agenda Setting.* Princeton, N.J.: Woodrow Wilson School of Public and International Affairs Monograph.

Newberger, E. J., and R. Bourne. 1985. *Unhappy Families: Clinical and Research Perspectives on Family Violence.* Littleton, MA: Publishing Sciences Group.

Nisbett, R. E., and S. Valins. 1972. "Perceiving the causes of One's Own Behavior." In E. E. Jones, D. E. Kanouse, H. H. Kelley, R. E. Nisbett, S. Valins, and B. Weiner, eds. *Attribution: Perceiving the Causes of Behavior.* Morristown, N.J.: General Learning Press.

Notman, M. T., and C. C. Nadelson. 1976. "The Rape Victim: Psychodynamic Considerations." *American Journal of Psychiatry* 4: 408–413.

Ottenberg, P. 1978. "The Battered Wife Syndrome." Paper presented at the Symposium on Violence in the Family, Teachers College, Columbia University, New York, October.

Pagelow, M. D. 1981. "Woman Battering: Victims and Their Experiences." *Sage Library Social Research,* 129. Beverly Hills: Sage Publications.

—— 1984. *Family Violence.* New York: Praeger.

Parke, R. D. 1977. "Socialization Into Child Abuse." In J. Tapp and F. Levine, eds. *Law, Justice and the Individual in Society.* New York: Holt, Rinehart and Winston.

Parke, R. D., and C. W. Collmer. 1975. "Child Abuse: An Interdisciplinary Analysis." In E. M. Hetherington, ed. *Review of Child Development Research,* 5. Chicago: University of Chicago Press.

Petchesky, R. P. 1980. "Reproductive Freedom: Beyond 'A Woman's Right to Choose.' " *Signs: Journal of Women in Culture and Society* 5(4): 661–683.

Petchesky, R. P. 1984. *Abortion and Women's Choice: The State, Sexuality, and Reproductive Freedom.* Boston: Northeastern University Press.

Peterson, C., S. M. Schwartz, and M. E. P. Seligman. 1981. "Self-Blame and Depressive Symptoms." *Journal of Personality and Social Psychology* 41: 253–259.

Pfouts, J. H. 1978. "Violent Families: Coping Responses of Abused Wives." *Child Welfare* 57(2): 101–111.

Piaget, J. 1928. *Moral Judgment and Reasoning in the Child.* New York: Harcourt, Brace.

Pittman, D. J., and W. Handy. 1964. "Patterns in Criminal Aggravated Assault." *Journal of Criminal Law, Criminology and Police Science* 55(4): 462–470.

Pizzey, E. 1974. *Scream Quietly or the Neighbors Will Hear.* London: If Books.

Pleck, E. 1981. "An Historical Perspective." Paper presented at the National Conference for Family Violence Researchers at the University of New Hampshire, Durham, July.

Queens Bench Foundation. 1975. *Rape Victimization Study.* San Francisco, California: Queens Bench Foundation.

Remsburg, B., and C. Remsburg. 1979. "The Case of Patricia Gross." *Family Circle* (April 24) 92(6): 52–54, 58–60.

Renvoize, J. 1978. *Web of Violence: A Study of Family Violence.* London: Routledge and Kegan Paul.

Rose, V. M. 1977. "Rape as a Social Problem: A Byproduct of the Feminist Movement." *Social Problems* 25(1): 75–89.

Rosenthal, R. and R. Rosnow. 1969. "The volunteer subject." In R. Rosenthal and R. Rosnow, eds. *Artifact in Behavioral Research.* N.Y.: Academic Press.

Ross, M., and D. Ditecco. 1975. "An Attributional Analysis of Moral Judgments." *Journal of Social Issues* 31: 91–109.

Rossi, P. H. 1972. "Testing for Success and Failure in Social Action." In P. H. Rossi, and W. Williams, eds. *Evaluating Social Programs.* New York: Seminar Press.

Rounsaville, B., and M. M. Weissman. 1978. "Battered Women: A Medical Problem Requiring Detection." *International Journal of Psychiatry in Medicine* 8(2): 191–202.

Roy, M. 1977. *Battered Women: A Psychosociological Study of Domestic Violence.* New York: Van Nostrand Reinhold Company.

Rubin, Z., and L. A. Peplau. 1975. "Who Believes in a Just World?" *Journal of Social Issues* 31(3): 65–90.

Russell, D. 1975. *The Politics of Rape: The Victim's Perspective.* New York: Stein and Day.

—— 1980. "The Prevalence and Impact of Marital Rape in San Francisco." Paper presented at the American Psychological Association meeting, New York, August.

—— 1981. "Preliminary Report on Some Findings Relating to the Trauma and Long-Term Effects of Intrafamily Childhood Sexual Abuse." Paper presented to Conference on Child Prostitution and Pornography. Boston.

—— 1982a. *Rape in Marriage.* New York: MacMillan.

—— 1982b. "Rape, Child Sexual Abuse, Sexual Harassment in the Workplace: An Analysis of the Prevalence, Causes and Recommended Solutions." Final report for the California Commission on Crime Control and Violence Prevention, March.

—— 1983. "Incidence and Prevalence of Intrafamilial and Extrafamilial Sexual Abuse of Female Children." *Child Abuse and Neglect,* 1: 133–146.

—— 1984. *Sexual Exploitation: Rape, Child Sexual Abuse and Sexual Harassment.* Beverly Hills: Sage.

Ryan, W. 1971. *Blaming the Victim.* New York: Vintage Books.

Sampson, E. E. 1975. "On Justice as Equality." *Journal of Social Issues* 31(3): 45–64.

Saxe, L., and M. Fine. 1981. *Social Experiments: Methods for Design and Evaluation.* Beverly Hills, CA: Sage.

Schechter, S. 1983. *Women and Male Violence.* Boston, Mass.: South End.

Scheppele, K. L., and P. B. Bart. 1983. "Through Women's Eyes: Defining Danger in the Wake of Sexual Assault." *Journal of Social Issues* 39(2): 63–81.

Schneider, E. 1986. "Describing and Changing: Women's Self Defense Work and the Problem of Expert Testimony on Battering." *Women's Rights Law Reporter* (Fall) 9(3/4) 195–222.

Schneider, E., and S. B. Jordan. 1978. "Representation of Women Who Defend Themselves in Response to Physical and Sexual Assault." Published by the Center for Constitutional Rights, 853 Broadway, New York, New York.

Schwartz, M. D., and T. D. Clear. 1978. "Toward a New Law on Rape." *Crime and Delinquency* 26(2).

Scroggs, J. R. 1976. "Penalties for Rape as a Function of Victim Provocativeness, Damage and Resistance." *Journal of Applied Psychology* 6: 360–368.

Seligman, M. E. P. 1975. *Helplessness: On Depression, Development and Death.* San Francisco: Freeman.

Shaver, K. G. 1970. "Defensive Attribution: Effects of Severity and Relevance on the Responsibility Assigned for an Accident." *Journal of Personality and Social Psychology,* 14: 101–113.

—— 1975. *An Introduction to Attribution Processes.* Cambridge, Mass.: Winthrop.

Shields, S. 1981. "The Legal Aspects of Marital Rape." Paper presented at the Association for Women in Psychology, Boston, March.

Shotland, R. L., and M. K. Straw. 1976. "Bystander Response to an Assault When a Man Attacks a Woman." *Journal of Personality and Social Psychology* 34: 990–999.

Silver, R. L., C. Boon, and M. H. Stones. 1983. "Searching for Meaning in Misfortune: Making Sense of Incest." *Journal of Social Issues* 39(2): 81–102.

Silverman, F. N. 1953. "The Roentgen Manifestations of Unrecognized Skeletal Trauma in Infants." *American Journal of Roentgenology* 69: 413–426.

—— 1974. "Radiologic Aspects of the Battered Child Syndrome:" In R. E.

Helfer and C. H. Kempe, eds. *The Battered Child.* Chicago: University of Chicago Press.

Smith, R. E., J. P. Keating, R. K. Hester, and J. Mitchell. 1976. "Role and Justice Considerations in the Attribution of Responsibility to a Rape Victim." *Journal of Research in Personality* 10: 346–357.

Snyder, J. C., and E. H. Newberger. 1986. "Consensus and Difference Among Hospital Professionals in Evaluating Child Maltreatment." *Violence and Victims* 1(2): 125–140.

Stark, R., and J. McEvoy. 1970. "Middle-Class Violence." *Psychology Today* 4(6): 330–32, 72–74.

Steele, B. F., and C. B. Pollock. 1968. "A Psychiatric Study of Parents Who Abuse Infants and Small Children." In R. E. Helfer and C. H. Kempe, eds. *The Battered Child.* Chicago: University of Chicago Press.

Steil, J. 1980. "Efficacy and the Response to Injustice by Relatively Advantaged and Disadvantaged Persons." Doctoral dissertation, Teachers College, Columbia University.

—— 1983. "The Response to Injustice: Effects of Varying Levels of Social Support and Position of Advantage or Disadvantage." *Journal of Experimental Psychology* 19: 239–253.

Steil, J., B. Tuchman, and M. Deutsch. 1978. "An Exploratory Study of Meanings of Injustice and Frustration." *Personality and Social Psychology Bulletin*, 4: 393–398.

Stern, D. 1985. *The Interpersonal World of the Infant.* New York: Basic Books.

Stokols, D., and J. Schopler. 1973. "Reactions to Victims Under Conditions of Situational Detachment: The Effects of Responsibility, Severity and Expected Future Interaction." *Journal of Personality and Social Psychology* 25: 199–209.

Straus, M. A. 1978. "Wife-Beating: How Common and Why?" *Victimology: An International Journal* 2(3-4): 443–458.

Straus, M. A., and R. J. Gelles, 1986. "Societal Change and Change in Family Violence from 1975 to 1985 as Revealed by Two National Surveys." *Journal of Marriage and the Family* (August)48: 465–479.

Straus, M. A., R. J. Gelles, and S. K. Steinmetz. 1980. *Behind Closed Doors: Violence in the American Family.* Garden City, New York: Doubleday/ Anchor.

Surrey, D. 1982. *Choice of Conscience: Vietnam Era Military and Draft Resisters in Canada.* New York: Praeger.

Sutherland, S., and D. Scherl. 1970. "Patterns of Response Among Victims of Rape." *American Journal of Orthopsychiatry*, 40: 503-511.

Svalastoga, K. 1962. "Rape and Social Structure." *Pacific Sociological Review*, 5: 48–53.

Symonds, M. 1975. "Victims of Violence: Psychological Effects and Aftereffects." *American Journal of Psychoanalysis*, 36: 19–26.

—— 1976. "The Rape Victim: Psychological Patterns of Response Among Victims of Rape." *American Journal of Psychoanalysis*, 36(1): 27–34.

Taylor, S. and S. Fiske. 1984. *Social Cognition.* Reading, Mass.: Addison-Wesley.

Taylor, S. E., J. V. Wood, and R. R. Lichtman. 1983. "It Could Be Worse: Selective Evaluation as Response to Victimization." *Journal of Social Issues* 39(2): 19–40.

United States Commission on Civil Rights. 1978. *Battered Women: Issues of Public Policy.* Washington, D.C.

Voltaire. 1924. *Philosophical Dictionary.* Selected and translated by H. I. Woolf. New York: Knopf.

Walker, L. E. 1979. *The Battered Woman.* New York: Harper and Row.

—— 1984. *The Battered Woman Syndrome.* New York: Springer.

Walker, L. and A. Browne. 1985. "Gender and Victimization by Intimates." *Journal of Personality* 53(2): 79–95.

Walster, E. 1966. "Assignment of Responsibility for an Accident." *Journal of Personality and Social Psychology* 3: 73–79.

Walster, E., E. Berscheid, and G. W. Walster. 1973. "New Directions in Equity Research." *Journal of Personality and Social Psychology* 25: 151–176.

Wardell, L., D. L. Gillespie, and A. Leffler. 1983. "Science and Violence Against Wives." In D. Finkelhor, R. Gelles, G. Hotaling, and M. Straus, eds. *The Dark Side of Families.* Beverly Hills: Sage Publications.

Warrior, B. 1976. *Wifebeating.* Somerville, Mass.: New England Free Press.

—— 1982. *Battered Women's Directory* (8th ed.). Cambridge, Mass.: Author, 46 Pleasant St., Cambridge, MA 02139.

Williams, C. C., and R. A. Williams. 1973. "Rape: A Plea for Help in the Hospital Emergency Room." *Nursing Forum* 12(4): 388–401.

Williams, W. and J. W. Evans. 1972. "The Politics of Evaluation: The case of Head Start." In P. H. Rossi, & W. Williams, eds. *Evaluating Social Programs.* New York: Seminar Press.

Wilt, M. 1977. *Domestic Violence and the Police.* Washington, D.C.: The Police Federation.

Witmer, H. and R. Kotinsky. 1952. *Personality in the Making.* New York: Harper and Row.

Woods, L. 1978. "Litigation on behalf of battered women." *Women's Rights Law Reporter.* 5 (1).

Women's Rights Convention 1848/1969. Seneca Falls, N.Y.: Arno.

Wortman, C. B. 1976. "Causal Attribution and Personal Control." In J. H. Harvey, W. J. Ickes and R. F. Kidd, eds. *New Directions in Attribution Research.* Hillsdale, N.J.: Lawrence Erlbaum.

Wortman, C. B., and J. W. Brehm. 1975. "Responses to Uncontrollable Outcomes: An Integration of Reactance Theory and the Learned Helplessness Model." In L. Berkowitz, ed. *Advances in Experimental Psychology* 8. New York: Academic Press.

Wortman, C. B., and C. Dunkell-Schetter. 1979. "Interpersonal Relationships and Cancer: A Theoretical Analysis." *Journal of Social Issues,* 35(1), 120–155.

Wouk, H. 1978. *War and Remembrance.* Boston, MA: Little, Brown and Co.
Young, L. R. 1964. *Wednesday's Children: A Study of Neglect and Abuse.*
   New York: McGraw Hill.
Zigler, E. 1979. "Controlling Child Abuse in America." In D. G. Gil ed.
   Child Abuse and Violence. New York: AMS Press, 37–48.

INDEX

———

American Educational Research Journal
Volume 53, Number 6—December 2016

S0-AXP-443

*Articles were accepted under the "Social and Institutional Analysis"
section editorship of Teresa L. McCarty.*

AMERICAN
EDUCATIONAL
RESEARCH
ASSOCIATION

American Educational Research Journal (*AERJ*) is the flagship journal of the American Educational Research Association, featuring articles that advance the empirical, theoretical, and methodological understanding of education and learning. It publishes original peer-reviewed analyses that span the field of education research across all subfields and disciplines and all levels of analysis. It also encourages submissions across all levels of education throughout the life span and all forms of learning. *AERJ* welcomes submissions of the highest quality, reflecting a wide range of perspectives, topics, contexts, and methods, including interdisciplinary and multidisciplinary work.

American Educational Research Journal (ISSN 0002-8312) (J589) is published bimonthly—in February, April, June, August, October, and December—on behalf of the American Educational Research Association, 1430 K Street NW, Washington, DC 20005, by SAGE Publications, 2455 Teller Road, Thousand Oaks, CA 91320. Periodicals postage paid at Thousand Oaks, California, and at additional mailing offices. POSTMASTER: Send address changes to AERA Membership Department, 1430 K Street NW, Washington, DC 20005.

Manuscript Submission: Authors should submit manuscripts electronically via SAGE Track: http://mc.manuscriptcentral.com/aerj. For more information regarding submission guidelines, please see the Manuscript Submission section of the *American Educational Research Journal*'s website: http://aerj.aera.net.

Member Information: American Educational Research Association (AERA) member inquiries, member renewal requests, changes of address, and membership subscription inquiries should be addressed to the AERA Membership Department, 1430 K Street NW, Washington, DC 20005; fax (202) 238-3250; phone (202) 238-3200; e-mail: members@aera.net; website: http://www.aera.net. AERA annual membership dues are $180 (Regular Members), $180 (Affiliate Members), $140 (International Affiliates), and $55 (Graduate Students and Student Affiliates). **Claims:** Claims for undelivered copies must be made no later than six months following month of publication. Beyond six months and at the request of the American Educational Research Association, the publisher will supply replacement issues when losses have been sustained in transit and when the reserve stock permits.

Subscription Information: All nonmember subscription inquiries, orders, back-issue requests, claims, and renewals should be addressed to SAGE Publications, 2455 Teller Road, Thousand Oaks, CA 91320; telephone (800) 818-SAGE (7243) and (805) 499-0721; fax (805) 375-1700; e-mail journals@sagepub.com; http://www.sagepublications.com. **Subscription Price:** Institutions $1,094; Individuals $79. For all customers outside the Americas, please visit http://www.sagepub.co.uk/customerCare.nav for information. **Claims (nonmembers):** Claims for undelivered copies must be made no later than six months following month of publication. The publisher will supply replacement issues when losses have been sustained in transit and when the reserve stock will permit.

Abstracting and Indexing: Please visit the journal's website (http://aerj.aera.net) and, under the "More about this journal" menu on the right-hand side, click on the Abstracting/Indexing link to view a full list of databases in which this journal is indexed.

Copyright Permission: Permission requests to photocopy or otherwise reproduce copyrighted material published in this journal should be submitted by accessing the article online on the journal's website, http://aerj.aera.net, and selecting the "Request Permission" link. Permission may also be requested by contacting the Copyright Clearance Center via their website at http://www.copyright.com, or via e-mail at info@copyright.com.

Advertising and Reprints: Current advertising rates and specifications may be obtained by contacting the advertising coordinator in the Thousand Oaks office at (805) 410-7763 or by sending an e-mail to advertising@sagepub.com. To order reprints, please e-mail reprint@sagepub.com. Acceptance of advertising in this journal in no way implies endorsement of the advertised product or service by SAGE, the journal's affiliated society(ies), or the journal editor(s). No endorsement is intended or implied. SAGE reserves the right to reject any advertising it deems as inappropriate for this journal.

Change of Address: Six weeks' advance notice must be given when notifying of change of address. Please send the old address label along with the new address to the AERA Membership Department (address above) to ensure proper identification. Please specify name of journal.

Printed on acid-free paper

American Educational Research Journal
December 2016, Vol. 53, No. 6, pp. 1491–1521
DOI: 10.3102/0002831216676569
© 2016 AERA. http://aerj.aera.net

Youth and Schools' Practices in Hyper-Diverse Contexts

Christine Brigid Malsbary
Vassar College

The article presents findings from a multisited ethnography in two public high schools in Los Angeles and New York City. Schools were chosen for their hyper-diverse student populations. Students came from over 40 countries, speaking 20 languages in one school and 33 languages in another. Results of analysis found that despite contrasting missions, policies, organizational structures, curricular techniques, and teachers' beliefs and attitudes across schools, youths' practices were similar. Youth enacted explicit transcultural repertoires of practice: multiplicities of talking, thinking, and acting that engaged the resources and opportunities of ethnically and linguistically diverse classrooms. The article theorizes the importance of recognizing hyper-diversity as a distinct cultural context that shapes and situates youths' practices and therefore their opportunities to learn.

KEYWORDS: anthropology, cultural analysis, diversity, equity, ethnography, immigration/immigrants, multisite studies, observational research, social context

Internationally and nationally, cities are experiencing the largest wave of international migration since the early 1900s. Currently, over 40.4 million immigrants[1] representing 13% of the U.S. population live in the United States; the nation's historic high has led to neighborhoods "characterized by multilayered, crisscrossing cultural, linguistic, religious, national, and racial/ethnic identifications" (McCarty et al., 2014, p. 5). While research on culture in education has proliferated (González, Moll & Amanti, 2005; Lee,

CHRISTINE BRIGID MALSBARY is an anthropologist of education, Vassar College, 124 Raymond Ave, Box 709, Poughkeepsie, NY 12604; e-mail: *chmalsbary@vassar.edu*. Her research is concerned with the negotiation and remaking of education spaces given the conflict between two social phenomena: rising cultural and linguistic hyper-diversity through student demographic changes on the one hand and restrictive acultural policies and practices given recent emphasis on education standardization on the other. Malsbary is faculty at Vassar College, where she teaches courses on the politics of language and race, qualitative research, and the making of culturally-saturated curricula.

2006), many studies are still focused on "single group studies" (Sleeter & Grant, 1987). Such studies are characterized by their attention to students' groups by race, class, or language affiliation in specific cultural communities. Single group studies remain critical to reparation efforts to reverse the "education debt" (Ladson-Billings, 2006) owed to communities given legacies of colonialism and slavery in the United States. But their proliferation runs the risk of our understanding of culture[2] in education becoming "overdeterministic," "solely" focused on the heritage practices of communities of color while ignoring their "evolving practices" (Paris & Alim, 2014).

I argue that hyper-diverse, multilingual cultural contexts shape and situate education sites, providing language and culture resources that lead youth to enact distinct practices. I make this argument to generate further research and dialogue about how schools can respond to and leverage youths' repertoires of practice for expanded opportunities to learn. Researchers grapple with the complexities of culture and identity in light of globalization, racist backlash toward immigrant and Black communities, and changing demographics in U.S. schools.

The goal of the work I present here is to document youths' evolving practices across differing school settings that are multilingual and transnational—settings that I term *hyper-diverse*. I use the term to refer to all school settings that serve mixtures of the following populations: bilingual populations, students with multiple racial affiliations, U.S.-born and immigrant/transnational students, and students with varying economic class backgrounds. What does the presence of more languages, more cultural affiliations, and blurring national, ethnic, and racial categories in schools mean for young people's social, cultural, and intellectual development?

Between 2009 and 2016, I conducted ethnographic research in two public high schools in hyper-diverse neighborhoods. Guadalupe High in Los Angeles and H.S. 245 in New York City (pseudonyms) had contrasting missions, policies, organizational structures, curricular techniques, and teachers' beliefs and attitudes. Guadalupe High sat in an English-dominant, gentrified neighborhood, H.S. 245 in a multilingual, working-class ethnic enclave. The schools absorbed differing regional immigration politics,[3] with California's proximity to the militarized U.S.-Mexico border and New York State's celebrated immigrant past as a gateway to the United States. And yet, an important aspect in common overshadowed the schools' contrasts. Both schools were microcosms of the powerful demographic shifts changing the cultural, linguistic, ethnic, and religious face of the United States over the past several decades. In addition to cultural, racial, and linguistic diversity, youth arrived at these schools with widely varying literacy skills, academic preparation, expectations of schooling norms, and differing documentation statuses. I ask the following research questions:

Research Question 1: How do schools respond to hyper-diverse contexts?

Research Question 2: What kinds of things do youth do and say to make sense of hyper-diversity?

Research Question 3: What does this mean for research?

Theorizing the Hyper-Diverse, Multilingual Cultural Context

Challenging the Concept of the Mainstream

Social scientists have theorized post-migration contact between immigrants and native-born populations as a process of *assimilation* (Gibson, 1988; Joppke, 1998; Portes, Fernandez-Kelly & Haller, 2005), emphasizing immigrants' linear and unidirectional movement into a homogeneous United States whereby the immigrant sheds his or her language and cultural practices to adopt American ways of being. Assimilation theory posits that social and cultural cohesion is necessary for economic and political stability (Gordon, 1964). More recently, the segmented assimilation model "gets rid of the concept of 'mainstream' except as a rhetorical device, and assert[s] that the key feature of American society at present is not its homogeneity but its diversity" (Portes, 2005, p. 7). The model of segmented assimilation stresses heterogeneity within the immigrant population, the host society itself, and the multiethnic mainstream. Yet the model remains limited, bluntly delineating how immigrants either become "White" or "Black" in the U.S. mainstream (Portes, Fernandez-Kelly, & Haller, 2005).

In the past decade, social scientists have examined integration into the mainstream beyond the Black/White polarity of racial constructs. Theories of *super-diversity* posit that post-migration contact is multivariant and dynamic as immigrant communities and native-born communities interact. The term underscores how human differences in global cities have reached complexity that has not been experienced before: multiple-origin, transnationally connected through new technological forms, socioeconomically differentiated, and legally stratified (im)migrants (Vertovec, 2007). This is not to ignore race as an overarching determinant, as in the United States racism and structural inequality persist, locating and positioning people according to longstanding racial hierarchies according to phenotype (Crenshaw, 1988). Indeed, assimilating people of color into "Whiteness" remains an established U.S. racial pattern (Omi & Winant, 2014). Still, social scientists work to find the language to express the new forms of identity markers people use given the complexities of globalization.

Transnationalism and Transculturalism

To understand culture in the 21st century, social scientists have turned to theories of transnationalism, transculturalism, and translanguaging. *Trans-* acts a heuristic for metaphors of movement and spatial frames containing both the global and the local (Pennycook, 2007). Such constructs privilege dynamics such as creativity, dynamism, and fluidity (Arnaut, 2012). Indeed, people and their cultural practices are "not confined to a fixed territory" but are "parts of multiple spatial networks and temporal linkages" (Salazar, cited in Glick-Schiller & Salazar, 2013). In transcultural spaces, forms fluidly change and are reused to fashion hybrid identities in diverse contexts, absorbing the "effects of the many encounters and hybrid co-productions of languages and cultures" (Pennycook, 2007, p. 6). Transcultural flows include not only "super-cultural commonalities," or cultural forms that transcend locality, but also processes of borrowing, blending, remaking, and returning to processes of alternative cultural production (Pennycook, 2007, p. 6).

Transnationalism studies in education have found that immigrant youth do not merely subjectively experience globalization but actively create globalization through their practices in transcultural spaces (Lam, 2006; Malsbary, 2016; Orellana, 2009a; Pennycook, 2007). Youth are "forging new diaspora and hybrid spaces of social and cultural activities through their growing economic and demographic presence and the use of instantaneous forms of communication," affecting how they "learn, play, work, and interact with the world around them" (Lam, 2006, p. 214). This repositioning of youth as agentive recognizes the work they do as empowered "cultural workers" who reshape and recontextualize global materials in their local communities (Lam, 2006, p. 223). Likewise, Orellana (2009a) contends that children's transcultural skills are not simply a rewording of borderlands theory or inter-culturality (e.g., moving between different, bounded cultural worlds) but are rather "efforts that are made by people living in contact zones to bring different world views together, grapple with, and reconcile their differences, or to 'translate' and actively mediate between them" (p. 2). She theorizes that youth who engage with transcultural flows have a "transcultural toolkit" that includes tools such as keen observation, attentive listening, and open, flexible dispositions: Transcultural toolkits develop while youth "shift alignments at different points in time and in distinct contexts, relationships and activities" (p. 5). In sum, recent education studies have documented how youth take cultural forms, grapple with their differences, translate between them, and produce and reconfigure materials. These practices require particular kinds of skills and lead to the creation of globalization in local spaces.

Translanguaging

Bilingual youth do not simply acquire language but actively do things with language ("languaging") in transnational language communities (Blommaert, 2013; Blommaert & Backus, 2011; García, 2011). García (2011) argues that translanguaging challenges traditional conceptualizations of bilingualism that position bilinguals as static receptacles filled with one container for native language and one container for English. This perspective on language learning has been made visible in bilingual programs that separate part of the school day for particular languages, with math taught in Spanish but history taught in English, for example. Rather, *translanguaging* describes bilinguals' fluid and creative use of any linguistic resources to make sense of communication (García, 2011), interweaving and intermeshing a range of resources across borders and boundaries (Blommaert & Backus, 2011; Cekaite & Björk-Willén, 2013; Rampton, 2011). Linguistic competence emerges out of local practices where multiple languages brought together through immigration are negotiated for their communicative purposes (Canagarajah, 2011).

Methods

To characterize hyper-diversity in schools, I turn to ethnography. Emerging from the traditions of cultural anthropology, ethnography traditionally has involved long-term participant observation in a local site; following on this, the researcher produces an intimate portrait of everyday life in one specific community. Transnationalism and transculturalism pose challenges to traditional ethnography. Marcus (1995) pushed the field of anthropology forward with his work on multisited ethnography, a technique meant to resolve the methodological need to capture transnational processes and people in motion in relation to globalization. In contrast to local ethnographies, multisited ethnographers *follow* a commodity, symbolic meanings, social problems, a biography, or a conflict through time or space. Hence, answering research questions involves comparative translation and tracing among sites (Marcus, 1995). Such tracing may change a long-held tenet of ethnography–time in the field–as the researcher travels to different sites following the social phenomenon. As related to schools, Vossoughi and Gutiérrez (2014) note how bringing a multisited sensibility to education problems may make visible the complexity and ingenuity of human development, particularly in the context of migration, diaspora, and other forms of transnational and intercultural movement.

Over a seven-year span (2009–2016), I ethnographically followed a "biography" and a "social problem," exploring the contours of what it means to live, learn, teach, and language in hyper-diverse cultural contexts and simultaneously delineating the ways in which power shifts and reshapes to limit the possibilities of transculturalism (Malsbary, 2012, 2014a, 2014b; Malsbary, Espinoza, & Bales, 2016). In this article, I analyze data collected across two substudies within the larger ethnographic project: Belonging in a Multiethnic, Multilingual High School, 2009–2011 and Teaching and Learning in Super-Diversity, 2013. The studies examined different parts of the contours of hyper-diverse cultural spaces. The first project focused on youths' sense of belonging and cultural lives in hyper-diversity. At completion, I designed the New York City project in order to deepen my understanding of youths' cultural practices in hyper-diversity comparatively, attending more to issues of learning and teaching in hyper-diversity. While I emphasize the creative possibilities and promises of hyper-diverse culture contexts in the present article, elsewhere (Malsbary, 2016), I look at racism and the reconfiguring of power in those same sites. (For further discussion of possibilities and a critique of research methods essential to understanding super-diversity, see Malsbary, 2016.)

Research Sites and Selection

I selected public schools located in the two top immigrant-receiving cities in the United States (Portes & Rumbaut, 2006). I used local metrics to select public schools in Los Angeles and New York City with a wide range of student body demographics; my selection criteria focused on the number of different languages spoken on site, ethnoracial affiliation, and multiplicity of national origins.[4] After entering the field, I identified differences in economic class and juridical/documentation status.

Guadalupe High had a high proportion of demographic student diversity in contrast to many segregated schools in the Los Angeles area. The comprehensive, traditional high school served approximately 1,000 students and reported that the student body spoke 33 different languages. The school's English as a second language (ESL) program separated immigrant students from their English-speaking peers, and their courses focused on English language development and sheltered content instruction. Administrators and ESL teachers struggled with the right way to create programs to best serve the youth, one year mainstreaming all youth labeled *English learners* (ELs). The next year, the administration created a separate ESL program again after general education teachers complained about it being challenging to teach the ELs and EL students expressed feeling unsafe and bullied by their English-speaking peers. Some subject areas did not have teachers who had training to teach "sheltered instruction," and some teachers taught in the program out of their certification and license areas.

Situated in a borough of New York City that receives the highest number of immigrants in the city, H.S. 245 was a different kind of school than Guadalupe High. The neighborhood surrounding the school had successive flows of immigrants from Taiwan and more recently from Fujian. H.S. 245 was a small school of approximately 400 students; the school was created to serve newcomer youth who had been in the United States for fewer than four years at the time of registration. The school reported that its students came from over 40 different countries, speaking 20 languages. Spanish and Chinese speakers made up the largest language groups, and there were also speakers of Arabic, Bangla, French, and Haitian/Creole, among many other languages. Students were academically heterogeneous as well, comprising youth who had uneven schooling experiences and who were designated as SIFE (Students With Interrupted Formal

Education), students speaking Indigenous languages, refugees, and students in need of both EL and special education services.

Following a progressive, teacher-developed model, school policy at H.S. 245 emphasized detracked, heterogeneous, collaborative learning. Teachers designed their own curriculum emphasizing integrated content and English language learning, with home language development as a critical part of the educational mission. Teachers collaborated to create innovative, interdisciplinary curricula and support each other to guide students through high-stakes district and city exams. Teachers had frequent professional development that supported their interdisciplinary curricula, leveraging both content and language instructional strategies. Administrators and the hiring committee prioritized hiring bilingual and trilingual teachers. Teachers reported feeling excited and confident about their abilities to effectively work with English-learning immigrant students.

Techniques of Data Collection

Participant Observation

Participant observation was the primary technique through which I collected data sources. I conducted time-extensive ethnography for 18 months at Guadalupe High,[5] visiting the school three to four times per week on average. I observed ESL, English language arts, and science systematically, choosing classes to attend that youth told me they enjoyed the most (following on that study's focus on how youth experienced a sense of belonging). In addition, I observed hallways, common areas, and neighborhoods surrounding the schools and participated in field trips, afterschool events, and parent meetings. Finally, I observed faculty meetings and teachers' co-planning and departmental meetings. When observing, I jotted down notes primarily describing youth interaction and talk and secondarily describing teachers' actions. I turned jottings into 400 pages of field notes.

Second, I conducted a time-intensive, ethnographic case study of the New York City high school. I visited the school daily for two months in spring 2013, with follow-up research in fall 2013 and fall 2014. In addition to written field notes, I videotaped classroom activity in interdisciplinary, 9th/10th mixed-grade English language arts and science classes, focusing on youth collaborative interactions around subject matter and their peer teaching practices. This resulted in 35 hours of video; I also collected approximately 50 pages of teacher-created curriculum and observed faculty planning and departmental meetings.

Interviews

Participant observation was triangulated with interview data; questions probed meanings in action (Erickson, 1985) such as participants' interpretations of their practices recorded in my field notes. First, at Guadalupe High, I engaged in longitudinal interviewing with four key informants—10th, 11th, and 12th graders from Mexico, Pakistan, Korea, and Iran. I spoke with each of the four youth informally each week and conducted three semi-structured interviews lasting one to three hours per interview over a two-year period. I asked questions about youths' belongingness, their peer interactions, and their perspectives on language, schooling, teachers' attitudes, and curricula. In addition to regularly speaking with many youth between classes, at lunch, and after school, I conducted 14 interviews with students in an ESL classroom at the Los Angeles site, a focus group interview (n = 25) at the Los Angeles site, and a focus group interview (n = 4) at the New York site. Interviews also probed youths' subjective and emotional stances. Finally, I regularly spoke with adults after classes and during faculty meetings about their intentions, perceptions, and beliefs. In formal interviews, I asked questions about their philosophies of schooling and goals of their institutions and their curriculum. In Los Angeles, I conducted an ethnographic survey (n = 68) and multiple semi-structured interviews with four teachers, two administrators, and a guidance counselor. In New York City, I conducted semi-structured interviews with three teachers and an administrator.

Secondary Techniques of Data Collection and Youth-Directed Research

To supplement primary sources, I collected visual information sources, both my own and through youth-directed visual research. Youth information sources helped me to see the cultural context through their eyes in what they chose to document and what was not photographed. In 2015, I returned to Los Angeles and New York City and conducted linguistic landscapes research (Gorter, 2006). Through this research, I sought to understand the power dynamics at play in a multilingual context, asking which languages were dominant in public space (including public education space) and why. Linguistic landscapes research aims to document the linguistic presence on walls and signs of a particular "scene," "made of streets, corners, circuses, parks, buildings—where society's public life takes place. As such, this scene carries crucial sociosymbolic importance as it actually identifies—and thus serves as the emblem of societies, communities and regions" (Ben-Rafael, Shohamy, Amara, & Trumper-Hecht, 2006, p. 8).

Second, I organized youth-directed research activities. At Guadalupe High, I taught a photography unit and gave cameras to students. Youth took photographs of spaces where they experienced a sense of belonging; I then interviewed youth about their photographs. At H.S. 245, I gave youth small video cameras and asked them to shoot interesting examples of youth interaction; the goal of this was deepen analysis around youth interaction across lines of difference. Finally, in fall 2014, I took a language and literacy walk in the area surrounding the school with undergraduate students. Students created and blogged video and soundscape studies of the multilingual semiotics present on the walls and shop windows of the neighborhood. Linguistic landscapes research supported my overall investigation, adding weight and depth to my analysis by situating the schools' responses to hyper-diversity within the larger sociolinguistic and immigration context of the surrounding community.

Ethnographic Data Analysis

I used a variety of qualitative analysis techniques to analyze field notes, videos, interview transcripts, survey results, curricular artifacts, and photographs of the school neighborhoods (Derry et al., 2010; Erickson, 1985; Miles & Huberman, 1994). First, I conducted pattern coding, establishing patterns of phenomena through iterative sorting, counting, and organizing of reoccurring evidence provided in data sources (Miles & Huberman, 1994). Each pattern was then labeled with a descriptor, becoming a code (e.g., bilingual talk). In general, the codes I chose to label phenomena were words that participants emically used in the field (e.g., "language isolates" to describe students who didn't speak anyone else's language; however, some descriptors were drawn from terms used by other researchers, e.g., "belonging") and applied to phenomena. In the second site, coding was both emic and etic as I applied codes generated from the first school site to what I was seeing in the second. For example, after I established that youth were engaging in "comparative knowing" in the first site, I looked for that phenomenon in the second and coded information sources accordingly.

To generate data reports, I created an index of all the codes, operationalized definitions of the codes, code examples, and locations of codes within the corpus of the data. By creating the code index, I was able to analyze how practices and phenomena related to one another and formed a narrative or larger argument. I developed tables and matrices that sorted codes hierarchically and in relation to one another. Some sorting, particularly for video data sources, occurred with the support of qualitative data analysis programs such as Atlas.ti. Developing matrices supported analysis of co-occurring phenomenon and predominance of particular youth practices. Finally, I wrote descriptive assertions (Erickson, 1985) to test the validity of findings against the overall corpus of the data. I then linked webs of assertions to my research questions to create data reports. Whenever possible, I shared key findings with participants to substantiate assertions and locate data reporting in local perspectives.

Insider/Outsider Positionality

I am a U.S. citizen, a biracial woman, and native English speaker raised transnationally across three countries. Like my youth participants, I learned a second language in adolescence through immersion in a public school. I had no relationship with Guadalupe High prior to the research there and was more of an outsider. Teachers and students saw me as a former teacher who worked for a university and had institutional capital. In New York City, I was an insider as I had taught in the same school consortium as H.S. 245 six years prior to the start of the study. Teachers located me as a former teacher and member of the extended consortium family. My insider-outsider positionality shaped my ability to collect data in that a deeper familiarity with H.S. 245's mission and teaching context lessened the time I needed in the field to make sense of participants' perspectives in order to design interview protocols (I needed more time at Guadalupe High to make sense of what I was seeing). At the same time, my love of H.S. 245 and its mission is an inherent bias in my work.

One of the limitations of the study is my own bilingualism: While I speak enough Spanish to write down Spanish-English interactions in my field notes, I did not speak the variety of other languages present at the site. Therefore, Spanish language interactions may be overrepresented in field notes taken in the first portion of the study (Guadalupe High) and in my data reporting. I attempted to reduce bias in the second portion of the study (H.S. 245) by relying on video to capture youth interaction across languages, which I could later hire bilinguals to transcribe.

In the next section, I report findings that engage the comparative translation of social phenomena observed across two sites. After characterizing and contextualizing two public high schools' responses to hyper-diversity, I showcase portraits of youths' repertoires of practice. In each school portrait, three sets of youths' practices are discussed. Youths' *assistance practices* involved expert immigrant youth who had lived in the United States longer assisting novice immigrant youth more recently arrived to access cultural norms and learning. In what I term *comparative knowing practices*, youth compared their experiences in countries where they had lived previous to the United States in relation to what they attentively observed in the United States, an action that I theorize here as an epistemic resource for learning. Finally, youth enacted *translanguaging* practices: a term that describes bilinguals' use of any and all available linguistic resources to make sense of information (Canagarajah, 2011; García, 2011).

Going to High School in Hyper-Diverse Cultural Contexts: Guadalupe High and H.S. 245

Guadalupe High

Guadalupe High served a newly gentrified neighborhood described by locals as lower- to lower-middle class. Visually, the neighborhood had a classic Los Angeles aesthetic, with an attractive suburban feel and green spaces and trees immediately surrounding the school. Closest to the school were single-family homes and a downtown area with shops and an upscale

Figure 1. **A typical street near Guadalupe High.**

farmer's market. This drew a young, mostly White crowd to the area, which a decade earlier had been mostly families of color. Many White students drove to school and parked in the school parking lot. Latino/a families mostly lived in apartment buildings on the outer reaches of the school zoning area, and students took the bus. Both in the surrounding neighborhood and at school, English was the dominant language of communication, with Spanish as an infrequent secondary presence. Shops displayed signs in English, although a few churches and a mosque had bilingual signs. This weak bilingualism indicated that Spanish-speaking community was not well represented (see Figure 1).

Mirroring their exclusion in the wider community, Spanish-speaking youth were marginalized at school, and non-English, non-Spanish speaking youth were even less included. In other words, the school's response to hyper-diversity was to create a racial-linguistic hierarchical structure that valued and centered the cultural and linguistic assets of some youth but not others.

In general, Guadalupe High responded more to diversity issues around race[6] and gender while transnationalism, immigrant status, and linguistic diversity were less visible. One of the symbolic details that came to illustrate the invisibility of the immigrant youths' transculturalism was a glass presentation box that sat in the front entry of the school. Every month, the case displayed a different topic related to diversity. Over one academic year, I saw a variety of displays in the case, including records of the accomplishments of women, African American civil rights, and the gay rights movement. Despite visiting the school three to four times a week that year, I never saw a display related to immigrant and immigrant-origin people or language diversity. The display case symbolized the wider exclusion of transnational and linguistic diversity.

Attempts to include linguistic diversity were met with resistance or did not come to fruition. At a faculty meeting early in the school year, I observed an administrator discussing the importance of creating multilingual signs, an effort that was never realized during the time I conducted fieldwork. In the crowd, two older White male teachers joked that if the school wanted to be multilingual, it should display signs in Welsh. Their joke indexed the kinds of tensions present in California, which, once part of Spanish-speaking Mexico, now saw Spanish-speaking immigrants routinely policed (Hayes-Bautista, 2004). To my knowledge, no students in the school spoke Welsh, and I interpreted the comment as an example of the kinds of linguistic microaggressions that students consistently reported to me. A teacher who worked closely with the immigrant students explained to me that few teachers in the general education program even knew who their immigrant students were, a sentiment I heard expressed regularly among teachers in the school's ESL program. Similarly, I never read about any of my participants in the school newspaper, and many immigrant students (but not all) told me they did not want to contribute in school activities or feel like they could.

The results of an ethnographic survey conducted with the teaching faculty and administration substantiated the impressions I recorded in my field notes. When asked, teachers reported that linguistic diversity was "more challenging" to deal with than racial diversity. This claim played out in complex ways. In part, the teachers' claim was that multilingualism was more complex than bilingual teaching contexts. As one teacher put it: "I knew how to work in bilingual New Mexico, but I don't know how to teach here with all the different languages." On the ethnographic survey, teachers used the words *frustrating, challenging*, and *overwhelming* to describing working with immigrant students. While the inclusion of transnational and linguistic diversity was primarily referred to as a pedagogical problem, an excerpt from an interview I conducted with a science teacher showed that linguistic diversity could also be seen as an impediment to integration into the multicultural—but English-speaking—mainstream:

> I don't think that [the immigrant students] are integrating well. When the bell rings, I can see usually the ESL kids—they tend to be the ones

that are talking to each other.. . . . And you know, speaking Spanish means that you will connect to one kind, one type of one person only. You need to make sure you are including everyone else.

In the interview, the teacher framed speaking Spanish as counter to the ethos of multiculturalism because it connected a person to "one kind, one type of one person only." What was sublimated was how speaking Spanish at the school gave young people access to a transnational world given that the youth I observed and interviewed were a diverse group of Spanish speakers from across North, Central, and South America, including Mexico, Chile, El Salvador, Colombia, and Guatemala. Indeed, within the transnational margins, speaking Spanish connected youth to an entire section of the world, introducing them to a wide array of culturally diverse practices, a finding to which I now turn.

Youths' Conceptualizations of Diversity and Their Practices

While adults at Guadalupe High ignored or problematized hyper-diversity, youth had a differing reaction. In the margins of their school and in their classrooms, students created a vibrant and (mostly) inclusive multilingual and transcultural community of practice. I observed students watching YouTube dance videos set in a variety of countries and learning to tie *hijab* in the different styles worn by girls from parts of Africa, the Middle East, and South Asia. When the World Cup was played, youth watched together at lunch and after school, ritually mocking each other's teams and countries in ways that seemed to unite rather than divide.

Participation in hyper-diversity played a critical role in youths' subjective experiences. When I asked about being a young Muslim woman on campus, my key informant responded: "How do I feel wearing a hijab here? Just fine. Some people have mohawks, I have a hijab." The young woman's dress was a critical part of her life as Sunni and her adherence to religious practices, including fasting. Yet, with the statement, the young woman placed mohawks—a style of hair originating among the Indigenous people of the Americas, and currently popular among U.S. urban youth—and her *hijab* as similar modes of representation in the transcultural space. Her interest in her classmates' identities included their various faith practices: "I like every religion in the world—even Christian, Jewish. Like here, I met so many people, I never met them before. Like Chinese people, practice their Buddhism and I like it so much." The girl explained her own faith practice, and as she rooted herself in her own faith, she was able to expand outwards, taking an interest in and open-minded stance toward other faith traditions. Likewise, another young woman from Guatemala explained bilingually: "Sometimes I go to the Muslim club. We. . . *organizada actividades* [organized activities]. I am not Muslim but I like to go. I like to see many cultures.

Muchas culturas de diferentes paises [Many cultures from different countries]." The student spoke in Spanish and English to describe her attendance at the school's Muslim club. While she herself was not Muslim, she attended to other cultural practices available to her given the hyper-diverse space. Carter (2010) has identified this kind of work as "cultural flexibility," and Orellana (2009a; 2009b) terms the ability of young people to seek out and understand others' differences in hyper-diverse, multilingual contexts as "transcultural perspective-taking."

Youths' Repertoires of Practice

Over the course of the ethnographic fieldwork at Guadalupe High, I observed youth enacting explicit *repertoires of practice*: multiplicities of talking, thinking, and acting that engaged the resources and opportunities of ethnically and linguistically diverse classrooms.

Assistance practices. While teachers reported that they didn't know how to navigate the multiple languages and transnational culture, youth did know. Students actively supported one another to access the unfamiliar cultural codes of the U.S. classroom and classroom materials in English. One key informant, a high school senior at Guadalupe High when I met him and an undergraduate at a university in California during our final interview, explained how assistance practices were enacted:

> When I came here some other Asian friends helped me. Aan Lee—she's Filipino. She helped me a lot. When I first came in I really didn't understand what they said. When they say, "Pass this paper," I did not understand at all, you know. She would help me to understand. I'm watching the processes and, like, imitating. So that's what I did at that time, but when the teacher started to solve the problem on the board, I didn't know what they doing. But when I stuck with the problem, Aan Lee tell me what am I suppose to do in English, very slowly, with easy vocabulary. She has been here for six or seven years already, so she knew what it was like.

Aan Lee explained how to navigate basic classroom processes such as passing in a paper or solving a problem on the board. My key informant "watched the process" and "imitated" his more expert peer who had been in the country for six or seven years. His account first lays bare the process of receiving assistance: A novice *imitates* the more expert peer, and the peer provides access points for the novice to ways of doing things in a new space. Later in the same interview, the young man contrasted how, without assistance practices, he was unable to engage in necessary tasks asked by the school. For example, he struggled to understand the loudspeaker announcements and had lost expensive books because he did not understand students should empty their lockers before the summer break. It is worth noting that

Aan Lee was from the Philippines and my key informant was from Korea. Elsewhere I have described the *transregional peer groups* youth participated in; here, assistance practices occurred in relation to a shared pan-Asian cultural identification (Malsbary, 2012) but across language difference.

Assistance practices mediated opportunities to learn across multilingual and transnational difference. When a 12th-grade Iranian student who spoke little English arrived in the spring semester, his more expert peers—in this case José, a key informant—supported him to access curriculum. In the spring of 2010, I recorded the following interaction in my field notes:

> José turned to Anoush: "Hey! Hey!" He explained the task to him. Anoush did not understand, so José opened up Anoush's folder, which was lying on his desk, and searched it. He went through a large stack of paper sandwiched into the folder before pulling out a worksheet. He looked at it closely and then grabbed a pencil and wrote: *He She It.* Then, José muttered to himself, "Oh no, no. Past tense. Was. Was." He showed Anoush what to do on the worksheet—take the subject and turn it into a pronoun, then pair it with the appropriate verb tense. Anoush went through the worksheet, occasionally referring to José's notes. José stood quietly next to him for some time, occasionally pointing at something or correcting. Anoush hesitatingly guessed a couple of past tense verbs aloud. He got several right, then stumbled over a pluralization. He picked up speed after about a third of the worksheet.

José explained a task to Anoush, and when he didn't understand, searched his belongings to find his work for him. He then created a model text for Anoush to imitate. Standing near him, José enacted the teacher's role in correcting and guiding Anoush through the activity. Their actions demonstrate how skilled peers may serve a function like that of adults, as Rogoff (2003) argues when describing on how the child care of infants and toddlers is conducted by 5-year-olds to 10-year-olds in many places around the world.

Life in the hyper-diverse margins of Guadalupe High was not utopian. While youth did engage regularly in practices of assistance across ethnonational categories and language barriers, there were ruptures. I observed a Spanish-speaking girl protest working with the only Thai speaker in the room. As I wrote in my field notes, the girl argued that she didn't want to work with the Thai speaker because *"ella no entiende nada* [she doesn't understand anything]"—despite both girls speaking about the same amount of English. The young woman used Spanish to make her case, which meant that only the teacher, who spoke some Spanish, and her Spanish-speaking friends could understand her. The teacher, who appeared to be at a loss for what to do, permitted the exclusion. Later, the Thai girl told me in an interview that she was frustrated with the extensive Spanish spoken in her ESL class. In an interview, a Spanish-English bilingual youth worried aloud to me about the non–Spanish-speaking students feeling lonely.

Comparative knowing. As youth worked to assist one another to make sense of the cultural logic of the U.S. classroom and curriculum, they engaged in comparative work. For example, in an exchange caught on audio recorder, two youth compared traffic patterns and festivals in Colombia and Mexico.

> **Youth 1**: Colombia. . . Bogotá. . . it has a lot of traffic. The city is small so there isn't a lot of space for cars. So there is a lot of public transportation. And taxis, but the taxis are expensive.
> **Youth 2**: It is the same in Mexico. Have you heard the saying that if you drive in Mexico City that you can drive every place in the world?
> **Youth 1**: In Colombia we say the same thing! Colombia has parties all year—festivales, carnivales.
> **Youth 2**: The same in Mexico.

This unprompted discussion took place during an interview with the first youth. The second was acting as a community research assistant and language broker, supporting my Spanish. With the youth from Mexico present, the first, from Colombia, admitted her homesickness, and the two began sharing stories about their national contexts, discussing traffic patterns and city festivals. Their knowing established a commonality of experience across their differing cultural-historical approaches. Knowing is conditioned by one's environment: As an Indigenous scholar explains it, "our empirical rapport with the environment is not something passive. We are active in our understanding. We are engaged in it. *Knowing something becomes something created*" (Meyer, 2001, p. 132). For the youth I observed and interviewed, their comparative knowing was something lived through transmigration and actively created in their new setting.

Youths' comparative knowing was never, to my knowledge, leveraged in curriculum at Guadalupe High. For example, one of my key informants told me during an interview that she wasn't authorized to talk about global poverty when topics came up in social studies. The transcript excerpt that follows demonstrates how her interest in the topic came out of her experience as a transmigrant:

> Saudi is more like California than Pakistan. In Saudi, people have good cars and enjoy their lives. It is middle class. The main difference between California and Saudi is that over there, people are Muslim and wear the long thing, you know? Here, everyone is wealthy. Saudi Arabia is a wealthy country too, I can say that. They have so much petrol over there. They have so much money. But, there are people here too that need help—the homeless people. Pakistan is very poor or very rich—we were middle class, normal, but there was poverty all around. Pakistan is like India, with no new technology, like cars. So much poverty there and in India—little children working.

The girl compared poverty and child labor in Saudia Arabia, Pakistan, India, and Los Angeles—places where she had lived by the time I met her at age 15. She cohered and made visible comparisons between disparate settings with an ease that may not be present in those who have not embodied migration. The young woman flowed in and out of cultural associations, endowing the far away with nearness of experience, reproducing, as Laoire, Carpena-Mendez, Tyrrell, and White (2010) have described, "deterritorialized frames of reference." The global political economy was something that this key informant and several other youth brought to my attention during interviews. In another example, a student from Mexico discussed the political landscape of his home state of Michoacán, comparing the safety of his life in Los Angeles to the violence of his hometown. After a summer in Mexico, he returned to Los Angeles troubled by the violence he had witnessed, such as shootings by the drug cartel in the streets of his small village—yet he was acutely aware of how U.S.-Mexico politics harmed Mexico. He also described crossing social class lines when he left Mexico and moved to the United States, describing the discrimination he faced as a Mexican immigrant in southern California and his subsequent repositioning as lower class.

Translanguaging practices. Youths' assistance practices and comparative knowing practices were delivered through playful, multilingual talk that engaged myriad linguistic resources present in hyper-diversity. In a representative example, youth enacted comparative knowing through their translanguaging work. José, from Mexico, leaned across and pulled on one of Claudia's curls, calling it a *"crespo."* Claudia, from Colombia, corrected him and termed the hair *"rizos,"* using a Colombian term. José leaned over to ask Paloma, a Chilean, how she said curl. "Si, crespo [Yes, curl]," she replied. José informed them, "Chinito en El Salvador [Little curl in El Salvador]." The conversation continued for some time, and someone offered the word *"colocho"* [curl] as another alternative. The incident demonstrated the linguistic diversity among transnational Latinos at Guadalupe High. As evidenced by the "curl conversation," youth frequently focused on the nature of language itself, comparing words from one dialect to words in others. Almost all youth reported to me that they had learned words from a variety of languages: José, it was reported, had learned the word for love in the 33 languages present at the school.

Access to multiple languages meant that youth had options for which language they chose to be their second language, engaging in a practice I have described elsewhere as *cultural adoption* (Malsbary, 2014a). While the institutional expectation was that English was the second language that ELs would learn, English was not always the youths' first choice. Youth adopted second languages other than English because they wanted to integrate into specific peer groups: A young Cantonese speaker learned Mandarin, a Portuguese speaker learned Spanish, and so on. In a relevant

xample of language adoption, a young Farsi/Persian-speaking woman from
ran struggled to find a peer group given that there were few other Farsi/
Persian speakers at Guadalupe High. She reported in an interview that she
looked for friends who had the same sense of independence, with cultural
practices similar to her own language, religion, class, national origin, and
regional pop culture. On her Facebook page, she played around in different
languages but concentrated on learning Portuguese to belong to the
Brazilian peer group who were "like Persians." She said:

> I hang out with Brazilians. . . and I am learning Portuguese. They are
> so warm, like first time when I met them, it was like they know me
> from—I don't know, three years ago. They were so good to me.
> They are—they are like Persians.

The young woman's friends "understood" her, and she "learned
Portuguese" in order to "talk with them." In this way, going to school in
this hyper-diverse, multilingual context afforded youth the opportunity to
develop robust and systematic transcultural repertoires of practice—languaging, knowing, and assisting one another in and across diversity.

H.S. 245

H.S. 245 drew on ethnic enclaves of Chinese, South Asians, and Mexican
and Central Americans, both established and new immigrant communities.
All students walked or took the subway to school. The clean-swept neighborhood had rows of tall, neat, brick apartment buildings surrounded by
railroads; bustling streets with small independent restaurants; and open-air
markets. Along central thoroughfares, crowded shops brightly advertised
bobo milktea, varieties of East Asian and Mexican foods and U.S. and non-
U.S. clothing options. The languages present on store fronts, posters, flyers,
graffitti and public murals, the subway, and even in the music heard in the
streets reflected the multilingual cultures of the area. Shops, churches, and
transportation stops displayed signs primarily in Chinese and Korean but
also in English and Spanish (see Figures 2 and 3). The local library had bilingual books and multiple languages on display as public pedagogy, with
phrases in 20 languages carved into the stairs leading to the library door.

In contrast to Guadalupe High, H.S. 245 responded to transnational and
linguistic diversity and racial diversity to a degree. Teachers were familiar
with the challenges students faced as immigrants in the United States, including health care, documentation status, family separation, racial profiling, and
religious discrimination. Teachers brought in outside organizations to provide wrap-around services for their immigrant students and their families,
characterizing themselves as activists and advocates as well as educators.
There was a student-led club for undocumented students, and I attended
an immigrant rights rally in front of the governor's office with teachers and

Figure 2. **A typical storefront near H.S. 245.**

Figure 3. **A handmade sign in Spanish near H.S. 245. Spanish speakers were newcomers to the area, and Spanish was less represented in formal signs in the neighborhood.**

students. Unlike English-only district policy fostered through practices like standardized testing (Menken, 2010), school policy at H.S. 245 positioned translanguaging as a fundamental part of the school's social justice mission. Teachers organized events such as science nights in a variety of home languages for parents to understand youths' learning. Reflecting the multilingual semiotics of the larger neighborhood, signs in multiple languages hung in the entry way of the school welcoming and directing visitors. Hallway walls in the school were decorated with students' multiliterate and multilingual classroom work. For example, underneath a set of paintings outside the art room, student-made signs read "don't touch the artwork" in English, Spanish, Chinese, Bangla, and Arabic. Every document issued to families went home in multiple languages, usually Spanish, Chinese, Bangla, Arabic, and French, although more infrequently spoken languages like Tagalog were not translated.

Youths' Repertoires of Practice

Assistance practices. Assistance practices occurred in the margins of the school and in classrooms at Guadalupe High but were formalized as policy and practice at H.S. 245 (Malsbary et al., 2016). Teachers organized students into collaborative groups with experts (10th graders, teachers, bilingual students) who supported novices (9th graders, emergent bilinguals) to access grade-level content. The following example is representative of the assistance work that was supported through collaborative groupings.

Three Chinese speakers and two Spanish speakers were clustered around a computer they had been directed to use to audio-record themselves reading aloud a paragraph from Hemingway's *The Old Man and the Sea*. Two expert bilingual students, a Chinese-speaking girl and a Spanish-speaking boy, took responsibility to get their classmates organized and on the right page.

> Felix introduced the activity, speaking slowly and clearly into the audio recording device: "Hi my name is Felix. We are going to talk page 81. Nico is going to read paragraph three." Felix turned to Nico and gestured for him to begin. Nico began: "He was dreaming he was in the village on his bed. . . ." Felix looked at Nico and slapped his hand to his forehead in dramatic horror. Nico pushed him away and continued to read. When Nico finished reading aloud Felix erupted in rapid Spanish, comically reprimanding him for reading the wrong paragraph. Nico tried to defend himself: "que dijo leyó la sentencia y lo hice. . . [*I read the paragraph!*]" Jin Li, a Chinese speaker, seemed to interpret the battle correctly. "Oh my god," she said, shaking her head in what appeared to be pretend disgust. Felix rebutted, throwing his hands up in the air with an air of resignation, "He did it wrong! Not my problem!" Jin Li leaned across the table, pointed a finger at Felix, and scolded him: "Just have him read the other paragraph, how will Miss Kipner know which paragraph you want him to read!"

In this exchange, the students interacted with one another playfully, yet their assistance practices also served to push their classmates forward and instruct them as to the correct way to do the activity. The expert Spanish-

English bilingual's mock horror both indicated the group's focus on getting the task right while simultaneously delivering the bad news to the novice Spanish-dominant speaker (that he did not follow Felix's direction) with a playfulness that may have softened the blow of the correction. Likewise, the expert Chinese-English bilingual took a stand and moved the entire group forward toward task completion by making sure that the novice student did not spend too much of the group's time on the choice of paragraph, a detail that she did not think mattered much. In this way, the two expert bilinguals inhabited the role of elders who inducted newer community members into the academic process.

Comparative knowing. The students' knowledge and experience were valued in the official classroom setting, allowing for comparative knowing practices to emerge in relation to subject-matter material. When I shared examples of comparative knowing from Guadalupe High with a teacher at H.S. 245, the teacher told me a story about discussing poverty with her students. Of their own accord, they brought up examples of having to go out to fetch water as there was no clean drinking water in their homes. "Around the room, heads were nodding," the teacher explained, struck by the how many of her students shared the experience of having no clean drinking water. Many of the teachers planned their curricula to respond to shared issues that the young people faced in contexts of globalization.

As the students had done at Guadalupe High, making traffic comparisons between Mexico City and Bogotá, youth at H.S. 245 also engaged in comparisons of daily life. For example, in a science classroom at H.S. 245, students compared foods eaten in relation to academic content during a science lesson on consumers and producers. The student who initiated the comparison was a vivacious young woman from China who loved food and who often recommended dishes from the local Chinese market in her neighborhood to me.

> The teacher walked over to the table of five students and asked them to clarify the food web they were creating. "Who is eaten by whom?" he asked, continuing: "Give me an example of a secondary consumer. Is it the loggerhead turtle?" After he left, the girls chatted about the food web they were sketching together. Then a student from China shared, "I don't know what animals eat. . . . Sometimes I eat something a little bad. Like dog." She giggled. "Dog?" her classmate from the Philippines asked. "Dog," the girl from China clarified, "wroof, wroof." "Mm-hmm," her classmate responded, nonplussed.

The girls continued to work quietly for a few minutes. Then, the classmate, without looking up from her work, asked the student from China if she had ever eaten a frog. The student from China denied it with a shiver and said she hated eating frog. The student from China associated her own eating practices with the biological concept of consumers and producers about which she was learning, repositioning herself as a consumer. It is important to note here how discussions of food can play into ugly stereotypes that cause harm when used to racialize groups; still, it is also critical to represent what youth do unedited. To the youth themselves, sharing food and talking about food was an important part of transcultural life.

Translanguaging. Similar kinds of translanguaging documented at Guadalupe High occurred regularly at H.S. 245. Youth translated for and assisted one another as they playfully engaged multilingualism. First, similarly to Guadalupe High, most students picked up fragments of each other's languages for use in this super-diverse setting. In my field notes, I captured a humorous instance of multilingual play at H.S. 245. A boy from the Dominican Republic bent over his classwork while a girl from China walked behind him and loudly encouraged him. *"Bien, bien,"* she said in French with a smirk. The boy looked up, momentarily disoriented. As the girl returned to her table, two trilingual Haitian Creole/French/English speakers, obvious instigators of the moment, broke into hilarious laughter.

Second, the same processes of cultural adoption that occurred at Guadalupe High also occurred at H.S. 245. For example, a Spanish-English bilingual at H.S. 245 converted to Islam one summer. Upon returning to school the following year, he made repeated and intentional overtures to the Muslim youth at the school, and I witnessed him trying to speak Arabic with them. I observed him practicing reading and writing Arabic during class hours. When I asked him about his literacy practices, he showed me a letter the school had sent home about the bedbug epidemic in New York City and the school. The letter had been translated into Arabic by the school, and the student translated and explained various words to me at length.

But, unlike Guadalupe High, translanguaging and translation at H.S. 245 were formally and consistently brought into subject-matter curricula. Teachers encouraged students to engage in translanguaging practices and leveraged translanguaging in learning tasks. A common practice was for teachers to start their instruction by asking students to translate the main ideas of the lesson into any of the home languages spoken by that particular student group (e.g., environmental issues was one such anchor concept). Students would then work with one another to translate the word environment into their home language and write it on the board for all students to see. Teachers also encouraged students to translanguage on written work. On one worksheet I photographed, a student had written: "because this word *son* very *inportant* this *nos enseño muchas cosas*" in response to the question of why he had picked a particular passage to share with his group. In his written work, he fluidly engaged Spanish and English, using whatever language necessary and accessible to him in order to create content and engage with curriculum.

Discussion

Much of the research to date has centered the study of culture on a single education site or a single cultural group. Researchers have done important work to map out the heritage practices that culture groups pass down generationally in order to propose ways that schools can protect and leverage the gifts of those cultural lineages (Moll, Amanti, Neff, & González, 1992; Lee, 2006). I build and elaborate this tradition of anthropology in education research by documenting youths' evolving practices newly forged in relation to hyper-diverse cultural spaces. Based on the empirical work I have presented in the present article, I theorize two constructs: the hyper-diverse school setting and transcultural repertoires of practice.

Finding 1: The Hyper-Diverse School Setting

Ethnographic research found that certain schools are *hyper-diverse* in that their student demographics are composed of youth with multiple and varying affiliations across national, linguistic, racial, economic, religious, and juridical lines. I develop the construct of hyper-diversity from studies in European sociology and sociolinguistics of super-diversity (Creese & Blackledge, 2010) and from the ethnographic evidence. What I take from the study of super-diversity is researchers' emphasis on looking at *both* language *and* ethnonational/racial affiliation.[7] Building on research in transculturalism, super-diversity, and translanguaging, I engage my own border crossing by bridging research areas marked by splits: Languaging is studied by language scholars, and diversity/multicultural studies are split between researchers who attend to groups by racial affiliation and others who attend to immigration. As Kubota and Lin (2006) argue, scholarship about racism is relatively absent in major fields such as Teaching English as a Second or Other Language (TESOL). These schisms in the research challenge researchers' ability to address intersectional identities of youth who live increasingly complex lives as racial minorities in some spaces but racial majorities in others, multilingual, with blurred immigrant "status" as families move back and forth across borders. Attending to hyper-diversity lends itself to ways of thinking and speaking about intersectional markers of identity, asking which markers are salient in which contexts and creating more accurate portraits of the demographic composition and cultural contexts of schools.

The schools I studied responded in different ways to their hyper-diverse contexts. One responded more to youths' racial affiliation stemming from the U.S. context but less to transnational diversity or linguistic diversity (or, indeed, to youths' racial affiliations in their countries of origin). Broadening out from the school, it was possible to see that this was a norm for the environment surrounding the school, where a weak Spanish-English bilingualism (which leaned toward English-only) dominated the physical landscape. The second school had a specific mission to serve immigrant youth and thus foregrounded linguistic and transnational diversity, as did the neighborhood surrounding the school. However, because the second school did not serve both immigrant *and* U.S.-born young people, results are inconclusive as to whether the school would have been able to continue its emphasis on linguistic diversity with a large English-speaking population. Still, the tools that teachers used to mediate hyper-diversity have broad implications for many different kinds of cultural contexts.

As a comparative analysis of two institutional contexts reaffirms, building on decades of scholarship, researchers are called on to grapple with the cultural politics of space. Cultural spaces can be as different as bilingual-bicultural borderlands of the U.S.-Mexico border, super-diverse and multilingual global cities where immigration has been sustained and continuous, and colonized sites such as African American enclaves in the postindustrial landscapes of Detroit and the south side of Chicago. In brief, scholars concerned with hyper-diverse, multilingual contexts must also be concerned with decolonizing and anti-racist education and engage actively with reparative and restorative schooling efforts. And yet, these cultural spaces can be treated in the aggregate, as diverse people of color are positioned under the U.S. racial project (Omi & Winant, 2014) as a single entity that exists only to be defined as something other than White. Again, collectivity is at times critical to leverage activist work and make policy claims, but to stay there is to work reductively, particularly in social science. We need more research on hyper-diverse contexts in order to accumulate and understand how and when power shape-shifts. The example of the teacher at Guadalupe High who believed Spanish speakers were not integrating well into "multiculturalism" because they spoke primarily to other Spanish speakers without accounting for the transnational diversity of the Central American and Latin American community at the school demonstrates such shape-shifting.

Finding 2: Transcultural Repertoires of Practice

I found that youth engaged in transcultural repertoires of practice in relation to their hyper-diverse environment *despite differences* in school policy and institutional practices. Across multiple sites, regular and identifiable youth practices were enacted that crossed borders of language, culture, and national origin and supported youth to experience a sense of belonging in a space of great cultural difference. In turn, their practices opened up opportunities for youth to learn. Importantly, youth also had a lot of fun: As it turns out, simply sitting next to someone in transnational diversity lends itself to messy, creative repertoires of practices. Drawing on Gutiérrez and Rogoff's (2003) description of "cultural repertoires of practice," I use the term *transcultural repertoires of practice* to illustrate the constellation of ways in which youth made sense of the hyper-diverse cultural context.

In their 2003 paper, Gutiérrez and Rogoff argue that cultural variation in approaches to learning is not reducible to a *trait* inherent to a particular ethnic group (e.g., all Asian youth are good at math) and that by thinking about cultural styles as ethnic group traits, researchers and educators run the risk of essentializing and overgeneralizing cultural communities. Rather, Gutiérrez and Rogoff argue, researchers can "examine people's usual ways of doing things, trying to understand individuals' history of involvement in the practices of varied communities, including ethnic or national communities as well as others such as academic or religious communities" (p. 22). Gutiérrez and Rogoff rely on a cultural-historical approach to construct their argument, noting how youths' repertoires can be characterized by "their familiarity with engaging in particular practices on the basis of what is known about their own or their communities' history" given the "usual, customary, habitual approaches" of particular cultural groups (p. 22).

In light of my findings, I build on and elaborate Gutiérrez and Rogoff's (2003) research as I characterize the ways in which hyper-diverse contexts foreground transculturality. Further, I argue, given the transcultural nature of the cultural context, researchers can examine how youths' repertoires of practice bridge and cross borders that are new to them rather than (or perhaps in addition to) youths' leveraging practices in alignment with the history of their cultural groups and what is "usual, customary and habitual" to them. In the following section, I elaborate this point.

In the hyper-diverse cultural contexts I studied, *transculturality* and movement across new languag(ing) and cultur(ing) forms (or rather, forms *that are new* to immigrant youth) was inherent to interaction and a valued activity. As Orellana (2015) writes so beautifully:

> As I examine movement across cultural, geographical, and linguistic lines, I use the "trans-" prefixed words that have become popular in this era of globalization: translanguaging, transnationalism, translation, transculturation. "Trans" puts the emphasis on *movement*, forcing us to consider what happens in the crossing. What is gained and what is lost? What prices are exacted? What competencies are cultivated? What feelings are evoked, as people cross in different ways? (p. 15)

By noting the movement and border crossing implicit to youths' practices and competencies, I advance that there is something about hyper-diversity and transculturation that lends themselves to the emergence of particular youth practices. Indeed, my comparative research demonstrates that youths' practices in relation to hyper-diversity were consistent even as the makeup of the ethnonational affiliations of individuals within the context changed from place to place. In the contexts I studied, one school served mostly youth from the Caribbean and China, while the other primarily served youth from Central America and the Middle East. Yet across both sites, as noted at the beginning of this discussion, regular and identifiable approaches to activities, learning, and languaging occurred. Through interactions with peers across what might have otherwise been overwhelming ethnonational, cultural, academic, and linguistic diversity, youth developed *transcultural* epistemic, linguistic, and assistance practices. Transcultural assistance practices were critical to the creation of belonging, occurring as youth with more time in the United States (elders) supported youth with less time in the United States (novices) to do the following things: access a new school culture, navigate unfamiliar institutional norms for academic and social behavior, understand teachers' talk and directions, and access academic content in English. At Guadalupe High and H.S. 245, assistance practices were transcultural when they fluidly engaged peers' resources across language, ethnonational group, documentation status, and social class. Youth drew on the epistemic and cultural historical resources available to them in their classrooms to act as bilingual language experts, knowledge/content experts, experts at navigating systems, and experts who understood the psychosocial experience of acculturation.

Across both sites, youths' *transcultural and comparative knowing* was at times humorous commentary on daily life and at times sociopolitical. The following topics were compared: poverty, plant life, differences in religious tolerance and intolerance, theology and belief systems, violence, war, traffic patterns, pop culture, music, foods eaten, adolescent sexual behavior and norms for sexual expectations, dress, dance, social class and its relationship to identity, and gender relations. Youths' engagement with transnationalism has led scholars to argue that by virtue of immigrant children's "diverse vantage points and transnational negotiations," they are uniquely positioned to educate their peers and teachers about the world (Campano & Ghiso, 2011, p. 166). Youths' comparative knowing practices become an epistemic stance demonstrated in youths' comparison-making between "here" and "there." Comparative knowing emerged from their embodied immigrant and transnational experiences, leveraging fluidity, movement, and change as repertoire and resource.

Conclusion

While youth engage and leverage the resources of the transnational era, public education moves further away from such cultural work. Around the United States, accountability and standardization education policies are "increasingly focused on managing, containing, and controlling certain kinds of diversity" and "governed by state-level standardizing regimes and language- and culture-restrictionist movements" (McCarty et al., 2014, p. 5). Across a web of institutional spaces, integration is down. In 2012, the Civil Rights Project at the University of California, Los Angeles reported that schools in the U.S. South were resegregating after decades in which civil rights law made it the section of the country with the highest levels of integration in its schools (Orfield, Kucsera, & Siegel-Hawley, 2012). Across the nation, a full 15% of Black students and 14% of Latino/a students attend "apartheid schools" where Whites make up 0% to 1% of the enrollment; segregation is even more profound for Latino/a students, particularly in California, New York, and Texas, all states that have been altered by immigration trends over the past half-century (Orfield et al., 2012). The detailed study of hyper-diversity as a form of cultural space that holds benefit for a society torn by persistent racial tensions is necessary to develop transcultural policy that centers culture, community, and context in everything we do.

Transcultural policy would be necessarily nuanced and complex. It could never be one size fits all. For instance, while we discuss forms of equity that engage historical reparations to specified groups who have been denied equity and educational access (e.g., Historically Black Colleges and Universities [HBCUs] for African Americans and bilingual schooling for Mexican-origin Spanish speakers), we must also discuss how to best further the brave cultural work that youth who attend schools that are hyper-diverse do. Second, while we hold as true that racial resegregation is a harm, we must also call the notion of segregation into question: Are schools serving 100% Spanish speakers segregated, or are they transnationally diverse? How can a single school recognize the intersectional needs of individuals while balancing the needs of cultural groups; identify, privilege, and leverage the new forms of cultural production that are forged in cultural translation between groups; *and* protect cultural-historical activities? Such equity is surely not easy to achieve. Still, such work is worth trying.

Results of this study show that youths' interaction across lines of difference—often vast cultural, religious, class, and linguistic difference—carries deep benefits. Youth developed social and political awareness, engaged as community members to support one another, and learned languages that in turn served to open them up to the histories, values, and perspectives of other cultural groups. Learning in hyper-diversity is a social good and one that surely leads to beneficial economic and civic outcomes. It is my hope that the study I have presented here is a starting point to generate more research on transcultural practices that could then substantiate renewed and vigorous attendance to the creation of national and state-level transcultural policy. Taking the example of H.S. 245, youths' transcultural practices can be tapped as exemplars to forge policies that link culture and subject matter, engage transnational literacies, and nurture youth as leaders and teachers of one another. Youth are getting on with the business of living in a globalized and transnational world. Scholarship and policy must follow their lead.

Notes

All research emerges from community, and the work that substantiates this article has had extraordinary community support. I began collecting data in 2009 and over the years received warm welcome and friendship from research participants in multiple schools; funding provided by the American Association of University Women, UCLA, University of Hawai'i College of Education, the Spencer Foundation, and Vassar College; anonymous reviewers' thoughtful feedback; and excellent editorial stewardship by Teresa McCarty. I am deeply grateful to: Barbara Rogoff and Kris Gutiérrez for inspiration and extraordinary mentorship; Danny Martinez, Shirin Vossoughi, Dafney Blanca Dabach, Nancy Hornberger, and Margaret Eisenhart for generously reading various drafts and providing compelling feedback; and Marjorie Orellana for everything—always.

[1]The term *immigrants* (synonymous for foreign born) refers to people residing in the United States who were not U.S. citizens at birth. This population includes naturalized citizens, lawful permanent residents, certain legal nonimmigrants (e.g., persons on student or work visas), those admitted under refugee or asylum status, and persons residing in the United States "illegally" without authorization. Unauthorized immigrants are also termed *undocumented* (without documents, or currently out of status) by those who wish to highlight broken immigration reform and law. Given that it can take over a decade, conservatively estimating, to receive a visa, many immigrants who migrate legally become undocumented as they wait for papers.

[2]The term *culture* is frequently misunderstood, conflated with "stable identities, categorical memberships, and holistic traits" (Lam, 2006, p. 217). The definition I use in this article builds on ideas that "culture" emerges through *practices*: "ways of acting and participating in diverse social groups and the heterogeneous sets of cultural knowledge, skills, and competence that are acquired in the process" (Lam, 2006, p. 217).

[3]As Keogan (2010) argues, based on his study that engages content analysis of newspapers, New York City has become the symbolic center for the commemoration of a nation of immigrants, but the history and cultural landscape of Southern California gives "little reminder of the positive contributions" immigrants made to the development of the area (p. 20).

[4]In order to provide a measure of confidentiality for my research participants, I do not share how I selected the public schools involved in the study because they would be too readily identifiable.

[5]All names are pseudonyms.

[6]While the school "responded" to race, there was no true anti-racist spirit. For example, when WASC visited the school for a quality review, "multiculturalism" was written down as one of the school's greatest strengths. Some teachers met this with some skepticism. As one teacher of color said of the outside assessor, "they praised us for something [e.g., multiethnic student population] that we really had nothing to do with." As the teacher noted, many Black and brown students remained underserved. Thus, while the physicality of Black and brown bodies on the school campus and in classrooms prompted outsiders and many teachers to call their school *multicultural*, a deeper and more critical, affirmative action-based multiculturalism (Torres, 1998) was absent.

[7]I have attended less to matters of race and racism in this particular article and point the reader to Malsbary (2014b).

References

Arnaut, K. (2012). Super-diversity: Elements of an emerging perspective. *Diversities*, *14*(2), 1–16.

Ben-Rafael, E., Shohamy, E., Hasan Amara, M., & Trumper-Hecht, N. (2006). Linguistic landscape as symbolic construction of the public space: The case of Israel. *International Journal of Multilingualism*, *3*(1), 7–30.

Blommaert, J. (2013). *Ethnography, superdiversity and linguistic landscapes: Chronicles of complexity*. Bristol, UK: Multilingual Matters.

Blommaert, J, & Backus, A. (2013). Superdiverse Repertoires and the Individual. In I. d. Saint-Georges & J.-J. Weber (Eds.), *Multilingualism and multimodality:*

Current challenges for educational studies (pp. 11–32). Rotterdam, the Netherlands: Sense Publishers.

Campano, G., & Ghiso, M. P. (2011). Immigrant students as cosmopolitan intellectuals. In P. Coates, P. Encisco, C. Jenkins, & S. Wolf (Eds.), *Handbook of research on children's and young adult literature* (pp. 164–176). New York, NY: Routledge.

Canagarajah, S. (2011). Translanguaging in the classroom: Emerging issues for research and pedagogy. *Applied Linguistics Review, 2*(1), 1–28.

Carter, P. L. (2010). Race and cultural flexibility among students in different multiracial schools. *Teachers College Record, 112*(6), 1529–1574.

Cekaite, A., & Björk-Willén, P. (2012). Peer group interactions in multilingual educational settings: Co-constructing social order and norms for language use. *International Journal of Bilingualism, 17*(2), 174–188.

Creese, A., & Blackledge, A. (2010). Towards a sociolinguistics of superdiversity. *Zeitschrift für Erziehungswissenschaft, 13*(4), 549–572.

Crenshaw, K. W. (1988). Race, reform, and retrenchment: Transformation and legitimation in antidiscrimination law. *Harvard Law Review, 101*, 1331–1387.

Derry, S. J., Pea, R. D., Barron, B., Engle, R. A., Erickson, F., Goldman, R., . . . Sherin, B. L. (2010). Conducting video research in the learning sciences: Guidance on selection, analysis, technology, and ethics. *Journal of the Learning Sciences, 19*(1), 3–53.

Erickson, F. (1985). Qualitative methods in research on teaching. In M. C. Wittrock (Ed.), *Handbook of research on teaching* (3rd ed., pp. 119–161). New York, NY: Macmillan.

García, O. (2011). *Bilingual education in the 21st century: A global perspective.* Malden, MA: Wiley-Blackwell.

Gibson, M. (1988). *Accommodation without assimilation: Sikh immigrants in an American high school.* Ithaca, NY: Cornell University Press.

Glick Schiller, N., & Salazar, N. B. (2013). Regimes of mobility across the globe. *Journal of Ethnic and Migration Studies, 39*(2), 183–200.

González, N., Moll, L. C., & Amanti, C. (Eds.). (2005). *Funds of knowledge: Theorizing practices in households, communities, and classrooms.* New York: Routledge.

Gordon, M. (1964). *Assimilation in American life: The role of race, religion, and national origins.* Oxford, UK: Oxford University Press.

Gorter, D. (Ed.). (2006). *Linguistic landscape: A new approach to multilingualism.* Clevedon, UK: Multilingual Matters.

Gutiérrez, K. D., & Rogoff, B. (2003). Cultural ways of learning: Individual traits or repertoires of practice. *Educational Researcher, 32*(5), 19–25.

Hayes-Bautista, D. (2004). *La nueva California: Latinos in the Golden State.* Los Angeles, CA: University of California Press.

Joppke, C. (1998). *Challenge to the nation-state: Immigration in Western Europe and the United States.* Oxford, UK: Oxford University Press.

Keogan, K. (2010), *Immigrants and the cultural politics of place: A comparative study of New York and Los Angeles.* El Paso, TX: LFB Scholarly Publications.

Kubota, R., & Lin, A. (2006). Race and TESOL: Introduction to concepts and theories. *TESOL Quarterly, 40*(3), 471–493.

Ladson-Billings, G. (2006). From the achievement gap to the education debt: Understanding achievement in US schools. *Educational Researcher, 35*(7), 3–12.

Lam, W. S. E. (2006). Culture and learning in the context of globalization: Research directions. *Review of Research in Education, 30*(1), 213–237.

Laoire, C. N., Carpena-Méndez, F., Tyrrell, N., & White, A. (2010). Introduction: Childhood and migration—Mobilities, homes and belongings. *Childhood, 17*(2), 155–162.

Lee, C. D. (2006). "Every good-bye ain't gone": Analyzing the cultural underpinnings of classroom talk. *International Journal of Qualitative Studies in Education, 19*(3), 305–327.

Malsbary, C. (2012). "Assimilation, but to what mainstream?": Immigrant youth in a super-diverse high school. *Encyclopaideia, 33*(1), 89–112.

Malsbary, C. B. (2014a). "It's not just learning English, it's learning other cultures": Belonging, power, and possibility in an immigrant contact zone. *International Journal of Qualitative Studies in Education, 27*(10), 1312–1336.

Malsbary, C. (2014b). "Will this hell never end?": Substantiating and resisting race-language policies in a multilingual high school. *Anthropology and Education Quarterly, 45*(4), 373–390.

Malsbary, C. (2016). Qualitative research in super-diverse schools. *International Journal of the Sociology of Language, 241*, 9–37.

Malsbary, C. B., Espinoza, S., & Bales, L. (2016). Liana's learning in a democratized classroom. *Pedagogies: An International Journal, 11*(3), 1–21.

Marcus, G. (1995). Ethnography in/of the world system: The emergence of multi-sited ethnography. *Annual Review of Anthropology, 24*, 95–117.

McCarty, T. L., Faircloth, S. C., Glass, G. V., Ladwig, J., Lee, S. J., McNaughton, S., . . . Villenas, S. A. (2014). As we embark on a new editorship: A statement from the *AERJ*-SIA editors. *American Educational Research Journal, 51*(1), 4–6.

Menken, K. (2010). NCLB and English language learners: Challenges and consequences. *Theory Into Practice, 49*(2), 121–128.

Meyer, M. A. (2001). Our own liberation: Reflections on Hawaiian epistemology. *The Contemporary Pacific, 13*(1), 124–148.

Miles, M. B., & Huberman, A. M. (1994). *Qualitative data analysis: A sourcebook of new methods* (2nd ed.). Thousand Oaks: Sage Publications.

Moll, L. C., Amanti, C., Neff, D., & Gonzalez, N. (1992). Funds of knowledge for teaching: Using a qualitative approach to connect homes and classrooms. *Theory Into Practice, 31*(2), 132–141.

Omi, M., & Winant, H. (2014). *Racial formation in the United States*. New York, NY: Routledge.

Orellana, M. (2009a, May). *From the borderlands to the center: Migrant youth as language brokers and the development of transcultural skills*. Keynote address, Migration and Memories Conference, London, UK.

Orellana, M. (2009b). *Translating childhoods: Immigrant youth, language, and culture*. London: Rutgers University Press.

Orellana, M. (2015). *Immigrant children in transcultural spaces: Language, learning, and love*. New York, NY: Routledge.

Orfield, G., Kucsera, J., & Siegel-Hawley, G. (2012). *E pluribus. . . separation: Deepening double segregation for more students*. UCLA: The Civil Rights Project / Proyecto Derechos Civiles. Retrieved from http://escholarship.org/uc/item/8g58m2v9

Paris, D., & Alim, H. S. (2014). What are we seeking to sustain through culturally sustaining pedagogy? A loving critique forward. *Harvard Educational Review, 84*(1), 85–100.

Pennycook, A. (2007). *Global Englishes and transcultural flows*. London: Routledge.

Portes, A. (2005, August). *To assimilate or not. . . and to what mainstream?* Paper presented for the Author Meets Critic meetings of the American Sociological Association, Philadelphia, PA.

Portes, A., Fernandez-Kelly, P., & Haller, W. (2005). Segmented assimilation on the ground: The new second generation in early adulthood. *Ethnic and Racial studies, 28*(6), 1000–1040.

Portes, A., & Rumbaut, R. G. (2006). *Immigrant America: a portrait.* Los Angeles: University of California Press.

Rampton, B. (2011). From "multi-ethnic adolescent heteroglossia" to "contemporary urban vernaculars." *Language and Communication, 31*(4), 276–294.

Rogoff, B. (2003). *The cultural nature of human development.* Oxford, UK: Oxford University Press.

Sleeter, C., & Grant, C. (1987). An analysis of multicultural education in the United States. *Harvard Educational Review, 57*(4), 421–445.

Torres, C. A. (1998). *Democracy, education, and multiculturalism: Dilemmas of citizenship in a global world.* New York, NY: Rowman and Littlefield.

Vertovec, S. (2007). Super-diversity and its implications. *Ethnic and Racial Studies, 30*(6), 1024–1054.

Vossoughi, S., & Gutiérrez, K. (2014). Studying movement, hybridity, and change: Toward a multi-sited sensibility for research on learning across contexts and borders. *National Society for the Study of Education, 113*, 603–632.

Manuscript received June 20, 2013
Final revision received August 23, 2016
Accepted September 14, 2016

American Educational Research Journal
December 2016, Vol. 53, No. 6, pp. 1522–1555
DOI: 10.3102/0002831216676568
© 2016 AERA. http://aerj.aera.net

"Just Let the Worst Students Go": A Critical Case Analysis of Public Discourse About Race, Merit, and Worth

Sabrina Zirkel
Santa Clara University & Mills College
Terry M. Pollack
Orinda Union School District

We present a case analysis of the controversy and public debate generated from a school district's efforts to address racial inequities in educational outcomes by diverting special funds from the highest performing students seeking elite college admissions to the lowest performing students who were struggling to graduate from high school. Widespread arguments against the proposed change emphasized the identification of highly successful students as "worthy" and others as "unworthy" of resources. Through an analysis of print and digital public texts, we identify a narrative cycle that informed public debate: (a) colorblind rhetoric, (b) academic performance is presumed to emerge solely from talent and effort, so (c) academic performance then becomes a measure of worth, and finally, (d) efforts to address racial disparities are "unfair." We argue that narratives identifying some students as worthy and others unworthy are highly influential in the outcomes of many educational policy and funding debates.

SABRINA ZIRKEL is dean of the School of Education and Counseling Psychology at Santa Clara University, 500 El Camino Real, Guadalupe Hall, Santa Clara, CA 95053; e-mail: *szirkel@scu.edu*. Her research interests focus on issues of race, ethnicity, and gender in schools, colleges, and universities using social identity theory, critical race theory, and anti-Blackness theory. Her recent publications can be found in *Educational Researcher, Teachers College Record, Race, Ethnicity and Education*, and *Urban Review*.

TERRY M. POLLACK is currently a fifth-grade teacher in the Orinda Union School District. Prior to that, she spent several years teaching in the educational leadership programs at San José State University and Mills College and teaching in elementary schools in the San Ramon Valley Unified School District. Her research interests include the perniciousness of narratives about race and ethnicity in schools, and her work has been published in *Race, Ethnicity, and Education; Urban Review; Multicultural Education*; and *Urban Education*.

KEYWORDS: race and education, merit, critical race theory, narrative theory

Those who endeavor to address racial inequities and injustices in education are often confronted with a stark and disturbing reality: These efforts are typically met with concerted, persistent, and often vociferous resistance. Again and again, we see this resistance in liberal as well as conservative communities (Brantlinger, 2003; Lee, 2005; Noguera, 2003; Noguera & Wing, 2008; Oakes & Lipton, 2002; Pollack & Zirkel, 2013). Resistance inevitably comes from the affluent parents of high-achieving children (Oakes & Lipton, 2002; Vaught, 2011), but it frequently comes from educators as well (Castagno, 2014; Gillborn & Youdell, 2000). This resistance can take many forms and can involve a variety of strategies—from the "White flight" from newly integrated schools in the 1950s and 1960s to modern, tech-savvy campaigns to change policy—but this resistance is nearly always framed as "simply" a concern about "quality" and "declining standards" (see e.g., Lee, 2005; Oakes, Wells, Jones, & Datnow, 1997; Pollack & Zirkel, 2013). Often, as in this case, the efforts to preserve resources utilized by the highest performing students from the most affluent families at the expense of resources for struggling, often lower-income students are successful. These efforts to protect funds for the highest performing students, then, become a central practice in the perpetuation of the racial, ethnic, and economic achievement gap in schools. In this article, we seek to uncover the narratives about race, merit, and worth that underlie many efforts to resist equity efforts in a wide range of educational settings.

We focus in on one such resistance effort by examining the narratives that informed public debates about a reform effort explicitly designed to address racial and ethnic disparities in educational outcomes. We analyze the public dialog and debate concerning a district proposal to move all required science lab instruction into the regular school day and to cease funding before and after school science lab instruction. The before and after school schedule was found to interfere with some students' ability to pass a required class and thus was harming their ability to graduate. This had a disproportionate effect on low-income students and thus students of color at this high school. Details about the proposed change and its rationale can be found below. Resistance to the reform came from parents and community members keen to protect the extra resources for high-achieving students who used the additional instructional time to take a large number of advanced placement (AP) science classes. The questions at stake were urgent and the money substantial.

The Story: Berkeley High, the "Achievement Gap," and the Science Lab Dilemma

Berkeley High School[1] (BHS) is the sole comprehensive public high school in Berkeley, California, and is racially, ethnically, and economically diverse. The school has been the site of much research and reporting on issues of race and the so-called achievement gap for more than 30 years (e.g., Noguera, 1994; Noguera & Wing, 2008). The city of Berkeley is a university town that sits within a geographic context that is highly racially and economically segregated and in which schools and districts vary enormously in terms of student test scores or other measures of how well students are learning (Noguera, 2003). The city is characterized by strong racial housing segregation, with expensive hills communities to the north and east and less expensive flatland communities in the south and west. Housing booms over the past 25 years have exacerbated existing economic disparities between racial and economic groups. Houses in the hills of Berkeley or in wealthier eastern streets at the time cost upwards of $1 million, but even small two-bedroom houses in the flatlands cost $500,000 or more. Even so, the city and BHS manage to maintain economic diversity through rent stabilization, public housing, and requirements that developers include below–market rate housing in their projects.

Berkeley High School has a large and persistent racial, ethnic, and economic achievement gap: Table 1 presents data from BHS's School Accountability Report Card (SARC) (Berkeley Unified School District [BUSD], 2013), showing racial, ethnic, and economic differences in academic performance at the time of these events. This racialized pattern has a longstanding and persistent history at Berkeley High (e.g., Noguera & Wing, 2008), and when Berkeley High was *once again* named the high school with the largest racial and ethnic achievement gap in California in 2009 (Barglow, 2009; Knobel, 2009), the BHS School Governance Council (SGC)[2] sought targeted ways to improve the educational outcomes of struggling students by focusing on specific barriers to student success. One particularly visible barrier, especially for low-income and African American and Latina/o students, involved the way in which science labs were scheduled at BHS.

The Science Laboratory Dilemma

Berkeley High had a longstanding commitment to provide additional instructional minutes for science education, more than virtually any other comprehensive public high school in the state. In the years leading up to these events, these extra instructional minutes had taken the form of required before- and after-school science labs. The district was proud of the extra instructional time it offered in science as this additional time allowed many high-performing students to complete several AP classes in science. However, the before- and after-school science labs were very poorly attended for a number of complex reasons, and this pattern was causing many poor students, typically students of color, to fail required science courses. This prevented them from receiving a high school diploma. Moreover, holding labs outside of the school day was a costly model because teachers had to be paid a salary supplement for the overtime work, and this limited the school's financial capacity to attempt other interventions.

Table 1

Berkeley High School Demographic and Student Achievement Information

	White	African American	Latino/a	Asian American	Native American	Filipino/Hawaiin/ Pacific Islander[a]	Multiracial	Unknown	Socioeconomically Disadvantaged[b]
Percentage of student body, overall	32.1	23.1	18.6	8.5	.3	1.0	9.1	6.3	29
Percentage scoring proficient or advanced on standardized STAR Test and CAHSEE (required for graduation)									
English/language arts	83	17	44	54	—[c]	41[a]	—	—	21
Science	79	22	39	54	—	—	—	—	29
Math	44	7	14	27	—	24[a]	40	—	12
Humanities/social sciences	71	12	27	39	—	—	53	—	17
CAHSEE pass rates	89	29	54	60	—	—	82	—	41

Source. Berkeley High School Accountability Report Card, 2013.

[a]Data reported here for Filipino students only; other students too few to report anonymously.
[b]Socioeconomically disadvantaged defined by State of California as meeting at least one of the following criteria: (a) Neither parent has a high school diploma or (b) student is eligible for a free or reduced-price lunch.
[c]The — in the table indicates that no data were reported, usually because there are too few students to report anonymously.

Over time, it became increasingly clear that the before- and after-school labs, designed to improve science learning, were actually *exacerbating* rather than *mitigating* the school's racial and ethnic achievement gap, leading the Governance Council to recommend eliminating the before- and after-school labs and integrating the laboratory curriculum into the regular class time. The rationale for this change was to: (a) increase access for *all* students to required science courses, (b) improve integration of the curricular content of the lab and lecture portions of the coursework, and (c) release funds to address what school leadership saw as an educational priority: improving the educational outcomes of the districts' large African American and Latina/o student populations. The decision would result in an overall reduction in the number of instructional minutes allocated for laboratory science classes but would free up a substantial amount of money used to pay science teachers for the additional work outside of the regular school day (for more detail, see Pollack & Zirkel, 2013). This decision was announced in December 2009 and was to be implemented at the beginning of the 2010–2011 school year.

Resistance and Resolution

A well-organized campaign to reverse the decision was quickly launched by a relatively small group of (predominantly White and more affluent) parents and teachers of the high-achieving students who had been especially well served by the before- and after-school labs. The before- and after-school lab arrangement gave this relatively small, elite group of students a clear competitive edge in admission to highly selective colleges. The additional instructional minutes had enabled BHS to get a waiver allowing students to take AP science classes without first taking the prerequisite high school courses (as is the case in most other high schools), thus enabling students to complete far more AP science classes than would be possible if AP students were required to take, for example, high school chemistry before AP chemistry as students are at other schools.

One especially effective aspect of this resistance was its successful engagement of several local news organizations. The story spread around the greater metropolitan area and to Southern California in a matter of days. Those opposed to the change effectively framed the way it was presented to news organizations and various education and science bloggers, who then presented the story as one in which "crazy," "liberal" school personnel were planning to cut science labs because "too many White students" were enrolled. This debate moved to a number of online comment boards with some comments containing a viciously racist tone. Over a period of months, the ideological battle over the proposed change reached a fevered pitch, with critics becoming increasingly vocal and vitriolic and some parents calling for the high school principal to step down. The district superintendent tried to tone down the public rhetoric by engaging the public in various ways, including a letter to the community pointing out that moving science labs to the regular school day could have many pedagogical benefits to off-set the loss of instructional time. The parents did not back down, however, and eventually Superintendent Huyett decided that a compromise with the parents and teachers of AP students was the only way forward. This plan kept the before- and after-school labs in place, but *only* for AP classes, thus ensuring that AP students retained additional resources. Some hoped this would calm the loud parental anger and angst about the proposal. Klein (2010) notes,

> a compromise proposal negotiated by Berkeley's school Superintendent William Huyett may help ease some of the anger generated by the original plan. . . . Huyett said in an interview that the "healthy debate" over the science labs issue was a good sign that the community cares a lot about the academic achievement of all of its kids. He only hopes now that things can cool down and a "less intense dialogue" will follow with a "focus on the issues."

By leaving intact the extra funding for AP science labs before and after school, three important changes resulted from the compromise: (a) The AP students retained the extra resources and additional instructional time they had always had; (b) to the extent that the before- and after-school labs were a problem for a subset of students (poor students, students of color), the barrier to their enrollment in AP classes was now codified with a formal barrier; and (c) the AP science teachers were able to keep their extra pay.

As two White women educators living in the area who are committed to creating racially just schools and colleges, we found ourselves shocked by both the tone of the debate and the near-complete silencing of voices in support of the proposal. As White women, we were also subject to vitriolic dialogs in a variety of situations in which others assumed that we "must see how stupid this is." We also taught educational leadership students struggling to make sense of similar parent dynamics as they were trying to make changes to address related needs in their schools. This article emerged from our exploration of that pattern, in which educational leaders propose changes to address what they see as injustices in their school's practices and affluent, privileged parents put up a successful resistance to those efforts. Our goal here is less to examine this particular change than to explore some of the narratives used to thwart these efforts to explore what these narratives reveal about how the public make meaning of efforts to create more equitable schools.

Conceptual Framework

Critical race theory (CRT), LatCrit theory, and the social construction of merit and worth provided the theoretical frames we used to guide our study.

We gave particular attention to CRT's conception of the ways that Whiteness is employed to access resources and material advantage (e.g., Crenshaw & Gotanda, 1995; Gillborn, 2008, 2010, 2013, 2014; Harris, 1993; Ladson-Billings, 2012) and the majoritarian narratives that support these efforts (e.g., Solórzano & Delgado Bernal, 2001; Solórzano & Yosso, 2002; Yosso, 2006).

Critical Race Theory

We highlight two ways that CRT can help us make sense of the public debates that we see in this case: (a) CRT's focus on the allocation of resources and educational CRT theorists' conceptualization of educational resources as both signals of and tools that protect advantage and (b) majoritarian narratives as a means by which differential access to educational resources is both explained and justified. A core insight from critical race theorists has been the role of race and racism in policing the allocation of resources. CRT theorists highlight the ways that racism is both centrally *concerned* with the distribution of resources and a *means* of distributing resources unequally. Education is no stranger to these processes (Bell, 1992; Gillborn, 2013, 2014; Ladson-Billings, 2012). Educational resources—be they teachers, curricula, technological, or physical—are seen as both scarce and highly desirable. In this present work, we examine public discourse about a proposed reallocation of a small portion of a school's resources from the most advantaged students to the least. CRT helps to illuminate the ways this specific debate is part of a larger struggle over access to advantage.

CRT has also highlighted the importance of stories as vehicles of racism (Bell, 1992). Solórzano and Yosso (2002; Yosso, 2006) coined the term *majoritarian narratives* to describe stories that reflect what Delgado and Stefancic (1993) refer to as the "bundle of presuppositions, perceived wisdoms, and shared cultural understandings persons in the dominant race bring to the discussion of race" (p. 462). Solórzano and Yosso note that because majoritarian narratives generate from a legacy of racial privilege, they are stories in which racial privilege seems "natural" (2002, p. 28). Such narratives support the status quo and explain, justify, rationalize, and support the existing pattern of racially unequal allocation of resources (see also Brantlinger, 2003; Castagno, 2014; Oakes & Lipton, 2002; Solórzano & Delgado Bernal, 2001; Vaught, 2011). In this article, we explore how majoritarian narratives inform debate about who "deserves" or "merits" financial support.

Social Construction of Merit

Baez (2006) reminds us that merit is a social construction whose meaning and purpose is determined by how it is used within schools and other institutions, and therefore, *merit practices* tell us much more about the society and institutions that use them than about the individuals who are subjected to them. The unchallenged acceptance and use of the concept of merit as a real and legitimate means for identifying individual *worthiness* formed a basic underlying assumption upon which the debate discussed in this article was staged and rationalized. "Merit" becomes an organizing principle for resource allocation by constructing and codifying some students as more "worthy" or "deserving" than others (see also El-Haj, 2006; Ladson-Billings, 2012; Oakes, 2008). Although merit is by definition a judgment of the observer and not an actual characteristic that resides within the person being judged, merit is made to appear legitimate because of how it is used to bind together meaning (deservingness) and utility (determining and measuring value or talent) in the service of a higher purpose (e.g., fairness, excellence, efficiency, and the health and prosperity of a democratic society) (Baez, 2006). Leonardo and Broderick (2011) highlight the way that "smartness" operates as an ideology and a form of property within educational settings. We build on these ideas to reveal how majoritarian narratives of smartness and merit render some students and their families as worthy and others unworthy of scarce educational resources (Castagno, 2014; El-Haj, 2006).

Overview

We analyze text and quotes from the public discussion that took place over a period of months in late 2009 and early 2010 concerning school officials' plans to cease funding before- and after-school science labs at Berkeley High School and divert those funds to struggling students in an effort to improve the overall high school graduation rate. The story and the subsequent debate about the decision was carried in every local newspaper, local and National Public Radio (NPR) talk shows featured the story and encouraged public debate about it, and it was picked up by media outlets across the state and even internationally. As a result, a tremendous amount of text was generated regarding the proposed change, its meaning, and public reactions to it. This text includes actual news stories, news headlines, content from blogs, public comments posted to websites, and letters to the editor. Using qualitative analysis, we examine this public discourse to reveal what we are terming a *narrative cycle of race, merit, and worth* in which stories are presented as arguments supporting the dedication of scarce educational resources to only the most high-achieving, typically affluent, students. Our purpose is to use this case study to explore how these narrative frames diverted attention away from the larger question of whether or not the schools in the district were serving all students adequately and instead focused attention on discussions of success, merit, race, and ultimately, worth.

Methods

We used a qualitative approach to analyze public comments made in reaction to the news stories. These comments are typically, though not exclusively, made anonymously, and as such they offer individuals an opportunity to express private views without concern for public sanctions (e.g., Bargh & McKenna, 2004; Zirkel et al., 2011). Given the social prescriptions about "race talk" in contemporary life (Myers & Williamson, 2001; Pollock, 2005; Villenas & Angeles, 2013), along with the public's increasing reliance on online platforms for news, commentary, and engagement in public debate on social issues (Purcell, Rainie, Mitchell, Rosenstiel, & Olmstead, 2010), we believe that anonymous online public forums represent an opportunity to explore ideas and perspectives that may not be openly expressed in other public contexts. We feel that this new public sphere in which issues of public import are discussed and debated (Taylor, 2004) represents an especially valuable source of data for examining views related to issues of race and equity, particularly because online environments can be so disinhibiting (Suler, 2004).

Materials and Sources

Through Internet searches using Google and Lexus-Nexus using the terms *Berkeley High School, science labs, science lab controversy*, and *Berkeley science labs*, we were able to find 39 news stories about the BHS controversy in print and/or online versions of 10 different news outlets, 4 of which identify as progressive papers (*East Bay Express, Berkeley Daily Planet, Berkeleyside*, and *Daily Californian*) and 6 as politically moderate or neutral (*San Francisco Chronicle, San Francisco Examiner, Contra Costa Times, Los Angeles Times*, KGO-TV Online, and *Berkeley High Jacket*). Readers posted 347 online comments in response to the BHS controversy. About one-third of these comments (123) were not identifying a position or were off topic.[3] Of the 224 news site comments that took a position on the proposed change, 188 comments (84%) were opposed to the change and/or critical of the underlying goal of the change (e.g., "So yet again, White students are forced to lower themselves instead of the minorities raising themselves. Praise multiculturalism!"). Thirty-six comments (16%) were in favor of or sympathetic to the proposed change (e.g., "I think this is a GREAT idea. White skin privilege rules our society and ought to be left at the door when students enter our public schools. As demographics change in our society, it is important that we are mindful of those changes and modify our curriculum accordingly").

In addition, 17 (non-newspaper) interactive websites posted a commentary or report on BHS's proposal to eliminate before- and after-school science labs. These include 1 politically progressive blog on huffingtonpost.com and 9 self-described conservative websites: Americanthinker.com, christopherfountain.com, freerepublic.com, humanevents.com, michellemalkin.com, thenewamerican.com, pajamasmedia.com, townhall.com, and eutimes.com. The remaining 7 websites focus on topics other than politics or express views that do not reflect one predominant political leaning. These are: techdirt.com and eGFI-k12.org (both focus on science and technology education), joanne-jacobs.com (general K–12 education), bayareaskeptics.org (science-based media analysis), richarddawkins.net (science-based critical thinking), perpetu-aofcarthage.blogspot.com (Anglican conservative), and creators.com ("Los Angeles media company that does content syndication, digital/audio publishing, and licensing content for film and TV"). We identified a total of 675 comments (including blog posts) on the BHS story posted to these websites, 129 of which were off topic or expressed no opinion. Of the 546 comments expressing an opinion, 19 (3%) were in favor of or sympathetic to the proposed change, and 527 (97%) were opposed to the change or critical of its goals.

Across both categories of sources, then, we identified 770 comments expressing an opinion, 715 of which were negative or opposed and 55 of which were supportive of the proposed change. Our focus from the start was exploring resistance to educators' change efforts, and so our analysis here is limited to the 93% of comments that opposed the change.

Data Analysis

Comments were downloaded from the Internet and stored electronically in folders to which each author had access. We awarded our attention on the negative comments because this was the largest category of comments by far. We began by reading and considering all 715 public comments opposed to the change. The process of analyzing the comments took place over a period of more than a year and was completed manually. Each author read through the comments repeatedly, and we met regularly to discuss what we were observing in the comments. We looked for themes that emerged in order to explore the extent to which our conceptual frameworks accounted for the totality of comments. Following Miles, Huberman, and Saldaña (2013), themes were identified, discussed, and collapsed into broader categories. Once a reasonable set of themes was identified, each author read through all comments and coded comments individually. Often, different sections of an individual comment might touch on more than one theme. We then came together to discuss our coding over many meetings covering several months. Our initial coding of material showed broad agreement: We agreed on 87% of the codes in our first round. Focusing on comments about which we differed, we found that we needed to revisit the codes we were using to more precisely understand what we were seeing. We discussed at length the precise meaning and labels of codes. Throughout this period, we discussed the codes with each other and with colleagues and made professional presentations of this work to ensure that our codes accurately reflected the comments reported. Having reworked the codes to more accurately reflect the data, we were in agreement on the coding of all comments, with a full understanding that qualitative data are inherently interpretive. The discursive themes that we identified were remarkably consistent across sites, with only a few exceptions: In a few cases, more liberal sources and more conservative sources presented different aspects of a similar theme (see the following). In identifying the four final themes noted in the following, we found that they formed a circular narrative. That is, rather than just four independent themes, we have identified what we see as a circular narrative in which each theme leads to the next to form a majoritarian narrative that both explains and justifies the allocation of greater resources to the most privileged students.

Narrative Themes Embedded in the Public Debate

Four narrative themes emerged from our analysis of the text and quotes from the public discussion that ensued in response to school officials' plans to cease funding before- and after-school science labs. These themes, typically presented as arguments, together form a circular majoritarian narrative that tells a story from a privileged perspective (Yosso, 2006) about who *deserves* access to scarce educational resources and who does *not*. We conceptualize these four themes as an explanatory majoritarian narrative and refer to them collectively as the narrative cycle of race, merit, and worth (see Figure 1). The four components of this narrative are: (a) *colorblind rhetoric,* in which it is argued that race and ethnicity should be ignored in discussions of educational policy; (b) *academic performance, deficit narratives, and the rhetoric of individual responsibility,* in which commenters emphasize that academic performance differences are to be expected and are grounded in individual effort, not social structures; and (c) *academic performance gaps render some students "worthy" and others "unworthy."* Because academic performance is linked primarily to individual or family effort, then we can use performance as a measure of "worth," and finally, (d) *equity efforts are unfair to White people*—therefore, any "change" proposal that gives resources to those who are doing less well in school must do so without taking away from the most "worthy" or it is inherently "unfair."

Colorblind Rhetoric

A strong colorblind rhetoric emerges in many of these comments, and it sets the stage for other parts of this narrative cycle. Many commenters to the different news stories argued that race "simply does not matter" and, in fact, suggested that all this focus on race was the "real" problem. Several people wrote about this general idea, including commenters to Right-wing blogs, Left-wing newspapers, and politically neutral science websites alike. For example, a person writes to the *East Bay Express*, a generally Left-leaning local weekly: "Try treating people as individuals and provide assistance on the basis of their individual abilities and needs instead of their skin color" (posted by zl1n0x on http://eastbayexpress.com, December 28, 2009).

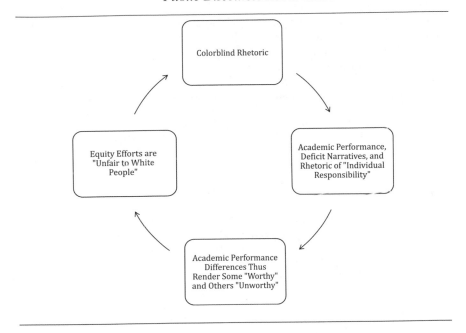

Figure 1. **Narrative cycle of race, merit, and worth.**

Similarly, another commenter to the relatively Left-leaning Huffington Post writes:

> The teachers and counselors [when I was in high school] were look-ing at the content of our characters. . . . There were plenty of debates about tracking back then. But as I recall, pursuing excellence won out, and no one had too much heartburn over race. (posted by ReasonIsMyReligion on http://huffingtonpost.com, February 20, 2010)

Bonilla-Silva (2006) has effectively argued that much colorblind rhetoric can and often does serve to support institutional racism, all while allowing the speaker to appear nonracist because he or she explicitly espouses equal-ity. In these comments, speakers suggest that "all" that needs to happen to ensure that all students have access to the highest quality education is to "treat them as individuals." This rhetoric harkens back to what King (1991) termed *dysconscious racism*, in which many White people have lim-ited and distorted understandings of racial inequality, uncritical acceptance of racial inequities, and therefore tend to espouse ideas suggesting that fair-ness and justice are served by ignoring issues of race and "treating everyone the same."

This colorblind view is not always innocuous or naively racist, however. Some comments reveal the more malicious aspects of a colorblind view in their sarcasm and assumptions. For example, another commenter to the local Left-wing weekly paper writes:

> If schools would stop pitting whites against blacks or brown against black, and instead pit the students against themselves and their own sense of acheivement [*sic*], maybe the cream would rise to the top and all the bickering would stop . . . no . . . wait . . . cream is white. Sorry. Never mind. (posted by "Mike Miller" on http://eastbayex press.com, December 27, 2009)

Similarly, a commenter on a conservative website posts:

> Wasn't the whole point of the de-segregation of schools in the U.S. to give all races the chance to learn together and enjoy the same opportunities? If student A (white) is smarter than student B (black), whose fault is that? (posted by Toronto Girl on http://pajamasmedia.com, January 15, 2010)

The colorblind rhetoric describing how things *ought* to be neatly morphs into an assumption that everyone *does* in fact have equal opportunity. For example, "Steven D" writes on Techdirt.com, a science-focused website:

> The issue with low and high performing kids is not one of race. The kids who get into AP classes apply for AP classes and voluntarily choose to be in science. NO ONE keeps any kid out because of racial bias. (http://techdirt.com, February 6, 2010)

In this version of the colorblind rhetoric, colorblindness is not presented just as an ideal but is presumed to describe "the way things are." This leads inevitably to the next theme we identify in these online comments—that differences in academic achievement are perceived to emerge solely from within individual students and families rather than from the structure, practices, policies, and curricula within schools.

Academic Performance, Deficit Narratives, and the Rhetoric of Individual Responsibility

The second theme that emerged from these public debates and discussions reveals a deep belief in immutable differences between individuals and groups—differences that are described as unchanging, often unchangeable, and that warrant different, separate, and largely unequal educational opportunities (Zirkel & Johnson, 2016). Commenters consistently insisted that large, persistent, group-based differences were to be expected and presumed "natural." Sometimes these ideas were expressed as frustration that schools would even try to address these disparities—since commenters frequently suggested that this was a futile effort and a waste of resources. For example, "Walled Lake Taxpayer" writes: "The black-white gap exists at EVERY school in the country, and is not a function of school structure" (http://sfexaminer.com, December 29, 2009).

The underlying assumption is that these racial disparities are perfectly normal *because* they are so pervasive and persistent throughout society. These comments reflect a whole category of public attitudes rooted in the uncritical acceptance of racial disparities in academic achievement as simply the "natural order" or things and therefore large performance differences should be both expected and accepted as unchangeable. This point was stressed repeatedly in an episode of the NPR show "Forum" that was devoted to this issue. A member of the BHS School Governance Council who voted against the change notes this in a larger quote about the diversity at Berkeley High:

> The achievement gap exists all over the United States. That is a tragic part of the past that is still with us today. . . . All our kids go to school together and that's part of what we love about living in Berkeley. . . . Kids at the top—many of them are children of academics—and we also have urban poor and a very diverse group of kids who are struggling and who didn't get a great start in school and those are the kids who are struggling at the bottom. (SGC member on Krasney, 2010)

By emphasizing that this is a problem of kids from different backgrounds coming together, she inadvertently de-emphasizes that these children are attending the same schools where some are "not getting a great start." "DavidShort" writes in response to a Left-leaning Huffington Post blog about these events:

> Of course there will always be a "gap" between students. There always have been, and always will be. There are those that are gifted, those that try harder, and those that just do not care. But working the system to "shrink" this gap is futile. (http://huffingtonpost.com, February 9, 2010)

These group-based performance differences are presumed to be "normal" and "natural" because they are explained through a large number of deficit narratives (Valencia, 1997, 2010; Valencia & Solórzano, 1997). School failure is attributed exclusively to a variety of internal attributes of those who are struggling. Students who are struggling (and sometimes their families) are described as lacking: They are lacking in "talent" (Bradbury, 2013; Gillborn & Youdell, 2000; Ladson-Billings, 2007; McKenzie & Scheurich, 2004), motivation, and effort (Bomer, Dworin, May, & Semingson, 2008; Foley, 1997) or suffering from a number of "cultural deficiencies" (e.g., Valencia, 1997, 2010) that prevent their succeeding in school.

Genetic Theories

Contemporary deficit thinking is a direct descendant of the blatantly racist, pseudo-scientific *genetic pathology theory* as described by Gillborn and Youdell (2000). It shares with it the same basic underlying assumptions about the immutability of group differences rooted in hereditarianism. Although discredited scientifically, such views maintain their hold on many members of the lay public as well as among a few controversial academics. Many of these comments, primarily posted to politically conservative websites, describe racial differences in disturbingly racist terms, and for that reason, they are difficult to read. These views are not generally given voice in public settings (Myers & Williamson, 2001)—however, the anonymous nature of many online comments allows for their expression (Bargh & McKenna, 2004; Suler, 2004). "Artichokegrower" writes: "The White and Asian kids will still find ways to study science. It's in their genes" (http://freerepublic.com, December 27, 2009). Others use discredited scientific evidence to support their views of the presumed genetic differences between students. The following comment was posted to the *San Francisco Chronicle*:

> Mr. Huyett [the District Superintendent] appears to be ignorant of the research and data concerning the fact that ethnoracial groups differ greatly in average levels of IQ. IQ-type intelligence is a highly heritable mental trait. Because Blacks and Hispanics have lower average IQ, they do worse than most Whites (and especially those Whites who inherited high-IQ genes from their brilliant Berkeley faculty parents). Similarly because high-caste Indians, Chinese and Jews tend to have higher IQs, they tend to do better than non-Jewish Whites. For the past 40 years, Arthur Jensen, UC Berkeley Professor Emeritus of Educational Psychology, has published research on ethnoracial differences in IQ-type intelligence. At UC Berkeley, Professor Jensen is one of their all-time most eminent scholars. (posted by rifraf on http://sfchronicle.com, February 21, 2010)

Still others used sarcasm to "flame" those who would think, naively, that racism played a role in these processes. "Morrisminor" posts on techdirt.com: "Math and science are so racist cause blacks and Hispanics sukk [*sic*] at it" (January 2, 2010). Such views, expressed here anonymously, are often hidden from publicly held policy debates, but we argue that they are still present— discussed in private settings and informing public opinion about how best to use public resources. Anonymous, online discussions are one of the few public places where one can hear such arguments being forcefully made.

Effort and Motivation

A second set of comments about the presumed cause for the group-based differences in performance concerns students' effort and motivation to succeed. Struggling in high school is seen as a *choice*—a choice not to spend time studying or a "choice" not to "care" about school. Because success in school is seen as wholly within the efforts and motivation of students, the emphasis here is on the presumed moral weakness of those who are not doing well. "Karen" posts on eastbayexpress.com: "Perhaps it's time to realize that those students who do poorly, do so mostly because it is their choice" (http://eastbayexpress.com, December 20, 2009). "Heymanoutdoors" explains the performance gap in this way: "So . . . the white kids choose to attend the labs and the 'non-whites' choose to find excuses not to attend" (http://abclocal.go.com/kgo/index, January 4, 2010). Another commenter also makes a similar argument, again suggesting that students have complete control over their performance: "Your outcome is the results of your inputs. Your life is what you make of it; it's not what someone gives you. If you want change, work at it" (posted by techies on http://sfchronicle.com, February 19, 2010). These comments were pervasive and represent a particular, culturally bound point of view that emphasizes personal control over all aspects of life (Savani, Stephens, & Markus, 2011). We see in many of these comments a very simplistic vision in which effort is the only factor that can explain group differences, along with the corresponding idea that those who do not "see" this "obvious" "fact" are simply being obstinate—a vision only made feasible if one believes that everyone has access to the same opportunities within a completely colorblind society.

> This decision mocks the concept of equality and transforms it into the rather specious notion of "equity." The author admits that the Berkeley school district has made great efforts to narrow the achievement gap between whites/asians and blacks/hispanics, yet the gap remains. Perhaps the district should conclude the obvious: blacks/hispanics are as intelligent as whites/asians but the former are not as willing to expend the effort in work and study. (posted by octavian on http://sfchronicle, February 13, 2010)

We see these and similar comments repeated regularly on a variety of sites reflecting a fairly broad political spectrum. Whereas comments invoking genetic differences were more common on conservative websites, an emphasis on students' presumed lack of effort was evident across a broader range of political contexts. In the narrative that emerges from these comments, motivation and effort are seen as emerging solely from within an individual and as "fixed" and easily discernable. That is, students are defined as either "motivated" or "unmotivated." Motivation and drive are seen as a characteristic of students' personality or self—as knowable, measurable, and most importantly, unchangeable (e.g., Rattan, Savani, Naidu, & Dweck, 2012)—and no allowance is made for the social context of motivation.

"Cultural" Deficits

Parents of struggling students came under tremendous criticism as well. "Uncaring parents," "a lack of value for education," and "laziness" were the most commonly cited cultural deficits used to explain group-based differences. Rather than blaming the effort of students, these commenters blame families for what are defined as "deficient" values, behaviors, or both. These explanations point to supposed cultural deficits as the source of the problem, that is, success is possible for every student but only if families would "care more," "try harder," and adopt the "right" values. The school itself is described as having little, if anything, to do with student performance. For example, Nancy, who called into the Forum radio show, speaks as a local: "I've lived in Berkeley since the '60s. My son went to Berkeley High and he has been teaching chemistry there for 11 years." She goes on:

> A lot of it has to do with the parents. Um, I know that it's very difficult to get a lot of those parents involved and I do not think that it is really all the school of even half the school's problem. It's just home situations and the school is doing an uphill battle. (Nancy on Krasney, 2010)

A commenter to the Huffington Post blog writes: "Life is unfair. Parents who care about their kids' education will work hard to ensure its quality" (posted by OldSchoolLiberal on http://huffingtonpost.com, February 10, 2009). Others make these arguments more aggressively: "The truth is that it's a hell of a lot easier and less politically incorrect to do away with classes than to hold minority parents and communities to task for not raising their damn children" (posted by Dark Helmet on http://techdirt.com, December 28, 2009). Another person writes:

> The so-called "achievement gap" is really a function of what I call "the concerned parent gap." Students who come from concerned two parent families will naturally score higher as a group than students who come from co-habitating or single parent families who do not have the time or resources to assist in the education of their children. (posted by martinfrosa on http://huffingonpost.com, February 10, 2010)

This blaming of parents was at times remarkably hostile and at other times extremely deterministic—often as deterministic as those who purported a "genetic" view of group-based differences. The following comment, posted by "Godric" on techdirt.com, is an example: "The adage is true: You can take them out of the projects, but you can't take the projects out of them. Sorry if this is not what you want to hear, but it is the truth" (December 28, 2009).

"Deprivation" and Other Deficits

Finally, some commenters laid blame for group-based performance differences on vague notions of "deprivation": Students of color who were not doing well were presumed to suffer from any number of "deprivations" that make their success impossible. Although such views did not presume that student failure emerged necessarily from genetic differences between groups or some presumed moral failing on the part of students, they were often just as fatalistic. These so-called deprivations were often ill-defined or ill-informed "moral panics" about so-called race-related social "pathologies." These moral panics inform the narrative of deprivation that permeates lay understanding of schools and students. Some, for example, exaggerated the social differences between White and Asian American students on the one hand and African American or Latina/o students on the other, suggesting White and Asian students are all the children of Nobel prize winners and African American and Latina/o students are "out-of-towner crack babies":

> The White and Asian students will continue to excel despite any efforts to ensure their failure on the part of the administration. The White students at BHS are the children of professors and intellectuals who are naturally bright and inquisitive. Many of the black students at BHS are the children of broken inner-city families in Oakland and Richmond who use a relative's address in Berkeley to fraudulently enroll their kids in a school that is at least better than the horrifying Oakland and Richmond schools. Will grown-up crack babies ever be able to compete with the children of Nobel Prize winners, regardless of the curriculum or how much money is thrown at them? Probably not. (posted by Old-school Berkeleyite on http://eastbayex press.com, February 4, 2010)

(In point of fact, the academic outcomes of Asian American students at Berkeley High are highly mixed and represent the diversity of Asian American experiences, as seen in Table 1; BUSD, 2013.)

These perspectives are disturbing in their fatalism. These social and economic patterns are not seen as something that can be addressed through, perhaps, access to specialized resources, such as the expensive professional tutors that are available to more affluent students. Instead, the issues are seen as somehow leading these students to be "unsalvageable"—regrettably perhaps, but "unsalvageable" nevertheless:

> The main issue of concern [is] the diversion of limited resources from one use to another for the sake of addressing the achievement gap. I would add that much of the frustration may stem from the concern that this diversion will likely, in the end, do little to alter the achievement gap. I believe schools have, in general, very limited power to address all the psychological and emotional challenges that students from disadvantaged backgrounds must overcome in order to excel. (posted by jy177 on http://berkeleyside.com, December 30, 2009)

Together, these models of group-based differences frame those differences as deeply embedded within students and their families and remarkably resistant to change. Across a broad political spectrum, we see commenters suggesting that for various reasons—genetic, moral, cultural, or economic—students who are struggling, poor students, and/or students of color who are not doing well are "beyond help." Large, group-based differences in performance are described as "natural" and expected, and fatalism pervades all of the explanations offered for why some students are doing well and some are not. This pessimism about schools' ability to have any influence on student outcomes—either because it is up to students and families alone to shape student outcomes or because some students "can" and some "cannot" leads to a social construction of some students as "worthy" and others "unworthy" of resources and attention.

Academic Performance Gap Renders Some Students "Worthy" and Others "Unworthy"

The debates expressed in this case example, like many in public discussions of education, are about how to allocate scarce resources, and ultimately these become conversations about which students and families are worthy and which are unworthy of these resources. Conversations move quickly from the initial equity concerns of the Governance Council (how best to allocate scarce resources and serve the greatest number of students) to questions about which students are "deserving" of these scarce resources and conversely, who is not. Many members of the public construed the proposed change as moving funds from "good," "motivated," "hardworking," "successful" students and giving them instead to "delinquent," "uncaring," "lazy," "failing" students. In this formulation, student success and student character are inextricably linked (for the persistence of these ideas in modern times, see Zirkel & Johnson, 2016).

This argument flows naturally to the next step in the narrative cycle we articulate in this article: that some students are *worthy* of time and investment (because of their talent, motivation, and effort) and others are *unworthy* (because of their lack of the same). This position is articulated by "Seanx," whose post to the Left-leaning *East Bay Express* forms the basis of this article's title: "It is time to just let the worst students go. With state and local budgets destroyed, it is time to save those worth saving. Regardless of race. Hurting the good students is obscene. And very possibly criminal fraud" (December 27, 2009). "Seanx" is not alone in his thinking. Several other people add similar comments to this and other publications running this story. "Tickyul" writes:

> The top 10 percent in this school are the ones who will make great advances for this country. . . . The biggest dollars should be poured into the brightest students, not the dummies or even the average

students. Take money away from the smartest and waste it on dumb-ells, not a good idea. (http://eastbayexpress.com, December 28, 2009)

Similarly, Nancy, the mother of a Berkeley High graduate who blamed the "parents of those kids" for their struggles, continues that "cutting the science labs for achieving students who really need this background in order to achieve in college is terrible" (Krasney, 2010). "NickEdee," another commenter to the same publication, articulates succinctly the way these two perspectives are linked. He argues that those who are not succeeding are not worthy of investment because they can never succeed:

> Whatever, they can try to knock the good students down as much as they want. It won't work. The dumb kids will still be dumb and the smart kids will still be smart and go on to have happy and successful lives. The crappy kids with their crappy parents will still be crappy. (http://eastbayexpress.com, December 28, 2009)

The anger in these comments is palpable and highlights the emotionally charged nature of the debate. Conversations about the allocation of resources are rarely dispassionate. Even so, many of these comments were particularly ugly, and the previous comments are only a few that indicated extreme levels of contempt and even disgust for students who were not performing well in school. For example, "Sycion" writes: "You people are making this overly complicated. Boot out the blacks/Hispanics and the problem is solved" (http://techdirt.com, January 3, 2010), and "VB-Pirate" suggests that

> If the underachievers can't hack the curriculum then put them on the short bus and put them in special education classes where they belong. But "DON'T" inhibit those students who are capable of achieving great things because the underachievers can't hack the curriculum. (http://techdirt.com, December 31, 2009)

Several commenters (posting to both mainstream and conservative websites) used particularly insulting language to express their opinions of students that they see as not just undeserving of public resources but also unworthy of basic human concern; for example: "Keep catering to the thug and (c)rap 'culture' and see where it gets the nation!! Usually those 'struggling' students are those who refuse to learn and disrupt the educational process for those who do want to learn" (posted by j davis on http://sfexaminer.com, January 4, 2010).

Equity Efforts Unfair to White People

The final narrative theme that we identify consists of a set of arguments suggesting that efforts to address racial equity in school are inherently unfair and ill-conceived because they redirect money from hardworking, successful, "worthy" students and direct them toward the needs of lazy, unsuccessful, "unworthy" students. Within these comments, we see two different aspects of the idea that efforts to address the racial achievement gap are inherently "unfair." One set of comments centers on the idea that efforts to divert funds to support struggling students are naïve, ill-conceived, and tantamount to "the pursuit of mediocrity." The second set of comments more explicitly state that these efforts are "unfair" and "anti-White."

Addressing Racial Inequities "Naïve and Ill-Conceived"

On a wide range of websites carrying this story, commenters routinely made the argument that the school's efforts to address the extensive and enduring racial achievement gap were naïve and ill-conceived and that the change proposal itself reflects a widespread and even deliberate "dumbing down" of American society. This point was made with remarkably similar language across websites and political communities—from the Left and the Right. For example, "Mary Eisenhart" writes: "So everyone's education should be dragged down to the level of the least successful? I don't think so. That's obscene" (http://eastbayexpress.com, December 23, 2009). "FMFDOC6" writes: "Rather than pursue excellence, we have chosen to pursue mediocrity; make everyone equally stupid!" (http://eastbayexpress.com, December 28, 2009). Another version of this comes from "san fran": "It seems to me that the advocates of 'social justice' are going beyond their usual promotion of mediocrity" (http://eastbayexpress.com, December 31, 2009). There were dozens of comments that made this point—it was in fact one of the most frequent points made in the comments.

Across a wide variety of websites, commenters also argued that redirecting resources in an attempt to raise the achievement of underperforming students is tantamount to punishing the more "deserving," high-achieving students. For example, the following comments were posted in local, politically moderate online newspapers: "Cutting off the legs of white children does not make black kids taller, but I do understand that it makes Liberals feel better to say that at least there will be less gap between the two" (posted by Bernie from Planck's Constant on http://berkeleyside.com, December 28,2009), and "It is unconscionable to penalize the academically inclined and motivated students because other students aren't doing as well as they are" (posted by hadji1966 on http://sfchronicle.com, February 21, 2010). Strikingly similar comments were posted to conservative websites; for example: "But if closing the achievement gap is what counts, the plan makes sense. After all, the gap can be closed by harming the more successful group, even if no benefits accrue to the less successful group" (posted by Don Bemont on http://joannejacobs.com, December 28, 2009), and "Unsaid (and unsayable in politically correct speech) in this debate is the obvious. If classes are open to all students, why should those students who choose the harder classes be punished in the name of students who did not choose to work as hard" (posted by "Ed Roger Hedgewick" on http://HumanEvents.com, January 29, 2010). These comments are reminiscent of those seen in response to other efforts to create greater educational equity, in which such efforts are feared to "bring down" successful students (e.g., Castagno, 2014; Lee, 2005; Oakes et al., 1997; Oakes & Lipton, 2002; Vaught, 2011; Welner & Burris, 2006).

Addressing Racial Inequities "Unfair" and "Anti-White"

Many of those commenting on these stories argued that the efforts of Berkeley High School to realign their science curriculum to meet the needs of students who were not doing well under the current system were not "fair." Appearing on the Forum radio broadcast, a member of the School Governance Council who had voted against the proposed change first expressed her surprise that far fewer Black and Latinx youth were taking lab science. She then dismisses educators' assessments of why that might be and instead changes the way we should frame "fairness":

> We really need to put this in context. Berkeley has a ten-year history of giving a lot of support to science and the parcel tax is the money we are talking about for this specific issue today. It is a parcel tax, and what that means is the people with the biggest houses in Berkeley are paying the highest parcel tax. (Krasney, 2010)

Others saw this effort as part of a "widespread" pattern of "discrimination against White people" that can be seen in many areas of society. These comments were especially prevalent on more conservative websites. "Just making sure. . . . It's OK to discriminate against whites, but bad to discriminate against blacks" (posted by "Mattm" on http://michellemalkin.com, January 1, 2010). "Marsh" writes: "[This is] the work of you leftist diversity mongers who think it's perfectly ok to discriminate against White people in the pursuit of 'diversity'" (http://pajamasmedia.com, January 15, 2010). Within this context, several people drew parallels between the overrepresentation of African Americans in sports on the one hand and science labs that educators had decided were not serving the needs of many students of color on the other. In drawing these parallels, commenters are implying that there is no difference in terms of educational or social benefit between students' participation in extracurricular athletic programs and academic subjects required for graduation. For example, "wingfat" writes: "Can they stop Basket Ball [sic] because no whites are taking it? No . . . so how do they do this . . . super lame" (http://techdirt.com, December 28, 2009). Another commenter, "Wrath of God," went to the trouble of investigating the racial makeup of sports teams at Berkeley High School:

> Just went to the [school newspapers'] website to check out the foot-
> ball and basketball programs. 3 or 4 token whites on the fb team and
> not a single white face on the bb team. I'm sure in the interest of
> diversity they'll be cutting those programs as well. (http://pajamas
> media.com, January 15, 2010).

Similarly, "BJ" writes: "I guess we had better get rid of the NBA. It's far too
black. That's discrimination against white people. Oh wait, I forgot. It's okay
to discriminate against white people" (http://thenewamerican.com, January
9, 2010).

Many of these comments were vicious or sarcastic in tone, as seen previously. Some were extreme in their arguments, including calling those who
proposed this policy change Nazis. "Foxtrot1" writes: "The administrators
demonstrated one thing, and that is that they are anti-White. They and the
authors of this [newspaper] article display the same attitude as the Nazis
and their obsessive genocidal ambitions targeting one group" (http://east
bayexpress.com, December 27, 2009). Others stated that these efforts were
part of an anti-White conspiracy, arguing that similar attention is never given
to the "needs" of White students and that White students are in fact "under
attack." "Civilwar2" argues: "Perhaps it's time for the White students to
demand a culturally sensitive curriculum that meets their cultural needs.
Like lab" (http://michellemalin.com, December 27, 2009). "RCL" states,
"When I left [Berkeley High School], the White kids were thinking of forming
a European Culture Club, clearly a reaction to feeling put upon by all the
other race oriented clubs out there" (http://pajamasmedia.com, January
18, 2010). "Moira" writes: "MOST OF THE FEEL-GOOD CLASSES ARE
DESIGNED TO FOSTER 'WHITE GUILT' WHICH IS AN ATTACK ON
WHITE STUDENTS" [capitalized in original] (http://pajamasmedia.com,
January 15, 2010). Finally, "spqr," writing on the more Left-leaning *East
Bay Express*, simply makes the direct claim: "Anti-racist is code for anti-
White" (http://eastbayexpress.com, December 27, 2010).

These comments reveal a tremendous amount of anger and frustration
with what are perceived to be policies and practices that somehow denigrate
or ignore the "needs" of White students in favor of the needs of students of
color. Institutional racism is neither understood nor given consideration.
Emerging from, and indeed building on, the logical progression of narratives
we discuss previously, this perspective leads naturally back to where we
began; that is, schools *ought* to be "colorblind." To the extent that school
personnel attend to race at all, the narrative goes, it is only to the detriment
of White people and to serve as an "artificial" raising of "other" students by
"lowering" White students. As these arguments unfold, we see a narrative
cycle that serves to protect White property and White interests. Any efforts
that question White students' entitlement to disproportionate educational
resources are ultimately deemed "reverse discrimination."

General Discussion

In this public discourse about the proposed BHS lab schedule change, we have identified several themes that together form what we refer to as a narrative cycle of race, merit, and worth. These themes build on each other to tell a story that forms a circular argument in which a particular way of understanding schools and the people in them is articulated. The arguments that form this narrative cycle represent a social imaginary—an understanding of the way the world works—one that simultaneously *emerges from* and *reinforces* a perspective that places tremendous value on ideals of individual agency and individually based models of talent, intelligence, effort, merit, and worth in educational settings. For this reason, the narrative cycle of race, merit, and worth represents a compelling explanatory story that renders alternative ideas and counternarratives invisible or implausible. Through implicit assumptions about the fixed nature and exclusive role of constructs such as *talent* and *effort* in learning and achievement, as well as explicit ridicule of ideas suggesting that school policies and practices can play a role in these outcomes, the narrative presented by these arguments suggests educators play no part in student motivation or outcomes. Such narratives actively endeavor to inhibit the social change and equity-oriented efforts of educators and instead blame individual students and families who are identified as undeserving and unworthy of educational resources.

Narratives, or Stories, as Carriers of "Social Imaginary" in Policy Debates

We are calling the cycle of themes identified here a narrative because the set of individual discursive themes or arguments link together to form a story—a story leading from an abstract idea (a "colorblind ideology") through a series of events with heroes ("successful," "hardworking," "motivated" students and their families) and villains ("unsuccessful," "lazy," and "unmotivated" students and their families and those who want to "reward" them) and concluding with a moral lesson about students and families and how schools should operate that leads right back to the abstract ideology of colorblindness. We argue that the narratives embedded within the comments presented here form a way of building an argument.

Narratives are a fundamental component of the way we think about and understand the world around us, and they form a central component of our cognitive processing of information. They are a means by which we communicate social imaginaries with each other (Taylor, 2004). By encoding implicit, often unexamined ideas, narratives form a means by which we can communicate understandings of how the world works in ways that would otherwise be difficult to articulate and communicate (e.g., Bonilla-Silva, Lewis, & Embrick, 2004; van Dijk, 1993). The story presented here is different than other stories that *could* be told—indeed than other stories that likely *are* told—in different social circles wherein different social imaginaries prevail. Represented here is a majoritarian narrative (Solórzano & Yosso, 2002; Yosso, 2006) that represents a particular point of view. We would encourage educational leaders to attend to stories—and to produce and highlight counterstories to these majoritarian narratives (see also Pollack & Zirkel, 2013; Zirkel et al., 2011). Although we cannot know the race or ethnicity of individual speakers, the people speaking here takes the *perspective of* the White middle-class or affluent parents who often wield enormous and disproportionate influence on schools and school policy (see e.g., Lee, 2005; Noguera & Wing, 2008; Oakes et al., 1997).

The study of the influence of narratives in policy debates forms an area of scholarship within public policy (e.g., Roe, 1994; Shanahan, McBeth, & Hathaway, 2011). Stories form much of the basis on which individuals both *make* arguments about policy and *make sense of* arguments about policy. Narrative policy analysts remind us that those who employ narratives typically prevail in policy debates as compared to those who put forward only abstract arguments (Shanahan et al., 2011). Similarly, sociologists have also highlighted the role that "stock stories" can play in politics and policy—framing debates by defining how groups of people are seen (see e.g., Skeggs, 2011). These stock stories need not be true (think Reagan's "welfare queens") or even consistent: Gillborn (2010) highlights two different conservative narratives about the White working class in Britain that existed simultaneously and were deployed in different contexts (White working class as victim of immigrants and White working class as degenerates and a threat to society). Counterstories, as CRT suggests, offer additional insights into how stories can powerfully be used to help educators frame the issues as they see them (Yosso, 2006). We see this pattern here—those arguing in favor of the change often appealed to abstract principals, whereas those opposed relied on narratives (majoritarian narratives) and prevailed.

In presenting a narrative of individual responsibility for the outcomes of one's life, the stories that undergirded the BHS debate were shaped by a social imaginary consistent with that of many who ultimately chose to support the concerns of AP students and their families, including school board members, district personnel, and teachers in the school. Gillborn and Youdell's (2000) insightful ethnography of two British secondary schools illuminates the way that even educators who wish to espouse a perspective of human potential and the power of teaching to transform young people often reveal deeper beliefs that some students "have it" and some just "do not." Bradbury (2013) demonstrates the same with teachers of very young students. Such views are pervasive in educational settings and undermine effective change efforts.

The Implicit and Explicit Influence of Neoliberal Models of Choice and Agency

Social constructions of merit in the United States is informed by culturally bound ideologies of individual agency and control in which individuals are seen as entirely responsible for their fate. Walkerdine (2003) refers to contemporary constructions of the individual as the *neoliberal subject*—in which individuals are construed as the sole architects or authors of themselves and their lives ("entrepreneurs of the self"). The work of Markus and her colleagues reveals that this ideology of individual agency and control represents a specific cultural frame—a frame that is primarily Western, White, and middle class (Savani et al., 2011; Stephens, Markus, & Fryberg, 2012). Conceptions of individual agency permeate the public narratives told about students of color and their families, here and elsewhere (e.g., Castagno, 2014; Lee, 2005; Vaught, 2011). In this article, we pay particular attention to the ways that some students (and their parents) are seen as "good" workers and "entrepreneurs of the self," while others are constructed as "bad" workers and "entrepreneurs" who do not take appropriate responsibility for their self-construction (Savani, Markus, Naidu, Kumar, & Berila, 2010; Walkerdine, 2003). This fits with what Taylor (2004) identifies as a core component of a *modern social imaginary*—seeing oneself as the primary influence on one's life. Within this frame, people are each individually responsible for making their own choices, and therefore, success and failure are seen as expressions of individual effort and talent. This *social imaginary* fits with a particularly Western view that only some people can be highly intelligent (Rattan et al., 2012), and therefore it is presumed to be most effective to target resources to those who can achieve the most.

We argue that the ideals of individual agency and control expressed in the narrative we have identified run so deep in American society and in the middle-class American psyche that educators themselves often abandon professional ideals about the role of educators and education in forming students' educational outcomes when they hear such arguments. Although much of the work of educators is based on the understanding that what happens in schools matters for young people and their lives, neoliberal ideals about personal talent, effort, and responsibility are so deeply and often implicitly held that educators themselves are often struck silent in the face of such arguments. In the case presented here, we saw a broad array of people from a range of political viewpoints argue fervently and consistently that student participation in advanced science classes and performance in science generally was *in no way* influenced by policies or pedagogies in the classroom. Educators' response to such critiques was largely silence. A few attempts were made to push back against the narrative embedded within the kinds of arguments presented here: The Berkeley Unified superintendent (Huyett, 2010) and school board president (Hemphill on Krasney, 2010) argued strongly that required labs for core academic courses should not happen outside of the school day, and a BHS teacher called in to voice support for the students the change was designed to support (Phillip, on Krasney, 2010). Very rarely, however, did members of the public voice support for the proposed change in any venue.

Theories of Ability and Motivation as Fixed and Known

The perspectives presented in these online comment boards point to a strong belief in both ability *and* motivation as *fixed* and *knowable*: fixed in the sense that each person has a certain amount of immutable talent, ability, or motivation and knowable in the sense that these individual characteristics can be measured and assigned value in some real and meaningful way. These characteristics, then, are seen as attributes of the students rather than as emerging from some interaction between individual students and their social environment. Based on their degree of academic success in school (i.e., test scores and grades), students are presumed to be either talented or not, motivated or not, and within the dominant narrative, these characteristics are not seen as something that are or can be influenced or developed by schools. This view stands in contrast to other perspectives from different cultural traditions in which many are seen as having the potential to become highly intelligent (for South Asian views, see Rattan et al., 2012), a view that would be consistent with a very different plan for allocating educational resources.

Pervasive assumptions, embedded within these comments, that students' motivation and effort were also relatively fixed capacities were surprising and disturbing. We repeatedly saw students' level of motivation described as a core attribute of students that schools and teachers can have little hope of influencing. The view expressed in this narrative is one in which student motivation comes from either within the student or perhaps from parents, but in either case, commenters seemed to see little opportunity to influence it. Viewing motivation as a fixed capacity seems even more potentially damaging to students than viewing intelligence that way. It is this conceptualization of motivation as a fixed attribute of the student rather than the outcome of a complex interplay of students and schools, curriculum, pedagogy, opportunities, student, and teacher relationships and expectations that leads to the construction of motivation as a *moral* judgment (i.e., some students *care* about education and bettering themselves, and some *do not*).

Limitations: A Note on Method

We wish to explore and discuss the strengths and limitations of our approach to studying public discussions. We do not mean to suggest that in analyzing public conversations that take place on newspaper comment boards we are observing the full range of views on a given issue. Undoubtedly, there are a number of selection factors at work—in terms of who reads particular media accounts online, who has access to the technology to post their views, who feels enough a part of a given community to contribute to the conversation, and finally, who has the time and inclination to do so. There is no question that all views or perspectives are not encapsulated in these comments. However, we argue that the perspectives offered on these comment boards are not those of people whose opinions are far removed from routine, mainstream, and conventional views. Public comment boards are becoming an increasingly mainstream way for members of the lay public to have debates and discussions about issues of concern. As technology becomes more ubiquitous, increasing numbers of people are participating in this process. A recent study by Purcell and her colleagues (2010) highlights the widespread and growing engagement with social and news media as a means of engaging in public debates, engagement that is beginning to reduce the long discussed *digital divide* in Internet use (Smith, 2014). Taylor (2004) described online public forums as the public sphere of our time.

There is no question that the tone of the anonymous online comments was certainly less civil and more vitriolic than comments made in less anonymous venues, but the sentiments expressed were similar to those that were expressed in other settings. The anonymous nature of these online comment boards had, we believe, a disinhibiting effect (Bargh & McKenna, 2004; Suler, 2004). As Castagno (2014) and Pollock (2005) demonstrate, "niceness" in conversations about race can obscure actions that speak otherwise. These ideas were expressed more politely in school board meetings, radio show call-ins, and parent and teacher conversations with school leadership, but they were nevertheless expressed. Although neither of us is affiliated with the school district, we live and work in the area and were privy to many conversations about the proposed change in personal and professional circles. These conversations mirrored many of the comments here in content, if not in tone. Moreover, similar views about students' educational worth have been seen in other responses to reform efforts (e.g., Lee, 2005; Oakes et al., 1997; Wells & Serna, 1996; Welner & Burris, 2006).

Although we contend that the views expressed in these public comments are fairly mainstream, we also argue that they primarily represent the views of those whose children were benefitting from the status quo. In a very few instances, people made comments empathetic with students and families who were struggling with the current system. However, in no case did we see commenters identify themselves as students or families who were struggling. No one ever identified himself or herself as a student or the parent of a student who was failing this science class or in danger of not graduating. Many, however, stated that they felt "persecuted" for being White—or that certain students were being "persecuted" for being high achieving. In other words, a few people spoke *on behalf of* poor students or students who were struggling in school, but no one spoke openly *as* a member of those groups. Ours is a study of resistance to social justice change efforts—but the participation (or lack thereof) of parents of struggling students in public debates about their schools' policies is worthy of further study: What are the contexts in which parents of students who are struggling in school can and do speak for their own needs? In what ways do schools close off these opportunities? Others have highlighted the pattern we see here in many racially integrated schools, in which more privileged parents exert disproportionate influence and—intentionally or not—parents of color are silenced, discounted, or dismissed (e.g., Bailey, 2011; Lee, 2005; Lewis & Diamond, 2015; Lewis, Diamond, & Forman, 2015; Noguera & Wing, 2008). We urge educators and researchers to further explore these issues and to help school leaders think about how to better engage a broader participation among parents in debates and discussions about school policies and practices.

Implications for School Policy and School Change

We conclude with an exploration of a few of the implications of these findings for educational policy, the process of educational change, and educational leadership. First, we wish to highlight the importance of anticipating resistance to school change efforts—particularly school change efforts that do not conform to middle-class notions of individual agency and control. We do not suggest that changes that go against the majoritarian narratives of socially powerful parents should not be attempted—indeed, we believe it is often essential to do so. Instead, we suggest that school leaders would do well to know their audience and anticipate and prepare for resistance to certain ideas or policies.

We also wish to emphasize the importance of narratives as a means of framing policy decisions and suggest that the power of narratives in policy discussions and debates can be harnessed and deployed in educational policy change efforts. As we note previously, the narrative that underlies the cycle we articulate here is only one possible narrative that could be presented to frame this policy debate. Other narratives went unspoken: narratives about students juggling many competing demands on their before- and after-school time, of students struggling to engage with lab material that seems divorced from the core material presented in lecture portions of classes, of an out-of-date science curriculum that doesn't integrate lab and lecture in daily learning, of families struggling to get adolescent students up and ready for a 7:00 a.m. science laboratory, or narratives about school resources being lavished on the most wealthy, privileged, and otherwise well-supported students who want another AP class to improve their chances at the Ivy League competing for resources with students struggling to graduate from high school. These real, everyday lived experiences form the kinds of counternarratives that were rarely, if ever, presented but that could have illuminated issues raised by these events. Where were these other narratives? Compelling stories could have been constructed for public debate but were not. We suggest that debates about educational policies often take place between and among members of the middle class, and it is middle-class narratives—and often White middle-class narratives—that are presented, listened to, and understood. To the extent that educators and educational leaders are often White and middle class themselves, these narratives have a certain verisimilitude and explanatory power among educational policymakers, even if educators struggle to hold and maintain other narratives simultaneously. We encourage educators to examine the extent to which policy debates are centered on the social imaginary of the middle class and focus on majoritarian narratives at the expense of other perspectives or ways of making sense of what is happening in schools.

Summary and Conclusions

We analyzed a series of public debates about a proposed change of resource allocation to reveal a series of racialized pubic narratives that protect the extensive use of educational resources in support of affluent and successful students' efforts to gain admission to elite universities rather than divert that money to efforts to help more students graduate from high school. The racialized nature of this debate is revealing and plays an important role in shaping which students are seen as worthy of educational resources and which are not. We see the arguments that members of the public use to frame this debate as forming a narrative cycle. Building on deficit narratives about students of color and/or students struggling in school, this narrative cycle becomes a self-perpetuating and self-justifying circular argument in which schools are seen as fair, except when they try to address the needs of struggling students, and every effort should be made to help struggling students as long as it does not take resources away from the most privileged students. We believe that this narrative cycle or ones like it influence many educational policy debates, and we highlight its use here in an effort to shine a light on the destructive nature these narratives have for students, families, schools, and communities.

Notes

Sabrina Zirkel is grateful to Mills College for sabbatical research support during part of the time this article was in development.

[1] Berkeley High School (BHS) is named because this is an article about a publicly debated story where the high school name was used routinely in the materials to be discussed. Comments by other public figures who expressed views about the proposals (e.g., the Berkeley Unified superintendent) are also named because they were involved in the conversation as public figures. We chose to protect the identities of members of the public whose names were identified in documents because they were speaking as citizens and therefore would not necessarily expect to be cited and quoted.

[2] A group that included most of the BHS leadership team as well as several teachers and parents.

[3] Such comments, for example, focused on general criticism of the school administration unrelated to this issue or asked questions of clarification. This also included comments that were censored by the news site for inappropriate content.

References

Baez, B. (2006). Merit and difference. *Teachers College Record, 108,* 996–1016.

Bailey, F. (2011). *"Where are their parents?" Rethinking, re-defining, and conceptualizing African American and Latino parental involvement, engagement, and empowerment in schols.* (Unpublished doctoral dissertation). Mills College, Oakland, CA.

Bargh, J. A., & McKenna, F. R. (2004). The Internet and social life. *Annual Review of Psychology, 55,* 573–590.

Barglow, R. (2009, December 17). Plan to eliminate science labs stirs controversy at Berkeley High. *The Berkeley Daily Planet.* Retrieved from http://www.berkeley dailyplanet.com/issue/2009-12-17/article/34289

Bell, D. (1992). *Faces at the bottom of the well: The permanence of racism.* New York, NY: Basic Books.

Berkeley Unified School District. (2013). *Berkeley High School 2011–12 school accountability report card.* Berkeley, CA: Author.

Bomer, R., Dworin, J. E., May, L., & Semingson, P. (2008). Miseducating teachers about the poor: A critical analysis of Ruby Payne's claims about poverty. *Teachers College Record, 110*(12), 2497–2531.

Bonilla-Silva, E. (2006). *Racism without racists: Color-blind racism and the persistence of racial inequality in the United States.* Lanham, MD: Rowman and Littlefield.

Bonilla-Silva, E., Lewis, A., & Embrick, D. G. (2004). "I did not get that job because of a Black man . . . ": The story lines and testimonies of color-blind racism. *Sociological Forum, 19*(4), 555–581.

Bradbury, A. (2013). *Understanding early years inequality: Policy, assessment and young children's identities.* New York, NY: Routledge.

Brantlinger, E. (2003). *Dividing classes: How the middle class negotiates and rationalizes school advantage.* New York, NY: Routledge.

Castagno, A. (2014). *Educated in Whiteness: Good intentions and diversity in education.* Minneapolis, MN: University of Minnesota Press.

Crenshaw, K., & Gotanda, N. (Eds.). (1995). *Critical race theory: The key writings that formed the movement.* New York, NY: The New Press.

Delgado, R., & Stefancic, J. (1993). Critical race theory: An annotated bibliography. *Virginia Law Review, 79,* 461–516.

El-Haj, T. R. A. (2006). *Elusive justice: Wrestling with difference and educational equity in everyday practice.* New York, NY: Routledge.

Foley, D. E. (1997). Deficit thinking models based on culture: The anthropological protest. In R. R. Valencia (Ed.), *The evolution of deficit thinking: Educational thought and practice* (pp. 113–131). London: Falmer Press.

Gillborn, D. (2008). *Racism and education: Coincidence or conspiracy?* New York, NY: Routledge.

Gillborn, D. (2010). The White working class, racism and respectability: Victims, degenerates and interest-convergence. *British Journal of Educational Studies, 58*(1), 3–25.

Gillborn, D. (2013). Interest-divergence and the colour of cutbacks: Race, recession and the undeclared war on Black children. *Discourse: Studies in the Cultural Politics of Education, 34*(4), 477–491.

Gillborn, D. (2014). Racism as policy: A critical race analysis of education reforms in the united states and england, *The Educational Forum, 78,* 26–41.

Gillborn, D., & Youdell, D. (2000). *Rationing education: Policy, practice, reform and equity.* Florence, KY: Routledge.

Harris, C. I. (1993). Whiteness as property. *Harvard Law Review, 106,* 1707–1791.

Huyett, W. (2010, February 19). Equity drives science lab decision in Berkeley. *San Francisco Chronicle.* Retrieved from http://www.sfgate.com/opinion/openfo rum/article/Equity-drives-science-lab-decision-in-Berkeley-3272624.php

King, J. E. (1991). Dysconscious racism: Ideology, identity, and the miseducation of teachers. *The Journal of Negro Education, 60*(2), 133–146.

Klein, E. (2010, February 3). Berkeley science labs compromise? East Bay Express.

Knobel, L. (2009, December 8). BHS schedule shift rumbles on. *Berkeleyside.* Retrieved from http://www.berkeleyside.com/2009/12/08/bhs-schedule-shift-rumbles-on/

Krasney, M. (Executive Producer). (2010). *Berkeley High School Science Labs in Forum.* Francisco, CA: KQED Radio.

Ladson-Billings, G.(2007). Pushing past the achievement gap: An essay on the language of deficit. *The Journal of Negro Education, 76*(3), 316–323.

Ladson-Billings, G. (2012). Through a glass darkly: The persistence of race in education research and scholarship. *Educational Researcher, 41,* 115–120.

Lee, S. (2005). *Up against Whiteness: Race, schooling, and immigrant youth.* New York, NY: Teachers College Press.

Lewis, A. E., & Diamond, J. B. (2015). *Despite the best intentions: How racial inequality thrives in good schools.* Oxford, UK: Oxford University Press.

Lewis, A. E., Diamond, J. B., & Forman, T. A. (2015). Conundrums of integration desegregation in the context of racialized hierarchy. *Sociology of Race and Ethnicity, 1,* 22–36.

Leonardo, Z., & Broderick, A. A. (2011). Smartness as property: A critical exploration of the intersections between whiteness and disability studies. *Teachers College Record, 113,* 2206–2232.

McKenzie, K. B., & Scheurich, J. J. (2004). Equity traps: A useful construct for preparing principals to lead schools that are successful with racially diverse students. *Educational Administration Quarterly, 40*(5), 601–632.

Miles, M. B., Huberman, A. M., & Saldaña, J. (2013). *Qualitative data analysis: A methods sourcebook.* Thousand Oaks, CA: Sage Publications.

Myers, K. A., & Williamson, P. (2001). Race talk: The perpetuation of racism through private discourse. *Race and Society, 4*(1), 3–26.

Noguera, P. A. (1994). Ties that bind, forces that divide: Berkeley High School and the challenge of integration. *University of San Francisco Law Review, 29,* 719.

Noguera, P. A. (2003). *City schools and the American dream.* New York, NY: Teachers College Press.

Noguera, P. A., & Wing, J. Y. (Eds.). (2008). *Unfinished business: Closing the racial achievement gap in our schools.* San Francisco, CA: Jossey-Bass.

Oakes, J. (2008). Keeping track: Structuring equality and inequality in an era of accountability. *Teachers College Record, 110,* 700–712.

Oakes, J., & Lipton, M. (2002). Struggling for educational equity in diverse communities: School reform as social movement. *Journal of Educational Change, 3*(3 4), 383–406.

Oakes, J., Wells, A. S., Jones, M., & Datnow, A. (1997). Detracking: The social construction of ability, cultural politics, and resistance to reform. *Teachers College Record, 98,* 482–510.

Pollack, T. M., & Zirkel, S. (2013). Negotiating the contested terrain of equity-focused change efforts in schools: Critical race theory as a leadership framework for creating more equitable schools. *The Urban Review, 45*(3), 290–310.

Pollock, M. (2005). *Colormute: Race talk dilemmas in an American school.* Princeton, NJ: Princeton University Press.

Purcell, K., Rainie, L., Mitchell, A., Rosenstiel, T., & Olmstead, K. (2010). Understanding the participatory news consumer: How Internet and cell phone users have turned news into a social experience. Retrieved from http://www.pe winternet.org/2010/03/01/understanding-the-participatory-news-consumer/

Rattan, A., Savani, K., Naidu, N. V. R., & Dweck, C. S. (2012). Can everyone become highly intelligent? Cultural differences in and societal consequences of beliefs about the universal potential for intelligence. *Journal of Personality and Social Psychology, 103*(5), 787–803.

Roe, E. (1994). *Narrative policy analysis: Theory and practice.* Durham, NC: Duke Universty Press.

Savani, K., Markus, H. R., Naidu, N. V. R., Kumar, S., & Berlia, N. (2010). What counts as a choice? US Americans are more likely than Indians to construe actions as choices. *Psychological Science, 21*, 391–398.

Savani, K., Stephens, N. M., & Markus, H. R. (2011). The unanticipated interpersonal and societal consequences of choice: Victim blaming and reduced support for the public good. *Psychological Science, 22*, 795–802.

Shanahan, E. A., McBeth, M. K., & Hathaway, P. L. (2011). Narrative policy framework: The influence of media policy narrataives on public opinion. *Politics & Policy, 39*, 373–400.

Skeggs, B. (2011). Imagining personhood differently: Person value and autonomist working-class value practices. *The Sociological Review, 59*, 496–513.

Smith, A. (2014). *African Americans and technology use: A demographic portrait.* Retrieved from http://www.pewinternet.org/2014/01/06/african-americans-and-technology-use/

Solórzano, D. G., & Delgado Bernal, D. (2001). Examining transformational resistance through a critical race and LatCrit theory framework Chicana and Chicano students in an urban context. *Urban Education, 36*, 308–342.

Solórzano, D. G., & Yosso, T. J. (2002). Critical race methodology: Counter-storytelling as an analytical framework for education research. *Qualitative Inquiry, 8*, 23–44.

Stephens, N. M., Markus, H. R., & Fryberg, S. A. (2012). Social class disparities in health and education: Reducing inequality by applying a sociocultural self model of behavior. *Psychological Review, 119*, 723–744.

Suler, J. (2004). The online disinhibition effect. *CyberPsychology & Behavior, 7*, 321–326.

Taylor, C. (2004). *Modern social imaginaries.* Durham, NC: Duke University Press.

Valencia, R. R. (1997). *The evolution of deficit thinking: Educational thought and practice.* London: Falmer Press.

Valencia, R. R. (2010). *Dismantling contemporary deficit thinking: Educational thought and practice.* New York, NY: Routledge.

Valencia, R. R., & Solórzano, D. G. (1997). Contemporary deficit thinking. In R. R. Valencia (Ed.), *The evolution of deficit thinking: Educational thought and practice* (pp. 160–210). London: Falmer Press.

van Dijk, T. A. (1993). Stories and racism. In D. K. Mumby (Ed.), *Narrative and social control: Critical perspectives* (pp. 121–142). London: Sage Publications.

Vaught, S. E. (2011). *Racism, public schooling, and the entrenchment of White supremacy: A crtical race ethnography.* Albany, NY: SUNY Press.

Villenas, S., & Angeles, S. L. (2013). Race talk and school equity in local print media: The discursive flexibility of Whiteness and the promise of race-conscious talk. *Discourse: Studies in the Cultural Politics of Education, 34*, 510–530.

Walkerdine, V. (2003). Reclassifying upward mobility: Femininity and the neo-liberal subject. *Gender and Education, 15*, 237–248.

Wells, A. S., & Serna, I. (1996). The politics of culture: Understanding local political resistance to detracking in racially mixed schools. *Harvard Educational Review, 66,* 93–118.

Welner, K. G., & Burris, C. C. (2006). Alternative approaches to the politics of detracking. *Theory Into Practice, 45,* 90–99.

Yosso, T. (2006). *Critical race counterstories along the Chicana/Chicano educational pipeline.* New York, NY: Routledge.

Zirkel, S., Bailey, F., Bathey, S., Hawley, R., Lewis, U., Long, D., . . . Winful, A. (2011). Isn't that what "those kids" need? Urban schools and the master narrative of the "tough, urban principal." *Race Ethnicity and Education, 14,* 137–158.

Zirkel, S., & Johnson, T. (2016). Mirror, mirror on the wall: A critical examination of the conceptualization of the study of Black racial identity in education. *Educational Researcher, 45,* 301–311.

Manuscript received February 5, 2014
Final revision received September 2, 2016
Accepted September 14, 2016

American Educational Research Journal
December 2016, Vol. 53, No. 6, pp. 1556–1587
DOI: 10.3102/0002831216670510
© 2016 AERA. http://aerj.aera.net

Racial/Cultural Awareness Workshops and Post-College Civic Engagement: A Propensity Score Matching Approach

Nicholas A. Bowman
University of Iowa
Nida Denson
Western Sydney University
Julie J. Park
University of Maryland

Racial/cultural awareness workshops constitute a salient form of co-curricular diversity engagement in higher education. Although these workshops are generally quite short in duration (often no more than two hours), previous research suggests that workshop participation is associated with undergraduate civic growth. The current study uses multilevel propensity score matching analyses to explore whether racial/cultural awareness workshops during college are associated with a variety of civic outcomes six years after graduation. Using a 10-year longitudinal sample of 8,634 alumni from 229 institutions, diversity workshop participation is significantly and positively related to 10 post-college behaviors, attitudes/beliefs, and skills/tendencies. Moreover, these effects are consistent regardless of participants' race/ethnicity, gender, and institutional affiliation.

NICHOLAS A. BOWMAN is an associate professor in the Department of Educational Policy and Leadership Studies as well as the director of the Center for Research on Undergraduate Education at the University of Iowa, N491 Lindquist Center, University of Iowa, Iowa City, IA, 52242; e-mail: *nick-bowman@uiowa.edu*. He uses a social psychological lens to examine various topics in higher education, including college diversity, student success, college admissions and prestige, and methodological issues for studying college impact.

NIDA DENSON is a senior research fellow in the School of Social Sciences and Psychology at Western Sydney University in Australia. Her research interests include diversity and diversity-related initiatives, racism, educational contexts, campus climates, and faculty work-life balance.

JULIE J. PARK is assistant professor in the Department of Counseling, Higher Education, and Special Education at the University of Maryland, College Park. Her work examines race, diversity, and equity in higher education, with a particular interest in Asian American college students. Other areas of focus include social capital, affirmative action, and the educational benefits of diversity.

KEYWORDS: civic engagement, college diversity experiences, college students, post-college outcomes, racial/cultural awareness workshops

As colleges and universities work to support racially diverse student populations, a common question is how these schools can promote meaningful engagement around diversity-related issues. Such engagement is critical in order to reap the educational benefits of diversity (Gurin, 1999). Over the past couple of decades, universities have increasingly institutionalized diversity initiatives in curricular and co-curricular spaces (Smith, 2009). While fostering diversity through interpersonal interactions and the curriculum receives a great deal of attention, educators also seek to maximize learning outside of the classroom by fostering co-curricular opportunities for engagement with diversity issues. One such initiative found at many college campuses is the racial/cultural awareness workshop. These workshops vary in scope but generally include content or programming that helps broaden and challenge students' understanding of issues related to race/ethnicity, diversity, inequality, and/or privilege, among other topics. While the content of workshops can be critiqued as overly simplistic (by providing a "one-stop shop" for students to learn about complex topics), numerous studies have found positive outcomes associated with workshop participation (e.g., Antonio, 2001; Astin, 1993; Cole & Zhou, 2014; Vogelgesang, 2001).

Although these studies document the potential benefits associated with racial/cultural awareness workshop participation during college, it is unknown whether the efficacy of these programs extends beyond the undergraduate years. Do these workshops constitute an experience that challenges students while in school but fades away with the passage of time? Or might there be effects that persist beyond graduation? As educators seek to understand how different curricular and co-curricular diversity opportunities enhance student learning, it is important to understand whether the impact of various diversity initiatives continues after college. Few data sets that contain information about student experiences during college also follow up with students after graduation. Therefore, this article examines the effect of participating in a racial/cultural awareness workshop on numerous civic outcomes six years beyond college.

Diversity Workshops in Higher Education

Given the increasing diversity of U.S. institutions and the United States as a whole, the majority of college campuses offer some type of diversity workshop for their students and/or faculty (McCauley, Wright, & Harris, 2000). Diversity workshops are "a small group situation in which a number of students and a group leader or facilitator discuss diversity-related issues" (McCauley et al., 2000, p. 102). With the goals of improving intergroup relations and reducing intergroup bias, diversity workshops are sometimes referred to as racial or cultural awareness workshops, prejudice reduction workshops, multicultural workshops, pluralism workshops, anti-bias workshops, or intergroup dialogues (McCauley et al., 2000; Schoem, Hurtado, Sevig, Chesler, & Sumida, 2001).

While diversity workshops appear to be present on most campuses, there is surprisingly little research about the prevalence of diversity workshops in higher education, when and how students might participate in them, and what they entail. One study by McCauley and colleagues (2000) has addressed these issues in depth. The authors conducted telephone interviews with almost 300 administrators from a random sample of over 350 U.S. four-year institutions (79% response rate). Although conducted a while ago, this study provides a snapshot of diversity workshops in higher education at the end of the past century; a summary of some of the key results is provided in Table 1. Even then, almost three-quarters (73%) of institutions reported currently offering diversity workshops on their campus, with the vast majority (81%) of institutions reported having offered diversity workshops on their campus either currently or in the past. Most diversity workshops were open to all students whenever the workshops were offered (61%); however, a substantial minority (36%) were available only to first-year students, typically during first-year orientation. Almost half (42%) of institutions that offered workshops required students to participate. The duration of the diversity workshops varied considerably, ranging from 45 minutes to 120 hours (median duration was 2 hours). The size of the workshop groups also varied, ranging from 4 to 1,080 students (median size was 25 students). Even for workshops that contained larger groups of students, institutions often reported using small group discussions as part of the larger session. Many institutions used more than one type of workshop facilitator; staff were the most common leaders (72%), but students (55%), faculty (41%), and outside consultants (32%) also served these roles at many schools.

There was considerable variation in the activities conducted in the workshops, with many institutions reporting using multiple activities. At least 80% of institutions reported that their workshop activities consisted of some form of written information or handouts along with activities to facilitate intergroup contact such as sharing personal experiences with bias or discrimination and/or group exercises for exploring racial/ethnic group differences. At least half of the institutions reported using other methods, such as role playing, videos, skits, and self-discovery exercises. Fewer than half of the institutions used case studies, and less than one-fifth of the institutions utilized stress reduction exercises or computer-based learning. While diversity workshops can cover a broad range of issues, the most frequent topics examined problems experienced by various minority groups, and these often covered more than one topic. The majority of the workshops explored challenges experienced by racial/ethnic/cultural minority groups, ranging from 61% that focused on Native Americans to 89% that focused on African

Table 1
**Summary of College Diversity Workshop Characteristics
From McCauley, Wright, & Harris (2000)**

Characteristic	Percentage
When are diversity workshops offered?	
First-year orientation only	31
First year only	5
Open to all whenever given	61
Who leads the diversity workshop?	
Staff	72
Students	55
Faculty	41
Outside consultants	32
What training methods are used in diversity workshops?	
Participants sharing stories of their own experience with bias or discrimination	92
Group exercises for exploring ethnic differences	87
Written information on handouts	86
Personal contact with minority participants	82
Lectures	75
Discussion of actual campus incidents	73
Role playing or behavioral training	71
Videos	68
Skits	67
Self-discovery exercises	53
What is the length of the typical diversity workshop?	
1 hour or less	19
1.25–1.75 hours	30
2.0–2.5 hours	29
3.0-3.5 hours	9
4 hours or more	12
What is the size of the typical workshop group?	
14 or less	14
15–19	10
20–24	18
25–29	17
30–39	14
40–59	10
60 or more	17

Americans. Diversity workshops also explored issues for gays/lesbians/bisexuals (77%), Jewish students (72%), international students (70%), people with disabilities (67%), other religious groups (48%), women (44%), and general cross-cultural topics (28%).

Theory and Research on Racial/Cultural Awareness Workshops and Civic Outcomes

With the goals of improving intergroup relations and reducing intergroup bias, racial/cultural awareness workshops are narrowly tailored to promote civic growth at a critical developmental stage for college students. Drawing on a number of psychological frameworks (e.g., Piaget, 1971, 1975/ 1985; Ruble, 1994), Gurin, Dey, Hurtado, and Gurin (2002) posit that many college students are at a developmental stage in which they are forming their values and identities, so they are particularly open to growth associated with diversity experiences. Given that many students are often from racially and socioeconomically homogeneous backgrounds (Orfield, 2009; Orfield, Kucsera, & Siegel-Hawley, 2012), college campuses provide students with greater opportunities to be exposed to opinions and situations different from their own home environments, which are often incongruous with their preexisting stereotypes and worldviews. As a result, students typically seek to resolve this discrepancy, which they may do either by reconciling these interactions with their current beliefs and conceptions or changing their views to incorporate this new information.

Dovidio and colleagues (2004) provided a framework through which diversity-related activities, such as racial/cultural awareness workshops, reduce racial bias. They argue that diversity-related activities operate through exposing students to content-related knowledge and/or intergroup contact approaches. The purpose of exposing students to knowledge is to increase understanding and empathy toward others or to one's own role and responsibilities in creating social change, whereas the purpose of intergroup contact is to provide students with structured interactions between majority- and minority-group members. These diversity activities stimulate important mediating processes, which include cognitive aspects (i.e., regarding the ways that students think about others) and emotional aspects (i.e., regarding the ways that students feel about others); in turn, these affect students' civic development by increasing cultural awareness and reducing racial bias.

Some research has directly examined the link between racial/cultural awareness workshops and college civic outcomes. Astin (1993) examined the extent to which workshop participation predicts 82 different outcomes when controlling for pretests, precollege characteristics, and other variables within a large, multi-institutional sample. He found that workshop attendance was associated with a variety of civic outcomes, including commitment to promoting racial understanding, cultural awareness, recognition of racial discrimination, and agency for effecting social change. Other studies have shown that these workshops significantly predict greater awareness of racism (Katz & Ivey, 1977), cultural knowledge/understanding and leadership ability (Antonio, 2001), civic mindedness (Cole & Zhou, 2014), motivation to promote inclusion and social justice (Zuniga, Williams, & Berger,

2005), commitment to promoting racial understanding (Antony, 1993; Hyun, 1994; Milem, 1994; Vogelgesang, 2001), openness to diversity and challenge (Pascarella, Edison, Nora, Hagedorn, & Terenzini, 1996; Whitt, Edison, Pascarella, Terenzini, & Nora, 2001), and attitudes toward diversity (Springer, Palmer, Terenzini, Pascarella, & Nora, 1996).

Additional research has examined outcomes associated with co-curricular diversity activities in general; this broader construct typically includes not only racial/cultural awareness workshops but also other campus events that explore issues of culture and difference. Several longitudinal studies have shown that co-curricular diversity experiences are positively associated with civic attitudes, values, and behaviors (e.g., Denson & Bowman, 2013; Engberg, 2007; Gurin et al., 2002; Hurtado, 2005; Taylor, 1994). Moreover, quantitative meta-analyses have shown that co-curricular and curricular diversity experiences are associated with not only increased civic outcomes (Bowman, 2011) but also improved cognitive skills and tendencies (Bowman, 2010) and reduced racial bias (Denson, 2009). The size and consistency of these positive effects are noteworthy. Within a meta-analysis of college diversity experiences and civic engagement, Bowman (2011) found that the average effect sizes for co-curricular diversity, diversity coursework, and intergroup dialogue were virtually identical.

An understudied issue is the extent to which the relationship between co-curricular experiences and civic outcomes varies as a function of student or institutional characteristics. Providing some indirect evidence, Denson's (2009) review found that studies with a higher proportion of students of color within the sample tended to have a weaker link between co-curricular/curricular activities and racial bias, which suggests that White students might benefit more than students of color. Moreover, the link between cross-racial interaction and civic growth also varies as a function of institutional diversity climate, such that this association is more positive at colleges and universities with poorer campus climates (Denson & Chang, 2009, 2015). Therefore, the potential presence of differential relationships between racial/cultural awareness workshops and civic outcomes also merits attention.

Sustained Effects of Short-Term College Experiences

Two additional studies have examined the extent to which racial/cultural awareness workshops during college predict outcomes well after graduation. Bowman, Brandenberger, Hill, and Lapsley (2011) found that undergraduate workshop participation was positively related to volunteer work 13 years beyond college among alumni from a single religiously affiliated university. Moreover, within a multi-institutional sample, Jayakumar (2008) found that workshop participation was positively and significantly associated with pluralistic orientation and leadership skills five years after college among White alumni (racial/ethnic minorities were not included within the study).

Is it really possible that this type of short experience—which may last only a couple of hours—can have such a lasting impact? Experimental evidence indeed suggests that other short-term interventions may have a sustained effect on college student outcomes. In a notable example, Walton and Cohen (2011) had Black and White first-year students take part in a one-hour laboratory session that was described as investigating the experiences and attitudes of first-year students. Participants who were randomly assigned to the treatment condition read survey results indicating that many students did not feel that they belong on campus at first but these concerns dissipated over time. Participants then wrote a short essay and gave a short speech (presumably to be given to future first-year students) about how their concerns about belonging had changed over time. The control group read results from a survey that was irrelevant to college sense of belonging (i.e., regarding changes in students' social-political views) and provided a short essay and speech on that topic. This intervention was intended to be most influential for Black students, who typically have greater concerns and challenges with campus belonging than do White students. When assessed three years later, Black students in the treatment condition had higher GPAs and reported being happier and healthier than Black students in the control condition, whereas there were no significant effects for White students. Other experimental studies with brief interventions (which involve either affirming students' deeply held values or changing their perceptions about the malleability of intelligence) have demonstrated achievement effects over the course of a college semester (Aronson, Fried, & Good, 2002; Harackiewicz, Canning, Tibbetts, Giffen, & Hyde, 2014; Miyake et al., 2010) and among K–12 students two or three years later (G. L. Cohen, Garcia, Purdie-Vaughns, Apfel, & Brzustoski, 2009; Sherman et al., 2013).

Short-term interventions may also have a sustained impact on civic attitudes and values. Brannon and Walton (2013) conducted a laboratory study in which they created a sense of social connection between a non-Latino participant and a Mexican American confederate (i.e., a student who was posing as another participant but was actually part of the study). Six months after this experiment, participants who had worked with the Mexican American student on a freely chosen Mexican cultural task were more interested in engaging with Mexican American peers and had more favorable attitudes toward undocumented Mexican immigrants than did participants who were randomly assigned to the control groups. Although this one-time experience (which combined intergroup contact with learning about another culture) lasted only about 15 minutes, its impact persisted through the end of the academic year.

How do these brief interventions maintain their long-term impact, especially when most participants forget that the intervention ever occurred and believe that it had no effect (Walton & Cohen, 2011)? According to multiple literature syntheses (G. L. Cohen & Sherman, 2014; Yeager & Walton, 2011), these approaches target recursive processes that lead to accumulated effects over time. That is, these interventions are designed so that students reattribute failure to unstable causes, believe that intelligence and academic performance are malleable (not innate), or perceive that difficulties with college adjustment and belonging are normal (and eventually reduced or eliminated). If the interventions are successful, then students are likely to develop better study skills and habits, greater self-efficacy for high achievement through hard work, and closer relationships with fellow students and faculty. Students benefit in the short term by thinking differently about—and usually undergoing immediate improvements in—academic success and social belonging. Moreover, they may then draw on these psychological and interpersonal resources throughout their college years. In sum, these interventions are effective because they are specifically designed to influence mechanisms and processes that shape student success. Similarly, racial/cultural awareness workshops may change students' perceptions, attitudes, and behaviors regarding diversity and other civic issues in the short term, which may then lead to psychological and behavioral tendencies that persist in the long term.

Limitations of College Diversity Research

However, given the available evidence, there may be no true causal relationship between college diversity experiences and post-college outcomes. The vast majority of studies on college diversity experiences and student outcomes are nonexperimental; as a result, it is unclear whether engaging in a racial/cultural awareness workshop (or other forms of engagement) actually *causes* civic engagement during the college years or beyond. Moreover, most of the analyses in Jayakumar (2008) and Bowman et al. (2011) did not use pretests for the outcome variables upon entering college, so the observed relationships do not reflect changes in civic engagement over time. It is extremely difficult to conduct a large-scale, real-world experiment in which some students are randomly assigned (and then required) to participate in diversity workshops, whereas other students are randomly assigned *not* to participate (and then prevented from attending even if they want to do so). Given that randomized experiments constitute the "gold standard" of causal inference (e.g., Campbell & Stanley, 1966; Shadish, Cook, & Campbell, 2002), research that falls short of that standard may yield different results than does experimental research. Indeed, in their meta-analysis of hundreds of studies on intergroup contact and intergroup bias, Pettigrew and Tropp (2006) observed differential effects for experimental versus nonexperimental studies. Self-selection into college diversity experiences may constitute a significant problem for drawing strong causal conclusions. In their seminal review, Feldman and Newcomb (1969) observed that students often choose college experiences that accentuate their preexisting attributes. In a recent diversity-related example, Bowman and Brandenberger (2012) showed that students who entered a service-learning course with higher levels of equality and social responsibility (ESR) orientation were more likely to have positive experiences with diversity during the course, which were then associated with increases in ESR orientation. In other words, a preexisting student characteristic (in this case, the pretest) was substantially related to both the experience and the outcome, which can lead to challenges for drawing causal conclusions from those observational data.

To help address this difficulty, educational researchers have increasingly begun to use quasi-experimental methods to provide a more rigorous examination of the causal impact of an intervention (see Shadish et al., 2002; Thyer, 2012). One quasi-experimental approach designed to address self-selection into experiences is propensity score matching (PSM; see Guo & Fraser, 2015; Holmes, 2013). The basic idea of PSM is to determine the likelihood that students (or others) will participate in a given experience (i.e., treatment) and then to "match" these students with other students who are equally likely to participate. If students in the treatment condition fare better on the outcome variable than their matched counterparts in the control condition (who did not participate in the experience), then one can be more confident that the treatment influenced the outcome. The strength of causal inference from a propensity score analysis depends on having variables that contribute both to selection into the treatment and to the level of the outcome. For example, a PSM analysis of the impact of a bachelor's degree on future earnings should include precollege socioeconomic status as one of the variables within the propensity score, since this precollege attribute is very likely related to degree attainment and future earnings.

Present Study

The purpose of this study is to examine the long-term effects of college participation in racial/cultural awareness workshops. The present study used PSM analyses to examine the relationships between participation in these workshops during college and numerous civic outcomes six years after graduation. Key constructs associated with the treatment and outcomes were used to create the propensity score, including pretests and proxy pretests for the outcomes, race-related attitudes, political orientation, intended college behavior, demographics, and institutional characteristics. All of these variables were collected when students entered college, so those attributes were precursors to both workshop participation and post-college outcomes. The use of a three-wave longitudinal study—with surveys administered upon entering college, end of the senior year, and six years after college—also ensures that students are more likely to remember their college experiences (as opposed to recalling their college experiences on an alumni survey). In addition to the quasi-experimental and longitudinal design, this study also improves on previous research by examining alumni behaviors (whereas most studies have focused on attitudes and self-perceptions), predicting civic outcomes that are both diversity related and not diversity related, considering conditional effects of workshop participation (i.e., whether these relationships vary by race/ethnicity, gender, or institution), using a large multi-institutional sample, and assessing post-college outcomes (as opposed to exploring gains during college and assuming that these will persist beyond graduation). Additional analyses also explored whether workshop participation predicts outcomes above and beyond interpersonal and curricular diversity engagement.

Method

Data Source and Participants

The data set was collected through the Cooperative Institutional Research Program, which is housed within the Higher Education Research Institute (HERI) at the University of California, Los Angeles. Three waves of data collection were included from students' entry into college in 1994 (Freshman Survey), end of their senior year in 1998 (College Senior Survey), and six years after college in 2004 (Civic Engagement Survey). The Freshman Survey contained information about students' demographics, attitudes, precollege experiences, and college intentions. The College Senior Survey asked about students' college experiences and other indicators (e.g., college satisfaction), and institutional data were linked to student records. Finally, the Civic Engagement Survey contained information about post-college experiences, attitudes, and behaviors. A total of 8,634 participants who graduated from 229 institutions completed surveys at all three timepoints. Because each college or university in the sample was responsible for administering the Freshman and Senior Surveys to its own students, the overall initial response rate and first retest response rate are unknown. In contrast, HERI directly administered the Civic Engagement Survey, which had a retest response rate of 50%. This sample was 67.6% female, 90.7% White, 3.5% Asian American/Pacific Islander, 3.1% Black/African American, 2.6% Latino/Hispanic/Chicano, 1.2% American Indian/Alaska Native, and 1.8% other race/ethnicity (the race/ethnicity figures add up to slightly more than 100% because participants were allowed to select multiple categories). Thirty-seven percent of participants reported having attended a racial/cultural awareness workshop in college. The institutional sample included five Historically Black Colleges and Universities (HBCUs) and 23 public institutions. The average institutional SAT score (verbal plus math) ranged from 615 to 1410, with a mean of 987.

Measures

Dependent Variables

A variety of post-college civic behaviors, attitudes/beliefs, and skills/tendencies were included as outcomes. For behaviors, community leadership was assessed with a three-item index (Cronbach's alpha = .76) regarding activities in which participants took a key civic role (e.g., "played a leadership role in improving your community"; 1 = *never*, to 4 = *frequently*). This variable was highly skewed such that about half of participants reported never having engaged in any of these behaviors. Since no transformation could yield even an approximately normal distribution, this variable was dichotomized into participants who had never participated in a community leadership experience since college (i.e., they had a mean of 1.0) and those with a mean greater than 1.0 (preliminary analyses showed that using different cut points yielded similar substantive results). Volunteer work was indicated with a single item regarding the number of hours per week spent volunteering during the past year (1 = *none*, to 8 = *over 20 hours*). Because this variable was also skewed, it was natural log transformed to yield an approximately normal distribution. Donating money to nonprofit organizations or political causes was indicated with a five-item index (1 = *never*, to 4 = *frequently*; α = .62). An 11-item index was used to measure the frequency of accessing various news sources through print, online, television, and radio formats (1 = *none*, to 4 = *5+ times per week*; α = .65). To allow for a more meaningful interpretation of effect size, the three continuous variables (news consumption, donating money, and volunteer work) were standardized with a mean of zero and a standard deviation of one. As a result, unstandardized multivariate coefficients predicting these outcomes can be interpreted as indicating the effect of racial/cultural workshop participation in standard deviation units (J. Cohen, Cohen, West, & Aiken, 2003). In addition, discussing racial issues and socializing with someone of another racial/ethnic group during the past year were each indicated with a single item (1 = *not at all*, to 3 = *frequently*).

For attitudes and beliefs, participants' personal value for keeping up to date on politics was measured (1 = *not important*, to 4 = *essential*). In addition, an item about how individuals can do little to change society (1 = *disagree strongly*, to 4 = *agree strongly*) was reverse-coded so that higher values indicate greater agency for effecting social change. Participants also reported the extent to which everyone in the United States has essentially the same opportunity to be successful (1 = *disagree strongly*, to 4 = *agree strongly*); this item was also reverse-coded so that higher values reflect a greater recognition of the presence of an unequal opportunity for success. Finally, for skills and tendencies, participants rated their leadership ability and cooperativeness relative to the average person their age (1 = *lowest 10%*, to 5 = *highest 10%*).

Independent Variables

Participation in a racial/cultural awareness workshop during college was measured on the College Senior Survey (0 = no, 1 = yes). All variables used to construct the propensity score were taken from the Freshman Survey; this decision is consistent with the conception of PSM as a technique that measures participants' preexisting proclivity to participate (or not) in a given intervention. Moreover, the use of variables from an earlier point in time ensures that these attributes may be causally related to participation in the intervention (as opposed to using a cross-sectional design, in which the values for the variables could be influenced by participation in the intervention). Our choice of measures to create the propensity score was influenced by conceptual considerations and previous research. We could only identify one study that examined racial/cultural awareness workshop participation as an outcome (Springer et al., 1996), and this study contained only a small number of predictors. According to their logistic regression analysis, political conservatism, degree aspirations, and parental education were all significantly related to workshop participation. We were not surprised by the significant effect of political orientation, since political orientation and affiliation predict the perceived importance of race within society (e.g., Sniderman, Crosby, & Howell, 2000). Therefore, we included political orientation (1 = *far right*, to 5 = *far left*) for creating the propensity score for this study. However, we were not sure why parental education or degree aspirations should logically be related to participation. Preliminary analyses showed that neither of these attributes significantly predicted workshop participation within the present data set; therefore, for both conceptual and empirical reasons, we did not include parental education or degree aspirations.

We chose the other propensity score variables through conceptual considerations and previous research on interpersonal interactions and friendships with diverse peers (e.g., Bowman & Park, 2014; Chang, Astin, & Kim, 2004; Milem, Umbach, & Liang, 2004; Saenz, 2010; Saenz, Ngai, & Hurtado, 2007). The pretest for the outcome variable is quite useful for creating a propensity score, since this variable is often substantially related to both the treatment and the outcome (Pascarella, Salisbury, & Blaich, 2013; Steiner, Cook, Shadish, & Clark, 2010). Therefore, several pretests and proxy pretests were included. The direct pretests were leadership ability, cooperativeness, agency for effecting social change, and time spent volunteering (also log transformed); the proxy pretests were discussing politics (1 = *not at all*, to 3 = *frequently*), belief that racial discrimination is a problem (1 = *strongly disagree*, to 4 = *strongly agree*), and a seven-item index (α = .80) measuring pluralistic orientation (e.g., importance placed on promoting racial understanding, being a community leader; 1 = *not important*, to 4 = *essential*). One of the items within this pluralistic orientation index was actually a direct pretest of an outcome variable (importance of keeping up to date with political affairs). Moreover, as another indicator of proclivity for civic engagement, students' anticipated likelihood of performing volunteer work during college was also included (1 = *no chance*, to 4 = *very good chance*).

Key demographics and precollege experiences that often predict college diversity engagement were used. Race/ethnicity was measured with several dummy variables (American Indian/Alaska Native, Asian American/Pacific Islander, Black/African American, Latino/Hispanic/Chicano, and other race/ethnicity, with White/Caucasian as the referent group), and sex was included (0 = male, 1 = female). Racial/ethnic difference in the precollege environment was indicated with a two-item index (α = .85) that indicated the proportion of high school classmates and neighbors who were from a different racial/ethnic group (1 = *none*, to 5 = *all*); we expected that students with more precollege diversity exposure would be more likely to participate in a racial/cultural awareness workshop.

Several institutional characteristics were also used; support for the selection of these variables is provided from studies that not only predict diversity interaction but also student satisfaction with campus diversity (Park, 2009) and diversity advocacy among faculty members (Park & Denson, 2009). The representation of faculty of color and female faculty were both expected to be positively related to workshop participation since faculty from these minority groups tend to perceive a greater need for diversity advocacy (Park & Denson, 2009). Because the distribution of faculty of color was notably skewed, a natural log transformation was conducted on the percentage of faculty of color. HBCUs were indicated with a dichotomous variable (1 = HBCU, 0 = non-HBCU) because both faculty and students at these institutions may be more cognizant of and concerned with racial issues. Given previous studies that showed institutional selectivity is positively related to diversity engagement (Bowman, Park, & Denson, 2015; Chang et al., 2004) yet negatively related to satisfaction with diversity (Park, 2009), the average total SAT score (verbal plus math or equivalent ACT composite score) was divided by 100 and included in the analyses.

However, we ultimately decided to exclude two other institutional variables that did not significantly predict workshop participation within the data set: racial diversity of the student body and institutional control. We anticipated that the structural racial diversity would be positively related to workshop participation, but this was not the case. Moreover, relative to public four-year schools, private schools have faculty who are more likely to advocate for diversity (Park & Denson, 2009), while students who attend private schools are less satisfied with diversity on campus (Park, 2009). Nonetheless, institutional control was not significantly associated with workshop participation within the present data set. Table 2 provides the descriptive statistics for all variables used within the study.

Although propensity scores should only be created with variables that occur before the treatment, control variables can be modeled independent of the PSM adjustment when predicting the outcomes (see Holmes, 2013). Therefore, we included three college diversity experiences as control variables. Positive cross-racial interaction was indicated with a four-item index of

Table 2
Descriptive Statistics

	Mean	*SD*	Minimum	Maximum
Outcome variables				
Community leadership	0.529	0.499	0.000	1.000
Discuss racial issues	2.146	0.591	1.000	3.000
Socialize across race	2.564	0.548	1.000	3.000
Donate money	2.147	0.666	1.000	4.000
News consumption	2.132	0.465	1.000	4.000
Volunteer work	0.641	0.533	0.000	2.079
Agency for effecting social change	3.067	0.777	1.000	4.000
Importance of keeping up to date on politics	2.368	0.912	1.000	4.000
Perceive unequal opportunity for success	2.756	0.903	1.000	4.000
Cooperativeness	3.936	0.708	1.000	5.000
Leadership skills	3.661	0.841	1.000	5.000
Key independent variable				
Racial/cultural awareness workshop	0.370	0.483	0.000	1.000
Control variables for select propensity score analyses				
Positive cross-racial interaction	1.906	0.468	1.000	3.000
Ethnic studies coursework	0.451	0.498	0.000	1.000
Women's studies coursework	0.275	0.446	0.000	1.000
Student characteristics used to create the propensity score				
Female	0.676	0.468	0.000	1.000
American Indian/Native American	0.012	0.109	0.000	1.000
Asian American/Pacific Islander	0.035	0.184	0.000	1.000
Black/African American	0.031	0.173	0.000	1.000
Latino/Hispanic/Chicano	0.026	0.159	0.000	1.000
Other race/ethnicity	0.018	0.132	0.000	1.000
Racial difference in precollege environment	2.121	0.968	1.000	5.000
Cooperativeness	3.972	0.709	1.000	5.000
Leadership ability	3.695	0.874	1.000	5.000
Agency for effecting social change	3.109	0.833	1.000	4.000
Time spent volunteering	0.816	0.569	0.000	2.079
Intentions for college volunteering	3.136	0.795	1.000	4.000
Pluralistic orientation	2.301	0.572	1.000	4.000
Believe racial discrimination is a problem	3.316	0.733	1.000	4.000
Discussed politics	2.035	0.641	1.000	3.000
Liberal political orientation	2.925	0.808	1.000	5.000
Institutional characteristics used to create the propensity score				
Institutional selectivity	9.870	1.300	6.150	14.100
Historically Black College or University	0.022	0.146	0.000	1.000
Representation of faculty of color	1.943	0.696	0.000	4.407
Representation of female faculty	0.360	0.121	0.100	0.830

Note. The continuous outcomes (donate money, news consumption, and volunteer work) were subsequently standardized for inclusion in the multilevel analyses.

the frequency with which participants studied, shared a meal, interacted in class, or dated someone from a different racial/ethnic group (1 = *not at all*, to 3 = *frequently*; α = .75). These forms of meaningful engagement across difference are more strongly related to college outcomes than is the mere frequency of cross-racial interaction (Denson & Chang, 2015; Hurtado, 2005; Nelson Laird, 2005), and interpersonal interactions are more strongly related to college civic and cognitive outcomes than are co-curricular and curricular diversity experiences (Bowman, 2010, 2011). As a result, including this interpersonal measure provides a strong test of the alternative hypothesis that the results for racial/cultural workshops can be explained by other forms of diversity engagement. Moreover, two dichotomous variables indicated taking at least one ethnic studies course and at least one women's studies course (0 = no, 1 = yes); such diversity coursework measures are consistently and positively related to civic outcomes in previous research (see Bowman, 2011; Denson & Bowman, in press).

Analyses

Because the current sample contained students/alumni nested within institutions, hierarchical linear modeling (HLM) analyses were used. This nesting violates a key assumption of ordinary least squares (OLS) multiple regression; HLM accounts for this issue by partitioning the variance within institutions (at Level 1) and between institutions (at Level 2) and adjusting standard errors accordingly (Raudenbush & Bryk, 2002). Intraclass correlation coefficients (ICCs) were examined to determine the proportion of variance that occurs between institutions; these can be computed for outcomes that are continuous (e.g., news consumption), ordinal (e.g., agency for effecting social change), and dichotomous (community leadership; for relevant formulas, see Snijders & Bosker, 2012). Although some scholars recommend that multilevel modeling be used if the ICC is at least 5% (Heck & Thomas, 2008), others do not provide a specific minimum ICC value (Luke, 2004; Raudenbush & Bryk, 2002), and single-level analyses cannot be performed on multilevel data if the predictor variables occur at both the individual and institutional levels (Thomas & Heck, 2001), which is the case here. In addition, multilevel analyses are simply considered unnecessary—not incorrect or inappropriate—if the ICC is low (Heck & Thomas, 2008). The ICCs for the post-college civic outcomes ranged from 1% (for cooperativeness and agency for effecting social change) to 7% (for perceiving unequal opportunity for success). As described later in this section, participation in a racial/cultural awareness workshop is also used as an outcome when creating the propensity score and determining whether this score sufficiently accounts for self-selection bias. The ICC for workshop participation was 12%. Listwise deletion was used to examine incomplete data. Participants with missing data on any variable (who comprised 14% of the total sample) did not differ significantly from those with complete data in terms of race/ethnicity, gender, attending a racial/cultural workshop, and 10 of the 11 post-college outcomes.

To select variables for the propensity score, each precollege variable was entered at the appropriate level (student or institution) as the lone predictor of workshop participation. Only significant predictors at $p < .05$ were used to create the propensity score; as noted earlier, structural racial diversity, institutional control, degree aspirations, and parental education did not meet this criterion. American Indian/Alaska Native was a nonsignificant predictor, but it was retained so that White/Caucasian would continue to serve as the racial/ethnic referent group. The remaining variables were entered simultaneously as predictors of workshop participation: sex, race/ethnicity, racial difference in the precollege environment, cooperativeness, leadership ability, agency for effecting social change, time spent volunteering, anticipated college volunteering, pluralistic orientation, belief that racial discrimination is a problem, discussing politics, and political orientation were modeled at Level 1, while institutional selectivity, HBCU, representation of faculty of color, and representation of female faculty were modeled at Level 2. The logit for each predictor was used to compute a single, linear propensity score for participation in a racial/cultural awareness workshop.

Consistent with the multilevel PSM analyses of Hong and Raudenbush (2005, 2006), stratification was used to match students with similar propensities to participate in the treatment. Stratification is one technique used for comparing the outcomes of students in the treatment and control conditions who are very similar in their predisposition to engage in the treatment. Alternative PSM approaches include matching each individual participant in the treatment group with one (or more) participants in the control group (see Guo & Fraser, 2015; Holmes, 2013; Rosenbaum, 2002). The linear propensity score variable was divided into five equal strata with 20% of participants included per stratum (Cochran, 1968; Guo & Fraser, 2015). This approach is designed to equate participants on the propensity score within each stratum; if this balancing is sufficient, then a two-way analysis of variance (ANOVA) predicting the linear propensity score with strata and treatment condition (workshop vs. no workshop) as independent variables should yield no significant main effect of treatment condition. However, there was a highly significant effect of workshop participation, indicating that workshop participants and nonparticipants did not have the same average propensity score within each stratum. Therefore, greater numbers of strata were tested to further reduce bias (Akers, 2010). A 15-strata solution performed much better, but it still exhibited a main effect of workshop participation and a significant Workshop $\times$ Strata interaction, $Fs > 8.00$, $ps < .001$. A visual inspection of the means suggested that the data were sufficiently balanced except for the lowest and the highest strata; the lowest stratum contained a large majority of non-workshop participants (some of

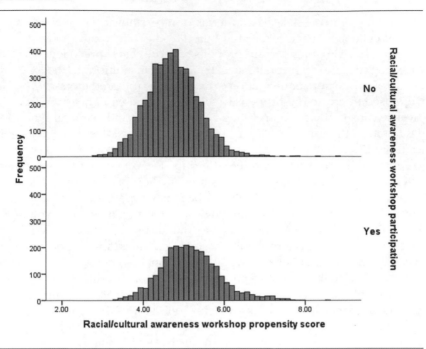

Figure 1. **Propensity score frequency distributions for students who did and did not participate in a racial/cultural awareness workshop.**

whom had very low propensity scores), and the highest stratum contained a large majority of workshop participants. Figure 1 provides an overall histogram of propensity scores by treatment group, which illustrates some of this mismatch within the distribution tails. Therefore, all participants from these lowest and highest strata were removed from the final analyses (preliminary analyses showed that this decision produced a somewhat more modest estimate of the effect of workshop participation than including these alumni). The removal of participants from these two strata resulted in a total reduction of 1,033 participants (13%); specifically, 517 and 516 participants were within the lowest and highest stratum, respectively. Within this truncated sample with participants from the 13 remaining strata, the two-way ANOVA found no main effect of workshop participation, $F(1, 6697) = 2.205$, $p = .138$, and no significant Workshop × Strata interaction, $F(12, 6697) = .997$, $p = .449$.

Another test of the effectiveness of the propensity score balancing examines whether each variable used to create the propensity score significantly predicts workshop participation when including the propensity score adjustment. If the propensity score succeeds in removing self-selection bias, then

Table 3
**Hierarchical Generalized Linear Modeling Analyses Predicting
Participation in a Racial/Cultural Awareness Workshop
Before and After Propensity Score Balancing**

Predictor	Before Balancing			After Balancing		
	B	*SE*	*p*	*B*	*SE*	*p*
Level 1 (student characteristics)						
Female	0.365	.050	<.001	.014	.061	.815
American Indian/Native American	0.111	.204	.586	−.043	.258	.867
Asian American/Pacific Islander	0.356	.138	.010	.096	.171	.575
Black/African American	1.334	.179	<.001	.207	.291	.477
Latino/Hispanic/Chicano	0.670	.146	<.001	−.184	.197	.348
Other race/ethnicity	0.475	.170	.005	.139	.228	.542
Racial difference in precollege environment	0.118	.028	<.001	−.005	.032	.879
Cooperativeness	0.114	.031	<.001	−.008	.037	.840
Leadership ability	0.282	.028	<.001	.043	.034	.203
Agency for effecting social change	0.239	.029	<.001	.021	.035	.549
Time spent volunteering	0.529	.040	<.001	.046	.053	.393
Intentions for college volunteering	0.493	.034	<.001	.073	.044	.096
Pluralistic orientation	0.677	.039	<.001	.091	.057	.108
Believe racial discrimination is a problem	0.201	.031	<.001	.026	.036	.472
Discussed politics	0.364	.043	<.001	.039	.050	.430
Liberal political orientation	0.222	.033	<.001	.032	.035	.374
Level 2 (institutional characteristics)						
Institutional selectivity	0.143	.044	.001	.019	.042	.651
Historically Black College or University	0.993	.290	<.001	.292	.374	.436
Representation of faculty of color	0.336	.071	<.001	.042	.079	.594
Representation of female faculty	2.009	.543	<.001	.552	.542	.310

Note. All predictors were measured upon entering college at Time 1.

the precollege variable should not significantly predict workshop participation when performing the propensity score adjustment (this adjustment occurs by including dummy variables for all but one stratum—leaving one out as a referent group—as additional independent variables within the HLM analysis). Table 3 provides a summary of these multilevel tests; the left-hand columns contain results when entering only the precollege predictor (as described earlier), and the right-hand columns display results that also include the strata within the models. None of the independent variables significantly predicted workshop participation when the PSM adjustment occurred (*ps* > .05), which indicates that the propensity score successfully removed bias associated with those variables.

The primary analyses predicted each of the 11 civic outcomes with workshop participation and the PSM strata entered as predictors. Volunteer work, donating money, and news consumption were treated as continuous outcomes through HLM analyses. Hierarchical generalized linear modeling (HGLM) analyses were used to predict the dichotomous outcome (community leadership) and the ordinal outcomes (discuss racial issues, perceive unequal opportunity for success, socialize across race, agency for effecting social change, importance of keeping up to date on politics, cooperativeness, and leadership ability). To explore whether the effect of racial/cultural awareness workshops varies across groups, additional analyses included interaction terms between workshop participation and several variables (gender and each racial/ethnic group in the model). Furthermore, to explore whether the effect of workshops might differ across institutions, the slope for workshop participation predicting each outcome was allowed to vary (i.e., it was not fixed to be identical across schools), and the potential presence of significant variance in slopes was examined.

Moreover, as a form of sensitivity analysis, positive cross-racial interaction, ethnic studies coursework, and women's studies coursework were added as control variables within propensity score analyses predicting the 11 post-college outcomes. This approach could possibly provide a skewed estimate of the impact of workshops, since all diversity experiences were measured at the same time. Thus, it is unclear whether these additional diversity experiences actually occurred before workshop participation (and therefore would constitute pretreatment control variables) or that the workshops caused students to engage in subsequent diversity experiences (and therefore the inclusion of these variables might obscure the relationship between participation and subsequent outcomes). Nonetheless, if the results of these analyses corroborate the findings from the analyses without control variables, then conclusions about the potential impact of racial/cultural awareness workshops would be strengthened, since these PSM analyses likely provide a more rigorous examination of the link between workshop participation and post-college outcomes.

Limitations

Some limitations should be noted. First, Whites/Caucasians, women, and private institutions were overrepresented within this data set relative to national norms (see *The Chronicle of Higher Education*, 2013). More than three-fourths of U.S. four-year colleges and universities are privately controlled (Council of Christian Colleges and Universities, 2010), so the overrepresentation of private schools is not as severe as one might think. In addition, moderation analyses determined whether the effect of workshops differs by race/ethnicity, gender, and institution. If the effects of workshop participation on civic outcomes are similar across students and institutions, then these sample characteristics are likely not a concern because they would not alter the relationships of interest. Thus, nonresponse bias would only be a problem for this study if the students and alumni who did not respond are affected differently by racial/cultural workshop participation than those who did respond. Second, the sample consisted entirely of four-year institutions, so it is unclear whether racial/ cultural workshops at two-year colleges would yield similar findings. Third, most of the outcome measures consist of single items rather than multi-item indices, which are generally considered to be preferable. However, the range restriction of these single items may mean that the relationships observed in this study constitute underestimates of the "true" effects of racial/cultural workshops. Clearly, considering the pattern of effects across these continuous, ordinal, and dichotomous outcomes will yield a clearer picture of the link between these workshops and post-college civic engagement.

Fourth, students who reported participating in a racial/cultural awareness workshop may have attended more than one workshop while in college. As a result, the analyses here reflect a comparison of students who participated in at least one workshop versus those who did not participate in any workshops. Fifth, participants simply reported whether they had engaged in this co-curricular activity, so the actual content and structure of each workshop is unknown. As a result, the analyses cannot determine whether certain types of workshops might be more effective at promoting long-term outcomes, which may be relevant as such practices have likely evolved since the college experiences in this data set were assessed. Finally, as discussed in more detail in a subsequent section, workshop participation may cause students to engage in other diversity-related activities while in college, so some of the relationships reported here may be indirect. Because all college experiences were assessed in the senior year, it is unclear in what order a student participated in various diversity experiences, so mediating processes cannot be explored directly in this study.

Results

Table 4 displays the results for HLM analyses predicting each dependent variable without the PSM adjustment (left-hand columns) and with the PSM adjustment (right-hand columns). In the unadjusted analyses, workshop participation is a significant, positive predictor of all 11 civic outcomes ($ps <$ .001). When propensity score adjustments are made, the HLM coefficients are smaller for all analyses; this reduction ranges from less than one-fourth (for perceiving unequal opportunity for success) to more than two-thirds (for importance of keeping up to date on politics). However, workshop participation is still a significant predictor for 10 out of 11 civic outcomes (the effect for keeping up to date on politics is positive but nonsignificant). These post-college outcomes cover a range of behaviors (e.g., community leadership, charitable giving), attitudes and beliefs (e.g., agency for social

Table 4
Results of Multilevel Analyses for Participation in a Racial/Cultural Awareness Workshop Predicting Civic Engagement Outcomes Six Years After College Graduation

Outcome variable	No PSM Adjustment			PSM Adjustment		
	B	*SE*	Odds Ratio	*B*	*SE*	Odds Ratio
Behaviors						
Community leadership	.588***	.056	1.800	.444***	.061	1.559
Discuss racial issues	.648***	.049	1.911	.398***	.055	1.489
Socialize across race	.483***	.050	1.621	.327***	.057	1.387
Donate money	.229***	.025		.135***	.027	
News consumption	.117***	.025		.075*	.030	
Volunteer work	.275***	.022		.174***	.024	
Attitudes/beliefs						
Agency for effecting social change	.407***	.045	1.502	.139**	.051	1.149
Importance of keeping up to date on politics	.302***	.043	1.352	.092	.051	1.096
Perceive unequal opportunity for success	.432***	.044	1.540	.331***	.050	1.392
Skills/tendencies						
Cooperativeness	.142***	.041	1.152	.094*	.047	1.098
Leadership skills	.337***	.045	1.401	.153**	.053	1.165

Note. Volunteer work, donate money, and news consumption were continuous outcomes examined with hierarchical linear modeling analyses, and all other variables were examined with hierarchical generalized linear modeling analyses (community leadership was a dichotomous outcome, whereas the remaining outcomes were ordinal). PSM = propensity score matching.
*$p < .05$. **$p < .01$. ***$p < .001$.

change, perceiving inequality), and skills and tendencies (e.g., leadership, cooperativeness) that are essential for the functioning of an effective society and workforce. The continuous dependent variables (volunteer work, donate money, and news consumption) were standardized with a mean of zero and a standard deviation of one, so the HLM coefficients can be interpreted as the adjusted Cohen's *d* for workshop participation. Because community leadership was a dichotomous outcome, a delta-*p* value can be calculated to determine the predicted change in probability of taking a community leadership role for alumni who did and did not participate in a racial/cultural awareness workshop (Cruce, 2009; Petersen, 1985). Using the workshop participation mean as the initial probability level, workshop participation is associated with a .107 increase in the probability of taking a community leadership role six years after graduation.

Table 5

**Results of Multilevel Propensity Score Analyses for Participation in
a Racial/Cultural Awareness Workshop Predicting Civic Engagement
Outcomes Six Years After College Graduation (With Control Variables Added)**

Outcome Variable	B	SE	Odds Ratio
Behaviors			
Community leadership	.382***	.065	1.466
Discuss racial issues	.270***	.054	1.310
Socialize across race	.199**	.061	1.221
Donate money	.136***	.028	
News consumption	.064*	.031	
Volunteer work	.167***	.026	
Attitudes/beliefs			
Agency for effecting social change	.119*	.053	1.127
Importance of keeping up to date on politics	.054	.051	1.056
Perceive unequal opportunity for success	.232***	.050	1.262
Skills/tendencies			
Cooperativeness	.070	.049	1.073
Leadership skills	.168**	.055	1.183

Note. Positive cross-racial interaction, ethnic studies coursework, and women's studies coursework during college were used as control variables in addition to the propensity score matching. Volunteer work, donate money, and news consumption were continuous outcomes examined with hierarchical linear modeling analyses, and all other variables were examined with hierarchical generalized linear modeling analyses (community leadership was a dichotomous outcome, whereas the remaining outcomes were ordinal).
*$p < .05$. **$p < .01$. ***$p < .001$.

Results from propensity score analyses that include interpersonal and curricular diversity experiences as control variables are provided in Table 5. Even with the addition of these well-established predictors of civic outcomes, workshop participation is positively and significantly related to 9 of the 11 post-college outcomes (only cooperativeness became nonsignificant when adding the control variables). Moreover, the reduction in the effect size when incorporating these control variables is typically modest; the median decrease in HLM coefficients across all outcomes is 14.7%, and two relationships actually become slightly larger when including control variables.

Additional analyses examined the extent to which the effect of racial/cultural awareness workshops might vary across students and institutions. First, the slope for workshop participation was allowed to vary across institutions to determine whether these workshops might be more effective at promoting post-college civic outcomes at some schools than at others. However, no significant variation in slopes was observed for any of the 11 analyses ($ps > .18$), which means that this effect is consistent across institutions. Second, additional models were examined to determine whether workshops might be more influential for some students than for others. All such analyses contained the following predictors: workshop participation, PSM strata, six demographic variables (American Indian/Alaska Native, Asian American/Pacific Islander, Black/African American, Latino/Hispanic/Chicano, other race/ethnicity, and female), and the interaction between workshop participation and each of the demographics. Across the 66 interaction terms included in these 11 moderation analyses, only 3 were statistically significant at $p < .05$, which is exactly what one would expect by random chance if no group differences were present in the population. As a result, these results are not presented in detail here.

Discussion

In summary, participation in a racial/cultural awareness workshop during college is significantly associated with numerous civic outcomes six years after graduation. This pattern is consistent for civic behaviors, attitudes/beliefs, and skills/tendencies; it occurs regardless of whether the outcome is diversity related or ostensibly unrelated to diversity, and it persists even in propensity score analyses that control for other forms of diversity engagement. When considering both the timing of the outcome assessment (6–10 years after the workshop) as well as the brevity of many of these workshops (which often last for no more than two hours), the magnitude of these effects is noteworthy. For instance, alumni who participated in a racial/cultural awareness workshop during college are over 10 percentage points more likely to take a leadership role in their post-college communities. Moreover, alumni who participate in these workshops fare about .15 standard deviations higher in terms of volunteer work and charitable/political donations than those who do not participate. The latter figure is considered "small" according to both J. Cohen's (1988) widely cited guidelines for social science research and recent guidelines for college student research (Mayhew, Rockenbach, Bowman, Seifert, & Wolniak, 2016). However, it is certainly not trivial when considered in context, as these short workshops are one of many potential ways to bolster long-term civic engagement among college students. This contextual consideration is consistent with J. Cohen's recommended use of these figures in light of relevant factors, which could include the substantial length of time between treatment and outcome. Moreover, effect sizes are often smaller in educational contexts than in other social science settings (Valentine & Cooper, 2003).

An important contribution of this study is its use of quasi-experimental design to more accurately estimate the effects of participating in a racial/cultural awareness workshop. Our findings show that employing PSM substantially reduces the estimates for all analyses (sometimes by more than half), which suggests that this method accounts for considerable self-selection bias. That is, students who choose to participate in a racial/cultural awareness workshop tend to have different attitudes, goals, personal attributes, and behaviors from those students who have chosen not to participate in these workshops. Even when accounting for self-selection bias, the attenuated effects of participating in racial/cultural awareness workshops have lasting effects six years after college graduation. The largest disparities between adjusted and unadjusted results occur within analyses predicting post-college attitudes and skills (not behaviors). Because most research on college diversity and civic engagement has examined nonbehavioral outcomes (Bowman, 2011), PSM may constitute a particularly important form of analysis for this line of inquiry and should be utilized when possible in future research.

Although the use of propensity score matching constitutes an improvement upon existing research, this quasi-experimental approach is generally perceived to be weaker than some others in terms of drawing causal conclusions (Shadish et al., 2002). Other quasi-experimental techniques are designed to deal with different means of selection into experiences (e.g., regression discontinuity is useful when the treatment assignment is determined by a cutoff score, such as remedial coursework or need-based financial aid). However, PSM is the best available approach for exploring the impact of many student experiences within large, multi-institutional data sets. Indeed, higher education researchers have begun to utilize PSM in recent years to control for self-selection bias in examining the impact of various college experiences on student outcomes (e.g., Clark & Cundiff, 2011; Malcom & Dowd, 2012; Melguizo, Kienzl, & Alfonso, 2011).

Another noteworthy aspect of these findings is that the observed effects are similar regardless of alumni's race/ethnicity, gender, and institution attended. Some previous evidence suggests that the potential impact of racial/cultural awareness workshops may differ as a function of students' race/ethnicity. For instance, Hyun (1994) found a larger effect of workshop participation on the commitment to promoting racial understanding for White students than for African American students. In addition, Engberg and Hurtado (2011) observed a larger direct effect of co-curricular diversity experiences on pluralistic orientation for Whites than for Asians but a larger indirect effect for Asians than for Latinos. However, other studies that have examined co-curricular diversity and civic outcomes have obtained similar effect sizes across racial/ethnic groups (Gurin et al., 2002; Kotori, 2009; Vogelgesang, 2001). Any similarity in the magnitude of these relationships does not imply that the processes through which these impacts occur are identical across groups, as the examination of direct effects in this study does not shed light on the specific mechanisms involved. Moreover, the lack of variation across more than 200 institutions in this sample may be the most surprising moderation finding; this result suggests that colleges and universities are about equally effective in providing diversity workshops that contribute to long-term civic outcomes. It is not necessarily the case that the length or content of these workshops are similar across schools; instead, institutions may be adept at designing workshops that are useful for the particular student populations that they serve.

An interesting issue that could not be explored directly within this study is whether students' motivation for workshop attendance might help shape their subsequent outcomes. Some students attend these workshops as part of a broader training program of which a racial/cultural awareness workshop is a required component (e.g., to become a resident assistant), whereas others attend these as a voluntary, stand-alone activity. Might the outcomes vary for these two types of students? Cognitive dissonance theory (Festinger, 1957) would suggest that students who choose to attend racial/cultural awareness workshops would then view their own participation as evidence that they care deeply about these issues, and their civic attitudes (and perhaps civic behaviors) would then change as a result. If students see themselves as being forced to participate, then these same benefits may not accrue. However, some evidence suggests that students' apparent receptiveness to diversity may not actually shape these outcomes; specifically, Denson and Bowman (2013) found that the relationships between curricular/co-curricular diversity and college civic outcomes do not differ as a function of students' openness to diversity or their precollege diversity exposure. Exploring possible differences in students' motivation for participating (or not) in racial/cultural awareness workshops would prove a fruitful avenue for future research.

Conclusion

Overall, racial/cultural awareness workshops appear to affect various civic outcomes six years after college graduation. This study identified positive and significant relationships for 10 of the 11 civic outcomes through propensity score matching techniques, which provide a rigorous analytic test of the potential impact of this experience. Taken together, the results suggest that participation in such workshops have a noteworthy effect on numerous attitudes and activities that are characteristic of a well-functioning workforce and democracy, such as volunteer work, donating money, community leadership, cross-racial interaction, and discussion of racial issues. Importantly, these results extend beyond usual examinations of outcomes toward the end of college to the critical years following graduation in which students are establishing life patterns around civic mindedness and community engagement.

Keeping in mind that many college students grow up in racially and socioeconomically segregated neighborhoods (Orfield, 2009; Orfield et al., 2012), these workshops may serve as an important first step in exposing students to diverse others and ideas. In turn, these workshops can nurture students' interest in diversity topics and subsequently enhance the proclivity of those exposed students to seek out more of those experiences or related knowledge. Interestingly, some evidence suggests that the apparent benefits of diversity experiences on various civic and intergroup outcomes are similar regardless of the difference in racial composition between students' high school and college environments as well as students' openness to diversity (Denson & Bowman, 2013). Thus, the significance of these workshops is even more compelling given that they may yield improvements even among students with little experience or interest in engaging across difference. This form of co-curricular involvement can provide students who have had limited precollege exposure to diversity a valuable opportunity for a brief but effective introduction to diversity, which can lead to more meaningful and sustained long-term interest in these issues. This approach would be consistent with Gurin et al.'s (2002) developmental perspective on college diversity experiences (which are often unusual and challenging for entering students) and subsequent outcomes.

While some workshops may be part of a broader and longer-term effort such as intergroup dialogue programs, this is often not the case. Thus, the results illustrate the positive and long-lasting role that brief interventions can play in enhancing civic and diversity-related outcomes. However, these workshops should not be a replacement for other critical curricular and co-curricular diversity activities that take place over a longer period of time, such as ethnic studies classes, intergroup dialogue programs, and student organizations that foster discussions around social issues. They can instead supplement and complement such efforts by enhancing student experiences around diversity with an influence that stretches beyond the college years. Racial/cultural awareness workshops may be an effective means of supporting student development because they can function as a bridge between the curricular and co-curricular spaces. Such workshops often contain information derived from academic content, so they may provide a space where material comes "alive" for students outside of the classroom, engaging students in a different way to enhance awareness of issues related to race, culture, and diversity. Workshops can also reach students who may not heavily engage with diversity issues in their major-related coursework.

Moreover, workshops may provide an effective impetus for students to engage in future interpersonal, curricular, and co-curricular diversity experiences. That is, attending these workshops may cause students to become more interested in and comfortable with issues of difference, which then leads them to engage more frequently and substantively with diversity. If this is true, then some of the relationships observed in this study may occur indirectly through these additional diversity experiences. Since few studies have examined the extent to which diversity experiences predict changes in other diversity experiences (see Bowman, 2012; Nelson Laird, Engberg, & Hurtado, 2005), this catalyzing potential of workshops merits attention in future research.

As a whole, colleges and universities are increasingly under pressure to show the worth of a postsecondary degree to the public. Although many consider classroom-based learning to be of utmost importance, this study suggests that co-curricular activities such as diversity workshops also have a marked influence on behaviors that are critical to societal flourishing and the functioning of a healthy diverse democracy. Therefore, as institutions seek to allocate their limited resources to maximize student learning outcomes, well-designed co-curricular activities may constitute a prudent (yet sometimes overlooked) investment. Universities often tout the impact their alumni have on society, and these workshops appear to be a key means of seeding the ground for social change and civic engagement during the post-college years.

Our findings are illuminating given recent events that magnify the continuing significance of race in society. During the writing of this article, the events in Ferguson sparked a national conversation about the persistent and systemic racial injustices that continue to permeate the country. More recently, at the University of Oklahoma, fraternity members were expelled for singing an egregiously racist song, showing how colleges still struggle to effectively engage students in understanding their responsibility and role in a diverse democracy. While racial/cultural awareness workshops as isolated events are not the sole remedy to alleviating these problems that plague college campuses and beyond, they can play a role in engaging students to think critically about the world around them. We recommend that workshops are accompanied by other curricular and co-curricular opportunities for students to spur active learning around these issues.

Notes

The authors thank the Higher Education Research Institute at the University of California, Los Angeles for the use of their Cooperative Institutional Research Program data.

References

Akers, A. (2010). Determination of the optimal number of strata for bias reduction in propensity score matching. *Dissertation Abstracts International, 71* (08), 58A. (UMI No. 3417726)

Antonio, A. L. (2001). The role of interracial interaction in the development of leadership skills and cultural knowledge and understanding. *Research in Higher Education, 42,* 593–617.

Antony, J. (1993, November). *Can we all get along? How college impacts students' sense of the importance of promoting racial understanding.* Paper presented at the annual meeting of the Association for the Study of Higher Education, Pittsburgh, PA. (ERIC Document Reproduction Service No. ED 365174).

Aronson, J., Fried, C., & Good, C. (2002). Reducing the effects of stereotype threat on African American college students by shaping theories of intelligence. *Journal of Experimental Social Psychology, 38,* 113–125.

Astin, A. W. (1993). Diversity and multiculturalism on the campus: How are students affected? *Change, 25*(2), 44–49.

Bowman, N. A. (2010). College diversity experiences and cognitive development: A meta-analysis. *Review of Educational Research, 80,* 4–33.

Bowman, N. A. (2011). Promoting participation in a diverse democracy: A meta-analysis of college diversity experiences and civic engagement. *Review of Educational Research, 81,* 29–68.

Bowman, N. A. (2012). Promoting sustained engagement with diversity: The reciprocal relationships between informal and formal college diversity experiences. *The Review of Higher Education, 36*(1), 1–24.

Bowman, N. A., & Brandenberger, J. W. (2012). Experiencing the unexpected: Toward a model of college diversity experiences and attitude change. *Review of Higher Education, 35,* 179–205.

Bowman, N. A., Brandenberger, J. W., Hill, P. L., & Lapsley, D. K. (2011). The long-term effects of college diversity experiences: Well-being and social concerns 13 years after graduation. *Journal of College Student Development, 52*(6), 729–239.

Bowman, N. A., & Park, J. J. (2014). Interracial contact on college campuses: Comparing and contrasting predictors of cross-racial interaction and interracial friendship. *Journal of Higher Education, 85,* 660–690.

Bowman, N. A., Park, J. J., & Denson, N. (2015). Student involvement in ethnic student organizations: Examining civic outcomes six years after graduation. *Research in Higher Education, 56,* 127–145.

Brannon, T. N., & Walton, G. M. (2013). Enacting cultural interests: How intergroup contact reduces prejudice by sparking interest in an out-group's future. *Psychological Science, 24,* 1947–1957.

Campbell, D. T., & Stanley, J. C. (1966). *Experimental and quasi-experimental designs for research.* Boston, MA: Houghton Mifflin.

Chang, M. J., Astin, A. W., & Kim, D. (2004). Cross-racial interaction among undergraduates: Some consequences, causes, and patterns. *Research in Higher Education, 45,* 529–553.

The Chronicle of Higher Education. (2013, August 19). Almanac issue 2013–14.

Clark, M. H., & Cundiff, N. L. (2011). Assessing the effectiveness of a college freshman seminar using propensity score adjustments. *Research in Higher Education, 52*(6), 616–639.

Cochran, W. G. (1968). The effectiveness of adjustment by subclassification in removing bias in observational studies. *Biometrics, 24,* 295–313.

Cohen, G. L., Garcia, J., Purdie-Vaughns, V., Apfel, N., & Brzustoski, P. (2009). Recursive processes in self-affirmation: Intervening to close the minority achievement gap. *Science, 324,* 400–403.

Cohen, G. L., & Sherman, D. K. (2014). The psychology of change: Self-affirmation and social psychological intervention. *Annual Review of Psychology, 65,* 333–371.

Cohen, J. (1988). *Statistical power analysis for the behavioral sciences* (2nd ed.). Mahwah, NJ: Lawrence Erlbaum.

Cohen, J., Cohen, P., West, S. G., & Aiken, L. S. (2003). *Applied multiple regression/correlation analysis for the behavioral sciences* (3rd ed.). Mahwah, NJ: Lawrence Erlbaum.

Cole, D., & Zhou, J. (2014). Do diversity experiences help college students become more civically minded? Applying Banks' multicultural education framework. *Innovative Higher Education, 39,* 109-121.

Council for Christian Colleges and Universities. (2010). *Profile of post-secondary education.* Retrieved from https://www.cccu.org/filefolder/Profile_US_Post-Secondary_Education-updated2010.pdf

Cruce, T. M. (2009). A note on the calculation and interpretation of the delta-p statistic for categorical independent variables. *Research in Higher Education, 50*(6), 608–622.

Denson, N. (2009). Do curricular and co-curricular diversity activities influence racial bias? A meta-analysis. *Review of Educational Research*, *79*, 805–838.

Denson, N., & Bowman, N. A. (2013). University diversity and preparation for a global society: The role of diversity in shaping intergroup attitudes and civic outcomes. *Studies in Higher Education*, *38*, 555–570.

Denson, N., & Bowman, N. A. (in press). Do diversity courses make a difference? A critical examination of college diversity coursework and student outcomes. In M. B. Paulsen (Ed.), *Higher education: Handbook of theory and research* (Vol. 32). New York, NY: Springer.

Denson, N., & Chang, M. J. (2009). Racial diversity matters: The impact of diversity-related student engagement and institutional context. *American Educational Research Journal*, *46*, 322–353.

Denson, N., & Chang, M. J. (2015). Dynamic relationships: Identifying moderators that maximize benefits associated with diversity. *Journal of Higher Education*, *86*, 1–37.

Dovidio, J. F., Gaertner, S. L., Stewart, T. L., Esses, V. M., Vergert, M., & Hodson, G. (2004). From intervention to outcome: Processes in the reduction of bias. In W. G. Stephan & W. P. Vogt (Eds.), *Education programs for improving intergroup relations* (pp. 243–265). New York, NY: Teachers College Press.

Engberg, M. E. (2007). Educating the workforce for the 21st century: A cross-disciplinary analysis of the impact of the undergraduate experience on students' development of a pluralistic orientation. *Research in Higher Education*, *48*, 283–317.

Engberg, M. E., & Hurtado, S. (2011). Developing pluralistic skills and dispositions in college: Examining racial/ethnic group differences. *The Journal of Higher Education*, *82*, 416–443.

Feldman, K. A., & Newcomb, T. M. (1969). *The impact of college on students*. San Francisco, CA: Jossey-Bass.

Festinger, L. (1957). *A theory of cognitive dissonance*. Stanford, CA: Stanford University Press.

Guo, S., & Fraser, M. W. (2015). *Propensity score analysis: Statistical methods and applications* (2nd ed.). Los Angeles, CA: Sage.

Gurin, P. (1999). Expert report. "Gratz et al. v. Bollinger, et al." No. 97-75321 (E.D. Mich.); "Grutter, et al. v. Bollinger, et al." No. 97-75928 (E.D. Mich.). *Equity & Excellence in Education*, *32*(2), 36–62.

Gurin, P., Dey, E. L., Hurtado, S., & Gurin, G. (2002). Diversity and higher education: Theory and impact on educational outcomes. *Harvard Educational Review*, *72*(3), 330–367.

Harackiewicz, J. M., Canning, E. A., Tibbetts, Y., Giffen, C. J., & Hyde, J. S. (2014). Closing the social class achievement gap for first-generation students in undergraduate biology. *Journal of Educational Psychology*, *106*, 375–389.

Heck, R. H., & Thomas, S. L. (2008). *An introduction to multilevel modeling techniques* (2nd ed.). New York. NY: Routledge.

Holmes, W. M. (2013). *Using propensity scores in quasi-experimental designs*. Los Angeles, CA: Sage.

Hong, G., & Raudenbush, S. W. (2005). Effects of kindergarten retention policy on children's cognitive growth in reading and mathematics. *Educational Evaluation and Policy Analysis*, *27*, 205–224.

Hong, G., & Raudenbush, S. W. (2006). Evaluating kindergarten retention policy: A case study of causal inference for multilevel observational data. *Journal of the American Statistical Association*, *101*, 901–910.

Hurtado, S. (2005). The next generation of diversity and intergroup relations research. *Journal of Social Issues, 61*, 595–610.

Hyun, M. (1994). *Helping to promote racial understanding: Does it matter if you're Black or White?* Paper presented at the annual meeting of Association of the Study of Higher Education, Tucson, AZ.

Jayakumar, U. M. (2008). Can higher education meet the needs of an increasingly diverse and global society? Campus diversity and cross-cultural work competencies. *Harvard Educational Review, 78*, 615–651.

Katz, J. H., & Ivey, A. (1977). White awareness: The frontier of racism awareness training. *Personnel and Guidance Journal* (April), 485–489.

Kotori, C. (2009). College impact on civic attitudes of Asian American and White undergraduate students: A comparative study. *Dissertation Abstracts International, 69*(07), 263A. (UMI No. 3315512)

Luke, D. A. (2004). *Multilevel modeling*. Thousand Oaks, CA: Sage.

Malcom, L. E., & Dowd, A. C. (2012). The impact of undergraduate debt on the graduate school enrollment of STEM baccalaureates. *The Review of Higher Education, 35*(2), 265–305.

Mayhew, M. J., Rockenbach, A. N., Bowman, N. A., Seifert, T. A., & Wolniak, G. C., with Pascarella, E. T., & Terenzini, P. T. (2016). *How college affects students (Vol. 3): 21st century evidence that higher education works*. San Francisco, CA: Jossey-Bass.

McCauley, C., Wright, M., & Harris, M. E. (2000). Diversity workshops on campus: A survey of current practice at U.S. colleges and universities. *The College Student Journal, 34*(1), 100–114.

Melguizo, T., Kienzl, G. S., & Alfonso, M. (2011). Comparing the educational attainment of community college transfer students and four-year college rising juniors using propensity score matching methods. *The Journal of Higher Education, 82*(3), 265–291.

Milem, J. E. (1994). College, students, and racial understanding. Thought and Action, 9(2), 51–92.

Milem, J. F., Umbach, P. D., & Liang, C. T. H. (2004). Exploring the perpetuation hypothesis: The role of colleges and universities in desegregating society. *Journal of College Student Development, 45*, 688–700.

Miyake, A., Kost-Smith, L. E., Finkelstein, N. D., Pollock, S. J., Cohen, G. L., & Ito, A. (2010). Reducing the gender achievement gap in college science: A classroom study of values affirmation. *Science, 330*, 1234–1237.

Nelson Laird, T. F. (2005). College students' experiences with diversity and their effects on academic self-confidence, social agency, and disposition toward critical thinking. *Research in Higher Education, 46*, 365–387.

Nelson Laird, T. F., Engberg, M. E., & Hurtado, S (2005). Modeling accentuation effects: Enrolling in a diversity course and the importance of social engagement. *Journal of Higher Education, 76*, 448–476.

Orfield, G. (2009). *Reviving the goal of an integrated society: A 21st century challenge*. Los Angeles, CA: The Civil Rights Project/Proyecto Derechos Civiles at UCLA.

Orfield, G., Kucsera, J., & Siegel-Hawley, G. (2012). *E pluribus. . . separation: Deepening double segregation for more students*. Los Angeles, CA: The Civil Rights Project/Proyecto Derechos Civiles at UCLA.

Park, J. J. (2009). Are we satisfied? A look at student satisfaction with diversity at traditionally White institutions. *The Review of Higher Education, 32*(3), 291–320.

Park, J. J., & Denson, N. (2009). Attitudes and advocacy: Understanding faculty views on racial/ethnic diversity. *Journal of Higher Education, 80*(4), 415–438.

Pascarella, E., Edison, M., Nora, A., Hagedorn, L., & Terenzini, P. (1996). Influences on students' openness to diversity and challenge in the first year of college. *Journal of Higher Education, 67*, 174–195.

Pascarella, E. T., Salisbury, M. H., & Blaich, C. (2013). Design and analysis in college impact research: Which counts more? *Journal of College Student Development, 54*, 329–335.

Petersen, T. (1985). A comment on presenting results from logit and probit models. *American Sociological Review, 50*, 130–131.

Pettigrew, T. F., & Tropp, L. R. (2006). A meta-analytic test of intergroup contact theory. *Journal of Personality and Social Psychology, 90*, 751–783.

Piaget, J. (1971). The theory of stages in cognitive development. In D. R. Green, M. P. Ford, & G. B. Flamer (Eds.), *Measurement and Piaget* (pp. 1–111). New York, NY: McGraw-Hill.

Piaget, J. (1985). *The equilibrium of cognitive structures: The central problem of intellectual development*. Chicago, IL: University of Chicago Press. (Original work published 1975)

Raudenbush, S. W., & Bryk, A. S. (2002). *Hierarchical linear models: Applications and data analysis methods* (2nd ed.). Newbury Park, CA: Sage.

Rosenbaum, P. R. (2002). *Observational studies* (2nd ed.). New York, NY: Springer.

Ruble, D. N. (1994). A phase model of transitions: Cognitive and motivational consequences. In M. P. Zanna (Ed.), *Advances in experimental social psychology* (Vol. 26, pp. 163–214). San Diego, CA: Academic Press.

Saenz, V. B. (2010). Breaking the segregation cycle: Examining students' precollege racial environments and college diversity experiences. *Review of Higher Education, 34*, 1–37.

Saenz, V. B., Ngai, H. N., & Hurtado, S. (2007). Factors influencing positive interactions across race for African American, Asian American, Latino, and White college students. *Research in Higher Education, 48*, 1–38.

Schoem, D., Hurtado, S., Sevig, T., Chesler, M., & Sumida, S. H. (2001). Intergroup dialogue: Democracy at work in theory and practice. In D. Schoem & S. Hurtado (Eds.), *Intergroup dialogue: Deliberative democracy in school, college, community, and workplace* (pp. 1–21). Ann Arbor, MI: The University of Michigan Press.

Shadish, W. R., Cook, T. D., & Campbell, D. T. (2002). *Experimental and quasi-experimental designs for generalized causal inference* (2nd ed.). Boston, MA: Houghton Mifflin.

Sherman, D. K., Hartson, K. A., Binning, K. R., Purdie-Vaughns, V., Garcia, J., Taborsky-Barba, S., . . . Cohen, G. L. (2013). Deflecting the trajectory and changing the narrative: How self-affirmation affects academic performance and motivation under identity threat. *Journal of Personality and Social Psychology, 104*, 591–618.

Smith, D. (2009). *Diversity's promise for higher education: Making it work*. Baltimore, MD: Johns Hopkins University Press.

Sniderman, P. M., Crosby, G. C., & Howell, W. C. (2000). The politics of race. In D. O. Sears, J. Sidanius, & L. Bobo (Eds.), *Racialized politics: The debate about racism in America* (pp. 236–279). Chicago, IL: University of Chicago.

Snijders, T. A. B., & Bosker, R. (2012). *Multilevel analysis: An introduction to basic and advanced multilevel modeling* (2nd ed.). Thousand Oaks, CA: Sage.

Springer, L., Palmer, B., Terenzini, P. T., Pascarella, E. T., & Nora, A. (1996). Attitudes toward campus diversity: Participation in a racial or cultural awareness workshop. *The Review of Higher Education, 20*(1), 53–68.

Steiner, P. M., Cook, T. D., Shadish, W. R., & Clark, M. H. (2010). The importance of covariate selection in controlling for selection bias in observational studies. *Psychological Methods, 15,* 250–267.

Taylor, S. H. (1994). Enhancing tolerance: The confluence of moral development with the college experience. *Dissertation Abstracts International, 56*(01), 114A. (UMI No. 9513291)

Thomas, S. L., & Heck, R. H. (2001). Analysis of large-scale secondary data in higher education research: Potential perils associated with complex sampling designs. *Research in Higher Education, 42,* 517–540.

Thyer, B. A. (2012). *Quasi-experimental research designs.* New York, NY: Oxford University Press.

Valentine, J. C., & Cooper, H. (2003). *Effect size substantive interpretation guidelines: Issues in the interpretation of effect sizes.* Washington, DC: What Works Clearinghouse, U.S. Department of Education.

Vogelgesang, L. J. (2001). *The impact of college on the development of civic values: How do race and gender matter?* Paper presented at the annual meeting of the American Educational Research Association, Seattle, WA.

Walton, G. M., & Cohen, G. L. (2011). A brief social-belonging intervention improves academic and health outcomes among minority students. *Science, 331,* 1447–1451.

Whitt, E. J., Edison, M. I., Pascarella, E. T., Terenzini, P. T., & Nora, A. (2001). Influences on students' openness to diversity in the second and third years of college. *Journal of Higher Education, 72,* 172–204.

Yeager, D. S., & Walton, G. M. (2011). Social-psychological interventions in education: They're not magic. *Review of Educational Research, 81,* 267–301.

Zuniga, X., Williams, E. A., & Berger, J. B. (2005). Action-oriented democratic outcomes: The impact of student involvement with campus diversity. *Journal of College Student Development, 46,* 660–678.

Manuscript received April 23, 2014
Final revision received January 11, 2016
Accepted August 1, 2016

American Educational Research Journal
December 2016, Vol. 53, No. 6, pp. 1588–1625
DOI: 10.3102/0002831216674805
© *2016 AERA. http://aerj.aera.net*

Social Mobility and Reproduction for Whom? College Readiness and First-Year Retention

Linda DeAngelo
University of Pittsburgh
Ray Franke
University of Massachusetts Boston

Completing college is now the minimum threshold for entry into the middle class. This has pushed college readiness issues to the forefront in efforts to increase educational attainment. Little is known about how college readiness improves outcomes for students traditionally marginalized in educational settings or if social background factors continue to impact students in the same way during college regardless of readiness. Examining first-year college retention using a nationally representative data set, this study asks if social background factors and financial resources for college differentially impact students based on readiness. Findings indicate that academic readiness matters and that parental income and college generation status differentially affect first-year college retention for less-ready students but not college-ready students. Students who begin college less prepared academically are also more disadvantaged than college-ready students by the funding sources they have for college. Implications for policy and practice are discussed.

LINDA DEANGELO is assistant professor of higher education and Center for Urban Education Fellow at the University of Pittsburgh, 5908 Posvar Hall, 230 S. Bouquet St., Pittsburgh, PA 15260, USA; e-mail: *deangelo@pitt.edu*. She studies stratification, equity, and diversity issues, investigating how social inequalities are produced within higher education. Her work examines the differential effect of institutions on students, pipeline and educational transitions, and outcomes for first-generation, low-income, and underrepresented students. Currently her scholarship focuses on retention, degree completion, and access to and engagement in faculty mentorship.

RAY FRANKE is an assistant professor of higher education in the College of Education and Human Development at the University of Massachusetts Boston. His research foci include higher education finance and financial aid, education policy, and organizational change in the United States and internationally. His recent work has examined how federal, state, and institutional financial aid programs and policy affect access to and success in higher education for students from different socioeconomic and racial/ethnic backgrounds.

Keywords: achievement gap, college readiness, effectively maintained inequality, higher education, retention, social stratification

Attending college and earning a degree have never been more important for social mobility. In fact, earning a degree is now the minimum threshold for entry into the middle class (Carnevale, Smith, & Strohl, 2010; Rothwell, 2012). In the higher education literature and on campuses across the United States, reform efforts and research have focused on increasing access to higher education for previously marginalized groups. This attention has contributed to dramatic increases in higher education attendance among underrepresented students (Astin & Osegura, 2004; Posselt, Jaquette, Bielby, & Bastedo, 2012). Despite these gains and a college-for-all ethos (Rosenbaum, 2001), degree attainment has not significantly increased (Alon, Domina, & Tienda, 2010; Roksa, 2010), and social inequality has actually grown (Dwyer, 2013; Grusky, Western, & Wimer, 2011; McCall, 2001). Attrition among students who begin college at a four-year institution is nearly 30% (American College Testing [ACT], 2013a) and has been increasing since 2009 (National Student Clearinghouse, 2013). These realities make additional research related to retention and educational attainment increasingly urgent.

The current study examines first-year retention focusing on the role of social status background factors among students of differing college readiness. College students do not arrive on campus equally prepared for academic success. Low-income and underrepresented students are less likely to begin college academically prepared for success and are the most likely to leave college prior to earning a degree (Adelman, 2006). While it is possible that differences in academic preparation explain higher rates of attrition in the first year of college and studies consistently find a relationship between prior academic achievement and retention (see Cabrera, Miner, & Milem, 2013), the interrelationships between academic preparation, social status background factors, and retention remain unclear. Prior research has yet to address these relationships directly.

We address this gap in the literature by explicitly investigating how the relationship between social status background and first-year retention may be different based on readiness. To do this, we examine influences of social status background on retention separately for college-ready students and students who begin higher education with less academic preparation, a departure from past studies that have examined readiness as one or more factors among many. With this modeling approach, we investigate the ways in which college readiness might interrupt the mechanisms that transmit the effects of social status across generations. Understanding the continuing and differential role of social status background factors in the status transmission process at this key transition along the educational attainment pipeline has important consequences for designing policy and practices that are consistent with increasing educational success.

Literature Review

This review begins with a discussion of the theoretical grounding that serves as the foundation for this study. A discussion of college readiness and the nascent literature emerging on the relationship of college readiness to retention and degree attainment follows. This section concludes with a review of recent retention and degree completion literature examining the role of social background factors and the financial resources students use to fund college. In doing so, we frame this study with six decades of theory and related research.

Theoretical Grounding

Two competing theoretical narratives have emerged in the educational and social attainment literature that influence the approach we take in this study. One narrative, status attainment theory, focuses on academic achievement and expectations for achievement as the primary mechanism for social mobility and success over the life course. The second encompasses critiques of that notion and centers on the continuing and predominant role of social status of origin and material circumstances despite educational achievement.

Status attainment theory emerged as a frame to examine social reproduction in the 1960s. Blau and Duncan (1967) developed it to examine how social status positions perpetuate across generations, and Sewell and colleagues (Sewell, Haller, & Ohlendorf, 1970; Sewell, Haller, & Portes, 1969) extended it to focus on the socialization processes through which family status background and relationships with significant others influence social status attainment in adulthood. The framework states that expectations for educational attainment and subsequent success and achievement in the educational arena are the central factors through which individuals achieve both social status (mobility) and maintain it (reproduction). The status attainment framework posits that interactions with family and significant others as well as self-assessment of one's potential based on academic performance form expectations for educational attainment (Knotterus, 1987). Signals from these sources combine and work together as students form expectations about their educational attainment.

In their critiques of status attainment theory, Kerckhoff (1984) and Bozick, Alexander, Entwisle, Dauber, and Kerr (2010) represent the alternative understanding of the status attainment process. Kerckhoff's critique focuses on the social allocation aspects of reproduction, whereas Bozick and colleagues focus on the explanatory power of status attainment theory to explain differences in attainment between individuals from higher and lower status families. Specifically, Kerckhoff argued that status attainment theory fails to acknowledge the role of material circumstances in molding outcomes. Thus, educational continuation decisions, despite expectations, could be constrained for lower status individuals by what an individual assesses can reasonably be achieved given both known and perceived constraints. For instance, the experience of attending college may give lower income students information about the achievability of a degree that they did not have previously, such as the difficulty of performing at a college level while working at a full-time job or the lack of support their particular institution provides, whether monetarily or otherwise. Thus, students who begin college expecting to earn a degree may find that they can reasonably project they will not complete their degree on the basis of information they gain in the first year and elect not to continue.

Bozick et al. (2010) argue that students receive different signals about their potential for college success depending on their social stratum of origin. In a study examining the socialization messages regarding college that students received from their families, these scholars find that students from high status families receive consistent messages that they are college material early on and throughout their schooling experiences, whereas lower status families provide mixed messages about prospects for college. They conclude that status attainment theory underestimates the force through which family structural location influences attainment over the life course through the allocation of these messages, arguing that mixed messages will influence some students to be easily deterred from achieving a college degree. Taken together, Kerckhoff's (1984) and Bozick et al.'s critiques address how signals in the environment about one's potential and limits on the realization of that potential take shape differently depending on social stratum of origin.

Focusing on how structural inequalities manifest themselves rather than status attainment among individuals, Lucas's (2001) theory of effectively maintained inequality posits that families and individuals with status will secure for themselves and their children some degree of advantage wherever the educational system affords that possibility. He argues that the site of conflict in securing advantage is determined at each level of education by the degree to which that level is universally obtained. When a particular level of education is near universally attained (in the United States earning a high school diploma), families of higher status will work to secure qualitatively better education at that level for their children, and when different levels of education are attained (in the United States earning a college degree), families will work to secure quantitatively more education for their children. Thus, higher status students will secure both better and more education based on their status position. In an effectively maintained inequality framework, students who are not fully college ready will nonetheless continue past their first year of college—and probably to obtaining a degree—*if* they have a higher social background, while students from lower social status backgrounds will not.

College Readiness

The large majority of college students today begin college not fully prepared for success (ACT, 2013b; College Board, 2013). Assessments of college readiness most often use three factors that have both overlapping and distinctive qualities: high school course-taking patterns, high school GPA, and standardized test scores. As Roderick, Nagaoka, and Coca (2009) explain, high school course-taking patterns provide a measure of exposure to the content knowledge needed in introductory college coursework, high school GPA measures the development of core academic skills and content knowledge, and test scores provide a standard measure of ability and core academic skills. Thus, high school course-taking patterns and high school GPA both assess content knowledge, and test scores and high school GPA both assess core academic skills. High school GPA also distinctively assesses noncognitive skills such as effort and study skills that students need to succeed in college. Gaps in readiness are more apparent using high school GPA rather than test scores as a measure of readiness, particularly in examining differences by sex and race/ethnicity (Roderick, Nagaoka, & Allensworth, 2006). In addition, high school GPA is a stronger predictor of academic achievement during the first college year (Cabrera et al., 2013; Roderick et al., 2009; Wolniak & Engberg, 2010), first-year retention (Cabrera et al., 2013), and degree completion (Geiser & Santelices, 2007; Roderick et al., 2006) than standardized test scores.

Current policy in the United States focuses on increasing college readiness through more rigorous course-taking patterns in high school (Roderick et al., 2009). Results from NCES's National Association of Educational Progress (NAEP) and from the Higher Education Research Institute (HERI) as well as data from ACT and SAT test takers document persistent and continuing gaps in course-taking patterns by race/ethnicity (ACT, 2009; College Board, 2012; Planty, Bozick, & Ingels, 2006; Pryor, Hurtado, DeAngelo, Blake, & Tran, 2009; Roderick et al., 2009), socioeconomic status (College Board, 2012; Planty et al., 2006), and first-generation status (Lohfink & Paulsen, 2005). These differences contribute to measured gaps in achievement on college entrance exams (ACT, 2009; College Board, 2012).

The connection between high school course-taking patterns and first-year retention has also begun to emerge as a focus of retention and degree completion studies. Warburton, Bugarin, Nunez, and Carroll's (2001) study of degree completion using NCES data found that students who took rigorous courses in high school were more likely to be retained to degree. Additionally, in examining their descriptive data they found that first-generation students who had completed a rigorous course sequence in high school were just as likely to complete a degree as continuing generation students. Studying the role of high school course-taking patterns separately for first-generation and continuing generation students with regression, Lohfink and Paulsen (2005), using Beginning Postsecondary Student (BPS) data, found that level of rigor in course-taking made no difference to retention within either group. These findings suggest that readiness for college might help to mitigate social background factors that are thought to put students at risk for attrition.

The Role of Socioeconomic Status and Financial Resources for College on Retention

The positive connection between socioeconomic status and retention and degree completion is one of the most consistent findings in the literature (Astin & Oseguera, 2005; Bozick, 2007; Cabrera, Burkum, & La Nasa, 2005; DeAngelo, Frank, Hurtado, Pryor, & Tran, 2011; Franke, 2012; Herzog, 2005; Hu & St. John, 2001; Ishitani, 2006; Leppel, 2002; Lohfink & Paulsen, 2005; Paulsen & St. John, 2002). Among these, Bozick's (2007) work using BPS data to study first-year retention is particularly relevant to the current study. He found that family income and family wealth had a direct and strong relationship with first-year retention and that family income and wealth mediate the experience students have on campus, which directly connects to retention. Thus, he identified a cumulative disadvantage for low-income students. Low-income students in the study were much more likely to have high intensity work schedules (more than 20 hours per week) than their high income peers and more likely to live with their parents, both of which connected directly to first-year attrition.

Other studies have confirmed the higher intensity work patterns in college of low-income students (Terenzini, Cabrera, & Bernal 2001; Walpole, 2003) and the effect of high intensity work on retention in the first college year (DeAngelo, 2014; Gilardi & Guglielmetti, 2011; Roksa, 2010). Intent to work full-time in college has also been negatively connected to degree completion (Astin & Oseguera, 2005; DeAngelo et al., 2011). On the other hand, Lohfink and Paulsen (2005) did not find a significant link between living on campus and first-year retention for either their first-generation or continuing generation student sample groups. In fact, first-generation students who chose the college they attended at least in part because it allowed them to live at home were more frequently retained. These findings challenge Bozick's (2007) results associating living with parents and college attrition.

Herzog's (2005) study addresses low-income students through a focus on financial aid. Using almost a decade's worth of cohort data from a single institution, Herzog found that when low-income students have a statewide scholarship paying full tuition in place, their likelihood of retention was higher than in years in which the scholarship was not in place and in which students had to use a combination of scholarships and loans to fund college. Thus, it seems these students benefited in terms of retention from having a single stable source of funding for college. At the same time, large amounts of grant aid did not entirely mitigate the disadvantage low-income students faced. They had lower odds of being retained at the end of the first year of college than high-income students regardless of funding.

Related directly to loans, Herzog's (2005) study found that loans in any amount were detrimental to first-year retention for low-income students. Other studies show the benefits of grants and detriments of loans to first-year retention for first-generation students (Ishitani, 2006; Lohfink & Paulsen, 2005) and the benefit of grants to first-year retention overall (Chen & DesJardins, 2010; DesJardins, Ahlburg, & McCall, 2002). However, Cabrera and colleagues (2005) found that loans facilitated degree completion, even among low-income students. More generally, studies demonstrate a negative connection between unmet financial need and concern about financing college and retention (Alon, 2007; DeAngelo, 2014; Herzog, 2005; Paulsen & St. John, 2002) as well as degree completion (Astin & Oseguera, 2005; DeAngelo et al., 2011).

In considering these findings as they relate to financial aid and educational attainment, it is important to recognize that the current policy context in the United States increasingly favors merit-based grants over need-based grants as well as a much heavier reliance on loans as an aid mechanism (Perna & Finney, 2014). The movement from need-based to merit-based grant aid has resulted in an increase in grant aid for high-performing, college-ready students regardless of need (Doyle, 2006; Perna & Finney, 2014). This direction is part of an overall policy context in which the large burden of funding the cost of college has shifted to the individual and away from the public in the form of state support for institutions and other public mechanisms of providing support for educational attainment.

Summary and Gaps in the Literature

Factors related to socioeconomic status clearly exert an influence on students during college, producing a substantial cumulative effect on the likelihood of degree completion. Further, research shows that socioeconomic status operates in part by influencing several specific decisions and conditions that affect degree attainment, including the number of hours students work, their place of residence, and the amount and type of financial aid they receive, all of which influence educational attainment decisions. The college readiness literature also reveals that socioeconomic status and other background factors influence who begins college prepared to succeed and that readiness factors may have the potential to level out the playing field for students once in college. Overall, the literature suggests that the processes through which readiness influences educational attainment may operate differently based on social status background and that both competing theoretical notions of social mobility and reproduction may be at play. College readiness may be a mediator in relation to first-year retention, interrupting mechanisms that transmit the effects of social status background across generations.

Although research to date suggests that social status background factors may predict retention differently based on readiness and that the transmission of social status across generations might be different for students who begin college academically prepared and those who begin with less preparation, research examining this link directly is limited. To address this gap from a methodological standpoint, studies need to take into account that readiness shares covariance in predicting retention with social status background factors. One way to do this is to disaggregate the data by college readiness. We disaggregate our data into two distinct readiness groups to focus on how the pattern of relationships predicting retention might be different for students whose preparation is above or below a critical readiness threshold as established in the literature (Planty et al., 2006; Pryor et al., 2008; Roderick et al., 2009) and as a means to study the social processes of status transmission related to first-year retention for these two groups.

By isolating and investigating the relationship between social status factors at a specific educational transition, this study supplements life course studies of educational attainment by reducing the likelihood of confounding the effects of socioeconomic status at a particular educational transition with earlier attainment points (Ewert, 2010). The theoretical and conceptual frames we bring to this study offer a rich analysis. As Lucas and Beresford (2010) assert, bringing theory-driven research to studies of educational transitions and success is the key to making progress to increase overall educational attainment.

Research Questions

Studying first-year retention separately for college-ready and less-ready students and focusing on how the processes related to educational attainment and social status transmission at this juncture differ based on social status background, we investigated the following research questions:

Research Question 1: How do college-ready and less-ready first-time, full-time students differ with respect to socioeconomic background, financial resources for college, and demographic characteristics?

Research Question 2: To what extent do socioeconomic background, financial resources for college, and demographic characteristics contribute to first-year retention differently for college-ready and less-ready students?

Methodology

Data Source and Sample

The Higher Education Research Institute (HERI) at the University of California, Los Angeles provided the data for this study. The data set draws from two main sources, the 2004 Freshman Survey (TFS) from the Cooperative Institutional Research Program (CIRP) at HERI and the National Student Clearinghouse (NSC). The TFS is a national survey of incoming college students designed to gather information about student background, high school experiences, financial resources for college, the college choice process, and expectations for experiences in college among other topics. NSC, which has been tracking enrollment and degree completion for participating institutions since 1993, provides data on student persistence. Through merging these data sources, HERI created a unique data set that allows for the study of the movement, persistence, and degree attainment of students at higher education institutions in the United States. To compensate for missing values, HERI carried out a multiple imputation method based on a multivariate normal approach in order to preserve the data set in its near entirety. The final, combined 2004 TFS/NSC data set that this study used encompasses 210,056 full-time, first-time students at 356 four-year colleges and universities (see DeAngelo et al., 2011, for details on data and imputation methodology). For analyses, the sample was weighted to be nationally representative for entering first-year students in 2004 following the procedures used at HERI for over 40 years (see DeAngelo et al., 2011, for details on weighting).

Based on our review of the literature, we define college readiness using a combination of high school course-taking patterns and high school GPA. We defined course-taking readiness based on readiness definitions adopted by HERI (Pryor et al., 2008) and NAEP (Horn & Kojaku, 2001). College-ready students have a B+ or better high school GPA and have completed four years of English, three years of math, two years of a foreign language, one year each of biological and physical sciences, plus an additional year of one or the other (in total three years of science), one year of history/government, and one year of arts. In our data set, 113,167 students (53.8%, unweighted) met our course-taking patterns requirements, and 151,937 students (72.3%, unweighted) met our GPA requirements. Taking both readiness factors together, 86,863 students (41.4%, unweighted) were college-ready. The remaining 123,193 students (58.6%, unweighted) did not meet at least one of the two necessary criteria and were classified as less-ready.

Measures

For the purposes of our study, we coded the dependent variable 1 for individuals who continued at their initial institution of enrollment after one year and 0 for those who did not. Although some students who leave their initial institution do successfully enter and graduate at other institutions, attrition from one's initial institution and student movement generally dampens one's chances of degree attainment and is especially troublesome for underrepresented populations (Kalogrides & Grodsky, 2011). Thus, we focus on persistence at the initial college or university into the second college year, the traditional dependent variable used to study retention in the higher education literature. See Appendix A for a full listing of the variables and coding schemes.

To address our research questions as they relate to relationships between socioeconomic status, financial resources for college, demographics, and first-year retention, we included a set of 15 variables in our model. To represent student socioeconomic status, we included parental income and first-generation status. We recoded the categorical parental income variable in the TFS into quartiles and inserted them as dummy variables. We determined first-generation status by parental educational attainment and inserted it as a dummy variable as well. If neither parent had college experience, we considered a student first generation. To examine the influence of the financial resources students use to fund college during the first year, we included measures for various sources of financial assistance, including family resources used to finance one's education, grants received, and loans. We recoded the categorical aid measures in the TFS into five dummy variables for each of these three financial aid sources. We incorporated a measure for students' financial concern, which we recoded into three dummy variables, each representing a different level of concern regarding having enough funds to complete college.

We incorporated students' SAT composite scores, which research shows correlate with family income (Bowen, Chingos, & McPherson, 2009) and are predictive of retention and degree completion. From the senior year of high school, we include hours per week spent studying and on household duties, both of which are known to be associated with family income (Fuligni & Pederson, 2002). Furthermore, hours per week spent studying is thought to indicate, in part, noncognitive habits of mind indicative of college readiness and predictive of college success (Conley, 2005, 2010). We also include measures of how students make the choice of which college they will attend; specifically, we include the degree to which a student chooses their institution because of cost and the degree to which they choose based on wanting to live near home. The distance the college attended is from home, the living arrangements students have made for their first college year, and intent to work full-time while attending college are also included. Lastly, we included an aggregated parental income measure at the institutional level to test if the overall socioeconomic status climate on campus had an effect on retention over and above any student level effects. Palardy's (2013) research on the significant role of aggregate socioeconomic status at high schools on college going supports this as an important variable for consideration.

To measure the relationship between student demographics and retention, we include student sex and race/ethnicity. Race/ethnicity is included as group of seven dummy variables in the analyses: African American, Asian American, American Indian, Latino/a, White (reference group), multiracial, and other.

To fully fill out our model based on the background literature on retention and degree completion in the higher education literature, we use Nora, Barlow, and Crisp's (2005) student/institution engagement model as a guide, focusing on the pre-college and intentions for college aspects of the model. By testing a fuller model, we can assess if factors of primary concern to this study are still significant even when other factors with a known connection to retention and degree completion are taken into account. At the student level based on this model, we include students' level of academic and social self-concept prior to the start of college, the hours per week in the senior year of high school devoted to student clubs/groups and volunteering, advanced degree aspirations, the intention to transfer to another college before graduating, having a declared major at the start of college, willingness to change one's major after starting college, and planning to be involved in campus life (for empirical validation of the inclusion of these variables, see Astin & Oseguera, 2005; DeAngelo et al., 2011). At the institutional level based on the research literature, we include selectivity, private or public institutional control, and aggregate transfer likelihood among the student population (Astin & Oseguera, 2005; DeAngelo, et al., 2011; Oseguera, 2005; Oseguera & Rhee, 2009). Lastly, we incorporated an indicator for Historically Black Colleges and Universities (HBCU control), due to the strong representation of African American students at these institutions in the data set.

Data Analysis

For our analyses, we evaluate models of first-year retention separately for the two readiness groups (college-ready, less-ready) using hierarchical generalized linear modeling (HGLM). This analytic strategy is consistent with the purpose of this study and recognizes that college readiness is derived from a discrete number of readily identifiable factors and that students are identified and understood by policymakers, practitioners, and administrators through a dichotomy as it relates to readiness. Modeling in a manner that is consistent with how students are understood helps to make our findings actionable by these external groups. Methodologically, although it might be argued that college readiness has elements of a continuous latent trait at the theoretical level and should be modeled as such with interaction terms used to identify significant differences between readiness and other key factors in the model, this strategy is problematic because it assumes that the potential mediating effect of college readiness in the relationship between social background factors and retention are similar and linear at different levels of readiness (Steinberg & Fletcher, 1998). Instead, the retention process may be substantially different above or below a critical readiness threshold. In addition, the complexity of interacting readiness with other key variables to identify significant differences can make interpreting main effects difficult (Warner, 2012) and is not the most efficient way to analyze the data for our purposes.[1]

The multilevel approach we carried out in this study has advantages over conventional analyses, such as ordinary least squares (OLS) or logistic regression, as it accounts for the dependence among students within colleges. It provides more efficient and reliable estimates in cases of unbalanced, nested data structures (Raudenbush, Bryk, Cheong, & Congdon, 2004). In building models within HGLM, analysts must ensure that the outcome significantly varies across institutions (Niehaus, Campbell, & Inkelas, 2014; Raudenbush & Bryk, 2004). To do this, we analyzed the random variance component from a fully unconditional model to determine whether the likelihood of retention at the end of the first year for both college readiness student groups varies significantly across institutions. The fully unconditional model suggested that institutions significantly differed in the average propensity of retention. Using the between-institution variance component to calculate the intraclass correlation (ICC), the results showed that 12.3% of the variability for less college-ready students is between institutions. For the college-ready students, the between-institution variability is only slightly lower at 10.2%, which indicates sufficient Level 2 variability to justify the use of a multilevel method. Considering the ICC results, we proceeded with building the full analytic models. We carried out all analyses using HLM 7.

For our analyses, we recoded categorical predictors in the data set into dummy variables before they were entered in the HGLM models. A series of diagnostic tests was carried out before the final analytic model was run, using procedures from Hosmer and Lemeshow (2004) and Tabachnick and Fidell (2007). All diagnostics were run on the full data set and separately for the two readiness groups under study. We also ran diagnostics separately for the original and all imputed data sets. First, we inspected all categorical variables for empty and low frequency cells but found no zero cells and no cells with expected frequency lower than five. Second, we examined the variance inflation factor (VIF) for each of the predictor variables, as a test of multicollinearity within the model, after visually inspecting coefficients and standard errors for exceedingly large values. All variables had a VIF below 2.0; thus, they were far below a critical threshold, and therefore all variables were retained in the analytical model. Third, we examined the linearity of the logit of the dependent variable for continuous predictors. For this, all continuous variables were transformed using the natural log and included together with the original predictors in the analysis. We inspected chi-square statistics in the likelihood ratio test but found no problematic values (using $p = .001$). Lastly, we plotted predicted probabilities against Cook's distance, a measure for multivariate outliers. For the group of college-ready students, we detected two data points that seemed distant from the rest of the distribution. However, when we excluded these points from the analysis, results did not change, thus we retained them in the data set.

To perform our main analyses, we specified the following within-college model. Due to the dichotomous nature of the outcome variable, the Level 1 (student-level) HGLM model uses a Bernoulli sampling distribution and logit link function:

$$\text{Prob}\,(Y_{ij} = |\beta_{ij}) = \Phi_{ij}. \tag{1}$$

The following equation characterizes the Level 1 (student-level or within-institution) model:

$$\text{Log}\left[\frac{\Phi_{ij}}{1 - \Phi_{ij}}\right] = \beta_{0j} + \beta_{1j} \times (\text{Demographics})_{ij} + \beta_{2j} \times (\text{Socioeconomic Status})_{ij}$$
$$+ \beta_{3j} \times (\text{Financial Resources \& Concern})_{ij} \tag{2}$$
$$+ \beta_{4j} \times (\text{Controls})_{ij} + e_{ij},$$

where i denotes the individual student and j represents the institution. The variable vectors included in the model represent characteristics and experiences we believe influence the outcome variable—retention at the end of the first year.

The Level 2 (institution-level or between-institution) model is represented by:

$$\beta_{0j} = \gamma_{00} + \gamma_{01} \times (\text{Aggregate Parental Income})_j$$
$$+ \gamma_{02} \times (\text{Institutional Characteristics})_j + u_{0j}, \tag{3}$$

where j denotes the institution, γ_{00} represents the average likelihood of retention across all institutions, and u_{oj} the random variance component for institution j. The variables included at the institution level describe how the context at four-year colleges and universities affect the student's average likelihood of first-year retention.

Multilevel modeling techniques require a consideration of how variables are centered (Raudenbush et al., 2004). For this study, all dichotomous predictors at the student and institutional levels have been inserted uncentered into the model. Continuous variables at the student level are group-mean centered, centered on their unadjusted institutional mean. Group-mean centering allows the intercept to represent the log-odds of being retained in the first college year for students who have average characteristics for the Level 1 variables at the same institution and is the appropriate centering technique given the purposes of this study and Level 2 controls. At the institutional level, continuous measures are grand-mean centered, the standard choice at Level 2.

Limitations

The use of TFS/NSC data presents a limitation to this study. Participation in the NSC has been increasing since its inception in 1993; more than 3,600 postsecondary education institutions submitted student enrollment and degree completion data for cohort 2004. Though coverage is widespread and continuously increasing, the quality of the data used in our study is affected by the proportion of data that can be matched between CIRP's 2004 Freshmen Survey and the NSC. Not all students that participated in 2004's administration of the TFS could be matched to NSC data, which could result in biases. However, from the 424,808 students that participated in the TFS, almost three-fifths (57.1% or 243,676) could be matched to NSC data (for a recent discussion of Clearinghouse data limitations, see Dynarski, Hemelt, & Hyman, 2013). Another limitation arises from the fact that the TFS survey relies on self-reported data for all its measures, which may also insert bias into the estimation.

Results

Descriptive Results

In the nationally weighted data set, 38% of students met the criteria for placement in the college-ready group. The remaining 62% did not meet at least one of the two necessary requirements and were thus classified into the less-ready group. These figures are on par with readiness figures from the College Board (2013), which classified 43% of incoming college students as ready for college. In our nationally weighted data set, 83% of the overall student population were retained into the second year. Among the college-ready group, the retention rate is higher at 88%, whereas among the less-ready group, the retention rate is lower at 78%; this difference is statistically significant ($p < .000$). This amounts to a loss of 58,041 students in the college-ready group and 178,468 students in the less-ready group in the first year. This means that students who begin college less-ready account for 75% of the attrition in the first year.

Table 1 provides the socioeconomic status, financial resources for college, and demographic characteristics of the college-ready and less-ready student groups in the weighted dataset. Female students have a higher representation in the college-ready group (60%) than in the less-ready group (52%). By race/ethnicity, more than 7 in 10 students (74%) are White in the college-ready group, whereas White students make up 66% of the population in the less-ready group. Asian American students likewise have a higher representation in the college-ready group (9%) and a lower representation in the less-ready group (6%). Group representation is equal among multiracial students (6% in each group), American Indian students (<1% in each group) and students of other race/ethnicity (2% in each group). On the

Table 1

Selected Descriptive Statistics (Weighted) by College Readiness Groups

	Less-Ready (N = 131,985)	College-Ready (N = 78,071)
Dependent variable: Retained into second year, %	78	88
Sex, %		
Female	52	60
Male	48	40
Race/ethnicity, %		
American Indian	1	1
Asian American	6	9
African American	14	5
Latino/a	6	4
White	66	74
Multirace/ethnicity	6	6
Other	2	2
First-generation status, %		
First generation	23	15
Not first generation	77	85
Financial resources (median in dollars)[a]		
Family income	66,270	77,680
Aid for first year from family	4,300	6,630
Grants for first year	2,720	3,680
Loans for first year	1,840	1,750

Note. Data from 2004 Freshmen Survey (TFS) and Cooperative Institutional Research Program (CIRP) and National Student Clearinghouse. Sample weighted to represent incoming first-time, full-time cohort in 2004 at all four-year institutions in the United States. Weighted sample includes N = 210,056 students attending n = 356 colleges and universities.

[a]Interpolated median, due to categorical nature of TFS survey data.

other hand, African American and Latino/a students have higher representation in the less-ready group than in the college-ready group. African American students in particular are overrepresented in the less-ready group, making up 14% of the student population but only 5% of the student population in the college-ready group. First-generation students also make up a larger percentage of the less-ready (23%) than the college-ready (15%) group.

The two groups' differences in socioeconomic status and financial resources for college reveal a noticeable, though not unexpected, association with academic preparation for college. Parental income is considerably higher in the college-ready group with a median income of $77,680, compared to $66,270 in the less-ready group. Students in the college-ready group also report more financial support from their families to pay for the first year of college ($6,630 median) than students who begin college less-ready for success ($4,300 median). College-ready students report larger median grant amounts ($3,680) and lower median loan amounts ($1,750) than students in the less-ready group for grants ($2,720) and loans ($1,840). Overall, the median amount college-ready students report they have available to fund their first year of college is almost one-third larger ($12,060) than the median amount among the less-ready group ($8,860).

Results From the HGLM

Table 2 contains results based on the full model but limited to the variables of interest in this study. Appendix B contains the complete results for all variables in the full model.

Socioeconomic and Financial Resources for College

Results demonstrate that social status factors have differential impact on first-year retention based on college readiness. Thus, the gaps in socioeconomic status and financial resources for college found in the descriptive results for the groups further compound into (dis)advantage in terms of retention to the second college year. Specifically, for less-ready students, as family income rises, so does retention. Lower-middle (odds ratio [OR] = 1.131), upper-middle (OR = 1.157), and high-income (OR = 1.114) students continue at a higher rate than low-income students. First-generation students (OR = 0.890) are also less likely to be retained among the less-ready group. Importantly, social status factors do not affect retention for students in the college-ready group. Thus, these results seem to indicate that if the playing field in terms of readiness can be leveled prior to students beginning college, the social status background factors that put students at risk of attrition once they begin college might be largely ameliorated. These results also indicate that the college environment itself appears to provide incomplete support for students who begin college less-ready.

Consistent with past research (Herzog, 2005, Lohfink & Paulsen, 2005), the results with regard to financial resources demonstrate a differential impact of these resources on retention by readiness. Using loans and higher amounts of loans in the first year puts students at an attrition risk during their first college year but to differing degrees based on readiness. Among the less-ready students, a loan to fund college of any amount is an attrition risk compared to no loans (OR = .892 <$2,999, OR = .817 $3,000–$5,999 and $6,000–$9,999, OR = .766 $10,000 or more), whereas college-ready students only incur a significant attrition risk with loans in amounts over $6,000 in the first year (OR = .776 $6,000–$9,999, OR = .742 $10,000 or more).

Findings related to the supportive nature of grants to first-year retention also accord with past research (Chen & DesJardins, 2010; DesJardins et al.,

Table 2

Parameter Estimates From Hierarchical Generalized Linear Modeling Analysis Predicting First-Year Retention, by College Readiness Groups (Study Variables)

	Less-Ready (N = 131,985)				College-Ready (N = 78,071)			
	Coefficient	SE	Significance	Odds Ratio	Coefficient	SE	Significance	Odds Ratio
Study variables								
Parental income (low-income reference group)								
Lower-middle income ($40,000–$74,999)	.123	.027	.000***	1.131	.042	.041	.306	1.043
Upper-middle income ($75,000–$149,999)	.146	.031	.000***	1.157	.108	.046	.019	1.114
High income (above $150,000)	.108	.038	.005**	1.114	−.011	.054	.834	0.989
First-generation status	−.117	.028	.000***	0.890	−.091	.042	.033	0.913
Financial resources for first year of college								
Aid for first year from family (no family resources reference group)								
Less than $2,999	.064	.041	.116	1.066	.042	.053	.426	1.043
$3,000–$5,999	.105	.044	.017	1.111	.076	.065	.247	1.078
$6,000–$9,999	.101	.042	.016	1.106	.132	.075	.079	1.142
More than $10,000	.091	.042	.033	1.095	.063	.064	.324	1.065
Grants for first year (no grants reference group)								
Less than $2,999	.105	.036	.011	1.110	.143	.049	.004**	1.153
$3,000–$5,999	.081	.041	.051	1.085	.139	.050	.006**	1.149
$6,000–$9,999	.095	.034	.006**	1.100	.152	.055	.006**	1.134
More than $10,000	.151	.036	.000***	1.162	.177	.057	.003**	1.194
Loans for first year (no loans reference group)								
Less than $2,999	−.115	.037	.004**	0.892	−.086	.042	.042	0.918
$3,000–$5,999	−.202	.044	.000***	0.817	−.111	.051	.034	0.895

(continued)

Table 2 (continued)

	Less-Ready (N = 131,985)				College-Ready (N = 78,071)			
	Coefficient	SE	Significance	Odds Ratio	Coefficient	SE	Significance	Odds Ratio
$6,000–$9,999	−.202	.038	.000***	0.817	−.254	.059	.000***	0.776
More than $10,000	−.267	.041	.000***	0.766	−.299	.051	.000***	0.742
Some financial concern (none reference group)	.026	.025	.297	1.027	−.043	.045	.345	0.958
Major financial concern (none reference group)	−.187	.038	.000***	0.829	−.305	.054	.000***	0.737
SAT composite score	.067	.012	.000***	1.069	.113	.015	.000***	1.119
Hours per week in high school senior spent studying/homework	.101	.008	.000***	1.106	.081	.013	.000***	1.084
Hours per week in high school senior spent on household duties	−.033	.009	.000***	0.968	−.029	.010	.006**	0.971
Choose institution because of costs	.109	.014	.000***	1.115	.151	.027	.000***	1.163
Choose institution wanted to live near home	.077	.018	.000***	1.080	.025	.025	.317	1.026
Distance college away from home	−.058	.013	.000***	0.944	−.146	.017	.000***	.864
Place of residence in the fall (on-campus reference group)								
Live with family	−.057	.049	.241	0.944	−.069	.070	.327	0.933
Other living arrangement	−.401	.067	.003***	0.670	−.501	.090	.000***	0.606
Plan to get full-time job to pay for college	−.111	.014	.000***	.895	−.087	.020	.000***	.916
Sex (female)	.134	.032	.000***	1.143	.106	.055	.054	1.111
Race (White reference group)								
American Indian	−.260	.115	.023	0.771	−.493	.222	.027	0.611
Asian	.348	.063	.000***	1.416	.394	.086	.000***	1.483
African American	.098	.065	.132	1.103	.117	.094	.213	1.124

(continued)

Table 2 (continued)

	Less-Ready (N = 131,985)				College-Ready (N = 78,071)			
	Coefficient	SE	Significance	Odds Ratio	Coefficient	SE	Significance	Odds Ratio
Latino/a	.045	.071	.528	1.046	.058	.082	.481	1.059
Other race/ethnicity	.280	.118	.020	1.323	.371	.126	.004**	1.449
Multi-ethnicity	-.161	.045	.001**	0.851	-.163	.054	.003**	0.850
Institutional context factor								
Institutional income/socioeconomic status (aggregate)	.116	.052	.026*	1.123	.071	.053	.184	1.074
Intercept	.819	.458	.074	2.268	1.681	.620	.007**	5.369

Note. Due to use of multiple imputation, parameter estimates are based on population-average models with robust standard errors. Weighted samples using $N = 131,985$ (Group 1) and $N = 78,071$ (Group 2) at $n = 356$ four-year institutions.

*$p < .05$. **$p < .01$. ***$p < .000$ (significance level at $p < .05$ only marked for Level 2 predictors).

2002) but again demonstrate differential impacts on retention by readiness (Herzog, 2005; Lohfink & Paulsen, 2005). Among college-ready students, students who received grant funding had increased odds of retention compared to students without grants, starting at 15% (OR = 1.153) for grants less than $2,999 and ending at 19% (OR = 1.194) for grants of more than $10,000. Thus, small grants, even those of $3,000 or less, serve to keep college-ready students matriculated at their institution of origin, while larger grants appear to have less marginal value. Students in the less-ready and less financially resourced group receive smaller amounts of grant funding than college-ready students (see Table 1). Moreover, grants of the size typically received by less-ready students have little impact on retention; a positive effect emerges only for grants in excess of $6,000 (OR = 1.100 $6,000-$9,999, OR = 1.162 $10,000 or more).

Unlike aid from loan and grant sources, financial support from the family was not a statistically significant predictor of retention for either readiness group, regardless of how much money the family provided toward the cost of college. This result should not be surprising since regardless of readiness, students without family support will be awarded Pell Grants and potentially other types of state or institutional grant aid, as well as packages that include loans, as necessary to fund college. Lastly, in examining financial resources for college, we found that students in both readiness groups who have major concerns about having enough funds to finance their college education are at a large attrition risk compared to those who report no concerns (OR = .829 for less-ready, OR = .737 college-ready). The known and perceived material circumstances that generate these concerns may serve as a signal that earning a degree is not a possibility (Kerckhoff, 1984). For the college-ready group, this factor has the largest effect on first-year retention of any we examined. For the less-ready group, among the financial supports and resources factors we studied, only a loan above $3,000 taken to fund the first year outpaces the deleterious effects of major financial concerns on retention. However, the difference between having no financial concerns about financing college and some concerns was not significant for either group.

In examining the relationship between first-year retention and student-level factors associated with socioeconomic status and financial resources for college, we find more similarity between readiness groups than difference in predictors of retention. For both readiness groups, higher SAT scores increase the likelihood of retention (OR = 1.069 less-ready, OR = 1.119 college-ready for each 100-point incremental score increase). Hours per week in senior year of high school spent on homework (OR = 1.106 less-ready, OR = 1.084 college-ready) was also positive for both readiness groups. On the other hand, time spent on household duties (OR = .968 less-ready, OR = .971 college-ready) shows a negative relationship for both groups. These results suggest a compounded impact on lower income students in both readiness groups since test scores (Bowen et al., 2009) and allocation of time to studying and household duties (Fuligni & Pederson, 2002) correlate with family income. In addition, students in both groups who placed greater importance in the college choice process on the cost of the college they selected (OR = 1.115 less-ready, OR = 1.163 college-ready) had higher retention rates, whereas students who planned to get a full-time job to pay for college (OR = .895 less-ready, OR = .916 college-ready) had lower rates.

In comparing students who were going to live on campus to those who were going live at home with family for the first year of college, we found no difference in terms of first-year retention. This adds to evidence from Lohfink and Paulsen (2005) that controlling for other factors—in this study readiness and in their study student generation status—there are no differences in first-year retention between living at home and living at campus. Conversely, students with living arrangements that were neither on campus nor with family were less likely to be retained (OR = 0.670 less-ready, OR = 0.606 college-ready). Distance between college and home (OR = 0.944 less-ready, OR = 0.864 college-ready) was also negative for both groups. Lastly, among less-ready students, those who placed importance on living near home in their college choice process (OR = 1.080) were more likely to be retained.

At the institutional level, we examined whether the overall socioeconomic status (SES) of the students on campus has an effect on individual retention. For college-ready students, institution-mean socioeconomic status was not significant, but less-ready students benefit from a campus environment with higher aggregate parental income levels among their students (OR = 1.123). Although this benefit in terms of retention from the institutional climate set on campuses with aggregate higher parental income levels accrues equally to less-ready students, this amounts to a kind of double SES advantage for higher income less-ready students that they receive on top of the benefit to retention they have based on their own family status and income backgrounds.

Sex and Race/Ethnicity

Among college-ready students, men are just as likely to be retained as women, but they are less likely to be retained in the less-ready group (OR = 1.143 for women). Race/ethnicity yields a more complex picture. Underrepresented racial minority students have a much higher representation in the less-ready group than in the college-ready group and therefore lower retention rates. But within each readiness group, American Indians, African Americans, and Latino/a students are just as likely to be retained as White students. Asian American students are more likely (OR = 1.416 less-ready, OR = 1.483 college-ready) and multiracial students less likely (OR = 0.851 less-ready, OR = 0.850 college-ready) to be retained than White students in both groups. College-ready students of other race/ethnicity are more likely to continue than their similarly ready White peers (OR = 1.449) but just as likely to be retained in the less-ready group.

Discussion and Implications

The key finding in this study is that not all lower income and first-generation students are equally at risk of attrition as they begin college. The transmission of social status across generations differs substantially depending on college readiness. Low-income and first-generation students who begin college academically prepared for success have as strong a chance of continuing past their first year as their equally prepared higher income and continuing generation peers. On the other hand, results show higher income and continuing generation students who are less ready for college have an advantage over similarly less-ready, lower income, and first-generation students. It is clear from these data that college readiness moderates retention for low-income and first-generation students. These results move our understanding of what contributes to educational attainment differences considerably beyond past studies that have found more generally that socioeconomic status (Astin & Oseguera, 2005; Bozick, 2007; Cabrera et al., 2005; DeAngelo et al., 2011; Herzog, 2005; Hu & St. John, 2001; Ishitani, 2006; Lohfink & Paulsen, 2005; Leppel, 2002; Paulsen & St. John, 2002) and first-generation status (Ishitani, 2006) significantly predict retention and degree completion. Specifically, results in this study, combined with prior research by Lofhink and Paulsen (2005) and Warburton, Bugarin, Nuñez, and Carroll (2001), solidify our understanding of the degree attainment process for students of differing readiness and social status background. In targeting efforts at a policy and practice level to improve first-year retention outcomes, the first important step is identifying not only which groups are at risk but why.

The main implication from this study, based on the findings related to family income and generation status, is that in the absence of academic readiness for college, current systems of higher education favor students from higher social status backgrounds. Higher income and continuing generation student characteristics thus amount to a distinct advantage in the college environment, which in the absence of beginning college ready for success, act as tacit markers of academic potential that are recognized, reinforced, and rewarded—and result in higher rates of first-year retention. For lower income and first-generation students who begin college-ready, readiness itself acts as a tacit marker of academic potential and a marker that they share equally with their higher income and continuing generation peers. All of this means that among the less-ready student group at this status transmission juncture, there are fewer possibilities for status mobility and more status maintenance or reproduction. Meanwhile, for all students who come to college prepared for academic success, both status mobility and status maintenance are possible.

Findings in this study also reveal that less-ready, first-generation, and lower income students benefit from a campus environment with higher aggregate parental income levels among students. This benefit likely stems from the higher expectations for success among the student peer group (Palardy, 2013), the higher expectations for student success overall on these campuses, and the climate for success that manifests itself through faculty, staff, and administrators' interactions with students as well as the services aimed at developing student potential (Stuber, 2011). Significantly, less-ready, higher income students benefit as much as their lower income peers from this climate. In totality, this means that advantages accumulate for less-ready, higher income students.

To promote equity, institutions must develop specific supports aimed at recognizing and developing the academic potential of less-ready, lower income, and first-generation students, part of what Rendón (1994) terms *validation*. Validation may be particularly important to less-ready, lower income, and first-generation students since the customs, traditions, and cultural values at college are more familiar to students with higher social status backgrounds (Reid & Moore, 2008).

Results in this study indicate that 75% of the attrition in the first college year is among students who begin college less-ready and that African American, Latino/a, lower income, and first-generation students have a much higher representation in the less-ready group than in the college-ready group. Thus, the very students who are most likely to have been dis-enfranchised at all earlier points in the educational pipeline (Adelman, 2006; Roderick et al., 2009) are also the most likely to leave college in the first year. This means that higher education institutions act as a lever of reproduction during the first college year, sorting out students who lack the desired markers of academic potential recognized by college communities. Given current policies and practices at the higher education level, ensuring lower income and first-generation students begin college academically ready for success has vast potential to raise retention. For elementary and secondary education reform, this finding suggests that efforts to increase readiness (Conley, 2005, 2010) can make a difference.

There are also important implications in this study for policymakers with respect to the differential role of readiness in retention based on the resources students have available to fund college. We found differences in retention between college-ready and less-ready students in the effect of using loans (for less-ready students, loans in any amount pose a retention risk; for college-ready, only loans over $6,000 pose a retention risk) and grants (less-ready students require $6,000 or more to see a retention benefit; college-ready students benefit from all amounts of grant aid). This means that current financial aid policies, which increasingly favor merit over need in grant-based aid, heavier reliance on loans, and tax credits that amount to regressive taxation (Perna & Finney, 2014), only increase differential retention rates for less-ready students. Our results buttress findings from past studies that current financial aid policies at all levels—institutional, state, and federal—are failing to support our national goal of increasing degree attainment. During the first college year, these aid policies also act as a mechanism of social reproduction or exceptionalism (rewarding the "few" academically ready, lower income, and first-generation students), both of which effectively maintain social inequality. Indeed, these policies very often reward students who would remain in the degree attainment pipeline regardless of aid or aid type received (Alon, 2011; Perna & Finney, 2014).

Other findings in this study related to the financial resources students have to fund college add to our implications for policymakers regarding financial aid. Specifically, the finding that a student's family financial contribution to funding the first year of college does not predict retention for either readiness group (controlling for other financial aid and perception of concerns about financing college), when coupled with our findings related to the overall positive relationship of grants and overall negative relationship of loans to retention, likely means that retention is supported by a stable source of non–loan based funds in general rather than a particular source. Herzog's (2005) findings for low-income students and retention confirm the importance of having a stable source of enough non–loan based aid to improving retention outcomes. The findings in this study that major concerns about the ability to finance college has a negative effect on retention for both groups further supports our conclusion about the need for enough available stable non–loan based aid and may be a strong additional signal to less-ready, lower income, and first-generation students about their actual potential for realizing a degree. Past research linking major financial concerns to attrition (Astin & Oseguera, 2005; DeAngelo, 2014; DeAngelo et al., 2011; Paulsen & St. John, 2002) mirror these findings. Additionally, findings in this study, with respect to college choice and the importance of various factors in the process of choosing which college to attend, also support the importance of amply funding marginalized groups in college. The more importance students place in the choice process on attending a college based on cost— which we believe encompasses having the appropriate type and amount of funds to cover costs—the higher the rates of first-year retention. Refocusing aid policies on need and providing enough aid to cover college costs irrespective of college readiness is an essential component of increasing degree attainment nationally.

How might the totality of results from this study inform basic theories of educational attainment? Findings from this study lend support both to the narrative that academic achievement and expectations for achievement are the primary mechanism for social mobility and success over the life course as well as narratives emphasizing the continuing and predominate role of social status of origin and material circumstances to social mobility and success over the life course. For students who begin college with less academic readiness, the weight of the evidence suggests that status begets status, with social status of origin and material circumstances prevailing (Kerckhoff, 1984). For students who begin college academically prepared, the evidence in this study suggests that social status of origin and material circumstances matter less to educational attainment at the first-year retention juncture. Academic readiness acts as a mediator to retention for lower income and first-generation students, interrupting mechanisms that transmit social status across generations.

Our findings may have further implications regarding the role of institutional signals in the status attainment process. We add to Bozick et al.'s (2010) push toward greater theoretical complexity in understanding the process through which individuals realize limits on the development of their potential. While the large-scale data employed here do not allow us to closely interpret students' experiences, we hypothesize that less-ready, lower income, and first-generation students receive signals that do not support their success from institutional actors, policies, and practices, some of which are related to financial aid. Our results suggest that these factors strongly relate to attrition for lower income and first-generation students who are not college-ready. It appears that these students choose not to continue to invest in a degree, perhaps taking them as a signal that they are unlikely to earn a degree (Beekhoven, De Jong, & Van Hout, 2002). For less-ready, lower income, and first-generation students, these messages become toxic to retention.

Extending Lucas's (2001) theory of effectively maintained inequality to higher education settings, our findings suggest the ways in which institutions recognize and support academic potential affect less-ready students in ways that effectively maintain societal inequality. Higher income and continuing generation less-ready students exhibit the markers of academic potential valued in higher education environments beyond readiness, and institutions invest in the retention of these students (Alon, 2011). Despite their lack of academic preparation, this gives higher income and continuing generation less-ready students a significant advantage that supports maintenance of their stratum of origin as adults. This advantage effectively maintains inequality in much the same way as tracking does at the primary and secondary levels. As Lucas describes it, tracking works as a system to maintain inequality earlier in the educational pipeline, with students from higher status backgrounds disproportionately dominating higher tracks.

In working to create more equitable practice once students begin college, we must recognize that the curricular and co-curricular reforms in higher education of the past 30 years aimed at improving outcomes in the first year of college (see Upcraft, Gardner, Barefoot, & Associates, 2005) have not been retaining less-ready, lower income, and first-generation students. For instance, many campuses have expanded on-campus housing and even required students to live on campus at least during their first college year as one measure of their efforts to increase retention (Zeller, 2005). Our finding that neither readiness group showed a difference in first-year retention if living on campus or living at home challenges the effectiveness of this effort. Lohfink and Palusen (2005) had similar results in their examination of retention by generation groups. While living on campus provides access to valuable resources and experiences that may be related to retention (see DeAngelo, 2014; Pike, Schroeder, & Berry, 1997; Schudde, 2011), our findings suggest that just living on campus makes little retention difference. In fact, given the additional cost of living on campus versus living at home, it is important to recognize that living at home with family does not itself put students at a disadvantage.

The challenge our study poses is for institutions to provide the on-campus experiences and access to resources that support retention to all students regardless of living arrangement. Currently, most institutions are organized to deliver the large majority of support and services to first-year students through mechanisms that work primarily for students who live on campus (Jacoby, 2014). Changing this will take a reimagining of co-curriculum to serve all students. This will only occur through a commitment to interrupting structures that reinforce the delivery of the benefits of the co-curriculum to students who have traditionally succeeded in higher education (Kezar, 2011). Certainly, results related to housing call on higher education professionals to consider more thoughtfully the purposes of housing investments and continued investment in increasingly more luxurious housing and amenities (Jacob, McCall, & Stange, 2013; Zeller, 2005). Specifically, we need to consider if these investments are about improving outcomes for all college students or wooing certain students to campus.

In developing practices to retain less-ready, lower income, and first-generation students, we also need to be mindful and supportive of family attachment and the importance and strength closeness with family confers (Guiffrida, 2005; Palmer, Davis, & Maramba, 2011; Stuber, 2011). Results in this study indicate that placing importance on living near home in their college choice process supports retention of less-ready students. Additionally, for both readiness groups, the further college is from home, the less likely a college is to retain the student. Guidance during the college choice process should reflect these realities.

Conclusion

One of the key strengths of this study is its use of a theory-rich analysis to examine the factors that contribute to retention in the first college year based on college readiness. As Lucas and Beresford (2010) discuss, studying significant educational transitions requires rich theoretical analyses. In this study, two theoretical narratives regarding the status attainment framework were employed to examine first-year retention separately for students who begin college academically ready for success and those who begin less ready. Although college degrees are increasingly necessary for entry into the middle class (Carnevale et al., 2010; Rothwell, 2012), degree attainment has not increased significantly among marginalized populations (Alon et al., 2010; Roksa, 2010). Increasing degree attainment in the United States depends on succeeding with students who begin college less academically ready and who are more vulnerable to attrition.

Findings from this study have revealed that academic readiness matters and that readiness mediates the relationships between social background factors and retention in the first college year. Specifically, our finding that academic readiness eliminates differences in retention for lower income and first-generation students while the relationship between family income and generation status remains significant for less-ready students adds significantly to our understanding of how status is transmitted across generations at this educational juncture. Evidence suggests that higher education environments contribute to social reproduction during the first college year, allocating students who begin college with less academic readiness toward different adult statuses based on social background factors. This means that the various policies and practices within and outside of the systems of higher education affect lower income and first-generation less-ready students in ways that their higher income and continuing generation peers do not experience. These processes effectively maintain inequality (Lucas, 2001). Mitigating these inequities will take a strong commitment at all educational levels. For policymakers and educators at the elementary and secondary level, the challenge from this study is to focus on readiness and practices that support success. Change within higher education will require a realignment and a reimagining of priorities, policies, and practices by all involved in the higher education effort. We must approach such reform holistically and creatively in order to fashion higher education environments conducive to broader student participation and success.

Descriptive Statistics for Variables Used in the Analysis (*N* = 210,056)

Variable	Minimum	Maximum	*M*	*SD*
Dependent variable: Retained into second year	0	1	.83	.375
Low income (<$40,000)	0	1	.21	.406
Lower-middle income ($40,000–$74,999)	0	1	.30	.456
Upper-middle income ($75,000–$149,999)	0	1	.32	.468
High income (>$150,000)	0	1	.17	.378
First-generation status	0	1	.18	.385
Aid for first year from family				
No family resources	0	1	.09	.290
Less than $2,999	0	1	.26	.441
$3,000–$5,999	0	1	.15	.361
$6,000–$9,999	0	1	.13	.340
More than $10,000	0	1	.36	.479
Grants for first year				
No grant aid	0	1	.19	.394
Less than $2,999	0	1	.29	.454
$3,000–$5,999	0	1	.17	.371
$6,000–$9,999	0	1	.13	.342
More than $10,000	0	1	.22	.413
Loans for first year				
No loans	0	1	.34	.472
Less than $2,999	0	1	.27	.446
$3,000–$5,999	0	1	.16	.371
$6,000–$9,999	0	1	.11	.312
More than $10,000	0	1	.12	.320
No financial concern	0	1	.34	.473
Some financial concern	0	1	.53	.499
Major financial concern	0	1	.13	.336
SAT score (range adjusted)	40.00	160.00	113.44	17.713
Hours per week spent studying for homework	0	4	2.10	1.270
Hours per week spent on household duties	0	5	1.82	1.320
Choose institution because of costs	0	2	.95	.783
Choose institution wanted to live near home	0	2	.62	.746
Distance of college away from home	0	4	2.24	1.224
Live with family	0	1	.12	.330
Live on campus	0	1	.84	.365
Other living arrangement	0	1	.03	.182
Sex (female)	0	1	.58	.494
Asian American	0	1	.07	.251
African American	0	1	.07	.262
American Indian	0	1	.01	.059
Latino/a	0	1	.05	.209

(continued)

Appendix A (continued)

Variable	Minimum	Maximum	*M*	*SD*
White	0	1	.74	.440
Other race/ethnicity	0	1	.02	.123
Multirace/ethnicity	0	1	.06	.232
Construct: academic self-concept	12.65	66.92	49.10	8.094
Construct: social self-concept	18.06	68.14	48.48	9.437
Hours per week spent on student clubs/groups	0	4	1.30	1.133
Performed volunteer work	0	2	1.13	.653
Highest degree aspirations	0	2	1.69	.504
Intention to transfer to another college	0	3	.99	.861
Major declared	0	1	.93	.257
Construct: college involvement	19.74	62.13	45.63	7.373
Plan to change major	0	3	1.50	.909
Plan to get a full-time job to pay for college	0	3	2.20	.905
Institutional income/socioeconomic status (student-level aggregate)	4.15	11.54	8.88	1.119
Selectivity (range adjusted)	80.00	151.00	112.76	12.510
Institutional control (private)	0	1	.51	.500
HBCU control	0	1	.03	.164
Institutional transfer climate (student-level aggregate)	1.33	2.81	1.98	.197

Note. Data based on 2004 Freshmen Survey (TFS) from Cooperative Institutional Research Program (CIRP) and National Student Clearinghouse.

Appendix B

Parameter Estimates Hierarchical Generalized Linear Modeling Analysis Predicting First Year Retention, by College Readiness Groups (Full Model)

	Less-Ready (N = 131,985)				College-Ready (N = 78,071)			
	Coefficient	SE	Significance	Odds Ratio	Coefficient	SE	Significance	Odds Ratio
Study variable, Level 1								
Parental income (low income reference group)								
Lower-middle income ($40,000–$74,999)	.123	.027	.000***	1.131	.042	.041	.306	1.043
Upper-middle income ($75,000–$149,999)	.146	.031	.000***	1.157	.108	.046	.019	1.114
High income (above $150,000)	.108	.038	.005**	1.114	-.011	.054	.834	0.989
First-generation status	-.117	.028	.000***	0.890	-.091	.042	.033	0.913
Financial resources for first year of college								
Aid for first year from family (no family resources reference group)								
Less than $2,999	.064	.041	.116	1.066	.042	.053	.426	1.043
$3,000–$5,999	.105	.044	.017	1.111	.076	.065	.247	1.078
$6,000–$9,999	.101	.042	.016	1.106	.132	.075	.079	1.142
More than $10,000	.091	.042	.033	1.095	.063	.064	.324	1.065
Grants for first year (no grants reference group)								
Less than $2,999	.105	.036	.011	1.110	.143	.049	.004**	1.153
$3,000–$5,999	.081	.041	.051	1.085	.139	.050	.006**	1.149
$6,000–$9,999	.095	.034	.006**	1.100	.152	.055	.006**	1.134
More than $10,000	.151	.036	.000***	1.162	.177	.057	.003**	1.194
Loans for first year (no loans reference group)								
Less than $2,999	-.115	.037	.004**	0.892	-.086	.042	.042	0.918
$3,000–$5,999	-.202	.044	.000***	0.817	-.111	.051	.034	0.895
$6,000–$9,999	-.202	.038	.000***	0.817	-.254	.059	.000***	0.776

(continued)

Appendix B (continued)

	Less-Ready (N = 131,985)				College-Ready (N = 78,071)			
	Coefficient	SE	Significance	Odds Ratio	Coefficient	SE	Significance	Odds Ratio
More than $10,000	−.267	.041	.000***	0.766	−.299	.051	.000***	0.742
Some financial concern (none reference group)	.026	.025	.297	1.027	−.043	.045	.345	0.958
Major financial concern (none reference group)	−.187	.038	.000***	0.829	−.305	.054	.000***	0.737
SAT composite score	.067	.012	.000***	1.069	.113	.015	.000***	1.119
Hours per week in high school senior spent studying/homework	.101	.008	.000***	1.106	.081	.013	.000***	1.084
Hours per week in high school senior spent on household duties	−.033	.009	.000***	0.968	−.029	.010	.006**	0.971
Choose institution because of costs	.109	.014	.000***	1.115	.151	.027	.000***	1.163
Choose institution wanted to live near home	.077	.018	.000***	1.080	.025	.025	.317	1.026
Distance college away from home	−.058	.013	.000***	0.944	−.146	.017	.000***	0.864
Place of residence in the fall (on-campus reference group)								
Live with family	−.057	.049	.241	0.944	−.069	.070	.327	0.933
Other living arrangement	−.401	.067	.000***	0.670	−.501	.090	.000***	0.606
Plan to get a full-time job to pay for college	−.111	.014	.000***	0.895	−.087	.020	.000***	0.916
Sex (female)	.134	.032	.000***	1.143	.106	.055	.054	1.111
Race (White reference group)								
American Indian	−.260	.115	.023	0.771	−.493	.222	.027	0.611
Asian	.348	.063	.000***	1.416	.394	.086	.000***	1.483
African American	.098	.065	.132	1.103	.117	.094	.213	1.124
Latino/a	.045	.071	.528	1.046	.058	.082	.481	1.059
Other race/ethnicity	.280	.118	.020	1.323	.371	.126	.004**	1.449

(continued)

Appendix B (continued)

	Less-Ready (N = 131,985)				College-Ready (N = 78,071)			
	Coefficient	SE	Significance	Odds Ratio	Coefficient	SE	Significance	Odds Ratio
Multi-ethnicity	−.161	.045	.001**	0.851	−.163	.054	.003**	0.850
Control variables, Level 1								
Construct: academic self-concept	.013	.002	.000***	1.013	.006	.002	.017	1.006
Construct: social self-concept	−.007	.002	.000***	0.993	−.005	.002	.007**	0.995
Hours per week spent on student clubs/groups	.058	.011	.000***	1.060	.043	.016	.006**	1.044
Performed volunteer work	.066	.017	.000***	1.068	.098	.027	.000***	1.103
Highest degree aspirations	.015	.022	.494	1.015	−.019	.039	.636	0.982
Intention to transfer to another college	−.247	.017	.000***	0.781	−.419	.027	.000***	0.658
Major declared	.005	.047	.924	1.005	−.005	.050	.915	0.995
Construct: college involvement	.012	.002	.000***	1.013	.011	.003	.000***	1.011
Plan to change major	.033	.012	.005**	1.034	.058	.022	.008**	1.060
Study variables, Level 2								
Institutional income/socioeconomic status (aggregate)	.116	.052	.026*	1.123	.071	.053	.184	1.074
Control variables, Level 2								
Selectivity	.030	.004	.000***	1.031	.027	.004	.000***	1.027
Control (private)	−.202	.060	.001**	0.817	−.139	.067	.038*	0.870
HBCU control	.682	.149	.000***	1.978	.740	.191	.000***	2.096
Institutional transfer climate (aggregate)	−.588	.148	.000***	0.556	−1.042	.200	.000***	0.353
Intercept	.819	.458	.074	2.268	1.681	.620	.007**	5.369

Note. Due to use of multiple imputation, parameter estimates are based on population-average models with robust standard errors. Weighted samples using N = 131,985 (Group 1) and N = 78,071 (Group 2) at n = 356 four-year institutions.

$*p < .05$. $**p < .01$. $***p < .000$ (significance level at $p < .05$ only marked for Level 2 predictors).

Acknowledgement

The authors thank Dr. Sean Kelly for his support and helpful feedback on this manuscript and the Higher Education Research Institute (HERI) at UCLA for allowing us data access.

Note

[1]We did, however, engage in preliminary model building using the full, undivided data set and a standardized and continuous college readiness measure. Using our full complement of study and control variables, we found the college readiness measure was significant, $t = 13.747$ ($p < .000$). We also tested a model with an interaction effect between college readiness and parental income, which was significant, $t = 2.764$ ($p < .01$).

References

American College Testing Service. (2009). *The condition of college readiness 2009.* Iowa City, IA: ACT, Inc.

American College Testing Service. (2013a). *2013 retention/completion summary tables.* Iowa City, IA: ACT, Inc.

American College Testing Service. (2013b). *The reality of college readiness 2013.* Iowa City, IA: ACT, Inc.

Adelman, C. (2006). *Toolbox revisited: Paths to degree completion from high school through college.* Washington, DC: U.S. Department of Education.

Alon, S. (2007). The influence of financial aid in leveling group differences in graduating from elite institutions. *Economics of Education Review, 26*(3), 296–311. doi: 10.1016/j.econedurev.2006.01.003

Alon, S. (2011). Who benefits most from financial aid? The heterogeneous effect of need-based grants on students' college persistence. *Social Science Quarterly, 92*(3), 807–829. doi: 10.1111/j.1540-6237.2011.00793.x

Alon, S., Domina, T., & Tienda, M. (2010). Stymied mobility or temporary lull? The puzzle of lagging Hispanic college degree attainment. *Social Forces, 88*(4), 1807–1832.

Astin, A. W., & Oseguera, L. (2004). The declining "equity" of American higher education. *The Review of Higher Education, 27*(3), 321–341. doi: 10.1353/rhe.2004.0001

Astin, A. W., & Oseguera, L. (2005). Pre-college and institutional influences on degree attainment. In A. Seidman (Ed.), *College student retention: Formula for student success* (pp. 245–276). Westport, CT: Greenwood Publishing Group.

Beekhoven, S., De Jong, U., & Van Hout, H. (2002). Explaining academic progress via combining concepts of integration theory and rational choice theory. *Research in Higher Education, 43*(5), 577–600. doi: 10.1023/A:1020166215457

Blau, P. M., & Duncan, O. D. (1967). *The American occupational structure.* New York, NY: John Wiley & Sons, Inc.

Bowen, W. G., Chingos, M. M., & McPherson, M. S. (2009). *Crossing the finish line: Completing college at America's public universities.* Princeton, NJ: Princeton University Press.

Bozick, R. (2007). Making it through the first year of college: The role of students' economic resources, employment, and living arrangements. *Sociology of Education, 80*(3), 261–285.

Bozick, R., Alexander, K., Entwisle, D., Dauber, S., & Kerr, K. (2010). Framing the future: Revisiting the place of educational expectations in status attainment. *Social Forces, 88*(5), 2027–2052.

Cabrera, A. F., Burkum, K. R., & La Nasa, S. M. (2005). Pathways to a four-year degree: Determinants of transfer and degree completion among socioeconomically disadvantaged students. In A. Seidman (Ed.), *College retention: A formula for success* (pp. 167–210). Westport, CT: Praeger Publishers.

Cabrera, N. L., Miner, D. D., & Milem, J. F. (2013). Can a summer bridge program impact first-year persistence and performance?: A case study of the New Start Summer Program. *Research in Higher Education, 54*(5), 481–498. doi: 10.1007/s11162-013-9286-7

Carnevale, A. P., Smith, N., & Strohl, J. (2010). *Help wanted.* Washington, DC: Georgetown University Center on Education and the Workforce.

Chen, R., & DesJardins, S. L. (2010). Investigating the impact of financial aid on student dropout risks: Racial and ethnic differences. *The Journal of Higher Education, 81*(2), 179–208. doi: 10.1353/jhe.0.0085

College Board. (2012). *The SAT report on college and career readiness: 2012.* New York, NY: Author.

College Board. (2013). *2013 SAT report on college & career readiness.* New York, NY: Author.

Conley, D. T. (2005). *College knowledge: What it really takes for students to succeed and what we can do to get them ready.* San Francisco, CA: Jossey-Bass.

Conley, D. T. (2010). *College and career ready: Helping all students succeed beyond high school.* San Francisco, CA: Jossey-Bass.

DeAngelo, L. (2014). Programs and practices that retain students from the first to second year: Results from a national study. *New Directions for Institutional Research, 2013*(160), 53–75.

DeAngelo, L., Franke, R., Hurtado, S., Pryor, J. H., & Tran, S. (2011). *Completing college: Assessing graduation rates at four-year institutions.* Los Angeles, CA: Higher Education Research Institute.

DesJardins, S. L., Ahlburg, D. A., & McCall, B. P. (2002). A temporal investigation of factors related to timely degree completion. *Journal of Higher Education, 73*, 555–581.

Doyle, W. R. (2006). Adoption of merit-based student grant programs: An event history analysis. *Educational Evaluation and Policy Analysis, 28*(3), 259–285.

Dwyer, R. E. (2013). The care economy? Gender, economic restructuring, and job polarization in the U.S. labor market. *American Sociological Review, 78*(3), 390–416.

Dynarski, S. M., Hemelt, S. W., & Hyman, J. M. (2013). *The missing manual: Using National Student Clearinghouse data to track postsecondary outcomes* (No. w19552). Cambridge, MA: National Bureau of Economic Research.

Ewert, S. (2010). Male and female pathways through four-year colleges: disruption and sex stratification in higher education. *American Educational Research Journal, 47*(4), 744–773. doi: 10.3102/0002831210374351

Franke, R. (2012). *Towards the education nation: Revisiting the impact of financial aid, college experience, and institutional context on baccalaureate degree attainment using a propensity score matching, multilevel modeling approach* (Doctoral Dissertation). University of California Los Angeles, Los Angeles, CA.

Fuligni, A. J., & Pedersen, S. (2002). Family obligation and the transition to young adulthood. *Developmental Psychology, 38*(5), 856.

Geiser, S., & Santelices, M. V. (2007). *Validity of high-school grades in predicting student success beyond the freshman year: High-school record vs. standardized tests as indicators of four-year college outcomes.* Berkeley, CA: Center for Studies in Higher Education.

Gilardi, S., & Guglielmetti, C. (2011). University life of non-traditional students: Engagement styles and impact on attrition. *The Journal of Higher Education, 82*(1), 33–53.

Grusky, D. B., Western, B., & Wimer, C. C. (Eds.). (2011). *The great recession.* New York, NY: Russell Sage Foundation.

Guiffrida, D. (2005). To break away or strengthen ties to home: A complex issue for African American college students attending a predominantly White institution. *Equity & Excellence in Education, 38*(1), 49–60. doi: 10.1080/10665680590907864

Herzog, S. (2005). Measuring determinants of student return vs. dropout/stopout vs. transfer: A first-to-second year analysis of new freshmen. *Research in Higher Education, 46*(8), 883–928. doi: 10.1007/sl1162-005-6933

Horn, L., & Kojaku, L. K. (2001). *High school academic curriculum and the persistence path through college.* Washington, DC: National Center for Education Statistics.

Hosmer, D. W., & Lemeshow, S. (2004). *Applied logistic regression.* New York, NY: John Wiley & Sons.

Hu, S., & St. John, E. P. (2001). Student persistence in a public higher education system: Understanding racial and ethnic differences. *Journal of Higher Education, 72*(3), 265–286.

Ishitani, T. T. (2006). Studying attrition and degree completion behavior among first-generation college students in the United States. *Journal of Higher Education, 77*(5), 861–885. doi: 10.1353/jhe.2006.0042

Jacob, B., McCall, B., & Stange, K. M. (2013). *College as country club: Do colleges cater to students' preferences for consumption?* (NBER Working Paper Series). Cambridge, MA: National Bureau of Economic Research.

Jacoby, B. (2014). Engaging commuter and part-time students. In S. R. Harper & S. J. Quaye (Eds.), *Student engagement in higher education: Theoretical perspectives and practical approaches for diverse populations* (pp. 289–305). New York, NY: Taylor & Francis.

Kalogrides, D., & Grodsky, E. (2011). Something to fall back on: Community colleges as a safety net. *Social Forces, 89*(3), 853–878.

Kerckhoff, A. C. (1984). The current state of social mobility research. *The Sociological Quarterly, 25*, 139–153.

Kezar, A. (2011). Rethinking postsecondary institutions for low-income student success: The power of post-structural theory. In A. Kezar (Ed.), *Recognizing and serving low income students in higher education: An examination of the institutional policies, practices, and culture* (pp. 3–26). New York, NY: Routledge.

Knotterus, J. D. (1987). Status attainment research and its image of society. *American Sociological Review, 52*, 113–121.

Leppel, K. (2002). Similarities and differences in the college persistence of men and women. *The Review of Higher Education, 25*(4), 433–450. doi: 10.1353/rhe.2002.0021

Lohfink, M. M., & Paulsen, M. B. (2005). Comparing the determinants of persistence for first-generation and continuing-generation students. *Journal of College Student Development, 46*(4), 409–428.

Lucas, S. R. (2001). Effectively maintained inequality: Education transitions, track mobility, and social background effects. *American Journal of Sociology, 106*(6), 1642–1690.

Lucas, S. R., & Beresford, L. (2010). Naming and classifying: Theory, evidence, and equity in education. *Review of Research in Education, 34*(1), 25–84.

McCall, L. (2001). *Complex inequality.* New York, NY: Routledge.

National Student Clearinghouse. (2013). *Snapshot report: Persistence-retention.* College Station, TX: National Student Clearinghouse Research Center.

Niehaus, E., Campbell, C. M., & Inkelas, K. K. (2014). HLM behind the curtain: Unveiling decisions behind the use and interpretation of HLM in higher education research. *Research in Higher Education, 55*(1), 101–122. doi: 10.1007/s11162-013-9306-7

Nora, A., Barlow, L., & Crisp, G. (2005). Student persistence and degree attainment beyond the first year in college. In A. Seidman (Ed.), *College student retention: Formula for success* (pp. 129–153). Westport, CT: Praeger.

Oseguera, L. (2005). Four and six-year baccalaureate degree completion by institutional characteristics and racial/ethnic groups. *Journal of College Student Retention: Research, Theory and Practice, 7*(1), 19–59.

Oseguera, L., & Rhee, B. S. (2009). The influence of institutional retention climates on student persistence to degree completion: A multilevel approach. *Research in Higher Education, 50*(6), 546–569. doi: 10.i007/s11162-009-9134-y

Palardy, G. J. (2013). High school socioeconomic segregation and student attainment. *American Educational Research Journal, 50*(4), 714–754. doi: 10.3102/0002831213481240

Palmer, R. T., Davis, R. J., & Maramba, D. C. (2011). The impact of family support on the success of black men at an historically black university: Affirming the revision of Tinto's theory. *Journal of College Student Development, 52*(5), 577–597.

Paulsen, M. B., & St John, E. P. (2002). Social class and college costs: Examining the financial nexus between college choice and persistence. *The Journal of Higher Education, 73*(2), 189–236.

Perna, L. W., & Finney, J. E. (2014). *The attainment agenda: State policy leadership in higher education.* Baltimore, MD: Johns Hopkins University Press.

Pike, G. R., Schroeder, C. C., & Berry, T. R. (1997). Enhancing the educational impact of residence halls: The relationship between residential learning communities and first-year college experiences and persistence. *Journal of College Student Development, 38*(6), 609–621.

Planty, M., Bozick, R., & Ingels, S. J. (2006). *Academic pathways, preparation, and performance: A descriptive overview of the transcripts from the high school graduating class of 2003.* Washington, DC: National Center for Education Statistics.

Pryor, J. H., Hurtado, S., DeAngelo, L., Blake, L. P., & Tran, S. (2009). *The American freshman: National norms, fall 2009.* Los Angeles, CA: Higher Education Research Institute.

Pryor, J. H., Hurtado, S., DeAngelo, L., Sharkness, J., Romero, L. C., Korn, W. S., & Tran, S. (2008). *The American freshman: National norms, fall 2008.* Los Angeles, CA: Higher Education Research Institute.

Posselt, J. R., Jaquette, O., Bielby, R., & Bastedo, M. N. (2012). Access without equity: Longitudinal analyses of institutional stratification by race and ethnicity, 1972–2004. *American Educational Research Journal, 49*(6), 1074–1111. doi: 10.3102/0002831212439456

Raudenbush, S. W., & Bryk, A. S. (2004). *Hierarchical linear models: Applications and data analysis methods.* Thousand Oaks, CA: Sage.

Raudenbush, S., Bryk, A., Cheong, Y. F., & Congdon, R. (2004). HLM 6: Hierarchical and nonlinear modeling [Computer software]. Lincolnwood, IL: Scientific Software International.

Reid, M. J., & Moore, J. L. (2008). College readiness and academic preparation for postsecondary education oral histories of first-generation urban college students. *Urban Education, 43*(2), 240–261. doi: 10.1177/0042085907312346

Rendón, L. I. (1994). Validating culturally diverse students: Toward a new model of learning and student development. *Innovative Higher Education, 19*(1), 33–51.

Roderick, M., Nagaoka, J., & Allensworth, E. (2006). *From high school to the future: A first look at Chicago Public School graduates' college enrollment. College preparation and graduation from four year colleges.* Chicago, IL: Consortium on Chicago School Research, University of Chicago.

Roderick, M., Nagaoka, J., & Coca, V. (2009). College readiness for all: The challenge for urban high schools. *The Future of Children, 19*(1), 185–210.

Roksa, J. (2010). Differentiation and work: Inequality in degree attainment in U.S. higher education. *Higher Education, 61*(3), 293–308. doi: 10.1007/s10734-010-9378-7

Rosenbaum, J. E. (2001). *Beyond college for all: Career paths for the forgotten half.* London: Russell Sage Foundation.

Rothwell, J. (2012). *Education, job openings, and unemployment in metropolitan America.* Washington, DC: Brookings.

Schudde, L. T. (2011). The causal effect of campus residency on college student retention. *The Review of Higher Education, 34*(4), 581–610.

Sewell, W. H., Haller, A. O., & Ohlendorf, G. W. (1970). The educational and early occupational status attainment process: Replication and revision. *American Sociological Review, 35*(6), 1014–1027.

Sewell, W. H., Haller, A. O., & Portes, A. (1969). The educational and early occupational attainment process. *American Sociological Review, 34*(1), 82–92.

Steinberg, L., & Fletcher, A. C. (1998). Data analytic strategies in research on ethnic minority youth. In V. C. McLoyd & L. Steinberg (Eds.), *Studying minority adolescents: Conceptual, methodological, and theoretical issues* (pp. 279–294). Mahwah, NJ: Lawrence Erlbaum Associates, Inc.

Stuber, J. M. (2011). *Inside the college gates: How class and culture matter in higher education.* Lanham, MD: Lexington Books.

Tabachnick, B. G., & Fidell, L. S. (2007). *Experimental designs using ANOVA.* Independence, KY: Thomson/Brooks/Cole.

Terenzini, P. T., Cabrera, A. F., & Bernal, E. M. (2001). *Swimming against the tide: The poor in American higher education.* New York, NY: The College Board.

Upcraft, M. L., Gardner, J. N., Barefoot, B. O., & Associates. (2005). *Challenging and supporting the first-year student: A handbook for improving the first year of college.* San Francisco, CA: Jossey-Bass.

Walpole, M. (2003). Socioeconomic status and college: How SES affects college experiences and outcomes. *The Review of Higher Education, 27*(1), 45–73.

Warburton, E. C., Bugarin, R., Nuñez, A. M., & Carroll, C. D. (2001). *Bridging the gap: Academic preparation and postsecondary success of first-generation college students* (NCES 2001–153). Washington, DC: U.S. Department of Education, National Center for Education Statistics.

Warner, R. M. (2012). *Applied statistics: From bivariate through multivariate techniques.* New York, NY: Sage.

Wolniak, G. C., & Engberg, M. E. (2010). Academic achievement in the first year of college: Evidence of the pervasive effects of the high school context. *Research in Higher Education, 51*(5), 451–467. doi: 10.1007/s11162-010-9165-4

Zeller, W. J. (2005). First-year student living environments. In M. L. Upcraft, J. N. Gardner, B. O. Barefoot, & Associates (Eds.), *Challenging and supporting the first-year student: A handbook for improving the first year of college* (pp. 410–427). San Francisco, CA: Jossey-Bass.

Manuscript received September 17, 2014
Final revision received September 20, 2016
Accepted September 22, 2016

American Educational Research Journal
December 2016, Vol. 53, No. 6, pp. 1626–1662
DOI: 10.3102/0002831216676572
© *2016 AERA. http://aerj.aera.net*

Devalued Black and Latino Racial Identities: A By-Product of STEM College Culture?

Ebony O. McGee

At some point most Black and Latino/a college students—even long-term high achievers—question their own abilities because of multiple forms of racial bias. The 38 high-achieving Black and Latino/a STEM study participants, who attended institutions with racially hostile academic spaces, deployed an arsenal of strategies (e.g., stereotype management) to deflect stereotyping and other racial assaults (e.g., racial microaggressions), which are particularly prevalent in STEM fields. These students rely heavily on coping strategies that alter their authentic racial identities but create internal turmoil. Institutions of higher education, including minority-serving schools, need to examine institutional racism and other structural barriers that damage the racial identities of Black and Latino/a students in STEM and cause lasting psychological strain.

KEYWORDS: stereotype management, STEM students of color, racial hostility in academia, STEM racial gap, cultural bias

> They [Rodney's White supervisors at a prestigious physics lab where he did a summer internship] didn't generally disvalue me, they questioned. . . . They were like, "Oh, okay, I didn't know there was any Black physicists," and then they would kind of lower their standards a little bit. And then after I told them I'm also Hispanic, they were like, "Oh, I didn't know there was any Hispanic physicists." So then they lowered their expectations a little bit more. So I strategically . . . started talking about my research, and then they went, "Oh, okay,

EBONY O. McGEE, assistant professor of diversity and STEM education at Vanderbilt University's Peabody College, studies the educational and career trajectories of historically marginalized students of color in science, technology, engineering, and mathematics (STEM), PMB 230 GPC 230 Appleton Place, Nashville, TN 37203; e-mail: *ebony.mcgee@vanderbilt.edu*. Her research also focuses on the role of racialized experiences and biases in STEM educational and career achievement, problematizing traditional notions of academic achievement and what it means to be successful in STEM yet marginalized in various ways.

you know your stuff," and I'm like, yeah, I thought y'all knew. [He pauses.] On second thought, I guess I was undervalued.

—Rodney,[1] college senior, physics major, future astrophysicist

Rodney's observation, above, came from one of 38 interviews I conducted with high-achieving Black and Latino/a science, technology, engineering, and mathematics (STEM) college students who were attending three types of postsecondary institutions: historically Black, historically White, and Hispanic-serving. Rodney was attending a historically Black university. He self-identified ethnically as both African American and Panamanian and racially as Black and Hispanic. Rodney felt that his supervisors doubted his intellectual abilities in physics, which triggered a response focused on proving his intellectual capacity by employing an evidencing tactic ("I strategically . . . started talking about my research"). His experience of being stereotyped was representative of the experiences of many students in this study. When students' employers, peers, teachers, and important others (e.g., administrators, campus police) showed racial bias in judging their capabilities, these participants responded with strategies that depended on a number of factors, including who delivered the racist assault; the classroom dynamics (STEM versus non-STEM courses); where the event took place; the number of Black, White, Asian, and Latino/a peers present; if it was a first racial offense; anticipated stress of a racially charged retort; and whether other racialized events occurred that week. These racialized events did not deter these Students of Color[2] from succeeding in a STEM field, contrary to what the research on stereotype threat would suggest (Aronson, Fried, & Good, 2002; Steele & Aronson, 1998). Instead, racial stereotypes served as a distressing motivation for the students to achieve in their chosen fields. However, racial stereotypes did have other consequences—heightened anxiety, increased bouts of anger, feelings of being an impostor, and compulsive work—as Students of Color were forced to prove they were fully capable of achieving in STEM (McGee, 2015).

This study investigated the experiences of STEM Students of Color who did not succumb to identity-related threats in ways that lower their academic performance or their likelihood of earning a STEM degree, as the theory of stereotype threat implies. My research shows that some high-achieving students know they are being stereotyped and can rearticulate the stereotypes and manage them to minimize their impact, at least to some degree (McGee & Martin, 2011). This method, which I call *stereotype management*, is both a process and a learned competency that enables students to recognize and negotiate social and psychological threats to their identities (McGee & Martin, 2011). It is an indispensable but unnerving practice for those who employ it, because the racial climate on many campuses—rather than favoring the elimination of racial stereotypes—reifies deficit ideologies about

Students of Color as unqualified, incompetent, and undeserving of opportunities in the STEM arena. I expand on stereotype management by investigating the experiences of Latino/a STEM college students, in addition to Black
students, to better explore the circumstances of the underrepresented in
STEM while attending to the differences in how Latino/a and Black students
manage stereotypes. Additionally, I expand the concept of stereotype management by introducing a primary strategy for negotiating stereotypes that the
students themselves call *frontin'*, which is an imitation of stereotypical forms
of Whiteness or anti-Whiteness—polarized opposites—to either defuse or further agitate the racialized situation.

I begin by examining how marginalization in education—and in STEM
in particular—limits the opportunities of Students of Color. I characterize
STEM departmental cultures, including STEM departments in institutions
designed to be affirming to Students of Color. Some theorists have made
intense efforts to increase the academic performance of Students of Color
through "grit" and other higher-order personality traits (e.g., personal
agency, self-efficacy, self-control; Duckworth & Gross, 2014). Given that
schooling is systemically inequitable and racially discriminatory, however,
Students of Color endure unique obstacles as they pursue advanced learning
opportunities (Mickelson, 2003). The "Implications and Conclusion" section
illuminates the role of institutions in systematically ostracizing Students of
Color while advocating that these very students create their own defensive
mechanisms, coping strategies, and techniques.

"Colored" Identities and Marginalized Experiences for Black and Brown College Students

Although institutions of higher education are characterized as places
where ethical and moral issues are considered highly significant and philosophical differences are welcomed, they fail to provide a complete and critical education for interrogating the nation's racial history, including the
historical and contemporary realities of racial prejudice, stereotyping, and
discrimination (Picca & Feagin, 2007). Racism in the educational experiences
of marginalized college students has been illuminated through the lens of
racial microaggressions (McCabe, 2009; Smith, Hung, & Franklin, 2011;
Solórzano, Ceja, & Yosso, 2000). As Pierce (1995) and Pierce, Carew,
Pierce-Gonzalez, and Wills (1978) argue, racism has transformed over time
from overt, blatant forms of discrimination and prejudice to more covert,
indirect, restrained, and ambiguous demonstrations, which they call racial
microaggressions. Both racial microaggressions and racial stereotypes serve
as racial stressors and products of racism, but neither term has been thoroughly operationalized in relation to each other, and so the terms are frequently used as synonyms. Sue and colleagues' (2007) research on
microaggressions does allude to the notion that racial microaggressions

are one way in which racial stereotypes are operationalized, but we need further constructions of the relationships and hierarchy of these two terms.

In the United States, racial stereotypes were fabricated in response to the need to provide evidence of the inhumanity of Black and Native American peoples so as to justify brutality against them. Racial stereotypes can exist in individual psyches. For example, Thomas Jefferson expressed fiercely racist stereotypes about enslaved Black Americans: They smell funny, are natural slaves, are less intelligent, are ugly in skin color, are lazy, are oversexed, are not as sophisticated in serious music, cannot learn advanced knowledge, and can never be integrated into White America (Marable, 2011). In current times, racial microaggressions (and other forms of bias) project an evolving form of racial stereotypes into the culture, policies, systems, and practices of U.S. society. *Racial microaggressions* produce "subtle, stunning, often automatic, and non-verbal exchanges which are 'put downs' of blacks by offenders" (Pierce et al., 1978, p. 66).

The findings of Pierce and colleagues prompted researchers to look not for the gross and obvious but for the subtle snubs, dismissive looks, and insulting tones when unpacking the racialized experiences of Students of Color. Microaggressions, both within and beyond the classroom, can leave Students of Color feeling disheartened and discouraged as their experiences are omitted, distorted, and stereotyped. In university settings, *racial microaggressions* grounded in racial stereotypes create assumptions about admission policies (e.g., being referred to as an "affirmative action student"), myths about the academic abilities of certain groups of students, segregation of in-class groups, and feeling personally diminished by White teachers and peers (Solórzano et al., 2000; Yosso, Smith, Ceja, & Solórzano, 2009). Racial stereotyping (e.g., assumptions of intellectual inferiority and criminality, pathologizing cultural values) systematically marginalizes Students of Color by endorsing negative expectations in a variety of educational situations (Sue et al., 2007). Racial stereotypes, enacted in part through racial microaggressions, are subtle yet persistent forms of racism that have pronounced adverse effects on the experiences (and not just the academic outcomes) of Students of Color in STEM, such as racial anxiety, minority status stress, and thoughts and actions of leaving STEM altogether (Cvencek, Nasir, O'Connor, Wischnia, & Meltzoff, 2014; Perna, Gasman, Gary, Lundy-Wagner, & Drezner, 2010).

In the course of their schooling, Students of Color have been taught in myriad ways that their identities—their very bodies—do not fit those of exemplary STEM students (Fries-Britt & Griffin, 2007; Malone & Barabino, 2009). Furthermore, successful minoritized students often find an identity that is an amalgam of their STEM and "colored" identities; however, this comes at the cost of altering their self-defined authentic (though evolving and fluid) identities and an overuse of personal grit, defined as perseverance and a passion for long-term goals (Golden, 2015; McGee & Stovall, 2015).

1629

Grit and resilience researchers who advocate habitually for Students of Color to "toughen up" and wear their survival calluses as badges of honor do not address the structural restraints perpetuated by everyday forms of racism and discrimination. This leaves many Students of Color exhausted and thinking twice about their place in STEM (McGee, 2015).

STEM College Values: Born of Whiteness

STEM higher education was born from White male supremacy. Scientific racism, including eugenics, which flourished in the late 19th and early 20th centuries, reflected socially constructed ideas of Black and Brown genetic inferiority that socially, materially, and scientifically advanced White hegemony (Roberts, 2013). Eugenics was created for White middle- to upper-class men and originated in military occupations (Riley, 2008). U.S. institutions of higher education acted on eugenic principles when they explicitly excluded underrepresented ethnic groups from participation in the production of scientific knowledge (Swartz, 2009). More than a century after eugenics was introduced in the United States, the typical STEM college student remains White, male, and middle class, along with some students of Asian descent (e.g., Chinese and Indian; National Science Board, 2012).

STEM higher education remains stratified by race, so that Blacks, Latinos/as, and Native Americans are on the bottom of a racialized STEM hierarchy (Martin, 2009; Nelson & Brammer, 2010). A host of historical and contemporary practices have negatively affected Black and Latino/a students, including lack of a critical mass of STEM Faculty of Color, impostor syndrome, unwelcoming institutional climates, institutional and social barriers in their departments, racial/ethnic stereotyping, a lack of role models or mentors, and high numbers of Black and Latino peers dropping out of college STEM fields (Cole & Espinoza, 2008; Malone & Barabino, 2009; Robinson, McGee, Bentley, Houston, & Botchway, 2016). Black students have been found to be among those most likely to report finding it hard to position themselves—and to be seen by others—as "properly" scientific (Carlone & Johnson, 2007). Similarly, Latino/a students' experiences point to a tradition of stereotypes that create low expectations, bias, and race discrimination as a primary cause of the loss of talent in STEM fields (Sevo, 2009). In a national analysis of tenure and tenure-underrepresented minorities in science and engineering faculties at research universities, in 2010, astronomy had no Black or Native American assistant professors. Moreover, the only Native American assistant professor in the top 50 physical sciences and engineering disciplines is in electrical engineering, which indicates a 7-year hiring lapse in the other disciplines (Nelson & Brammer, 2010).

Despite this well-documented stratification, the field has not mobilized against the trend. For instance, an influential report (Cullinane, 2009) raised concern about the lack of support from STEM faculty and senior leadership for the goal of increasing access and success in STEM education for under-represented Students of Color and low-income students. A White engineering professor pulled me aside after my presentation on racist and sexist experiences of Black female engineering doctoral students at a national conference on engineering education and provided commentary that exposed racism and sexism within his engineering college:

> Look, I'm going to tell you what they [his fellow White engineering professors] won't say. We are competitive with each other. We will cut each other's throat in a heartbeat if it benefits our research. We don't care about failing half of our students, and they are most likely White or foreigners, so why would we care about failing Black students? Honestly, we just call them [Black students] quota kids anyway. Besides, we already got diversity 'cause we got a few women [engineering faculty]. But they are both bitches... [laughs out loud].
> (White engineering professor, August 14, 2015)

In line with this White professor's claim, research has shown that STEM college departments are cutthroat environments, and often members of disfavored groups are included as an annoying afterthought (Fabert, Cabay, Rivers, Smith, & Bernstein, 2011; Wyer, Schneider, Nassar-McMillan, & Oliver-Hoyo, 2010).

With this backdrop, the historical legitimization of race-based stereotypes, biases, and other forms of legalized social stratification (e.g., policies, laws, and commonplace practices) strongly communicate to Students of Color that they are underqualified and incapable of STEM intellectual endeavor (Martin, 2009). The stereotypes and assumptions about groups that are or are not competent in STEM can dictate differential treatment based on racial classification. This construction has perpetuated a lengthy, documented history of the suppression of STEM access and opportunities for college Students of Color (Allen, 2015; González, 2009). This reality was qualified in December 2015, when the U.S. Supreme Court Chief Justice Roberts challenged the notion that a Student of Color is inherently valuable as he posed the following question during *Fisher v. University of Texas*: "What unique perspective does a minority student bring a physics class?" An open-letter response to the Supreme Court from the Equity & Inclusion in Physics & Astronomy Group (2016), comprising more than 2,400 physicists, astrophysicists, and supporters, powerfully rebuts theories that place Students of Color in deficit frameworks (Herrnstein & Murray, 2010; Jencks & Phillips, 2011) by rejecting the premise that racial segregation in STEM should be normalized as acceptable. In asking why physics education routinely fails brilliant minority students, the letter's authors cited the manuscript on stereotype management to allude to the harmful culture that exists in many STEM college environments (McGee & Martin, 2011).

A Strategy for Managing Stereotypes: High
STEM Achievement, Racial Battle Fatigue

Emergent research explores the ways students cope with racial stereotypes and other forms of bias while maintaining high achievement in STEM fields (Cole & Espinoza, 2008; Museus, Palmer, Davis, & Maramba, 2011). A considerable proportion of the research on the academic outcomes of African Americans in STEM fields has focused on stereotype threat. Through a series of experiments with college students, Steele and Aronson (1998) discovered that when race was underscored in pretest guidelines, Black college students performed more poorly on standardized tests than White students. When race was perceived as neutral, however, Black students performed more equally with White students, thereby giving rise to the notion of "stereotype threat" as a common social experience (Steele & Aronson, 1998). This work provided evidence that test achievement outcomes in academic contexts can be impaired by the recognition that one's perceived performance might be viewed through the lens of racial stereotypes (Aronson & Steele, 2005; Taylor & Walton, 2011).

College Students of Color give a wide array of responses when prompted about how they react to being stereotyped, but the pathways and outcomes that do not lead to academic disengagement have been given far too little attention (Block, Koch, Liberman, Merriweather, & Roberson, 2011). One outcome, racial battle fatigue, was brought to the forefront by Smith and colleagues to describe the stress associated with being Black in predominantly White educational environments (Smith, 2004; Smith et al., 2011). Racial battle fatigue refers to race-related stressors and the time and energy African American, Latina/o, and Native American students expend to function among stereotypes; it can lead to detrimental psychological and physiological stress (Nelson & Brammer, 2010; Yosso et al., 2009). However, some Students of Color have developed strategies to help protect themselves from *some* of the damage that racial battle fatigue inflicts; thus, despite being frequently stereotyped, they can maintain their academic success (Fries-Britt & Griffin, 2007; Maton, Pollard, McDougall Weise, & Hrabowski, 2012). These strategies are detailed in the next section.

How Do College Students of Color Cope With Stereotypes in STEM?

As a result of the persistent racism manifested in the form of racial stereotypes and microaggressions, some minoritized STEM students have learned how to succeed academically even while weathering various forms of oppression in racially challenging STEM environments (Maton, Hrabowski, & Schmitt, 2000; Reddick, Welton, Alsandor, Denyszyn, & Platt, 2011). My previous work demonstrates that, as a tactical response to the ongoing presence of racial threats, stereotype management emerged along overlapping paths of racial, gender, and STEM identity development (McGee & Martin, 2011). Although stereotype management allowed for STEM success, these students maintained an intense and perpetual state of awareness that their racial identities were undervalued and negatively conceptualized, and they continually sought to substantiate their intellectual and academic credibility to teachers, peers, administrators, and the larger STEM educational community. STEM success for these students was tempered when important figures (e.g., STEM professors, peers, employers) presumed these students were inferior, based largely on the color of their skin and sometimes in concert with their gender.

Learning to Manage Stereotypes

In previous work, I have documented how high-achieving African American students in STEM majors react to racial stereotypes (see McGee, 2015; McGee & Martin, 2011 for more detailed descriptions). All students ($N = 23$) were interviewed in college and asked about their first recollections of managing stereotypes. For some students, the process began early in life, when they noticed certain oddities. For example, their first mathematics teachers never called on them or assumed they did not know the difficult mathematics problems, frequently giving preference to White and Asian students. Students who attended predominantly Black and Latino/a elementary and middle schools were frequently paraded as the "smart minority kids," whereas their same-race peers with worse performance in mathematics and science were berated or ignored. For some students, working against stereotypes began in high school, when tracking placed them in classes in which their racial groups were underrepresented and racial stereotypes persisted. A few students claimed they were not aware they were managing stereotypes until college. Their realization was usually precipitated by a jarring college experience such as going from the top high school mathematics classes to remedial mathematics in college. For some students, one racist act was all it took for them to initiate strategies to circumvent stereotypes. Other students acted only after a series of racialized events in which their silence or verbal backlash proved to be inefficient in deflecting stereotypes and created or exacerbated stress. The students learned how to transform their shame, anger, and feelings of hopelessness and despair into strategies that minimized or deflated the blow of the stereotype. However, many of these students still felt disheartened in spite of having stellar grades and other achievement-based accolades, and they questioned their future in STEM.

Reactions to Racial Stereotypes While Maintaining STEM Success

Students who engage in stereotype management employ an array of strategies to either preempt or lessen the likelihood of being stereotyped, based on prior STEM classroom experiences. These include coming to class prepared to be challenged on their intellectual capacity because of the perception of always having to know more than their peers, being hypervigilant about negative perceptions of Black behavior and being preemptive (e.g., getting to class early to circumvent the stereotype of Black people always being late), and excelling in STEM to show others that they are worthy of their STEM GPA (McGee, 2015; McGee & Martin, 2011). The present study expands on the stereotype management strategy of *frontin'*, or the performance of acts that are socially acceptable to the dominant culture but demand the sacrifice of aspects of one's racial, cultural, and/or ethnic identity. Students in my earlier work often used the term *frontin'* to describe minimizing, overemphasizing, or altering their racial or cultural identity as a strategy to prove themselves in their STEM majors (McGee & Martin, 2011). Unlike biculturalism or code switching (Toomey, Dorjee, & Ting-Toomey, 2013), which are often described as moving seamlessly between the dominant culture and one's own home culture, frontin' engenders a fair amount of personal agony and the devaluation of parts of one's racial or ethnic identity. Whereas previous research has outlined the pressures for talented Black collegians to avoid the exhibition of stereotypically Black behaviors (Fries-Britt & Griffin, 2007), frontin' encompasses instances of students who demonstrate stereotypical traits of Blackness as an act of defiance of being stereotyped. Thus, frontin' includes altering the characteristics and mannerisms they associate with being their authentic Black selves. For example, a recurrent coping response was to act stereotypically Black to prove that one could be ostensibly Black yet successful. Students repeatedly reported not being true to their authentic selves, as they were playing into negative stereotypes about what it means to be Black (McGee & Martin, 2011). Frontin' therefore encompasses purposeful functioning in various ways that perpetuate scripted standards of Whiteness and Blackness.

The act of performing Blackness also makes frontin' different from code switching or performing biculturally, because students react to racialized situations by performing identities that work to either confirm or negate the stereotype. Even when behavior considered appropriate in a Black cultural context was not acceptable in mainstream settings, proving Blackness appeared to be just as important as proving smartness through White posturing. Research supports the finding that some African American students actively reject the opportunity to move fluidly between cultural contexts, such as the culture of origin and the mainstream (White middle-class) culture (Klingner et al., 2005). However, some students who perform stereotypical notions of Blackness that will not be accepted by their institutions (whether traditionally White or not) still purposefully choose to do this as an act of resistance (Johnson, 2003). Consequently, students sometimes exhibit a resistance to code switching even when it may be the optimal response strategy because it often emulates White norms and behaviors. Nonetheless, the need to engage in frontin' can result in emotional and psychological injury despite academic success.

This description of stereotype management comes out of a body of work that focuses on one minoritized STEM population, Black students. To better understand it as a social strategy for navigating postsecondary education, I expand my investigation of this phenomenon through a comparison of successful Black and Latino/a STEM students in a range of institutional settings. By looking at both Black and Latino/a students, I can better understand the shared and unique ways that they cope with being racialized within and beyond STEM contexts. In addition, by looking at both historically minority-serving institutions (MSIs) as well as predominantly White institutions, this research illuminates the operationalization of stereotype management found in institutions that traditionally serve Students of Color. To that end, this study asked the following questions:

1. What, if any, are the similarities among high-achieving Black and Latino/a STEM college students in identifying and responding to being stereotyped?
2. How does the process of managing and coping with stereotypes differ between Black and Latino/a students, if at all?

The third question emerged through the analytic process, as is common in qualitative research. Additional theoretical insights emerged from my team's recognition of patterns of stereotype management in all institutional contexts. To that end, I asked:

3. How, if at all, does the process of managing and coping with stereotypes differ at universities serving predominantly Students of Color versus those serving predominantly White students?

This study sought to add to the approaches other researchers advanced and to promote an appreciation of what it means to be academically successful in contexts where these historically marginalized students are few and where negative racialized beliefs about their abilities and motivations maintain credibility (Berry, Thunder, & McClain, 2011; Conchas, 2006; Perry, Steele, & Hilliard, 2004). The study also affirms the pursuit of education by Black and Latino/a students in spite of institutional and structural obstacles and reveals the tenuous pathways that Students of Color must navigate in STEM college disciplines.

Methods

Research Context

This study was part of a larger study conducted at six postsecondary institutions across the country during the 2010–2014 academic years; it investigated the experiences and career trajectories of 61 high-achieving Asian, Black, and Latino/a STEM college students. I interviewed 38 high-achieving sophomores, juniors, and seniors who self-identified as Black and Latino/a on their campuses between 2010 and 2012; 19 of the 38 students were interviewed for a second time by telephone in 2013 and 2014. Surprisingly, the telephone interviews were more impersonal and revealed much less about students' racialized experiences than I had anticipated. Although I have insider status as a former practicing electrical engineer with bachelor's and master's degrees in engineering, the rapport I had developed in person did not seem to transfer to telephone conversation. This experience emphasized the importance of in-person interviews for unearthing narratives associated with being stereotyped. I interpret the difference between the in-person and telephone interviews as a sign that although my identification (Black, former engineer) would aid their willingness to communicate, face-to-face interviews were more conducive to revealing racially sensitive topics. Thus, the majority of the data analyzed come from the original interviews. Of the six institutions in the larger study, five institutions were included: One is a historically White institution (HWI), two are Hispanic-serving institutions (HSIs), and two are historically Black institutions (HBIs). Table 1 shows the student racial and ethnic breakdown and identifies the five universities they were attending.

Data Collection

I recruited students through engineering diversity/minority program directors who agreed to distribute flyers to students who fit the following criteria: high-achieving within a STEM major (a minimum of a 2.8 on a 4.0 scale in STEM courses), at least a second-semester sophomore, and self-identified as Black, African American, Latino/a, or Hispanic. I wrote interview protocols that focused on their interactions with administrators, teachers, and peers in a variety of contexts (e.g., labs, internships, classroom, conferences) and how they reflected and responded to these encounters. Additionally, I used an augmented life-story approach (McAdams, 2013) to understand their subjective narratives throughout their schooling and gain a glimpse into their future trajectories. The interviews were audiotaped and transcribed. To standardize my inquiry into their demographic backgrounds, I also administered a two-page questionnaire completed prior to the interview. Semistructured life-story interviews were conducted with all 38 participants (average interview time: 79 minutes).

Data Reduction and Analysis

I and a research team composed of three doctoral students and one master's student went through the transcribed interviews and corrected minor errors in the transcripts. Following Saldaña's (2015) coding manual for

Table 1

Characteristics of the 38 Student Participants

Pseudonym	♀♂	Institute Type	GPA in Major	Major or Graduate Program	College Level	Greatest scientific discovery?	Career Aspirations
Black or African American, not Hispanic or Latino/a [further ethnic identity in brackets]							
ANNETTA	♀	HBI	—	Biomedical engineering/chemistry and math	F s J S	"Nothing stands out"	Medical career, helping community
BRANDY	♀	HBI	3.06	Biochemistry/biology	F s J S	Open heart surgery	MD/PhD in nanotechnology
CHARLOTTE	♀	HBI	3.7	Computer science/security	F s J S	Internet	Computer programming, computer forensics, mentor
CIARA [Creole]	♀	HBI	3.1	Chemistry/math	F s J S	Medication	Research scientist
DAMON	♂	HBI	—	Chemistry	F s J S	—	Pediatrician and researcher
ELISE	♀	HBI	3.6	Electrical engineering	F s J S	Light bulb	MS in engineering, PhD in education
JAMILLA	♀	HBI	—	Applied math/computer science	F s J S	Microscope	PhD, government
JANET	♀	HBI	4.0	Chemistry	F s J S	Airplanes	MD—pediatrics or cardiology
JOHARI [Jamaican]	♂	HEI	—	Chemistry/biology (minor)	F s J S	Chromatography	Pharmacognosist
JOY	♀	HBI	4.0	Chemistry	F s J S	Chemotherapy	Pharmaceutical scientist
KAMI	♀	HBI	3.1	Chemistry/math	F s J S	Blackbody radiation	Cosmetic chemist
LATASHA	♀	HBI	3.85	Chemistry	F s J S	Microscope	PhD in public health or public health policy
LATOYA	♀	HBI	—	Biochemistry	F s J S	The hot comb	MD/PhD—cancer biology, molecular biology, or biochemistry
TIMOTHY	♂	HBI	3.48	Secondary math education	F s J S	—	Math teacher

(continued)

Table 1 (continued)

Pseudonym	♀♂	Institute Type	GPA in Major	Major or Graduate Program	College Level	Greatest scientific discovery?	Career Aspirations
VITA [Haitian]	♀	HBI	3.75	Physics	(F)(S)(J)(S)	X-ray	Research—nanoscience/biomaterial, international healthcare policy
JASON	♀	HSI	3.2	Chemistry/biology	(F)(S)(J)(S)	Nuclear magnetic resonance	Pharmaceutics of drug design
CHRIS	♂	HWI	3.1	Aerospace engineering	(F)(S)(J)(S)	Electricity	Working in research and development in aerospace
JEENA	♀	HWI	2.9	Chemistry/biology	(F)(S)(J)(S)	Light bulb	Clinical health administrator
JERROD	♂	HWI	2.86	Nuclear engineering	(F)(S)(J)(S)	$E = mc^2$	Career revolving around self-help and inspiring others
NNAKEME [Nigerian]	♂	HWI	3.0	Aerospace engineering	(F)(S)(J)(S)	Flying a plane	—
Black or African American and Hispanic or Latino/a [further ethnic identity in brackets]							
KAREN [Mexican]	♀	HBI	3.0	Chemistry/math	(F)(S)(J)(S)	Einstein and Newton	Environmental chemist
RODNEY [Panamanian]	♂	HWI	—	Physics/visual arts	(F)(S)(J)(S)	Integrated circuits	Astrophysician
Black or African American, no response on Hispanic ethnic identity [further ethnic identity in brackets]							
GRANT	♂	HBI	3.5	Computer engineering	(F)(S)(J)(S)	Microprocessor/micro controller	PhD, CEO of a robotics company
MATTHEW	♂	HWI	2.9	Chemical engineering	(F)(S)(J)(S)	iPad	Chemical engineer
White and Hispanic or Latino/a [further ethnic identity in brackets]							
BEL	♀	HSI	3.23	Biology/chemistry	(F)(S)(J)(S)	—	PhD research scientist
CAITLYN [Columbian/Guatemalan]	♀	HSI	2.89	Biology/chemistry	(F)(S)(J)(S)	DNA manipulation	Pediatric oncologist
EARLENA	♀	HSI	2.8	Physics/international studies	(F)(S)(J)(S)	—	Pilot, international diplomacy, or related field

(continued)

Table 1 (continued)

Pseudonym	♀♂	Institute Type	GPA in Major	Major or Graduate Program	College Level	Greatest scientific discovery?	Career Aspirations
GILBERTO	♂	HSI	3.5	Computer science	Master's student	Internet	PhD in society and technology; professor
HECTOR	♂	HSI	2.8	Mathematics	F s J S	Integral and differential calculus	Scientist, mathematician, or a combination of the two
RICARDO	♂	HSI	3.5	Math	F s J S	Music recording	PhD in mathematics education
JAVIER	♂	HWI	3.4	Aerospace engineering	F s J S	$F_{net} = ma$	MBA in consulting, supply chain management, aerospace
More than one race; Hispanic or Latino/a [further ethnic identity in brackets]							
JOSE	♂	ESI	3.7	Physics	F s J S	Internet	Industry/research
No response to race identity; identify ethnically as Hispanic or Latino/a [further ethnic identity in brackets]							
ALICIA	♀	HSI	3.6	Biology and math/chemistry and computer science	F s J S	—	MD/PhD; "love" research
ANTONIO	♂	HSI	4.0	Aerospace engineering	F s J S	The pencil	Research manager or electric propulsion developer
EDUARDO	♂	HSI	4.0	Biology/chemistry	F s J S	—	Biomedical researcher, bioengineer, or pharmaceutical research
GERALDO [Mexican American]	♂	HSI	3.6	Mathematics	F s J S	Software like Maplesoft	Math teacher or actuary
JUAN	♂	HSI	3.1	Electrical engineering	F s J S	Hubble's deep field picture	Research lab—space propulsion laboratory
MIGUEL	♂	HWI	3.6	Biology/physics	F s J S	Quantum mechanics	PhD, physicist

Note. HBI = historically Black institution; HSI = Hispanic-serving institution; HWI = historically White institution.

qualitative researchers, we developed two sets of codes to address the first two research questions, after the open coding phase. First, to understand the students' narratives of their *responses to structural and social challenges* they encountered in higher education institutions, we coded to label these strategies relative to each student's perceptions based on his or her experiences rather than on prescribed traditional definitions of stereotypes and student agency (Miles, Huberman, & Saldaña, 2013). For example, we developed codes around the theme of structural barriers: (a) lack of same-race students being recruited and retained in participants' STEM department (student response: work twice as hard, become the ideal "token" student), (b) professors who doubt the STEM abilities of Black and Latino/a students (student response: prove themselves, at times studying to the point of exhaustion), and (c) administration that is unresponsive to or that minimizes participants' complaints about microaggressions (student response: "tough it out" or share their concerns with confidants outside the institution). Next, we developed codes to document *racial stereotypes* students encountered. Although some of these codes were built on the interviews, we also drew on prior work on Black students' experiences with stereotypes on predominantly White campuses and on Students of Color in STEM to link our codes with the literature (we could not find many articles detailing racial stereotypes on campuses primarily serving Students of Color; exceptions include Harper & Gasman, 2008; Kynard & Eddy, 2009). This gave us language to label and aggregate students' mostly descriptive accounts of their experiences (e.g., Aronson & Steele, 2005; Beasley & Fischer, 2012; Block et al., 2011; Cokley, 2014; Fries-Britt & Griffin, 2007; Harris-Perry, 2011; Malone & Barabino, 2009). We investigated the first research question by scrutinizing the students' transcripts for the shared ways both racial groups experience stereotypes, including how the students might respond to and develop from these racialized depictions. Table 2 lists some of the codes relevant to the theme of being racially stereotyped as a college Student of Color.

Coding took place in two stages. The first stage involved creating a preliminary code list, creating operational definitions for each code, and coding 10 interviews (five students who self-identify as Black/African American and five students who self-identify as Hispanic or Latino/a) using the existing code list until all codes were identified. Two doctoral students and I separately coded the same six interviews. In the second stage of coding, we validated the usefulness of the code list by checking the codes' reliability at meetings held after each interview was individually coded, during which codes were negotiated (Miles et al., 2013). After the 12th interview, we had established about 85% of all the codes, at which time saturation was nearly achieved; that is, the number of people who had to be interviewed or observed before no new data emerged had been met, which indicated that we had reached the boundaries of the phenomenon. My team coded the remaining 25 interviews, adding only 14 new codes to our established

Table 2
Partial Schema of Racial Stereotyping Codes

7.0	Codes under the theme of racial stereotype
7.1	Reflections/perceptions of racial stereotypes (general)
7.2	Perceptions of a particular ethnicity/racial/gender group being stereotyped
7.3	Difficulties/pressure of being racially/ethnically stereotyped or how being stereotyped negatively affected the respondent
7.4	Stereotypes, racialized remarks, perceptions about race and/or gender groups outside of the respondent's race and/or gender
7.5	Perceptions of university-based programs that cater to underrepresented groups
7.6.1	Reactions/responses to racialized experiences that produce temporary academic setbacks
7.6.2	Reactions to racialized experiences that produce negative emotional wear and tear
7.8	Coping strategies specifically related to racial bias in STEM fields
7.9	Reflections about racial stereotyping in their future STEM careers
7.10	Perceptions of the long-term damage of being stereotyped in STEM

set of 113. The coding team achieved consensus, and the cross-checking and auditing process improved the trustworthiness of the data analysis (Richards, 2014).

In attending to the second research question, we differentiated the strategies employed by Black and Latino/a students in responding to and reflecting on the stereotype. For the Latino/a students in particular, but not exclusively, there was much discussion of ethnicity and their migration to the United States (or perceived migration, as some students were born in the United States but were often assumed to be born elsewhere). Therefore, the ethnicity codes proved to be relevant to understanding the role racial stereotypes played for several Latino/a students and the two Black students who were born and raised outside the United States (Table 3).

Through our analysis, we unearthed an unanticipated aspect of racial stereotyping: Institutions described as culturally affirming overall had a microculture in the STEM departments that appeared to be almost identical to that of HWIs. Thus, to better assess the institutions' role, a third research question emerged as we looked at the institution (department, faculty members, campus climate) for clues about how the environment might contribute to perpetuating stereotypes. For example, Black and Latino/a students at both MSIs and HWIs desired courses with professors who matched their racial background, but this proved difficult due to the lack of Black or Latino/a professors.

Among the 38 participants, there were three disconfirming cases. One Latino male student exclaimed that he was lucky to never have been

Table 3
Partial Schema of Ethnicity Codes

4.0	Codes Under the Theme of Ethnicity
4.1	Non-U.S. cultural context (first or second generation)
4.2	Family traditions/customs/ideologies related to ethnicity
4.3	Reconciling ethnicity/race identity with an Americanized identity
4.4	Thoughts/reflections about being Black or Latino/a with immigrant or presumed immigrant status
4.5	Responses to being treated like a Black or Latino/a with immigrant or presumed immigrant status
4.6	International communities as resources/assets
4.7	Definitions, perceptions, and descriptions of racial/ethnic identity
4.8	Ethnic language of family/community/household
4.9	Skin color dynamics/skin color stratification (colorism)
4.10	Ethnic and cultural practices that were purposefully minimized as a coping strategy
4.11	Thoughts/reflections about being perceived as a "White" American

stereotyped and said he did not see stereotypes playing any role in his future as a STEM professional. The other two students, one Black female and one Black male, reported training themselves to become detached and anesthetized from being stereotyped. Johari (all names are pseudonyms) said, "I get stereotyped every day, but I'm so used to it. It's like I go numb." Although a total of nine students in this study mentioned numbness as one of their coping strategies, only these two students claimed it as their sole strategy for disregarding stereotypes.

Researcher Role

Although my bachelor's degree in electrical engineering is about 20 years old and much has changed since then, studying people whose experience was so much like mine (i.e., processing racial experiences while pursuing a STEM undergraduate degree) required me to acknowledge and discuss my own position and subjectivity. I attended an HBI for my undergraduate electrical engineering degree, where at least half my professors were of African descent, but I had no Black female STEM professors. I recognize that my research has been influenced by how and why race and racism operate in STEM higher education, which has contributed to my understanding that power, privilege, race, class, and sexual oppression are at the root of many of the academic experiences minoritized students withstand. Thus, I am committed to carrying out this research from a race-conscious perspective and to problematizing the success of STEM Students of Color by giving voice to these students through their counternarratives. At the same time, I acknowledge the position of Henry and Generett

(2005) that "all scholarship is veiled autobiography" (p. 1). As a researcher, my empirical commitments lead me to seek disconfirming evidence for emerging conjectures and to engage with atypical cases in reporting my findings.

Limitations

This study had several limitations. Participants were selected based on their self-identification of race/racial identity, but they included students whose ethnicities within their races were culturally distinctive. For example, the Latino/a students were from different countries and regions of the world (e.g., Colombia, Mexico, and Guatemala). Teasing out the complexities within and between these ethnicities would have added another layer of identity to this study. In addition, although I had developed rapport with the participants during the in-person campus interviews, the follow-up phone interviews did not yield robust findings about the ongoing role of managing stereotypes and other forms of bias. Another limitation is the variance in MSIs. In 2009, HBIs graduated 80% of all Black STEM undergraduates, whereas only 6% of the STEM undergraduate degrees from HSIs went to Latino/as and Hispanics. Thus, the institutional impact of MSIs on Students of Color in STEM is greater for Black college students (Stage, Lundy-Wagner, & John, 2013). The unique roles HBIs and HSIs play in the production of degrees and experiences of STEM Students of Color warrant more attention.

Findings

The successful STEM Students of Color used a range of stereotype management strategies that enabled them to maneuver and in some cases subdue the full impact of racial stereotypes; however, protection was short lived, as the variety and frequency of stereotyping served as an unrelenting competitor. The central research question examines the shared approaches that Black and Latino/a STEM students exercised to manage racial stereotypes and that enabled them to thrive academically while becoming emotionally fatigued as a result of defending themselves against multiple forms of racial bias in and around their STEM settings. Managing stereotypes necessitated the students' adoption of defensive strategies to protect their academic identities yet often resulted in disrupting their racial identities. Attending to the question that explores the differences in three institutional types (HWI, HBI, and HSI), we found that stereotypes were rampant in the STEM departments of both HWIs and MSIs, and students responded to those stereotypes in similar ways. Thus, the results are organized to show the similarities of managing stereotypes by institution. The final section of these findings explores the unique ways each racial group contended with stereotypes, with some Latinos/as adopting White racial schemas that advantage Whites to minimize the effects of racialized bias. Although this article primarily discusses the role of stereotypes, students shared perspectives on how they balanced stereotypes with forms of endorsement received from organizations and institutional programming such as the National Society of Black Engineers, Society of Hispanic Engineers, Minority Engineering Program Directors, national conferences that affirmed the identities of Black and Latino/a students, and faculty who encouraged these students' brilliance and provided a sense of belongingness (see McGee & Martin [2011] for a more detailed discussion of these sources of support).

Shared Strategies Among STEM Students of Color

The first research question investigated and compared how participants identified and then responded to being stereotyped, in which 35 of the 38 students are represented. As these Students of Color shared details on the ways in which stereotypes were enacted and their responses, another microgroup emerged: students of lower socioeconomic class, who encounter an additional layer of negative categorization due to stereotypes associated with both their class and race. Thirty-one of the 35 students purposely gave up parts of their racial/cultural identity to perform mainstream mannerisms, behaviors, and ideologies as a defensive strategy to minimize the effects of racism. Global strategies to manage racial stereotypes are based on students' knowledge of their race being devalued in STEM contexts, which required them to disconnect from parts of their racial/cultural identity.

Participants raised in same-race low-income neighborhoods. Students of Color said that racial stereotypes caused emotional injury and harmed their overall college STEM experience, but students coming from low-income families revealed an additional layer of inequity. Coming from racially homogeneous, low-income neighborhoods was associated with adding class-based insults to racial injury. Eleven of the 38 participants (6 Black, 5 Latino/a) attested to being raised in ethnically and racially homogeneous neighborhoods and admitted to minimal prior experiences operating in predominantly White spaces. Among these students was Miguel (biology/physics), who explained that he was always scared that "my *barrio* [the Spanish word for 'hood, slang for neighborhood] culture might slip out." He was raised in a neighborhood he described as "Hispanic, economically depressed, but culturally and spiritually rich," a fact he was proud of until he arrived at his HWI. His mentors and professors told him how lucky he was to fulfill the "American Dream" of being the first person in his family to attend college. One of Miguel's professors said he should quickly forget where he came from and embrace his more "respectable lifestyle." In other words, when Miguel revealed his roots, he learned that the department considered him only marginally acceptable. Miguel managed the stereotype associated with "barrio life" by obtaining a new address to avoid assumptions about his home neighborhood:

I was sort of, kinda, somewhat accepted, until they [White peers and professors] asked me about the crib [his home neighborhood]. Then they backed off big time and started treating me like a statistic. So now I say I'm from the 'burbs. I even got a PO box address, so they don't have to know where I'm really from.

Miguel was surprised at the number of times he had to tell university people his home address: for scholarships, awards, internships, and financial aid. He preferred that these individuals retain the impression that he was from a middle-class community instead of a low-income, mostly Latino/a community—and he went to great lengths to maintain the façade.

Jeena (chemistry/biology) exclaimed that she was the pride of her densely populated, low-income, predominantly Black community after being awarded a full scholarship to attend a prominent university associated with prestige and success. Despite being, in her words, "academically unstoppable," Jeena felt it was impossible to succeed at her HWI without frontin', or adopting traits and behaviors that her college community deemed appropriate. She described this process as happening over the course of her first two years in college. When Jeena first arrived at the HWI, she strutted proudly across campus with her curly red weave and the bright, tight-fitting clothes she was accustomed to wearing, which was revered as "bussin' gear" (appealing dress style) in her community. In the second semester of her freshman year, she replaced her long, red, kinky-curl weave with a straight, brown, "Whitish-looking" hair weave. She explained that she did this after "the White and some uppity Black girls teased me about my hair and outfits, basically my whole body, being too ghetto and too trashy." Jeena's White female freshman roommate bluntly clarified this point: "I know you are smart, but nobody is going to believe you are smart with that fake red hair and your boobs hanging out all the time." The professor who taught Jeena's freshman mathematics for computer science class was very rude to her; he frequently walked in another direction to avoid coming into close contact with her. Jeena was horrified by the myriad strategies he took to avoid her and blamed it on her colorful self-expression, which she later defined as her "too-Black street style."

In her sophomore year, Jeena felt compelled to appear less sexy and opted to dress more like the "smart kids do." She got rid of her favorite outfits, which were mostly short and multicolored, and replaced them with plain-colored, "neat" clothes. After several months of Jeena's new, more assimilated look, this same mathematics professor eagerly approached Jeena, telling her, "Now you actually look presentable. I bet you are making better grades too." Jeena was consistently an A student—including the A she earned in this professor's class—but her racialized and gendered experiences at this HWI made her feel increasingly insecure about expressing herself. The less she looked like herself, the more her teachers and peers valued her intellect, likely because she looked more assimilated and, I would argue, less culturally defiant and expressive. Jeena's story also illustrates how Black and Latina women have been framed and misrepresented by stereotypes about their sexuality and presumed promiscuity (Flores & Garcia, 2009; Harris-Perry, 2011).

Of the 11 students raised in low-income, predominantly Black and Latino/a neighborhoods, seven attended MSIs and yet three of the seven students also spoke of race and class oppression. The denial of racial and class privilege creates a tendency in the middle class, or among those who wish to have middle-class status, to see lower-income Blacks and Latino/as as personally failing and to judge those who defy White cultural values as undeserving (McFarlane, 2009; Wiggins, 2001). The social construction of classism embraces prejudicial attitudes and stereotypes that denigrate the culture of the very poor and of working-class people, including students. Ironically, the Black and Latino/a middle classes are fragile, because, despite having some class privileges, they are never fully free from concern over how they might be perceived because of the stereotypes associated with their racial group (Omi & Winant, 2014).

HBIs, for example, have a legacy of attendance by generations of elite Black families, which copy the ideologies of the White middle class and take part in organizations and activities that distinguish them from other classes in the Black community; this class segregation is imitated on those campuses (Frazier, 1997; Harper & Gasman, 2008). MSIs host racial stereotypes of low-income Blacks and Latino/as (e.g., laziness, sexual promiscuity, irresponsible parenting, disinterest in education, and disregard for the law). Thus, those who are entrenched or holding on to their middle-class status can be some of the biggest critics of low-income individuals within their own racial group (Banner-Haley, 2010). Thus, some of the students in this section were further marginalized because of their low-income cultural status at institutions that are classified as racially affirming.

Sacrificing one's cultural identity as a tactic to elude stereotyping. Nineteen students discussed the ways in which Blackness and Brownness were devalued or Whiteness was aligned with being privileged. Eduardo attended an HSI, where he felt the main purpose of the institution was to "take us in Brown and turn us out White." Eduardo's success in biology and chemistry included associating with a different class of friends: He was "advised" to stop hanging out with his friends from his hometown, teased and told to tone down his accent, and told in class, by the professor, that if he stayed out of the Latino Caucus (a progressive campus-based organization), he would have a better chance of securing employment. Eduardo regretfully admitted that as a result of this advice, he limited public contact with his hometown Latino/a friends, which ultimately strained those friendships. He also became an inactive member of the Latino Caucus and eliminated all forms of activism from his college life.

Jerrod (nuclear engineering) was frontin' when he pretended that he had not studied for a test in order to create "maximum shock value" when he scored in the high 90s. In his words, "no matter how many A's I get in physics, he [Jerrod's European physics professor] always seems surprised." As a result, Jerrod just pretended that he was "their definition of Black and gifted," which he described this way:

> [A] Black dude who can just do physics without studying. But that's not really me. I study my butt off, but my professor thinks that the only conceivable way I could actually score that high is that I must be a semi-genius. I really don't think he believes that Black males can really be successful any other way. It pains me, but I just go along with the program. And it's better than him accusing me of cheating.

One semester, Jerrod made excellent grades in chemistry and his professor accused him of cheating. To avoid repeating that painful experience, he fronted and played into the genius label that his physics professor bestowed on him. For Jerrod's professor, being Black and in STEM was operationalized to denote that if Jerrod made excellent grades, he must be a prodigy.

Jose was a member of a chemical engineering lab at an HSI, but the majority of the lab members were of Asian descent, except for two White males. In this lab, each student took turns playing the music of his/her choice. When Jose's turn arrived, he brought in his favorite salsa CD and turned up the music. The first 30 seconds of the song was met with stunned silence. Then, as if someone had told a joke, his lab members busted out in unabashed laughter. They started very badly imitating salsa dancing and somehow this led to calling each other *ese* (or, "Hey bro," in slang) and then to pantomiming a gang gun battle. Jose was horrified, grabbed his CD, and left the lab. Although satisfied with the research in the lab, he realized after three long weeks of constant teasing that he had to leave. His new lab welcomed him, but only after his new principal investigator warned Jose about "being too sensitive about jokes and good-natured fun." Before that incident, Jose had felt sheltered from stereotypes; afterward, however, he actively avoided conversations about his Latino culture. Jose's frontin' included not playing his music when he was riding with his engineering classmates and hiding his girlfriend's pregnancy to avoid being subjected to stereotypes about young unmarried Latinas bearing children. Jose's distress over the experience continued partly because he had finally felt accepted in his original lab group, only to discover that his culture was ripe for racial insult. Jose was one of 12 study participants who were considering opting out of a STEM career entirely.

Black and Brown universities: White and Asian STEM faculty. Regarding the third research question on the differences in managing and coping with stereotypes at universities serving predominantly Students of Color versus those serving predominantly White students, more than half the participants who attended MSIs had similar racialized experiences in their STEM departments as the students who attended HWIs. Students of Color have long said they have to prove their academic competence while attending HWIs (Moore, Madison-Colmore, & Smith, 2003). Thirty of the 38 Black and Latino/a students who attended HBIs and HSIs attested to having college experiences similar to what research reports about MSIs: Their college experiences fostered cultural, spiritual, and intellectual affirmations of themselves, including racial pride and a sense of community (Bettez & Suggs, 2012; Cokley, 2014). This section details how half the Black and Latino/a students who attended HBIs or HSIs witnessed contemporary forms of older ideologies borrowed from HWIs that were based on racial subservience, assimilation of mainstream ideologies, and obedience to White ideals within their STEM departments.

William H. Watkins (2001), in *The White Architects of Black Education: Ideology and Power in America, 1865–1945*, provides detailed historical archive analysis maintaining that HBIs were created and continue to be maintained as a reflection of the dominant class. Indeed, Booker T. Washington's advocacy of Black acceptance of segregation in exchange for economic advancement was fundamental to the development of HBIs (Harper & Gasman, 2008). Watkins contended that this "mis-education" persists at MSIs, where the philosophical and ideological orientation continues to reinforce White privilege and supremacy.

Brandy (biochemistry) attended an HBI but was disappointed that most of her STEM professors were of Asian descent. She felt that her Asian professors had low expectations for their Black students. Brandy extended her schooling for an extra semester by securing a cooperative internship so that she could avoid taking an advanced statistics class from an Asian professor who had a reputation for openly berating his Black students.

Geraldo (mathematics), who attended an HSI, was also dissatisfied that he could not see himself in his professors:

> I chose to come here because I really wanted to be taught by Latino professors. I did get that as a freshman, but now as a junior I'm heavy in my chemistry and engineering classes [and] I have no Latino professors. It's true. I mean, no Hispanic professors. From now until the time I will graduate, none of my teachers will look like me.

According to just under half of the students in this study who attended HBIs and HSIs, which have an institutional reputation for being culturally and racially affirming, these places fell short of achieving a sense of warmth and affinity in their STEM departments. It emerged that the STEM departments in some HSIs and HBIs were eerily similar to those at HWIs. Kynard and Eddy (2009) examined university power structures to explain why institutional racism can and does occur at colleges and universities designed to serve the needs of Students of Color. Asian and European STEM faculty members were a dominant presence, and many subscribed to negative racial stereotypes and biased ideologies against Students of Color, as revealed by subtle and not-so-subtle acts of discrimination (McGee, 2014). Students complained about the increasing number of Asian students in their STEM classes, whom the Asian professors seemed to favor as research and teaching assistants and for other mentoring opportunities. In short, almost half the students at MSIs described the tension between the overall racial warmth and solidarity of the HBI or HSI and the sense of being stereotyped or undervalued by STEM department faculty; this tension contributed to feelings of intellectual inferiority among Students of Color.

Latino/a Students Negotiating American Whiteness

In addressing the second question of this study—whether Black and Latino/a students manage stereotypes differently—I found that the two groups employed strategies similar to those detailed above, with one exception: Of the 16 students who identified (partly or fully) as Latino/a in this study, 8 espoused negotiating forms of Whiteness as a strategy for minimizing bias, and sometimes merely for convenience, in ways that the students who identified (partly or fully) as African American/Black did not. These same eight students identified their racial identity as exclusively White, or as White and, for example, Colombian, Mexican, or Costa Rican, along with their ethnic identity of Hispanic and Latino/a.[3]

While both racial groups were involved with embodying White practices and behaviors, Latino/a students were able to switch into "being White" in certain situations to eliminate the chance of being stereotyped. Eight of the Latino/a students in this study used the frontin' strategy, mostly by using their light complexions and European features to gain entry into contexts that are privileged by skin color and to avoid being subject to discriminatory practices. Some Latino/a students across skin shades negotiated their identities by eliminating markers that once showcased their racial pride and identity. For example, one student had a Cinco de Mayo tattoo removed, and another stopped wearing a pendant her grandmother had given her that displayed the Puerto Rican map. Other strategies involved checking the "White only" race/ethnicity category on a college application but claiming Hispanic race/ethnicity for minority scholarship applications; being less than honest about their family's employment status and job titles, particularly if they were in the cleaning and landscaping industries, even if their family members were entrepreneurs living a middle-class lifestyle; pretending not to speak Spanish; and straightening their naturally curly hair. These reactions appear to be a response to the persistence of discrimination (e.g., attacks on immigrants, the United States' racialized classification system, and continued racism against middle-class, college-educated Latino/as) and not an acceptance of assimilation or acculturation (Flores & Garcia, 2009; Sanchez, 2008).

Javier (aerospace engineering), a Colombian male who racially identifies as White and Latino, described how he struggled with "always" being identified as Mexican:

> I really feel like Hispanics are stereotyped, except, you know, people always say jokes they think represent the Mexican culture. It's like a Mexican gangster. They're the ones that shave their heads, California, tattoos, mustache. And it's always, [people say] like, "Do you speak Mexican?" That's like the one and only thing that really makes me mad is, "Hey, are you Mexican? Oh, you speak Mexican?" So that, you know, kind of like that American focus just on themselves sometimes makes me mad.

Javier revealed that he sometimes tells people he is White, in part to distance himself from stereotypes associated with being Mexican. Javier attended an HSI, but he strategically associated with his non-Mexican peers. Javier manages this stereotype by actively avoiding Mexican students to minimize the potential associations his peers and teachers might make with Mexican culture, thereby reducing his chances of being the victim of Mexican ethnic stereotypes. Javier said he was proud of being Latino but resented being a target of Mexican-based stereotypes and other bias. Javier blamed U.S.-born citizens, particularly his White college peers and professors, for being ignorant of other Latino/a ethnicities and cultures.

Caitlyn (biology/chemistry) is a Colombian and Guatemalan woman who racially identifies as White and Hispanic. She emphasized her White identity as a strategy to avoid being negatively stereotyped. Caitlyn added gender to her analysis:

> You constantly have to prove yourself as a Hispanic woman. You have to prove yourself to someone who just doesn't know. I mean, how's an old White guy [referring to her White male chemistry professor] going to know what it's like to be a Hispanic young adult, young female? First of all, he never got raised Hispanic, so there's presumptions he doesn't know, not because he's ignorant, but just because he doesn't know what it's like to be a young Hispanic woman because he's an old man, and you can't expect them to just know. It still feels super awkward.

Caitlyn said that in response to those awkward situations, she decided to conceal the Hispanic part of her identity:

> Being White helps me to avoid so many uncomfortable conversations . . . like, about where my family is from and what kind of domestic work my mother does, and what type of gardener is my father, how many of my relatives live in my house, how many brothers do I have in gangs, do I have a U.S. passport, am I worried about getting

deported, or do I have a baby yet and all those other stupid asinine questions.

Caitlyn confirmed that her science major also helped her to maintain her White identity, as it was difficult for others to believe that a Hispanic woman could even aspire to become a doctor.

Ricardo (mathematics), a Mexican American male who racially identifies as Latino, revealed that he often gets mistaken for a non-Latino White. After a series of experiences in which he was mistaken for White, he thought it was sometimes best to, in his words, "just keep quiet, not revealing nor denying my race." Ricardo felt culturally and racially safe at his HSI but added that unhealthy reminders of his second-class status were "everywhere." Ricardo was having a conversation with his elderly White mathematics professor about the increased numbers of "undesirables" on the professor's block:

> It was that feeling . . . I'll never forget when I realized that the racism would never end, when I spoke to my [White] professor about the history of her block. She was telling me how great the neighborhood was and how everything was great and you knew everybody, but then the Mexicans moved in. I don't think she realized I was Mexican. So, I was, "Oh, okay."

Ricardo wondered whether she forgot that he was Latino, although his name was "authentically" ethnic-sounding. His frontin' involved actively avoiding any further conversations with her and with others who revealed similar ideologies about Mexicans because he was afraid they might find out that he was Mexican and apply their negative stereotypes to him. In the case of his mathematics professor, her assumptions about Mexican people could pose a threat to his A– grade in her class.

Earlena (physics/international studies), whose name is ethnically Latina, said she could not help but notice that once her name was revealed, some conversations would take unexpectedly negative, uncomfortable, or awkward turns. Thus, when talking to professors, speaking with potential employers, or engaging in similar activities, Earlena put her "White-girl voice on." She said that most situations "unfortunately go easier that way." Hector, Gilberto, and Javier disclosed similar strategies of deflecting stereotypes with their phenotypically White or light skin and European facial features. They described it as another layer of protection against being stereotyped.

None of the students were comfortable with negotiating Whiteness as though they were thoroughly assimilated. They seemed highly conflicted, as Eduardo (biology/chemistry) revealed:

> I wish I could just be myself. But in this country being yourself can get you hurt, ignored, and feeling like a nuisance just because you

are Latino. So, if White kids can benefit from the privilege of being White, then why can't I?

Eduardo's ultimate goal was to diversify the chemistry field by opening pathways and opportunities for Latino/as. The Latino/a students featured in this section appeared to feel conflicted but obligated to play into the ways American culture rewards Whiteness in order to deflect potential stereotyping and to capture a small sense of belonging in social and academic spaces.

Discussion

The principal research question explored the role and impact of racial stereotypes in experiences and lives of Black and Latino STEM students attending universities that are predominantly Black, Latino, or White. The findings indicate that these students have to wrestle, prioritize, and respond to negative assumptions, biases, and derogatory, often toxic, stereotypes and microaggressions about their intellectual aptitude and STEM identity. Stereotypes helped to shape their academic worlds, and their response strategies allowed them to ensure high levels of STEM achievement, but at the cost of limiting their racial/cultural, and in some cases socioeconomic class or gender identities. These findings suggest that racial stereotyping and other biases were functions of STEM education at the university level and that academic success for Students of Color included learning how to navigate racism cleverly and with a set of tools that soften the blow of stereotyping but never eliminate it.

The participants reported frequently feeling deflated and exhausted by the effort of trying to manage the quantity and variety (from subtle to blatant) of racial bias they endured. Along the way, they learned and manipulated White ways of knowing and doing by performing the social and racial practices that are commonplace in postsecondary institutions. The students attempted to deflect the force of ever-present stereotypes by shifting their identities—for example, by frontin'—while remaining keenly aware of Americanized notions of race and capitalizing on strategies that gave them an advantage or that purposefully challenged the notion of being disadvantaged. Although frontin' by definition includes both acts of assimilation of White norms and acts of resistance that accentuate stereotypical demonstrations of Blackness, I found that these students did not use the latter aspect of frontin'. Perhaps they did not need additional trumped-up presentations of Blackness or Brownness because their own authentic racial identities were viewed as sufficiently deviant from mainstream White values and behaviors. Recall that Jeena's tight and bright fashion and hair style were deemed "ghetto" enough without any additional markers of Blackness. Therefore, frontin' could be reconceptualized such that the very bodies of Black and Brown people are viewed by their STEM departments, and to some extent by their universities and colleges, as acts of resistance, mediated by the extent to which they enact their own racialized identities. Low socioeconomic class status further complicates the way students are viewed: Stereotypes often thrive on the identities of lower socioeconomic class within a particular racial group (Kirschenman & Neckerman, 1991). To sum up, the students in this study negotiated racial stereotypes through the choices they made about their appearance, spoken dialect, and behavior that sought to mimic White ways of knowing and doing. For the majority of the participants, this was characterized as a type of social performance, an attempt to situate themselves as socially and academically acceptable.

Stereotype management focuses on responding to stereotypes rather than ending them; the majority of the participants in this study attested to suffering psychological strain, despite their academic success. Once the stereotype has been activated and the recipients perceive it as a racialized threat, its effects persist long after the situation in which the student was stereotyped (McGee & Martin, 2011). These findings therefore demonstrate the value of stereotype management for affirming academic competency, but the tactic does not keep students from enduring racialized stress and anxiety. Most, but not all, students had long given up on the goal of ending stereotypes. In fact, most of the students viewed the stereotypes as inescapable and concluded that they will always be burdened by having to prove they are intellectually capable in their STEM fields.

The racial composition of their STEM departments' faculty offered little help to Black and Latino/a students who attended MSIs, although their overall university experience was culturally affirming. The strategies they used to circumvent racial stereotypes were similar to those of students in HWI settings because the MSI STEM departments' microculture had similar characteristics: high numbers of Asian students and faculty; a competitive, even cutthroat environment; overburdening of the few Black and Latino/a STEM faculty with serving and mentoring Students of Color; and racially segregated study and laboratory groups. The practices and policies of STEM departments help to control structural possibilities, and so the departments marginalize Students of Color and regulate how they should behave and what behavior is deemed misbehaving. Issues of conservatism at HBIs and HSIs are often invisible in literature that situates these institutions as universally supportive and nurturing (notable exceptions include Gasman, 2012; Harper & Gasman, 2008; Watkins, 2001). More research on sociocultural norms at MSIs that endorse the values and ideologies of the dominant culture at the expense of low-income Blacks and Latino/as will complicate the cultural affirmation that MSIs are assumed to possess. There appears to be a microculture in STEM departments at MSIs that is, a set of values, beliefs, and behaviors based on a common history of racial stereotyping and discrimination that varies systematically from the larger, often affirming cultural milieu of the MSI (Lynch, 2001). Some participants did not find nurturing STEM environments or access to Black and Latino/a STEM faculty, which affected their satisfaction with their college experience. Instead, they encountered non-Black STEM faculty and middle-class Asian, White, and non-U.S.-born students and faculty who appeared to hold biases against the Students of Color, particularly those of lower socioeconomic status. The MSIs, as Juan suggested, "turn White and Asian" in the upper level STEM courses, referring to the White and Asian students and faculty that dominated his advanced STEM courses. Some MSIs espoused mainstream behaviors, such as a business-class dress code, corporate and industrial funding (e.g., in 2014, the billionaire industrialist Koch brothers, known for funding conservative causes and candidates, gave $25 million to the United Negro College Fund), and restrictive institutional policies. Thus, even students at institutions that are traditionally racially affirming sometimes experience the power of racial stereotypes through racialized experiences in their STEM programming. Black and Latino/a STEM students at MSIs therefore might require different forms of negotiation and support in their STEM programs to maintain the feelings of cultural affirmation that characterize their MSIs as a whole.

Students did not share their on-campus experiences of being racially stereotyped with campus leaders. A couple of students who did speak out said they were told to stay strong and continue to be resilient, or they were shamed into silence. Institutional leaders appeared to be advocating for constructs like grit, perseverance, and mental toughness without properly acknowledging the multiple forms of suffering Black and Latino/a students continue to experience. I contend that current research on grit and resilience, at least as these concepts are sometimes defined and operationalized, does not explore the toll societal racism takes on Students of Color, particularly those who may be viewed as successful (McGee & Stovall, 2015). The majority of this research refers to static definitions of resilience, such as the innate ability to bounce back from obstacles, without properly acknowledging how structural racism breeds the racial practices, policies, and ideologies that force Black and Latino/a students to adopt unhealthy levels of racial mental toughness in order to pursue traditional forms of STEM educational advancement.

The second research question concerns the differences in how Black and Latino/a students manage stereotypes; that is, some Latino/a students utilized the tactic of passing as White while the Black students did not. Historians tend to think of passing for White as an individualistic and opportunistic practice, a tool for getting ahead, an instrument for survival; however, the Latino/a students in this study negotiated American Whiteness with a heavily conflicted conscience. Hobbs (2014) suggests that researchers should not concentrate on what is gained by passing for White but on what is lost by partial or full rejection of one's racial and cultural identity. Thus, investigations should be undertaken into these students' social and academic worlds and how negotiating Whiteness affects their decision-making and their STEM career trajectories. Furthermore, the feeling of being obligated to limit parts of one's cultural and racial identity illuminates enduring societal issues of race and White privilege. For these students, managing their ability to gain White privilege is not simply an individual choice; it is a socially constructed act with significant emotional, social, and academic consequences. Colorism, or discrimination based on skin color, in the lives and educational experiences of Latino/a and Black students also needs further inquiry (Gans, 2013; Monroe, 2013), particularly since some of the Latino/a students reported they could negotiate Whiteness in ways the Black students either could not or did not. However, it is important to note that, in response to slavery and as reinforced by Jim Crow, light-skinned African Americans with phenotypically White features chose to present themselves as White. Thus, the practice of passing for White has occurred in both Black and Latino/a racial groups (Hobbs, 2014). Since Whiteness is the cultural, historical, and sociological default identity associated with having a positive educational and social life, future research should focus on how colorism affects Students of Color who could exploit Whiteness and how some Students of Color use their phenotypically White features to manipulate concepts of Whiteness while others resist conforming to it. Lastly, as the debate on immigration intensifies, particularly the rhetoric positioning immigration from Mexico and Latin America as a threat to American national identity, Latino/a identity in America becomes complicated, which can increase the pressure to assimilate. Thus, students can use the fact that forms of Whiteness are beneficial and, simultaneously, be distraught over the obligation of performing Whiteness. There is evidence of a relationship between frontin' and passing for White. Exploring why STEM Students of Color cannot be their fully authentic racial selves and the long-term consequences of frontin' in STEM (e.g., racial battle fatigue [Smith, 2004]) could reveal an underexplored influence on STEM retention issues in educational and career trajectories of Students of Color.

Black and Latino/a students in STEM should have educational settings that affirm rather than problematize their identities. If these Students of Color continue to succeed in STEM at the expense of their own cultures, often as a far-from-ideal compulsory accommodation, we will need to rethink the way STEM college programs are complicit in the structural practices that marginalize underrepresented students in STEM.

Implications and Conclusion

Based on the findings from this study, I offer several implications for practice and research. College faculties and administrators can benefit from gaining a better understanding of underrepresented students' experiences on campus and from working with these groups, individually and collectively, to find ways to reduce the burden of stereotyping they confront. Extensive examination of the impact of stereotyping is needed to fully understand its impediments to a STEM college and career trajectory for marginalized students. Stereotyping can create structural and institutional shortcomings that permanently damage the career paths of Students of Color, particularly those pursuing STEM degrees (McGee, 2013). Since racial bias is omnipresent in the STEM arena, racial stereotyping may be the reason Black and Latino/a recipients of STEM bachelor's degrees are disproportionately leaving their STEM careers 10 years after receiving their degrees, in contrast to their White and Asian counterparts (National Science Board, 2012).

Some college faculty members perpetuate a climate that is conducive to the endurance of racial stereotypes. Students reported that their STEM faculty overheard or witnessed racial microaggressions and stereotyping but did nothing in response. Indifferent faculty can be just as disturbing as unsupportive faculty. Institutional leaders should commit to minimizing racial bias, which includes faculty speaking up against various forms of marginalization, even when they are not the direct perpetrators. STEM colleges and departments could benefit from presenting evidence that "diversity trumps ability" (Page, 2008, p. xiv) in studies that showcase examples of different races, cultures, religions, genders, and other identity traits engaging in award-winning STEM innovation. Page's (2008) research provides strong support for developing an antistereotyping STEM college culture, wherein authentic racial and ethnic identities can be openly incorporated and embraced as being critical to accomplishing creative technological innovation. Positioning the power of difference as an asset for the development of more innovative STEM technologies can improve the overall performance of STEM programs.

Additionally, encouraging Black and Latino/a students to share their racial or gendered experiences can help them realize they are not alone in contending with negative stereotypes. Only two students in this study spoke of forming partnerships with Black, Latino/a, and other minority students in an effort to change assumptions and stereotypes about race (Sanchez, 2008). Further research could explore the outcomes of Black and Latino/a student organizations merging strategies and sharing tactics to build collective agency and to unravel the complex forms of discrimination found on college campuses.

Stereotype management is not ideal; it is a pragmatic strategy to combat the persistent, complex barrier of being perceived as a problem. It is a temporary resolution for the persistent structural framing that positions Students of Color at the bottom of STEM educational and career hierarchies. STEM leaders, researchers, educators, and politicians in the United States seek to enhance the postsecondary-to-career STEM pipeline by inviting marginalized students to rise above their challenges and roadblocks, but they do this without recognizing the stresses associated with surviving the racism endemic to this branch of academia. At present, an equitable, holistic, and culturally affirming experience in STEM, in which the activation of stereotype management is no longer needed, does not appear to be attainable. While we fight for the structural changes in policies, practices, and ideologies to remove the deficit paradigms that allow racial stereotyping to prosper in STEM education, my fear is that if Black and Latino/a students do not learn how to manage stereotypes in ways that reduce the distress over being unfairly judged, their experiences and possibly their long-term outcomes in STEM will remain in jeopardy.

Notes

[1]The names of the participants and universities are pseudonyms. Names have been changed to ensure confidentiality.

[2]*Students of Color* is primarily used to describe students who are not White, but in this article, the term is limited to Students of Color who have been historically marginalized in STEM education and attainment (e.g., African Americans, Latino/as, Native Americans). This term is ideal because it unites disparate racial and ethnic groups into a larger collective in solidarity and in shared forms of marginalization.

[3]*Colorism*, the skin color stratification that associates light skin with societal privilege, is found throughout the world. In Black and Latino/a cultures, a color caste system exists in which lighter skin is perceived as ideal and privileged and darker skin seen as deficit and inferior (Johnson, 2003). Thus, historically there are gains associated with individuals of any racial background who can pass for White and, to a lesser extent, those who are considered fair in skin color (Montalvo, 2005). While colorism is a worldwide phenomenon, in the United States skin color stratification has its roots in slavery. When the first Africans arrived in Virginia in 1619, however, there was no "White" racial classification (Allen, 2012). Racial classification came 60 years later, when America's ruling classes created the category of the "white race" as a means of social control. Since that early invention, the privileged Whites enforced the myth of racial superiority and thus began the preferential treatment of enslaved people with lighter complexions. Other racial features, such as hair texture and eye color, further complicate the phenotype game, particularly in U.S. society, where guesses are habitually formed about the social, economic, and educational status of persons based on phenotype, in addition to style of dress and mannerisms.

More than 18 million Latino/as checked the "other" racial box in the 2010 census, up from 14.9 million in 2000. Reasons for the increase are said to be the result of the sharp disconnect between how Latino/as view themselves and how the government insists on counting this ethnically and racially diverse group (Lee, Batalova, & Leach, 2004). Around the world, including countries where descendants of the Latin and African diasporas reside, Latino/as identify themselves as White, often because of colorist dynamics at play in their countries of birth (Vidal-Ortiz, 2004). White racial identification is a widely accepted self-designation throughout Latin America and the United States, but skin color bias and discrimination greatly affect Latino/as who live in the United States (Golash-Boza & Darity, 2008).

References

Allen, T. A. (2012). *On the invention of the White race, "White privilege," and the working class*. New York, NY: Verso Books.

Allen, Q. (2015). Race, culture and agency: Examining the ideologies and practices of US teachers of Black male students. *Teaching and Teacher Education, 47*, 71–81.

Aronson, J., Fried, C. B., & Good, C. (2002). Reducing the effects of stereotype threat on African American college students by shaping theories of intelligence. *Journal of Experimental Social Psychology, 38*(2), 113–125.

Aronson, J., & Steele, C. M. (2005). Stereotypes and the fragility of human competence, motivation, and self-concept. In C. Dweck & E. Elliot (Eds.), *Handbook of competence and motivation* (pp. 436–456). New York, NY: Guilford.

Banner-Haley, C. T. (2010). *The fruits of integration: Black middle-class ideology and culture, 1960–1990.* Jackson: University Press of Mississippi.

Beasley, M. A., & Fischer, M. J. (2012). Why they leave: The impact of stereotype threat on the attrition of women and minorities from science, math and engineering majors. *Social Psychology of Education, 15*(4), 427–448.

Berry, R. Q. III, Thunder, K., & McClain, O. L. (2011). Counter narratives: Examining the mathematics and racial identities of Black boys who are successful with school mathematics. *Journal of African American Males in Education, 2*(1), 10–23.

Bettez, S. C., & Suggs, V. L. (2012). Centering the educational and social significance of HBCUs: A focus on the educational journeys and thoughts of African American scholars. *The Urban Review, 44*(3), 303–310.

Block, C. J., Koch, S. M., Liberman, B. E., Merriweather, T. J., & Roberson, L. (2011). Contending with stereotype threat at work: A model of long-term responses. *The Counseling Psychologist, 39*(4), 570–600.

Carlone, H. B., & Johnson, A. (2007). Understanding the science experiences of successful women of color: Science identity as an analytic lens. *Journal of Research in Science Teaching, 44*(8), 1187–1218.

Cokley, K. O. (2014). *The myth of Black anti-intellectualism: A true psychology of African American students.* Santa Barbara, CA: Praeger, an imprint of ABC-CLIO, LLC.

Cole, D., & Espinoza, A. (2008). Examining the academic success of Latino students in science, technology, engineering, and mathematics (STEM) majors. *Journal of College Student Development, 49*(4), 285–300.

Conchas, G. Q. (2006). *The color of success: Race and high-achieving urban youth.* New York, NY: Teachers College Press.

Cullinane, J. (2009). *Diversifying the STEM pipeline: The model replication institutions program.* Washington, DC: The Institute for Higher Education Policy.

Cvencek, D., Nasir, N. S., O'Connor, K., Wischnia, S., & Meltzoff, A. N. (2014). The development of math–race stereotypes: They say Chinese people are the best at math. *Journal of Research on Adolescence, 25*(4), 630–637.

Duckworth, A., & Gross, J. J. (2014). Self-control and grit related but separable determinants of success. *Current Directions in Psychological Science, 23*(5), 319–325.

Equity Inclusion in Physics Astronomy Group. (2016). *An open letter to SCOTUS from professional physicists.* GitHub, http://eblur.github.io/scotus [http://web.archi ve.org/web/20160408051826/http://eblur.github.io/scotus/].

Fabert, N., Cabay, M., Rivers, M., Smith, M. L., & Bernstein, B. L. (2011). Exaggerating the typical and stereotyping the differences: Isolation experienced by women in STEM doctoral programs. In *ASEE Annual Conference and Exposition, Conference Proceedings* (pp. 2011-704). Washington, DC: American Society for Engineering Education.

Flores, J., & Garcia, S. (2009). Latina *testimonios*: A reflexive, critical analysis of a "Latina space" at a predominantly White campus. *Race Ethnicity and Education, 12*(2), 155–172.

Frazier, E. (1997). *Black bourgeoisie.* New York, NY: Free Press Paperbacks.

Fries-Britt, S., & Griffin, K. (2007). The Black box: How high achieving Blacks resist stereotypes about Black Americans. *Journal of College Student Development, 48*(5), 509–524.

Gans, H. J. (2013). "Whitening" and the changing American racial hierarchy. *Du Bois Review: Social Science Research on Race, 9*(2), 267–279.

Gasman, M. (2012). *The changing face of historically Black colleges and universities.* Philadelphia, PA: Center for MSIs, Graduate School of Education, University of Pennsylvania.

Golash-Boza, T., & Darity, W.Jr. (2008). Latino/a racial choices: The effects of skin colour and discrimination on Latinos' and Latinas' racial self-identifications. *Ethnic and Racial Studies, 31*(5), 899–934.

Golden, N. A. (2015). "There's still that window that's open": The problem with "grit." *Urban Education.* doi: 10.1177/0042085915613557

González, J. C. (2009). Latinas in doctoral and professional programs: Similarities and differences in support systems and challenges. In M. F. Howard-Hamilton, C. L. Morelon-Quainoo, S. M. Johnson, R. Winkle-Wagner, & L. Santiague (Eds.), *Standing on the outside looking in: Underrepresented students' experiences in advanced degree programs* (pp. 103–123). New York, NY: Grove Press.

Harper, S. R., & Gasman, M. (2008). Consequences of conservatism: Black male undergraduates and the politics of historically Black colleges and universities. *Journal of Negro Education, 77*(4), 336–351.

Harris-Perry, M. (2011). *Sister citizen: Shame, stereotypes, and the Black woman in America.* New Haven, CT: Yale University Press.

Henry, S. E., & Generett, G. G. (2005). Guest editor's introduction: The problem of colorblindness in US education: Historical trajectories and contemporary legacies. *Educational Studies, 38*(2), 95–98.

Herrnstein, R. J., & Murray, C. (2010). *Bell curve: Intelligence and class structure in American life.* New York, NY: Simon and Schuster.

Hobbs, A. (2014). *A chosen exile: A history of racial passing in American life.* Cambridge, MA: Harvard University Press.

Jencks, C., & Phillips, M. (Eds.). (2011). *The black-white test score gap.* Washington, DC: Brookings Institution Press.

Johnson, E. P. (2003). *Appropriating blackness: Performance and the politics of authenticity.* Durham, NC: Duke University Press.

Kirschenman, J., & Neckerman, K. M. (1991). "We'd love to hire them, but...": The meaning of race for employers. In C. Jencks & P. E. Peterson (Eds.), *The urban underclass* (pp. 203–232). Washington, DC: Brookings Institution Press.

Klingner, J. K., Artiles, A. J., Kozleski, E., Harry, B., Zion, S., Tate, W., Duran, G. Z., & Riley, D. (2005). Addressing the disproportionate representation of culturally and linguistically diverse students in special education through culturally responsive educational systems. *Education Policy Analysis Archives, 13*(38), 1–39.

Kynard, C., & Eddy, R. (2009). Toward a new critical framework: Color-conscious political morality and pedagogy at historically Black and historically White colleges and universities. *College Composition and Communication, 61*(1), 24–44.

Lee, J., Batalova, J., & Leach, M. (2004). *Immigration and fading color lines in America.* New York, NY: Russell Sage Foundation.

Lynch, S. (2001). "Science for all" is not equal to "one size fits all": Linguistic and cultural diversity and science education reform. *Journal of Research in Science Teaching, 38*(5), 622–627.

Malone, K. R., & Barabino, G. (2009). Narrations of race in STEM research settings: Identity formation and its discontents. *Science Education, 93*(3), 485–510.

Marable, M. (2011). *Living Black history: How reimagining the African-American past can remake America's racial future*. New York, NY: Basic Books.

Martin, D. B. (2009). Researching race in mathematics education. *Teachers College Record, 111*(2), 295–338.

Maton, K. I., Hrabowski, F. A., & Schmitt, C. L. (2000). African American college students excelling in the sciences: College and postcollege outcomes in the Meyerhoff Scholars Program. *Journal of Research in Science Teaching, 37*(7), 629–654.

Maton, K. I., Pollard, S. A., McDougall Weise, T. V., & Hrabowski, F. A. (2012). Meyerhoff Scholars Program: A strengths-based, institution-wide approach to increasing diversity in science, technology, engineering, and mathematics. *Mount Sinai Journal of Medicine: A Journal of Translational and Personalized Medicine, 79*(5), 610–623.

McAdams, D. P. (2013). *The redemptive self: Stories Americans live by* (revised and expanded ed.). New York, NY: Oxford University Press.

McCabe, J. (2009). Racial and gender microaggressions on a predominantly-White campus: Experiences of Black, Latina/o and White undergraduates. *Race, Gender & Class, 16*(1–2), 133–151.

McFarlane, A. G. (2009). Operatively White: Exploring the significance of race and class through the paradox of Black middle-classness. *Law & Contemporary Problems, 72*(4), 163–196.

McGee, E. O. (2013). High-achieving Black students, biculturalism, and out-of-school STEM learning experiences: Exploring some unintended consequences. *Journal of Urban Mathematics Education, 6*(2), 20–41.

McGee, E. O. (2014). When it comes to the mathematics experiences of Black preservice teachers . . . race matters. *Teachers College Record, 116*(6), 1–50.

McGee, E. O. (2015). Robust and fragile mathematics identities: A framework for exploring racialized experiences and high achievement among Black college students. *Journal of Research in Mathematics Education, 46*(5), 599–625.

McGee, E. O., & Martin, D. B. (2011). "You would not believe what I have to go through to prove my intellectual value!": Stereotype management among academically successful Black mathematics and engineering students. *American Education Research Journal, 48*(6), 1347–1389.

McGee, E. O., & Stovall, D. O. (2015). The mental health of Black college students: A call for critical race theorists to integrate mental health into the analysis. *Educational Theory, 65*(5), 491–511.

Mickelson, R. A. (2003). When are racial disparities in education the result of discrimination? A social science perspective. *Teachers College Record, 105*(6), 1052–1086.

Miles, M. B., Huberman, A. M., & Saldana, J. (2013). *Qualitative data analysis: A methods sourcebook*. Thousand Oaks, CA: Sage Publications.

Monroe, C. R. (2013). Colorizing educational research: African American life and schooling as an exemplar. *Educational Researcher, 42*(1), 9–19.

Montalvo, F. F. (2005). Surviving race: Skin color and the socialization and acculturation of Latinas. *Journal of Ethnic and Cultural Diversity in Social Work, 13*(3), 25–43.

Moore, J. L., Madison-Colmore, O., & Smith, D. M. (2003). The prove-them-wrong syndrome: Voices from unheard African-American males in engineering disciplines. *The Journal of Men's Studies, 12*(1), 61–73.

Museus, S. D., Palmer, R. T., Davis, R. J., & Maramba, D. (2011). *Racial and ethnic minority student success in STEM education: ASHE Higher Education Report*. New York, NY: Wiley.

National Science Board. (2012). *Science and engineering indicators 2012* (NSB 12-01). Arlington, VA: National Science Foundation.

Nelson, D. J., & Brammer, C. N. (2010). *A national analysis of diversity in science and engineering faculties at research universities.* Washington, DC: National Organization for Women.

Omi, M., & Winant, H. (2014). *Racial formation in the United States.* New York, NY: Routledge.

Page, S. E. (2008). *The difference: How the power of diversity creates better groups, firms, schools, and societies.* Princeton, NJ: Princeton University Press.

Perna, L. W., Gasman, M., Gary, S., Lundy-Wagner, V., & Drezner, N. D. (2010). Identifying strategies for increasing degree attainment in STEM: Lessons from minority-serving institutions. *New Directions for Institutional Research, 148,* 41–51.

Perry, T., Steele, C., & Hilliard, A. G. (2004). *Young, gifted, and Black: Promoting high achievement among African-American students.* Boston, MA: Beacon Press.

Picca, L., & Feagin, J. (2007). *Two-faced racism.* New York, NY: Routledge.

Pierce, C. (1995). Stress analogs of racism and sexism: Terrorism, torture, and disaster. In C. Willie, P. Rieker, B. Kramer, & B. Brown (Eds.), *Mental health, racism, and sexism* (pp. 277–293). Pittsburgh, PA: University of Pittsburgh Press.

Pierce, C. M., Carew, J. V., Pierce-Gonzalez, D., & Wills, D. (1978). *An experiment in racism: TV commercials.* In C. M. Pierce (Ed.), *Television and education* (pp. 62–88). Beverly Hills, CA: Sage.

Reddick, R. J., Welton, A. D., Alsandor, D. J., Denyszyn, J. L., & Platt, C. S. (2011). Stories of success: High minority, high poverty public school graduate narratives on accessing higher education. *Journal of Advanced Academics, 22*(4), 594–618.

Richards, L. (2014). *Handling qualitative data: A practical guide.* Thousand Oaks, CA: Sage Publications.

Riley, D. (2008). Engineering and social justice. Synthesis Lectures on Engineers, *Technology and Society, 3*(1), p. 1–152.

Roberts, D. (2013). *Fatal invention: How science, politics, and big business re-create race in the twenty-first century.* New York, NY: The New Press.

Robinson, W. H., McGee, E. O., Bentley, L. C., Houston, S. L., & Botchway, P. K. (2016). Addressing negative racial and gendered experiences that discourage academic careers in engineering. *Computing in Science & Engineering, 18*(2), 29–39.

Saldaña, J. (2015). *The coding manual for qualitative researchers.* Thousand Oaks, CA: Sage.

Sanchez, G. R. (2008). Latino/a group consciousness and perceptions of commonality with African Americans. *Social Science Quarterly, 89*(2), 428–444.

Sevo, R. (2009). The talent crisis in science and engineering. In B. Bogue & E. Cady (Eds.), *Apply Research to Practice (ARP) resources.* Retrieved from http://www.engr.psu.edu/AWE/ARPResources.aspx

Smith, W. A. (2004). Black faculty coping with racial battle fatigue: The campus racial climate in a post-civil rights era. In D. Cleveland (Ed.), *A long way to go: Conversations about race by African American faculty and graduate students* (pp. 171–190). New York, NY: Peter Lang.

Smith, W. A., Hung, M., & Franklin, J. D. (2011). Racial battle fatigue and the miseducation of Black men: Racial microaggressions, societal problems, and environmental stress. *Journal of Negro Education, 80*(1), 63–82.

Solórzano, D., Ceja, M., & Yosso, T. (2000). Critical race theory, racial microaggressions and campus racial climate: The experiences of African-American college students. *Journal of Negro Education, 69*(1/2), 60–73.

Stage, F. K., Lundy-Wagner, V. C., & John, G. (2013). Minority serving institutions and STEM. In R. Palmer, D. Maramba, & M. Gasman (Eds.), *Fostering success of ethnic and racial minorities in STEM: The role of minority serving institutions* (pp. 16–32). New York, NY: Routledge.

Steele, C. M., & Aronson, J. (1998). Stereotype threat and the test performance of academically successful African Americans. In C. Jencks & M. Phillips (Eds.), *The Black-White test score gap* (pp. 401–427). Washington, DC: Brookings Institution Press.

Sue, D. W., Capodilupo, C. M., Torino, G. C., Bucceri, J. M., Holder, A., Nadal, K. L., & Esquilin, M. (2007). Racial microaggressions in everyday life: Implications for clinical practice. *American Psychologist, 62*(4), 271–286.

Swartz, E. (2009). Diversity: Gatekeeping knowledge and maintaining inequalities. *Review of Educational Research, 79*(2), 1044–1083.

Taylor, V. J., & Walton, G. M. (2011). Stereotype threat undermines academic learning. *Personality and Social Psychology Bulletin, 37*(8), 1055–1067.

Toomey, A., Dorjee, T., & Ting-Toomey, S. (2013). Bicultural identity negotiation, conflicts, and intergroup communication strategies. *Journal of Intercultural Communication Research, 42*(2), 112–134.

Vidal-Ortiz, S. (2004). On being a white person of color: Using autoethnography to understand Puerto Ricans' racialization. *Qualitative Sociology, 27*(2), 179–203.

Watkins, W. H. (2001). *The White architects of Black education: Ideology and power in America, 1865–1954.* New York, NY: Teachers College Press.

Wiggins, M. J. (2001). Race, class, and suburbia: The modern Black suburb as a race-making situation. *University of Michigan Journal of Law Reform, 35*(4), 749–808.

Wyer, M., Schneider, J., Nassar-McMillan, S., & Oliver-Hoyo, M. (2010). Capturing stereotypes: Developing a scale to explore U.S. college students' images of science and scientists. *International Journal of Gender, Science and Technology, 2*(3), 382–415.

Yosso, T., Smith, W., Ceja, M., & Solórzano, D. (2009). Critical race theory, racial microaggressions, and campus racial climate for Latina/o undergraduates. *Harvard Educational Review, 79*(4), 659–691.

Manuscript received October 1, 2014
Final revision received June 11, 2016
Accepted September 9, 2016

American Educational Research Journal
December 2016, Vol. 53, No. 6, pp. 1663–1697
DOI: 10.3102/0002831216675719
© 2016 AERA. http://aerj.aera.net

Restorative Interventions and School Discipline Sanctions in a Large Urban School District

Yolanda Anyon
University of Denver
Anne Gregory
Rutgers, The State University of New Jersey
Susan Stone
University of California, Berkeley
Jordan Farrar
Jeffrey M. Jenson
Jeanette McQueen
University of Denver
Barbara Downing
Eldridge Greer
John Simmons
Denver Public Schools

A large urban district (N = 90,546 students, n = 180 schools) implemented restorative interventions as a response to school discipline incidents. Findings from multilevel modeling of student discipline records (n = 9,921) revealed that youth from groups that tend to be overrepresented in suspensions and expulsions (e.g., Black, Latino, and Native American youth; boys; and students in special education) had similar, if not greater, rates of participation in restorative interventions than their peers. First-semester participants in restorative interventions had lower odds of receiving office discipline referrals (OR .21, p < .001) and suspensions (OR .07, p < .001) in the second semester. However, the suspension gap between Black and White students persisted. Implications for reform in school discipline practices are noted.

KEYWORDS: office discipline referral, restorative intervention, restorative justice, school discipline, suspension

A collective challenge to conventional wisdom about school discipline has been issued at local, state, and federal levels. No longer is it assumed that suspension should remain the "go to" response to student misconduct and school safety concerns. A growing body of evidence indicates that exclusionary discipline practices, such as out-of-school suspension (OSS) and expulsion, are not effective or equitable approaches to improving student behavior and school safety (American Academy of Pediatrics, 2013). School officials also recognize that aggregated discipline rates obscure disparities between student groups. Many educators are now scrutinizing their

YOLANDA ANYON is an assistant professor in the Graduate School of Social Work at the University of Denver, 2148 S. High Street, Denver, CO 80208, USA; e-mail: *yanyon@du.edu* Her research draws on mixed methods and critical theories to consider the roles of schools and community-based organizations in shaping the life outcomes of low-income youth of color.

ANNE GREGORY is an associate professor at the Graduate School of Applied and Professional Psychology at Rutgers University. Her research has focused on the persistent trend that African American adolescents are issued school suspension and expulsion at higher rates than adolescents from other groups. Through program development and evaluation, she aims to improve educational settings for students from diverse racial and ethnic backgrounds.

SUSAN STONE is the Catherine Mary and Eileen Clare Hutto Professor of Social Services in Public Education. Her work is focused on social work in education and its impact on the academic progress of vulnerable youth in schools.

JORDAN FARRAR is a doctoral candidate at the Graduate School of Social Work at the University of Denver. Her research interests include youth involved in armed conflict, restorative justice and indigenous healing practices, and global social work research.

JEFFREY M. JENSON is the Philip D. & Eleanor G. Winn Professor for Children and Youth at Risk at the Graduate School of Social Work at the University of Denver. His teaching and research interests address the etiology and prevention of childhood and adolescent problems of bullying, aggression, school dropout, and juvenile delinquency.

JEANETTE MCQUEEN is an assistant professor and director of the online MSW program at the Graduate School of Social Work at the University of Denver. She has worked in a variety of clinical settings with children, youth, and families, including community-based services, residential treatment, and public schools.

BARBARA DOWNING is a district partner in the Office of Social-Emotional Learning at Denver Public Schools. She is responsible for monitoring the implementation of district discipline policy, improving student information system technology, and training and facilitation of school staff.

ELDRIDGE GREER is the associate chief of student equity and opportunity at Denver Public Schools, where his focus is removing structural barriers that negatively impact educational opportunity. He has been nationally recognized for his work in Denver for discipline reform efforts, with a particular focus on eliminating the racial disparities in discipline.

JOHN SIMMONS is the former associate chief of the Division of Student Services at Denver Public Schools. He oversaw division decision-making on resource allocation, policy, professional development opportunities, and assessment and monitoring systems.

data to detect disproportionality along the lines of student race, gender, and special education status (e.g., Public Schools of North Carolina, 2013).

Indeed, there is consensus among many researchers, policy makers, educators, and school-based mental health professionals that exclusionary school discipline practices rarely improve school safety and, in fact, exacerbate racial inequalities in education and incarceration. In 2014 alone, national reports about school discipline were issued from the U.S. Departments of Education and Justice (U.S. Department of Education, 2014), the Council of State Governments Justice Center (Morgan, Salomon, Plotkin, & Cohen, 2014), and the Discipline Disparities Research to Practice Collaborative (Carter, Fine, & Russell, 2014). The reports converge in their recommendations to reduce suspension through alternative practices that have a greater chance of changing student behavior, keeping youth in school, and maintaining a positive school climate.

These recent calls for change reflect evidence that suspension has deleterious effects on student well-being and school safety. Schools with high rates of suspensions, expulsions, and law enforcement referrals are perceived by students, teachers, and parents to be less safe than other schools (Osher, Poirier, Jarjoura, & Brown, 2014; Steinberg, Allensworth, & Johnson, 2014). Moreover, youth who have been suspended or expelled are more likely than students who do not receive disciplinary sanctions to be pushed out of school and into criminal justice systems; this process is often referred to as the "school-to-prison pipeline" (Fabelo et al., 2011; Rausch, Skiba, & Simmons, 2004; Skiba et al., 2014). For instance, a longitudinal study of Florida ninth graders found that each suspension decreased students' odds of graduating high school by an additional 20% and decreased their odds of enrolling in postsecondary schooling by 12% (Balfanz, Byrnes, & Fox, 2015). Moreover, a Texas statewide study found that students suspended or expelled for a discretionary school violation were about three times more likely than other youth to have contact with the juvenile justice system in the next school year (Fabelo et al., 2011).

Patterns of dropout and juvenile justice involvement are of particular concern given racial disparities in exclusionary school discipline outcomes. Latino, Native American, and Black youth are significantly more likely than students of other backgrounds to be referred to school administrators for discipline problems and to receive OSS, expulsion, or a referral to law enforcement as punishment (Hannon, DeFina, & Bruch, 2013; Payne & Welch, 2010). These students tend to be disciplined more harshly than White students for the same type and number of offenses (Anyon et al., 2014; Bradshaw, Mitchell, O'Brennan, & Leaf, 2010) but are less likely to have access to much needed support services (Reyes, Elias, Parker, & Rosenblatt, 2013). The interlocking nature of the discipline, achievement, and incarceration gaps suggests that, over the long term, whole groups of students who are disproportionately suspended and have lower achievement are less likely to obtain a range of positive life outcomes (Gregory, Skiba, & Noguera, 2010).

Concerns about equity and the detrimental effects of suspension have driven educators to seek alternatives to traditional suspension practices and policies. The U.S. Departments of Education (DOE, 2014) and Justice recommend that students should not only be held accountable for conduct but should also have opportunities to learn from discipline incidents and build social and emotional skills. They note that schools may decide to use restorative interventions (RIs) to enhance and teach a range of individual skills. Similarly, the Council of State Governments Justice Center (Morgan et al., 2014) suggests that after conflict or rule infractions, educators should utilize a "restorative follow-up." The follow-up, they explain, provides students with opportunities to discuss incidents, accept responsibility for harmful actions, and identify ways to repair harm. Recommendations from these reports reflect a wave of initiatives sweeping the United States (following the lead of many other countries such as New Zealand, Australia, and England) in which schools have implemented RIs as alternatives to suspension (Drewery, 2013; McCluskey et al., 2008; Schiff, 2013). Despite reduced suspension rates in individual schools and descriptive accounts of improvements in districts that implement RIs (e.g., Encarnacao, 2013; Karp & Breslin, 2001; Schiff, 2013; Stinchcomb, Bazemore, & Riestenberg, 2006), multivariate analyses of implementation data that account for between-school variability and the nature of student offenses are rare and have not been published in peer-reviewed journals.

Restorative Interventions

Arising from a humanist philosophy and with historical roots in a range of diverse cultures (e.g., Native American, Maori) and religions (e.g., Judaism), restorative approaches assume that subjective experiences of harmful acts need to be acknowledged and that it is worthwhile to harness the power of the collective for resolution and repair (Drewery, 2013; Zehr, 2002; Zehr & Toews, 2004). Restorative approaches to school discipline include a variety of practices on the prevention-intervention continuum. Namely, some practices aim to prevent infractions and other practices intervene after infractions have occurred (e.g., Amstutz & Mullet, 2005; Blood & Thorsborne, 2005; McCluskey et al., 2008; Wachtel, Costello, & Wachtel, 2009). At the intervention end of the continuum, restorative approaches have two core features: (a) Those affected by an infraction or crime come together to identify how people were impacted by the incident, and (b) they jointly problem-solve and identify actions that will repair the harm (Coates, Umbreit, & Vos, 2003; McGarrell & Hipple, 2007).

In essence, RIs are problem-solving processes held in a small conference or a larger circle format, which may include people affected by the incident directly and indirectly. Typically, conferences for serious incidents follow a formal procedure. First, a preconference meeting is held whereby a facilitator meets with a disputant to orient him or her to restorative approaches. At this meeting, a disputant can decline to participate in an RI or a facilitator can determine a conference is not appropriate if the disputant will not accept any responsibility or acknowledge his or her role in the incident and/or is not willing to repair the harm (Wachtel, O'Connell, & Wachtel, 2010). Second, if the conference is to proceed, a range of parties are invited to voluntarily attend, including the disputant, the disputant's supporters, and all those negatively impacted by the incident (McCluskey et al., 2008).

Third, in the conference itself, participants sit in a circle facing one another, and a facilitator uses a structured set of questions to guide the exchange among all the participants. The goal is for everyone (including the victim and the disputant) to voice their perspectives. The set of questions facilitate reflection on the link between actions and subsequent consequences. Typical questions include the following: "What happened?"; "Who has been harmed/affected by what you have done?"; "What part are you responsible for?"; and "How will the harm be repaired?" (Teachers Unite, 2014). Questions also solicit sharing of the emotional experience of the incident to further empathy and understanding (Nathanson, 1997; Wachtel et al., 2010).

Fourth, the participants jointly develop a plan to repair the harm and prevent future incidents. The aim is to hold disputants accountable for breaching trust with the community and at the same time reintegrate those students back into the community (Braithwaite, 1989, 2001; Costello, Wachtel, & Wachtel, 2010). Agreements to repair the harm can take many forms, including the disputant making amends through his or her actions (e.g., community service or repair damaged property). Typically, agreements are written down and agreed upon by all conference participants.

RIs and Positive Outcomes

Most prior research on restorative practices has examined school-wide reductions in office discipline referrals (ODRs) and OSSs using single group, pre-, and posttest designs (Schiff, 2013). These studies lack comparison groups and seldom use any statistical controls to account for potential confounders. That said, numerous international studies have reported reductions in school-wide ODRs and OSS rates after restorative practices were introduced, including in New Zealand (Buckley & Maxwell, 2007), Scotland (Kane et al., 2007), and China (Wong & Mok, 2011). Studies of school-based restorative practices in the United States have shown similar declines, including in Denver, Colorado (González, 2015), Minneapolis, Minnesota (Riestenberg, 2013), and Philadelphia, Pennsylvania (Lewis, 2009). In addition, in Oakland, CA, the suspension rate of Black students declined at a sharper rate than the suspension rate of White students after the introduction of a range of interventions including restorative approaches to discipline, Schoolwide Positive Behavioral Intervention Supports, and the Manhood Development Program (Jain, Bassey, Brown, & Kalra, 2014). In Denver, during years when RIs initially spread to schools throughout the district, González (2015) reported a 4 percentage point decrease in the Black/White suspension gap. These trends are only suggestive of the promise for restorative approaches to reduce exclusionary practices and narrow the racial discipline gap.

Findings from experimental research addressing student outcomes resulting from school-based conferences have yet to be published. However, research on adult and youth restorative conferencing in the criminal justice system suggests that similar programming in school settings may be beneficial. Randomized controlled trials in the United States, Australia, and Great Britain, in which juvenile offenders were assigned to restorative conferences, other diversion programs, or typical court procedures, have found that some restorative conference programs have the ability to reduce rates of reoffense, whereas other programs have no long-term effects on reoffending (Larsen, 2014; Latimer, Dowden, & Muise, 2005). Specifically, Strang, Sherman, Mayo-Wilson, Woods, and Ariel (2013) analyzed results from 10 controlled trials on three continents with a total of 1,879 offenders and 734 interviewed victims. Their results showed that among cases in which both offenders and victims were willing to meet, restorative justice conferences reduced future crime. That said, using propensity score matching with samples of youth offenders in Australia, Smith and Weatherburn (2012) revealed no difference in future offense rates between youth who participated in a conference and those who participated in a business-as-usual condition. Further, although a controlled trial in Indianapolis found that participants randomly assigned to conferencing or to other diversion programming experienced short-term benefits in terms of reduced rates of reoffense after 2 years (McGarrell & Hipple 2007), the benefits were not sustained in a 10-year follow-up (Jeong, McGarrell, & Hipple, 2012). The researchers conclude that conferences may result in short-term (not long-term) reduction in risk.

The experimental literature from juvenile justice suggests that research on both distal and proximal outcomes of school-based RIs are needed. Moreover, research on the impact of RIs in educational settings is warranted because of the unique dynamics of school environments compared to community systems. For example, it is possible that the impact of RIs on youth outcomes could be stronger than what has been found from criminal justice studies. In schools, it is likely that RIs are used with a much more diverse group of young people with lower risk profiles than community-based offenders and could also lead to changes in relationships between youth, their peers, and the school adults with whom they interact on a more consistent basis than police officers or crime victims (Anyon, 2016).

School and Student Participation in RIs

Schools often vary tremendously in their adoption of new initiatives (Forman, 2015). One measure of program diffusion is the degree to which an intervention is used by practitioners (Durlak & Dupre, 2008; Schulte, Easton, & Parker, 2009). Several studies have shown that schools' use of restorative approaches to discipline can differ throughout a district, which may weaken their impact on student outcomes (Jain et al., 2014; McClusky et al., 2008). Lower use of RIs in response to discipline incidents can indicate practical barriers such as lack of training or staffing, poor alignment between a restorative philosophy and the norms or values of school personnel, and/or limited opportunities for practitioners to improve their skills (Anyon, 2016; Durlak & Dupre, 2008). Yet no studies have examined the relationship between school-level rates of RI use and individual student outcomes after receiving an RI.

Moreover, given consistent evidence that schools contribute to sorting and labeling students (Weinstein, 2002), a concern about the implementation of alternatives to suspension would be that participation in RIs would reflect typical dynamics related to power and privilege. This would parallel consistent patterns in the child welfare and juvenile justice systems whereby more disadvantaged youth and their families receive harsher consequences, and fewer support services, than their privileged counterparts (Chapin Hall Center for Children, 2008; Derezotes, Testa, & Poertner, 2005). In fact, using data from a national survey of principals in the late 1990s, Payne and Welch (2010) found that the proportion of Black students at the school level was negatively associated with the site's reported use of restorative practices in response to student misbehavior. Thus, there is a need for new research using actual discipline records to assess whether students from disadvantaged groups similarly participate in RIs when they receive a discipline referral compared to more advantaged student groups. Equitable participation is especially needed for Black, Latino, Native American, and male students as well as students in special education—all groups of students who tend to receive suspension at higher rates than more advantaged peers (Losen & Martinez, 2013).

The Current Study

RIs in school settings appear to be a promising response to discipline problems. However, to date, few studies have analyzed RI implementation results using statistical approaches that account for the hierarchical nature of these datasets, in which students are nested within schools, or control for confounds like the type of student offense (Schiff, 2013). The current study controls for a range of covariates, most notably students' socioeconomic status and their number/type of ODRs, to assess the relationship between participation in RIs and adverse student discipline outcomes during the spring semester. The study builds on prior analyses conducted in the same school district (Anyon et al., 2014) by using time-ordered data from a subsequent school year linked to school-level rates of RI use. Specifically, current analyses examine whether receiving RIs in the first semester is associated with lower odds of disciplined students receiving additional ODRs or OSSs in the second semester. Scholars have argued that students from disenfranchised groups could benefit the most from RIs focused on building relationships, soliciting student voice, promoting an ethic of care, and reintegrating students back into the school community (Drewery, 2004). Therefore, an exploratory analysis also examines whether the association between RI participation and discipline is moderated by student racial background (Losen & Martinez, 2013).

The study also builds on prior findings indicating that the implementation of restorative programming varies widely across schools (Jain et al., 2014; McClusky et al., 2008). To this end, it examines whether school-level variation in RI use is associated with student-level discipline outcomes (Schulte et al., 2009). We postulate that the relationship between student participation in RIs and subsequent discipline outcomes will be stronger in schools that use RIs more often. Prior theory and research guides this hypothesis: Relative to schools relying more on exclusionary discipline and less on RIs, schools with higher rates of RI participation may reflect staff members' commitment to, preparation for, and/or skill in implementing high-quality RIs (Cross et al., 2011; Forman, 2015). Through an equity lens, the study also considers whether marginalized and disadvantaged groups have similar patterns of participation in RIs. To our knowledge, no studies have compared the sociodemographic characteristics of students who have or have not participated in RIs.

In summary, the following questions guide this study: (1a) Is a student's participation in one or more RIs in the first semester associated with lower odds of ODRs and/or OSSs in the second semester? (1b) Is the association between participation in RIs and later discipline incidents moderated by student racial background or school-level use of RI? (2) Do disciplined students from disadvantaged backgrounds have equitable participation in RIs?

Method

School District and Study Participants

Study Site

The study site for this investigation is Denver Public Schools (hereafter referred to as "the District"). The District is uniquely situated as a site to examine the influence of RIs on school discipline outcomes. First, following a major discipline policy reform in 2008 that aimed to reduce the use of exclusionary discipline sanctions, increase alternative approaches such as RIs, and eliminate racial disparities in suspension and expulsion, the

District has witnessed sustained reductions in rates of OSS, expulsion, and law enforcement referral (Anyon et al., 2014). These results are impressive because they have taken place during a time when the overall District population has increased by 14%, making the District among the fastest growing urban school districts in the nation (Department of Planning and Analysis, 2013). Second, despite these successes, District data indicate that reform goals have not yet been fully realized and that disparities in race, class, gender, and special education status persist in school discipline outcomes (Anyon et al., 2014). These trends prompted District leaders' interest in evaluating the impact of RIs on ODRs and OSSs to assess whether additional resources should be invested in this approach.

In the 2012–2013 school year, the District served a student population (N = 90,546) that was 57.31% Latino, 20.83% White, 14.47% Black, 3.35% Asian, 2.99% Multiracial, 0.81% Native American, and 0.24% Pacific Islander. Forty-nine percent were female, and 51% were male. Close to half (44%) of District students were English Language Learners (ELLs). The District serves predominantly low-income students, as over two thirds of the students in the District were eligible for free and reduced lunch (68.8%) and 2.2% of students were identified as being homeless. In addition, 11.5% of District students participated in special education, and 1.1% were identified as having an emotional disability (ED).

School District Discipline Reform

After overhauling the District's school discipline policy reform in 2008, school officials began offering voluntary staff training in restorative approaches. The training was, and continues to be, available to any employee of the District. Staff members can choose to sign up to participate via an online registration system where all professional development opportunities are listed. During monthly meetings with school-based staff, District leaders strongly recommended that principals, disciplinarians, teachers, and special service providers (such as social workers and psychologists) participate in the training. Two types of training are provided to staff. The first is an introductory training that is 4 hours long and focuses on preventive RIs (e.g., classroom community-building circles). Relevant to the current study, the second training is 2 days long and emphasizes RIs in response to discipline incidents. The following content is covered in the 2-day trainings: (a) overview of the origins and key principles of RIs (including their use in response to concerns about racial disparities in OSS), (b) review of empirical evidence of the effectiveness of restorative approaches in the District and beyond, (c) RIs as they relate to District discipline policy and schools' student codes of conduct, (d) brief introduction to prevention-oriented restorative practices (dialogues and proactive circles), (e) lengthy introduction to intervention-oriented restorative practices (reactive circles, mediations, and conferences), (f) overview of core features of all restorative practices (e.g., problem solving, paraphrasing, reframing), and (g) strategies to monitor the implementation and success of restorative approaches. Each content area is supplemented with interactive role-play scenarios and case studies (DPS, 2012).

At the end of the training, participants are provided with a handbook that details all content from the training, including example codes of conduct and forms for implementing restorative approaches (e.g., agreements, action plans, parent letters, and evaluative surveys). On-site coaching and support from the district coordinator is available following the training. Since August 2008, more than 2,700 district educators have participated in the 2-day training. In the 2012–2013 school year (the focus of the current study), 126 staff members (37 teachers, 28 administrators, and 61 support service providers) represented 53 District schools at the trainings.

District policy strongly recommends that students be offered a RI for behavior that leads to a discipline action. Restorative conferencing is an option for Type 2 (e.g., severe defiance of authority/disobedience) through Type 5 (e.g., first degree assault) infractions (DPS, 2008). The policy suggests RIs may be provided independently (e.g., RI only), as alternatives to each other (e.g., RI or 1-day suspension), or in conjunction with each other (e.g., RI and in-school-suspension) (DPS, 2008). These decisions are made by school administrators and vary depending on their site's specific code of conduct. Therefore, it is not known if RIs were offered as options in a similar manner to students at all schools. This limitation is common in school discipline research because most discipline policies rely on the discretion of administrators in determining consequences, which are often inconsistently implemented (Hannon et al., 2013; Morris, 2005; Shaw & Braden, 1990).

If an administrator does decide to incorporate a RI as part of resolving a discipline incident, District protocol is that the student then meets with the trained staff member. If the student is willing to "take responsibility for his or her part of the situation" after reflecting on the incident, a restorative circle, mediation, or conference with all affected parties is held (DPS, 2012, p. 13). If not, the student is referred back to the school administrator for a different consequence. In the framework of a tiered system of support (RtI), circles, mediations, and conferences are considered targeted (Tier 2) and intensive (Tier 3) interventions, as opposed to Tier 1 universal supports (Berkowitz, 2012; Corrigan, 2012). Restorative conferences in the District typically involve those directly involved in the conflict (typically a two-party dispute). Reactive circles include individuals indirectly affected by an incident—an incident can indirectly affect others through disruptions to instruction or community well-being (González, 2015). At the end of a RI, participants develop an agreement or action plan for "making things right," and all involved parties sign the agreement.

Student Sample

The student sample included all youth (n = 9,921) in Grades K–12 across all District schools (n = 180 schools) who were issued one or more ODRs in the 2012–2013 school year (see Table 1). These disciplined students comprised 11% of all youth in the District. Mirroring trends observed by other researchers, disciplined students were disproportionately Black, Latino, Native American, male, low-income, eligible for special education, and classified as ED. Findings from chi-square tests shown in Table 1 indicate that subgroup differences in discipline rates were statistically significant. For example, Black students comprised 14.5% of the general student population versus 25.2% of the population with at least one ODR. Students who identified as Asian, Pacific Islander, White, or ELL were issued ODRs at significantly lower rates than their enrollment. Suspension rates had similar patterns of significant over- and underrepresentation of varying student groups. Table 1 also indicates that RIs were most often utilized with students who were referred to the office for midrange offenses such as disobedience or defiance and detrimental behavior.

Table 2 presents disproportionality figures for ODRs and OSSs for all racial groups in the District that parallel the patterns evident in Table 1. Risk indices capture rates of suspension and referrals for each subgroup. They were calculated by dividing the number of one group of students who have been referred or suspended by the number of that same group in the population of the district (Skiba et al., 2008). Relative risk ratios (RRRs) were calculated as the ratio of the risk indexes of two groups (IDEA Data Center, 2014; Shaw, Putnam-Hornstein, Magruder, & Needell, 2008). In other words, the RRR is a ratio of ODR or suspension rates per 1,000 between two groups of students (Shaw et al., 2008). For example, in the case of ODRs, Black students had a risk index of 19.02% and RRRs of 3.41 compared to White youth and 1.99 compared to all other students. Among Latinos, the ODR rate was 11.22%, and the RRRs were 2.00 compared to White students and 1.06 compared to all other students. For OSSs, Black students had a suspension rate of 9.64% and the RRRs were 4.95 compared to White students and 2.55 compared to all other students. In contrast, the suspension rate for Latino students was 4.46%, whereas the RRRs were 2.29 compared to White students and .92 compared to all other students.

Measures

Sociodemographic and discipline records were downloaded from the District's electronic student information system (Infinite Campus). Downloaded datasets included school-level characteristics (e.g., enrollment size), student background information, and student-level discipline records.

Table 1

Sample Characteristics of Students Who Received One or More Office Discipline Referrals (ODRs) Across One School Year

	All Students (N = 90,546)	Disciplined Students[a,b] (n = 9,921)	Received an OSS[c] (n = 4,184)	Participated in RI[d] (n = 1,277)	Did Not Participate in RI[e] (n = 8,644)
Student sociodemographics (%)					
Race					
Native American (n = 735)	0.8	0.99*	1.0	.8	1.02
Asian (n = 3,036)	3.4	1.5***	1.3	1.2	1.5
Black (n = 13,098)	14.5	25.2***	30.2***	26.9	24.9
Latino (n = 51,893)	57.3	58.7***	55.3***	59.2	58.6
White (n = 18,858)	20.8	10.6***	9.0***	9.6	10.8
Pacific Islander (n = 216)	0.2	0.14*	0.1	0.1	0.2
Multiracial (n = 2,710)	3.0	2.9	3.1	2.2	3.0
Boys (n = 46,235)	51.1	65.8***	66.9***	67.3	65.6
Eligible for free/reduced lunch (n = 62,321)	68.8	84.8***	87.6***	85.4	84.7
ELLs (n = 39,871)	44.0	37.8***	33.5***	34.0**	38.4**
Students in special education (n = 10,422)	11.5	20.28***	25.7***	21.5	20.1
ED (n = 954)	1.1	4.0***	7.2***	4.0	4.1
Grade level					
Elementary (n = 35,916)	39.7	22.5***	15.9***	17.2***	23.33***
Middle (n =12,924)	14.3	28.2***	28.2***	32.0***	27.6***
High (n=19,034)	21.0	26.2***	25.9	20.2***	27.1***
Alternative grade configuration (n = 22,632)	25.0	23.1***	23.8	30.7***	22.0***
Referral reasons[e,f,g]					
Bullying (n = 823)		8.3	8.3	11.0***	7.9***
Destruction of school property (n = 200)		2.0	3.1***	2.4	2.0
Disobedient/defiant (n = 3,212)		32.4	34.6***	37.7***	31.6***
Other code of conduct violation (n = 2,474)		24.9	26.5 **	32.6***	23.8***
Detrimental behavior (n = 5,415)		54.6	63.0***	69.0***	52.5***

(continued)

Table 1 (continued)

	All Students (N = 90,546)	Disciplined Students[a,b] (n = 9,921)	Received an OSS[c] (n = 4,184)	Participated in RI[d] (n = 1,277)	Did Not Participate in RI[e] (n = 8,644)
Third degree assault (n = 247)		2.5	4.4***	3.8**	2.3**
Unlawful sexual behavior (n = 23)		1.4	1.7	1.1	1.4
Drug possession or distribution (n = 730)		7.4	13.2***	4.5***	7.8***
Dangerous weapon (n = 173)		1.7	3.3***	2.1	1.7
Number of discipline consequences[i]		M (SD)	M (SD)[b]	M (SD)[i]	M (SD)[i]
OSS		.68 (1.12)	1.60 (1.25)[n/a]	.79 (1.31)**	.66 (1.10)**
In-school suspension		.61 (1.18)	.69 (1.45)***	.79 (1.41)***	.59 (1.14)***
Behavior contract		.03 (.20)	.07 (.30)***	.08 (.33)***	.02 (.18)***
RI		.17 (.52)	.18 (.56)	1.30 (.79)[n/a]	0 (0)[n/a]
Referred to law enforcement		.08 (.32)	.17 (.00)***	.11 (.01)***	.08 (.00)***
Expulsion		.01 (.09)	.02 (.00)***	.02 (.00)**	.01 (.00)***

Note. ED = emotional disability; ELL = English Language Learners; ODR = office discipline referrals; OSS = out-of-school suspension; RI = restorative interventions.

[a]Disciplined students received one or more ODRs during the 2012–2013 school year.

[b]Significant differences were determined by chi-square tests, compared with all students in the District who did not receive one or more office referrals.

[c]Significant differences were determined by chi-square tests, compared with all disciplined students not suspended.

[d]Significant differences were determined by chi-square tests, compared with all disciplined students who did not receive a RI.

[e]Significant differences were determined by chi-square tests, compared with all disciplined students who did receive a RI.

[f]Percentages of referral reasons do not add up to 100 because 42% of students received more than one ODR over the course of a school year. The complete data for all referral reasons are available upon request from the authors.

[g]Due to space limitations, only the nine most common reasons for referral are presented in the table.

[h]Significant differences were determined by independent-samples t tests, comparing students who did not receive an OSS to those who did.

[i]Significant differences were determined by independent-samples t tests, comparing students who did not receive a RI to those who did.

[j]Discipline consequences are not mutually exclusive. For one discipline incident, a student may receive multiple consequences as part of the resolution to his or her offense. Forty-eight percent of students also have more than one discipline incident, so they also can receive a consequence more than once.

*p < .05. **p < .01. ***p < .001.

Table 2
Risk Indices[a] and Relative Risk Ratios[b] for Office Disciplinary Referrals and Out-of-School Suspension

Student Race	Office Disciplinary Referrals All Year			OSS All Year		
	Risk Index	RRR Compared to White Students	RRR Compared to All Other Students	Risk Index	RRR Compared to White Students	RRR Compared to All Other Students
Black	19.08%	3.41	1.99	9.64%	4.95	2.55
White	5.60%	1.00	0.45	1.95%	1.00	0.37
Latino	11.22%	2.00	1.06	4.46%	2.29	0.92
Asian	4.74%	0.85	0.42	1.81%	0.93	0.38
Multiracial	10.55%	1.88	0.96	4.80%	2.46	1.04
Native American	13.33%	2.38	1.22	5.85%	3.01	1.27
Pacific Islander	6.48%	1.16	0.59	2.31%	1.19	0.50

Note. RRR = relative risk ratio.
[a]The risk index is the proportion of students from one racial group who have been suspended. It is computed by dividing the number of students suspended from one group by the total number of students from that group (Skiba et al., 2008).
[b]The relative risk ratio is computed by taking a ratio of the rates per 1,000 between two groups (IDEA Data Center, 2014; Shaw et al., 2008).

Student Discipline Records

The District's discipline database included information for each ODR issued to a student in 2012–2013; this information included the reason for each referral and related consequences. These data are entered by a school staff member trained to indicate the reason for the referral based on the categories in the District's discipline policy (DPS, 2008). ODRs reflect a multistep process whereby educators assess student misconduct, complete the formal discipline referral paperwork, and record it in the school's database. Despite educators' varying approaches to addressing student behavior or misconduct, and their inconsistent use of the legally mandated discipline record keeping, research has established that ODRs are consistent correlates of teachers' perceptions of problematic behavior, poor teacher–student relationships, future misconduct, and future academic difficulties (e.g., Pas, Bradshaw, & Mitchell, 2011). For example, students' receipt of one or more ODRs is associated with negative teacher behavioral ratings (Pas et al., 2011) and, years later, with being off-track for graduation (Tobin & Sugai, 1999)—evidence for the concurrent and predictive validity of ODRs.

The ODR referral categories represent the total number of times a student was referred to the office for each particular ODR reason (0 = student was not referred to the office for this reason, 1 or more = number of referrals a student received for this behavior). This coding method was necessary because almost half of disciplined students (42%) were referred to the office more than once during the school year, often for different behaviors. Therefore, ODR reasons at the student level are not mutually exclusive; as a result, the reference group for each referral category is all other reasons. The nine most common reasons for an ODR (comprising 98% of all discipline incidents) were detrimental behavior (54.58% of disciplined students), disobedience or defiance (32.38%), other violations of the school's code of conduct (24.94%), bullying (8.30%), possession and/or distribution of drugs (7.36%), third degree assault (2.49%), destruction of school property (2.02%), unlawful sexual behavior (1.38%), and weapons possession (1.74%). An additional seven reasons for referral were included in the dataset but were infrequently issued (e.g., alcohol violation [.97%], robbery [0.60%], tobacco violation [0.50%], gang affiliation [0.32%], first degree assault [.23%], witness intimidation [0.14%], other felonies [0.14%]) (see Table 1).

For each student ODR, the District's discipline database indicated the type of consequences assigned by the administrator (one discipline incident may have multiple consequences). As shown in Table 1, among all disciplined students (defined as students who experienced an ODR at least once during the academic year), 13% received RIs and 43% received OSSs. In the current study, we distinguished between consequences received in the first or second semester. To answer Research Question 1, we created a dichotomous dependent variable to indicate whether, in the second semester, a student received one or more ODRs (1) or none at all (0). We also indicated whether a student in the second semester received an OSS (1) or not (0)—a group that included those students who never received another ODR. All analyses conducted to answer Research Question 1 included an independent variable that accounted for the total number of RIs a student received in the first semester (among those who participated in an RI; M = 1.30, SD = .79, minimum = 0; maximum = 8). To answer Research Question 2 regarding the equitable access to RIs, we created a dichotomous dependent variable to indicate whether, in the first semester as a consequence for an ODR, a student received one or more RIs (1) or no RIs (0). RIs included circles, mediations, and conferences; the dataset did not distinguish between these three practices.

Student Characteristics

The District's electronic student information system included sociodemographic information for each student issued a discipline referral in 2012–2013. Student racial categories used by the District are as follows: (1) Native American or Alaska Native, (2) Native Hawaiian or other Pacific

Islander, (3) Asian or Asian American, (4) Black or African American (non-Hispanic), (5) Hispanic or Latino/Latina, (6) White or Caucasian, and (7) Multiracial. Each racial category was recoded into dummy variables with White students as the reference group. Additional student-level variables available in the dataset were all dichotomous and included gender (male or not), free and reduced lunch eligibility (eligible or not), special education status (active Individualized Education Program or not), designation as seriously emotionally disabled (ED or not), and ELL or not.

School Characteristics

School-level covariates were selected based on prior research consistently linking them to discipline outcomes (e.g., Arcia, 2007; Payne & Welch, 2010; Skiba et al., 2014), including proportion of the student body that was Black and the proportion eligible for free and reduced lunch, along with grade configuration and school size (divided by 100). Grade configuration was dummy coded with K–5 elementary schools as the reference group relative to middle schools, high schools, and schools with alternative combinations of grade levels (e.g., grades K–8). We also calculated school-wide use of RI by dividing the number of students who received RIs in each school by the number of students with ODRs from that site. The resulting RI rate ranged across schools from 0% to 75% (M = 8.31%, SD = 13.10%).

Data Analytic Plan

Multilevel logistic regression methods were used to assess study outcomes.[1] Using STATA 13 software, hierarchical modeling techniques accounted for the nested structure of the dataset (Level 1 = students; Level 2 = schools) and were used to estimate the relationships between (a) student sociodemographic characteristics, (b) participation in RIs during the first semester of the school year, and (c) discipline outcomes in the second semester (Rabe-Hesketh & Skrondal, 2008; Steenbergen & Jones, 2002). For research Questions 1a–c, we ran a set of models predicting the dependent variables (one or more second-semester ODRs and OSSs). The first models examined the overall association between student participation in RIs and subsequent discipline outcomes. The second models included interaction terms testing whether the correlation between participation in RIs and subsequent discipline outcomes varied by student race or by school-level rates of RI use. For Research Question 2, we ran a single model with sociodemographic characteristics predicting participation in one or more RIs.

In all analyses, we covaried number of referrals for each discipline category, as the District requires schools to implement a graduated discipline system in which consequences increase with the seriousness and number of student offenses. This practice is consistent with empirical evidence from other school districts indicating that ODR reason is related to the severity of consequence (Skiba et al., 2014). All possible reasons for referral were included as covariates in analyses, but regression estimates were only tabled for the nine most common reasons due to space constraints. The complete data and model output for all referral reasons are available upon request. To improve the precision of our estimates, we also covaried student characteristics (e.g., free and reduced lunch eligibility) and school characteristics (i.e., school size, proportion Black student enrollment).

Results

While reviewing the results below, the reader must keep in mind that this correlational study examines the association between RIs and students' future discipline outcomes, without accounting for all relevant confounds. Therefore, findings do not indicate causality or provide strong evidence of intervention efficacy or effectiveness. Moreover, because the study dataset does not include implementation process data, the circumstances under which certain groups came to participate in RIs more or less than others are not known. Results should therefore be interpreted to add depth to prior findings from descriptive, qualitative, and single case research on RIs and identify patterns and relationships that provide direction for future studies.

RIs and Second-Semester ODRs and OSSs

Tables 3 and 4 show the results of a multilevel logistic regression model predicting the odds of receiving at least one ODR or OSS in the second semester of the same year for students who participated in RIs during the first semester. The odds ratio (OR) for each predictor and the 95% confidence intervals for each OR represent the association of an individual predictor (e.g., number of RIs received) with the dependent variable (e.g., ODR), accounting for all other covariates. An OR larger (or smaller) than 1.00 indicates an increase (or decrease) in the odds of an RI participant receiving future discipline, compared to his or her referred peers who did not receive a RI. Findings reveal that, after accounting for students' reasons for and frequency of ODRs and a range of school and student characteristics, students who received RIs as consequences for referrals in the first semester had lower odds than their peers of being referred back to the office for misconduct in the second semester (OR = .21, $p < .001$; Model 1, Table 3); these students were also less likely to receive an OSS (*OR* = .07, $p < .001$; Model 3, Table 4) in the second semester.

The next statistical models included interaction terms to determine if the strength of this correlation varied by student or school characteristics. The results indicate that results were equivalent across racial groups for second-semester ODRs (Table 3, Model 2) and OSSs (Table 4, Model 4). Specifically, the interaction terms (e.g., Black × Participation in RIs) testing

Table 3

Multilevel Logistic Regression Model of the Relationship Between Participation in RIs and Second-Semester Office Disciplinary Referrals (*n* = 9,921)

	Model 1		Model 2	
	OR	95% CI	OR	95% CI
Participation in RI				
First-semester RI	0.21***	.09, .51	.15***	.05, .43
Student sociodemographics				
Race (comparison group = White youth)				
Latino	0.95	.79, 1.14	.96	.80, 1.15
Black	1.09	.90, 1.32	1.09	.90, 1.32
Native American	1.22	.73, 2.04	1.22	.73, 2.04
Asian	0.93	.61, 1.41	.88	.57, 1.36
Multiracial	0.88	.64, 1.21	.89	.65, 1.22
Pacific Islander	2.71	.58, 12.79	2.65	.56, 12.49
Gender (male)	0.95	.86, 1.05	.96	.86, 1.06
Eligible for free/reduced lunch	0.97	.84, 1.12	.97	.84, 1.12
ELL	1.09	.97, 1.23	1.09	.96, 1.22
Special education	0.92	.81, 1.06	.92	.80, 1.05
ED	0.71*	.53, .95	.69*	.51, .92
Referral reason[a]				
Bullying	2.12***	1.76, 2.55	2.11***	1.78, 2.54
Destruction of school property	1.81**	1.25, 2.63	1.81**	1.25, 2.63
Disobedient/defiant	2.10***	1.93, 2.29	2.06***	1.90, 2.24
Other code of conduct violation	1.97***	1.77, 2.20	1.95***	1.75, 2.17
Detrimental behavior	1.89***	1.75, 2.03	1.87***	1.73, 2.01
Third degree assault	2.55***	1.84, 3.53	2.55***	1.85, 3.56
Unlawful sexual behavior	1.68*	1.10, 2.55	1.67*	1.10, 2.54
Drug possession or distribution	1.67***	1.40, 1.98	1.64***	1.38, 1.95
Dangerous weapon	2.07***	1.37, 3.12	2.04***	1.36, 3.08
School context				
% Black students	0.40*	.16, 1.00	.40+	.16, 1.01
% eligible free/reduced lunch	1.64	.89, 3.02	1.65	.89, 3.04
High schools (Grades 9–12)	0.43***	.29, .64	.43***	.29, .64
Middle schools (Grades 6–8)	0.87	.60, 1.26	.87	.60, 1.27
Other grade configurations	0.68**	.49, .95	.68*	.49, .94
School size	1.07**	1.03, 1.12	1.07**	1.03, 1.12
Rate of RI use	.98	.40, 2.36	1.08	.45, 2.65
Interactions				
Native American × Participation in RI			1.68	.31, 9.19
Black × Participation in RI			1.41	.70, 2.86
Latino × Participation in RI			1.08	.56, 2.09

(continued)

Table 3 **(continued)**

	Model 1		Model 2	
	OR	95% CI	OR	95% CI
Asian × Participation in RI			.36	.04, 3.93
Multiracial × Participation in RI			1.55	.45, 5.36
Pacific Islander × Participation in RI			—[b]	
Participation in RI × School RI Rate			.86***	.80, .93
Model statistics				
Constant	2.75***	1.48, 5.10	2.62***	1.41, 4.86
Variance component[c]	−.64	−.97, −.32	−.64	−.96, −.31
ICC[d]	.14	.10, .18	.14	.10, .18
Log likelihood	−5,148.02		−5,133.92	

Note. CI = confidence interval; ED = emotional disability; ELL = English Language Learners; ICC = intraclass correlation; OR = odds ratio; RI = restorative interventions.
[a]Additional low-frequency reasons for referral were included in the statistical model, but estimates are not presented in the table. The complete output for all models is available upon request from the authors.
[b]No Pacific Islander students received a RI in the first semester.
[c]Log of the school-level random effect variance component.
[d]Residual intraclass correlation, or the total variance contributed by the school-level random effect variance component.
$+p < .10.$ $*p < .05.$ $**p < .01.$ $***p < .001.$

whether student race moderated the link between participation in RIs and second-semester discipline outcomes were all nonsignificant.

Interaction terms were also included to examine whether the negative association between participation in RIs and adverse discipline outcomes was moderated by school-wide RI use (Participation in RI × School RI Rate). As shown in Table 3, Model 2 indicates that RI participants had lower odds of receiving a second-semester ODR in schools that had higher school-wide RI rates (OR = .86, $p < .001$). These results suggest that school-level use of RI relates to the probability of a student receiving an ODR after participating in the intervention. Holding all other variables in the model constant, a referred student who did not participate in an RI during the first semester and attended a school with an average first-semester RI rate (M = 8.31%) had a 72% probability of receiving one or more ODRs in the second semester (Huang, 2014; Huang, Invernizzi, & Drake, 2012). A referred student who did participate in at least one RI in the first semester and attended a school with an average first-semester RI rate had a much lower (28%) probability of receiving one or more ODRs in the second semester. A referred student who

Table 4
Multilevel Logistic Regression Model of the Relationship Between Participation in RIs and Second-Semester Out-of-School Suspension (*n* = 9,921)

	Model 3		Model 4	
	OR	95% CI	OR	95% CI
Participation in RI				
First-semester RI	0.07***	.01, .31	.10**	.02, .50
Student sociodemographics				
Race (comparison group = White youth)				
Latino	1.16	.95, 1.43	1.16	.94, 1.42
Black	1.33**	1.08, 1.65	1.32**	1.07, 1.64
Native American	1.54	.89, 2.66	1.47	.84, 2.55
Asian	1.31	.81, 2.12	1.33	.81, 2.16
Multiracial	1.31	.92, 1.85	1.27	.90, 1.81
Pacific Islander	1.14	.30, 4.35	1.17	.31, 4.44
Gender (male)	0.97	.87, 1.08	.97	.87, 1.08
Eligible for free/reduced lunch	1.28**	1.08, 1.51	1.27**	1.08, 1.50
ELL	0.91	.80, 1.04	.91	.80, 1.03
Special education	1.16*	1.00, 1.33	1.16*	1.01, 1.33
ED	1.39**	1.06, 1.83	1.37*	1.04, 1.81
Referral reason[a]				
Bullying	1.45***	1.24, 1.70	1.46***	1.25, 1.72
Destruction of school property	2.08***	1.50, 2.87	2.07***	1.50, 2.87
Disobedient/defiant	1.29***	1.23, 1.34	1.29***	1.23, 1.34
Other code of conduct violation	1.47***	1.35, 1.59	1.47***	1.36, 1.60
Detrimental behavior	1.62***	1.54, 1.70	1.62***	1.54, 1.70
Third-degree assault	3.05***	2.29, 4.06	3.10***	2.33, 4.13
Unlawful sexual behavior	1.86**	1.26, 2.74	1.88**	1.27, 2.77
Drug possession or distribution	3.26***	2.75, 3.86	3.27***	2.76, 3.87
Dangerous weapon	4.75***	3.32, 6.80	4.75***	3.32, 6.80
School context				
% Black students	2.07	.51, 8.17	2.06	.52, 8.22
% eligible free/reduced lunch	4.12**	1.61, 10.52	4.11**	1.61, 10.50
High schools (Grades 9–12)	0.80	.43, 1.49	.80	.43, 1.49
Middle schools (Grades 6–8)	1.86*	1.05, 3.29	1.86*	1.05, 3.29
Other grade configurations	1.49	.91, 2.43	1.49	.91, 2.43
School size	1.08*	1.01, 1.16	1.08*	1.01, 1.16
Rate of RI use	.13**	.03, .53	.13**	.03, .54
Interactions				
Native American × Participation in RI			.14	.01, 1.91
Black × Participation in RI			.80	.36, 1.80
Latino × Participation in RI			.62	.29, 1.34

(continued)

Table 4 **(continued)**

	Model 3		Model 4	
	OR	95% CI	OR	95% CI
Asian × Participation in RI			1.23	.13, 11.86
Multiracial × Participation in RI			.39	.09, 1.76
Pacific Islander × Participation in RI			—[b]	
Participation in RI × School RI Rate			.98	.91, 1.05
Model statistics				
Variance component[c]	.33	.05, .60	.32	.05, .60
ICC[d]	.30	.24, .36	.30	.24, .36
Log likelihood	−4,698.72		−4,695.00	

Note. CI = confidence interval; ED = emotional disability; ELL = English Language Learners; ICC = intraclass correlation; OR = Odds ratio; RI = restorative interventions.
[a]Additional low-frequency reasons for referral were included in the statistical model, but estimates are not presented in the table. The complete output for all models is available upon request from the authors.
[b]No Pacific Islander students received a RI in the first semester.
[c]Log of the school-level random effect variance component.
[d]Residual intraclass correlation or the total variance contributed by the school-level random effect variance component.
$*p < .05.$ $**p < .01.$ $***p < .001.$

participated in at least one RI but attended a school with a school-wide RI rate that was 1 *SD* above the mean (*SD* = 13.10%) had an even lower (18%) probability of receiving one or more ODRs in the second semester. In contrast, moderation by school-level rate of RI use was not statistically significant when predicting second-semester OSSs (Table 4, Model 4, Participation in RI × School RI Rate = *ns*). That said, the school-level RI rate was negatively correlated with receiving OSSs for all students (OR = .13, $p < .01$).

The models also revealed that even after accounting for RI participation at the student and school level, Black students and those eligible for free lunch, classified as having an ED, or receiving special education services still had higher odds of receiving second-semester OSSs relative to their peers (ORs ranged from 1.16 to 1.37, $p < .05$). This finding held no matter the seriousness and frequency of ODRs or the type of school setting (e.g., grade level, school size), indicating that despite RI participation, disparities in exclusionary discipline remained for Black students, low-income students, and students in special education.

Equitable Participation in RIs

Table 5 presents the results of the multilevel logistic regression model predicting student participation in at least one RI. Results indicate that, accounting for students' number of ODRs in each referral category and school-level covariates, only one student group of interest—youth designated as ELL—had lower odds of participating in an RI (OR = .81, $p <$ .05) compared to non-ELL students. On the other hand, many student groups that tend to be overrepresented in exclusionary discipline outcomes were equally likely to participate in a RI as their peers. Specifically, Native American students, males, low-income students, students in special education, and students classified as having an ED had similar odds of participating in a RI as other, more advantaged groups of students. Results also indicate that two marginalized and disadvantaged groups were more likely to participate in RIs. Of interest was that Latino (OR = 1.40, $p < .05$) and Black (OR = 1.36, $p < .05$) students had higher odds of participating in a RI relative to White students.

As shown in Table 5, findings from the statistical models also reveal important information about the type of offenses that are associated with RI participation. For example, students who were referred for a greater number of offenses involving interpersonal conflict had the highest odds of participating in RIs; these offenses included bullying, detrimental behavior, and third-degree assault (ORs ranged from 1.35–2.14, $p < .01$). In contrast, students referred for drug possession or distribution were less likely than other students to engage in a RI (OR = .72, $p < .05$). Other referral reasons, such as destruction of school property, disobedience or defiance, and weapons possession, were not statistically significant predictors of participation in RIs. Also noteworthy was the finding indicating that students in schools with alternative grade configurations (relative to elementary schools) had over three times higher odds of participating in RIs (OR = 3.50, $p < .05$).

Discussion

The study suggests that RIs may be a useful alternative to punitive, exclusionary consequences. Findings corroborate prior research (Anyon et al., 2014) and address methodological limitations by (a) controlling for a range of student and school characteristics using a multilevel modeling approach and (b) using time-ordered discipline records of individual students across a school year. Specifically, with each RI students received (circles, mediations, or conferences) during the first semester, their odds of receiving another ODR or OSS in the second semester were lower. This association held after accounting for sociodemographics (e.g., race, gender, free/reduced lunch eligibility), educational placements (e.g., general or special education), frequency or seriousness of office referrals (e.g., detrimental behavior, third-degree assault,

Table 5
Multilevel Logistic Regression Model Predicting Participation in a Restorative Intervention (*n* = 9,921)

	OR	95% CI
Student sociodemographics		
Race (comparison group = White students)		
Latino	1.40*	1.07, 1.83
Black	1.36*	1.02, 1.81
Native American	0.89	.40, 1.96
Asian	1.24	.65, 2.36
Multiracial	0.88	.53 1.47
Pacific Islander	1.47	.29, 7.37
Gender (male)	1.04	.89, 1.21
Eligible for free or reduce price lunch	1.03	.83, 1.28
ELLs	0.81*	.69, .97
Special education	0.92	.76, 1.12
ED	0.82	.54, 1.23
Referral reason[a]		
Bullying	1.35**	1.11, 1.63
Destruction of school property	1.03	.65, 1.63
Disobedient/defiant	1.04[+]	.99, 1.09
Other code of conduct violation	1.31***	1.19, 1.44
Detrimental behavior	1.37***	1.30, 1.44
Third-degree assault	2.14***	1.47, 3.09
Unlawful sexual behavior	.86	.58, 1.28
Drug possession or distribution	0.72*	.55, .93
Dangerous weapon	1.24	.76, 2.03
School context		
% Black students	0.13	.01, 2.58
% eligible for free or reduced price lunch	1.26	.18, 8.81
High school	2.27	.60, 8.60
Middle school	3.29[+]	.94, 11.45
Alternative grade configuration	3.50**	1.21, 10.11
School size	1.10	.95, 1.27
Model statistics		
Variance component[b]	1.78	.1.43, 2.13
ICC[c]	.65***	.56, .72

Note. CI = confidence interval; ED = emotional disability; ELL = English Language Learners; ICC = intraclass correlation; OR = odds ratio.
[a]Additional low-frequency reasons for referral were included in the statistical model, but estimates are not presented in the table. The complete output for all models is available upon request from the authors.
[b]Log of the school-level random effect variance component.
[c]Residual intraclass correlation or the total variance contributed by the school-level random effect variance component.
+*p* < .10. *p < .05. **p < .01. ***p < .001.

dangerous weapon possession), and diverse school environments in terms of grade level (e.g., elementary school, high school), size of the student body, proportion of Black and low-income students, and school-level RI rate. The study also found that the negative association between participation in RIs and adverse discipline outcomes was similar across racial groups; in other words, student race did not have a moderating role.

Our ability to interpret these results or make claims about the impact of RIs on discipline outcomes is highly constrained by lack of random assignment (by school or student) to RIs and the limited covariates in our dataset. The associations between receipt of RIs in the first semester and fewer ODRs/OSSs in the second semester did not account for a range of student and school characteristics that could influence RI participation and/or subsequent discipline incidents. For example, there is emerging evidence that students' likelihood of participating in a restorative conference is influenced by their trust or relationship with the person who will be implementing the intervention (Anyon, 2016). Other influences could include students' propensity to take responsibility for their actions, a disciplinarian's willingness to offer students the opportunity to participate in a RI, or a school leader's commitment to proactive or preventative approaches to addressing misbehavior (e.g., Payne & Welch, 2010; Skiba et al., 2014). Since we were not able to account for these confounding factors, study results cannot be interpreted to mean that first-semester RI participation caused a reduction in second-semester ODRs and OSSs. Nevertheless, the finding of a negative association between these two variables is promising and warrants further investigation.

Variability in School Use of RIs

The study demonstrated that schools varied considerably in the rates at which referred students in the school participated in circles, mediations, and conferences. For example, the full range of school-wide RI rates was 0% to 75% ($M = 8.3\%$, $SD = .13$), with 13% of all disciplined students in the district having participated in at least one RI. Referred students in schools with higher rates of RI use, in general, had lower odds of receiving an OSS than students in schools with lower RI rates. In the case of office referrals, school-wide RI rate also moderated the relationship between individual RI participation and subsequent ODRs. This might suggest that schools implementing circles, mediations, and conferences are generally seeking to steer students out of the discipline system and limit the use of suspension when they do. Many schools in this district are engaging in a broad set of prevention and intervention initiatives to keep students in the classroom and the school building (Anyon, 2016; Anyon et al., 2016). This in and of itself is a worthy goal given that negative academic and behavioral trajectories of referred students are exacerbated when they are excluded from instruction (e.g., Balfanz et al., 2015).

Also noteworthy was that results at the student level held no matter the school's overall rate of RI use. Whether or not schools regularly or rarely engaged students in circles, mediations, or conferences, the negative correlation between RI participation in the first semester and exclusionary practices (ODRs and OSSs) in the second semester remained. Finally, the study found school-level use of RIs moderated the relationship between student-level participation in RIs and another discipline incident in the second semester. In other words, high program use at the school level (a facet of treatment delivery; Schulte et al., 2009) strengthened the negative relationship between RI participation and subsequent office referrals at the student level. This suggests that school-level participation rates relate to the probability of a student experiencing an office disciplinary referral after participating in the intervention. These findings are consistent with arguments some RI scholars and practitioners have made that the depth of school community engagement with these practices is critical to maximizing their benefits (Anyon, 2016; Anyon et al., 2016). Indeed, as innovations spread and take hold through a school building, educators' attitudes, beliefs, and skills related to the new programming may actually strengthen the quality of implementation and resulting effects on student outcomes (Rogers, 2003). On the other hand, it is also plausible that school capacity to implement RIs meaningfully operates as a crucial driver of disciplinary outcomes.

RIs and Equity Issues

Results of this study demonstrate that in a large urban district many disadvantaged youth had similar rates of RI participation as more privileged students, with the noteworthy exception of ELL students. Relative to their peers, low-income students, Native American youth, males, and students with special education services or an ED classification participated comparably in RIs. Black and Latino students were more likely to participate in RIs than White students. Moreover, the only school-level predictor of student-level RI participation was the grade configuration of the school; students at sites with non-traditional formats (e.g., K–12, K–8) had significantly higher odds of participating in this alternative to suspension. These findings are surprising in light of experimental studies indicating that disadvantaged groups may consciously (or unconsciously) be issued harsher sanctions for similar behavior than more advantaged groups (Okonofua & Eberhardt, 2015). More specifically, results stand in contrast to previous research by Payne and Welch (2010) indicating that, at the school level, the proportion of Black students was a negative predictor of a school's use of student conferences, peer mediations, restitution, and community service in response to discipline incidents. It is possible that the unique dynamics of service access in this study reflect the District's focus on eliminating racial disparities in school discipline, as articulated by board policy, professional development trainings on RIs, and district officials' public statements (DPS, 2008, 2012). However, it is concerning that ELLs were less likely to participate in RIs. This finding is consistent with prior research demonstrating that students' access to school-based programs can be limited for students for whom English is not their native language (Anyon et al., 2013). Taken together, findings suggest that educators need to be vigilant in ensuring fair access to less punitive alternatives when implementing new discipline initiatives, such as RIs. In other words, the recent push for schools to disaggregate their ODR and suspension data should be extended to the use of RIs.

Despite a higher likelihood of participation in RIs relative to White students, Black students remained at heightened risk of being suspended in the second semester. Likewise, despite having comparable participation in RIs, low-income students, youth in special education, and those with an ED classification also had higher odds of being issued a second-semester suspension than their more advantaged peers. Comparable participation in RIs for these groups did not correspond with eliminating heightened risk among these populations for a future second-semester OSS across the district—a risk that persisted even after controlling for participation in RIs and frequency and seriousness of referral reasons. In other words, discipline disparities were not eliminated in the District despite its use of restorative alternatives to suspension. It therefore seems likely that additional forms of prevention and intervention, in addition to individual RIs, are needed to fully address equity concerns (Anyon, 2016; Anyon et al., 2016).

The persistence of disparities may be due to a number of reasons. RIs were issued as consequences for a wide range of referral reasons including detrimental behavior, bullying, and third-degree assault. That said, only 12.52% of all those referred for discipline in the first semester in the District (n = 652) received a RI. Implementation may need to be much more widespread and frequent to significantly reduce or eliminate disparities in discipline. The infrequent use of RIs in many schools reflects the challenge of integrating alternative disciplinary strategies in large urban school districts. Although the District offers voluntary training about RIs, additional resources like school-based RI coordinators may be necessary to increase implementation and reduce racial discipline gaps district-wide (Anyon, 2016; Anyon et al., 2016; Durlak & Dupre, 2008).

Schools may make additional gains in reducing discipline disparities by increasing their prevention efforts (while maintaining the focus on restorative approaches to intervention; Anyon, 2016; Anyon et al., 2016). Building community, creating positive social bonds, and fostering investment in school rules before conflict arises may be among the keys to reducing disparities, especially for students in groups who are alienated from school (Gregory, Bell, & Pollock, 2016). Moreover, preventive interventions can also occur by training teachers to strengthen the motivating and engaging qualities of instruction and by preventing negative teacher–student interactions from occurring in the first place (Gregory, Hafen et al., 2016). Finally, staff training about culturally responsive practices and racial justice may reduce the likelihood of misreading or mislabeling students' body language or speech and may decrease overly punitive responses to students of color (Anyon, 2016; Anyon et al., 2016; Davis, Lyubansky, & Schiff, 2015; Monroe, 2005).

Study Limitations and Implication for Future Research

Several limitations related to study design suggest that caution in interpreting study findings is warranted. First and foremost, we must reiterate that neither disciplined students nor school sites were randomly assigned to participate in RIs. Instead, the District policy recommends that RIs be used in response to midrange offenses when a student is willing to accept some responsibility for his or her actions. This potential of individual and school sorting of students toward or away from a RI suggests multiple potential sources of selection bias. For example, at the student level, those who were able to acknowledge their role in an offense may have already been less likely to reenter the discipline system. In other words, a student's lack of ability to acknowledge his or her contributing role in a discipline incident is likely a risk for future discipline contacts but was not measured in this study. Moreover, the study was not able to directly measure and account for a school's or administrator's propensity to offer students RIs or punitive consequences in response to a discipline incident.

Whereas the current study found a significant association between RI participation and positive discipline outcomes, a crucial goal for future research is to move beyond a conditional analysis such as this to begin to identify design or analytic strategies to mitigate the influence of key selection processes. We anticipate that there may be barriers in implementing experimental designs to estimate the effects of RI (e.g., ethical considerations in differentially offering less exclusionary disciplinary options to students, given evidence of the harm of OSSs). If researchers must rely on observational designs, crucial first steps include more specific identification of (1) the RI intervention (e.g., what are the essential components of the intervention at school and student levels and at what intensity); (2) the student, educator, and school characteristics that are predictive of RI participation beyond basic sociodemographic characteristics (e.g., student verbal communication, emotional regulation, externalizing behaviors, history of disciplinary interactions, prior relationships with school staff, peer norms about the acceptability of RI, and a school or district's willingness to implement RIs); and (3) how such characteristics contribute to exclusionary discipline outcomes of interest (Hemphill, Plenty, Herrenkohl, Toumbourou, & Catalano, 2014; Skiba et al., 2014). If such factors can be observed and measured reliably, propensity score matching methods may be a viable option for understanding the impact of RIs (see Hong & Raudenbush, 2005, as an exemplar).

The low incidence of RI use among disciplined students also raises questions about the capacity for widespread dissemination of this approach in school settings. When the district policy was passed in 2008, only 4% of all disciplined students participated in RIs. Four years later, the incidence of RI use increased to 12.52%, as reported in this study. Although this rate is low, it is important to note that district policy mandates were not accompanied with financial incentives or new site staff. The increased use of RIs is more impressive in this context, in which the only implementation supports offered to schools have been voluntary training and technical assistance led by one district coordinator. Future research should consider whether the diffusion of RIs in schools could be more widespread, with attention to other factors that affect the implementation of interventions like work climate, staff norms, the support of organizational leaders, and the development of "program champions" (Durlak & Dupre, 2008).

Another study limitation is that our dataset provided no information to assess the process or quality of RI implementation. Schools did not track whether, for example, disciplinarians adhered to eligibility protocols when offering RIs to students with discipline incidents or if participants were motivated by threats for more severe repercussions if they did not engage in an RI. Moreover, the dataset did not indicate to what degree each school experienced pressure to implement this approach or the degree to which educators felt motivated or skilled to do so.

Future research would be substantially strengthened by the inclusion of indicators that measure multiple and multilevel (student/school) factors related to implementation fidelity. Of particular relevance to school-based RIs are compatibility or fit between school leaders' discipline philosophies and the principles that guide RIs, the degree to which school staff buy in to the approach, staff capacity (in particular the presence or absence of a person trained and available to facilitate formal mediations or conferences), and school personnel's participation in RI trainings (Anyon, 2016; Anyon et al., 2016; Payne & Welch, 2010). Such process and quality characteristics and the development of measures thereof have great potential to enhance both observational and experimental designs.

To further elucidate the finding of moderation by school-level rate of RIs, future research might compare schools with high versus low rates to ascertain if high participation schools have (1) better skilled facilitators of circles, mediations, and conferences due to practice; (2) positive peer norms related to RIs that influence individual students' commitment to the restorative process; and/or (3) positive staff attitudes and expectancies related to RIs that impact their commitment to providing behavioral supports and following through with RI participants. These studies should also explore in a more multifaceted way the quality, quantity, and the degree to which RI needs to be implemented school wide in order to be maximally effective. More broadly, study findings highlight the need to account for school-level contextual factors in future studies of RIs.

Similarly, there are potentially multiple decision-making points that could result in the finding of varying RI participation rates across diverse student groups. School staff may tend to refer to RIs students who are from certain racial groups more than from other racial groups. Once referred and oriented to the restorative process, students from certain groups may tend to consent to participate more than their peers from other groups. Given this complexity, the current study's focus on participation in RIs is only a first step in understanding disparate or comparable patterns of use of a promising alternative to suspension. Future research might seek to explain why Black and Latino students were more likely to participate in RIs than White students in this study. Qualitative research from schools with low and equitable suspension rates in Denver indicates that many school staff members are aware of racial disparities in school discipline and are actively encouraging the use of less punitive practices among students of color (Anyon, 2016; Anyon et. al., 2016), but these findings are not generalizable and further study is warranted. Studies might also seek to explain our finding that ELL students' RI participation was low relative to non-ELL students. Such research might examine whether schools inadvertently deny access to RIs for students whose first language is not English because of cultural barriers or limited language capacity on the part of school staff.

The study's singular focus on discipline outcomes also limits the scope of the findings. ODRs and OSSs reflect school staff's use of formal discipline procedures and paperwork or data entry. The degree to which an ODR or OSS reflects student misconduct, staff's tendency to use the formal discipline procedures, or poor classroom management skills is unknown (Morrison, Redding, Fisher, & Peterson, 2006). Future studies should include other school outcomes such as academic engagement, attendance, and achievement. This much-needed research would build on findings from Oakland where schools implementing RI, along with a range of other interventions, had significantly greater improvements in reading proficiency and greater reductions in absenteeism and dropout than non-RI schools (Jain et al., 2014).

Conclusion

Study findings advance current knowledge about patterns and correlates of student participation in school-based RIs. Using discipline records from a large urban district, results indicate that students who received a RI in the first semester had lower odds of receiving another ODR or suspension in the second semester of the same school year. This finding held after accounting for student racial background, special education status, free or reduced lunch eligibility, and frequency and seriousness of disciplinary referrals. The study also showed that school-wide RI rates were negatively associated with exclusionary discipline outcomes. In fact, for ODRs, the strength of association between RI participation and adverse discipline outcomes was more pronounced in schools with high rates of RI use. Finally, participation in RIs was comparable across many disadvantaged groups, with the notable exception of ELL students. However, Latino and Black students, two groups with disproportionally high rates of suspension in many regions in the United States, had greater odds of receiving RIs than their White peers. This suggests that for most disadvantaged groups in the District, schools implemented RIs in a manner that provided them equal access to an alternative, problem-solving approach to conflict. These findings are encouraging but do not provide causal evidence of the utility of this approach to reducing students' risk of exclusionary discipline infractions. Experimental research with robust implementation process measures is sorely needed to identify the mechanisms underlying the patterns identified in this study.

Note

[1]We considered implementing a propensity score matching strategy guided by the methods of Hong and Raudenbush's (2005) multilevel study of the effects of grade retention practices in schools. We ultimately ruled out such an approach for two reasons. First, we could not be completely certain, given the structure of the dataset, that key student-level predictors (ODRs) actually preceded receipt of RI, which is a fundamental condition for propensity score matching in intervention studies. Thus, the only available student matching variables were sociodemographic characteristics, which are unlikely to generate less biased results (Cook, Shadish, & Wong, 2008). As a comparison, Hong and Raudenbush's (2005) multilevel propensity methods benefited from an extensive body of prior research on the student- and school-level attributes that predict grade retention. Moreover, their rich dataset had over 200 multilevel covariates to use in generating propensity scores. There is no comparable prior research on correlates of RI participation, and the dataset employed in this study only included a limited number of control variables.

References

American Academy of Pediatrics. (2013). Out of school suspension and expulsion. *Pediatrics, 131*, 1000–1007. Available at http://pediatrics.aappublications.org/content/131/3/e1000.full.pdf+html

Amstutz, L., & Mullet, J. H. (2005). *The little book of restorative discipline for schools.* Intercourse, PA: Good Books.

Anyon, Y. (2016). *Taking restorative practices school-wide: Insights from three schools in Denver.* Denver, CO: Denver School-Based Restorative Justice Partnership.

Anyon, Y., Horevitz, L., Moore, M., Whitaker, K., Stone, S., & Shields, J. (2013). Risk behaviors, race, and use of school-based health centers: Policy and service recommendations. *Journal of Behavioral Health Services and Research, 40*, 457–468.

Anyon, Y., Jenson, J., Altschul, I., Farrar, J., McQueen, J., Greer, E., Downing, B., & Simmons, J. (2014). The persistent effect of race and the promise of alternatives to suspension in school discipline outcomes. *Children and Youth Services Review, 44*, 379–386.

Anyon, Y., Wiley, K., Yang, J., Pauline, M., Grapentine, J., . . . Pisciotta, L. (2016). *Spotlight on success: Changing the culture of discipline in Denver Public Schools.* Denver, CO: Office of Social and Emotional Learning, Division of Student Services, Denver Public Schools.

Arcia, E. (2007). Variability in schools' suspension rates of black students. *The Journal of Negro Education*, 76(4), 597–608.

Balfanz, J., Byrnes, V., & Fox, J. (2015). Sent home and put off track: The antecedents, disproportionalities, and consequences of being suspended in the 9th grade. In D. J. Losen (Ed.), *Closing the school discipline gap: Equitable remedies for excessive exclusion* (pp. 17–30). New York, NY: Teacher's College Press.

Berkowitz, K. (2012). *Restorative practices whole-school implementation guide*. San Francisco, CA: San Francisco Unified School District.

Blood, P., & Thorsborne, M. (2005). *The challenges of culture change: Embedding restorative practice in schools*. Paper presented at the Sixth International Conference on Conferencing, Circles and other Restorative Practices: Building a Global Alliance for Restorative Practices and Family Empowerment, Sydney, Australia.

Bradshaw, C. P., Mitchell, M. M., O'Brennan, L. M., & Leaf, P. J. (2010). Multilevel exploration of factors contributing to the overrepresentation of Black students in office disciplinary referrals. *Journal of Educational Psychology*, 102, 508–520.

Braithwaite, J. (1989). *Crime, shame and reintegration*. New York, NY: Cambridge University Press.

Braithwaite, J. (2001). Restorative justice and a new criminal law of substance abuse. *Youth and Society*, 33, 227–248.

Buckley, S., & Maxwell, G. (2007). *Respectful schools: Restorative practices in education. A summary report*. Wellington, New Zealand: Office of the Children's Commissioner and the Institute of Policy Studies, School of Government, Victoria University.

Carter, P., Fine, M., & Russell, S. (2014). *Discipline disparities series: Overview*. Bloomington, IN: The Equity Project at Indiana University. Available at http://rtpcollaborative.indiana.edu/briefing-papers/

Chapin Hall Center for Children. (2008). *Racial and ethnic disparity and disproportionality in child welfare and juvenile justice: A compendium*. Chicago: Chapin Hall Center for Children at the University of Chicago.

Coates, R. B., Umbreit, M., & Vos, B. (2003). Restorative justice circles: An exploratory study. *Contemporary Justice Review*, 6, 265–278.

Cook, T. D., Shadish, W. R., & Wong, V. C. (2008). Three conditions under which experiments and observational studies produce comparable causal estimates: New findings from within-study comparisons. *Journal of Policy Analysis and Management*, 27(4), 724–750.

Costello, B., Wachtel, J., & Wachtel, T. (2010). *Restorative circles in schools: Building community and enhancing learning*. Bethlehem, PA: International Institute for Restorative Practices.

Corrigan, M. (2012). *Restorative practices in New Zealand: The evidence base*. Wellington, New Zealand: Ministry of Education.

Cross, D., Epstein, M., Hearn, L., Slee, P., Shaw, T., & Monks, H. (2011). National safe schools framework: Policy and practice to reduce bullying in Australian schools. *International Journal of Behavioural Development*, 35(5), 398–404

Davis, F. E., Lyubansky, M., & Schiff, M. (2015). Restoring racial justice. In R. Scott & S. Kosslyn (Eds.), *Emerging trends in the social and behavioral sciences* (pp. 1–16). Hoboken, NJ: John Wiley & Sons, Inc.

Denver Public Schools. (2008). *Policy JK-R—Student conduct and discipline procedures*. Available at http://sts.dpsk12.org/dps-school-board-policies/

Denver Public Schools. (2012). *Restorative approaches training manual*. Denver, CO: Mental Health and Assessment, Division of Student Services.

Department of Planning and Analysis. (2013). *5 year enrollment trends*. Denver, CO: Denver Public Schools.

Derezotes, D., Testa, M., & Poertner, J. (Eds.). (2005). *Race matters in child welfare: The overrepresentation of African American children in the system*. Washington, DC: Child Welfare League of America.

Drewery, W. (2004). Conferencing in schools: Punishment, restorative justice, and the productive importance of the process of conversation. Journal of Community & Applied Social Psychology, *14*, 332–344.

Drewery, W. (2013). Restorative justice practice: Cooperative problem-solving in New Zealand's schools. *FORUM, 55*, 209–216.

Durlak, J., & Dupre, E. (2008). Implementation matters: A review of research on the influence of implementation on program outcomes and the factors affecting implementation. *American Journal of Community Psychology, 41*, 327–335.

Encarnacao, J. (2013, September 3). Sharp drop in suspensions as Boston schools try 'restorative' approach. *Boston Herald*.

Fabelo, T., Thompson, M. D., Plotkin, M., Carmichael, D., Marchbanks, P., III, & Booth, E. A. (2011). *Breaking schools' rules: A statewide study of how school discipline relates to students' success and juvenile justice involvement*. Council of State Governments Justice Center Publications. Accessible at http://justicecen ter.csg.org/resources/juveniles

Forman, S. G. (2015). *Implementation of mental health programs in schools: A change agent's guide*. Washington, DC: American Psychological Association.

González, T. (2015). Socializing schools: Addressing racial disparities in discipline through restorative justice. In D. J. Losen (Ed.), *Closing the school discipline gap: Equitable remedies for excessive exclusion* (pp. 151–165). New York, NY: Teachers College Press.

Gregory, A., Bell, J., & Pollock, M. (2016). How educators can eradicate disparities in school discipline: Issues in intervention. In R. J. Skiba, K. Mediratta, & M. K. Rausch (Eds.), *Inequality in school discipline: Research and practice to reduce disparities* (pp. 39–58). New York, NY: Palgrave MacMillan.

Gregory, A., Hafen, C. A., Ruzek, E. A., Mikami, A. Y, Allen, J. P., & Pianta, R. C. (2016). Closing the racial discipline gap in classrooms by changing teacher practice. *School Psychology Review, 45*, 171–191.

Gregory, A., Skiba, R. J., & Noguera, P. A. (2010). The achievement gap and the discipline gap: Two sides of the same coin? *Educational Researcher, 39*, 59–68.

Hannon, L., DeFina, R., & Bruch, S. (2013). The relationship between skin tone and school suspension for African Americans. *Race and Social Problems, 5*, 281–295.

Hemphill, S. A., Plenty, S. M., Herrenkohl, T. I., Toumbourou, J. W., & Catalano, R. F. (2014). Student and school factors associated with school suspension: A multilevel analysis of students in Victoria, Australia and Washington State, United States. *Children and Youth Services Review, 36*, 187–194.

Hong, G., & Raudenbush, S. W. (2005). Effects of kindergarten retention policy on children's cognitive growth in reading and mathematics. *Educational Evaluation and Policy Analysis, 27*(3), 205–224.

Huang, F. L. (2014). Further understanding factors associated with grade retention: Birthday effects and socioemotional skills. *Journal of Applied Developmental Psychology, 35*, 79–93.

Huang, F. L., Invernizzi, M. A., & Drake, E. A. (2012). The differential effects of preschool: Evidence from Virginia. *Early Childhood Research Quarterly, 27*, 33–45.

IDEA Data Center. (2014). *Methods for assessing racial/ethnic disproportionality in special education: A technical assistance guide* (revised). Rockville, MD: Data

Accountability Center, U.S. Department of Education's Office of Special Education Programs.

Jain, S., Bassey, H., Brown, M. A., & Kalra, P. (2014). *Restorative justice in Oakland Schools. Implementation and impact: An effective strategy to reduce racially disproportionate discipline, suspensions, and improve academic outcomes.* Retrieved from www.ousd.k12.ca.us/

Jeong, S., McGarrell, E. F., & Hipple, N. K. (2012). Long-term impact of family group conference son re-offending: The Indianapolis restorative justice experiment. *Journal of Experimental Criminology, 8,* 369–385.

Kane, J., Lloyd, G., McCluskey, G., Riddell, S., Stead, J., & Weedon, E. (2007). *Restorative practices in Scottish schools.* Edinburgh, UK: Scottish Executive.

Karp, D. R., & Breslin, B. (2001). Restorative justice in school communities. *Youth & Society, 33,* 249–272.

Larsen, J. J. (2014). *Restorative justice in the Australian criminal justice system.* Canberra, Australia: Australian Institute of Criminology. Available at http://www.aic.gov.au/publications/current%20series/rpp/121-140/rpp127.html

Latimer, J., Dowden, C., & Muise, D. (2005). The effectiveness of restorative justice practices: A meta-analysis. *The Prison Journal, 85,* 127–144.

Lewis, S. (2009). *Improving school climate: Findings from schools implementing restorative practices.* Bethlehem, PA: International Institute of Restorative Practices. Retrieved from http://www.iirp.edu/pdf/IIRP-Improving-School-Climate.pdf

Losen, D. J., & Martinez, T. E. (2013). *Out of school and off track: The overuse of suspensions in American middle and high schools.* Los Angeles, CA: University of California, Los Angeles.

McClusky, G., Lloyd, G., Kane, J., Stead, J., Riddell, S., & Weedon, E. (2008). Can restorative practices in schools make a difference? *Educational Review, 60,* 405–417.

McGarrell, E. F., & Hipple, N. K. (2007). Family group conferencing and re-offending among first-time juvenile offenders: The Indianapolis experiment. *Justice Quarterly, 24,* 221–246.

Monroe, C. R. (2005). Understanding the discipline gap through a cultural lens: Implications for the education of African American students. *Intercultural Education, 16,* 317–330.

Morgan, E., Salomon, N., Plotkin, M., & Cohen, R. (2014). *The school discipline consensus report: Strategies from the field to keep students engaged in school and out of the juvenile justice system,* New York, NY: The Council of State Governments Justice Center.

Morris, E. W. (2005). 'Tuck in that shirt!' Race, class, gender and discipline in an urban school. *Sociological Perspectives, 48,* 25–48.

Morrison, G. M., Redding, M., Fisher, E., & Peterson, R. (2006). Assessing school discipline. In S. R. Jimerson & M. J. Furlong (Eds.), *Handbook of school violence and school safety: From research to practice* (pp. 211–220). Mahwah, NJ: Lawrence Erlbaum Associates.

Nathanson, D. (1997). Affect theory and the compass of shame. In M. Lansky & A. Morrison (Eds.), *The widening scope of shame* (pp. 339–354). Hillsdale, NJ: Analytic Press.

Okonofua, J. A., & Eberhardt, J. L. (2015). Two strikes: Race and the disciplining of young students. *Psychological Science, 26,* 617–624.

Osher, D. M., Poirier, J. M., Jarjoura, G. R., & Brown, R. C. (2014). Avoid quick fixes: Lessons learned from a comprehensive districtwide approach to improve conditions for learning. In D. J. Losen (Ed.), *Closing the school discipline gap:*

Equitable remedies for excessive exclusion (pp. 192–206). New York, NY: Teachers College Press.

Pas, E. T., Bradshaw, C. P., & Mitchell, M. M. (2011). Examining the validity of office discipline referrals as an indicator of student behavior problems. *Psychology in the Schools, 48,* 541–555.

Payne, A. A., & Welch, K. (2010). Modeling the effects of racial threat on punitive and restorative school discipline practices. *Criminology, 48,* 1019–1062.

Public Schools of North Carolina. (2013). *Annual report on the use of corporal punishment session law 2011-282.* Raleigh, NC: State Board of Education Department of Public Instruction. Available at http://www.ncpublicschools.org/

Rabe-Hesketh, S., & Skrondal, A. (2008). *Multilevel and longitudinal modeling using stata.* College Station, TX: Stata Press.

Rausch, M. K., Skiba, R. J., & Simmons, A. B. (2004). *The academic cost of discipline: The relationship between suspension/expulsion and school achievement.* Bloomington, IN: Center for Evaluation and Education Policy, School of Education, Indiana University.

Reyes, J. A., Elias, M. J., Parker, S. J., & Rosenblatt, J. L. (2013). Promoting educational equity for disadvantaged youth: The role of resilience and social-emotional learning. In S. Goldstein & R. B. Brooks (Eds.), *Handbook of resilience in children* (pp. 349–370). New York, NY: Springer.

Riestenberg, N. (2013). Challenges to education: Restorative approaches as a radical demand on conservative structures of schooling. In H. Cremin, G. McCluskey, & E. Sellman (Eds.), *Restorative approaches to conflict in schools: Interdisciplinary perspectives on whole school approaches to managing relationships* (pp. 207–216). London: Routledge.

Rogers, E. M. (2003). *Diffusion of innovations.* New York, NY: Free Press.

Schiff, M. (2013). *Dignity, disparity and desistance: Effective restorative justice strategies to plug the "school-to-prison pipeline."* Paper presented at the Center for Civil Rights Remedies National Conference "Closing the School to Research Gap: Research to Remedies Conference," Washington, DC.

Schulte, A. C., Easton, J. E., & Parker, J. (2009). Advances in treatment integrity research: Multidisciplinary perspectives on the conceptualization, measurement, and enhancement of treatment integrity. *School Psychology Review, 38,* 460–475.

Shaw, S. R., & Braden, J. P. (1990). Race and gender bias in the administration of corporal punishment. *School Psychology Review, 19,* 378–384.

Shaw, T. V., Putnam-Hornstein, E., Magruder, J., & Needell, B. (2008). Measuring racial disparity in child welfare. *Child Welfare, 87,* 23–36.

Skiba, R. J., Chung, C., Trachok, M., Baker, T. L., Sheya, A., & Hughes, R. L. (2014). Parsing disciplinary disproportionality: Contributions of infraction, student, and school characteristics to out-of-school suspension and expulsion. *American Educational Research Journal, 51,* 640–670.

Skiba, R. J., Simmons, A. B., Ritter, S., Gibb, A. C., Rausch, M. K., Cuadrado, J., & Chung, C. G. (2008). Achieving equity in special education: History, status, and current challenges. *Exceptional Children, 74*(3), 264–288.

Smith, N., & Weatherburn, S. (2012). Youth justice conferences versus children's court: A comparison of re-offending. Contemporary Issues in Crime and Justice, *160,* 1–23.

Steenbergen, M. R., & Jones, B. S. (2002). Modeling multilevel data structures. *American Journal of Political Science, 46,* 218–237.

Steinberg, M. P., Allensworth, E., & Johnson, D. W. (2014). What conditions support safety in urban schools? The influence of school organizational practices on student and teacher reports of safety in Chicago. In D. J. Losen (Ed.), *Closing the school discipline gap: Equitable remedies for excessive exclusion* (pp. 118–131). New York, NY: Teachers College Press.

Stinchcomb, J. B., Bazemore, G., & Riestenberg, N. (2006). Beyond zero tolerance: Restorative justice in secondary schools. *Youth Violence and Juvenile Justice, 4*, 123–147.

Strang, H., Sherman, L., Mayo-Wilson, E., Woods, D., & Ariel, B. (2013). Restorative justice conferencing (RJC) using face-to-face meetings of offenders and victims: Effects on offender recidivism and victim satisfaction. A systematic review. *Campbell Systematic Reviews, 9*(12). Available at http://www.campbellcollabor ation.org/lib/download/3066/

Teachers Unite. (2014). *Growing fairness toolkit.* Available at http://www.teachersu nite.net/toolkits

Tobin, T. J., & Sugai, G. M. (1999). Using sixth-grade school records to predict school violence, chronic discipline problems, and high school outcomes. *Journal of Emotional and Behavioral Disorders, 7*, 40–53.

U.S. Department of Education. (2014). *Guiding principles: A resource guide for improving school climate and discipline,* Washington, DC: Author.

Wachtel, T., Costello, B., & Wachtel, J. (2009). *The restorative practices handbook for teachers, disciplinarians and administrators.* Bethlehem, PA: International Institute of Restorative Practices.

Wachtel, T., O'Connell, T., & Wachtel, J. (2010). *Restorative justice conferencing: Real justice and the conferencing handbook.* Bethlehem, PA: International Institute for Restorative Practices.

Weinstein, R. S. (2002). *Reaching higher: The power of expectations in schooling.* Cambridge, MA: Harvard University Press.

Wong, D. S., & Mok, L. W. (2011). Restorative justice and practices in China. *Journal of Community Justice, 8*, 23–35.

Zehr, H. (2002). *The little book of restorative justice.* Intercourse, PA: Good Books.

Zehr, H., & Toews, B. (2004). *Critical issues in restorative justice.* Monsey, NY: Criminal Justice Press.

Manuscript received November 23, 2014
Final revision received September 25, 2016
Accepted September 26, 2016

American Educational Research Journal
December 2016, Vol. 53, No. 6, pp. 1698–1731
DOI: 10.3102/0002831216675403
© *2016 AERA. http://aerj.aera.net*

Joint Inquiry: Teachers' Collective Learning About the Common Core in High-Poverty Urban Schools

Elizabeth Leisy Stosich
Stanford Center for Opportunity Policy in Education

Recent research on the relationship between standards and teachers' practice suggests that teachers are unlikely to make changes to practice without extensive opportunities for learning about standards with colleagues. This article extends this line of research, using a comparative case study of three high-poverty urban schools to examine the nature of teachers' collaborative work around the Common Core State Standards and the conditions that support this work. It argues that collaborative practices that encourage joint examination of instruction and student learning against standards support teachers in noticing and attending to differences between their current practice and standards. In addition, it examines the role of teachers' instructional knowledge and principals' leadership in supporting teachers' collaboration around standards.

KEYWORDS: accountability policy, inquiry, professional learning, standards, teacher collaboration

The Common Core State Standards (CCSS) were designed to set ambitious expectations for what students should know and be able to do in grades K–12. Beginning in the 1980s, the standards movement sought to foster excellence and equity in student learning outcomes by institutionalizing high expectations for all students while allowing teachers to have professional discretion in deciding how to support students in meeting these goals (Payne, 2008). As explained in the introduction to the CCSS,

ELIZABETH LEISY STOSICH is a research and policy fellow at the Stanford Center for Opportunity Policy in Education (SCOPE), 505 Lasuen Mall, Stanford, CA 94305, USA; e-mail: *stosich@stanford.edu*. Her research focuses on the challenge of growing the capacity of educators and organizations to productively respond to policies and programs designed to improve equity and excellence in educational opportunities. She applies sociological, organizational, and sociocultural learning theories to understand the role of leadership, learning, and collaboration in systems change.

> By emphasizing required achievements, the Standards leave room for teachers, curriculum developers, and states to determine how those goals should be reached. . . . Teachers are thus free to provide students with whatever tools and knowledge their professional judgment and experience identify as most helpful for meeting the goals set out in the Standards. (Common Core State Standards Initiative, 2010, p. 4)

Helping students meet these standards presents a major challenge for teachers since they ask students and consequently teachers to learn to work in new and challenging ways.

Research suggests that previous standards failed to produce widespread improvements in teaching and learning because teachers had few opportunities to fully understand the ideas behind standards and their implications for practice (Cohen & Ball, 1999; Cohen & Hill, 2001; Spillane, 2004). Decades of educational reform reveal that policies calling for ambitious change on the part of teachers have frequently been paired with limited support for learning (Cohen & Barnes, 1993; Elmore, 2004). One explanation is that deep divisions in American politics led policymakers to adopt vague policy goals and learning supports. Although still politically divisive, standards have gained broad support by institutionalizing high expectations for all students without dictating the methods that would be used to meet standards (Rothman, 2011). Notably, urban districts have struggled to respond to standards-based accountability policies (Payne, 2008), and the ineffective implementation of standards in urban districts threatens the potential for common standards to enhance educational equity.

I conducted a comparative case study of 26 teachers in three high-poverty schools in a large urban district in the Northeastern United States. Educators in these schools were some of the first in the country to begin teaching to the CCSS; thus, learning from their experience presents a timely opportunity as teachers across the country seek to respond to these new standards. My goal was to understand in some detail the collaborative practices and school conditions that support teachers in learning how to support students in meeting the CCSS. Despite a long history of teacher isolation (Lortie, 1975), opportunities for teacher collaboration have become prevalent in schools since the introduction of standards-based accountability policies (Earl & Timperley, 2009; Wei, Darling-Hammond, & Adamson, 2010).

My findings suggest that collaborative practices that encourage joint examination of instruction and student learning support teachers in noticing and attending to differences between their current practice and standards. All teachers in the study worked with colleagues to plan instruction, select resources, and use data on student learning; however, the degree to which this collaboration supported teachers in understanding the gap between current practice and the expectations of the CCSS varied greatly across and within schools. I examine the collaborative practices of teachers and the conditions that support these practices in three high-poverty schools: Bay, Park, and Sunnyside Elementary.[1]

Theoretical Framework: Policy Implementation as Teacher Learning

There is growing agreement among scholars that educational policy is better understood as a challenge of teacher learning than as a challenge of "implementation" since the success of any policy is largely determined by the individual and collective capacity of teachers to meet the policy's goals (Cobb & Jackson, 2012; Gallucci, 2003; Little, 1999; Spillane, Reiser, & Gomez, 2006). The policy logic behind the CCSS presumes that teachers will produce superior and more equitable student outcomes if expectations for student learning are clear at each grade level, build progressively toward career and college readiness, and all students are held to these same high expectations. However, many teachers may not know how to support students in reaching these standards or may not believe that their students are capable of meeting these expectations. Recent research suggests that teachers fail to align their instruction with standards because they misunderstand the underlying principles behind policy and their implications for practice (Spillane, 2004; Spillane, Reiser, & Reimer, 2002). This misunderstanding of policy is unsurprising. Meeting new standards requires teachers to comprehend the meaning of the standards themselves, the way their instruction would need to change to support students in meeting these standards, and ultimately, they must learn how to work in these new ways.

Opportunities for teacher learning are essential because the expectations outlined in the CCSS require students to engage in more critical thinking and less routine learning than previous state standards and thus represent a major shift for teachers' instructional practice. Porter, McMaken, Hwant, and Yang (2011) conducted a comparative analysis of the CCSS and state standards, assessments, and teachers' reports of their instructional practice from 31 states, including the state in which these three schools were situated. Their findings revealed that the CCSS placed more emphasis on cognitively demanding processes than previous state standards and assessments. For example, a higher proportion of the CCSS required students to "demonstrate understanding" in mathematics and "analyze" in English language arts and reading (ELAR) than prior state standards. Teachers may lack the knowledge and skills needed to engage in more complex practices. Researchers find that teachers' practice is weakest in areas that involve more complex tasks, such as problem solving and asking high-level questions (Kane & Staiger, 2012; Sartain, Stoelinga, & Brown, 2011). Thus, teachers will need not only to adjust to the higher level of cognitive demand of the standards but also learn how to effectively lead high-level instruction.

Framing the standards as a challenge of teacher learning runs counter to recent federal "turnaround" efforts. So-called turnaround policies call for firing and replacing principals and teachers in low performing schools. This approach is based on questionable evidence, disproportionately affects low-income communities of color (Trujillo & Reneé, 2012), and alienates the very people who must solve the challenge of improving student performance. Supporting students, particularly children living in poverty, in meeting the demands of the CCSS requires much more than hiring new personnel. It requires changing the way teachers think about instruction and how they carry out their work with students each day.

Making Sense of Standards, Transforming Practice

Scholars have applied a cognitive framework to understand how teachers engage in "learning," "interpretation," or "sensemaking" about policy (Coburn, 2005; Spillane et al., 2002). This line of research reveals that teachers' understanding of and actions related to policy are influenced by their prior knowledge, beliefs about instruction and students' abilities, social interactions, and connections with messages about policy (Coburn, 2004, 2005; Cohen & Ball, 1999; Spillane et al., 2006; Stosich, 2016; Weick, 1995). Standards and the curriculum, assessments, and professional development (PD) that are designed to align with these standards communicate information about what teaching to these standards would look like in practice. Cohen and Hill (2001) surveyed teachers about their experiences with new mathematics standards in California. The teachers they surveyed were more likely to report implementing standards-aligned practices, and students achieved at higher levels in schools that provided substantial opportunities for teachers to learn about standards-aligned curriculum and assessments. However, only a small proportion of schools—about 10%—fostered these intensive and practice-based opportunities for learning. Further research is needed to identify the specific learning experiences that support teachers in revising their instructional practice in ways that lead to improvements in teaching and learning.

Research that examines the experience of individual teachers with educational policies suggests that teachers are likely to ignore, misunderstand, or only superficially adopt policies that depart from their current practice (Coburn, 2004; Spillane, 2004). Teachers make sense of policies through the lens of their existing knowledge and beliefs, "supplementing" rather than "supplanting" existing knowledge and practice (Cohen & Weiss, 1993, p. 227). In fact, teachers may layer new practices on top of existing practices in ways that do not fully address the goals of policy or that conflict with policy principles (Coburn, 2004; Spillane, 2004), which Cuban (1984) calls "conservative progressivism." For example, Cohen (1990) described a teacher who adopted new topics but taught them using a traditional pedagogical approach, which failed to encourage the deep conceptual understanding that the mathematics policy was designed to foster.

The process of learning to teach to standards is challenging because it requires "developing new understandings of familiar ideas such as problem solving" (Spillane, 2004, p. 157). Teachers must forsake previous practices and beliefs and develop alternative ones to meet the goals set by new standards (Strike & Posner, 1992). Teachers who accept the logic behind new and higher standards risk harming their self-concept (Spillane et al., 2002) because these standards imply that current practice is inadequate for reaching expectations for student learning (Cohen, Moffitt, & Goldin, 2007). Instead, teachers may attribute the challenge of meeting reform goals to their students' characteristics, including students' abilities, socioeconomic status, or English learner status, rather than their own instructional practice (Anagnostopoulos & Rutledge, 2007; Coburn, 2005; Gallucci, 2003). Moreover, teachers often view new policies as similar to their existing practice (Cohen, 1990; Hill, 2001; Spillane & Callahan, 2000; Spillane et al., 2006). Viewing reforms as familiar can lead to misinterpretation and rejection of information that conflicts with current beliefs about instruction or students' abilities and consequently make restructuring knowledge and practice all the more difficult. This presents a paradox: Teachers are both the targets of policy and the ones tasked with determining how to meet policy goals.

Intensive and ongoing collaboration with colleagues around standards may be essential for translating abstract standards into explicit changes in instructional practice (Coburn, 2001, 2008; Cohen & Hill, 2001). Spillane (2004) found that teachers whose practice most closely aligned with ambitious mathematics standards all described learning about standards as a social endeavor. The teachers he studied engaged in ongoing collegial deliberation about standards, such as conversations about standards-based curriculum and ideas from PD. However, this collective sensemaking process does not guarantee that teachers will adopt practices that align with policy goals. In fact, teachers who collaborate with colleagues who hold beliefs and practices that conflict with policy goals may be more likely to reject policy than teachers who work in isolation (Gallucci, 2003). Coburn (2001) found that teachers in a school serving mostly poor and minority students dismissed policy messages about reading that they viewed as too difficult for their students when working with colleagues. Thus, collaboration among colleagues has the potential to reinforce teachers' deficit views of students.

Nonetheless, Spillane (1999) argues that teachers are unlikely to "notice opportunities for learning, or stimuli for change in their environment" when working in isolation (p. 169). To date, however, scholars have not closely examined the collaborative practices that support teachers in learning how to teach to new standards. Little (1990) argues that interactions among teachers exist along a continuum from complete independence to interdependence. Teachers' practice becomes public and differences in beliefs and practices are more likely to surface when teachers work interdependently with colleagues, what Little describes as "joint work." However, widespread norms of autonomy and privacy among teachers (Donaldson et al., 2008; Lortie, 1975; Stosich, 2016) make engaging in interdependent work challenging. Instead, teachers are likely to engage in "sharing" when they collaborate (Little, 1990), openly exchanging information and materials while maintaining individual autonomy over instructional decisions.

Coburn and Stein (2006) describe "policy implementation as a process of learning that involves gradual transformation of practice via the ongoing negotiation of meaning among teachers" (p. 26). Working with colleagues to select instructional approaches and materials, try them out, and reflect on their effectiveness in supporting students to meet standards may be an important part of identifying and beginning to bridge the gap between policy and practice. Correspondingly, research on teachers' professional learning suggests that engaging in sustained inquiry with colleagues encourages teachers to question underlying assumptions and current practices (Earl & Timperley, 2009; Gallimore, Ermeling, Saunders, & Goldenberg, 2009). This line of research has generally explored whether using particular protocols for investigating instruction with colleagues leads to improvement in teaching and learning over time. However, requiring teachers to use particular inquiry protocols can result in what Hargreaves (1994) calls "contrived collegiality," which does not lead to any meaningful change in practice. I explore teachers' collaborative practices more broadly to understand the specific processes and conditions that support teachers in learning about standards and how to support all students in meeting these expectations. Specifically, I seek to answer the following questions:

Research Question 1: How do teachers come to understand the CCSS?
Research Question 2: How do teachers enact practices related to the CCSS?
Research Question 3: How, if at all, does teachers' collaboration with colleagues relate to the way teachers say that they come to understand and enact practices related to the CCSS?

Research Design and Methods

I conducted a comparative case study of three schools, using a nested design in which I consider individual teachers' responses within their school context. I examined teachers' work with standards using direct observation as well as ex situ accounts in interviews, assuming that teachers actively make sense of messages about the CCSS in the context of their school environment and in collaboration with colleagues. Although their experiences are not generalizable, close examination of teachers' experiences has the potential to contribute to theory about how teachers learn about standards (Yin, 2009).

Context of the Study

At the time of the study (January–December 2013), teachers in all three schools had been teaching to the CCSS for three years. The district in which these schools were situated adopted the CCSS in 2010, required teachers to begin integrating the CCSS in their instruction in fall 2011, administered the first CCSS-aligned assessments in spring 2013, and adopted CCSS-aligned curriculum in fall 2013. The district's instructional expectations stated that collaboration in teacher teams was a central process for teachers to learn about the new standards. On these teams, they would: (1) analyze student work to adjust teaching practice and instructional planning, (2) plan CCSS-aligned curricular units, (3) plan for changes in instruction based on the CCSS, and (4) adjust lessons, units, and classroom assessments to address the gap between what the new standards required and what their students knew and were able to do.

In addition, the district formed the Common Core Innovation Network (CCIN), a network of 35 schools that volunteered to be early adopters of the CCSS and receive additional support in teaching to the new standards. The CCIN was led by central office administrators who worked with teachers from each school to develop shared expectations for instruction and student performance through discussions of student work and collaborative development of curriculum units aligned with the CCSS. The work of the CCIN reinforced and extended the district's focus on professional learning in teacher teams. The district had supported teacher teams in engaging in collaborative inquiry for the five years prior to the beginning of the study. The inquiry team process called for teachers to work with colleagues to analyze student and teacher work, identify a learning challenge, select a research-based instructional approach to address this challenge, implement the approach, and evaluate its success.

Sample

I used purposive sampling (Seidman, 2006) to select schools with a history of success in supporting student achievement, comparable student populations, and membership in the CCIN. Three of the four schools that met these criteria chose to participate. All three schools performed the same or higher, on average, on previous state assessments than schools in the district with similar student populations; thus, they may have been more likely to meet the goals of the CCSS than schools that had made little progress in meeting prior state standards. Nevertheless, meeting the high expectations set by the CCSS presented a major challenge for teachers in these schools since about half of students in each school failed to meet previous state standards in mathematics and ELAR, as measured by the state assessment (see Table 1). More than 95% of students at each school were Black or Latino, and more than 80% of students received free or reduced-price lunch;

Table 1
School Demographics and Performance Profiles

Student Demographics and Performance	Bay	Park	Sunnyside
Total students	244	521	226
% Free and reduced price lunch	86	81	95
% Limited English proficient	12	6	4
% Special education	23	20	14
% African American	57	80	85
% Hispanic	39	16	14
% Asian	2	1	0
% White	2	1	1
% Proficient ELAR 2012	31.4	47.1	32.8
% Proficient math 2012	53.7	57.1	56.6
% Proficient ELAR 2013 (CCSS)	11.5	18.3	13.9
% Proficient math 2013 (CCSS)	14.8	24.1	12.9

Note. ELAR = English language arts and reading; CCSS = Common Core State Standards.
Source. State Education Data 2012–2013.

thus, all three schools were considered high-poverty schools where at least 75% of students were low-income (Aud et al., 2010). Growing gaps in achievement and college attainment between low-income and high-income students (Bailey & Dynarski, 2011; Reardon, 2011) make the need for understanding how educational policies can support high achievement among low-income students all the more pressing.

To better understand teachers' opportunities for learning about standards, including opportunities for learning in grade-level teams, I invited principals and teachers in Grades 3, 4, and 5 to participate in the study. These teachers faced pressure from state testing to meet the new standards, taught similar content, and met regularly in grade-level teams. Study participants included regular and special education teachers who worked in self-contained classes as well as special education teachers who co-taught with regular education teachers Most (81%) teachers who were invited chose to participate in the study. However, the purposive sampling of teachers and schools precludes me from generalizing about all teachers in any one school, the district, or elementary educators more broadly.

Notably, almost all teachers who participated in the study were highly experienced, most teachers were people of color, and all principals were people of color who had been in their position 10 or more years. Teachers participating in the study had from 2 to more than 25 years of teaching experience; half had more than 15 years of experience, and most had taught at the same school for more than 10 years. Thus, this study examines how experienced teachers working in stable organizations respond to new and higher standards for students' learning.

Table 2
Data Collection

Data Source	Participants	Interviews	Observations
Bay Elementary			
Principals	1	2	2 faculty meetings
Teachers	7	10	2 team meetings
			5 classroom observations
Park Elementary			
Principals	1	3	1 faculty meeting
Teachers	12	20	3 team meetings
			7 classroom observations
Sunnyside Elementary			
Principals	2[a]	3[a]	0 faculty meeting
Teachers	7	6	2 team meetings
			5 classroom observations
Common Core Innovation Network			5 PD observations

[a]Includes assistant principal.

Data Collection and Analysis

Teacher interviews and observations were the primary focus of data collection. In total, 26 teachers, 3 principals, and 1 assistant principal participated in the study (see Table 2). I conducted 36 teacher interviews, 8 principal interviews, 17 classroom observations, 10 teacher meeting observations, and 5 PD observations. I interviewed third-, fourth-, and fifth-grade teachers in each school using a semi-structured interview protocol (Seidman, 2006) to examine how they learned about and enacted practices related to the CCSS. Specifically, I asked teachers about how they made instructional decisions and how the CCSS, students, resources, colleagues, administrators, and opportunities for learning influenced their instructional practice. In addition, I interviewed principals to learn how they influenced teachers' opportunities to learn about new standards, including how they provided instructional feedback, selected resources, organized opportunities for learning and collaboration, or connected teachers with external support.

Research suggests that opportunities for learning about policy include both formal structures for collaboration, such as team meetings and PD, and informal conversations with colleagues (Spillane, 2004). Therefore, I spent five days in each school observing formal and informal opportunities for teacher collaboration and professional learning. I also observed five half- or full-day PD opportunities hosted by the CCIN. Additionally, I observed participating teachers' instruction to better understand how the practices they reported employing related to the CCSS. I supplemented interviews and observations with the collection and review of documents related to standards, professional learning opportunities, and instruction, including but not limited to instructional plans, students' work, protocols, and meeting agendas. Most interviews were audio recorded and transcribed verbatim, detailed field notes were taken during observations, and major themes were captured in interpretive memos.

I engaged in data collection and analysis concurrently (Miles & Huberman, 1994). During initial readings of transcripts, field notes, and interpretive memos, I used Dedoose qualitative data analysis software to code the data for teachers' opportunities to learn about standards, including learning about standards-based curriculum and assessments, formal PD, collaborative team processes, and principals' support for teachers' collaboration. As part of this, I included codes for the specific collaborative practices that district policy and the CCIN encouraged teachers to carry out, including developing curricular units, using curricular units and tasks provided by the district, and using inquiry team protocols.

Additionally, I used weighted codes from 1 (*not at all*) to 4 (*completely*) to analyze the level of described and observed alignment of practice with the changes in practice recommended by the district for meeting the CCSS. The district communicated the increased level of cognitive demand emphasized in the CCSS through policy documents that highlighted the following instructional changes in ELAR and math: balancing informational and literary texts, reading and writing grounded in text evidence, building academic vocabulary, fluency with calculations, deep focus on conceptual understanding, and application of mathematical concepts to "real-world" situations. I used these descriptions to code teachers' self-reported and observed practice. For example, during an ELAR lesson observed at Park, the teacher asked students to use evidence from a literary text to support their arguments and then accepted a student's response that was based on general information about the plot. Thus, the teacher's question was rated as completely aligned to the CCSS (4) because it called for reading grounded in text evidence. However, the student's response was rated as somewhat aligned (3) with the CCSS because it was based on the text but not specific evidence. I calculated an average CCSS-alignment score for each lesson observed based on all lesson segments (e.g., teacher question, teacher description of assignment, student response) coded.

I analyzed cross-case patterns, looking for themes, comparisons, and variation in how teachers reported learning about the CCSS and how their learning related to their collaboration with colleagues (Miles & Huberman, 1994; Yin, 2009). For example, I created graphs to visualize how variation in teachers' opportunities for learning about standards related to the observed alignment of teachers' practice with the CCSS. I then used matrices to develop codes inductively, examining how teachers described their collaborative practices and how this collaboration related to teachers' practice (Miles & Huberman, 1994). I engaged in an iterative coding process, revisiting data, emergent themes, and my initial hypothesis about the relationship between collaborative practices and teacher understanding and enactment of the CCSS.

I sought to reduce the risk of systematic bias and enhance the validity of my findings by drawing on multiple data sources and collection methods (Maxwell, 2012) to understand how teachers came to understand and enact the CCSS. I collected data from teachers and principals to analyze teachers' experiences with the CCSS and the context in which they occur from multiple perspectives. I used multiple data collection methods, including interviews, observations, and document analysis, to understand teachers' experiences. While coding, developing matrices, and writing memos, I remained attuned to disconfirming evidence and evaluated my findings against rival explanations (Yin, 2009). Finally, I conducted a member check (Merriam, 1995) by sharing initial findings with participants to allow for input and further verify the accuracy of my interpretations.

Findings

As teachers made sense of the CCSS, they turned to their colleagues for resources, expertise, and partnership in inquiry. All three schools included in this study had basic structures and processes in place to support the work of teacher teams, including a weekly meeting time, a team leader on every grade-level team, student assessment data available to inform instruction, and training in inquiry practices. On the surface, teachers all engaged in similar collaborative work. They planned curricular units, shared resources and ideas, and used assessments to monitor student learning. However, their collaborative practices appeared to differ in the extent to which they encouraged the interdependent decision making described by Little (1990) as "joint work" or more superficial forms of information and resource "sharing" that allowed teachers to retain individual authority for making instructional decisions. Figure 1 illustrates the specific collaborative practices teachers engaged in at each school and how these practices varied in the degree to which they encouraged more independent or interdependent instructional decision making among teachers. I find that teachers who worked more interdependently, all Bay teachers and four fourth-grade teachers at Park, were observed enacting practices that were more aligned with the CCSS shifts, on average, than teachers who worked more independently, including all Sunnyside teachers and most Park teachers (see Table 3). In the sections that follow, I analyze these distinct approaches to collaboration to better understand the nature of teachers' collaboration and its implications for their learning about and enactment of policy. I describe the collaborative practices and school conditions that supported or constrained teachers' learning about standards in each school.

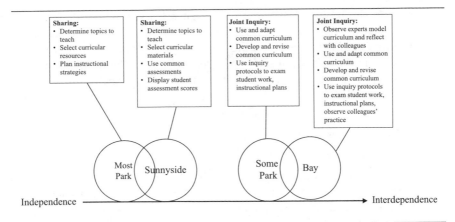

Figure 1. **Continuum of collaborative practices. Adapted from "The Persistence of Privacy: Autonomy and Initiative in Teachers' Professional Relations," by J. W. Little, 1990, *Teachers College Record*, 91(4), 512.**

Table 3
**Average Alignment of Teachers' Instructional Practice
With Common Core State Standards**

| | Grade Level | | | |
School	Third	Fourth	Fifth	Schoolwide
Bay	3.3	2.6	2.5	2.9
Park	1.3	2.4	1.6	1.8
Sunnyside	1.6	1.7	1.4	1.6

Note. 1 = not at all aligned, 2 = slightly aligned, 3 = somewhat aligned, 4 = completely aligned.

Joint Inquiry

All teachers at Bay Elementary and four fourth-grade teachers at Park Elementary engaged in what I call *joint inquiry*, working with colleagues to investigate their instruction and students' work and determine the changes they would need to make to support students in meeting standards. These collegial interactions combined the collective action described by Little (1990) as "joint work" with an orientation toward improving instructional practice. Specifically, engaging in joint inquiry included analyzing curriculum with support from experts and colleagues, developing or revising curriculum to meet the new standards, and using inquiry protocols. Teachers at Bay Elementary and the small group of teachers at Park Elementary described viewing the new standards as similar to their current practice initially; however, they reported that engaging with colleagues in close analysis of curriculum, instruction, and student work led them to view the new standards as requiring, as one said, "a really different way of teaching." In the following sections, I describe the collaborative practices that involved joint inquiry and how they influenced teachers' instructional beliefs and practices.

Using Standards-Based Curriculum With Support From Colleagues and Experts

The teachers at Bay and the fourth-grade teachers at Park described ana-lyzing and experimenting with curricular materials as experiences that changed their instruction and in many cases their fundamental beliefs about what they and their students could do. Five of the seven Bay teachers inter-viewed reported that having models—model curricular units, student work based on these curricular materials, and observing experts demonstrate the use of curricular materials—helped them understand the changes they needed to make in their practice to meet the CCSS. In fact, two teachers described the opportunity to observe models of standards-based practice with colleagues as their most meaningful opportunity for learning about the CCSS. A fifth-grade teacher said that when curricular units were "explained and student work was shown," she and her colleagues "had an idea of what the standard would be." Similarly, a fourth-grade teacher described observing an expert use the new math curriculum with students as "extremely beneficial" because he had not been using the curriculum very effectively initially. This teacher said that he had witnessed improve-ment in his students' performance as a result of this learning experience. I observed him ask students to explain and justify their approach to solving multistep problems and assign questions in the newly adopted math text-book that reflected the balance of procedural fluency and conceptual under-standing called for in the CCSS.

The Bay principal supported teachers in learning from standards-based curriculum by bringing in leaders from the CCIN to demonstrate how to use these curricular materials with students. A teacher explained that she and her grade-level colleagues had looked at the new mathematics standards and thought they were "doing it right." However, seeing an expert demonstrate how to use the new standards-based curricular materials made her realize that she and her colleagues had to "totally revamp" the way they planned instruction.

> Instead of . . . just trying to impose all your knowledge, you have to really question [students] and get them thinking. . . . You have to be trained and you have to reflect on yourself as a teacher. "What do I do that's maybe not so conducive to Common Core?" I think a lot of us, when we sat back and reflected, realized that we had it all

> wrong. . . . When you saw how really deep the questions were, then you realized you have to really start planning the questioning into your lesson plan rather than just going with the flow. . . . In this community . . . you just want to do the GPSing—guide them all the way—but you have to step back and give [students] a chance to be independent and be accountable for their thinking.

Notably, the experience of observing an expert demonstrate how to use the standards-based curriculum with students supported this teacher in changing the way she thought about instructional planning, the kinds of questions she asked, and the role of students in learning. Specifically, this teacher shifted from viewing students as the recipients of knowledge to viewing students as independent thinkers. According to Bay teachers, opportunities for learning from models of instruction, curriculum, and student work were especially helpful for learning about the CCSS when paired with opportunities to reflect on how these models related to their current practice with colleagues.

At Park Elementary, four fourth-grade teachers reported that witnessing the success of their students in doing work that they had not thought possible changed their beliefs about what they and their students could do. These four teachers described working together to teach a standards-based curricular unit on child labor, which they all viewed as too difficult for their students initially. Nonetheless, they agreed to try it and then worked together to adapt it to meet their students' needs. A special education teacher on the team described how the experience changed her beliefs:

> We did a [curriculum unit] last year on child labor that was based on the Common Core. . . . The students had to look at political cartoons. They had to read articles. My first thought was, "This is way too hard for my students." But [our grade-level team] spent months on it. We just picked apart every article. . . . We used graphic organizers. Then [my students] were able to meet those Common Core Standards of writing opinion pieces using evidence from the articles. I was very shocked at how well my students did. I feel like the Common Core holds you to these high standards and these high expectations. You'd be surprised what you can do and what your students can do if you stick to these standards.

This example illustrates the intense collaborative work—months determining how to support students in comprehending specific texts—that went into learning how to support all students in meeting the ambitious new standards. This process assisted teachers in enacting practices related to two core elements of the CCSS: reading complex texts and using text evidence.

One Park teacher said that working with her colleagues made them less "fearful" of experimenting with new standards-based curricular materials. When teachers view messages about reform as being too difficult for their students, they are likely to reject or ignore these messages (Coburn, 2001).

Team norms of experimentation and mutual responsibility appeared to support these teachers in trying out and persisting with standards-based curricular units, even when they initially viewed them as "too difficult" or "too much" for their students. Their collective commitment to experimentation was particularly important since using these new materials was a choice made by the individual teachers in this grade level rather than a systematic practice at the school.

Developing and Revising Standards-Based Curriculum

Teachers at Bay and most fourth-grade teachers at Park used standards-based curricular materials to learn how to meet standards, but they also worked with colleagues to revise these materials or develop new materials to more effectively support students in meeting standards. The Bay principal regularly asked teacher teams to revisit and revise their curricular plans. Correspondingly, teachers called their curricular plans "living documents" and described the process of revising unit plans as one of integrating new learning from experience, PD, inquiry team work, as well as student needs into their shared plans. For example, one grade-level team used Webb's (2007) Depth of Knowledge framework to evaluate whether their curricular plans included the high-level questions necessary for students to do the kind of thinking called for by the standards. Much like the Bay teachers' joint observation of an expert's model lesson, using Webb's framework provided a shared framework for evaluating the rigor of their curricular plans in an effort to more closely align their plans with new and higher standards.

The results of shared decision making in teacher teams were evident in classrooms at Bay. For example, three third-grade teachers decided to use informational videos to model how to draw conclusions from evidence and use this evidence in informational essays to prepare students for drawing conclusions from complex texts, a focus of the new standards. I observed all three teachers using this instructional approach in their classrooms. Similarly, three fifth-grade teachers described working together to design a social studies unit that required students to use evidence from videos and text in their informational essays. During classroom observations, all three fifth-grade teachers asked questions and assigned tasks that required students to interpret evidence from videos and develop written arguments based on this evidence. A fifth-grade teacher described the team's instructional planning process: "One teacher is not allowed to do it. . . . Everything is collaborative to meet the needs of students." This process reflected the sense of mutual accountability (Katzenbach & Smith, 1993), or shared responsibility, for the work of the team described by all teachers at Bay.

Fourth-grade teachers at Park credited the experience of using standards-based curricular materials for helping them learn how to develop and adapt curriculum to support their students in meeting the new standards. A teacher on the team explained, "Learning how to scaffold, learning how to break things down and ask these questions of the students as they're reading to get them to understand it, all of that came from the child labor unit." Through their collaborative analysis, adaptation, and development of curriculum, teachers were better able to understand the actions they could take to teach to standards. Unlike Bay, joint development and revision of curricular plans was not a regular practice at Park. In fact, the principal required each grade-level team to work together to develop and use one common CCSS-aligned curricular unit as part of their involvement in the CCIN.

Nevertheless, the fourth-grade teachers' learning from their experience with the child labor unit appeared to transfer to the development of additional shared curricular units and their instructional practice more broadly. For example, two teachers displayed student work from a recent unit the team had created on the pros and cons of homework. Students had read multiple articles on the topic and used evidence from the articles to support their views, a focus of the CCSS in ELAR. Similarly, a third teacher asked students to infer what a fictional character's actions revealed about his feelings and regularly prompted students to go back to the text to identify evidence to support their responses. All four teachers reported that they were committed to continuing to support students with the higher level learning called for by the new standards because they had witnessed the impact of their efforts in their students' daily work and on the state test. The fourth-grade students had outperformed, on average, the other grade levels in the school and schools in the district despite serving a higher proportion of students living in poverty than most other schools.

With the support of their shared commitment to their colleagues, these four Park teachers worked together to improve their instruction and students' learning by analyzing, developing, and adapting standards-based curricular materials. However, the changing focus at the school site and the principal's limited attention to team work seemed to make sustaining their work difficult. For example, the teachers continued to use some of the units they had developed the following school year, but they did not teach the unit on child labor despite the great influence this unit had on their understanding of the new standards. One reason for this was that the teachers were beginning to use new ELAR and math curricula adopted by the school and had received little or no training in how to use these materials. When the school adopted new curricula and stopped requiring teachers to plan curricular units, these teachers continued to use and develop new standards-based units because they viewed them as important for meeting the new standards; however, there was no longer dedicated time in faculty or team meetings for working on unit plans. Their experience suggests that teachers who engage in collaborative efforts to design and adapt standards-based curriculum in schools with weak supports for this work may find it difficult to sustain and build on their learning over time.

Engaging in Inquiry Protocols

When teachers at Bay and fourth-grade teachers at Park worked with colleagues to revise curriculum and instructional practices or respond to student needs, they often used inquiry protocols from the district or CCIN. Inquiry protocols encouraged teachers to ask questions about their goals for instruction and compare them with the goals of standards. Bay teachers asked, "What do we want them to get out of the curriculum?" and "How can we get them there?" For example, a Bay teacher said that the curriculum required students to write their own informational book, but she had found that her students were not prepared to meet the standards for writing informational essays after this experience. She shared her students' work with her colleagues in order to investigate what it would take to support students in meeting the writing standards as part of their inquiry team work.

> I brought my work to the [table]. We sat. We did an inquiry about—What are [students] doing? How much work do we need to really get to where we need to go? We actually evaluate each other's students. We just come with our students' [essays]. . . . We look at each other's work. And then we say, "This is what we need to work on, just getting the introduction." We might do another cycle of writing an essay. Then we come back the following week and we say, "We still need to work on it." Half way through, we realize—okay—we're not going to worry about the book. We're just going to try to [have students write] . . . maybe 2 or 3 more essays because that's where we really need to focus. That's what the students need.

Inquiry team protocols called for teachers to come together to examine student work, try out an instructional approach, and circle back to revise their approach based on their analysis of students' work. Inquiry team protocols focused teachers' attention on the specific actions they could take to support students in meeting standards. In this case, for example, they found that their students made more progress toward meeting writing standards when they had many opportunities to write informational essays with direct support on different aspects of writing (e.g., introductions) rather than writing an informational book, as called for in the curriculum. Teachers at Bay credited the inquiry team processes with supporting their understanding of how curricular materials could be used to best promote students' learning.

At Bay, teachers received direct support and feedback on how they used inquiry team protocols in their grade-level teams. During a third-grade team meeting, for instance, the grade-level leader shared the "warm" and "cool" feedback the team had received on their inquiry work from the administrators and teachers on the leadership team. All the teachers had their packets documenting their inquiry work, which included the team's focus question, their timeline for collecting student work and adjusting instruction, and the graded samples of student work they had collected to track students' progress. The team's focus question asked whether they had seen evidence of growth in essay structure in students' writing. The leadership team's feedback suggested that their focus question should probe into specific challenges that students faced in writing and how to address them. In response, the third-grade teachers discussed how to improve their focus question and, specifically, how to tailor it to address the needs of their English learners. This meeting highlighted the great attention given to the inquiry process at Bay.

All Bay teachers said that protocols for examining instruction and student learning, including inquiry team protocols, were helpful for learning how to teach to the new standards. Notably, only at Bay did teachers use inquiry protocols to observe their colleagues' practice, a practice that directly challenges norms of privacy and autonomy over instructional decisions. Two teachers described using a fishbowl protocol with support from an expert from the CCIN as a meaningful learning experience that occurred during faculty meetings. The fishbowl protocol required a teacher to set a goal for the lesson (e.g., ask high-level questions), present the lesson in front of colleagues, listen to warm and cool feedback from their colleagues on how well the lesson met the goal, and identify next steps for improving the lesson. One teacher described this experience:

> We had a fishbowl where we all just had to say something positive, and then we'd have to say something negative. So you have to hear it all. There were some tears, but we learned from it. That was the intention, for us to do better and to improve our craft. I think it helped. It really did.

Another teacher noted, "We don't want to be critical, but we want to be honest. . . . We're cautious in how we talk—professional—but we give constructive criticism." The design of the protocol was intended to create a safe space for giving improvement-oriented feedback to colleagues. As described in greater detail below, the use of this fishbowl protocol for observing colleagues was made possible by the strong relationships among the faculty and the principal, who created opportunities for learning from colleagues during whole-faculty meetings.

The fourth-grade teachers at Park used protocols from the district's inquiry team initiative and the CCIN to support them in analyzing whether their instructional plans and the work of their students met the expectations of the new standards. Unlike Bay, however, decisions about whether and how to use these protocols were made by individual teachers rather than a schoolwide expectation set by the principal. In fact, the fourth-grade teachers described inviting a leader from the CCIN to attend several of their grade-level meetings to share new protocols and support them in using these protocols. Protocols from the CCIN focused the teachers' attention on the gap between students' work and the expectations of the CCSS and the actions teachers could take to close this gap. For example, one protocol asked them to consider the following questions when reviewing students' work: (1) To what degree does the student's work present evidence of meeting the CCSS? (2) Does the task provide the opportunity for students to present evidence of meeting the CCSS? If not, what improvements need to be made? (3) What pedagogical strategies can a teacher (or teacher team) employ to address the gaps between current student performance and the performance required by the task/CCSS? Through systematic discussions of instructional plans and student work, teachers developed shared expectations for student performance and determined instructional practices for promoting student mastery of the new standards.

Although these teachers believed that meeting the CCSS presented a major challenge, the four Park teachers viewed the assistance of their colleagues as essential for responding to this challenge. For example, one teacher described using a protocol for analyzing student work in an effort to get ideas from her team about how to address a student's challenge with academic vocabulary.

> A case that we had last meeting, I had a student who was struggling with some vocabulary words. I pulled the Tuning Protocol where I spoke first and explained the situation. Then my colleagues were able to ask me clarifying questions about the student. . . . They were able to give me some feedback about what I should try out with the student to see how that would help whatever issues he was having. After I try those out, I come back to the team and say, "This worked, and that didn't work." Then we take notes on that, and they can make more suggestions. . . . You feel like you're not alone.

The protocol assisted her and her colleagues in analyzing the student's challenge with vocabulary, determining an instructional approach, and following up as a team to see if the approach was effective.

Sharing Information and Resources

In contrast to the interdependent work of teachers who engaged in joint inquiry, all teachers at Sunnyside Elementary and the eight other teachers interviewed at Park Elementary described engaging in what Little (1990) characterizes as "sharing." These teachers discussed instructional ideas and exchanged resources with colleagues in ways that made their practice public. Yet they still maintained professional norms of individual autonomy over instructional decisions (Lortie, 1975) and, in doing so, constrained the influence of their colleagues. These teachers viewed teaching to the CCSS primarily as a challenge of figuring out *what* to teach rather than *how* to teach, and their collaboration with colleagues reflected this focus. In fact, most teachers characterized the challenge of supporting students in meeting the new standards as one that could be met without substantially altering their existing beliefs or practice. In the words of one Park teacher, "It's really not that different from what we were already doing. It's just another name." Unlike teachers who engaged in joint inquiry, these teachers worked more superficially with colleagues to select topics to teach, resources to use, and instructional strategies to employ. I describe in the following the limited influence that these collaborative practices had on teachers' beliefs and practices.

Choosing Topics to Teach

For most teachers at Park and Sunnyside, instructional planning was viewed through the lens of existing practice and beliefs. To illustrate, four third-grade teachers at Park all described starting with a lesson they wanted to teach and then "plugging in" or "matching" the new standards to their lesson objectives. A teacher described their planning process:

> The Common Core, the way it's laid out—we know what to do, what topics we must cover for the entire school year. So we break down the topics according to months for the ten months. . . . It's not really how they teach. We can make our [own lesson] plans, and your teaching style may be different from mine when you get to your room. . . . It's what to teach. It's not how.

This description highlights how teachers maintained norms of autonomy by focusing on what to teach rather than how to teach. Teachers at Park all described their colleagues as being willing to share ideas and materials. This openness to sharing can encourage the open exchange of ideas but also maintains teachers' individual autonomy over instruction (Little, 1990).

Similarly, almost all Park teachers described working with colleagues to develop at least one curricular unit aligned to the new standards; however, their unit plans included little information about what would actually occur in each classroom. For example, the third-grade team's unit plan about mystery literature in ELAR included a list of the standards students would meet and broad objectives about making predictions and identifying the elements of a mystery. However, it lacked any description of the lessons teachers would carry out, the texts students would read, or the tasks students would complete. This unit plan revealed the limited effort put into creating unit plans by many teachers but also reflected the limited knowledge and experience of Park teachers with unit planning.

After participating in classroom observations at Park, one third-grade teacher noticed, "Even though teachers plan on grade, they don't normally teach what they are asked to teach." She viewed this as a problem because it led teachers to "blame" students for poor performance rather than teachers' instruction. For example, she and her colleagues agreed to work on opinion writing, but one of her colleagues did not follow through with their plans, and thus, the students in her colleague's class received little support in writing an opinion piece.

> We give that monthly writing piece where they were to do it by themselves, on-demand writing. I might look at my class—they've done well. I might look at another class—it's not done well. I'm blaming the students: "These students are not learning anything." I should be blaming the teacher. It doesn't give you a true reflection of what the students can or can't do because the students were not taught how to write that opinion piece.

The superficial nature of collaboration—focused on what topics to teach—seemed to foster little accountability to peers for following through with team decisions. Consequently, collaboration seemed to lead to little change in teachers' practice or beliefs about students.

At Sunnyside, teachers described working with colleagues to select topics to teach or "re-teach." Using student assessment data to make instructional decisions was a major focus at the school. Teachers described revisiting lessons, re-teaching skills, or spending more time on topics that they identified as challenging for students. Each of these approaches to using data with colleagues focused on matching lessons and topics to student scores rather than examining the underlying causes for students' performance. Nevertheless, re-teaching standards with which students struggled was challenging because students' scores were very low. In fact, most students scored 1 out of 4, the lowest possible score on the interim assessments designed to mirror the state's CCSS-aligned end-of-year assessments. Thus, teachers would need to re-teach nearly every topic if they were to simply re-teach topics that students failed to pass on the test.

Selecting Curricular Resources

Park teachers looked to newly adopted curriculum described as aligned to the CCSS, online resources (e.g., worksheets) labeled as *CCSS-aligned*, and questions that mirrored those in standards-based assessments as they planned instruction. Teachers said that they had little PD preparing them to use the new curricula, but they did not view this as a problem. As one teacher explained, "They just gave us the program. This is it. Just open it up. Read it on your own, and try to figure it out on your own. . . . It's pretty self-explanatory, I think."

Classroom observations, however, revealed that Park teachers often used the curriculum in ways that failed to meet the goal of these standards. These teachers broke down multiple-step problems for students, neglected to ask questions requiring students to explain their answers, divided text into small chunks, focused on lower-level recall questions about text, and asked questions that required information about students' personal experience rather than text evidence. At times, teachers appeared to ignore aspects of curriculum that conflicted with their existing beliefs about instruction. For example, one teacher said the CCSS-aligned math curriculum was "not really different" from her existing practice. However, she broke down complex problems into discrete steps during a classroom observation, reducing the challenge of the task. In addition, she failed to ask questions in the textbook that required students to explain their thinking, which was part of the focus on conceptual understanding in the CCSS.

Sunnyside teachers also described working with colleagues to decide what they would teach from their newly adopted CCSS-based curriculum, how long they would need to teach the material, and to select additional resources to supplement the curriculum. Two fourth-grade teachers described the CCSS-based curricular materials as "too much" for their students. These teachers decided to use the resources over a longer period of time than the curriculum suggested. On the other hand, these same teachers reported that the curriculum was not "enough" to prepare their students to meet the standards. These teachers were observed using supplemental workbooks purchased by the school, which seemed to focus on low-level recall and execution tasks. For example, they were observed asking students to identify and underline the narrator and examples of dialogue in a passage in the workbook. Decisions about what to teach were influenced by teachers' beliefs about their students' abilities and often focused on breaking down the CCSS-aligned curriculum that the school had adopted or using simpler materials, which failed to meet the more ambitious demands of the new standards.

All teachers at Sunnyside described using the CCSS-based ELAR and math curricula adopted by the school during instruction, but some teachers were more successful than others in using them to meet the more demanding goals set by standards. In contrast to Park, classroom observations at Sunnyside suggested that teachers in grade-level teams did follow through with decisions about what to teach; thus, they worked more interdependently than most Park teachers. Nevertheless, the way in which teachers used curricular materials differed in important ways. For example, three third grade-teachers were observed using the same lesson from the ELAR curriculum on using text evidence to determine a character's motivation. In one class, the two co-teachers planned to ask questions about character motivation and had written these questions on the board. However, they never asked them because their students struggled to simply recall what happened in the chapter they had read. In contrast to the two fourth-grade teachers described previously, these two teachers described their students as capable of engaging with the new and more challenging curriculum. However, they did not seem to know how to use the curriculum effectively given their students' current abilities.

In a different third-grade class at Sunnyside, the teacher asked students to quickly reread the chapter and then begin discussing the following prompts with others at their table: "Describe Doyle's traits, motivations, and feelings. What do these details reveal about his character?" As students discussed the character, the teacher walked around the room asking students to explain their ideas and prompting them to look back at the text. She asked, "Why is he angry?" Then she prompted students to look in the text where it described him as angry. With some support from their teacher, students in this class learned how to use text evidence to develop arguments about the character. The questions and text from the curriculum and the questioning of the teacher in this class reinforced the goal of using text evidence to support an argument, a central focus of the new standards in ELAR. Yet this teacher was the only one whom I observed engaging in practices that reflected the goals of the CCSS at Sunnyside. During classroom observations, all six other teachers asked questions or assigned tasks that required almost exclusively low-level recall of information, such as defining terms from the textbook, answering questions based on personal experience, or executing simple arithmetic procedures.

Planning Instructional Approaches

Similar to their use of curriculum, teachers at Park and Sunnyside applied instructional strategies intended to support students in meeting the new standards in ways that conformed to their existing beliefs about students' abilities. For example, three third-grade teachers at Park described learning about techniques for higher-level questioning and choosing complex texts and agreeing to use these approaches in their classrooms. However, these teachers all believed the approaches were inappropriate for students they all described as "low functioning." Instead, these teachers described matching students they viewed as less academically capable with lower level questions and texts. Thus, instructional approaches designed to increase the level of learning for all students were implemented in ways that contradicted policy goals.

As part of the school focus on using assessment to drive instruction, Sunnyside teachers at each grade level worked together to create and administer weekly assessments to monitor students' progress in meeting standards. However, the content of these assessments did not reflect the changes in student learning called for by the new standards. For example, a third-grade assessment included eight items, all but one of which required simple recall of information or using single-step procedures. The test included a spelling test, dictation, and two questions about a text to measure their performance in ELAR. Students were asked: How does Jessie feel about Evan? How do you know this? Students could use text evidence to support their answer to the second question, which was a focus in the CCSS; however, the question did not explicitly require students to use text evidence to justify their response.

Regularly scheduled grade-level meetings at Sunnyside had the potential to support teachers in developing a shared understanding of effective approaches for teaching to the new standards. However, observations of team meetings and interviews with teachers suggested that there was little discussion of instruction during these meetings. Although teachers, the data specialist, and administrators all described the work of grade-level teams as "inquiry team work," they did not seem to use inquiry protocols or other processes for structuring their work with student data. For example, one week the data specialist reported that the grade-level meetings focused on improving the performance of "target groups," students who scored in the bottom third of students in the school on the CCSS-aligned state test. During two grade-level team meetings that week, I observed the data specialist give teachers a list of students who scored in the bottom third and communicate the expectation that teachers were to improve their scores. When a teacher asked the data specialist to help him use the new online system to find examples of the problems his students got wrong on the test, the data specialist agreed to look into this. This interaction ended with a commitment from the data specialist to locate additional problems that were similar to the ones frequently missed by students but no discussion of why these problems might be difficult for students or how the concepts were taught.

At Sunnyside, teachers shared openly about the topics they would teach, the resources they would use, and the performance of their students on assessments. They shared this information by coming together to plan and posting their instructional plans and student assessment scores on bulletin boards inside and outside of their classrooms. Although their instructional plans and student outcomes were public, their specific instructional practices remained private. The privacy surrounding teachers' instructional approaches protected teachers' practice from scrutiny but also appeared to prevent the spread of effective approaches for teaching to the new standards among colleagues.

School Conditions

Overall, my findings suggest that three school conditions influenced the nature of teachers' collaboration around standards: the level of principal support for collaboration, the use of particular processes or protocols to structure collaboration, and relationships among colleagues. Notably, the conditions in each school varied greatly, and these differences appeared to influence whether all, some, or no teachers in each school described engaging in joint inquiry around standards.

Bay Elementary

At Bay, teachers described collaboration among colleagues as central to their learning about standards and described the principal as the "driving force" behind this emphasis on collaboration. As I describe in greater detail in Stosich (in press), the principal at Bay made inquiry work a priority by sitting in on inquiry team meetings, using team and whole-faculty meetings for teams to engage in the inquiry team process, providing feedback on each grade-level team's inquiry work during team leader meetings, and setting school goals focused on inquiry. The school goals, which were posted in classrooms and referenced by teachers, made clear that all teachers were expected to use the district's inquiry team process: "By June 2014, 100% of teachers will be involved in inquiry work around the Common Core in ELA and math." In addition, the principal brought in leaders from the CCIN to model how to use new CCSS-aligned curriculum and support teachers in engaging in collaborative protocols for developing curricular plans and critiquing their colleagues' instructional plans and practice.

At Bay, the use of protocols to structure difficult conversations and the collegial relationships among the staff supported teachers in speaking honestly about how to improve their practice. Two teachers said that they were able to give critical feedback on each other's practice because the faculty was a "family" of educators who were committed to getting better. Another teacher noted that they had "been working on the culture of [their] school for a long time." This teacher was the union chapter leader and a member of the school's social committee, which had been "trying to have the staff be more of a family" by organizing staff lunches, retirement parties, baby showers, and pulling together resources when there was a death in a family. She explained, "If we can all play together, we can all work together."

Importantly, the level of knowledge and skill of the faculty also contributed to teachers' collective learning about standards at Bay. As teachers analyzed curricular resources, revised instructional plans, solicited feedback from colleagues, and engaged in inquiry protocols, they relied significantly on the knowledge and skills of their colleagues to improve their instructional practice. All teachers at Bay described the feedback of their colleagues as an important and useful resource for learning to teach to the new standards. In schools with teachers with lower levels of instructional capacity, feedback from colleagues may be viewed as less valuable for improving instruction, which would limit the usefulness of joint inquiry.

Park Elementary

The principal at Park described his strategy for meeting the new standards as "forming teacher teams at every grade level and building . . . a community of learners. Inquiry process at every level." In contrast to Bay, however, the principal at Park was not directly involved in teachers' work in teams and, consequently, had little influence on how teachers worked together. According to the principal, one challenge for teacher collaboration was that meeting with colleagues more than once a month was "voluntary," according to the union's contract. However, he encouraged teachers·to meet weekly, and many did. In fact, the four fourth-grade teachers described meeting almost daily. To encourage other teachers to work closely with colleagues, the principal invited the fourth-grade teachers to share about how they collaborated around curriculum and students' work during faculty meetings.

The principal at Park held all teachers accountable for following through with district policies, including working in grade-level teams to develop a curricular unit that aligned with the CCSS and using standards-based curriculum in instruction. Accordingly, all teachers described developing at least one curricular unit aligned with the CCSS, and student work from these units was displayed on teachers' bulletin boards. Unlike Bay, however, developing curriculum was not a regular practice, and the principal had little influence on the processes teachers used during collaboration. A fourth-grade teacher explained that the "administrators were there to push" unit planning. Teachers would "do the work, but they were not really doing it as they should." According to this teacher, the superficial nature of some teachers' efforts to develop curriculum units limited the value of this collaborative process.

The strength of personal relationships among teachers varied greatly in the school, and this had direct implications for teachers' work with colleagues. Almost all teachers described their colleagues as "friendly" and willing to share resources or ideas. The four fourth-grade teachers, by contrast, described themselves as a "connected" and "close-knit group" that was committed to working together to improve their practice and students' learning. Interestingly, one fourth-grade teacher said that his negative personal relationships with colleagues left him working mostly in isolation. A teacher on the team said that they would "let him know" what they were teaching, but they did not plan curricular units or engage in inquiry work with this colleague. His colleagues may have excluded him from their joint work due to his low level of teaching skill. Although his colleagues did not describe him as incompetent, he was concerned about receiving an unsatisfactory performance rating from the principal. He explained,

> I'm not going to be able to write the lesson plan effective enough for what [the administrators] expect. I don't want them to give me a U rating. . . . We should be exposed to [information about new instructional approaches] from another colleague. I think it's unfair that I'm struggling. I have to run around asking [colleagues] instead of being told.

In contrast to Bay, decisions about how teachers worked together, with whom they worked, and whether they followed through with the decisions made by the team were left to the discretion of individual teachers, leaving some teachers to fend for themselves.

Sunnyside Elementary

Unlike Bay and Park, teachers and administrators at Sunnyside did not describe collaboration among colleagues as a central aspect of their strategy for meeting the expectations of the new standards. Although grade-level teams were scheduled to meet weekly, these meetings were often cancelled or ended early. Instead, the principal and assistant principal described the focus of the school as using data on students' performance to inform instruction. The principal held teachers accountable for using data to guide instruction by requiring teachers to administer weekly assessments, posting the results of these assessments in their classrooms, and grouping students based on their performance during instruction. In every classroom, teachers had data boards with student scores from assessments, including reading levels and scores from assessments in ELAR, math, social studies, and science. Every Friday, teachers assessed students and used their scores to change student groupings during instruction. The school even had one teacher who acted as a "data specialist" and facilitated all grade-level team meetings.

Notably, the principal and assistant principal both expressed uncertainty about whether the CCSS were "developmentally appropriate" for their students. According to the principal, the new standards required them to teach material that was too difficult for students: "Basically, we were told to expose children to material two grade levels above their level." Interviews with teachers and classroom observations suggested that most Sunnyside teachers viewed the new standards and the standards-based curricula as too difficult for their students. The school adopted challenging, new math and ELAR curricula from a list of choices approved by the district. In response to teachers' input, the school also purchased "practice" workbooks and test preparation materials. By purchasing these materials, the administrators endorsed their use in classrooms in addition to or in place of the more rigorous core curricula. In fact, the principal did not hold teachers accountable for closely following the new curricula and described these resources as providing "merely a suggestion" for how to teach to the new standards. Correspondingly, attention to how teachers could use the more rigorous curricular materials to support their students in meeting the CCSS was limited.

Despite the lack of principal support for collaboration, all teachers interviewed described working with their colleagues in their grade level and, in many cases, across grade-level teams to develop assessments, plan instruction, select curricular resources, or share best practices. As one teacher explained, "We are not in isolation. As a grade-level we share best practices, information. . . . Teachers learn from each other." The lack of close collaboration around standards at Sunnyside did not appear to be related to a lack of collegial relationships among teachers. Instead, the superficial level of collaboration among teachers seemed related to the absence of specific processes for supporting collaboration. For example, teachers and administrators described weekly grade-level team meetings as "inquiry team work," but they did not describe and were not observed using inquiry team protocols for structuring these meetings. Instead, discussion among colleagues seemed to have little structure and focused primarily on sharing information and resources.

Discussion

This study aims to explain how teachers come to understand new and more ambitious academic standards, how they enact these standards in their classrooms, and how their understanding and enactment of these standards is influenced by opportunities for collaboration with colleagues. Similar to previous research (e.g., Hill, 2001; Spillane et al., 2006), I find that teachers' initial reaction to the new standards was to view them as similar to current practice. However, I find that teachers were more likely to revise their instructional beliefs and practices in ways that reflected the goals of standards when their collaborative work was focused on designing, adapting, and improving specific instructional plans, curricular resources, and students' work rather than more superficial discussions of practice. These findings connect prior research on the collaborative practices that support changes in teachers' instructional practice and beliefs about students (e.g., Earl & Timperley, 2009; Gallimore et al., 2009) to the unique challenge of learning to teach to standards.

Most teachers in the study came to understand the new standards as similar to their current practice, and their collaborative practices failed to challenge these beliefs. All teachers at Sunnyside and most teachers at Park shared information with colleagues about the topics and resources they would use in instruction, leaving individual teachers to figure out how to integrate these ideas and resources in classroom practice. Consequently, these teachers adopted new practices and resources in ways that reinforced rather than contested their existing beliefs about what was appropriate for their low-income students. They were observed and described simplifying complex problems, assigning tasks that required merely recall of information, and matching low-level questions and texts to low performing students. Without working with colleagues to critically evaluate their practice against the expectations of standards, teachers may be more likely to enact practices that reinforce their beliefs about the abilities of their low-income students and are constrained by their existing pedagogical knowledge.

By contrast, all teachers at Bay and four fourth-grade teachers at Park approached their work together as joint inquiry, a shared investigation of what it would take to support students in meeting standards. This inquiry-oriented approach to collaboration seemed to support teachers in understanding the ways in which the new standards differed from their current practice and how to bridge the expectations of the new standards to the current abilities of their students. Specifically, these teachers analyzed standards-based curricular materials, developed and revised curricular units, and engaged in inquiry team protocols. All of these collaborative practices supported teachers in analyzing and adapting instruction to better meet the goals of the new standards and their students' needs. During classroom observations, these teachers carried out instruction aligned with the goals of the CCSS; they asked questions and assigned tasks that required students to use evidence from texts and videos to support their ideas orally and in writing, build procedural fluency in mathematics, and justify their mathematical reasoning.

Strong principal leadership, collegial relationships among teachers, the use of protocols for guiding their work, and the valued instructional knowledge and skills of their colleagues acted as enabling conditions for joint inquiry. Joint inquiry in teams is not something that can be mandated by principals because it requires a collective commitment to action among teachers. Nevertheless, principals can influence whether and how teams collaborate (Coburn, 2005; Stosich, in press). The principal at Bay provided explicit direction for how teachers were expected to collaborate, which focused on using specific protocols to engage in inquiry cycles to improve instructional plans and student performance. In contrast, neither the Park principal nor the Sunnyside principal provided direction for how teachers worked with colleagues. Without explicit attention to teachers' collaborative work from the principal, joint inquiry may occur in small pockets of volunteers but may be unlikely to become widespread.

Teachers at Bay and Park described detailed protocols for structuring their collaboration as essential for engaging in difficult conversations about the changes they would need to make to their instruction for all students to meet the new standards. By contrast, no teachers at Sunnyside described or were observed using protocols during collaboration. Notably, all teachers had been trained in using inquiry protocols by the district and CCIN, but only those teachers with strong relationships with colleagues and support from the principal or a leader in the CCIN used these protocols to make significant changes to their practice. Only at Bay did the faculty describe actively cultivating the relationships among teachers by celebrating and supporting important life events (e.g., weddings, family death) and carefully focusing opportunities for feedback from colleagues on constructive criticism (Bryk & Schneider, 2002).

Furthermore, teachers are unlikely to choose to collaborate with colleagues whom they view as unknowledgeable about instruction. For example, one fourth-grade teacher at Park described himself as "struggling" to teach to standards and said he was excluded from his team's collective work. Additionally, teachers may avoid collaborating with colleagues around academic content about which they are less knowledgeable. Although some teachers worked with colleagues to develop and adapt curricular units in ELAR, no teachers in the study described engaging in this deep collaborative work in mathematics. Instead, Bay teachers described the opportunity to learn from an expert modeling the use of the new math curriculum as beneficial. High-poverty schools typically employ higher proportions of teachers with weak levels of mathematical knowledge for teaching than schools serving more affluent students (Hill & Lubienski, 2007). Thus, efforts to enhance teachers' instructional capacity, particularly in mathematics, may be necessary for joint inquiry to flourish in high-poverty schools.

There are several important limitations to these findings. By design, the study focused on a limited number of teachers in three high-poverty schools to understand differences in teachers' collaboration around standards in some detail. These schools all had highly experienced and stable faculties who had volunteered to be early adopters of the new standards. High-poverty schools are more likely to have large concentrations of inexperienced educators (Goldhaber, Lavery, & Theobald, 2015) and experience high rates of teacher turnover (Simon & Johnson, 2015) than schools serving more affluent students. Thus, weak instructional knowledge among novice teachers and instability among the faculty may make it difficult for joint inquiry to take root in many high-poverty schools. Furthermore, teachers may be more resistant to teaching to the CCSS in schools that have not made an early commitment to meeting these new standards.

Implications for Research, Policy, and Practice

These findings raise questions about how we can foster collective commitments among teachers to transform instructional practice to meet new standards. Specifically, the collaborative practices of the teachers at Bay and the four fourth-grade teachers at Park reflected Hargreaves and Fullan's (2012) conception of professional autonomy as a collective commitment to shared knowledge, standards of practice, and ongoing improvement. Notably, these teachers said that they chose to make shared decisions about instructional practice based on close collaboration with colleagues because of their sense of commitment to colleagues, the value they placed on the input of their colleagues, and the improvements they witnessed in their instructional practice and students' work as a result of their efforts.

Schools and districts can foster meaningful learning about standards among teachers by providing substantial support for teachers' collaborative practices. When teachers adopt new practices and resources without engaging in systematic inquiry into the effectiveness of the new approach, it is unlikely that teachers will experience the success that might change their beliefs about practice (Spillane et al., 2006). Specific protocols, such as the inquiry team protocols used in this district, can support the learning process.

However, my findings suggest that productive engagement in inquiry-oriented collaborative practices is unlikely without direct support from school leaders and external partners. Given the important role of principals in setting the direction for teacher collaboration, districts should consider providing training and support for principals in leading the work of teacher teams. Future research can explore whether this approach to teacher collaboration as joint inquiry could become more widespread with targeted professional development and support from school leaders.

Supporting learning about standards through teacher collaboration requires strong collegial relationships among teachers and sufficient instructional capacity to support teachers in productively responding to information about standards. Direct support for collaborative practices in conjunction with opportunities for building productive relationships with colleagues may be sufficient for fostering joint inquiry among experienced educators. However, efforts to support collaborative learning around standards may be more successful when paired with explicit training in pedagogical content knowledge. As states adopt new standards, including the Next Generation Science Standards, researchers may identify additional areas of weak instructional capacity for intervention.

As was the case at Sunnyside and Park, teachers' collaboration often has little influence on practice (e.g., Gallucci, 2003; Little, 1990). Nevertheless, the work of the teachers at Bay and fourth-grade teachers at Park presents a promising vision for the ambitious teaching and learning that can take place in high-poverty urban schools when teachers engage in joint inquiry around specific curriculum, instructional plans, and student work. Their students were learning from complex texts, using evidence from text to support their arguments, solving multiple-step mathematical problems, and explaining their reasoning with limited support from teachers. At the same time, findings from this study provide additional evidence that the success of ambitious educational policies depends on the degree to which schools and districts foster meaningful teacher learning (Cohen & Barnes, 1993; Cohen & Hill, 2001; Elmore, 2004). This district's focus on collaboration in teacher teams and support for the use of inquiry team protocols made it a promising context for teacher learning about policy. Nevertheless, the experience of these teachers reveals the need for training in collaborative practices that foster shared inquiry, explicit efforts to foster collegial relationships among teachers, investments in teachers' instructional capacity, and support from principals for collaboration among teachers to influence teachers' understanding of standards and their implications for practice.

Note

[1]Pseudonyms.

References

Anagnostopoulos, D., & Rutledge, S. (2007). Making sense of school sanctioning policies in urban high schools: Charting the depth and drift of school and classroom change. *Teachers College Record, 109*(5), 1261–1302.

Aud, S., Hussar, W., Planty, M., Snyder, T., Bianco, K., Fox, M., . . . Drake, L. (2010). *The condition of education 2010* (NCES 2010-028). Washington, DC: National Center for Education Statistics, Institute of Education Sciences, U.S. Department of Education.

Bailey, M. J., & Dynarski, S. M. (2011). *Gains and gaps: Changing inequality in US college entry and completion* (No. w17633). Cambridge, MA: National Bureau of Economic Research.

Bryk, A., & Schneider, B. (2002). *Trust in schools: A core resource for improvement.* New York, NY: Russell Sage Foundation.

Cobb, P., & Jackson, K. (2012). Analyzing educational policies: A learning design perspective. *Journal of the Learning Sciences, 21*(4), 487–521.

Coburn, C. E. (2001). Collective sensemaking about reading: How teachers mediate reading policy in their professional communities. *Educational Evaluation and Policy Analysis, 23*, 145–170.

Coburn, C. E. (2004). Beyond decoupling: Rethinking the relationship between the institutional environment and the classroom. *Sociology of Education, 77*(3), 211–244.

Coburn, C. E. (2005). Shaping teacher sensemaking: School leaders and enactment of reading policy. *Educational Policy, 19*(3), 476–509.

Coburn, C. E. (2008). The role of nonsystem actors in the relationship between policy and practice: The case of reading instruction in California. *Education Evaluation and Policy Analysis, 27*(1), 23–52.

Coburn, C. E., & Stein, M. K. (2006). Communities of practice theory and the role of teacher professional community in policy implementation. In M. I. Honig (Ed.), *New directions in educational policy implementation* (pp. 25–46). Albany, NY: State University of New York Press.

Cohen, D. K. (1990). A revolution in one classroom: The case of Mrs. Oublier. *Educational Evaluation and Policy Analysis, 12*(3), 311–329.

Cohen, D. K., & Ball, D. L. (1999). *Instruction, capacity, and improvement* (CPRE Research Report Series RR–43). Philadelphia, PA: Consortium for Policy Research in Education.

Cohen, D. K., & Barnes, C. A. (1993). Pedagogy and policy. In D. K. Cohen, M. W. McLaughlin, & J. E. Talbert (Eds.), *Teaching for understanding. Challenges for policy and practice* (pp. 207–239). San Francisco, CA: Jossey-Bass.

Cohen, D. K., & Hill, H. (2001). *Learning policy: When state education reform works.* New Haven, CT: Yale University Press.

Cohen, D. K., Moffitt, S. L., & Goldin, S. (2007). Policy and practice: The dilemma. *American Journal of Education, 113*(4), 515–548.

Cohen, D. K., & Weiss, J. (1993). The interplay of policy and prior knowledge in public policy. In H. Redner (Ed.), *Studies in the thought of Charles E. Lindblom* (pp. 210–234). Boulder, CO: Westview.

Common Core State Standards Initiative. (2010). *Common Core State Standards for English language arts & literacy in history/social studies, science, and technical subjects.* Retrieved from http://www.corestandards.org/assets/CCSSI_ELA%20Standards.pdf

Cuban, L. (1984). *How teachers taught: Constancy and change in American classrooms, 1890–1980.* New York, NY: Longman Inc.

Donaldson, M., Johnson, S. M., Kirkpatrick, C., Marinell, W., Steele, J., & Szczesiul, S. (2008). Angling for access, bartering for change: How second-stage teachers experience differentiated roles in schools. *Teachers College Record, 110*(5), 1088–1114.

Earl, L., & Timperley, H. (Eds.). (2009). *Professional learning conversations: Challenges in using evidence for improvement.* New York, NY: Springer.

Elmore, R. F. (2004). *School reform from the inside out: Policy, practice and performance.* Cambridge, MA: Harvard Education Press.

Gallimore, R., Ermeling, B. A., Saunders, W. M., & Goldenberg, C. (2009). Moving the learning of teaching closer to practice: Teacher education implications of school-based inquiry teams. *The Elementary School Journal, 109*(5), 537–553.

Gallucci, C. (2003). Communities of practice and the mediation of teachers' responses to standards-based reform. *Education Policy Analysis Archives, 11*(35), 1–30.

Goldhaber, D., Lavery, L., & Theobald, R. (2015). Uneven playing field? Assessing the teacher quality gap between advantaged and disadvantaged students. *Educational Researcher, 44*(5), 293–307.

Hargreaves, A. (1994). *Changing teachers, changing times: Teachers' work and culture in the postmodern age.* New York, NY: Teachers College Press.

Hargreaves, A., & Fullan, M. (2012). *Professional capital: Transforming teaching in every school.* New York, NY: Teachers College Press.

Hill, H. C. (2001). Policy is not enough: Language and the interpretation of state standards. *American Educational Research Journal, 38*(2), 289–318.

Hill, H. C., & Lubienski, S. (2007). Teachers' mathematics knowledge for teaching and school context: A study of California teachers. *Educational Policy, 21*(5), 747–768.

Kane, T. J., & Staiger, D. O. (2012). *Gathering feedback for teachers: Combining high-quality observations with student surveys and achievement gains.* Seattle, WA: Bill and Melinda Gates Foundation.

Katzenbach, J., & Smith, D. (1993). *The discipline of teams.* Boston, MA: Harvard Business Press.

Little, J. (1990). The persistence of privacy: Autonomy and initiative in teachers' professional relations. *Teachers College Record, 91*(4), 509–536.

Little, J. W. (1999). Organizing schools for teacher learning. In L. Darling-Hammond & G. Sykes (Eds.), *Teaching as the learning profession: Handbook of policy and practice* (pp. 233–262). San Francisco, CA: Jossey-Bass.

Lortie, D. C. (1975). *Schoolteacher: A sociological study.* Chicago, IL: University of Chicago Press.

Maxwell, J. A. (2012). *Qualitative research design: An interactive approach.* Thousand Oaks, CA: SAGE Publications.

Merriam, S. (1995). What can you tell from an N of 1? Issues of validity and reliability in qualitative research. *PAACE Journal of Lifelong Learning, 4*, 51–60.

Miles, M. B., & Huberman, A. M. (1994). *Qualitative data analysis* (2nd ed.). Thousand Oaks, CA: SAGE Publications.

Payne, C. M. (2008). *So much reform, so little change: The persistence of failure in urban schools.* Cambridge, MA: Harvard Education Press.

Porter, A., McMaken, J., Hwant, J., & Yang, R. (2011). Common Core standards: The new unintended curriculum. *Educational Researcher, 40*(3), 103–116.

Reardon, S. F. (2011). The widening academic achievement gap between the rich and the poor: New evidence and possible explanations. In G. J. Duncan & R. J. Murnane (Eds.), *Whither opportunity?: Rising inequality, schools, and children's life chances* (pp. 91–116). New York, NY: Russell Sage Foundation.

Rothman, R. (2011). *Something in common: The Common Core standards and the next chapter in American education.* Cambridge, MA: Harvard Education Press.

Sartain, L., Stoelinga, S., & Brown, E. R. (2011). *Rethinking teacher evaluation in Chicago: Lessons learned from classroom observations, principal-teacher conferences, and district implementation.* Chicago, IL: Consortium on Chicago School Research. Retrieved from http://ccsr.uchicago.edu/publications/Teacher%20 Eval%20Report%20FINAL.pdf

Seidman, I. (2006). *Interviewing as qualitative research: A guide for researchers in education and the social sciences.* New York, NY: Teachers College Press.

Simon, N. S., & Johnson, S. M. (2015). Teacher turnover in high-poverty schools: What we know and can do. *Teachers College Record, 117*(3), 1–36.

Spillane, J. P. (1999). External reform initiatives and teachers' efforts to reconstruct their practice: The mediating role of teachers' zones enactment. *Journal of Curriculum Studies, 31*(2), 143–176.

Spillane, J. P. (2004). *Standards deviation: How schools misunderstand educational policy.* Cambridge, MA: Harvard University Press.

Spillane, J. P., & Callahan, K. A. (2000). Implementing state standards for science education: What district policy makers make of the hoopla. *Journal of Research in Science Teaching, 37*(5), 401–425.

Spillane, J. P., Reiser, B. J., & Gomez, L. M. (2006). Policy implementation and cognition. In M. I. Honig (Ed.), *New directions in educational policy implementation* (pp. 47–64). Albany, NY: State University of New York Press.

Spillane, J. P., Reiser, B. J., & Reimer, T. (2002). Policy implementation and cognition: Reframing and refocusing implementation research. *Review of Educational Research, 72*(3), 387–431.

Stosich, E. L. (2016). Building teacher and school capacity to teach to ambitious standards in high-poverty schools. *Teaching and Teacher Education, 58*, 43–53.

Stosich, E. L. (in press). Leading in a time of ambitious reform: Principals in high-poverty urban elementary schools frame the challenge of the Common Core State Standards. *Elementary School Journal.*

Strike, K. A., & Posner, G. J. (1992). A revisionist theory of conceptual change. In R. Duschl & R. Hamilton (Eds.), *Philosophy of science, cognitive psychology, and educational theory and practice* (pp. 147–176). Albany, NY: State University of New York Press.

Trujillo, T., & Reneé, M. (2012). *Democratic school turnarounds: Pursuing equity and learning from evidence.* Boulder, CO: National Education Policy Center. Retrieved from http://nepc.colorado.edu/publication/democratic-school-turnarounds.

Webb, N. L. (2007). Issues related to judging the alignment of curriculum standards and assessments. *Applied Measurement in Education, 20*(1), 7–25.

Wei, R. C., Darling-Hammond, L., & Adamson, F. (2010). *Professional development in the United States: Trends and challenges.* Dallas, TX: National Staff Development Council.

Weick, K. E. (1995). *Sensemaking in organizations.* Thousand Oaks, CA: Sage Publications.

Yin, R. K. (2009). *Case study research: design and methods* (4th ed.). Thousand Oaks, CA: Sage Publications.

Manuscript received February 12, 2015
Final revision received September 14, 2016
Accepted September 27, 2016

American Educational Research Journal
December 2016, Vol. 53, No. 6, pp. 1732–1758
DOI: 10.3102/0002831216674804
© 2016 AERA. http://aerj.aera.net

Greater Engagement Among Members of Gay-Straight Alliances: Individual and Structural Contributors

V. Paul Poteat
Boston College
Nicholas C. Heck
Marquette University
Hirokazu Yoshikawa
New York University
Jerel P. Calzo
San Diego State University

Using youth program models to frame the study of Gay-Straight Alliances (GSAs), we identified individual and structural predictors of greater engagement in these settings with a cross-sectional sample of 295 youth in 33 GSAs from the 2014 Massachusetts GSA Network Survey (69% LGBQ, 68% cisgender female, 68% White, M_{age} = 16.07). Multilevel modeling results indicated

V. Paul Poteat is associate professor in the Department of Counseling, Developmental, and Educational Psychology at Boston College, Campion Hall 307, 140 Commonwealth Ave., Chestnut Hill, MA 02467, USA; e-mail: *PoteatP@bc.edu*. His research on Gay-Straight Alliances (GSAs) has identified specific individual, group, advisor, and school factors that contribute to youth members' experiences in GSAs and the mechanisms by which GSAs promote youths' well-being.

Nicholas C. Heck is an assistant professor in the Department of Psychology at Marquette University. His research centers on the identification and reduction of health disparities that exist among lesbian, gay, bisexual, and transgender people.

Hirokazu Yoshikawa is the Courtney Sale Ross University Professor of Globalization and Education at New York University's Steinhardt School of Culture, Education and Human Development. He studies Gay-Straight Alliances and their associations with youth development. In addition, he examines the effects of programs related to immigration, early childhood development, and poverty reduction on children and youth in the United States as well as in low- and middle-income countries.

Jerel P. Calzo is associate professor in the Division of Health Promotion and Behavioral Science at San Diego State University Graduate School of Public Health. His research examines the development of gender and sexual orientation health disparities in adolescence and young adulthood and evaluates school- and community-based programs to promote the health and positive youth development of gender and sexual minority adolescents and young adults.

that members who perceived more support/socializing from their GSA, had more LGB friends, were longer serving members, and were in GSAs with more open and respectful climates reported greater engagement. Further, there was a curvilinear association between organizational structure in the GSA and engagement: Perceptions of more structure were associated with greater engagement to a point, after which greater structure was related to less engagement.

KEYWORDS: engagement, Gay-Straight Alliance, lesbian, gay, bisexual, transgender, organizational structure, youth programs

Many youth participate to varying degrees in a wide range of programs in schools or the broader community that can promote positive development (Catalano, Berglund, Ryan, Lonczak, & Hawkins, 2004; DuBois, Holloway, Valentine, & Cooper, 2002; Eccles & Gootman, 2002). Nevertheless, studies have given little attention to the experiences of sexual and gender minority youth (e.g., lesbian, gay, bisexual, or transgender youth; LGBT) or to programs that specifically address sexual orientation–related issues. Given that many schools and communities remain unsafe for LGBT youth and that many LGBT youth and some heterosexual youth face homophobic victimization at school (Poteat, Scheer, DiGiovanni, & Mereish, 2014; Russell, Everett, Rosario, & Birkett, 2014), there is a pressing need for greater consideration of such programs and youths' engagement in them.

Gay-Straight Alliances (GSAs) are school-based groups across the United States that provide a setting for youth to receive support and engage in advocacy around issues related to sexual orientation and gender identity (e.g., coming out, bias-based harassment; Griffin, Lee, Waugh, & Beyer, 2004; Russell, Muraco, Subramaniam, & Laub, 2009). They can be described within the framework of youth program models, which identify characteristics of successful youth programs such as safe and structured environments, opportunities to foster peer connection, building on youths' strengths to promote self-confidence, empowering youth by placing them in positions of responsibility, and providing adult support and role modeling (Damon, 2004; Eccles & Gootman, 2002). Consistent with these models, GSAs are youth-driven and supported by an adult advisor, with a major aim of providing social support and opportunities to engage in advocacy (Griffin et al., 2004). Nonexperimental studies show that youth in schools with GSAs report lower health and academic risks than youth in schools without GSAs (Davis, Stafford, & Pullig, 2014; Heck, Flentje, & Cochran, 2011; Poteat, Sinclair, DiGiovanni, Koenig, & Russell, 2013; Walls, Kane, & Wisneski, 2010). Additionally, qualitative studies suggest that multiple factors, such as bullying and a desire to improve the school climate for LGBT students, influence youths' decisions to join a GSA (Heck, Lindquist, Stewart, Brennan, &

Cochran, 2013; Sweat, 2004). However, few studies have considered the experiences among youth who have joined GSAs and, in particular, how youth who are GSA members vary from one another in their levels of engagement. As such, we move from studying GSA involvement as a dichotomous indicator (i.e., members vs. nonmembers) to look at varying levels of active engagement specifically among GSA members. Within the present study, we consider youth engagement to be reflected by behaviors such as consistently attending GSA meetings, contributing to conversations, helping with projects, and taking leadership roles. Using data from the 2014 Massachusetts GSA Network Survey, we examine whether student demographics, membership duration, level of support received, having LGBT friends, organizational structure, and GSA climate are associated with greater levels of engagement among GSA members.

There are important reasons to identify factors that may promote or impede levels of engagement among GSA members. Youth who are more actively engaged and invested in youth programming in general derive greater academic, developmental, and economic benefits relative to those who are less engaged (Busseri & Rose-Krasnor, 2009; Dawes & Larson, 2011; Kuhn & Weinberger, 2005; Pearce & Larson, 2006). For example, youth program involvement is associated with greater empowerment and college attendance (Mahoney, Cairns, & Farmer, 2003; McMahon, Singh, Garner, & Benhorin, 2004). Specific to GSAs, youth membership is connected to greater empowerment and lower substance use, depressive symptoms, and suicidality (Russell et al., 2009; Toomey, Ryan, Diaz, & Russell, 2011). Thus, it is important to not simply identify predictors of whether youth become members in these programs but also to consider how engaged members are within them. Also, as GSAs are largely youth-driven, it is incumbent on youth members to take an active role in order to ensure that the group remains a stable resource within the school. Together, these issues underscore the importance of identifying individual and group characteristics that relate to higher levels of GSA engagement.

Individual Factors Related to GSA Engagement

Drawing on models from the youth program literature (Eccles & Gootman, 2002) and from the intergroup relations literature, we consider individual characteristics that could relate to variability in members' GSA engagement. First, we consider demographic patterns based on sexual orientation, gender, and race/ethnicity. GSAs are intended to be a supportive setting for both sexual minority and heterosexual youth (Griffin et al., 2004), and GSAs appear beneficial for both groups (Poteat, Sinclair, DiGiovanni, Koenig, & Russell, 2013; Russell et al., 2009). As such, we expect that sexual minority and heterosexual GSA members, on average, will not differ in their level of GSA engagement. Regarding gender, cisgender females could be more engaged than cisgender males because male adolescents often face peer pressure to prove their heterosexuality and conform to masculine norms that stigmatize sexual minorities (Pascoe, 2007). Yet, cisgender male GSA members may be a unique group of youth who may feel less pressured to conform to these norms. Thus, while cisgender females and males in the general student population could differ in their likelihood to join a GSA, those who do join may not differ in their level of engagement. Also, it would be important to consider whether transgender members differ from cisgender members in their GSA engagement. Transgender youth face similar stressors as lesbian, gay, and bisexual (LGB)[1] youth as well as unique barriers in school (Grossman & D'Augelli, 2006; McGuire, Anderson, Toomey, & Russell, 2010). These unique barriers could either impede transgender youth members' level of engagement or galvanize them to be even more engaged in GSAs to make use of this setting as a means to address these issues. Finally, scholars have called for attention to racial/ethnic minority youths' experiences in youth programs (Fredricks & Simpkins, 2012; Perkins et al., 2007). In a recent finding, racial/ethnic minority GSA members reported feeling less supported in their GSA than White GSA members (Poteat et al., 2015). We anticipate, then, that racial/ethnic minority GSA members will report lower engagement than White GSA members because they may feel less welcomed.

Youth program models indicate that supportive relationships are a critical element of successful programs (Dawes & Larson, 2011; Eccles & Gootman, 2002; Serido, Borden, & Wiggs, 2014); thus, we hypothesize that the amount of support and socializing that youth receive from their GSA will relate to greater levels of engagement. One of the primary aims of GSAs and youth programs in general is to provide a safe context in which youth can socialize with one another and provide mutual support (Griffin et al., 2004; Jarrett, Sullivan, & Watkins, 2005). Perceived levels of GSA support are related to greater self-esteem, mastery, and sense of purpose among GSA members (Poteat et al., 2015). This could be due to the fact that youth who perceive greater support from their GSA also engage more in their GSA, thus leading to these positive outcomes.

In addition to youth program models emphasizing the need for supportive relationships, having LGBT friends may be a major factor related to heterosexual and sexual minority youths' greater engagement in programs such as GSAs that focus on issues of diversity. The intergroup contact literature has shown that having intergroup friendships is linked to lower prejudice (Pettigrew & Tropp, 2006). Similarly, heterosexual adults have noted that their LGB friends influenced their engagement in advocacy (Duhigg, Rostosky, Gray, & Wimsatt, 2010; Goldstein & Davis, 2010). We expect that heterosexual GSA members with more LGBT friends will be more engaged in the group because they may wish to support their LGBT friends or engage in advocacy to counter discrimination that their LGBT friends experience. Likewise, as an intragroup dynamic, we expect that LGBT members with more LGBT friends will have an even greater investment and motivation to be engaged in their GSA. Notably, LGBT youth who socialize with LGBT peers may be less susceptible to the negative effects of stigma (Frable, Platt, & Hoey, 1998). Additionally, LGBT GSA members may wish to build a larger community with LGBT youth at other schools when their GSA participates in multi-GSA events (e.g., conferences).

Finally, we anticipate that longer membership duration will relate to greater engagement in the GSA. Findings from other youth-driven programs show that youth in these programs have a distinct sense of ownership compared to those in adult-driven programs (Larson, Walker, & Pearce, 2004). Longer-serving GSA members may be more engaged because they may have a greater sense of ownership after having invested in their GSA over time. Longer-serving members could also represent a more selective sample of youth who had positive experiences within their GSA, whereas youth with less positive experiences may have discontinued their involvement. In that case, it would be likely for membership duration to relate to engagement levels. As such, we include membership duration as a covariate and focus on whether our other primary set of variables relate to engagement levels even while controlling for youths' membership duration.

Organizational Structure and Climate Related to GSA Engagement

A systems framework maintains that the organizational structure and climate of social settings have significant effects on youths' experiences in these settings (Tseng & Seidman, 2007). These dimensions are therefore important to consider in addition to individual factors. We expect that elements related to how GSAs are structured and run as groups will relate to how engaged members are in the GSA. Youth program models underscore the need for adequate organizational structure within these settings in order for them to be successful (Catalano et al., 2004; Eccles & Gootman, 2002; Wood, Larson, & Brown, 2009). Organizational structure—represented in this study by factors such as agenda setting, continuity across meetings, and group facilitation—can enhance programs' capacity to promote positive youth development (Catalano et al., 2004). At the same time, too much structure could stifle organic discussions from emerging or could be monotonous, which could lead youth to disengage in their GSA.

Organizational structure within work settings appears to have a curvilinear relationship with work engagement (Tanskanen, Taipale, & Anttila, 2016). Research has identified a similar curvilinear relationship between parental control and adolescent problem behavior (Mason, Cauce, Gonzales, & Hiraga, 1996). Such findings, although not directly from the youth program literature, suggest that the connection between structure and youth engagement in GSAs may be complex, and we anticipate a similar curvilinear relationship. This is because GSAs attempt to serve a variety of functions and meet a range of needs (Griffin et al., 2004; Russell et al., 2009). GSAs may need to provide some structure to ensure multiple needs and interests can be voiced and larger goals can be addressed while also allowing sufficient flexibility to accommodate unanticipated events or for new discussions to emerge.

We also consider youth engagement levels in association with the climate of the GSA as one that allows members to voice different views respectfully and have a say in what is done in the group. These qualities have been examined as attributes of open classroom climates, and findings show them to be associated with outcomes such as civic engagement and social competence (Brock, Nishida, Chiong, Grimm, & Rimm-Kaufmann, 2008; Campbell, 2008). Open climates could be particularly important in settings such as GSAs where issues of diversity are addressed directly among members from different backgrounds. Indeed, intergroup dialogue research has emphasized the need for safe and respectful group norms in order for dialogues to be effective (Dessel & Rogge, 2008; Sorensen, Nagda, Gurin, & Maxwell, 2009). Youth in GSAs without such norms may feel silenced or fear judgment from other members and thus may be less actively engaged in the group. Further, this issue aligns with youth program models that underscore the need for positive social norms (Eccles & Gootman, 2002; Roth & Brooks-Gunn, 2003). Thus, we expect that youth in GSAs where these norms are more apparent will report more active engagement because they feel more assured that their views will be respected.

Current Study and Hypotheses

As studies continue to suggest the benefit of having GSAs in schools, research must look carefully at members' actual levels of engagement in GSAs and identify factors that promote more active engagement. This knowledge will be crucial to help GSAs maximize their potential benefits for members. In this study, we consider individual and group characteristics that could account for variability among members of GSAs in their levels of engagement. As individual characteristics, we consider demographic factors, perceived support and socializing received from the GSA, having LGBT friends, and membership duration. As group characteristics, we consider youths' perceived levels of organizational structure within their GSAs and their perceptions of an open climate within their GSAs.

In relation to individual characteristics, we hypothesize that sexual minority and heterosexual youth and cisgender male and female youth will not differ significantly in their levels of engagement in their GSAs; for exploratory purposes, we examine whether transgender youth report more or less engagement than cisgender youth. Also, we hypothesize that racial/ethnic minority youth will report less engagement than White youth based on emerging findings that racial/ethnic minority youth in GSAs perceive less support from their GSAs than White youth (Poteat et al., 2015). In addition to these demographic comparisons, we further hypothesize that youth who perceive receiving more support and socializing from their GSA, have more LGBT friends, and have been longer serving members of their GSA will report greater engagement in their GSA. We base these hypotheses on established youth program models and intergroup contact theory (Dawes & Larson, 2011; Eccles & Gootman, 2002; Pettigrew & Tropp, 2006).

In relation to GSA characteristics, we hypothesize a curvilinear association between youths' perception of organizational structure within their GSA and their level of engagement in the GSA: Greater organizational structure may be linked to greater engagement among GSA members to a point, after which it may then relate to less engagement. We base this hypothesis on research conducted in work and family settings (Mason et al., 1996; Tanskanen et al., 2016) and youth program models indicating the need for adequate structure in order to promote youth engagement in these settings (Catalano et al., 2004; Eccles & Gootman, 2002; Wood et al., 2009). We consider this association as it relates to each individual's own perception of structure in the GSA as well as the collective perception of structure based on the composite average perceptions of all the members in the same GSA. We consider each individual's perception of structure because each youth may perceive structure differently; some youth may find a given level of organizational structure to be rigid while other youth may find it to be desirable. Thus, the effect may be more evident at the individual level than group level. At the same time, the composite index of organizational structure for each GSA could account for variability across GSAs as a whole in their youths' level of engagement. Finally, we hypothesize that youth in GSAs with a more open climate will report greater engagement. We base this hypothesis on the open classroom climate and intergroup dialogue literature as well as youth program models (Campbell, 2008; Roth & Brooks-Gunn, 2003; Sorensen et al., 2009).

Method

Data Source and Procedures

In collaboration with the Massachusetts GSA Network, we conducted secondary data analyses using the 2014 Massachusetts GSA Network Survey of GSA members. The GSA Network is sponsored by the Massachusetts Commission on LGBTQ Youth and the Massachusetts Safe Schools Program for LGBTQ Students. It gathers data for needs assessments, program evaluations, and identification of youths' experiences in their GSAs. The 2014 data were collected at five regional conferences throughout

Massachusetts and through postings to GSA advisors on their GSA-based list-serv. At the conferences, surveys were made available at the start of the meetings. Through the listserv, GSA advisors requested surveys be sent to them, which they then made available to and collected from youth (the surveys were sent to GSAs that had not attended regional conferences). For both outlets, youth voluntarily completed the anonymous survey if their GSA advisor granted adult consent. The GSA Network uses adult consent over parent consent to avoid potential risks of outing LGBT youth to parents. This method is common in research among LGBT youth to protect their safety and confidentiality (Mustanski, 2011). The youth were told that their responses would be anonymous and that data would be used for program evaluation and potentially for research purposes to produce reports or articles. Youth who did not want to take the survey at the conferences could do other activities. Youth who did not want to complete the survey available through their GSA advisor could elect not to ask for a survey from their advisor. We secured Institutional Review Board approval for our secondary data analysis.

Participants

The full sample included 308 youth in 42 GSAs; however, because of our focus on individual and group factors and because we considered the youth nested within their GSAs, we only included youth who were in GSAs with three or more members represented in order to avoid complications with limited or no variability in scores within GSAs. This produced a final sample size of 295 youth in 33 GSAs (M_{age} = 16.07, SD = 1.14). The average membership duration of youth in their GSA was 1.56 years (SD = 1.22 years). Descriptive demographic data are presented in Table 1.

Measures

Demographics

Youth reported their age, grade, sexual orientation, gender identity, and race/ethnicity. We dichotomized the sexual orientation responses as heterosexual or sexual minority because of the limited number of youth represented in each specific sexual minority group (write-in responses represented nonheterosexual identities such as pansexual or queer). For gender, because of the limited number of youth represented in the specific transgender, gender-queer, and other write-in responses, we considered them together in a trans/gender-queer group for our analyses (write-in responses were largely reflective of gender-queer identities such as gender-fluid or nonbinary/pangender). We dichotomized the race/ethnicity responses as White or racial/ethnic minority because of the limited number of youth represented in each specific racial/ethnic minority group.

Table 1
Participant Demographic Information

Demographic Factor	*N* (%)
Grade level	
Grade 8	4 (1.4)
Grade 9	47 (15.9)
Grade 10	90 (30.5)
Grade 11	95 (32.2)
Grade 12	55 (18.6)
Not reported	4 (1.4)
Sexual orientation	
Heterosexual	87 (29.5)
Lesbian or gay	73 (24.8)
Bisexual	59 (20.0)
Questioning	18 (6.1)
Other self-reported sexual orientations	55 (18.6)
Not reported	3 (1.0)
Gender	
Cisgender female	200 (67.8)
Cisgender male	66 (22.4)
Gender-queer	9 (3.0)
Transgender	11 (3.7)
Other self-reported gender identities	7 (2.4)
Not reported	2 (0.7)
Race/ethnicity	
White	201 (68.1)
Biracial/multiracial	32 (10.9)
Latino/a	18 (6.1)
Asian/Asian American	16 (5.4)
Black or African American	16 (5.4)
Native American	4 (1.4)
Other self-reported racial/ethnic identities	5 (1.7)
Not reported	3 (1.0)

Note. Total sample size: *n* = 295.

Membership Duration

Youth reported the number of months and/or years they had been involved in their GSA. We converted responses to be expressed in the number or fraction of years.

LGB and Transgender Friends

Youth reported their number of close friends who identified as lesbian, gay, or bisexual. Response options were *zero, one, two, three, four,* or *five or more* (scored 0–5). Youth also reported their number of close friends who identified as transgender, with identical response options.

Support and Socializing Received

Youth reported the amount of support and socializing they received from their GSA across seven items, which were preceded by a stem asking them to report the extent to which they personally felt they got each thing from their GSA. The items were: (a) a place of safety, (b) emotional support, (c) validation and reassurance, (d) a place where I share any concerns, (e) hang out with others, (f) just be myself with others, and (g) meet new people or make new friends. Response options ranged from 1 (*not at all*) to 5 (*a lot*). An exploratory factor analysis with principal axis factor extraction indicated a unidimensional factor structure for these items (eigenvalue: 4.02; factor loadings: .84, .83, .82, .77, .77, .63, and .62, respectively). Higher average scores represent greater support and socializing youth perceived they received from their GSA. Coefficient alpha reliability was α = .90.

Perceived Level of GSA Organizational Structure

Youth reported the extent to which they perceived a level of organizational structure to their GSA meetings based on four items, preceded by the stem, "How often does your GSA do these things": (a) We do check-ins at the beginning of GSA meetings, (b) we follow up about things that were discussed in the last GSA meeting, (c) our GSA meetings follow an agenda, and (d) there is someone who leads our GSA meetings. Response options were *never, rarely, sometimes, often*, and *all the time* (scaled 0–4). An exploratory factor analysis with principal axis factor extraction indicated a unidimensional factor structure for these items (eigenvalue: 1.46; factor loadings: .76, .62, .52, and .48, respectively). Higher average scores represent greater perceived organizational structure within GSA meetings. Coefficient alpha reliability was α = .68. Individual perceptions of structure were included as a predictor at Level 1 (the individual level), and a composite score for each GSA derived from the mean of all the students in that GSA was included as a predictor at Level 2 (the GSA level) in our multilevel model.

Perceived Open GSA Climate

Youth used the Open Classroom Climate Scale (Flanagan, Syvertsen, & Stout, 2007) to report whether they perceived an open climate in their GSA that encouraged members to express their beliefs, have input on GSA projects, and express disagreements respectfully. The four items were preceded by the stem, "In my GSA, students . . . ": (a) have a voice in what happens; (b) can disagree with the advisor, if they are respectful; (c) can disagree with each other, if they are respectful; and (d) are encouraged to express opinions. Response options ranged from 1 (*strongly disagree*) to 5 (*strongly agree*). Higher average scores represent a more open GSA climate. Past coefficient alpha reliability has been reported at α = .86 (Flanagan et al., 2007) and the scale is associated with factors such as trusting others and group solidarity (Flanagan & Stout, 2010). The coefficient alpha reliability from the current data was α = .91. Individual perceptions of the GSA climate were included as a predictor at Level 1 (the individual level), and a composite score for each GSA derived from the mean of all the students in that GSA was included as a predictor at Level 2 (the GSA level) in our multilevel model.

Engagement Level in GSA

Youth reported their level of active engagement in the GSA based on five items, preceded by the stem, "Please consider your own GSA involvement in responding to these items": (a) I attend GSA meetings or other GSA events, (b) I participate in conversations at GSA meetings, (c) I take leadership roles in activities and events in my GSA, (d) I have discussions with my GSA advisor(s) about GSA-related matters, and, (e) I help with events or projects in my GSA. These items have been piloted and refined over several iterations by the GSA Network prior to this current version. Response options were *never, rarely, sometimes, often*, and *all the time* (scaled 0–4). An exploratory factor analysis with principal axis factor extraction indicated a unidimensional factor structure for these items (eigenvalue: 3.19; factor loadings: .86, .84, .84, .81, and .63, respectively). Higher average scale scores represent greater engagement in the GSA. Coefficient alpha reliability was α = .89.

Analytic Strategy

We conducted MANOVAs to test for demographic group differences on our main predictors and the outcome of engagement based on sexual orientation, gender identity, and race/ethnicity. We also examined simple bivariate associations among the variables prior to testing our multilevel model.

We used HLM 7.0 with restricted maximum likelihood (REML) estimation to test our hypothesized model in which our set of factors accounted for variability in youth members' level of engagement in their GSA. We used multilevel modeling to account for the interdependence of respondents, where youth were nested within their respective GSAs. As we later note, there was a significant amount of interdependence among youth in the same GSA, making multilevel modeling an appropriate analytic approach. In our models, individual youth data were included at Level 1, and GSA-level data were included at Level 2. First, we tested the unconditional null model to determine whether there was significant variance across GSAs in youths' level of engagement. Next, we tested a model with our Level 1 independent variables, including youths' demographics (i.e., sexual orientation, gender, race/ethnicity) and their number of LGB friends, transgender friends, membership duration, perceived support and socializing received from the GSA, their own perception of organizational structure within their GSA (including linear and quadratic effects), and their own perception of open climate within their GSA, all of which were group-mean centered. Finally, we tested the full multilevel model in which we added our Level 2 independent variables. The composite average scores of perceived open climate and structure (linear and quadratic effects) of all the youth in each GSA, as well as the number of youth participants in each GSA (simply as a control variable), were included at Level 2 as predictors of the Level 1 intercept (i.e., to account for differences across GSAs in average levels of youth engagement).

Results

Group Differences and Bivariate Correlations

The MANOVA for sexual orientation was significant, Wilks' Λ = .81, $F(7, 252)$ = 8.53, $p < .001$, η_p^2 = .19. Follow-up ANOVAs indicated that sexual minority youth reported receiving more support and socializing from the GSA, having more LGB friends and transgender friends, longer membership duration, perceived a more open GSA climate, and greater engagement in the GSA than heterosexual youth (Table 2). The MANOVA for race/ethnicity also was significant, Wilks' Λ = .93, $F(7, 252)$ = 2.72, $p = .01$, η_p^2 = .07. Follow-up ANOVAs indicated that White youth reported having more LGB friends and transgender friends and greater engagement in the GSA than racial/ethnic minority youth (Table 2). Finally, the MANOVA for gender was significant, Wilks' Λ = .85, $F(14, 504)$ = 2.99, $p < .001$, η_p^2 = .08. Follow-up ANOVAs indicated gender differences for number of transgender friends, membership duration, and engagement level (Table 3). Tukey post hoc comparisons indicated that trans/gender-queer youth reported having more transgender friends than cisgender male youth ($p < .05$, d = 0.66) and cisgender female youth ($p < .05$, d = 0.78); cisgender male youth reported shorter membership duration than cisgender female youth ($p < .05$, d = 0.39) and trans/gender-queer youth ($p < .05$, d = 0.70); and trans/gender-queer youth reported greater engagement in the GSA than cisgender female youth ($p < .05$, d = 0.59).

All the independent variables were significantly associated with level of engagement in the GSA as hypothesized (we tested for the curvilinear effect of organizational structure in the multilevel model in the following section). Youth who reported greater engagement in their GSA than others reported higher levels of perceived support and socializing received from their GSA ($r = .34$, $p < .001$), more LGB friends ($r = .25$, $p < .001$), more transgender friends ($r = .21$, $p < .001$), longer membership duration ($r = .47$, $p < .001$), perceived more organizational structure within their GSA ($r = .18$, $p < .01$),

Table 2
Descriptive Data for Demographic Comparisons: Sexual Orientation and Race/Ethnicity

	Sexual Orientation				Race/Ethnicity			
	Sexual Min. (n = 181)	Heterosexual (n = 79)	F	η_p^2	Racial Min. (n = 76)	White (n = 184)	F	η_p^2
Engagement	2.92 (0.94)	2.55 (1.01)	8.45**	.03	2.47 (1.13)	2.95 (0.87)	13.51**	.05
M. duration	1.75 (1.22)	1.14 (1.08)	14.52**	.05	1.41 (1.22)	1.65 (1.20)	2.09	—
LGB friends	3.76 (1.47)	2.57 (1.64)	33.64***	.12	3.03 (1.54)	3.55 (1.62)	5.90*	.02
Trans friends	1.00 (1.22)	0.39 (0.71)	17.07***	.06	0.55 (0.92)	0.93 (1.18)	6.18*	.02
Sup/soc received	4.53 (0.58)	4.30 (0.86)	6.30**	.02	4.36 (0.82)	4.49 (0.61)	1.93	—
Structure	3.12 (0.73)	2.94 (0.69)	3.55	—	2.93 (0.78)	3.10 (0.70)	2.77	—
Open climate	4.73 (0.51)	4.39 (0.89)	15.49***	.06	4.51 (0.87)	4.68 (0.56)	3.38	—

Note. Values represent the means and standard deviations (in parentheses) of scores for each demographic group. Engagement = level of youth engagement in the GSA; M. duration = membership duration in number of years; LGB friends = number of LGB friends; trans friends = number of transgender friends; sup/soc received = amount of support/socializing received from the GSA; structure = perceived level of structure within the GSA; open climate = perceived level of open climate within the GSA; sexual min. = sexual minority youth; racial min. = racial/ethnic minority youth; GSA = Gay-Straight Alliance.
*p < .05. **p < .01. ***p < .001.

Table 3

Descriptive Data for Demographic Comparisons: Gender

	Male (n = 59)	Female (n = 176)	Trans/G-Queer (n = 26)	F	η_p^2	Tukey Post Hoc Comparisons
Engagement	2.79 (1.03)	2.74 (0.95)	3.29 (0.90)	3.79*	.03	T/G > F
M. duration	1.19 (1.06)	1.64 (1.23)	2.00 (1.24)	5.03**	.04	M < T/G, F
LGB friends	3.27 (1.67)	3.42 (1.59)	3.62 (1.65)	0.43	—	—
Trans friends	0.80 (1.14)	0.68 (0.93)	1.77 (1.73)	11.52***	.08	T/G > M, F
Sup/soc received	4.59 (0.47)	4.41 (0.74)	4.56 (0.58)	1.86	—	—
Structure	3.16 (0.71)	3.03 (0.71)	3.02 (0.86)	0.74	—	—
Open climate	4.68 (0.65)	4.59 (0.71)	4.77 (0.34)	1.07	—	—

Note. Values represent the means and standard deviations (in parentheses) of scores for each demographic group. Engagement = level of youth engagement in the GSA; M. duration = membership duration in number of years; LGB friends = number of LGB friends; trans friends = number of transgender friends; sup/soc received = amount of support/socializing received from the GSA; structure = perceived level of structure within the GSA; open climate = perceived level of open climate within the GSA; trans/g-queer = trans/gender-queer youth. For Tukey post hoc comparisons, T/G = trans/gender-queer youth, M = cisgender male youth, and F = cisgender female youth. GSA = Gay-Straight Alliance.
*p < .05. **p < .01. ***p < .001.

Table 4
Bivariate Correlations among the Variables

	Engagement	M. Duration	LGB Friends	Trans Friends	Sup/Soc Received	Structure
Engagement	—					
M. duration	.47***	—				
LGB friends	.25***	.19**	—			
Trans friends	.21***	.22***	.36***	—		
Sup/soc received	.34***	.05	.19**	.19**	—	
Structure	.18**	.02	.22***	.14*	.42***	—
Open climate	.35***	.09	.13*	.16**	.56***	.31***

Note. Engagement = level of youth engagement in the GSA; M. duration = membership duration; LGB friends = number of LGB friends; trans friends = number of transgender friends; sup/soc received = amount of support/socializing received from the GSA; structure = perceived level of structure within the GSA; open climate = perceived level of open climate within the GSA; GSA = Gay-Straight Alliance.
*$p < .05$. **$p < .01$. ***$p < .001$.

and perceived a more open climate within their GSA ($r = .35$, $p < .001$). All bivariate correlations among the independent variables are included in Table 4.

Multilevel Model of Engagement Levels in GSAs

The initial unconditional null model without independent variables indicated that there was significant variance across GSAs in youths' level of engagement (i.e., on average, some GSAs had more engaged members than others; $\chi^2 = 104.13$, $p < .01$, deviance = 788.97). The amount of variance within GSAs was 0.81, and the amount of variance across GSAs was 0.18. The intraclass correlation coefficient thus indicated that 18% of the total variance in youths' level of engagement was across GSAs. Next, we tested our Level 1 model (Table 5). At the individual level, multiple factors accounted for variability among youth in their level of engagement in the GSA. First, longer-serving members reported greater engagement than those who more recently had joined (b = 0.31, $p < .01$). A year longer membership was associated with roughly a third of a point greater GSA engagement—which could be interpreted as an engagement level roughly one-third of a standard deviation higher as the standard deviation for engagement was about one point. Second, youth who perceived receiving more support and socializing from their GSA reported greater engagement than others (b = 0.23, $p < .05$). A one unit increase in perceived amount of support and socializing received from the GSA was associated with nearly a quarter of a point greater level of engagement (again, comparable to a quarter standard deviation greater

Table 5

Individual and Gay-Straight Alliance (GSA) Factors Associated With Level of Youth Engagement in GSAs

	Level 1 Model		Multilevel Model	
	Coefficient	SE	Coefficient	SE
Level 1: Individual level				
Sexual orientation	0.03	0.12	−0.02	0.11
Male	0.04	0.12	0.06	0.11
Trans/gender-queer	0.47**	0.17	0.45**	0.16
Race/ethnicity	−0.26*	0.12	−0.28**	0.10
Membership duration	0.31**	0.05	0.31**	0.05
LGB friends	0.11**	0.04	0.11**	0.04
Trans friends	0.00	0.05	0.00	0.05
Support/socializing received	0.23*	0.09	0.23*	0.09
Individual perception of structure (lin. fx)	−0.02	0.09	−0.02	0.09
Individual perception of structure² (quad. fx)	−0.14**	0.04	−0.13**	0.04
Individual perception of open climate of GSA	0.12	0.09	0.13	0.09
Level 2: GSA level				
Number of participants in the GSA			−0.06**	0.01
Collective perception of structure (lin. fx)			0.02	0.14
Collective perception of structure² (quad. fx)			0.04	0.05
Collective perception of open climate of GSA			0.52*	0.20
Deviance statistic	623.65		603.72	

Note. Values are unstandardized coefficient estimates and their standard errors (*SE*). Sexual orientation is dichotomized as 1 = sexual minority; race/ethnicity is dichotomized as 1 = racial/ethnic minority. Lin. fx = linear effect; quad fx = quadratic effect.
*$p < .05$. **$p < .01$.

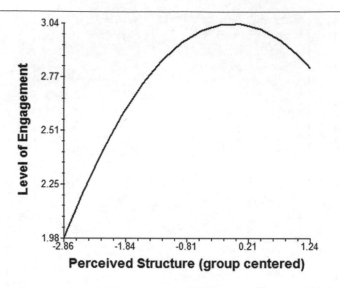

Figure 1. **Curvilinear association between perceived organizational structure within the Gay-Straight Alliance (GSA) and members' levels of engagement in the GSA.**

engagement). Third, youth who had more LGB friends reported greater engagement (b = 0.11, p < .05). A one unit increase in a member's number of LGB friends (e.g., from having one friend to having two friends) related to about a tenth of a point greater level of engagement. For exploratory purposes, we tested whether individuals' sexual orientation moderated this association; it did not, indicating that having more LGB friends was associated with engagement levels for both heterosexual and sexual minority youth members. Also for exploratory purposes, we tested the potential interaction of sexual orientation with all other individual-level factors. None of these interaction effects were significant. Fourth, the quadratic effect of perceived organizational structure was significant (b = −0.14, p < .01). Figure 1 displays the association between organizational structure and level of youth engagement in their GSA. As hypothesized, perceptions of greater organizational structure were associated with more engagement in the GSA to a point, which was followed by a decrease in engagement as perceptions of structure further increased. Fifth, trans/gender-queer youth reported greater engagement in the GSA than cisgender female youth (b = 0.47, p < .01). Trans/gender-queer youths' engagement was close to a half of a point greater (and comparable to a one-half standard deviation greater) than non-trans/gender-queer youth. Finally, racial/ethnic minority youth reported less engagement in the GSA than White youth (b = −0.26, p < .05). Racial/ethnic minority youths' level of engagement was about a quarter of a point lower than White youths' level of engagement. The amount of variance at Level 1 was reduced to 0.53 with these variables included, and the pseudo R^2 value indicated that our model accounted for 35% of the variance at this level.

Finally, we tested our full multilevel model (Table 5), displayed in the Appendix. At the GSA level, youth in GSAs who collectively perceived a more open climate in their GSA reported greater engagement than youth in GSAs who collectively perceived a less open climate in their GSA (γ = 0.52, p < .05). At the group level, a one unit increase in youths' collective perceptions of a more open climate in their GSA was associated with half of a point greater level of engagement among youth in that GSA—or a collective engagement level roughly one standard deviation higher, as the standard deviation for engagement at the group level was about half of a point. Also, related to our control variable, youth in GSAs that had more participants reported less engagement (γ = -0.06, p < .01). An increase of one member in the GSA was associated with an overall decrease of less than a tenth of a point in level of engagement among members of that GSA. The amount of variance at Level 2 was reduced to 0.01 with these variables included, and the pseudo R^2 value indicated that our model accounted for 94% of the variance at this level.

Discussion

As studies suggest the benefits of GSA presence in schools, research needs to focus on the varied experiences of GSA members. We focused on members' engagement levels because more engaged youth derive greater benefits from their involvement in youth programming (Busseri & Rose-Krasnor, 2009; Dawes & Larson, 2011; Kuhn & Weinberger, 2005; Pearce & Larson, 2006). As hypothesized, youth who reported greater engagement were those who perceived receiving more support and socializing from their GSA, had more LGB friends, were longer serving members, and were in GSAs with a more open climate. We also documented demographic differences. Also as hypothesized, there was a curvilinear association between perceived organizational structure in the GSA and engagement. These findings can be used to provide empirically based recommendations for how GSAs might increase members' engagement, which in turn could maximize the benefits that members derive.

Patterns of GSA Engagement Across Demographic Groups

Because GSAs aim to include youth from different social backgrounds, it is important to identify whether members from certain groups report less engagement. We identified initial differences between sexual minority and heterosexual youth, but they were not significant in the full multilevel model. This may be because by their name and historical precedence, GSAs are expressly intended for both sexual minorities and heterosexual allies (Griffin et al., 2004). Similarly, there were no differences between cisgender male or female youth. Trans/gender-queer youth reported greater engagement than cisgender females but no significant difference from cisgender males. Given the added barriers that transgender youth face in school (Grossman & D'Augelli, 2006; McGuire et al., 2010), it is possible that transgender GSA members were aware of these additional inequalities and were galvanized to be active and address these issues. Within the context of Massachusetts, and historically around the time during which these data were collected, there were legislative efforts to extend explicit protections to transgender youth in schools. Transgender GSA members may have been able to use the GSA setting to contribute to these efforts, which might explain this difference. Yet, because we focused entirely on GSA members, it would be important for research to consider how transgender nonmembers perceive their school's GSA to ensure that GSAs are equally welcoming of transgender youth and whether this difference reflects one that would either be stable or variant over time.

Racial/ethnic minority GSA members reported less engagement than White members. We anticipated this pattern because racial/ethnic minority youth have reported less perceived support from their GSA than White youth (Poteat et al., 2015), and adequate support provision is a key necessity for youth programs (Dawes & Larson, 2011; Eccles & Gootman, 2002). Other factors could also account for this finding. For example, certain engagement styles may be differentially valued across cultures, and this may not have been adequately captured with the measure in this survey.

The general youth program literature has called for greater focus on the experiences of racial/ethnic minority youth in these settings (Fredricks & Simpkins, 2012; Perkins et al., 2007), and our findings underscore that this need extends to GSAs. Whereas GSAs may be known for their focus on sexual orientation issues, this perception may not extend to race and racial discrimination. Racial/ethnic minority youth, whether heterosexual or LGB, may have perceived GSAs as less inclusive of their needs that intersect with their racial/ethnic background, leading them to engage less in their GSA. Alternatively, they may have faced added barriers to accessing their GSA or youth programs in general (Perkins et al., 2007; Serido et al., 2014). Advisors could play a role in addressing this issue by being intentional in raising issues of race or racism and ensuring that an intersectional lens is applied to discussions and activities within GSAs. Doing so could foster greater engagement among racial/ethnic minority youth by ensuring the relevance of such discussions or activities and demonstrating affirmation of their personal experiences.

Individual Factors Related to Variability in GSA Engagement

We drew from youth program models and the intergroup relations literature to identify several individual factors associated with greater engagement. Congruent with youth program models that emphasize the importance of supportive relationships in these settings (Dawes & Larson, 2011; Eccles & Gootman, 2002; Jarret et al., 2005), members who perceived receiving more support and socializing from their GSA were more engaged. Perceived GSA support has been linked to positive development among GSA members (Poteat et al., 2015), and our findings add to this by showing that support is strongly connected to engagement. There could be a potential mediational process among these factors: Youth who perceive more initial support may become more engaged, which could lead them to experience greater well-being. This finding adds weight to one of the central aims of GSAs, which is to provide support (Griffin et al., 2004). As such, although GSAs often attempt to serve multiple functions within a limited scope of time, it would be important that these functions not overshadow this fundamental provision.

Youth settings such as GSAs that place a specific emphasis on issues of diversity may need to draw not only from general youth program models but also from the intergroup relations literature to identify ways to fully engage their members. To this point, as hypothesized, GSA members with more LGB friends reported more active engagement, which did not differ for heterosexual or sexual minority members. For heterosexuals, having LGBT friends is associated with more favorable attitudes toward and more advocacy on behalf of LGBT people (Duhigg et al., 2010; Goldstein & Davis, 2010; Herek & Capitanio, 1996). Within the present sample, LGB friendships may have strengthened heterosexual youths' motivation to be actively engaged in the GSA in order to support their friends. For LGB members, friendships with LGB peers could have prompted their greater engagement in order to strengthen their connection to others in the community and because these intragroup connections could promote their own well-being (Frable et al., 1998). This finding highlights the unique nature of GSAs as an intergroup setting and suggests that this could be viewed as an asset for fostering engagement among members and potentially other positive outcomes that should be examined in future research.

In contrast, having more transgender friends was not associated with greater GSA engagement in the multilevel model. This difference could partly be due to the restricted response range in that most youth reported having relatively few transgender friends. It is also possible that GSAs may give less focus to transgender-related issues than LGB issues, and thus youth with more transgender friends may not have seen the GSA as ideal an outlet in which to become involved as they may have seen it for addressing issues faced by their LGB friends.

Longer-serving GSA members reported more engagement in their GSA. These members may have felt a greater sense of ownership to contribute to the GSA or take on leadership roles. These youth attributes are particularly evident in youth-driven programs (Larson et al., 2004). At the same time, these youth could have been a rather selective sample, especially when considering the sampling methodology of this project. These youth may have had initially more positive experiences than others, leading them to stay, whereas other youth may have discontinued their membership. Still, while controlling for the effects of membership duration, our other factors accounted for significant variance in members' levels of engagement.

The Importance of Organizational Structure and Open Climates Within GSAs

We identified two important elements related to how GSAs operated that were associated with greater engagement among members. First, we documented a curvilinear association between youths' perception of organizational structure in the GSA and their level of engagement: Perceptions of more structure were associated with greater engagement to a point, after which stronger perceptions of structure were related to less engagement. This finding aligned with a foundational point of youth program models that adequate structure is an essential element of successful programs (Catalano et al., 2004; Eccles & Gootman, 2002; Wood et al., 2009). The curvilinear effect captured further nuance and may suggest that excessive or rigid structure could stifle youth participation; this finding appears consistent with the literature on structure and work engagement as well as the family literature on parental structure and youth behavior (Mason et al., 1996; Tanskanen et al., 2016). GSAs fulfill quite varied functions (e.g., socializing, support, advocacy) and work with youth from diverse backgrounds (Griffin et al., 2004). Thus, GSAs may have all the more need for flexible structure to ensure that multiple needs and interests can be voiced and acted on in a way that is neither too rigid to prevent unanticipated issues from being addressed nor inadequate for a necessary level of cohesion. Some of these dynamics have been noted in observational findings (Poteat et al., 2015), and our quantitative findings add to this within a larger model of factors related to engagement. Building on this finding, at a practical level, the items comprising this measure suggest several concrete ways in which GSA advisors or youth leaders could provide structure within their group. For example, they could reserve time for members to do check-ins and follow-ups at the beginning of meetings, or they could prepare a flexible agenda for some of their meetings.

We identified this pattern for structure at the individual level but not the group level. We anticipated this result because individual youth in the same GSA may perceive or react to organizational structure differently. Thus, collective perceptions of greater organizational structure among members of a GSA did not distinguish those GSAs that, on average, had more engaged members than other GSAs. Rather, it appeared that individual youths' own perception of the amount of organizational structure was more important in accounting for their level of engagement. As such, advisors or youth leaders may want to check with youth members individually and not only collectively about whether they perceive the current level of structure in the group as helpful or restrictive.

Finally, GSAs whose members perceived them to have more open climates had more engaged members. This finding aligns with those related to open classroom climates (Brock et al., 2008; Campbell, 2008). This finding also aligns with the intergroup dialogue literature showing that safe and respectful norms must be present for dialogues to be effective (Dessel & Rogge, 2008; Sorensen et al., 2009). Especially in GSAs and in other youth settings that bring together youth from different social backgrounds, open climates may be essential. Youth who perceived a more open climate in their GSA may have felt more assured that their views and experiences would be respected, even if they differed from those of others; as a result, they may have been more motivated to actively engage in their GSA. It could be valuable, then, for members of GSAs to occasionally discuss their perceptions of the group's climate and identify ways to cultivate and maintain respectful dialogues and interactions, even when youth hold different beliefs or have different goals or expectations for the group.

Strengths, Limitations, and Future Directions

To date, most GSA research has focused on comparisons of youth based on GSA presence in their school or dichotomous GSA membership status. Although this has offered support for the importance of GSAs, there has been little research on the varied experiences of GSA members. As such, the major contribution of the current study was to identify a range of factors associated with youths' greater engagement levels as members of GSAs. Further, we applied established youth program and intergroup relations models to identify major factors that could account for variability in youths' experiences in GSAs. As additional strengths, our study included several hundred youth from across multiple GSAs located in diverse settings (e.g., rural, suburban, and urban settings; economically diverse settings). Finally, we were able to use multilevel modeling of youths' data for a more rigorous test of individual and group factors associated with their engagement.

Along with these strengths, there were several limitations to the study. First, despite the number of GSAs and their geographic diversity, they were all located in Massachusetts, and the GSAs were not randomly sampled. As such, there may be limitations to the representativeness of the sample (e.g., average levels of engagement in this sample may be higher than in other GSAs). The generalizability of our findings across other parts of the country should be considered. In relation to this, it would be important to consider how broader social factors might account for further variability in youths' ability to engage within the GSA (e.g., the political climate or legislative policies—affirming or discriminatory—in certain districts or states; the economy or resource availability within certain districts). Second, our primary GSA organizational variables were aggregated individual perceptions at the GSA level. Aggregate individual perceptions are in fact important features of social settings that predict individual-level outcomes. However, future research should add advisor-reported data and direct observations of GSA functioning. For example, a smaller recent study of GSAs found that using participant-observation methods, there was meaningful variation in aspects of GSA structure and climate and that advisor reports of GSA characteristics were associated with positive youth development (Poteat et al., 2015). Third, some items were not from preestablished scales, such as those assessing organizational structure. At the same time, the items comprising these scales were concrete and directly relevant to GSAs. In this manner, they could be directly translatable into practice (e.g., items for structure pointed to specific actions such as offering check-ins and follow-ups). Fourth, although there was a degree of sexual orientation, racial/ethnic, and gender diversity, the number of youth from specific minority group backgrounds was insufficient to conduct specific comparisons or examine patterns related to the intersection of these identities (e.g., racial/ethnic minority LGB youth). Attention to this level of specificity will be important as GSAs seek to tailor their services to diverse members (Poteat & Scheer, 2016). In addition, it would be beneficial for future research to include other demographic indicators such as measures of social class. Fifth, our data were cross-sectional and nonexperimental. Thus, we cannot attribute causality between our independent variables and level of engagement. Still, our identification of these associations can inform the development of interventions to be tested within GSAs that incorporate these factors and examine their potential causal effects. Sixth, we could not distinguish in this article between non–GSA-involved students in the same schools and the GSA members who participated. Certainly this basic level of involvement (whether one is a GSA member or not) determines the composition of GSAs, which may in turn affect level of engagement of GSA members. Future work could sample both populations and include prediction of any involvement simultaneously with level of engagement among members. Finally, we focused on behavior-based engagement. Future research should consider emotional and cognitive indices of engagement as well (Fredricks, Blumenfeld, & Paris, 2004).

Our findings suggest several areas for continued research and for programming efforts with GSAs and similar youth settings. For instance, future studies should consider how advisors promote greater engagement among youth members. Longitudinal studies should also examine youths' engagement in GSAs over time and identify factors that might account for periodic fluctuations in their engagement. Further, studies should consider links between youths' GSA engagement and developmental outcomes. In terms of programming, our findings point to several strategies that could be implemented in GSAs to promote engagement. For instance, GSAs might adopt approaches reflected in the items of our measures. Similarly, GSAs should be mindful to be inclusive and supportive of all members, particularly those who may be more underrepresented and have specific concerns and strengths (e.g., Black, Latino, and Asian youth). Ultimately, this expanded and more nuanced approach to studying GSAs and the experiences of youth involved in them will provide empirically based knowledge on how GSAs can be structured and tailored to maximize their benefits for a wide range of youth.

Appendix

The tested multilevel model is presented in the following:

$$\text{Engagement}_{ij} = \beta_{0j} + \beta_{1j}(\text{Sexual minority}_{ij}) + \beta_{2j}(\text{Male}_{ij}) +$$

$$\beta_{3j}(\text{Trans/Gender-queer}_{ij}) + \beta_{4j}(\text{Racial minority}_{ij}) + \beta_{5j}(\text{LGB friends}_{ij}) +$$

$$\beta_{6j}(\text{Transgender friends}_{ij}) + \beta_{7j}(\text{Membership duration}_{ij})$$

$$+ \beta_{8j}(\text{Support/socializing received}_{ij}) + \beta_{9j}(\text{Perceived organizational structure}_{ij}) +$$

$$\beta_{10j}(\text{Perceived organizational structure}_{ij})^2 + \beta_{11j}(\text{Perceived open climate}_{ij}) + r_{ij}$$

$$\beta_{0j} = \gamma_{00} + \gamma_{01}(\text{Group size})_j + \gamma_{02}(\text{Composite organizational structure})_j +$$

$$\gamma_{03}(\text{Composite organizational structure})^2_j +$$

$$\gamma_{04}(\text{Composite open climate})_j + u_{0j}$$

Notes

Support for the writing of this manuscript was partially based on funding awarded from the National Institute of Minority Health and Health Disparities (NIMHD), R01MD009458, to Poteat (Principal Investigator) and Calzo and Yoshikawa (Co-Investigators). Additional support for the second author (Calzo) was provided by funding from the National Institute on Drug Abuse (NIDA), K01DA034753.

[1]In the current article, we use the LGBT acronym when referring to studies and findings focused on both sexual and gender minority youth, and we use the LGB acronym for those specifically referring to sexual orientation. Because the data in this current study assessed sexual orientation and gender identity separately, as well as LGB and transgender friends separately, we use the LGB acronym when we refer to findings in this study specific to sexual orientation.

References

Brock, L. L., Nishida, T. K., Chiong, C., Grimm, K. J., & Rimm-Kaufman, S. E. (2008). Children's perceptions of the classroom environment and social and academic performance: A longitudinal analysis of the contribution of the Responsive Classroom approach. *Journal of School Psychology, 46*, 129–149.

Busseri, M. A., & Rose-Krasnor, L. (2009). Breadth and intensity: Salient, separable, and developmentally significant dimensions of structured youth activity involvement. *British Journal of Developmental Psychology, 27*, 907–933. doi:10.1348/026151008X397017

Campbell, D. E. (2008). Voice in the classroom: How an open classroom climate fosters political engagement among adolescents. *Political Behavior, 30*, 437–454.

Catalano, R. F., Berglund, M. L., Ryan, J. A. M., Lonczak, H. S., & Hawkins, J. D. (2004). Positive youth development in the United States: Research findings on evaluations of positive youth development programs. *Annals of the American Academy of Political and Social Science, 591*, 98–124.

Damon, W. (2004). What is positive youth development? *Annals of the American Academy of Political and Social Science, 591*, 13–24.

Davis, B., Stafford, M. B. R., & Pullig, C. (2014). How Gay-Straight Alliance groups mitigate the relationship between gay-bias victimization and adolescent suicide attempts. *Journal of the American Academy of Child & Adolescent Psychiatry, 53*, 1271–1278.

Dawes, N. P., & Larson, R. (2011). How youth get engaged: Grounded-theory research on motivational development in organized youth programs. *Developmental Psychology, 47*, 259–269.

Dessel, A., & Rogge, M. E. (2008). Evaluation of intergroup dialogue: A review of the empirical literature. *Conflict Resolution Quarterly, 26*, 199–238.

DuBois, D. L., Holloway, B. E., Valentine, J. C., & Cooper, H. (2002). Effectiveness of mentoring programs for youth: A meta-analytic review. *American Journal of Community Psychology, 30*, 157–197.

Duhigg, J. M., Rostosky, S. S., Gray, B. E., & Wimsatt, M. K. (2010). Development of heterosexuals into sexual-minority allies: A qualitative exploration. *Sexuality Research and Social Policy, 7*, 2–14.

Eccles, J., & Gootman, J. A. (2002). *Community programs to promote youth development*. Washington, DC: National Academy Press.

Flanagan, C. A., & Stout, M. (2010). Developmental patterns of social trust between early and late adolescence: Age and school climate effects. *Journal of Research on Adolescence, 20*, 748–773. doi:10.1111/j.1532-7795.2010.00658.x

Flanagan, C. A., Syvertsen, A. K., & Stout, M. D. (2007). *Civic measurement models: Tapping adolescents' civic engagement* (CIRCLE Working Paper 55) Retrieved from http://www.politicipublice.ro/uploads/adolescents.pdf.

Frable, D. E. S., Platt, L., & Hoey, S. (1998). Concealable stigmas and positive self-perceptions: Feeling better around similar others. *Journal of Personality and Social Psychology, 74*, 909–922. doi:10/1037/0022-3514.74.4.909

Fredricks, J. A., Blumenfeld, P. C., & Paris, A. H. (2004). School engagement: Potential of the concept, state of the evidence. *Review of Educational Research, 74*, 59–109.

Fredricks, J. A., & Simpkins, S. D. (2012). Promoting positive youth development through organized after-school activities: Taking a closer look at participation of ethnic minority youth. *Child Development Perspectives, 6*, 280–287.

Goldstein, S. B., & Davis, D. S. (2010). Heterosexual allies: A descriptive profile. *Equity & Excellence in Education, 43*, 478–494.

Griffin, P., Lee, C., Waugh, J., & Beyer, C. (2004). Describing roles that Gay-Straight Alliances play in schools: From individual support to social change. *Journal of Gay & Lesbian Issues in Education, 1*, 7–22.

Grossman, A. H., & D'Augelli, A. R. (2006). Transgender youth: Invisible and vulnerable. *Journal of Homosexuality, 51,* 111–128.

Heck, N. C., Flentje, A., & Cochran, B. N. (2011). Offsetting risks: High school Gay-Straight Alliances and lesbian, gay, bisexual, and transgender (LGBT) youth. *School Psychology Quarterly, 26,* 161–174.

Heck, N. C., Lindquist, L. M., Stewart, B. T., Brennan, C., & Cochran, B. N. (2013). To join or not to join: Gay-Straight Student Alliances and the high school experiences of lesbian, gay, bisexual, and transgender youths. *Journal of Gay and Lesbian Social Services, 25,* 77–101.

Herek, G. M., & Capitanio, J. P. (1996). "Some of my best friends": Intergroup contact, concealable stigma, and heterosexuals' attitudes toward gay men and lesbians. *Personality and Social Psychology Bulletin, 22,* 412–424.

Jarrett, R. L., Sullivan, P. J., & Watkins, N. D. (2005). Developing social capital through participation in organized youth programs: Qualitative insights from three programs. *Journal of Community Psychology, 33,* 41–55.

Kuhn, P., & Weinberger, C. (2005). Leadership skills and wages. *Journal of Labor Economics, 23,* 395–436. doi:10.1086/430282

Larson, R., Walker, K., & Pearce, N. (2004). A comparison of youth-driven and adult-driven youth programs: Balancing inputs from youth and adults. *Journal of Community Psychology, 33,* 57–74.

Mahoney, J. L., Cairns, B. D., & Farmer, T. W. (2003). Promoting interpersonal competence and educational success through extracurricular activity participation. *Journal of Educational Psychology, 95,* 409–418.

Mason, C. A., Cauce, A. M., Gonzales, N., & Hiraga, Y. (1996). Neither too sweet nor too sour: Problem peers, maternal control, and problem behavior in African American adolescents. *Child Development, 67,* 2115–2130.

McGuire, J. K., Anderson, C. R., Toomey, R. B., & Russell, S. T. (2010). School climate for transgender youth: A mixed method investigation of student experiences and school responses. *Journal of Youth and Adolescence, 39,* 1175–1188.

McMahon, S. D., Singh, J. A., Garner, L. S., & Benhorin, S. (2004). Taking advantage of opportunities: Community involvement, well-being, and urban youth. *Journal of Adolescent Health, 34,* 262–265.

Mustanski, B. (2011). Ethical and regulatory issues with conducting sexuality research with LGBT adolescents: A call to action for a scientifically informed approach. *Archives of Sexual Behavior, 40,* 673–686.

Pascoe, C. J. (2007). *Dude, you're a fag: Masculinity and sexuality in high school.* Los Angeles, CA: University of California Press.

Pearce, N. J., & Larson, R. W. (2006). How teens become engaged in youth development programs: The process of motivational change in a civic activism organization. *Applied Developmental Science, 10,* 121–131.

Perkins, D. F., Borden, L. M., Villarruel, F. A., Carlton-Hug, A., Stone, M. R., & Keith, J. G. (2007). Participation in structured youth programs: Why ethnic minority urban youth choose to participate—or not to participate. *Youth & Society, 38,* 420–442.

Pettigrew, T. F., & Tropp, L. R. (2006). A meta-analytic test of intergroup contact theory. *Journal of Personality and Social Psychology, 90,* 751–783.

Poteat, V. P., & Scheer, J. R. (2016). GSA advisors' self-efficacy related to LGBT youth of color and transgender youth. *Journal of LGBT Youth, 13,* 311–325.

Poteat, V. P., Scheer, J. R., DiGiovanni, C. D., & Mereish, E. H. (2014). Short-term prospective effects of homophobic victimization on the mental health of heterosexual adolescents. *Journal of Youth and Adolescence, 43,* 1240–1251.

Poteat, V. P., Sinclair, K. O., DiGiovanni, C. D., Koenig, B. W., & Russell, S. T. (2013). Gay-Straight Alliances are associated with student health: A multi-school comparison of LGBTQ and heterosexual youth. *Journal of Research on Adolescence, 23,* 319–330.

Poteat, V. P., Yoshikawa, H., Calzo, J. P., Gray, M. L., DiGiovanni, C. D., Lipkin, A., . . . Shaw, M. P. (2015). Contextualizing Gay-Straight Alliances: Student, advisor, and structural factors related to positive youth development among members. *Child Development, 86,* 176–193.

Roth, J. L., & Brooks-Gunn, J. (2003). What exactly is a youth development program? Answers from research and practice. *Applied Developmental Science, 7,* 94–111.

Russell, S. T., Everett, B. G., Rosario, M., & Birkett, M. (2014). Indicators of victimization and sexual orientation among adolescents: Analyses from youth risk behavior surveys. *American Journal of Public Health, 104,* 255–261.

Russell, S. T., Muraco, A., Subramaniam, A., & Laub, C. (2009). Youth empowerment and high school Gay-Straight Alliances. *Journal of Youth and Adolescence, 38,* 891–903.

Serido, J., Borden, L. M., & Wiggs, C. B. (2014). Breaking down potential barriers to continued program participation. *Youth & Society, 46,* 51–69.

Sorensen, N., Nagda, B. A., Gurin, P., & Maxwell, K. E. (2009). Taking a "hands on" approach to diversity in higher education: A critical-dialogic model for effective intergroup interaction. *Analyses of Social Issues and Public Policy, 9,* 3–35.

Sweat, J. W. (2004). Crossing boundaries: Identity and activism in gay-straight alliances. *Dissertation Abstracts International, 65*(9-A). (UMI No. 3148503)

Tanskanen, J., Taipale, S., & Anttila, T. (2016). Revealing hidden curvilinear relations between work engagement and its predictors: Demonstrating the added value of generalized additive model (GAM). *Journal of Happiness Studies, 17,* 367–387. doi:10.1007/s10902-014-9599-z

Toomey, R. B., Ryan, C., Diaz, R. M., & Russell, S. T. (2011). High school Gay-Straight Alliances (GSAs) and young adult well-being: An examination of GSA presence, participation, and perceived effectiveness. *Applied Developmental Science, 15,* 175–185. doi:10.1080/10888691.2011.607378

Tseng, V., & Seidman, E. (2007). A systems framework for understanding social settings. *American Journal of Community Psychology, 39,* 217–228.

Walls, N. E., Kane, S. B., & Wisneski, H. (2010). Gay-Straight Alliances and school experiences of sexual minority youth. *Youth & Society, 41,* 307–332.

Wood, D., Larson, R. W., & Brown, J. R. (2009). How adolescents come to see themselves as more responsible through participation in youth programs. *Child Development, 80,* 295–309.

Manuscript received May 20, 2015
Final revision received June 1, 2016
Accepted August 22, 2016

American Educational Research Journal
December 2016, Vol. 53, No. 6, pp. 1759–1791
DOI: 10.3102/0002831216678320
© *2016 AERA. http://aerj.aera.net*

Knowledge Globalization Within and Across the People's Republic of China and the United States: A Cross-National Study of Internationalization of Educational Research in the Early 21st Century

Robert J. Tierney
University of British Columbia
University of Sydney
Beijing Normal University
Wei Kan
Beijing Normal University

The study examines globalization within and across China and the United States in conjunction with a portrayal of the nature of the scholarly endeavors over the past 10 years in the two preeminent educational research journals of these countries. By extensive analyses of topics, methodology, and citations the research clarifies the global and local forces at work within and across countries, including the types of internationalization occurring between the United States and People's Republic of China. The findings suggest that globalization involves forces in transaction with one another—local forces addressing national interests and international forces seeking a comparative perspective primarily tied to local interests. The findings highlight

ROBERT J. TIERNEY is a professor of language and literacy education at the University of British Columbia, a Distinguished Visiting Professor at Beijing Normal University, and Honorary Professor at the University of Sydney, Australia; e-mails: *rob.tierney@ubc.ca*, *rob.tierney@sydney.edu.au*. Rob's interests are focused upon global research developments often in the area of literacy and especially as they pertain to historical ways of knowing.

WEI KAN is an associate professor of the Institute of Curriculum & Teaching, Faculty of Education, Beijing Normal University. He has published more than 20 papers in Chinese educational journals and a book by Springer in English Constructivist Teaching in China: Transformation in the Chinese High School System. His main research interests lie in the comparative curriculum and teaching theories and practices, classroom sociology and studies on teachers and pupils voices.

the insularity of each country's scholarly endeavors and how research is skewed toward western scholarship.

KEYWORDS: globalization, internationalization, comparative, epistemologies

Our study occurs at the confluence of studies of the sociology of global knowledge—especially east-west constructions (e.g., Bourdieu, 1998; K. H. Chen, 2010; Collins, 1998), historical analyses of epistemologies (e.g., Elman, 1984), comparative studies of educational research developments (e.g., Manzon, 2011), contrastive rhetoric (Kubota & Lehner, 2004) and a transnational accounting of the mobility of people and ideas (e.g., Charle, Schriewer, & Wagner, 2004; Popkewitz & Rizvi, 2011). Our goal is to examine the epistemological leanings of western and eastern educational research in conjunction with critical reflections on the scholarly trajectories, especially related to internationalization and the interplay between local and global forces that are being manifested within the People's Republic of China (China) and the United States (US) over the past decade. To this end, we pursue comparative analyses of the internationalization of educational research within a corpus of research articles published over the past decade within preeminent journals of China and the US.

Some Background

What is often referred to as the global knowledge economy, in this age of connectedness and increasing global management, includes a shift toward expansive economic and social developments simultaneously intersecting at various levels. This shift involves individuals, institutions, and nations positioning themselves locally as well as within regional and global networks as they trade in the production and consumption of ideas. It is in this era of globalization that previous forms of imperialism are being replaced by what appears to be global government and media-driven western influences (K. H. Chen, 2010; Stack, 2016).

Contributing momentum to these developments are international agencies such as the World Bank, the Organisation for Economic Co-operation and Development (OECD)—originally the Office for European Economic Co-Operation—the United Nations Educational, Social and Cultural Organization (UNESCO), the International Association for the Evaluation of Educational Achievement, and other foundations. These groups have spurred new forms of global governance, national alignments and oversight of education tied to measures of knowledge production (Robertson & Dale, 2009; Rizvi & Lingard, 2010). As Ka Ho Mok of the University of Hong Kong has suggested:

> Against an increasingly competitive global context . . . schools and universities in different parts of the globe have been under

tremendous pressures from governments and the general public to restructure or reinvent the way that they are managed in order to adapt to the ever-changing socio-economic and socio-political environments and to maintain individual nation-states' global competitiveness. (2007, p. 307).

This managerialism is multilateral in nature and quite coercive. For example, it has involved the adoption, by international organizations such as OECD, the World Bank, and others, of forms of management based upon governments "buying into" indices to calibrate national and institutional performance that in turn may influence funding and institutional identity. The World Bank has introduced a *Knowledge Index* that attempts to measure and compare the ability of countries to generate, adopt, and diffuse knowledge, as well as a *Knowledge Economic Index* to assess and compare the economic readiness of countries (World Bank, 2012). Both indices afford countries a basis for assessing themselves based upon the state of education and human services, investment, and infrastructure, including information and communications technology. Likewise, OECD oversees the periodic tracking, development, and use of various educational indices and outcome measures (e.g., Programme for International Student Assessment, 2012) to monitor education progress in various countries. These indices and measures are used within and across countries to leverage change. Various international rankings groups (e.g., Times Higher Education's *World University Ranking*, 2015; QS's *World University Rankings*, 2015; Center for World-Class Universities' *Academic Ranking of World Universities*, 2014) and advisory groups (e.g., Academic Analytics) provide corollary support to institutions vying to advance their international rankings based upon their scholarlyship and reputations.

Simultaneous developments have occurred at the national level (in the United Kingdom (UK), Australia, Canada, and now increasingly in the US and China) with universities being subjected to detailed institutional or government-run audits of funding success and scholarly output to monitor and reward universities based upon their knowledge production. The influence is palpable, with research journals touting their international status based upon impact, university departments advertising their rankings in promotional material, and national media headlines declaring the advance or decline of higher education and future economic and social development based upon these rankings. The repercussions within and across the knowledge sector reflect an alignment of scholarly productivity with these developments as universities and various disciplines argue their raison d'être and basis for investment and decisions on faculty continuation and support. Given that the stakes are high, these measures become priorities with the potential to define, shift, displace, supplement, eliminate, or narrow the scholarship of universities, researchers, professional societies, journals, and publishing houses. Citations indices (e.g., Thomson Reuter's Social Science Citation Index) serve as proxies to judge the quality and quantity of scholarly outputs of institutions and individual faculty members and, in turn, benchmarks which become rewards. In China and in some other countries, universities will provide financial rewards for faculty based upon its prestige as determined by its ranking (Shao & Shen, 2011). In the US, promotion and tenure deliberations on the quality and impact of a faculty member's research will be informed by such indices. Indeed, even skeptical examinations of their merit have offered pragmatic pronouncements of their worth. As James Ladwig (2008) concluded, despite the psychometric limitations of such measures, they have become equivalent to a form of important third party assessment. Ladwig went on to note that nations, especially Australia and others vying to advance, should recognize that "standing on the side-lines or playing the role of the critic is a luxury only the already dominant can afford" (2008, p. 13).

To a large extent, the currency of the realm is tied to western indices that equate success to an alignment with western intellectual traditions and not with eastern, southern, or indigenous. As Malaysian-born scholar Sayed Farid Alatas in his book *Alternative Discourses in the Asian Social Sciences* argued, "There is a Eurocentric bias in that ideas, models, problem selection, methodologies, techniques and even research priorities tend to originate from American, British, and to some extent, French and German works" (2006, p. 32). As Alatas suggested, Asian epistemologies are in danger of being trivialized as they travel across borders. As he stated, "There is a general neglect of local literacy and philosophical traditions. While there may be studies on local literature or philosophy, these traditions remain objects of study and are not considered as sources of concepts in the social sciences" (2006, p. 32).

Ka Ho Mok (2007), Simon Marginson (2000), and others lament the adverse effects of a form of western neoliberal and hierarchical hegemony whereby the education knowledge sector is heavily influenced by national government influences tied more to a western dominated market economy than to their historic traditions and local contexts. Drawing upon his comparative work in Asia, Mok has suggested: "The extreme form of globalization along the 'Anglo-Saxon' line may produce adverse effects and threaten the social, economic, political, and cultural developments of East Asian states." (pp. 312–313). Further, as Mok conjectured, globalization under western influences has the power to shift cultural and historical alignment or allegiances:

> Against an increasingly competitive global context . . . universities in different parts of the globe have been under tremendous pressures from governments and the general public to restructure or reinvent the way that they are managed in order to adapt to the ever-changing socio-economic and socio-political environments and to maintain individual nation-states' global competitiveness. (Mok, 2007, p. 307)

In a similar vein, African (Zululand) scholar Dennis Ocholla has discussed that there may be marginalization of Indigenous African Knowledge (IK). As he stated:

> in order for an individual/community to be admitted into "civilized" or modern society, that individual/community had to abandon practicing and using IK. IK was vindicated, illegitimated, illegalized, suppressed and abandoned by some communities, and the countries and peoples practicing it were condemned and associated with out datedness, a characteristic most people find demeaning. This form of marginalization produced a generation that for the most, does not understand, recognize, appreciate, value or use IK. Arguably, this situation has produced an intellectually "colonized" mindset. (Ocholla, 2007, p. 239)

Similarly, as Raewyn Connell (2007) discussed in her book, *Southern Theory: The Global Dynamics of Knowledge in Social Science*, social science at its core is an undemocratic enterprise in its preference for the traditions of northern scholars. Fazal Rizvi and Robert Lingard (2010) offer a counterargument in suggesting that global developments are occurring in a form that is more filtered and negotiated than sometimes imagined by the colonial lens. They suggest that transformation rarely occurs purely in the image of the dominant partner, but happens in a fashion that is more transactional—akin to a form of hybridization of global influences. As they stated: "While the local is always transformed as a result of engagement with others, this transformation is never uniform across cultural sites; globalization produces new hybrid formations that are highly context-specific and localized." (p. 167). Rizvi and Lingard concur with Piterese (2005), who has contended that the suggestion of homogenization and enculturation:

> overlooks the counter-currents—the impact that the non-Western cultures have been making on the Western cultural practices. It downplays the ambivalence of the globalizing momentum and ignores . . . the indigenization of Western elements (Piterese, 2005, p. 87).

Further illustrating the multifaceted nature of the forces at play and the complex transactional and differentiated nature of these developments, a number of studies have examined shifts in the nature of educational scholarship across time by scholars (e.g., Schriewer, 2004; Schriewer & Martinez, 2004; Yang & Chang, 2009; Zhao, Zhang, Yang, Kirkland, Han, & Zhang, 2008). Taken together, these studies suggest a complex relationship between internationalization, transnational, and intranational developments. In short, there are variations in response within the same community befitting the deep-rooted and complex histories and relationships to ideas, people, and places. For example, in a study of the topics addressed and citations across the articles within selected journals publishing Russian, Spanish, and

Chinese educational research, Schriewer and Martinez (2004) and Schriewer (2004) demonstrated marked differences over time within and across countries that appear to align with political developments within those countries. For example, in China, their topical analyses of articles in three of the leading educational research and policy journals (*Jiaoyu Zazhi* [Education Review], 1901–1949 excluding the war years; *Renmin Jiaoyu* [People's Education], 1950–present; and *Jiaoyu Yanjiu* [Educational Research], 1979–present) indicated an expansion and retraction in international topics versus historical topics from 1921 to 1997. Prior to 1957, predominately international topics accounted for more than 50% of the discussions; from 1964 through 1997, historical topics predominated, accounting for almost 100% of the articles from 1964 to 1965 and approximately 60% from 1995 to 1997. Schriewer and Martinez discerned that the orientation to internationalism in China before the 1950s was tied to an interest in John Dewey and the progressive educational movement; the alignment shifted toward socialism in the postwar period; and finally, with the opening of China in 1978, it shifted toward western and global developments. When Schriewer and Martinez compared scholarly references across the journals (1970–1990) against the *International Encyclopedia of Education* (Husén & Postlethwaite,1994), their data suggested that there were major differences in terms of the origin of the references enlisted. In particular, very few non-western references were among the 31 baseline reference points in *The International Encyclopedia of Education* (Husén & Postlethwaite, 1994). *The International Encyclopedia of Education* included two references that were international organizations, 27 that were European or American, but none by Chinese scholars. In terms of instances of these reference points in China's journals, most were never referenced and only eight (John Dewey, Jean Piaget, Robert Glaser, Marlaine Lockhead, Benjamin Bloom, John Keeves, OECD, UNESCO) more than once.

The lack of correspondence between the citations in the *International Encyclopedia of Education* with citations in the Chinese, Spanish, and Russian journals suggests that it would be mistaken to assume that educational scholarship has the same antecedents across different countries. As Schriewer and Martinez (2004) concluded, educational knowledge is "refracted by each society's internal selection thresholds and needs for interpretation, which are the outcome of cultural traditions and collective mentality, as well as political forces and dominant ideologies." (p. 50)

In a similar study, Yong Zhao et al. (2008) examined a subsample of articles published in 2003–2004 from *Jiaoyu Yanjiu* [Educational Research] (*JYYJ*) and the *American Educational Research Journal* (*AERJ*) in an attempt "to understand epistemological and methodological differences and similarities across countries" (p. 2). Their study reinforced the view that international issues receive considerably less emphasis than domestic matters (especially in the US) and that there are significant differences in scholarly approaches across countries. They found that the proportion of empirical versus conceptual articles across the two journals was marked, with the majority of Chinese articles being more conceptual and aligned with more eastern traditions than western. Drawing extensively upon Nisbett's (2003) discussion of eastern versus western traditions, Zhao and colleagues speculated there was a tendency to enlist a "holistic" Chinese tradition versus the "analytic" western tradition. As they stated:

> At a deeper level, empirical investigation and logical argumentation, which are integral to the western empirical tradition, are often at odds with the Chinese habits of mind, which is characterized by holistic, dialectal thinking that relies on personal experiences, wisdom and reflection. . . . Easterners inculcated with a holistic and dialectal mental habit tend to pay more attention to contexts and relationships than objects. They prefer experience- and context-based reasoning over applying pure logical rules. (Zhao et al., 2008, p. 15)

The impact of the predisposition to the local extends to the manner in which international scholarship is considered. A study of the infiltration of western critical educational thought upon China over time illustrates the refractive nature and overriding influence of local filters upon studies from abroad. Guang-cai Yang and Yin Chang, in an article entitled "The circumstances and the possibilities of Critical Educational Studies in China" (2009), explored the circumstances that contribute to China's selective consideration, and sometimes dismissal of western critical theory and Marxist scholarship. They detailed the historical conditions that have contributed to how Chinese scholars positioned western critical theories. Despite the interest that Chinese translations of their work have received, they claim that American Marxist scholarship is not seen as transferable. Instead, the work of Dewey (Dewey, 1916/2001; Wang, 2007) and constructivists has been given more prominence in terms of applicability to China's development. Yang and Chang emphasize the situatedness of scholarship within countries and the global knowledge systems across countries, including their ideological orientations across time, space, and circumstances. They offer a view of knowledge transfer, which is akin to complex, site-based forms of selective consideration and differential use rather than universal applicability.

Further highlighting the interplay between local and global forces, Yoshiko Nozaki's (2009) article, "Orientalism, the west and non-west binary, and postcolonial perspectives in cross-cultural research and education," argues that the creation of a "we" versus "you" characterizations of peoples represent forms of hegemonic categorizations. Nozaki suggests that cross-national research has a tendency to perpetuate a view of cultures and peoples as binaries, highlighting uniformity rather than complex hybridity that brings to the fore variability consistent with intranational differences versus cross-national elements befitting a more orientalist view. She further argues, "researchers need to stress the variations, multiplicities, and contradictions within all Asian nations, peoples, and cultures. . . . Just like an individual's identity, a national identity is multiple and contradictory" (Nozaki, 2009, p. 486).

Consistent with this view, a number of Asian scholars have discussed the complex nature of Asian identities, across different regions, over the past 50 years. For example, stemming from his analyses of different Asian regions, Taiwanese scholar Kuan-Hsing Chen (2010), in his book, *Asia as Method: Toward Deimperialization*, argues for the unpacking of the development of new forms of colonization and power relations in conjunction with the advent of forces across and within Asia. Chen describes the advent of new forms of imperialism on multiple fronts tied to historical antecedents and current circumstances, including emerging global forces, an amalgamation of western and eastern styles, and shifting power relationships across and within societies. In a different vein, Leo Ching (2000) in *Globalizing the Regional, Regionalizing the Global: Mass Culture and Asianism in the Age of Late Capital*, draws upon a consideration of cultural forces at play within and across nations in conjunction with mass media to suggest a form of globalization involving a conflating of global, regional, and local forces. He posits a form of cultural integration emerging not from colonization or imperialism, but in alignment with global, regional, and local transactions of mass identity

Our Study

The current study reports our efforts to delve into these issues by undertaking a comparative analysis of educational research from China and from the US, enlisting a framework that extends the analyses of Schriewer and Martinez (2004) and Zhao et al. (2008) to address not only differences in goals, practices, methodological tendencies, specific topics, and citations, but also the extent and nature of internationalization within and across two of the most preeminent education journals in the US and China. In particular, we were keen to determine the nature and extent of international scholarship and how international pursuits were positioned alongside the local forces—especially the nuanced influences of local upon global and global upon the local. Our goal was to delve into how local traditions and internationalization interfaced with one another.

Our overriding questions were: What are the scholarly trajectories, especially related to internationalization, that are being manifested within China and the US over the past decade? What is the nature of the interplay between local and global forces? We posited that educational research publications would help us understand the forces at play in the high-status world of global dominance of information not unlike that which Pierre Bourdieu (1998) described in his analysis of the French academic world in *Homo Academicus*. As he stated:

Only a sociological self-analysis of this kind, which owes and concedes nothing to self-indulgent narcissism, can rally help to place the scholar in the position where he is able to bring the familiar word the detached scrutiny which, with no special vigilance, the ethnologist brings to bear on any world to which he is not linked by the inherent complicity of being involved in its social game, its *illusio*, which creates the very value of the objectives of the game, as it does the game itself. (Bourdieu, 1998, p. xii)

For this study, we presumed that the *American Educational Research Journal* (*AERJ*) would be representative of educational research in the US and *Jiaoyu Yanjiu* [Educational Research] (*JYYJ*) would be representative in China. They are parallel in many ways: both involve blind review of articles and are highly selective, with acceptance rates less than 20% of their submissions. *AERJ* is published four to six times per year by the American Educational Research Association, a nonprofit professional society with more than 25,000 members. The National Institute publishes *JYYJ* monthly for Educational Studies, a research office for the Ministry of Education of the People's Republic of China. Apart from advancing government policy deliberations, *JYYJ* represents the premier venue for independent educational research of relevance to China.[1] We chose to examine all the articles published in each journal at the turn of the 21st century and 10 years later. This included 139 journal articles plus occasional editorials across 20 issues of *AERJ* (2002–2003, 2013–2014) and 464 articles across 12 issues of *JYYJ* (2003, 2013).

As we have stated, we directed our analyses toward uncovering the visible manifestations of internationalization based upon and compared with the aspirations as declared by the editors of the journals, the composition of the editorial board, and actual articles examining international issues that reached across countries. We were especially keen to address the nature, type, and amount of international research appearing in the two journals and how such work is positioned. Were there parallels or crossover in the scholarship within and across the two journals, the topics covered, and the methodologies employed?

To these ends, our analyses involved extracting and presenting the key features of the two journals from the information provided by the editors, from fact sheets included on the official websites or front matter of the journals. Some of the analyses were tied to simple counts such as page numbers or the nature and number of references and other material, all of which were checked and easy to verify. The categories and coding employed to assess topic coverage and methodologies involved an iterative process with the two researchers developing, redeveloping, and revising categories based upon an initial scoping of categories from related research. We adjusted the categories based upon our observations of the characteristics of the articles that we encountered. As our discussion of findings suggest, the coding systems were applied consistently; however, the complexity of their development and nuances brought to the fore some notable cross-national differences. Based upon a check of our coding across 10% of the articles in both journals, we agreed upon our categorization at a level of 92%. Whenever we differed, we reached a consensus on the application of a single category while noting factors that might account for the disagreement, especially if they were rooted in cultural constructions. As David Clarke (2015) has elucidated, tensions reflecting cultural differences arise whenever one is making comparisons across countries using categories or measures fitted to one and not quite to the other. As he stated, "The danger is that the commensurability demands of such comparisons conceal major conceptual differences" (p. 5). Indeed, in our study, matters of fit often revealed differences that we were keen to discern.

Our examinations of internationalization are threaded throughout our various analyses. We listed all instances of studies that we deemed international—that is, studies that reference data from countries other than the home country of the journal. Second, we examined how these studies served the interests of the home country. Indeed, oftentimes international work exists on the seams of the local as a way of supplementing, confirming, or comparing and contrasting local inquiries. Third, we examined the crossover in terms of topics, methodology, and citations between the two countries and the extent to which scholarship from another country (especially the US and China, respectively) informed the other. Fourth, we examined the editorial philosophy and infrastructure of each journal.

Findings

Stated Purpose of the Journals, Especially in Terms of Internationalization

By examining the front matter and occasional editorial comments in each journal, we were able to extract declarations that espoused the overall goals of each journal, including whether and how internationalization might be a goal. We found explicit statements that suggest that internationalization represents a stated goal, but, as a pursuit, we noted that it appeared to take a "backseat" to, or is not viewed as, serving the core goal to publish original research of relevance to their own countries.

The website of the National Institute of Education Studies makes clear that the focus of *JYYJ* is China. As they state:

> Since its foundation in 1979, Educational Research has played a leading role in disseminating knowledge of educational policies of the Communist Party of China (CPC) and the Ministry of Education, and has provided theoretical support and underpinning for China's educational reform and development. Educational Research offers deep insight into educational theory, advocates academic innovation and pays close attention to and focuses on key educational issues.

The journal functions as a platform for significant academic discussion and numerous high-quality articles on educational theory have been published. (National Institute of Education Studies, 2015)

The editors of *JYYJ* state that their goal is to address the significant problems of Chinese educational reform and development, promoting the publishing of original educational research that attends to localized challenges. To this end, they advocate for educational science with Chinese characteristics: educational science that is informed rather than governed by communications with foreign educational studies (Zeng & Gao, 2009). In terms of the latter, they stress the importance of learning from other nations' educational policies and practices, understanding their strengths and weaknesses of education in the service of identifying areas of improvement for China. Befitting this orientation, a number of articles including international references were published in *JYYJ* in the 1990s, as was a recurring column entitled "Comparative Education." This column was replaced in 2010 by a new section entitled "International Perspectives." We would conjecture that this partitioning into a column or section was a means of also dealing with international perspectives, but in the interest of supporting local development.

Over the past 10 years *AERJ*'s editorial teams has explicitly declared that their overriding goal was the publication of original reports of theoretical and empirical work. Their website states:

The *American Educational Research Journal* (*AERJ*) publishes original empirical and theoretical studies and analyses in education. The editors seek to publish articles from a wide variety of academic disciplines and substantive fields; they are looking for clear and significant contributions to the understanding and/or improvement of educational processes and outcomes (*AERJ*, 2015).

This goal has been maintained under the leadership of different editorial teams as well as during shifts in the journal itself. In terms of internationalization, *AERJ* recognizes that a large proportion of its subscribers (individual and institutional) are from overseas, including a significant number of Asians and Africans.[2] Relative to scholarship, efforts to internationalize have been voiced especially with *AERJ* editors offering broad statements about the merits of internationalization, but in the interest of, or complementary to, the local. For example, in 2006, in an editorial overview of the "Social and Institutional Analyses" section of the journal, incoming editors Sandra Hollingsworth and Margaret Gallego stated "their deep commitment to diversity across geographical and cultural spaces . . . and international perspectives" (p. 3). In 2014, the new editors of the "Social and Institutional Analyses" section declared an interest in publishing articles that dealt with how the local is "intertwined with the global" in responding to "global phenomena," and suggested the need for "a view of schooling as a world cultural phenomena" (McCarty et al., 2014, p. 5) and for scholarship to be "making a difference in the world" (p. 6). In 2014, Harold O'Neil, Jr., the new editor of the "Teaching and Learning" section, made some mention of internationalization in conjunction with suggesting areas of research, including issues of privacy on a global scale and noted that they would expect "a probable increase" in articles from scholars outside of the US (O'Neil, 2014, p. 114).

Composition of Editorial Boards Especially in Terms of International Representation

Our examination of the nature of the commitment to internationalization extended to an analysis of the editorial board of each journal. We were interested in the countries or international regions represented by the institutional affiliation of those scholars listed as the editors and editorial review board members. We questioned whether there was significant representation of scholars from outside the US for *AERJ* and from outside of China for *JYYJ*, and whether the selection of editors and the editorial review board members of *AERJ* and *JYYJ* extended beyond Euro-American representation.

We found that neither the listed institutional affiliations of the editors nor the editorial board of either *AERJ* or *JYYJ* suggested that a conscious or concerted effort had been made to internationalize. Both journals have had a very limited number of editorial associates and editorial board members with international backgrounds, but rarely do they reach beyond Euro-Americans or the American continent. Indeed, international representation appeared very limited across both journals. In particular, despite the recent appearance of scholars from outside North America as associate editors of *AERJ*, the number of international scholars from nonwestern countries as members of the *AERJ* editorial board and inclusive of any non-American country has been less than 10 percent for some time. In 2014, *AERJ*, for one of the two sections (i.e., Social and Institutional Analysis) appointed two associate editors from overseas: an American-born Australian and a New Zealander. For the second section (i.e., Teaching and Leaning), *AERJ* appointed a New Zealander and a Korean. But the international editorial board representation has remained limited to a handful of international scholars. Furthermore, with only a couple of exceptions, over the past 12 years, all of the scholars serving as editorial team members have been from western countries. In terms of *JYYJ*, the editorial team included only two international scholars, who were Hong Kong academics.

International Scope of the Journals in Terms of Articles

Based upon the aforementioned analyses, we would suggest that neither *AERJ* nor *JYYJ* has been overt in their support of international submissions.

Hence, we were not surprised that the journals tend to include only international pieces that served national perspectives or interests. In *JYYJ*, discussions of educational developments in other countries or comparative studies were focused upon the implications for China; likewise, in *AERJ* studies of educational developments in other countries or comparative studies were focused on the relevance to the US alone. With few exceptions, international comparisons published in *JYYJ* were focused on the US with occasional comparisons to other western countries; in *AERJ*, international work extended to Canada, North and South America, and other western nations. Comparison rarely extended to Asia or African countries. Again, it is as if there are strong local forces at play and the global forces have a predominately western bias.

In *JYYJ*, articles that are international or comparative have a small foothold and are relatively stable with 24 (12.5%) international in 2003 and 28 (10.5%) in 2013, with approximately 3% of these articles involving comparative studies.[3] In terms of the specific character of the international topics, as we have suggested, *JYYJ* mainly focused on themes deemed relevant to China and restricted international discussions to a few countries—usually the UK and the US.[4] For example, in 2003, *JYYJ* published international studies that focused on topics of interest to the Chinese (e.g., moral education, higher education, educational finance, and rural education). They included studies with the following foci:

- Characteristics of western moral education in the 20th century,
- Shifts in the moral education system at American elementary schools,
- Curricula (e.g., art education) and curriculum reform in the UK,
- History of western higher education, and
- Educational investment—Europe & the US.

In 2013, 28 articles focused on developments outside of—but aligned with—issues also arising in China of interest to Chinese scholars (e.g., school reform: K–12, higher education, assessment matters, international organization, and teacher education) including:

- Higher education in the US (e.g., student-based assessment, reviews systems),
- American teacher education professional standards,
- International organizations (e.g., UNESCO),
- Strategies and approaches of international aid organization, and
- School improvement pursuits in New York schools.

For *AERJ*, the number and nature of international studies represented a similar percentage and the same bias toward comparisons with western countries. Over the past 10 years, *AERJ* did not publish a substantial number of articles with an international focus. The number of articles dealing with non-US or non-Canadian matters represented only 10% of the articles published in 2002–2003. Only one article dealt with a nonwestern country. In 2013–2014, international pieces accounted for 12.5%, but again only one included data from a nonwestern country.

During the period 2002–2003, *AERJ* articles dealing with international matters included the following: a study on class size by four UK authors; a paper coauthored by Canadian and US scholars on alternative assessment reform; a paper by US authors on tracking in the US, Germany, and Japan; a study focused on Hong Kong students' self-concept by an Australian and Hong Kong authors; two studies by Canadian authors on programs for young women and a study dealing with issues of pacing in teaching skills; a study by an Israeli author on cooperative learning; and a paper on globalization and citizenship by a US-located author.

In 2013–2014, the number of international contributions or non-American studies appearing in *AERJ* was slightly higher at 12.5%, but again only one study included a nonwestern country. Topics appeared to be tied to US interests (e.g., streaming) and some issues that also had some resonance with global developments or concerns (e.g., indigenous education, immigration, teacher education). Specifically, the international contributions included a study by a New Zealand and an Australian author on a Maori-based educational model; a German study on preservice teachers; a Dutch study on teacher development; a UK historical analysis of examinations; a German development study of young migrant children; a paper focusing on educational researchers and "practicality"; a study by a Singaporean and Australian-based scholars on streaming in Singapore; and a cross-national comparison by US and Mexican scholars of US and Mexican students learning to read in Spanish.

If one compares the state of international scholarship across the two journals, there is a sense of the local overriding the global currents. Additionally, global currents, if they exist, tend to flow between or toward western countries. For example, in the US, most international work was western, originating in Canada, Europe, Australia, or New Zealand; in China, comparisons and international benchmarking were tied to western versus other Asian or southern countries. Without discounting the difficulty journals might have in procuring international submissions, we would posit there is a form of national-centrism and western bias in knowledge exchange verging on free-trade zones among western countries and especially between selected countries (e.g., Canada).[5] We would speculate that the failure to facilitate exchanges with eastern and southern scholars is limiting. Indeed, we would suggest that there are unrealized potentials as authors and editors fail to connect to scholars pursing similar issues across the globe—east and west, north and south. Overall, across both journals there appeared to be a limited commitment to international articles, and those that appeared were subordinated to the domestic interests of the country of origin of the journal.

Areas of Study

A subset of articles from both journals was read by both researchers as we formulated topic areas and in conjunction with checks on our reliability. Once the topic areas were agreed upon, each of us was responsible for discerning the primary topic of each article based upon a reading of each article published within *AERJ* or *JYYJ* for four years. The discernment was based upon the full text, abstract, and listing key words.

Our examinations of the areas of study across all the articles within each journal during these time periods helped us delve into the nature of the scholarship within each country and possible parallels. In both countries, our analyses supported the view that educational research was inextricably tied to and served an important role in addressing national matters. The primary topics across the two journals appeared to signal the importance of educational research studies in China and the US and recognition of their role as tools for and barometers of societal developments aligned with the values and policies of each country.

In both countries, there was a similar emphasis upon teacher education, school reform, higher education, and curriculum, instruction, and learning across the two journals. At the same time, there were some areas such as moral education, educational finances, and rural education that represented a major focus of China versus the US. For the US, there was a strong interest in issues of diversity, with a large percentage of papers across the various topics focused upon race, gender, minority groups, economic differences, and matters of equity and cultural differences.

As shown in Table 1, *JYYJ* covered a wide range of topics. Teacher education (7.7% in 2003; 7.1% in 2013), higher education (10.7% in 2003; 15.1% in 2013) was the focus of a substantial number of studies along with the emergence of studies focused upon K–12 education (especially if one combines the research on schooling with the emergence of papers describing projects in local schools). Educational psychology (7.1% in 2003; 2% in 2013) declined perhaps with the emergence of other outlets for this work in China. Comparative educational studies declined in terms of the relative number of overall percentage of articles, but not in terms of the actual number (17 or 10.1% in 2003; 22 or 8.7% in 2013).

As shown in Table 2, *AERJ* had a similarly large number of teaching and teacher education articles as well as articles on school management, curriculum, instruction, and learning. At times these areas overlapped. For example, educational policy, educational reform, and school management overlapped with one another and sometimes with other categories. Missing from *AERJ* were studies focused on moral development.

Essentially, the scholarship in both countries focused on policy and reform, but *AERJ* seem to reflect shifts in the focus of the reform agenda in the US (e.g., increased attention to the role of teachers). We would

Table 1
Areas of Study for *JYYJ*

Topics	*JYYJ* 2003		*JYYJ* 2013	
	Frequency	Percent	Frequency	Percent
Educational philosophy & theory	25	14.8	29	11.5
Teacher education & teaching	13	7.7	18	7.1
Moral education/schooling	9	5.3	7	2.8
Higher education	18	10.7	38	15.1
School management & policy	8	4.7	8	3.2
Professional education	4	2.4	12	4.8
Continuing education	0	0	3	1.2
Rural education	5	3.0	1	0.4
Non-gov't education & charter ed.	5	3.0	2	0.8
Educational psychology & dev.	12	7.1	6	2.4
Educational technology	0	0	2	0.8
Early childhood	0	0	4	1.6
Basic education (K–12) & policy	0	0	26	10.3
Educational assessment	3	1.8	5	2.0
Educational economy & finance	8	4.7	0	0
Educational history studies	11	6.5	12	4.8
Comparative educational studies	17	10.1	22	8.7
Other Arguments	8	4.7	19	7.5
Essays	8	4.7	6	2.4
Book reviews	4	2.4	6	2.4
Conference/review	11	6.5	7	2.8
Projects	0	0	19	7.5
Total	169		252	

contend that in both 2002–2003 and again in 2013–2014, the number of articles dealing with educational policy and reform was significant, but distributed slightly differently. To judge the stability of a focus on policy and reform, we combined some of the categories (e.g., school management, educational policy, and educational reform) and also extended the combination in 2013–2014 to include teacher studies, which became part of the reform agenda in the US during this period. If combined, the number of articles dealing with interrelated policy/management/reform issues in 2002–2003 and 2013–2014 would approach 33%—that is, they remained similar across the decade.

Perhaps the most salient feature in this analysis of *AERJ* was the sustained focus on equity, poverty, and differences. While this is not reflected directly in the categories, we found ourselves making special note of the significant number of papers that adopted a critical lens in examining schooling

Table 2
Areas of Study for *AERJ*

Topics	*AERJ* 2002–2003		*AERJ* 2013–2014	
	Frequency	Percent	Frequency	Percent
Educational philosophy & theory	10	16.9	3	3.9
Teacher education & teaching	7	11.9	11	14.3
Moral education/schooling	0	0	1	1.3
Higher education	3	5.1	14	18.2
School management & policy	10	16.9	14	18.2
Professional education	0	0	1	1.3
Continuing education	0	0	0	0
Rural education	0	0	1	1.3
Non-gov't funded, charter schools	3	5.1	2	2.6
Educational psychology & dev.	0	0	4	5.2
Educational technology	4	6.8	0	0
Early childhood	5	8.5	6	7.8
Basic education (K–12) & policy	0	0	2	2.6
Educational economy & finance	0	0	0	0
Curriculum & teaching	12	20.3	12	15.6
Educational history studies	3	5.1	5	6.5
Comparative educational studies	2	3.4	1	1.3
Other: arguments, essays, projects etc.	0	0	0	0
Total	59		77	

across genders, race, language minority groups (including Asian-American, Mexican-American, or other immigrant groups), and economic circumstances in conjunction with discussions of schools and society, especially matters of equity, access, opportunity, and difference. Indeed, more than 50% of the articles delved into the data across diverse learners, particularly in the context of research focused on curriculum, school reform, teaching and teacher education, and school management.[6] In terms of cross-national differences, whereas in the US, research studies were interfaced with concerns around ethnicity, gender, and poverty, in China, studies were often coupled with concerns around rural issues and economic disparities. The findings befit the trend identified by past comparative studies—namely, the nature of and variations in topics addressed in the key research journals reflect historical developments within nations, including governmental leanings and local concerns (Cheek, 2016; Schriewer, 2004; Schriewer & Martinez, 2004). They also align with the sentiments of educational leaders—including journal editors—in China and the US who tout local and national interests as priorities ahead of international pursuits unless directed to serve local needs. Such notions are not inconsistent with perhaps China's leading comparative

Table 3
**The Number of Separate *JYYJ* Citations of Western Authors:
Top 10 Frequently Cited**

Rank	2003	Citation Frequency	2013	Citation Frequency
1.	Marx, K.	20	Burton, R. C.	17
2.	Dewey, J.	17	Dewey, J.	17
3.	Hegel. F. G. W.	7	Marx, K.	12
4.	Tyler, W. R.	6	Whitehead, A. N.	7
5.	Foucault, M.	5	Fullan, M.	9
6.	Pinar, W.	5	Hegel. F. G. W.	8
7.	Bell, D.	4	Bourdieu P.	6
8.	Burton, R. C.	4	Leithwood, K.	5
9.	Giddens, A.	4	Hallinger, P.	5
10.	van Manen, M.	4	Bridges, E.	5

educator, Mingyuan Gu (2014), who in his discussion of the future of Chinese scholarship, has argued that there is need to balance respect for education's cultural roots with a form of integration of selected western ideas with Chinese thought and practice.

Citations

The insularity and biases of each country were most apparent in their enlistment or lack thereof of nonwestern scholars. Our analyses of the citations provided evidence of national-centric tendencies within the two countries, but especially for the US. Whereas American scholars appearing in *AERJ* did not cite Chinese scholars (i.e., scholars located in the People's Republic of China), Chinese scholars in *JYYJ* did cite a small, but slightly increasing number of American scholars and other western sources.

Table 3 lists a subset of the most cited western scholars in *JYYJ* for 2003 and for 2013. They tend to be western scholars whose work has been translated for Chinese audiences and aligned with Chinese interests in social philosophy, curriculum theory, and school leadership.

It is important to note that the local filters in effect influence not only what scholarship might be cited, but also how it is used. Chinese authors tend to mention and adapt rather than impose foreign frameworks upon their work. Western thinking, methods, and findings are selectively considered and, if enlisted, adjusted in ways that befit Chinese circumstances and Chinese ways of knowing. For example, Marx and Engels along with Foucault tend to be referenced as broad ideological perspectives befitting China's underlying values. As Yang and Chang (2009) argued in their assessment of the influence of western sociological studies, such work is seen as relevant, but not directly or "mechanically" since they fail to "fit the reality of Chinese society and education" (p. 375).

As we have specified, our examination of the citations within *AERJ* indicated that authors located in the People's Republic of China were not cited. Instead, *AERJ* authors cited other American scholars or scholars from other western countries. They did so in a manner that was quite focused—that is, many of the citations were specific to the nature of the study itself. For instance, studies of history education might cite Peter Seixas and other history educators; in mathematics education, studies might cite mathematics educators such as Hilda Borko, Alan Schoenfeld, or others. Likewise, studies of teaching and teacher education tended to cite research related to teacher education scholars such as Marilyn Cochran-Smith, Kenneth Zeigler, and Virginia Richardson. Studies of reform in this period drew from David Tyack and John Dewey, but more recently from David Berliner, Michael Fullan, Andy Hargreaves, Linda Darling-Hammond, and Anthony Bryk.

Given the prevalence of *AERJ* articles dealing with diversity, school reform matters, and matters of equity, many of the articles drew upon sociocultural theorists, including critical theorists focused upon race, gender, and class, as well as discussions of diversity. Across the decade, *AERJ* authors drew upon critical theorists such as Michael Apple, Paulo Freire, Henry Giroux, Joseph Kincheloe, Patti Lather, Peter McLaren, Thomas Popkewitz, Shirley Steinberg, and others. Their perspectives were informed by North American and South American critical theorists as well as a number of European scholars, including Basil Bernstein, Pierre Bourdieu, Norman Fairclough, Michel Foucault, Mikhail Bakhtin, Gilles Deleuze, and others who had unpacked dimensions of power and identity. Selected articles involved critical discussions related to the following: issues of race with citations from scholars such as Gloria Ladson-Billings, Carol Lee, Stuart Hall, Carl Grant, bell hooks, Hillary Jenks, Michelle Fine, and Carol Weiss; matters of cultural diversity drawing upon Kris Gutiérrez, James Banks, J. Hill, G. Valdes, Norma Gonzales, Luis Mull, A. Valenzuela; issues of gender drawing extensively upon Bronwyn Davies and Nancy Fraser; issues of class and poverty drawing upon a range of authors including David Berliner, Henry Ginsburg; critical treatments of a combination of race and class issues tied to matters of choice, tracking, privatization, desegregation, immigration, and urban–rural divide, drawing upon Larry Cuban, Linda McNeil, Jeannie Oakes, James Coleman, and others; and most recently indigenous research drawing upon the work of scholars such as Teresa McCarty, Graham Hingangaroa Smith, and Linda Tuhiwai Te Rina Smith. It should be noted that many American studies drew upon media reports; scholars in both China and the US drew upon Chinese government or US government reports respectively. In the US, a great deal of secondary analyses of national data sets was apparent as well as some involving the Trends in International

Mathematics and Science Study or the Programme for International Student Assessment.

Taken together, the findings for the US are quite stark especially if one considers differences between the length and number of citations of the articles in *AERJ* versus *JYYJ*. Each *AERJ* article was significantly longer with three to four times the number of citations as compared with the *JYYJ* articles. *AERJ* articles include a significant number of citations per article (25 to 100+). Compared with the citations of *AERJ*, only three out of 21 articles (less than 15%) sampled from *JYYJ* had more than 25 citations. Most of the articles (slightly over 60%) cited six to 20 references. As we mentioned, in the January 2014 issue of *JYYJ*, for example, 13 papers (62%) listed fewer than 10 citations. In addition, seven articles (nearly 33%) had lists of fewer than five citations. Due to the brevity of the articles and the lack of extensive reference lists in articles published in *JYYJ*, discerning patterns among citations was difficult. Most of the articles (slightly over 60%) cited just six to 20 references. For example, in the January 2014 issue of *JYYJ*, the majority of articles had fewer than seven citations.

Given the sparseness of references in *JYYJ*, citation patterns within *JYYJ* over the past decade are more suggestive than definitive. Nonetheless, we would argue that Chinese scholars are less national-centric, even taking into account their preference for citing other Chinese scholars. In terms of the latter, among Chinese scholars, two books by Zhongying Shi were most highly cited in 2013 by Chinese educational researchers: *Transformation in Knowledge Growth Mode and Educational Reform* (2000) and *On the Logic of Educational Practices* (2006), which was cited 23 times in *JYYJ*. In addition, in the area of teacher education and educational methodology, Xiangming Chen's works were frequently cited: X. M. Chen (2000; 2003) were cited 20 times in *JYYJ* in 2013.

Methodologies

As we have indicated, we were keen to explore the scholarly traditions in some depth. To do so, we wanted to go beyond what was explored and who informed the research, to how it was studied. To this end, we attempted to sort the articles by the methods employed. We did so while recognizing that pigeonholing almost any study was quite problematic, as increasingly studies employed a variety of methods tied to different theoretical frameworks (sociocultural, critical, etc.). Methodologies were interfaced with the nature of the arguments offered and the role of research from an epistemological perspective.[7]

Our examinations of the methodologies employed yielded interesting findings for each country and across the two countries. For the US, we had anticipated that the behavioristic vestiges of the past would be apparent in *AERJ*, especially along with the reappearance of positivistic

Table 4
AERJ Methodologies

Methodology	AERJ 2002–2003		AERJ 2013–2014	
	Frequency	Percent	Frequency	Percent
Experimental	6	10.00	9	11.39
Case study	20	33.33	15	18.98
Discourse analysis, document & historical study	10	16.66	9	11.39
Comparative research	3	5.00	8	10.13
Survey	0	0	5	6.33
Ethnographic study	3	5.00	5	6.33
Secondary analysis	13	21.67	20	25.31
Mixed methodology	4	6.67	7	8.86
Reflections, interpretation	1	1.67	1	1.26
Total	60		79	

experimentation as a result of a narrowed view of research mandated by governments and the privileging of randomized trials of interventions. Instead, we found a rich mix of research pursuits within *AERJ*, including a mix of qualitative and quantitative methodologies. Qualitative studies often enlisted ethnographic tools coupled with historical analyses and discourse analysis. In terms of quantitative leanings, *AERJ* authors appeared to be more intent on advancing understandings by delving into issues with more of a case study orientation that involved explorations of large-scale data, a region, school, or select populations. Many of the articles focused on the generation and testing of complex, multidimensional models based upon a composite of variables. Indeed, approximately 50% of the case studies, comparative research, survey research, and secondary analyses involved testing and building hierarchical models or were examined against qualitative data from interviews or follow-up surveys. In turn, the articles were provocative and historical rather than claiming wide generalizability. Again, over the past decade, *AERJ* published only a limited number of traditional empirical intervention studies focused upon specific teaching strategies or approaches. More common were studies involving surveys or existing data sets, which are subjected to more extensive analyses and follow-up, oftentimes enlisting a mix of qualitative probes of a subset of the participants related to the broader quantitative findings of the fuller population. It is noteworthy that many of the articles appearing in *AERJ* referenced or drew upon national or regional data sets and findings. Across most *AERJ* articles, various national and state reports released by government authorities or private foundations as well as the media were often cited.

Table 5
JYYJ Methodologies

Methodology	JYYJ 2002–2003		JYYJ 2013–2014	
	Frequency	Percent	Frequency	Percent
Experimental	3	1.53	6	2.21
Case study	4	2.04	12	4.48
Discourse, historic analysis	4	2.04	10	3.73
Comparative research	6	3.06	19	7.09
Survey	1	0.51	7	2.61
Ethnographic study	0	0	3	1.12
Secondary analysis	9	4.59	16	5.97
Mixed methodology	2	1.02	17	6.34
Reflections/interpretations[a]	167	85.20	178	66.42
Total	196		268	

[a]Most of these papers are theoretical interpretations or reflections on the researchers' arguments without statistics, data, or other qualitative or quantitative evidences.

In contrast, our analyses of *JYYJ* suggested a more limited range of research in the Chinese journal than was found in *AERJ*—especially the extent to which American scholars engage in data-based examinations, mixed methods design, and model testing. We discerned that the majority of the *JYYJ* articles were not empirical or data-based studies, especially in 2003. The overwhelming majority (close to 85%) of the articles published in *JYYJ* were essays, reviews of the literature, or interpretative or argumentative pieces. In 2013, despite a significant reduction in those numbers, 178 articles, some 66%, were still interpretative essays. In 2013, nearly 17% papers reported experiments, case studies, discourse analyses, or mixed methodology studies; 7% were case studies and surveys. Most data-based studies in *JYYJ* lacked the mix of qualitative and quantitative data that is now common in *AERJ*.

The results of our attempt to examine the various scholarly dimensions (topics, citations, and methodologies) yielded what we contend are some provocative findings, including significant differences across *AERJ* and *JYYJ*. While there was some overlap in areas of study, there were significant differences in the methodologies employed and the scholarly works framing their inquiries—including their use or lack of use of foreign scholarship. Our data substantiated differences in research practices aligned with each country's historical disposition and antecedents, not unlike those discussed in efforts to portray and trace Chinese scholarly traditions by Lloyd and Sivin (2003) and Nisbett (2003). As they have argued, Chinese scholarship has a tendency toward pursuing persuasion aligned with public interest, rather than western forms of rationalistic empiricism in competition with existing ideas (see Lloyd and Sivin, 2003).

They also suggest changes may be afoot as new dynamics emerge. For example, the increase in the proportion of empirical studies in China appearing in *JYYJ* may reflect the shifting goals of the journal in terms of its competitiveness globally. It may also represent an attempt by the journal to respond to and accommodate Chinese scholars returning from the west equipped with western tools and dispositions. However, these differences may also have their antecedents in mundane elements. For example, some of the prevailing differences may be reinforced or accounted for by editorial practices. For instance, there are major differences in the length of articles: *AERJ* articles are three to four times the length of *JYYJ* articles.

Discussion

What are the scholarly trajectories, especially related to internationalization, that are being manifested within China and the US during what we deemed as a period of heightened global forces over the past decade? Although there is voiced support for internationalization and globalization among those editing educational research journals, there are similar forces in US and China that are shaping the nature of the internationalization of scholarship. The primary forces in effect are local forces tied to expectations that the primary audience of the journal remains American or Chinese, rather than a global or regional audience. Predominately, the two journals publish work that is tied to national agendas often based upon national data sets, but with minimal reference to global developments. Even when international scholarship appears, it is viewed as supporting the advancement of American or Chinese education and is expected to relate to education issues in those countries. Global forces exist but are subjected to local filters; for example, whereas Chinese scholars attend to developments in the US and around the globe, they do so in a fashion that is selective and differentiated. *JYYJ* articles include occasional references and discussions of American scholarship, but in a fashion that is discerning with consideration to its fit or relevance to Chinese circumstances. *AERJ* advances some global research, but very little or none at all from China. Indeed, the exclusion of Asian and African work from *AERJ* is notable and stark. We found no research originating from mainland Chinese scholars among any of the articles appearing in the four years examined for the present study. That is, no mainland Chinese scholar was referenced across the 139 *AERJ* articles analyzed. It seems that local forces dominated and filtered the international forces at play. Further, across both journals, these international forces should not be considered truly global as they represent mostly European and American endeavors rather than research from eastern or southern nations.

Essentially, assuming our analyses of *JYYJ* and *AERJ* are credible and representative of current practice, internationalization seems on the margin of scholarship in the US and China. Scholars seem to publish in *JYYJ* and *AERJ* without substantial regard for one another's scholarship and without the apparatus needed to shift their positioning of international scholarship in each of their journals. Despite global trends and a large proportion of non-US subscribers, very little accommodation of nonwestern scholarship has occurred within *AERJ*. With *JYYJ*, the incorporation of international perspectives seems to be occasional, differentiated, and occurring in a manner that is refractive. Mostly, they seem indifferent to the possibilities that knowledge of one another's scholarship might yield.

We would posit that the end result of such insularity is unrealized potential. Scholars proceeding without regard for one another or their pursuits or advances—uninformed and unsupportive of the possibilities that knowledge of one another's scholarship might yield and the merits of advancing a global disposition that advances diversity and situation-specific differences versus the exclusivity of the west.

While the editors of the journals extol the merits of international studies and comparative work, their pursuit of this goal verges on the disingenuous as it is skewed toward self-interest and has a strong bias toward western scholarly endeavors and form. While China may have revealed more cross-fertilization than the US, both countries operate in ways that appear more insulated than either collective or integrated. We would suggest that our broad analyses revealed forms of globalization that remain skewed in both countries. International studies appear to be interpreted, filtered, or published if the national interests of the journal of origin are served. Additionally, there appears to be a preference, if not reverence, for Euro-American scholarship. *AERJ* appears to be quite American-centric and certainly dominated by western scholarship and is either ignorant or neglectful of nonwestern scholarship. *JYYJ* appears to be China-centric but again with some infiltration of western scholarship applied in ways distinctive to China. For instance, critical theoretic work in the US is referenced but in a fashion tethered to American circumstances. As in the US, there seems to be a reverence or preference for Euro-American scholarship with no references to either scholarly endeavors of other Asian (non-Chinese) scholars or African countries. If we can generalize from *JYYJ* to China, then China seems to be on course to selectively consider and incorporate western scholarship without discounting its own practices and local circumstances (Mingyuan, 2014).

If we can generalize from *AERJ* to the state of academic educational publishing in the US, then the US appears to be quite insulated. Apart from occasional references to European scholarship, *AERJ* seems to exclude nonwestern or international work done for non-US purposes. Why is this the case? Is there a failure to recognize the merits of global work? Does it not serve local needs? And if not, why not? Whereas Chinese scholars appear to be informed of American scholarship (as a result of translations of selected works,[8] their English language abilities, studies in western countries or exchanges with western scholars) and their reputational aspirations as participants in the global economy, their American counterparts seem to be mostly stymied despite increasing contacts with Chinese scholars and memoranda of understanding declaring support for collaboration. We surmise that, unfortunately, American scholars are poorly informed and their current approach to China is largely grounded in a form of detachment from "other" as they focus on the problems and issues of education development within their respective countries. Indeed, we would surmise that the conditions have yet to emerge for the US to make the significant shifts needed to move beyond what appears to be a rather insular, skewed approach to internationalization and forms of transnationality anchored in one's own country.

Certainly global rankings and reputational measures appear to be tied to maintaining the status and the privilege of western journals, a sidelining of other voices and scholarly sources, and the perpetuation of a tolerance of ignorance for others. As Arjun Appadurai (2002) suggests in his article, "Grassroots Globalization and the Research Imagination," western and northern scholars tend to take for granted their ways of knowing and proceed with others without examining their own epistemologies. Along the same vein, Keita Takayama contends:

> Given that the existing unequal structure automatically warrants Western scholars the right to speak "on behalf of the world," they have ethical responsibility to bring in sophisticated theoretical work from the margin that should immensely contribute to the discussion in the center. . . . Democratic space must be generated . . . where non-Western scholars and activists can participate in theoretical knowledge production on an equal footing with Euro-American counterparts. (2009, p. 364)

If we could accept an imaginary place where internationalization became an aspiration for the US, there are other matters that need to be addressed. For instance, we suspect that there are differences in the rhetorical expectations for Chinese versus American publications that will make the exchange more difficult. The work of Zhao et al. (2008), Lloyd & Sivin (2003), and our ongoing work (Tierney & Kan, 2014) with Chinese authors suggest that there are differences in how claims or proclamations are warranted that represent historical traditions of authorship, author intentionality, and audience that have a bearing on persona and ethos. Whereas American authors are expected to warrant each claim with detailed arguments or data, Chinese authors often will make claims tied to historic values and reverence for noted scholars. While American authors tend to adopt an objective, somewhat detached, third-person stance, Chinese scholars would often enlist "we" as if to align with a societal or collective persona. Whereas Chinese scholars tend to make pronouncements to justify their research, American scholars tend to offer a more incremental, expanded, and detailed rationale, including findings and approaches to related studies leading to the need for the current study. Likewise, Chinese scholars presented findings without as much or the same type of backup evidence compared with American scholars.

We would surmise that the publishing apparatus across the two countries might account for some of these tendencies. Whereas the *JYYJ* publishes a large number of articles, their length is restricted and hence the articles are briefer and contain fewer elaborations, citations, background, explication, and exploration of findings. In contrast, *AERJ* publishes a limited number of articles of considerable length, which affords more expansive description of the research endeavor and typically more extensive analyses. Whereas *JYYJ* publishes a large number of essays, *AERJ* publishes the exploration ideas typically accompanied by data-based examination of these issues, including exploration of viability of models that might account for complex data based upon a combination of qualitative and quantitative analyses. Also, size, nature, the frequency of editorial and editorial board shifts, the philosophies, and the narrowness of both groups should be considered. While there are no notable differences in international representation, or lack thereof, on their editorial boards, there are differences in the tenure and size of their boards. Whereas the tenure for *AERJ* editors has involved three sets of turnovers in the past 10 years, with corresponding shifts in a sizeable editorial board, the editor, associate editors, and editorial board for *JYYJ* have remained the same across the past 10 years. Twenty-four persons participate in *JYYJ*'s editorial boards, compared with 100+ editorial board members on *AERJ*.

Despite strong global pressures at the national level, local traditions are deep rooted. Indeed, our study highlights the cultural specificity of studies with ties to foci, norms, and expectations of their disciplinary traditions and form of inquiries. The cross-national integration and filtered hybridization of foreign ideas witnessed in the internationalization movement in China seem to befit forms of "glocalization" (Robertson, 1992)—that is, organic antecedents anchored in local and national historic developments. The need, as Schriewer has noted, is to "reckon with varying relations between the globalized communication of the sciences . . . and . . . educational system-reflection's commitment to processing meanings that are deeply rooted in distinctive political and cultural settings." (2004, p. 532)

Perhaps there is the possibility of significant change with some of the key forces emerging. In the physical and natural sciences, as Juana Moiwo and Fulu Tao (2013) have noted, citations of Chinese research have increased significantly as Chinese scientists have begun to position their work through translations, westernization of editorial boards etc. As

Anthony Welch (2015) noted, while we have yet to see a large number of Chinese journals in English, there is a growth of other Chinese publications intended for western audiences.[9] Within Chinese faculties of education there is an increase in foreign faculty and the number of faculty with overseas credentials and experiences. Likewise, we see western institutions with faculty having Chinese scholarly backgrounds. Chinese institutions are increasing their recruitment of international students and faculty as well as offering courses focused on western scholarship. Western institutions are competing for Asian students and are adjusting their offerings in a fashion that suggests there is some accommodation of scholarly traditions. For example, in Australia we are seeing deliberate attempts to integrate Asian knowledge with western knowledge in the doctoral experiences of Asian students enrolled in western institutions (see Singh, 2011). In addition, a number of studies are serving to introduce western scholars to Chinese educational leaders, scholarly developments, and educational developments (Hayhoe, 1999; Yongling & Hayhoe, 2004). Pinar (2014) has been attempting to trace the history of curriculum development in China by unpacking the intellectual history of Chinese scholars. Schulte (2004) has unpacked the emergence of cultural linguistics in China; others are focusing upon forms of transnational socialization drawing upon contrastive linguistics to examine the complexity of learning to engage in different scholarly discourse communities (e.g., Kubota & Lehner, 2004). A number of books explore China's own history of science including China's historic influence upon the west (e.g., Goody, 2010; Hobson, 2004).

The present study raises questions with a degree of currency for the US—in particular, at a time of heightened embrace of global developments, it questions whether and how the west and particularly the US is embracing internationalization. Certainly the US and other western universities are actively engaging in recruiting international students from eastern and southern countries. Growing numbers of Asian and other international attendees participate at annual meetings located in the US. As noted earlier (see footnote 2) institutional subscriptions for the American Educational Research Association and other western journals are nowadays predominately African and Asian. Despite growing numbers of scholars and publications touting global and transnational interests as well as the establishment of the World Educational Research Association, it remains to be seen whether these shifts and other changes in practice will result in the internationalization of scholarship beyond the current Eurocentric disposition. Based upon our interviews of select recognized Chinese scholars, many have reservations about writing for a western audience. They have suggested that they would be unlikely to have an article accepted for publication in the west without western citations, stylistic adjustments, and background information on China for a western readership. Given their speculation on the lack of wide international representation on the editorial boards of western journals, they are unsure as to whether their submission would be considered by empathetic reviewers with the cultural knowledge to provide a credible review.

Closing Remarks

Our study befits a tradition of studies on the history of science over time, but it also responds to these times in this place. We concur with Connell (2007), who suggests that there is a need to learn from, of, about, and with those who are historically marginalized, such as eastern and southern scholars, as well as to increase our understanding of how the intersecting local and international forces operate to contribute to or detract from a form of collective accommodation. We would argue with some urgency for a fuller interrogation of these issues and additional research. In particular, we would hope for research that builds upon and extends the present study and responds to some of the calls by leading comparative educators, sociologists, and global epistemologists. As Maria Manzon (2011) has argued in her most recent discussion of the future of comparative education, we would hope that other studies are launched that interrogate the sociological and epistemological dynamics occurring across time and place and shaping intellectual endeavors specifically and institutionally. As sociologists Randall Collins (1998) and Jürgen Schriewer (2004) posit, drawing upon Niklas Luhmann's (1982) suggestion of self-referential systems, we see a need for further ongoing reflexive forensic work to ascertain the dialogical connections between regionalization and globalizations across societies and ways of knowing.

Certainly, the political nature of this work should not be overlooked. We fear that internationalization will remain skewed without a fuller interrogation of how it is positioned. The interrogation needs especially to address the international forces that marginalize others and the local forces in countries such as the US that result in apparent insularity, and perhaps ignorance and lack of respect for "non-western" scholarship. Boaventura de Sousa Santos (2007a, 2007b, 2013) argues we should move beyond a representational orientation to a form of ecological intervention. He suggests that there is need for an ecological approach to epistemologies that challenge the hegemony of the west and support epistemological diversity. In the name of what de Sousas Santos has termed "cognitive justice," the politics of colonialization, domination, and violence against the epistemologies of non-western groups should be made visible and challenged. To do so, de Sousa Santos argues that we need to position epistemologies as interventions of the present and future rather than as just representations or relics of the past. Cross-national research on ways of knowing should recognize the interface with language diversity and the shifts to status and use of knowledges occurring in nonwestern settings—their value or loss of worth and possible extinction, or as de Sousa Santos suggests, the possibility of epistemocide (de Sousa Santos, 2007a, 2007b, 2013).

As Kuan-Hsing Chen proposed in *Asia as Method: Toward Deimperialization* (K. H. Chen, 2010), we may be at a pivotal global time for both Asia and the west for interrogating, deliberating developing, and recognizing our own as well as each other's diverse epistemologies—shifting our gaze to embrace each other as subjects rather than objects—in ways that are not colonizing or imperialistic. To do so through our venues for scholarship might become a "third space" that affords a form of fertile diversity (Bhabha, 2004; Gutiérrez, 2008) and a space that studies, nurtures, and develops the enlisting of a range of approaches that might help us unravel, understand, but not override the local, organic mutations, meanings, coalitions, and networking (e.g., Abbott, 1999; Cheek, 2016; Collins, 1998).

We would hope that our study prompts a recognition that change needs to occur on all sides (east-west, north-south) and at different levels (government, institutional, disciplinary fields, and the engagements of scholars) synergistically and complementarily to one another rather than in fashion that is competitive, marginalizing, or exclusionary.

Notes

[1]Further, we wished to link to Schriewer & Martinez (2004) who chose *JYYJ* and Zhao et al. (2008) who chose *AERJ* and *JYYJ* for their comparative analyses.

[2]In 2011, institutional subscribers included Africa (24%), Europe (23%), Asia (17%), the US (16%), South America (12%), the Middle East (5%), Australasia (2%), and Canada (1%). In terms of submissions, the greatest number of manuscripts came from the US (73% with an acceptance of 10%), followed by Europe (10% with an acceptance rate of 10%), Australasia (2.4% with 0% acceptance), the Middle East (3.5% with 0% acceptance), Asia (5.2% with 0% acceptance), and other countries (> 1% of total submissions) (Sage, 2012).

[3]The international articles in *JYYJ* include two categories: (1) foreign authors translated into Chinese by Chinese researchers and (2) the papers focused on international issues. The comparative articles are defined as two types in *JYYJ*: (1) comparative studies between China and other countries and (2) studies of international issues applicable to China.

[4]The comparative studies in 2003 only focused on developed nations, e.g., the UK, the US, Korea, or Japan. There were no comparative studies between China and other southeast Asian countries or any African countries.

[5]Despite differences in Canadian educational research developments, US scholars enlist the work of selected Canadian scholars extensively (e.g., Michael Fullan) as if the countries are less bordered and differences less profound.

[6]Our topical assessments were hampered by our attempt to pigeonhole each study into a single primary topic. Most articles deal with more than one topic (e.g., school management, curriculum, teaching in rural areas, etc.).

[7]The authors examined each article to ascertain its methodology. A subset was reviewed for reliability.

[8]As Li (2015) reports, 28, 500 books were translated into Chinese during 1978 to 1990, 94,400 during 1995—2003 and 12,000 in 2011.

[9]Currently, the only social science international journal in English published in China is the *Frontiers of Education in China*. It is not covered by SSCI.

References

Abbott, A. (1999). [Review of the book *The sociology of philosophies: A global theory of intellectual change*]. *American Journal of Sociology, 105*(2), 528–531.

Alatas, F. S. (2006). *Alternative discourses in Asian social science. Responses to Eurocentrism*. New Delhi: Sage.

American Educational Research Journal. (2015). *American Educational Research Journal* statement. Retrieved from http://www.aera.net/Publications/Journals/AmericanEducationalResearchJournal/tabid/12607/Default.aspx

Appadurai, A. (2002). Grassroots globalization and the research imagination. In A. Appadurai (Ed.) *Globalization* (pp. 2–21). Durham, NC: Duke University Press.

Bhabha, H. K. (2004). *The location of culture*. Abingdon, UK: Routledge.

Bourdieu, P. (1998). *Homo Academicus*. Cambridge, UK: Polity.

Center for World-Class Universities of Shanghai Jiao Tong University. (2014). Academic ranking of world universities. Retrieved from http://www.shanghairanking.com/index.html

Charle, C., Schriewer, J., & Wagner, P. (2004). *Forms for academic knowledge and the search for cultural identities*. Chicago, IL: University of Chicago Press.

Cheek, T. (2016). *The intellectual in modern Chinese history*. Cambridge, UK: Cambridge University Press.

Chen, K. H. (2010). *Asia as method: Toward deimperialization*. Durham, NC: Duke University Press.

Chen, X. M. (2000). *Qualitative methodology and social science research*. Beijing: Educational Science Publishing House.

Chen, X. M. (2003). Practical knowledge: Basement of teachers' professional development. *Educational Review of Beijing University, 14*(1), 12–19.

Ching, L. T. S. (2000). Globalizing the regional, regionalizing the global: Mass culture and Asianism in the age of late capital. *Public Culture, 12*(1), 233–257.

Clarke, D. (2015). The challenge of international comparison: Seven variants of the validity-comparability compromise. Paper presented at the annual meeting of the American Educational Research Association, Chicago, IL.

Collins, R. (1998). *The sociology of philosophies: A global theory of intellectual change*. Cambridge, MA: Harvard University Press.

Connell, R. (2007). *Southern theory: The global dynamics of knowledge in social science*. Cambridge, UK: Polity.

de Sousa Santos, B. (Ed.). (2007a). *Another knowledge is possible*. London: Verso.

de Sousa Santos, B. (2007b). Beyond abyssal thinking: From global lines to ecologies of knowledge. *Eurozine, 33*, 45–89.

de Sousa Santos, B. (2013). *Epistemologies of the south: Justice against epistemicide*. London: Paradigm.

Dewey, J. (1916/2001) *Democracy and education: An introduction to the Philosophy of Education* (Chinese translation). Beijing: People's Education Press. (Originally published in 1916 in New York by the Macmillan Company).

Elman, B. A. (1984). *From philosophy to philology: Intellectual and social aspects of change in late imperial China*, Cambridge, MA: Council on East Asian Studies, Harvard University, distributed by Harvard University Press.

Goody, J. (2010). *The Eurasian miracle*. Cambridge, UK: Polity.

Gutiérrez, K. D. (2008). Developing a sociocritical literacy in the third space. *Reading Research Quarterly, 43*(2), 148–164.

Hayhoe, R. (1999). *China's universities 1895–1995: A century of cultural conflict.* Hong Kong Comparative Education Research Centre, The University of Hong Kong, 1999.

Hobson, J. (2004). *The Eastern origins of Western civilization.* Cambridge, UK: Cambridge University Press.

Hollingsworth, S., & Gallego, M. A. (2006). A Message From the New *AERJ/SIA* Editors *American Educational Research Journal, 43,* 3–4.

Husén, T., & Postlethwaite, T. N. (Eds.) (1994). *The international encyclopedia of education.* Oxford, UK: Pergamon Press.

Kubota, R., & Lehner, A. (2004). Toward critical contrastive rhetoric. *Journal of Second Language Writing, 13,* 7–27.

Ladwig, J. G. (2008). *The paper tiger, the waking giant and the ants: On the international ranking of higher education and its implications for the Antipodes.* Paper presented at the American Educational Research Association Annual Meeting, New York, NY.

Li, J. R. (2015). Translation projects on western social and culture books since 1990s, China Pulising (in Chinese), 9(5), 74–19.

Lloyd, G., & Sivin, N. (2003). *The Way and the word: Science and medicine in early China and Greece.* New Haven, CT; Yale University Press.

Luhmann, N. (1982). The world society as a social system. *International Journal of General Systems, 8*(3), 131–138.

Manzon, M. (2011). *Comparative education: The construction of a field.* Comparative Education Research Centre, The University of Hong Kong.

Marginson, S. (2000). Entrepreneurial universities. *Comparative Education Policy Occasional Paper Series 1,* 1–15, Comparative Education Policy Research Unit, City University of Hong Kong, Hong Kong.

McCarty, T. L., Faircloth, S. C., Glass, G. V., Ladwig, J., Lee, S. L., McNaughton, S., . . . Villenas, S. A. (2014). As we embark on a new editorship: A statement from the AERJ-SIA editors. *American Educational Research Journal, 51,* 4–6.

Mingyuan, G. (2014). *Cultural foundations of Chinese education.* Leiden, the Netherlands: Brill.

Moiwo, J. P., & Tao, F. (2013). The changing dynamics in citation index publication position China in a race with the USA for global leadership. *Scientometrics, 95*(3), 1031–1050.

Mok, K. H. (2007). Withering the state? Globalizations, challenges and the changing higher education governance in East Asia. In W. T. Pink & G. W. Noblit (Eds.), *International handbook of urban education* (pp. 305–320). Dordrecht, the Netherlands: Springer.

National Institute of Education Studies. (2015). National Institute of Education Studies statement. Retrieved from English.nies.net.cn/Publications/Journals_and_Newspapers/201405/t20140523_314983.html

Nisbett, R. (2003). *The geography of thought: How Asians and westerners think differently . . . and why.* New York, NY: Free Press.

Nozaki, Y. (2009). Orientalism, the west and non-west binary, and postcolonial perspectives in cross-cultural research and education. In M. Apple, W. Au, & L. Gandin (Eds.), The Routledge *international handbook of critical education* (pp. 382–390). New York, NY: Routledge.

Ocholla, D. (2007). Marginalized knowledge: An agenda for indigenous knowledge development and integration with other forms of knowledge. In proceedings of the first African Information Ethics conference. *International Review of Information Ethics, 7,* 236–245.

O'Neil, Jr., H. F. (2014). Editorial. *American Educational Research Journal, 51,* 114–116.

Pinar, W. F. (2014). *Curriculum studies in China: Intellectual histories, present circumstances.* New York, NY: Palgrave Macmillan.

Piterese, J. N. (2005). Globalization and culture. London: Routledge.

Popkewitz, T., & Rizvi, F. (Eds.) (2011). *Globalization and the study of education. Yearbook of the National Society for the Study of Education, 108*(2), Malden, MA: Wiley-Blackwell.

Programme for International Student Assessment. (2012). The programme for international student assessment. Retrieved from http://www.oecd.org/pisa/aboutpisa/

QS. (2015). QS world university rankings. Retrieved from http://www.topuniversities.com/university-rankings

Rizvi, F., & Lingard, B. (2010). *Globalizing educational policy.* New York, NY: Routledge.

Robertson, R. (1992). Globalization: Social theory and global culture. Thousand Oaks, CA: Sage.

Robertson, S. L., & Dale, R. (2009). The World Bank, the IMF, and the possibilities of critical education. In M. Apple, W. Au, & L. Gandin (Eds.), *The Routledge international handbook of critical education* (pp. 23–35). New York, NY: Routledge.

Schriewer, J. (2004). Multiple internationalities: the emergence of a word-level ideology and the persistence of idiosyncratic world-views. In C. Charle, J. Schriewer, & P. Wagner (Eds.), *Transnational intellectual networks: Forms of academic knowledge and the search for cultural identities* (pp. 473–533). Frankfurt: Campus Verlag.

Schriewer, J., & Martinez, C. (2004). Constructions of internationality in education. In G. Steiner-Khamsi (Ed.), *The global politics of educational borrowing and lending* (pp. 29–53). New York, NY: Teachers College Press.

Schulte, B. (2004). East is east and West is west? Chinese academia goes global. In C. Charle, J. Schriewer, & P. Wagner (Eds.), *Transnational intellectual networks: Forms of academic knowledge and the search for cultural identities* (pp. 307–322). Frankfurt: Campus Verlag.

Shao, J., & Shen, H. (2011). The outflow of academic papers from China: Why is it happening and can it be stemmed? *Learned Publishing, 24,* 95–97.

Shi, Z. Y. (2000). *Transformation of knowledge and educational reform.* Beijing: Educational Science Publishing House.

Shi, Z. Y. (2006). *On the logic of educational practices.* Beijing: Educational Science Publishing House.

Singh, M. J. (2011). Learning from China to internationalise Australian research education: Pedagogies of intellectual equality and 'optimal ignorance' of ERA journal rankings. *Innovations in Education and Teaching International, 48*(4), 355–365.

Stack, M. (2016). *Global university rankings and the mediatization of higher education.* New York, NY: Palgrave Macmillan.

Takayama, K. (2009). Progressive education and critical education scholarship in Japan: toward the democratization of critical educational studies. In M. Apple, W. Au, & L. Gandin (Eds.), *The Routledge international handbook of critical education* (pp. 354–367). New York, NY: Routledge.

Tierney, R. J., & Wei, K. (2014). *Confronting global knowledges: Chinese and US educational researchers in the 21st century.* Paper presented at World Educational Research Association, Edinburgh, Scotland, November 21, 2014.

Times Higher Education. (2015). World university rankings. Retrieved from http://www.timeshighereducation.co.uk/world-university-rankings

Wang, J. C-S. (2007) *John Dewey in China: To teach and to learn*. Albany: State Universities of New York Press.

Welch, A. (2015). A new epistemic silk road? The Chinese knowledge diaspora, and its implications for the Europe of knowledge. *European Review, 23*(S1), S95–S111.

World Bank. (2012). Knowledge assessment methodology. Retrieved from https://knoema.com/WBKEI2013/knowledge-economy-index-world-bank-2012. Retrieved November 3, 2016.

Yang, G.-C., & Chang, Y. (2009). The circumstances and the possibilities of critical educational studies in China. In M. Apple, W. Au, & L. Gandin (Eds.), *The Routledge international handbook of critical education* (pp. 368–385). New York, NY: Routledge.

Yongling, Y., & Hayhoe, R. (2004). Chinese higher learning: The transition process from classical knowledge patterns to modern disciplines, 1860–1910. In C. Charle, J. Schriewer, & P. Wagner (Eds.), *Transnational intellectual networks: Forms of academic knowledge and the search for cultural identities* (pp. 269–306). Frankfurt: Campus Verlag.

Zeng, T. S., & Gao, B. L. (2009). Analysis on the current research findings and their influences (in Chinese), *Educational Research (JYYJ), 30*(8), 34–41.

Zhao, Y., Zhang, G., Yang, W., Kirkland, D., Han, X., & Zhang, J. (2008). A comparative study of educational research in China and the US. *Asia Pacific Journal of Education, 28*(1), 1–17.

Manuscript received June 18, 2015
Final revision received July 25, 2016
Accepted September 29, 2016

American Educational Research Journal
December 2016, Vol. 53, No. 6, pp. 1792–1833
DOI: 10.3102/0002831216675404
© *2016 AERA. http://aerj.aera.net*

Leveled and Exclusionary Tracking: English Learners' Access to Academic Content in Middle School

Ilana M. Umansky
University of Oregon

This study examines the characteristics and determinants of English learners' (ELs') access to academic content in middle school (Grades 6–8). Following 10 years of data from a large urban school district in California, I identify two predominant characteristics of EL access to content: leveled tracking in which ELs are overrepresented in lower level classes and underrepresented in upper level classes and exclusionary tracking in which ELs are excluded from core academic content area classes, particularly English language arts. Using regression analysis and two regression discontinuity designs, I find evidence that ELs' access to content is limited by a constellation of factors, including prior academic achievement, institutional constraints, English proficiency level, and direct effects of EL classification. This study contributes to understanding of the experiences and opportunities of students learning English as well as theory regarding educational tracking.

KEYWORDS: course-taking, English learners, regression discontinuity, tracking

Introduction

For students learning English, as for any student, success in school depends in large part on exposure to instruction and content. Policy and law regarding the education of English learners (ELs) are structured around the concept of enabling full and meaningful integration in school. Yet a large body of research suggests that ELs face inequitable opportunity to learn (Dabach & Callahan, 2011). A critical determinant of opportunity

ILANA M. UMANSKY is an assistant professor at the University of Oregon, 102Q Lokey Education Building, Eugene OR 97403, e-mail: *ilanau@uoregon.edu*. Her research uses quantitative methods and sociological theory to examine the educational opportunities and outcomes of immigrant students and students classified as English learners.

to learn and subsequent educational achievement is students' access and exposure to academic content. In this article, I empirically examine ELs' course placement in middle school (Grades 6–8) and the factors that limit ELs' course access.

Using longitudinal data from a large urban school district in California, the article is divided into two analytic sections. In the first section, I offer a descriptive analysis of EL course-taking in middle school, comparing patterns between EL and non-EL students as well as patterns between subgroups of EL students of different English proficiency levels and academic achievement levels. I propose a conceptual framework describing EL course-taking, identifying two main features of EL access to content. The first is leveled tracking, in which ELs are disproportionately in lower track classes. The second is exclusionary tracking, in which ELs disproportionately are not enrolled in academic content area classes.

In the second analytic section, I hypothesize and test the causes of ELs' inferior access to courses compared with English speakers. I examine the role of four theoretically derived factors that may limit ELs' access: (1) academic performance, (2) institutional barriers, (3) English proficiency level, and (4) EL classification. I find evidence that ELs' access to content is structured by each. These findings suggest that ELs may face multiple barriers to content. The implications of ELs' limited course access are likely to be profound, potentially contributing to low academic performance, high drop-out rates, and low college eligibility and enrollment (Fry, 2007; Gándara & Contreras, 2009).

English Learner Course-Taking and Access to Academic Content

Students who are deemed to be acquiring English have two essential rights that have been delineated through a series of court cases and federal and state regulations. First, schools must provide English language instruction so that EL students acquire English proficiency. Second, schools must provide accessible academic content instruction so that EL students can reach grade-level standards in the academic curriculum (*Castañeda v. Pickard*, 1981; Every Student Succeeds Act of 2015, 2015; *Lau v. Nichols*, 1974; Lhamon & Gupta, 2015; Moran, 2005; No Child Left Behind Act of 2001, 2002; Wiley, 2009).

Paralleling federal law, ELs' courses in middle school can be thought of in two categories. The first is direct instruction in the English language, typically in the form of one or more designated class periods for English language development (ELD). The second consists of core academic courses. Federal guidelines on EL education specify that core academic curriculum includes English language arts (ELA), math, science, and social studies (Lhamon & Gupta, 2015). Furthermore, federal law specifies that core academic content must be provided in a way that is accessible to students who are not yet proficient in English. Most districts comply with this law by offering academic classes that employ specific instructional techniques and methods to increase accessibility (these classes are often referred to as specially designed academic instruction in English—SDAIE—classes).

Middle school is a critical period in students' lives, a time that is credited with establishing academic identities and setting in motion course sequences that continue through high school and beyond (Eccles, Lord, & Midgley, 1991; Kurlaender, Reardon, & Jackson, 2008). Increasingly, the stakes are high when it comes to middle school course-taking, with important implications for career, education, and life outcomes (Rumberger & Lim, 2008; Wang & Goldschmidt, 2003; Williams et al., 2010).

Existing research has found numerous ways in which ELs' access to academic content in school is problematic. ELs have been found to be overrepresented in lower level classes and underrepresented in upper level classes (Callahan, 2005; Gándara, Rumberger, Maxwell-Jolly, & Callahan, 2003; Solorzano & Ornelas, 2004; Wang & Goldschmidt, 1999; Zuniga, Olson, & Winter, 2005). ELs are also less likely than non-ELs to complete graduation and college preparatory coursework (Callahan & Shifrer, 2016; Xiong, 2010) and face barriers to enrollment in academic content areas such as math (Estrada, 2014; Gándara et al., 2003; Lillie, Markos, Arias, & Wiley, 2012; Nord et al., 2011; Olsen, 1997). Evidence suggests that ELs' course access may be limited by factors that other students do not encounter. Several analyses, for example, indicate that EL classification and the services and treatments that EL classification triggers may create barriers to academic course-taking or delay progress through school (Callahan, Wilkinson, & Muller, 2010; Callahan, Wilkinson, Muller, & Frisco, 2009; Carlson & Knowles, 2016; Hodara, 2015; Umansky, 2016; Zuniga et al., 2005).

While research suggests that ELs tend to have inferior access to content in school compared to English-speaking students, this article address two main gaps in the literature. First, I propose a framework for analyzing and understanding ELs' access to academic content, delineating two main forms of tracking: leveled and exclusionary. Second, I analyze the role of key factors that contribute to limiting ELs' access to academic content. This allows for targeted policy and practice implications to improve ELs' course access.

Conceptual Framework

Educational Tracking and Dimensions of EL Course-Taking

Educational tracking refers to the placement of students in separate and hierarchically tiered classes or instructional settings. Scholars have long discussed how tracking disproportionately impacts African American, Latino, and poor students (Gamoran, 2010; Oakes, 2005), and increasingly, the term is being used by policymakers, practitioners, and researchers with regard to EL students. In fact, the original Supreme Court case *Lau v. Nichols* (1974), which frames EL students' rights in school, itself employed the concept of tracking, warning that EL services "must not operate as an educational dead-end or permanent track."

Scholars have analyzed EL course placement as a form of educational tracking, parallel to academic ability grouping, but based instead on stratification of students by English proficiency or language classification (Callahan, 2005; Callahan & Shifrer, 2016; Gándara et al., 2003; Harklau, 1994; Valdés, 1998; Valenzuela, 1999; Wang & Goldschmidt, 1999). Like traditional ability-based tracking, these scholars discuss the ways in which EL course placement can contribute to limiting ELs' access to academic content as well as their exposure to English-speaking and/or high-achieving peers.

Course availability and course assignment policies and practices can differ from school to school, district to district, and state to state (Estrada, 2014; Garet & DeLany, 1988; Spade, Columba, & Vanfossen, 1997). In part due to flexible federal policy regarding the rights of ELs in schools as described previously, variation in EL course-taking patterns and exposure to content is likely to be considerable across settings.

Leveled Tracking

I theorize that EL course-taking may differ from that of non-ELs along two key dimensions.[1] First, ELs may be enrolled in classes that differ, on average, in level from non-ELs. Zuniga and colleagues (2005), for example, examining one rural high school, find that ELs are placed into low track science classes regardless of prior achievement. Similarly, Kanno and Kangas (2014) document the course placement practices of a large suburban high school, finding that ELs, when able to exit from SDAIE classes, are placed automatically into low track classes. These are examples of the traditional notion of tracking, in which students are placed into hierarchically leveled classes according to measured or perceived ability or prior performance. In this article, I refer to this as *leveled tracking* because course placement is structured by levels.

Honors, grade level, and remedial classes constitute the three traditional levels in a leveled tracking system. Honors classes (referred to as upper level classes) offer grade-level content but are geared toward high-achieving students, usually covering additional content or delving more deeply into content. Remedial classes (referred to as lower level classes) are below grade level classes that focus on basic concepts in order to support struggling students. Importantly, several studies have found that student characteristics, such as race and socioeconomic status, predict level placement after controlling for prior achievement, suggesting that level placement is not distributed solely by ability/prior performance (Kelly, 2009; Oakes, 2005).

Leveled tracking is commonplace throughout the country at the middle and high school levels. The central argument for leveled tracking is that students' educational needs are better met if classes are tailored to their ability levels and if teachers can focus instruction on a specific band of ability levels. Research suggests that while tracking often benefits high track students, it penalizes low track students, thereby exacerbating gaps between high and low performers (Attewell & Domina, 2008; Gamoran, 2010; Garrett & Hong, 2015; Nomi & Raudenbush, 2016; Oakes, 2005). Compared to upper track classes, lower track classes typically offer slower pacing and less rigorous content, are characterized by fewer higher-order thinking activities, employ more authoritarian and discipline-oriented instruction, and build weaker student-teacher relationships (Harklau, 1994; Oakes, 2005; Page, 1991).

Exclusionary Tracking

The second form of course-taking difference is that ELs may differ from non-ELs in the amount of access they have to certain subject areas. For example, ELs may be less likely to be enrolled in science classes compared to non-ELs. This form of differentiated access to academic content has not been examined in prior tracking literature but instead emerges from in-depth, often school-level examinations of ELs' course access (Callahan, 2005; Estrada, 2014; Olsen, 1997; Valdés, 1998). Analyzing EL students' high school course schedules, Gándara et al. (2003) find frequent cases of students with empty class periods, multiple electives, and missing core content areas such as science and social studies. Estrada (2014) documents middle school class placement policies in four schools and finds that some schools systematically exclude low English proficiency ELs from core academic content areas. In this article, I propose that this is a distinct form of tracking, and I call it *exclusionary tracking* given that it pertains to students' inclusion or exclusion from academic subject areas.

Beyond these two dimensions of course-taking difference, it deserves mention that merely being placed in the same classes as non-ELs does not guarantee that ELs have equal access to academic content. If instruction in mainstream classes is inaccessible or incomprehensible to EL students, then they will have less access to content despite equal allocation to courses. Although this issue lies at the heart of the *Lau v. Nichols* Supreme Court case, it does not relate to course-taking per se and is not examined in this study.

Why ELs May Have Inferior Access to Courses Than Non-ELs

ELs may have inferior access to courses compared to English proficient students for four main reasons: (1) prior academic achievement, (2) institutional constraints, (3) English proficiency, and (4) EL classification. While this list is not exhaustive, these are the factors that I examine in this study.

Prior Academic Achievement

EL students may have inferior access to content in middle school as a result of having lower levels of academic preparation and achievement than fluent English speakers upon entry into middle school. ELs have lower achievement profiles than non-ELs, on average, for complex reasons. First, because academic performance is a common criterion for exiting EL status, selection into EL status, by definition, is linked to lower academic achievement (Hopkins, Thompson, Linquanti, Hakuta, & August, 2013; Saunders & Marcelletti, 2012). Second, outcomes on academic assessments administered in English are often downwardly biased when taken by ELs (Abedi & Lord, 2001; Bialystok & Hakuta, 1994; Martiniello, 2008; Parker, Louie, & O'Dwyer, 2009). Third, EL students often attend under-resourced schools (discussed in the following section on institutional constraints) and come from low-income families, characteristics that are correlated with lower academic achievement (Alba, Massey, & Rumbaut, 1999; Dronkers & Levels, 2007; Fry, 2008; Kao, Tienda, & Lafield, 2005; Portes & MacLeod, 1996). Finally, ELs may reach middle school with lower average levels of academic preparation than fluent English speakers because of systematic differences in their educational experiences in elementary school that result in lower academic achievement (Umansky, 2016). While non-ELs are also placed in classes based on prior academic achievement, ELs' average lower academic achievement could result in disproportionate constraints on ELs' course access.

Institutional Constraints

Institutional constraints, from limited or insufficient resources, may result in tracking that limits ELs' access to content in school. While there is considerable variation by locale, socioeconomic status, and national origin, a large body of research documents the relative segregation of many immigrant families and their children in low-income neighborhoods, neighborhoods frequently served by under-resourced schools (Alba et al., 1999; Dronkers & Levels, 2007; Ellen et al., 2002; C. Lee, 2006; Portes & MacLeod, 1996; Reardon, Yun, & Eitle, 2000; Rumberger & Gándara, 2004; Suárez-Orozco, Suárez-Orozco, & Todorova, 2009). These schools—whose composition is often largely comprised of students of color and immigrant students—have been shown to offer fewer high track academic classes on average than more economically advantaged schools in more affluent communities (Chang, 2000; Iatarola, Conger, & Long, 2011; Monk & Haller, 1993; Oakes, 2005; Spade et al., 1997). As a result, many ELs may face more constrained access or no access at all to specific academic classes, most notably honors or advanced placement (AP) classes (Fry, 2008; Garet & DeLany, 1988; C. Lee, 2006).

English Proficiency Level

ELs may have different access to academic content in middle school on account of their English proficiency, irrespective of their academic achievement levels. Course-placement policy or administrator/teacher beliefs may confound English proficiency with academic ability, placing lower English proficient students into lower track classes or excluding them from academic content (Bruna, Vann, & Escudero, 2007; García, 1992; Yoon, 2008). Closely related, the content of specific classes may be deemed (either in policy or in practice) linguistically inaccessible to students with lower English proficiency levels (Harklau, 1994; Olsen, 1997). Exclusionary and leveled tracking based on English proficiency may be subjective rather than objective; course placement may be based on assumptions about ELs' proficiency levels rather than accurate knowledge of students' English language abilities.

EL Classification

Finally, EL students may have limited access to content as a direct effect of EL classification. Again, this could happen for multiple reasons depending on how individual schools or districts structure services for ELs. A likely mechanism in many schools is crowding-out due to ELD. The requirement that ELs have designated ELD instruction often removes one or more periods from students' schedules. If students' schedules become sufficiently constrained, this may result in exclusion from academic content areas (Estrada, 2014). State policy in Arizona, for example, places ELs in a four-hour ELD block, amounting to 80% of students' instructional time, severely constraining students' ability to take academic classes (August, Goldenberg, & Rueda, 2010; Lillie et al., 2012). While the aforementioned is an example of exclusionary tracking, schools may also structure students' access to course level by EL classification. Schools' institutionalized course sequences may feed ELs from SDAIE classes into remedial classes, essentially barring access to grade level, honors, and AP classes (Kanno & Kangas, 2014).

Data and Context

I use longitudinal administrative data from a large urban school district in California. This is a useful school district in which to examine EL course-taking for several reasons, including having a large and diverse EL population, having a strong historical focus on EL opportunity and achievement, and being located in California, a state that often leads the United States in EL policy and has the highest proportion of EL students (IES, 2015).

The data consist of student course-taking panel data over a 10-year period spanning from fall 2002 to spring 2012. The district annually enrolls between 60,000 and 70,000 students. Over 50% of the student population speaks a language other than English at home. These students come from multiple linguistic and national backgrounds.

District Language Classification Policy

Policies in this district reflect federal and California state law.[2] When a new student arrives in the district, his or her parents complete an intake form that includes questions regarding language use at home. The district identifies language minority students (students who have a primary language other than English) from these questions and gives them an English language assessment. Over the time period examined, the assessment was the California English Language Development Test (CELDT), comprised of speaking, listening, reading, and writing subtests. Students who score below established thresholds on the CELDT are classified as EL. The overall CELDT and each subtest is scored along five proficiency levels (1–5), each of which represents a distinct band of scale scores. The five levels are: beginning, early intermediate, intermediate, early advanced, and advanced. During the time period examined, incoming kindergarten language minority students who scored below a 4 (early advanced) on the overall CELDT were to be classified as EL (CELDT subtest scores were not determining factors for the cohorts examined).

Aside from EL classification, students in the district can fall into three other language categories (California Department of Education [CDE], 2006). Students who have no primary language other than English, according to the parental intake form, do not have their English level assessed and are classified as English only (EO) (Abedi, 2008; Linquanti, 2001). Language minority students who take the CELDT for initial identification and score above the EL thresholds are classified as initially fluent English proficient (IFEP). IFEP therefore describes students who speak a language other than English at home but enter school already proficient in English. The final language classification is reclassified fluent English proficient (RFEP); this classification describes language minority students who are classified as ELs when they enter the school district, receive services as ELs, and then test out of EL status based on annual assessments (CDE, 2015a; Linquanti, 2001; Ragan & Lesaux, 2006). Collectively, I refer to EO, IFEP, and RFEP students as non-ELs. Non-EL students are mainstreamed in school while EL students receive specialized ELD, bilingual, and/or SDAIE instructional services.

According to district policy, every EL student should be assessed annually to determine eligibility for reclassification. To be reclassified, over the time period examined, students needed to reach set thresholds on the CELDT as well as on the state English language arts test. Specifically, students needed to attain a minimum of early advanced (Level 4) on the CELDT with no CELDT subscore below intermediate (Level 3). Students also needed to score at least mid-basic (scale score 325) on the California standards test in English language arts (CST ELA). In addition to these test criteria, the district also considered a set of more localized criteria, including grade point average, teacher recommendation, and parent approval.

District EL Course Placement Policy

According to district policy, middle school EL students should take ELD and a full academic course load of classes each semester. Following federal guidelines, the district considers a full academic course load to include ELA, math, science, and social studies (Lhamon & Gupta, 2015).

As mentioned earlier, ELD classes are classes specifically designed to teach ELs the English language, often focusing on oral English skills (Saunders, Goldenberg, & Marcelletti, 2013). The English skills taught in ELD classes can pertain to nonacademic areas (e.g., life skills) or can relate to any academic subject area (math, science, etc.). Importantly, ELD is not designed to take the place of ELA, a core academic subject area focused on literacy, genre, and literature. Instead, ELD and ELA are designed to be offered "in tandem . . . [for] ELs at all English proficiency levels" (CDE, 2015b, p.7). As evidence, ELD courses do not count toward ELA requirements for higher education eligibility in California.[3] Furthermore, California state policy underscores the importance of designated (i.e., separate and focused) ELD instruction (CDE, 2015b). I elaborate on the tension between ELD and ELA as well as designated versus integrated ELD in the discussion section.

Procedures for course placement in this district, as in many districts in California, are determined at the school level (Estrada, 2014; Zuniga et al., 2005). Some schools allow for student and parent choice in course enrollment, others use a computerized course placement system, while others still rely on school administrators to determine students' schedules.

During the time period examined, the district offered middle school classes in each of the three traditional tracking levels: remedial, grade level, and honors. One difference in this district compared to traditional leveled tracking systems is that remedial classes are designed to be taken in addition to, rather than in place of, a grade-level class of the same content area. This policy is enacted most of the time: In the data examined here, 91% of students in remedial ELA classes and 88% of students in remedial math classes are simultaneously enrolled in grade-level classes of the same content areas.

Data

Table 1 presents descriptive statistics, by language classification, of the analytic sample. In total, the sample includes 42,790 individual students and 189,013 student-semester observations in Grades 6–8 (see Table A in the online version of the journal for a table of observations by year and grade). Because so many of the variables of interest vary over time, Table

Table 1
**Descriptive Statistics of Analytic Sample, in First
Observed Semester in Grades 6-8**

		Language Classification			
	Total	EL	EO	IFEP	RFEP
Latino (%)	21	39	11	27	17
Chinese (%)	36	40	11	37	63
Other ethnicity (%)	43	20	78	36	20
Female (%)	51	46	53	54	53
U.S. born (%)	71	36	91	79	74
CST-ELA proficiency level (1–5)	3.40	2.33	3.58	3.92	3.89
CST-math proficiency level (1–5)	3.44	2.82	3.35	3.80	3.95
Level enrollment (leveled tracking)					
Grade level credits	11.34	12.70	11.38	10.59	10.34
Honors credits	3.53	0.61	4.08	4.73	4.97
Remedial credits	0.96	1.33	1.09	0.73	0.54
Algebra by eighth grade (%)	47	37	44	55	58
Subject enrollment (exclusionary tracking)					
Total credits	21.99	25.01	21.44	20.87	20.46
Total academic credits	15.83	14.65	16.56	16.05	15.85
ELA credits	5.21	3.72	5.88	5.63	5.49
Math credits	5.43	5.74	5.45	5.25	5.19
Science credits	5.20	5.20	5.23	5.16	5.17
ELD credits	1.86	6.33	0.36	0.40	0.40
Full academic course load (%)	85	52	96	96	97
N (students)	42,790	10,651	15,639	4,419	12,081

Note. EL = English learner student; EO = English only student; IFEP = initially fluent English proficient student; RFEP = reclassified fluent English proficient student; ELA = English language arts; ELD = English language development; CST = California Standards Test. The total academic credits row sums math, science, and ELA credits. Full academic course load indicates enrollment in math, science, and ELA. A full credit course is five credits.

1 describes the sample in each student's first observed middle school semester (fall of sixth grade for most students). I removed students who were ever classified for special education services from the sample (17.6% of middle school students) due to prior research suggesting that special education students often have course-taking patterns that are substantially different than non–special education students, coupled with research suggesting disproportionality of EL representation in special education (Artiles, Rueda, Salazar, & Higareda, 2005; Shifrer, Callahan, & Muller, 2013; Thompson, Umansky, Martinez, & Díaz, 2016).

Table 1 illustrates key differences between EL and non-EL students. Average academic performance, as measured by the ELA and math CST tests, is lower for ELs than for all other student subgroups. Table 1 also shows that ELs enroll in more credits overall compared to non-EL groups but fewer academic credits and fewer honors level credits. In this district, a full credit course is five credits. Credit averages below five indicate that some students are not enrolled in that category while averages above five suggest that some students are enrolled in more than one class in that category.

In order to provide more information on the EL population analyzed in this study, Table B in the online version of the journal presents descriptive data on the EL population (again in their first observed semester of middle school), subdivided by English proficiency level. Following district definitions, just over one-third of the EL sample is considered newcomer students (students who enter U.S. schools post-kindergarten and have been in the United States for less than two years). Newcomer students are clustered in the lower English proficiency levels, particularly Level 1. Roughly one-fifth of the EL sample is considered by the district to be long-term ELs (i.e., having been classified as ELs for more than five years without reaching reclassification criteria), with that proportion somewhat higher at the higher English proficiency levels.[4] The remaining 43% of EL students are considered in this district to be developmental ELs (having been in the district between two and five years). These three subgroups of ELs have diverse educational needs and outcomes (Francis, Rivera, Lesaux, Kieffer, & Rivera, 2006; Kleyn, Menken, Ascenzi-Moreno, & Chae, 2009), and where possible, I note how findings relate to these different subgroups. However, a full analysis of EL course-taking by years in U.S. schools is not possible in this article.

Sixty-four percent of the EL sample is born outside the United States, again concentrated in the lower English proficiency levels. The two largest ethnic groups are Chinese (40%) and Latino (39%), with the remaining students coming from many different ethnic and linguistic backgrounds. While research has shown very different patterns of outcomes for ELs of different national origins (J. Lee & Zhou, 2015; Lew, 2006; Portes & Rumbaut, 2006; Valentino & Reardon, 2015), a differentiated analysis of course-taking patterns by ethnicity is beyond the scope of this article.

Data are complete with the exception of test scores. The CELDT, taken only by EL-classified students, is missing for 6.8% of EL students, roughly evenly distributed across academic years and grade levels. Math and ELA CST tests, taken by all students in Grades 2 through 11, are missing in 2% to 3% of cases, roughly evenly distributed across years and grades. Missingness of CELDT and CST is significantly associated with certain predictor variables, including ethnicity and in the case of CST, language classification. However, the differences are small in magnitude and are unlikely to bias results. I do not impute missing test scores.

Key Variables

Outcome variables were created from student course-taking data. Over the course of a year, I worked with a team from the school district to classify courses by level and subject area. This process involved several checks by different district departments for accuracy. Leveled tracking outcome variables include the number of credits taken in remedial, grade level, and honors classes per semester. I also created dummy variables indicating whether a given level (e.g., grade level) is the highest level a student takes in a given semester. Finally, I include a dummy variable indicating whether a student takes algebra by the end of eighth grade. Algebra has been found to be a gatekeeper course that, if completed by the eighth grade, facilitates access to advanced coursework in high school (Smith, 1996). The timing of algebra relates to students' exposure to more or less advanced content in middle school, and as such, I include it as a measure of leveled tracking.

Outcome variables for exclusionary tracking include the number of credits a student takes in ELD, ELA, math, and science classes per semester as well as dummy variables for whether a student takes any credits in each content area in a given semester. Due to data limitations, I cannot reliably examine social science course-taking in this district. Finally, I created a dummy variable indicating whether a student is enrolled in a full academic course load in a given semester. I define a full academic course load as enrollment in ELA, math, and science (I do not include ELD because it is not considered an academic course).

Key predictor variables relate to the hypothesized explanatory variables: CST scores (academic achievement), school of attendance (institutional factors), CELDT scores (English proficiency level), and language classification variables (EL, EO, IFEP, and RFEP). Control variables include student ethnicity, generational status, gender, and cohort. Unfortunately, I do not have a control for family socioeconomic status. The only data the district systematically collects on this is free and reduced-priced lunch eligibility. This variable is both problematic as a proxy for socioeconomic status (Harwell & LeBeau, 2010) and unavailable because the district considers it to be private, non-shareable data under federal law.

Comparison Groups

In this article, I use several methods to examine the characteristics and determinants of EL course-taking patterns, each of which calls for a specific comparison group. In the descriptive portion of the analysis, I compare EL course-taking to that of every other language classification (EO, IFEP, and RFEP) as well as comparing course-taking between ELs of different English proficiency and academic achievement levels. In looking at the roles of prior academic achievement and institutional constraints, I compare EL course-taking to that of EOs. EOs are an important comparison group because they represent traditionally mainstream students. In looking at how English proficiency structures course access, I compare ELs with higher English proficiency levels to ELs with lower English proficiency levels. Annual English proficiency testing among ELs allows me to look at how course-taking changes across the continuum of English proficiency levels. Finally, in looking at the role of EL classification, I compare students who are classified as ELs to those with similar characteristics but who are not classified as ELs. Therefore, I use the comparison groups of IFEPs and RFEPs, language minority students who are not EL-classified. Taken together, these analyses and comparison groups provide multiple lenses and a comprehensive and comparative picture of EL course-taking in this school district.

Methods

Descriptive Analyses

In the descriptive portion of this study, I compare course-taking outcomes across subgroups of interest. These analyses include the full analytic sample of 42,790 students. Data for all semesters of middle school are combined. I compare ELs to EOs, IFEPs, and RFEPs, as well as comparing ELs with different English proficiency levels and academic achievement levels.

Explanatory Analyses

In the second part of the study, I examine the role of the four hypothesized causes of ELs' limited access to content. Analyses were conducted using Stata version 13.

Prior Academic Achievement

To examine the role of prior academic achievement, I use ordinary least squares (OLS) regression to examine the extent to which prior academic achievement explains differences between EL and EO course-taking. The sample for this analysis includes all EL and EO students for whom I have fifth-grade achievement data (the main control variable) and who are present in the data in sixth grade. This results in a sample size of 15,911 students. The model is presented in Equation 1. Outcomes (Y) include leveled and exclusionary course-taking outcomes in the sixth grade (combining fall and spring credits). I do not include seventh- or eighth-grade outcomes in this analysis since they would introduce endogeneity. In order to control for prior achievement, I include A, students' fifth-grade ELA and math CST scores. *EL* indicates a student is EL rather than EO; X includes a vector of student characteristics including ethnicity, gender, and generational status; and Δ_y are fixed effects for academic year. Academic year fixed effects are included to control for any cohort effects or changes over time in the district.

The coefficient β_E represents the difference between EL and EO course-taking, controlling for prior academic achievement (and other covariates). If prior achievement explains the differences between EL and EO course-taking, I would expect β_E to be small and nonsignificant (and $\boldsymbol{B_A}$ to be significant and large), indicating that differences in leveled and exclusionary tracking disappear once controlling for student achievement. As an OLS model, causal inference is limited. In other words, if the inclusion of prior achievement variables diminishes course-taking differences, I cannot conclude that this is directly because of prior achievement. However, it gives preliminary evidence of the role of prior achievement.

$$Y_i = \beta_0 + \boldsymbol{B_A A_i} + \beta_E EL_i + \boldsymbol{B_X X_i} + \Delta_y + e_i. \tag{1}$$

As a sensitivity check, I also ran the model controlling for a vector containing each student's third-, fourth-, and fifth-grade CST scores. This is a more robust set of prior achievement variables, but it cuts the sample size down considerably and changes the sample characteristics to include only students who have been present in the district from at least the third grade.

Institutional Constraints

To examine the role of institutional constraints, I add school fixed effects (Λ_s) to Model 1 (see Equation 2). This allows me to compare EL to EO course-taking for students with the same prior academic achievement who attend the same school. In effect, this allows me to examine the extent to which differences in course offerings or course placement practices across schools explain differences in EL and EO course-taking. If these differences across schools play a role, I would expect leveled tracking, specifically differences in honors level enrollment, to diminish, as prior research has shown that low-income schools, such as those attended by many ELs, tend to offer fewer upper track classes (Oakes, 2005).

$$Y_i = \beta_0 + \boldsymbol{B_A A_i} + \beta_E EL_i + \boldsymbol{B_X X_i} + \Delta_y + \Lambda_s + e_i. \tag{2}$$

The sample for this analysis is the same as in the prior analysis (15,911 students). The coefficient of interest remains β_E. If institutional constraints limit ELs' course-taking, I hypothesize that β_E will diminish once including school fixed effects, specifically for the honors enrollment outcome. Again, this is an OLS model, and causal inference is limited.

English Proficiency Level

To examine the extent to which students' English proficiency level structures ELs' access to core content in middle school, I compare course-taking patterns of ELs with different English proficiency levels, holding other factors constant (see Equation 3). As in the prior analyses, I only examine sixth-grade course-taking outcomes because my main independent variable—English proficiency level—is taken from Grade 5. The sample for this analysis therefore includes EL students in Grade 6 who have fifth-grade CELDT and CST scores (3,883 students).

$$Y_i = \beta_0 + \boldsymbol{B_A A_i} + \beta_C CELDT_i + \boldsymbol{B_X X_i} + \Delta_y + \Lambda_s + e_i. \tag{3}$$

The model controls for prior achievement (fifth-grade math and ELA CST scores) $(\boldsymbol{A_i})$; student characteristics, including ethnicity, gender, and generational status $(\boldsymbol{X_i})$; academic year (Δ_y); and school (Λ_s). In this model, the coefficient of interest, β_C, identifies the estimated OLS association of one additional CELDT proficiency level in Grade 5 on a range of sixth-grade course-taking outcomes. In this analysis, I use CELDT proficiency levels rather than CELDT scale scores in order to facilitate the interpretation of regression results. If course access is structured by English proficiency level, I would expect to see significant and meaningful point estimates on the CELDT coefficient indicating greater access among students with greater English proficiency. Again, this is an OLS analysis, so causal inference is limited.

EL Classification

I measure the effect of classification as an EL on middle school course-taking using two regression discontinuity (RD) designs. RD takes advantage of the essentially random assignment of certain individuals when treatment is assigned based on one or more cut-points on known distributions. In this case, students who speak a language other than English at home are assigned to language classifications based on cut-points on the CELDT and, for reclassification, CST ELA. This is true both for initial classification (EL or IFEP) and subsequent classifications (EL or RFEP). While EL students are not the same, on average, as IFEP or RFEP students across the continuum, they are the same, in expectation, right at the cut-point. For example, students who fall just short of reaching reclassification criteria in a given grade are, in expectation, identical to those who just manage to reach those same criteria. Following these two, otherwise identical groups of students over time, RD takes advantage of these natural experiments to estimate the impact of treatment (EL classification in this case), for those just above and below the thresholds. In this article, I conduct two regression discontinuity analyses; the first exploits the assignment of students to EL versus IFEP status when students first enter school in kindergarten, and the second exploits the assignment to remain EL versus reclassify to RFEP that occurs in the transition from fifth to sixth grade. In the following, I describe both, including their samples, model specifications, and assumptions.

The first RD method provides a strong causal estimate of the direct effect of initial EL versus IFEP classification in kindergarten on middle school course-taking among language minority students who enter kindergarten just above or below the IFEP cut-point (I refer to these students as marginal students). The sample for this analysis includes language minority kindergarten entrants in the years 2002–2005. These are the cohorts in the dataset that reach the middle school grades by spring 2012 when the data ends. The analysis does not include any students who enter the district after kindergarten (and therefore includes no newcomer students). While the analytic sample is limited, a strength of this analysis is that it compares a group of EL students to an otherwise identical group of students who never experience EL classification. A weakness, however, is that most (78%) of the EL-classified students in the sample are reclassified as RFEP by the time they reach middle school. To the extent that RFEP students have fuller access to content than EL students, the estimands from this analysis may dilute the true effect of EL classification among students who remain EL.

Compliance with the EL-IFEP classification policy (reaching 4 on the CELDT) is high; 90% of students at the EL-IFEP margin are appropriately classified based on their CELDT score (see Figure A in the online version of the journal). I examine course-taking outcomes in sixth through eighth grade and embed the RD in a growth model to account for students moving through grades. Equation 4 specifies the model. Level 1 represents how each student's course-taking outcomes change across semester, and Level 2 represents how students' course-taking outcomes differ based on EL or IFEP classification (Reardon & Robinson, 2010; Singer & Willett, 2003).

In Level 1, *Spring6, Fall7,* and so on, are dummy variables for each semester of middle school (omitting fall of sixth grade), and *Grade* is a linear term for each semester of Grades 6–8, centered in the fall of sixth grade. The model includes dummy variables for each semester to allow for nonlinear variation in course-taking by semester. It includes a linear grade term in order to estimate a linear effect of EL (vs. IFEP) status on course-taking.

Key variables for the RD design are in Level 2. *Rating* is a standardized, centered transformation of each student's CELDT score. *EL* is a dummy variable indicating whether the student should be classified as EL based on their CELDT score. In developing this final model, I compared goodness of fit of different models as well as considered how one would expect EL status to influence course-taking. Outcomes, Y, include the set of leveled and exclusionary tracking outcomes. I cluster standard errors to account for the coarseness of the rating variable and include control variables (X_i) for student ethnicity, gender, cohort, and generational status.

Level 1:

$$Y_{it} = \beta_{0i} + \beta_{1i} Spring6_{it} + \beta_{2i} Fall7_{it} + \beta_{3i} Spring7_{it} + \beta_{4i} Fall8_{it}$$
$$+ \beta_{5i} Spring8_{it} + \beta_{6i} Grade_{it} + e_{it}$$

Level 2:

$$\beta_{0i} = \gamma_{00} + \gamma_{01} Rating_i + \gamma_{02} EL_i + \gamma_{03} Rating_i \times EL_i + \boldsymbol{B_0 X_i} + u_{0i}$$
$$\beta_{1i} = \gamma_{10}$$
$$\beta_{2i} = \gamma_{20}$$ \hfill (4)
$$\beta_{3i} = \gamma_{30}$$
$$\beta_{4i} = \gamma_{40}$$
$$\beta_{5i} = \gamma_{50}$$
$$\beta_{6i} = \gamma_{61} Rating_i + \gamma_{62} EL_i + \gamma_{63} Rating_i \times EL_i + \boldsymbol{B_6 X_i} + u_{6i}.$$

In this model, γ_{02} is the first parameter of interest, representing the average effect of initial EL (vs. IFEP) status on marginal students' course-taking outcomes in the fall of sixth grade. γ_{62} is the second parameter of interest. It represents the average effect of initial EL (vs. IFEP) status on the incremental change in marginal students' course-taking outcomes, by semester, for each semester after fall of sixth grade through spring of eighth grade. For each outcome, I run a test of joint significance of γ_{02} and γ_{62} to test the hypothesis that EL classification (compared to IFEP classification) impacts marginal students' course-taking. This model is an intent-to-treat model. It estimates the effect of EL classification on course-taking outcomes for all marginal students irrespective of whether a given student was actually assigned to EL or IFEP status correctly. As such, it is a lower bound estimate of the effect of EL classification among compliers (i.e., students who are assigned to EL and IFEP classification in compliance with district policy).

For all outcomes, I run the models using a range of bandwidths of data on each side of the cut-score from .5 to 1 standard deviations (*SD*s). A .75 bandwidth means that I use data from .75 *SD*s on the rating variable below the cut-score through .75 *SD*s above the cut-score. I use the Imbens and Kalyanaraman (2012) method to calculate, for each outcome, the optimal bandwidth that balances precision with lack of bias. The optimal bandwidths cluster around .75 *SD*s (see Table C in the online version of the journal), so while I present results from the range of bandwidths, I focus the discussion on the .75 bandwidth results. In general, the point estimates are similar in direction and size across bandwidths.

In order to interpret the RD estimates causally, the model must meet certain assumptions. Key among these is the assumption that nothing other than language classification varies at the cut-score. If other variables vary at the cut-score, then it is difficult to determine whether estimated effects are due to the treatment (EL classification) or due to some other factor that changes at the cut-score. In testing this assumption, I find that while no other pretreatment covariates vary at the cut-score, the proportion of Latino students varies at a marginally significant level (see Table D in the online version of the journal). Specifically, there are 6 percentage points fewer Latino students just above the IFEP threshold than just below it. This may indicate possible manipulation of the EL-IFEP classification system or differential sample attrition that is related to student ethnicity. To account for this possible assumption violation, I include student ethnicity variables in the model (Robinson-Cimpian & Thompson, 2016). With these variables included, EL and IFEP assignment, at the margin, is random in expectation.

The second RD estimates the impact of entering sixth grade as an EL compared to entering sixth grade as an RFEP on course-taking outcomes for students just above and below the reclassification thresholds in fifth grade. The sample analyzed in this method is of considerable interest given that fifth grade is when the largest proportion of EL students is reclassified (Umansky & Reardon, 2014). This sample also includes a broader range of EL students than the previous RD since EL students who enter the district after kindergarten (and before the sixth grade) are included. A limitation of this method is that RFEP students may experience barriers to content as a result of having previously been ELs (Kanno & Kangas, 2014; Umansky, 2016). If this is the case, the estimands from this analysis will likely obscure some of the ways in which ELs face barriers to access.

As described earlier, reclassification criteria in this district are substantially more complex than initial classification criteria. The main criteria are CELDT overall scores, CELDT subtest scores and CST ELA scores, but the district also takes into account students' grades, teacher recommendation, and parental opinion. Of these criteria, I have access to CELDT (overall and subtest) scores and CST ELA scores, meaning that I cannot perfectly model reclassification eligibility. Using the test scores, I calculate a 46% compliance rate at the threshold (see Figure B in the online version of the journal). This means that just reaching these criteria, as opposed to just missing them, results in a 46 percentage point jump in likelihood of RFEP classification. While considerably lower than the 90% compliance I find at the EL-IFEP threshold, this rate is on par with other studies of reclassification (Robinson-Cimpian & Thompson, 2016).

$$Y_i = \beta_0 + \beta_1 Rating_i + \beta_2 EL_i + \beta_3 Rating_i \times EL_i + \boldsymbol{B_X X_i} + e_i. \tag{5}$$

The model is presented in Equation 5. Outcomes, Y, include leveled and exclusionary tracking outcomes in the sixth grade; *Rating* is a standardized, centered transformation of each student's lowest contributing test score (the lowest test score is the determining score for whether a student should be classified as EL or not; see Reardon & Robinson, 2010). *EL* is a dummy variable indicating whether a student should be classified as an EL based on *Rating*. Standard errors are clustered to account for the coarseness of the rating variable and control variables, X_i, are included for student ethnicity, gender, cohort, and generational status. I conducted the same checks on this analysis as on the prior RD, and there are no assumption violations in this analysis (see Table E in the online version of the journal). β_2 is the coefficient of interest, representing the estimated impact of EL versus RFEP eligibility at the end of fifth grade on students' sixth-grade course-taking outcomes, among students at the margin. As with the prior RD, this is an intent-to-treat model. Optimal bandwidths cluster around .5 (see Table F in the online version of the journal), so I present findings from a range of bandwidths of data on each side of the cut-score from .25 to .75 standard deviations, focusing on the .5 results.

Results

Descriptive Results

ELs Compared to Non-ELs

Table 2 compares EL course-taking to that of EOs, IFEPs, and RFEPs. ELs have inferior access to content compared to students in all other language classifications with regard to both leveled and exclusionary tracking. ELs are in lower level classes, on average, compared to EOs, IFEPs, and RFEPs. For example, ELs are enrolled in one-ninth the number of honors credits, compared to EOs. ELs are also less likely than any other group to take algebra by the eighth grade.

In terms of exclusionary tracking, ELs are less likely to be enrolled in math, science, and ELA compared to EOs. In math and science, an additional 3% and 9% of ELs are not enrolled, respectively. Results are particularly striking with regard to ELA; 42% of ELs are not enrolled in ELA in a given semester compared to 1% to 2% of non-ELs. The full academic course load row also shows ELs' exclusion from academic content areas. While over 95% of students in the non-EL categories are enrolled in math, science, and ELA in a given semester, the corresponding figure for ELs is 53%. This means that in a given semester, close to one in two ELs is not enrolled in at least one academic content area.

Contrary to state and district policy, 32% of ELs are not enrolled in ELD in a given semester of middle school. ELD and ELA are largely used as substitutes rather than complements to each other. Supplementary analysis (see Table G in the online version of the journal) shows that only about one in four ELs is in both ELA and ELD. The remaining three out of four are in either ELD or ELA, with a very small proportion (<1%) of ELs not enrolled in either.

Table 2

Descriptive Course-Taking Statistics, by Language Classification, Semester Averages Grades 6–8

	Language Classification			
	EL	EO	IFEP	RFEP
Total credits	25.2	22.2	21.4	21.1
Total academic credits	14.9	16.6	16.0	15.8
Level enrollment (leveled tracking)				
Grade level credits	12.6	10.8	10.0	10.1
Honors credits	0.5	4.5	5.2	5.0
Remedial credits	1.8	1.2	0.8	0.6
Algebra by eighth grade (%)	37	44	55	58
Subject area enrollment (exclusionary tracking)				
ELA credits	4.0	5.8	5.6	5.4
Math credits	6.1	5.6	5.3	5.3
Science credits	4.8	5.1	5.1	5.0
ELD credits	5.5	0.3	0.3	0.3
No ELA (%)	42	1	1	2
No math (%)	4	1	1	1
No science (%)	10	1	1	1
No ELD (%)	32	94	95	94
Full academic course load (%)	53	98	98	97
N (students)	10,651	15,639	4,419	12,081

Note. EL = English learner; EO = English only; IFEP = initially fluent English proficient; RFEP = reclassified fluent English proficient; ELA = English language arts; ELD = English language development. The total academic credits row sums math, science, and ELA credits. Full academic course load enrollment indicates enrollment in math, science, and ELA. A full credit course is five credits.

ELs of Different English Proficiency Levels

The first set of columns in Table 3, titled "English Proficiency Level (CELDT)," presents descriptive statistics on course enrollment among ELs, by English proficiency level. As predicted, leveled and exclusionary tracking characterize the course-taking of ELs with low levels of English proficiency more than those with higher English proficiency levels.

Lower proficiency ELs are in fewer honors credits than higher proficiency ELs but also in fewer grade-level and remedial credits. These results are driven by exclusionary tracking patterns, most specifically that large proportions of lower proficiency ELs are not enrolled in ELA (85% at Level 1 and 63% at Level 2). Exclusionary tracking in ELA appears to be strongly linked to English proficiency while the same is not the case with exclusion from math and science. In those subjects, ELs with higher English proficiency

Table 3

Descriptive Course-Taking Statistics, Among ELs, by English Proficiency Level and Math and ELA Performance Level, Semester Averages Grades 6–8

	English Proficiency Level (CELDT)						Math Performance Level (CST Math)						ELA Performance Level (CST ELA)					
	Beginning	Early Intermediate	Intermediate	Early Advanced	Advanced	Missing	Far Below Basic	Below Basic	Basic	Proficient	Advanced	Missing	Far Below Basic	Below Basic	Basic	Proficient	Advanced	Missing
Total credits	27.1	25.9	25.5	24.6	23.8	23.5	26.6	26.0	25.2	24.3	24.2	24.7	26.6	25.8	24.6	23.4	22.3	25.2
Total academic credits	12.0	13.5	15.4	16.0	16.0	16.1	15.2	15.6	15.3	14.2	14.1	14.1	13.3	14.9	15.5	15.5	15.6	15.0
Leveled tracking																		
Grade level credits	10.7	11.6	13.1	13.4	13.1	12.8	12.6	12.9	13.0	12.1	11.1	12.2	11.5	12.6	13.2	12.7	9.9	12.7
Honors credits	0.1	0.1	0.3	0.6	1.2	1.6	0.1	0.2	0.4	0.8	2.3	0.3	0.1	0.2	0.5	1.7	5.2	0.4
Remedial credits	1.3	1.8	2.0	2.0	1.7	1.7	2.4	2.5	1.9	1.2	0.7	1.5	1.7	2.1	1.8	1.1	0.5	2.0
Algebra by eighth grade (%)	36	35	36	39	42	41	32	32	41	61	79	13	31	32	43	59	69	18
Exclusionary tracking																		
ELA credits	0.9	2.5	4.4	5.2	5.5	5.2	3.9	4.5	4.2	3.5	3.3	3.7	2.3	3.9	4.7	4.8	4.9	4.3
Math credits	6.3	6.4	6.2	6.0	5.6	6.0	6.5	6.3	6.2	5.8	5.7	5.8	6.3	6.2	6.0	5.6	5.5	6.0
Science credits	4.8	4.6	4.9	4.9	4.9	5.0	4.8	4.8	4.9	4.9	5.1	4.7	4.7	4.8	4.9	5.1	5.2	4.7
ELD credits	10.5	7.8	5.1	3.6	2.8	2.6	6.4	5.5	5.1	5.4	5.3	5.9	8.6	6.0	4.2	2.9	1.5	5.3
No ELA (%)	85	63	36	26	19	20	45	39	38	45	44	45	67	45	31	23	14	43
No math (%)	5	2	3	4	6	2	5	4	3	3	2	5	5	4	3	3	1	4
No science (%)	10	13	10	10	8	7	11	10	9	8	5	13	12	11	9	5	2	11
No ELD (%)	5	15	30	41	50	66	26	30	33	34	40	30	13	26	39	56	76	37
Full academic course load (%)	13	33	58	68	73	77	48	55	56	51	53	50	29	49	63	73	84	52
N (students)	2,623	1,137	2,667	2,265	802	1,157	776	1,906	2,381	1,777	820	2,991	2,487	3,018	3,467	894	177	608

Note. Math CST test is measured in seventh grade (the only grade in middle school when there is only one test type) rather than by semester in order to avoid confusing test score with test type. The total academic credits row sums math, science, and ELA credits. Full academic course load enrollment indicates enrollment in math, science, and ELA. A full credit course is five credits. CELDT = California English Language Development Test; CST = California Standards Test; EL = English learner; ELA = English language arts; ELD = English language development.

levels are roughly as likely as ELs with lower English proficiency levels to not be enrolled.

ELs of Different Math and ELA Performance Levels

Leveled and exclusionary tracking characterize access to content more for EL students with lower math levels than those with advanced math skills (see the second set of columns in Table 3, titled "Math Performance Level [CST Math]"). EL students with low math scores are almost never in honors classes whereas students with advanced math scores take, on average, 2.3 honors credits per semester.

ELs with low math performance are also more likely than their higher achieving peers to not be enrolled in math and science. ELs of all levels of math performance face exclusionary tracking in ELA, however. Between one in two and one in three ELs is not enrolled in ELA across math performance levels. Even among high performers, nearly one in two is not in a full course load of classes in any given middle school semester.

The final set of columns in Table 3 shows results by ELA performance levels (columns titled "ELA Performance Level [CST ELA]"). Patterns here are similar to those of math, with leveled and exclusionary tracking limiting course access particularly among ELs with low CST ELA scores. One notable difference is that ELs with high CST ELA scores are rarely excluded from ELA classes or other core content areas. As a result, while 29% of CST ELA "far below basic" EL students are in a full course load, 84% of "advanced" EL students are.

Analyses of Explanatory Factors

The descriptive results reveal that ELs have very different access to content compared to non-ELs and that access to content among ELs is structured along lines of English proficiency level and academic performance level. It also underscores the prominence of both leveled and exclusionary tracking—both of which limit ELs' access to content in middle school. This next section analyzes possible causes of ELs' inferior course access.

Prior Academic Achievement

In Table 4, Model 1 looks at the raw differences between ELs and EOs and confirms that there are large and highly significant differences in the course-taking patterns of ELs and EOs across leveled and exclusionary outcomes. Model 2 assesses the extent to which lower academic achievement explains ELs' comparatively limited access to content. Unlike some of the subsequent analyses, this analysis relates to the full spectrum of EL students in the district, including newcomers, developmental ELs, and long-term ELs.

Table 4

Ordinary Least Squares Estimates of Effect of EL Language Classification Compared to EO Classification on Sixth Grade Leveled and Exclusionary Tracking Outcomes

	Model 1		Model 2		Model 3	
Leveled tracking						
Honors credits	−7.97***	(0.25)	−2.50***	(0.24)	−2.18***	(0.21)
Grade level credits	3.48***	(0.28)	−2.28***	(0.27)	−2.39***	(0.24)
Remedial credits	1.41***	(0.10)	−0.33**	(0.11)	−0.57***	(0.10)
Highest class: honors	−0.21***	(0.01)	−0.02*	(0.01)	−0.01	(0.01)
Highest class: grade level	0.21***	(0.01)	0.02*	(0.01)	0.00	(0.01)
Highest class: remedial	0.00~	(0.00)	0.00	(0.00)	0.00	(0.00)
Exclusionary tracking						
Total credits	3.54***	(0.27)	−0.12	(0.28)	−0.24	(0.27)
Total academic credits	−3.08***	(0.19)	−5.12***	(0.20)	−5.14***	(0.20)
ELA credits	−2.73***	(0.11)	−3.32***	(0.12)	−3.46***	(0.12)
Math credits	0.21*	(0.08)	−0.91***	(0.09)	−0.85***	(0.09)
Science credits	−0.56***	(0.05)	−0.90***	(0.05)	−0.83***	(0.05)
ELD credits	7.86***	(0.13)	6.00***	(0.14)	5.86***	(0.14)
No ELA	0.25***	(0.01)	0.20***	(0.01)	0.19***	(0.01)
No math	0.01~	(0.00)	0.00	(0.00)	−0.01**	(0.00)
No science	0.00	(0.00)	0.00	(0.00)	0.00	(0.00)
Full academic course load	−0.43***	(0.01)	−0.40***	(0.01)	−0.39***	(0.01)
Student characteristics	X		X		X	
Year FE	X		X		X	
Achievement			X		X	
School FE					X	
N (student-semesters)	15,911		15,911		15,911	

Note. Standard errors shown in parentheses. EL = English learner; EO = English only student; FE = fixed effects; ELA = English language arts; ELD = English language development. Student characteristics include variables for student ethnicity, gender, and generational status. Year FE include dummy variables for each academic year. Achievement controls include fifth-grade math and ELA California Standards Test (CST) scores. School FE include dummies for each middle school. The total academic credits row sums math, science, and ELA credits. Full academic course load indicates enrollment in math, science, and ELA. A full credit course is five credits.
~$p < .10$. *$p < .05$. **$p < .01$. ***$p < .001$.

Controlling for prior academic achievement dramatically attenuates ELs' exposure to leveled tracking. With achievement controls, ELs take far fewer credits at all three levels (honors, grade level, and remedial) compared to EOs with the same achievement profiles. This indicates the presence of exclusionary tracking since ELs do not make up for fewer credits at one level with more credits at another level. A limited degree of leveled tracking may remain; ELs remain 2 percentage points less likely to have an honors level class as their highest level class, compared to EOs with the same prior achievement.

By contrast, controlling for prior achievement exacerbates many of the exclusionary tracking patterns in the base model. Once controlling for prior achievement, ELs take 5.12 fewer academic credits, on average, compared to EOs with the same achievement profiles. While the bulk of this is accounted for by ELA (3.32 credits), ELs also take fewer math (.91) and science (.90) credits compared to EOs with the same prior achievement. Likewise, controlling for prior achievement has little effect on differences in full course load enrollment; ELs are 40 percentage points less likely to be in a full academic load compared to similarly achieving EOs.

In summary, prior achievement explains much of the pattern of ELs enrolling in fewer upper level classes and more lower level classes, but it does not explain differences in enrollment between ELs and EOs in academic subject areas. As discussed earlier, I conducted a sensitivity check using Grades 3–5 ELA and math CST scores as predictor variables. The results are very similar to those presented here (see Table H in the online version of the journal), indicating that fifth-grade test scores are a good proxy for a more extensive set of prior achievement variables.

Institutional Constraints

Model 3 in Table 4 tests the hypothesis of institutional constraints: namely, that ELs have inferior course access because they are disproportionately enrolled in schools with fewer upper track classes.

The results show modest support for this hypothesis. As predicted, including school fixed effects modestly diminishes ELs' under-enrollment in honors level classes (from 2.5 fewer credits to 2.18 fewer credits). A similar pattern can be seen with regard to students' highest level class: While ELs are significantly less likely to have an honors level class as their highest class compared to EOs with the same prior achievement, this difference drops slightly to 1 percentage point and nonstatistical significance when comparing ELs to similar EOs in the same schools. This suggests that the schools that ELs attend may offer fewer honors level classes, on average, compared to those that EOs attend.

English Proficiency Level

English proficiency is predictive of students' course-taking, after controlling for school, prior achievement, cohort, and student background characteristics (see Table 5). Point estimates in that table reflect the association of a one unit change in English proficiency level (measured from Levels 1–5) on a given course-taking outcome. ELs with lower English proficiency levels in middle school—most of whom are newcomer students—experience clear

Table 5

Ordinary Least Squares Estimates of Effect of English Proficiency Level (CELDT Performance Level) on Sixth-Grade Course-Taking Outcomes

	Coefficient on CELDT Performance Level	
Leveled tracking		
Honors credits	0.28***	(0.07)
Grade level credits	0.82***	(0.16)
Remedial credits	0.27***	(0.08)
Highest class: honors	0.03***	(0.01)
Highest class: grade level	−0.04***	(0.01)
Highest class: remedial	0.00*	(0.00)
Exclusionary tracking		
Total credits	−0.47*	(0.23)
Total academic credits	1.36***	(0.18)
ELA credits	1.30***	(0.11)
Math credits	0.00	(0.07)
Science credits	0.06	(0.05)
ELD credits	−1.81***	(0.13)
No ELA	−0.11***	(0.01)
No math	−0.01*	(0.00)
No science	0.00	(0.00)
Full academic course load	0.09***	(0.01)
N	3,883	

Note. This model controls for fifth-grade math and ELA CST scores, student ethnicity, gender, and generational status, middle school fixed effects, and academic year fixed effects. ELA = English language arts; ELD = English language development; CST = California Standards Test; CELDT = California English Language Development Test. The total academic credits row sums math, science, and ELA credits. Full academic course load indicates enrollment in math, science, and ELA. A full credit course is five credits.
*$p < .05$. ***$p < .001$.

patterns of leveled and exclusionary tracking as compared to ELs with higher English proficiency—most of whom are developmental EL students.

For every one-unit gain in English proficiency level, ELs are 3 percentage points more likely to have an honors class as their highest level class. This means that a Level 5 EL is 12 percentage points more likely to have an honors level class as their highest level class compared to a Level 1 EL with the same prior achievement in the same school.

With regard to exclusionary tracking, EL students at higher proficiency levels take significantly more academic credits. Each additional proficiency level is associated with 1.36 more academic credits and an 11 and 1 percentage point gain in the likelihood of ELA and math course enrollment, respectively. Taken together, these differences have large implications for students' enrollment in full academic course loads. A Level 1 EL is a full 36 percentage points less likely to be enrolled in a full academic load than a Level 5 EL with the same prior achievement in the same school.

EL Classification

The two regression discontinuity analyses reveal that EL classification may also limit students' course access. As described in the methods section, the first model examines the impact of EL as compared to IFEP classification in kindergarten on middle school course-taking, among students at the margin of EL classification in kindergarten. Results are presented in Tables 6 (leveled tracking outcomes) and 7 (exclusionary tracking outcomes). While the results are largely in the expected direction (providing less access to EL- than IFEP-classified students at the margin), most are not statistically significant. No leveled tracking results reach standard levels of significance. Exclusionary tracking results suggest that EL classification, among marginal students, results in greater ELD enrollment in middle school, a difference that diminishes over time. In addition, this analysis suggests that EL classification, among marginal students, results in enrollment in fewer core academic content area credits in middle school, a difference that grows over time. The test of joint significance for this outcome is only marginally significant, and the effect size is small, however, amounting to only a fraction of a credit each semester.

The second RD method looks at the impact of remaining an EL as compared with being reclassified at the end of fifth grade on sixth-grade course-taking. Results are presented in Table 8. There are no significant results with regard to leveled tracking. With regard to exclusionary tracking, there are clear and immediate effects of remaining an EL versus being reclassified, for marginal students. Namely, remaining an EL results in higher credit enrollment in ELD and science and lower enrollment in ELA (.88 fewer credits) and a full academic load (7 percentage points).

Discussion

In this section, I first discuss the two prevailing characteristics of EL course access: leveled tracking and exclusionary tracking. I then discuss findings regarding the causes of ELs' limited access to academic courses.

Leveled Tracking

This study adds to a growing body of research showing that ELs take fewer high track credits and more lower track credits compared with students of any other language classification (Callahan, 2005; Gándara et al., 2003; Nord et al., 2011; Solorzano & Ornelas, 2004; Wang & Goldschmidt, 1999; Zuniga et al., 2005). Underrepresentation in honors classes is particularly acute among ELs with low academic achievement and/or low English

Table 6
Regression Discontinuity Estimates, Impact of EL Versus IFEP Classification in Kindergarten on Middle School Leveled Tracking Outcomes

	BW.5		**BW.75**		BW1	
Grade level credits						
Intercept	0.61	(0.65)	**0.13**	**(0.55)**	−0.05	(0.51)
Slope	−0.11	(0.13)	**0.04**	**(0.11)**	0.08	(0.10)
Joint test *p* value	0.63		**0.81**		0.70	
Honors credits						
Intercept	−0.34	(0.64)	**0.02**	**(0.51)**	0.14	(0.47)
Slope	−0.05	(0.13)	**−0.13**	**(0.10)**	−0.14	(0.09)
Joint test *p* value	0.57		**0.36**		0.27	
Remedial credits						
Intercept	−0.22	(0.14)	**−0.15**	**(0.11)**	−0.09	(0.09)
Slope	0.05	(0.06)	**0.01**	**(0.05)**	0.00	(0.04)
Joint test *p* value	0.28		**0.26**		0.46	
N	7,419		**11,039**		13,593	
Algebra by eighth grade						
Algebra	0.00	(0.02)	**−0.02**	**(0.02)**	−0.02	(0.02)
N	1,737		**2,577**		3,146	

Note. Optimal bandwidth in bold. Standard errors shown in parentheses. The intercept value represents the estimated impact of EL versus IFEP status on fall of sixth-grade course-taking outcomes. The slope value represents the estimated change in the impact of EL versus IFEP status on each subsequent middle school semester after fall of sixth grade. EL = English learner; IFEP = initially fluent English proficient; BW = bandwidth.

proficiency. While this finding is not surprising given ELs' lower average academic performance compared to other students, there is ample evidence that placement into low track classes can depress achievement and likelihood of graduation (Oakes, 2005; Slavin, 1990; Walqui & Van Lier, 2010). High track placement and exposure to advanced content, by contrast, benefits disadvantaged students' achievement, self-esteem, college enrollment, college completion, and labor market earnings (Engel, Claessens, Watts, & Farkas, 2016; Kettler, Shiu, & Johnsen, 2006; Long, Conger, & Iatarola, 2012). Some of this research shows effects of content exposure specifically for ELs (Aguirre-Muñoz & Boscardin, 2008; Garrett & Hong, 2015).

Leveled tracking might be particularly problematic for ELs. First, many factors combine to exacerbate the potential that ELs are placed in inappropriately low track classes (e.g., downwardly biased test results due to English language barriers) (Kieffer, Lesaux, Rivera, & Francis, 2009). Therefore, ELs may be less likely than English speakers to reap benefits from purposeful differentiated instruction that undergirds leveled tracking systems.

Table 7

Regression Discontinuity Estimates, Impact of EL Versus IFEP Classification in Kindergarten on Middle School Exclusionary Tracking Outcomes

	BW.4		**BW.7**		BW1	
Total credits						
Intercept	0.14	(0.45)	**0.09**	**(0.40)**	0.08	(0.36)
Slope	−0.18	(0.15)	**−0.15**	**(0.13)**	−0.14	(0.11)
Joint test *p* value	0.28		**0.17**		0.19	
Total academic credits						
Intercept	0.05	(0.22)	**0.00**	**(0.21)**	0.01	(0.17)
Slope	−0.11	(0.09)	**−0.09**	**(0.08)**	−0.08	(0.07)
Joint test *p* value	0.14		**0.09~**		0.17	
ELA credits						
Intercept	−0.11	(0.14)	**−0.14**	**(0.12)**	−0.11	(0.11)
Slope	−0.01	(0.05)	**−0.01**	**(0.04)**	0.00	(0.04)
Joint test *p* value	0.23		**0.15**		0.28	
Math credits						
Intercept	0.02	(0.10)	**0.05**	**(0.09)**	0.05	(0.07)
Slope	−0.04	(0.04)	**−0.04**	**(0.04)**	−0.04	(0.03)
Joint test *p* value	0.48		**0.40**		0.34	
Science credits						
Intercept	0.15*	(0.07)	**0.09**	**(0.07)**	0.07	(0.06)
Slope	−0.06**	(0.02)	**−0.04~**	**(0.02)**	−0.03	(0.02)
Joint test *p* value	0.03*		**0.15**		0.30	
ELD credits						
Intercept	0.36*	(0.16)	**0.32***	**(0.13)**	0.30**	(0.11)
Slope	−0.07~	(0.04)	**−0.07***	**(0.03)**	−0.07*	(0.03)
Joint test *p* value	0.06~		**0.05***		0.02*	
Full academic course load						
Intercept	−0.01	(0.01)	**−0.02**	**(0.01)**	−0.01	(0.01)
Slope	0.00	(0.00)	**0.00**	**(0.00)**	0.00	(0.00)
Joint test *p* value	0.31		**0.55**		0.60	
N	6,004		**10,443**		13,593	

Note. Optimal bandwidth in bold. Standard errors shown in parentheses. The intercept value represents the estimated impact of EL versus IFEP status on fall of sixth-grade course-taking outcomes. The slope value represents the estimated change in the impact of EL versus IFEP status on each subsequent middle school semester after fall of sixth grade. EL = English learner; IFEP = initially fluent English proficient; BW = bandwidth; ELA = English language arts; ELD = English language development. The total academic credits row sums math, science, and ELA credits. Full academic course load indicates enrollment in math, science, and ELA. A full credit course is five credits.
~$p < .10$. *$p < .05$. **$p < .01$.

Second, lower track classes do not simply provide less advanced content. Rather, lower track classes are characterized by fewer opportunities

Table 8

Regression Discontinuity Estimates, Impact of End-of-Fifth-Grade EL Versus RFEP Classification on Sixth-Grade Leveled and Exclusionary Tracking Outcomes

	BW.25		**BW.5**		BW.75	
Leveled tracking						
Honors credits	1.10~	(0.66)	**0.77**	**(0.52)**	0.49	(0.45)
Grade level credits	−1.77~	(0.94)	**−1.06**	**(0.67)**	−0.90	(0.57)
Remedial credits	−0.16	(0.40)	**0.07**	**(0.31)**	0.33	(0.29)
Exclusionary tracking						
Total credits	1.67	(1.02)	**3.05*****	**(0.75)**	3.62***	(0.67)
Total academic credits	−0.83	(0.79)	**−0.22**	**(0.58)**	−0.09	(0.50)
ELA credits	−1.15*	(0.48)	**−0.88***	**(0.35)**	−0.64*	(0.30)
Math credits	0.04	(0.33)	**0.33**	**(0.24)**	0.30	(0.21)
Science credits	0.28	(0.21)	**0.33***	**(0.16)**	0.25~	(0.13)
ELD credits	1.90**	(0.68)	**2.52*****	**(0.49)**	3.12***	(0.43)
No ELA	0.18*	(0.07)	**0.18*****	**(0.05)**	0.17***	(0.04)
No math	−0.02	(0.01)	**−0.01**	**(0.01)**	0.01	(0.01)
No science	−0.01	(0.01)	**0.00**	**(0.01)**	0.01	(0.01)
Full academic course load	−0.07~	(0.03)	**−0.07***	**(0.03)**	−0.09***	(0.02)
N	1,802		**3,315**		4,390	

Note. Optimal bandwidth in bold. Standard errors shown in parentheses. This model includes controls for student ethnicity, gender, cohort, and generational status. EL = English learner; RFEP = reclassified fluent English proficient; ELA = English language arts; ELD = English language development. The total academic credits row sums math, science, and ELA credits. Full academic course load indicates enrollment in math, science, and ELA. A full credit course is five credits.
$\sim p < .10.$ $*p < .05.$ $**p < .01.$ $***p < .001.$

for meaningful content-based language use as well as less supportive student-teacher relationships (Harklau, 1994; Katz, 1999; Page, 1991; Raudenbush, Rowan, & Cheong, 1993; Valenzuela, 1999). Opportunities for meaningful content-based language use and supportive student-teacher relationships have both been posited as key ingredients for EL success in school (Saunders et al., 2013; Stanton-Salazar & Dornbusch, 1995; Stanton-Salazar & Spina, 2003). As such, ELs' disproportionate placement in lower track classes is an important barrier to their opportunity to learn.

Exclusionary Tracking

A contribution of this study is the finding that ELs' course access is characterized by a dimension that has rarely been examined in general studies of course access and tracking. Namely, large proportions of ELs are not enrolled in a full course of study in middle school. ELs most commonly lack enrollment in English language arts classes, but exclusion from academic content also occurs in math and science.

Districts across the country face an underlying challenge: how to provide both English language development support and access to grade-level academic content within the confines of the school day. Regulations regarding the requirement to provide English language instruction tend to be relatively straightforward. In California, for example, schools are required to provide daily designated ELD instruction to all EL students (California Department of Education, 2015b). This requirement is substantiated in part through reporting requirements in which districts annually report how they provide ELD to their EL students (American Civil Liberties Union of California & Asian Pacific American Legal Center, 2013).

However, federal and state guidance regarding the requirement to provide ELs with equitable access to academic content has been less defined and delineated. While federal law is clear that ELs must have "parity of participation" in academic instruction (*Castañeda v. Pickard*, 1981, p. §1703(f)), federal regulation allows for schools to temporarily disrupt ELs' access to academic content in favor of concentrated English language instruction so long as they "recoup any deficits that they may incur in other areas of the curriculum as a result of spending extra time on ELD" (Lhamon & Gupta, 2015, p. 17). California law parallels federal law, stating:

> Districts must ensure that all students meet grade-level core curriculum standards within a reasonable amount of time. If a district chooses to emphasize ELD before full access to the core curriculum or if the student does not comprehend enough English to allow full access to the core curriculum, the district must develop and successfully implement a plan for ELs to recoup any and all academic deficits before the deficits become irreparable. (CDE, 2006, p. 4)

Federal and state regulation do not, however, specify when, for whom, or for how long academic delays are allowable or appropriate. Nor are there guidelines on how schools must compensate for any delays that occur or reporting requirements that pertain to ELs' access to academic content. As such, ELs' right to English language support may be more fully realized than their right to equitable access to content (Callahan & Shifrer, 2016; Walqui et al., 2010).

While allowable, ELs, with few exceptions (e.g., recently arrived ELs with weak or absent prior formal education), benefit from simultaneous rather than sequential access to content (Estrada, 2014; Rios-Aguilar, Canché, & Sabetghadam, 2012; Walqui & Van Lier, 2010). As a result, the district examined here specifies that all ELs should be placed in a full load of academic classes each semester. Other large California districts have similar policies (Los Angeles Unified School District, 2015; San Bernadino City Unified School District, 2010). Despite district policy, this analysis suggests that many ELs do not have full access to academic content. Exclusionary tracking, albeit more pervasive among lower performing and lower English proficiency ELs, is quite common even among high performing and English proficient ELs. Many of these middle school ELs with higher English proficiency have been in U.S. schools since kindergarten, suggesting that exclusionary tracking is not, at least for some, a temporary practice.

In this district, ELA and ELD are, in practice, largely used as substitutes rather than complements. This may, in part, be due to the fact that the lines between ELD, ELA and other academic content areas have been blurring. States, including California, promote the implementation of both designated and integrated ELD (CDE, 2015b). Designated ELD is ELD instruction in a protected and separate block of time. Integrated ELD, by contrast, is ELD support provided within the context of academic or elective content instruction. Furthermore, designated ELD can focus on English skills that are targeted toward a specific content area, such as math or science. Finally, there has been limited movement in some locales to fully integrate ELD with ELA for EL students with relatively high levels of English proficiency, particularly for those EL students who qualify as long-term ELs (Los Angeles Unified School District, 2015).

Regardless of these trends, exclusion from ELA can have serious implications for ELs that last well beyond K–12 education. For example, the university system in California requires that students take four full years of ELA in high school in order to be eligible to apply to a four-year college. If the pattern I observe in middle school continues into high school, a large proportion of EL students may be ineligible to apply to college due to exclusion from ELA.

ELs are not only underrepresented in ELA, they are also underrepresented in math and science courses. Exclusion from math and science is relatively evenly distributed across ELs of different English proficiency levels, suggesting that this exclusion is not a temporary disruption for newcomer students or those with low English proficiency levels. Indeed, the English proficiency group with the highest proportion of students not enrolled in math is actually those with the highest English proficiency level.

This article revealed a somewhat paradoxical finding in math and science enrollment: EL students can be, at one and the same time, enrolled in more math or science credits than non-EL students and more likely to be excluded from math or science than non-EL students. This paradox is created because while EL students are more likely than non-ELs to not take math or science, they are also more likely to be enrolled in grade-level science or math with supplementary remedial support. This suggests a possible bifurcated response to ELs in these content areas: Some schools or administrators may respond to EL status or low English proficiency by providing a double dose of content, while others respond by delaying or blocking access to content.

Like ELA, lack of enrollment in math and/or science in middle school has grave repercussions for students' opportunity to learn. Middle school coursework introduces concepts and skills that are used in high school, and courses are sequenced throughout secondary education (Wang & Goldschmidt, 2003). Missing math or science in one semester, therefore, often results in long-term delays that can block students from being able to graduate or apply to college (Zuniga et al., 2005).

Causes of ELs' Limited Course Access

Grounded in the rich literature on ELs' experiences and opportunities in school, I posited four hypotheses for why ELs have limited course access. These are: academic achievement, institutional constraints, English proficiency, and EL classification. I find at least limited support for each of these four hypotheses.

The findings from this study, taken together, suggest that ELs face multiple barriers to academic content in school. Some of these barriers, namely, academic achievement and institutional constraints, are in place for all students but disproportionately impact ELs. In other words, access to content is structured for all students based on their prior achievement and the school they attend, but due to the characteristics of ELs and the schools they attend, these structures impact a disproportionate number of ELs (Fry, 2007, 2008). The other barriers, English proficiency level and EL classification, impact only EL students because they pertain to characteristics that only EL students have.

While these findings shed light on factors that may limit ELs' access to content, they do not address how, specifically, these barriers are operationalized. Prior research, however, has articulated how prior achievement and school and residential segregation operate. Prior achievement, in schools with leveled tracks, is used to determine students' course level placement (Oakes, 2005). Segregation influences students' access to course level because schools with greater resources and those in more affluent communities tend to offer a greater number of high track classes (Oakes, 2005; Solorzano & Ornelas, 2004). The findings in this article are confirmatory of these processes: Prior achievement and school of attendance explain nearly all of EL students' disproportionate placement in lower track classes. The findings are also confirmatory in that prior achievement and school of attendance are not predictive of exclusionary tracking outcomes. In other words, theory and research on how prior achievement and segregation limit students' access to content deal overwhelmingly with access to high track classes rather than access to core academic instruction.

We know less about how course access is operationalized along the lines of English proficiency and EL classification. The findings from this study indicate that structuring access by English proficiency and EL classification may relate as much or more to exclusionary tracking than to leveled track-ing. This is particularly the case with EL classification. In the two analyses related to EL classification, being identified as an EL impacted exclusionary tracking outcomes but not leveled tracking outcomes. In the case of English proficiency level, students with lower proficiency levels had less access to core academic subjects and less access to higher track classes.

While research on tracking by English proficiency level and EL classifi-cation is less abundant, it is gaining momentum. A growing body of work is identifying ways in which administrators and teachers, at times, make assumptions about ELs' academic capacity to succeed in mainstream classes based on their English skills (Bruna et al., 2007; Yoon, 2008). Research fur-ther documents how these practices may bar students from accessing high track classes and entire academic subjects (Callahan, 2005; Dabach, 2009; Harklau, 1994; Valdés, 1998). These assumptions can be formalized in school or district policy or programs, or they can be the informal decisions of indi-viduals (Estrada, 2014; Kanno & Kangas, 2014).

Likewise, research is growing on how EL classification may impact course access and how this varies based on local policies, practices, and beliefs about EL students' needs and abilities. In several of these studies, EL classification operates to limit course access through crowding out due to ELD instruction or other EL services (August et al., 2010; Estrada, 2014; Lillie et al., 2012).

Policy and Practice Implications of ELs' Limited Course Access

This study has several implications for education policy and practice. The first relates to the importance of clear regulations and monitoring of ELs' access to academic content. As stated earlier, federal and state guidelines have inadvertently created a weakness in EL students' right to academic con-tent by allowing for sequential or delayed provision of academic content without clear guidance on when and for whom this is appropriate and with-out monitoring requirements to ensure that delays are fully compensated. Research findings are clear that simultaneous provision of ELD and academic content is preferable to sequential provision, and federal, state, and local education authorities should move to create regulations limiting the condi-tions under which districts can delay access to academic content. Likewise, they should monitor ELs' access to content and hold schools accountable for providing that access.

Closely related, schools and districts will need resources as they seek solutions to reduce the tension between language and content instruction. These tensions create formidable challenges in staffing, scheduling, and funding for schools (Gándara et al., 2003). Some schools and districts have found ways of extending the school day or school year for ELs (Farbman, 2015). Others, including the district examined here, are considering creative ways of integrating ELD into elective courses such as art, music, or computer science in order to reduce crowding-out effects of ELD. Technical, professional, and financial resources should be available to schools and districts as they seek to minimize EL exclusionary tracking, reduce the crowding-out of content due to ELD, and ensure that ELD complements rather than duplicates other content area classes.

Finally, schools and districts need to address ELs' disproportionate placement in lower track classes. Some districts are moving to offer open enrollment in honors classes or de-track at the middle school level (Oakes & Lipton, 1992; Winebrenner, 2006; Yonezawa, Wells, & Serna, 2002). In schools that continue to use course levels, the development and use of valid assessment and placement practices that do not negatively bias results for students acquiring English is critical, as is the need to ensure the quality of lower track classes. Finally, teachers need ample support and preparation to work with ELs within their academic classes and to differentiate their English skills from their academic knowledge and ability.

Limitations and Future Research

The analyses presented in this article have several limitations. First and foremost, they are from one school district and only cover middle school grades. Course access patterns are likely to differ according to local and state policy and practice. Future work should be done documenting EL course access patterns in terms of both leveled and exclusionary tracking in different locales and at different grade levels. Second, the analyses of the roles of achievement, institutional resources, and English proficiency are descriptive rather than causal, and the RD analyses of the role of EL classification provide causal estimates only for students near the margin of EL-IFEP and EL-RFEP classification. More quasi-experimental and qualitative research is needed on the factors that influence EL students' access to academic content and, in particular, on how these factors operate to influence EL students' access. This article also did not explore several key issues with regard to EL access to content, including: (1) how access differs for students of different ethnic and linguistic backgrounds and for students with different amounts of time in U.S. schools, (2) how language of instruction may mediate access to content, (3) the extent to which ELs are enrolled in parallel (SDAIE) classes and the academic rigor of those classes, (4) ELs' access to social studies and electives, and (5) the extent to which course completion (as opposed to enrollment) differs between ELs and non-ELs. Importantly, research is needed on the effectiveness of policies and services, some of which are suggested previously, designed to increase EL students' equitable access to content.

Conclusion

English learners arrive in school with unique sets of strengths and vulnerabilities. They bring with them remarkable linguistic assets and cross-cultural and international knowledge and skills (Callahan & Gándara, 2014; González, Moll, & Amanti, 2013; Kolker, 2011). All too often, however, schools interpret these assets as weaknesses as schools become focused on students' lack of English proficiency and the implications this may have on students' ability to participate in schools that are structured for native English speakers (Ruiz, 1984; Valenzuela, 1999). This process undermines students' strengths and exacerbates their vulnerabilities. One of the key ways in which ELs' opportunities are limited in school is stratification in course access.

Despite a legal and regulatory framework that guarantees ELs' equal access to content in school, this article finds that ELs undergo substantial tracking in middle school. The characteristics of this tracking include overrepresentation in lower track classes and underrepresentation in upper track classes as well as exclusion from core academic subject areas. ELs likely have limited course access for a constellation of reasons. In this article, I find evidence that academic achievement, school and residential segregation, English proficiency level, and EL classification all may play a role in limiting EL students' opportunity to learn. These barriers are likely to have negative implications for students' educational outcomes and their lives beyond school. Fortunately, many of the factors that are limiting ELs' access to content are malleable to changes in policy and practice. Addressing these barriers and inequities and implementing policies and practices to ensure ELs' equitable access to content is of urgent importance.

Notes

This research was supported by two Institute of Education Sciences grants (award numbers R305B090016 and R305A11067), the Stanford Graduate Fellowship, the Karr Family Fellowship, and the National Academy of Education/Spencer Dissertation Fellowship.

I extend enormous thanks to Sean Reardon as well as to Kenji Hakuta, Claude Goldenberg, Tomás Jimenez, Martin Carnoy, Rachel Valentino, Adam Gamoran, and Jessica Vasquez. I also wish to thank the individuals that I worked closely with at the school district examined in this study. I will leave them unnamed in order to protect the anonymity of the district, but this article would not have been possible without them. Any remaining errors are my own.

[1]There is a third way in which English learners' (EL) course-taking may differ from that of non-ELs: ELs may be placed into classes that parallel non-EL classes but are designed for or populated by ELs specifically. Bilingual and specially designed academic instruction in English (SDAIE) classes are the primary examples of these. Due to space constraints, however, I do not analyze this form of tracking in this article. For this article, I consider both SDAIE and bilingual courses to be grade-level courses in their respective content areas.

[2]Throughout this article, I refrain from citing policy documents from the school district examined. I do this in order to protect district anonymity. I did, however, review this district's policy documents, and wherever appropriate I cite state and federal policy documents.

[3]California policy does allow up to one year of advanced level English language development (ELD) to count toward the four years of required high school English language arts (ELA) to be eligible to apply to the University of California system (University of California, n.d.). Following that guideline, this district gives ELA credit for select advanced level ELD classes that are designed for ELs who have not reclassified after five years. In this analysis, I count those specific courses as both ELA and ELD.

[4]While the term *long-term EL* is used by the district and will be used in this article to differentiate this subgroup of students, I use it with recognition of the problematic nature of this label (Brooks, 2015; Thompson, 2015).

References

Abedi, J. (2008). Classification system for English language learners: Issues and recommendations. *Educational Measurement: Issues and Practice, 27*(3), 17–31.

Abedi, J., & Lord, C. (2001). The language factor in mathematics tests. *Applied Measurement in Education, 14*(3), 219–234.

Aguirre-Muñoz, Z., & Boscardin, C. K. (2008). Opportunity to learn and English learner achievement: Is increased content exposure beneficial? *Journal of Latinos and Education, 7*(3), 186–205.

Alba, R., Massey, D., & Rumbaut, R. G. (1999). *The immigration experience for families and children*. Washington, DC: American Sociological Association.

American Civil Liberties Union of California & Asian Pacific American Legal Center (2013). *Opportunity lost: The widespread denial of services to California English learner students*. Los Angeles, CA: ACLU.

Artiles, A., Rueda, R., Salazar, J. J., & Higareda, I. (2005). Within-group diversity in minority disproportionate representation: English language learners in urban school districts. *Exceptional Children, 71*(3), 283–300.

Attewell, P., & Domina, T. (2008). Raising the bar: Curricular intensity and academic performance. *Educational Evaluation and Policy Analysis, 30*(1), 51–71.

August, D., Goldenberg, C., & Rueda, R. (2010). Restrictive state language policies: Are they scientifically based? In P. Gándara & M. Hopkins (Eds.), *Forbidden language: English learners and restrictive language policies* (pp. 139–158). New York, NY: Teachers College Press.

Bialystok, E., & Hakuta, K. (1994). *In other words: The science and psychology of second-language acquisition*. New York, NY: Basic Books.

Brooks, M. D. (2015). "It's like a script": Long-term English learners' experiences with and ideas about academic reading. *Research in the Teaching of English, 49*(4), 383.

Bruna, K. R., Vann, R., & Escudero, M. P. (2007). What's language got to do with it?: A case study of academic language instruction in a high school "English Learner Science" class. *Journal of English for Academic Purposes, 6*(1), 36–54.

California Department of Education. (2006). *English learners frequently asked questions*. Sacramento, CA: State of California.

California Department of Education. (2015a). *CELDT frequently asked questions*. Retreived from http://www.cde.ca.gov/ta/tg/el/celdtfaq.asp

California Department of Education. (2015b). *English language arts/English language development framework for California public schools*. Sacramento, CA: State of California.

Callahan, R. (2005). Tracking and high school English learners: Limiting opportunity to learn. *American Educational Research Journal, 42*(2), 305–328.

Callahan, R., & Gándara, P. (Eds.). (2014). *Bilingual advantage: Language, literacy, and the labor market*. Clevedon, UK: Multilingual Matters.

Callahan, R., & Shifrer, D. (2016). Equitable access for secondary English learner students course taking as evidence of EL program effectiveness. *Educational Administration Quarterly, 53*, 463–496.

Callahan, R., Wilkinson, L., & Muller, C. (2010). Academic achievement and course taking among language minority youth in US schools: Effects of ESL placement. *Educational Evaluation and Policy Analysis, 32*(1), 84–117.

Callahan, R., Wilkinson, L., Muller, C., & Frisco, M. (2009). ESL placement and schools: Effects on immigrant achievement. *Educational Policy, 23*(2), 355–384.

Carlson, D., & Knowles, J. (2016). The effect of English language learner reclassification on student ACT scores, high school graduation, and postsecondary enrollment: Regression discontinuity evidence from Wisconsin. *Journal of Policy Analysis and Management, 35*, 559–586.

Castañeda v. Pickard (United States Court of Appeals for the Fifth Circuit 1981).

Chang, M. J. (2000). The relationship of high school characteristics to the selection of undergraduate students for admission to the University of California-Berkeley. *Journal of Negro Education, 69*, 49–59.

Dabach, D. (2009). *Teachers as a context of reception for immigrant youth: Adaptations in "sheltered" and "mainstream" classrooms.* Unpublished doctoral dissertation. University of California, Berkeley.

Dabach, D., & Callahan, R. (2011). Rights versus reality: The gap between civil rights and english learners' high school educational opportunities. *Teachers College Record 16558*, 113.

Dronkers, J., & Levels, M. (2007). Do school segregation and school resources explain region-of-origin differences in the mathematics achievement of immigrant students? *Educational Research and Evaluation, 13*(5), 435–462.

Eccles, J. S., Lord, S., & Midgley, C. (1991). What are we doing to early adolescents? The impact of educational contexts on early adolescents. *American Journal of Education, 99*, 521–542.

Engel, M., Claessens, A., Watts, T., & Farkas, G. (2016). Mathematics content coverage and student learning in kindergarten. *Educational Researcher, 45*(5), 293–300.

Ellen, I. G., O'Regan, K., Schwartz, A. E., Stiefel, L., Neal, D., & Nechyba, T. (2002). Immigrant children and New York City schools: Segregation and its consequences. In *Brookings-Wharton papers on urban affairs* (pp. 183–214). Washington, DC: Brookings Institution Press.

Estrada, P. (2014). English learner curricular streams in four middle schools: Triage in the trenches. *The Urban Review, 46*(5), 535.

Every Student Succeeds Act of 2015, Pub. Law No. 114-95 §1177 (2015).

Farbman, D. (2015). *Giving English language learners the time they need to succeed: Profiles of three expanded learning time schools.* Boston, MA: National Center on Time and Learning.

Francis, D., Rivera, M., Lesaux, N., Kieffer, M., & Rivera, H. (2006). *Research-based recommendations for serving adolescent newcomers. Practical guidelines for the education of English language learners.* Retrieved from https://www2.ed.gov/about/inits/ed/lep-partnership/newcomers.pdf.

Fry, R. (2007). *How far behind in math and reading are English language learners?* Retrieved from http://www.pewhispanic.org/2007/06/06/how-far-behind-in-math-and-reading-are-english-language-learners/.

Fry, R. (2008). *The role of schools in the English language learner achievement gap.* Washington, DC: Pew Hispanic Center.

Gamoran, A. (2010). Tracking and inequality: New directions for research and practice. In *The Routledge international handbook of the sociology of education* (pp. 213–228). Abingdon, UK: Routledge.

Gándara, P., & Contreras, F. (2009). *The Latino education crisis: The consequences of failed social policies.* Boston, MA: Harvard University Press.

Gándara, P., Rumberger, R., Maxwell-Jolly, J., & Callahan, R. (2003). English learners in California schools: Unequal resources, unequal outcomes. *Education Policy Analysis Archives, 11*(36), 1–54.

García, E. (1992). *Teachers for Language Minority Students: Evaluating Professional Standards.* Paper presented at the Focus on Evaluation and Measurement: Proceedings of the National Research Symposium on Limited English Proficient Student Issues, Washington DC.

Garet, M. S., & DeLany, B. (1988). Students, courses, and stratification. *Sociology of Education, 61,* 61–77.

Garrett, R., & Hong, G. (2015). Impacts of grouping and time on the math learning of language minority kindergartners. *Educational Evaluation and Policy Analysis, 38,* 222–224.

González, N., Moll, L. C., & Amanti, C. (2013). *Funds of knowledge: Theorizing practices in households, communities, and classrooms.* New York, NY: Routledge.

Harklau, L. (1994). Tracking and linguistic minority students: Consequences of ability grouping for second language learners. *Linguistics and Education, 6*(3), 217–244.

Harwell, M., & LeBeau, B. (2010). Student eligibility for a free lunch as an SES measure in education research. *Educational Researcher, 39*(2), 120–131.

Hodara, M. (2015). The effects of English as a second language courses on language minority community college students. *Educational Evaluation and Policy Analysis, 37*(2), 243–270.

Hopkins, M., Thompson, K., Linquanti, R., Hakuta, K., & August, D. (2013). Fully accounting for English learner performance a key issue in ESEA reauthorization. *Educational Researcher, 42*(2), 101–108.

Iatarola, P., Conger, D., & Long, M. C. (2011). Determinants of high schools' advanced course offerings. *Educational Evaluation and Policy Analysis, 33*(3), 340-359.

IES. (2015). Retrieved from https://nces.ed.gov/programs/digest/d13/tables/dt13_204.20.asp.

Imbens, G., & Kalyanaraman, K. (2012). Optimal bandwidth choice for the regression discontinuity estimator. *The Review of Economic Studies, 79*(3), 933–959.

Kanno, Y., & Kangas, S. (2014). "I'm not going to be, like, for the AP": English language learners' limited access to advanced college-preparatory courses in high school. *American Educational Research Journal, 51*(5), 848–878.

Kao, G., Tienda, M., & Lafield, B. S. (2005). Optimism and achievement: The educational performance of immigrant youth. In *The new immigration: An interdisciplinary reader* (pp. 331–343). Abingdon, UK: Routledge.

Katz, S. (1999). Teaching in tensions: Latino immigrant youth, their teachers, and the structures of schooling. *Teachers College Record, 100*(4), 809–840.

Kelly, S. (2009). The Black-White gap in mathematics course taking. *Sociology of Education, 82*(1), 47-69.

Kettler, T., Shiu, A., & Johnsen, S. K. (2006). AP as an Intervention for middle school Hispanic students. *Gifted Child Today, 29*(1), 39–46.

Kieffer, M. J., Lesaux, N. K., Rivera, M., & Francis, D. J. (2009). Accommodations for English language learners taking large-scale assessments: A meta-analysis on effectiveness and validity. *Review of Educational Research, 79*(3), 1168–1201.

Kolker, C. (2011). *The immigrant advantage: What we can learn from newcomers to America about health, happiness and hope.* New York, NY: Simon and Schuster.

Kurlaender, M., Reardon, S., & Jackson, J. (2008). *Middle school predictors of high school achievement in three California school districts.* Santa Barbara, CA: California Dropout Research Project, University of California, Santa Barbara.

Lau v. Nichols, United States Supreme Court (1974).

Lee, C. (2006). *Denver public schools: Resegregation, Latino style*. Cambridge, MA: Harvard University, Civil Rights Project.

Lee, J., & Zhou, M. (2015). *The Asian American achievement paradox*. New York, NY: Russell Sage Foundation.

Lew, J. (2006). Burden of acting neither White nor Black: Asian American identities and achievement in urban schools. *The Urban Review, 38*(5), 335–352.

Lhamon, C., & Gupta, V. (2015, January 7). *Dear colleague letter*. Washington, DC: U.S. Department of Justice, Civil Rights Division and Department of Education, Office for Civil Rights.

Lillie, K. E., Markos, A., Arias, M. B., & Wiley, T. G. (2012). Separate and not equal: The implementation of structured English immersion in Arizona's classrooms. *Teachers College Record, 114*(9), 1–33.

Linquanti, R. (2001). *The redesignation dilemma: Challenges and choices in fostering meaningful accountability for English learners*. Berkeley, CA: The University of California Linguistic Minority Research Institute.

Long, M. C., Conger, D., & Iatarola, P. (2012). Effects of high school course-taking on secondary and postsecondary success. *American Educational Research Journal, 49*(2), 285–322.

Los Angeles Unified School District. (2015). *Placement, scheduling and staffing of English learners in middle school and high school 2015–16* (Memorandum). Los Angeles, CA: Author.

Martiniello, M. (2008). Language and the performance of English-language learners in math word problems. *Harvard Educational Review, 78*(2), 333–368.

Monk, D. H., & Haller, E. J. (1993). Predictors of high school academic course offerings: The role of school size. *American Educational Research Journal, 30*(1), 3–21.

Moran, R. F. (2005). Undone by law: The uncertain legacy of *Lau v. Nichols*. *Berkeley La Raza Law Journal, 16*.

No Child Left Behind Act of 2001, Pub. L. No. 107–110, §115, Stat. 1425 (2002).

Nomi, T., & Raudenbush, S. W. (2016). Making a success of "algebra for all": The impact of extended instructional time and classroom peer skill in Chicago. *Educational Evaluation and Policy Analysis, 38*(2), 431–451.

Nord, C., Roey, S., Perkins, R., Lyons, M., Lemanski, N., Brown, J., & Schuknecht, J. (2011). *America's high school graduates. Results of the 2009 NAEP high school transcript study*. Washington, DC: National Center for Education Statistics.

Oakes, J. (2005). *Keeping track: How schools structure inequality*. Princeton,NJ: Yale University Press.

Oakes, J., & Lipton, M. (1992). Detracking schools: Early lessons from the field. *The Phi Delta Kappan, 73*(6), 448–454.

Olsen, L. (1997). *Made in America: Immigrant students in our public schools*. New York, NY: The New Press.

Page, R. N. (1991). *Lower-track classrooms: A curricular and cultural perspective*. New York, NY: Teachers College Press.

Parker, C. E., Louie, J., & O'Dwyer, L. (2009). *New measures of English language proficiency and their relationship to performance on large-scale content assessments*. Washington, DC: National Center for Education Evaluation and Regional Assistance, Institute of Education Sciences, US Deptartment of Education.

Portes, A., & MacLeod, D. (1996). Educational progress of children of immigrants: The roles of class, ethnicity, and school context. *Sociology of Education, 69*(4), 255–275.

Portes, A., & Rumbaut, R. G. (2006). *Immigrant America: A portrait*. Berkeley, CA: University of California Press.

Ragan, A., & Lesaux, N. (2006). Federal, state, and district level English language learner program entry and exit requirements: Effects on the education of language minority learners. *Education Policy Analysis Archives, 14*, 20.

Raudenbush, S. W., Rowan, B., & Cheong, Y. F. (1993). Higher order instructional goals in secondary schools: Class, teacher, and school influences. *American Educational Research Journal, 30*(3), 523–553.

Reardon, S., & Robinson, J. (2010). Patterns and trends in racial/ethnic and socioeconomic academic achievement gaps. In H. F. Ladd & E. B. Fiske (Eds.), *Handbook of research in education finance and policy* (pp. 497–516). New York, NY: Routledge.

Reardon, S., Yun, J., & Eitle, T. (2000). The changing structure of school segregation: measurement and evidence of multiracial metropolitan-area school segregation, 1989–1995. *Demography, 37*, 351–364.

Rios-Aguilar, C., Canché, M., & Sabetghadam, S. (2012). Evaluating the impact of restrictive language policies: The Arizona 4-hour English language development block. *Language Policy, 11*(1), 47–80.

Robinson-Cimpian, J., & Thompson, K. (2016). The effects of changing test-based policies for reclassifying English learners. *Journal of Policy Analysis and Management, 35*(2), 279–305.

Ruiz, R. (1984). Orientations in language planning. *NABE: The Journal for the National Association for Bilingual Education, 8*(2), 15–34.

Rumberger, R., & Gándara, P. (2004). Seeking equity in the education of California's English learners. *The Teachers College Record, 106*(10), 2032–2056.

Rumberger, R. W., & Lim, S. A. (2008). *Why students drop out of school: A review of 25 years of research* (California Dropout Research Project Report 15). Santa Barbara, CA: University of California Santa Barbara.

San Bernadino City Unified District. (2010). *Master plan for English learners*. San Bernadino, CA: Author.

Saunders, W., Goldenberg, C., & Marcelletti, D. (2013). English language development: Guidelines for instruction. *American Educator, 37*(2), 13.

Saunders, W., & Marcelletti, D. (2012). The gap that can't go away: The catch-22 of reclassification in monitoring the progress of English learners. *Educational Evaluation and Policy Analysis, 35*(2), 139–156.

Shifrer, D., Callahan, R. M., & Muller, C. (2013). Equity or marginalization? The high school course-taking of students labeled with a learning disability. *American Educational Research Journal, 50*, 656–682.

Singer, J. D., & Willett, J. B. (2003). *Applied longitudinal data analysis: Modeling change and event occurrence*. New York, NY: Oxford University Press.

Slavin, R. E. (1990). Achievement effects of ability grouping in secondary schools: A best-evidence synthesis. *Review of Educational Research, 60*(3), 471–499.

Smith, J. B. (1996). Does an extra year make any difference? The impact of early access to algebra on long-term gains in mathematics attainment. *Educational Evaluation and Policy Analysis, 18*(2), 141–153.

Solorzano, D. G., & Ornelas, A. (2004). A critical race analysis of Latina/o and African American advanced placement enrollment in public high schools. *High School Journal, 87*(3), 15–26.

Spade, J. Z., Columba, L., & Vanfossen, B. E. (1997). Tracking in mathematics and science: Courses and course-selection procedures. *Sociology of Education, 70*, 108–127.

Stanton-Salazar, R. D., & Dornbusch, S. M. (1995). Social capital and the reproduction of inequality: Information networks among Mexican-origin high school students. *Sociology of Education, 68*(2), 116–135.

Stanton-Salazar, R. D., & Spina, S. U. (2003). Informal mentors and role models in the lives of urban Mexican-origin adolescents. *Anthropology & Education Quarterly, 34*(3), 231–254.

Suárez-Orozco, C., Suárez-Orozco, M. M., & Todorova, I. (2009). *Learning a new land: Immigrant students in American society.* Boston, MA: Harvard University Press.

Thompson, K. D. (2015). Questioning the long-term English learner label: How classification and categorization can blind us to students' abilities. *Teachers College Record, 117.*

Thompson, K. D., Umansky, I., Martinez, M., & Díaz, G. (2016, March). *Both over and under-identification: The mysterious case of english learner students with disabilities.* Paper presented at the Oregon English Language Learner Alliance Conference, Eugene, OR.

Umansky, I. (2016). To be or not to be EL: An examination of the impact of classifying students as English learners. *Educational Evaluation and Policy Analysis, 38*(4), 714–737.

Umansky, I., & Reardon, S. (2014). Reclassification patterns among Latino English learner students in bilingual, dual immersion, and English immersion classrooms. *American Educational Research Journal, 51*(5), 879–912.

University of California. (n.d.). *A-G guide.* Retreived from http://www.ucop.edu/agguide/a-g-requirements/b-english/index.html

Valdés, G. (1998). The world outside and inside schools: Language and immigrant children. *Educational Researcher, 27*(6), 4–18.

Valentino, R., & Reardon, S. (2015). Effectiveness of four instructional programs designed to serve English language learners: Variation by ethnicity and initial English proficiency. *Educational Evaluation and Policy Analysis, 37,* 612–637

Valenzuela, A. (1999). *Subtractive schooling: US-Mexican youth and the politics of caring. SUNY Series, The Social Context of Education.* Albany, NY: State University of New York Press.

Walqui, A., Estrada, P., Koelsch, N., Hamburger, L., Gaarder, D., Insurralde, A., . . . Weiss, S. (2010). *What are we doing to middle school English learners?: Findings and recommendations for change from a study of California EL programs* (Research report). Oakland, CA: WestEd.

Walqui, A., & Van Lier, L. (2010). *Scaffolding the academic success of adolescent English language learners: A pedagogy of promise.* San Francisco, CA: WestEd.

Wang, J., & Goldschmidt, P. (1999). Opportunity to learn, language proficiency, and immigrant status effects on mathematics achievement. *Journal of Educational Research, 93*(2), 101–111.

Wang, J., & Goldschmidt, P. (2003). Importance of middle school mathematics on high school students' mathematics achievement. *The Journal of Educational Research, 97*(1), 3–17.

Wiley, T. G. (2009). *The education of language minority immigrants in the United States.* Bristol, UK: Multilingual Matters.

Williams, T., Kirst, M., Haertel, E., Rosin, M., Perry, M., Webman, B., & Woodward, K. M. (2010). *Gaining ground in the middle grades: Why some schools do better.* Mountain View, CA: EdSource.

Winebrenner, S. (2006). Effective teaching strategies for open enrollment honors and AP classes. *Prufrock Journal, 17*(3), 159–177.

Xiong, Y. S. (2010). State-mandated language classification: A study of Hmong American students' access to college-preparatory curricula. *AAPI Nexus: Policy, Practice and Community, 8*(1), 17–42.

Yoon, B. (2008). Uninvited guests: The influence of teachers' roles and pedagogies on the positioning of English language learners in the regular classroom. *American Educational Research Journal, 45*(2), 495–522.

Yonezawa, S., Wells, A. S., & Serna, I. (2002). Choosing tracks: "Freedom of choice" in detracking schools. *American Educational Research Journal, 39*(1), 37–67.

Zuniga, K., Olson, J. K., & Winter, M. (2005). Science education for rural Latino/a students: Course placement and success in science. *Journal of Research in Science Teaching, 42*(4), 376–402.

Manuscript received June 24, 2015
Final revision received September 13, 2016
Accepted September 27, 2016

American Educational Research Journal
December 2016, Vol. 53, No. 6, pp. 1834–1868
DOI: 10.3102/0002831216671864
© 2016 AERA. http://aerj.aera.net

What Can Student Perception Surveys Tell Us About Teaching? Empirically Testing the Underlying Structure of the Tripod Student Perception Survey

Tanner LeBaron Wallace
University of Pittsburgh, Pittsburgh
Benjamin Kelcey
University of Cincinnati
Erik Ruzek
University of Virginia

We conducted a theory-based analysis of the underlying structure of the Tripod student perception survey instrument using the Measures of Effective Teaching (MET) database (N = 1,049 middle school math class sections; N = 25,423 students). Multilevel item factor analyses suggested that an alternative bifactor structure best fit the Tripod items, and preliminary evidence suggests that both the general responsivity and the classroom management–specific dimensions are positively associated with teacher value-added scores. In our discussion, we consider the distinct characterizing features of adolescents as raters of teaching, the implications for teacher professional learning opportunities, and key areas for future research.

TANNER LEBARON WALLACE is an associate professor of applied developmental psychology and co-chair of the Motivation Center (MC) at the University of Pittsburgh, 230 S. Bouquet Street, WWPH 5948, Pittsburgh, PA 15260; e-mail: *twallace@pitt.edu*. She studies adolescents' interpretations of instructional interactions and how these affect learning outcomes.

BENJAMIN KELCEY is an associate professor in the Quantitative Research Methodologies Program at the University of Cincinnati. His research interests focus on causal explanation and inference and measurement methods within the context of classrooms and schools.

ERIK RUZEK is a research assistant professor at the Center for Advanced Study of Teaching and Learning at the University of Virginia. His research integrates information on students and teachers from different measurement traditions, including classroom observations, student reports, teacher reports, and direct assessments. His work combines data from these different sources to describe how students' motivation, engagement, and learning are influenced by their experiences in classrooms.

KEYWORDS: multilevel confirmatory factor analysis, student perceptions, teacher evaluation

Advancing theories of effective teaching on the basis of adolescent mean-ing-making (within the context of a teacher evaluation system) necessi-tates several acts of translation. First, adolescents' daily experiences of exposure to particular teacher actions that affect student outcomes must be translated into high-quality survey items. Then, translation must proceed from the data generated from those items into informed individualized pro-fessional learning opportunities for teachers. Indeed, policy-relevant find-ings and guidelines for teaching are predicated on issues of validity—actually knowing the specific nature of what is being measured —so that clear practices and policies to support the improvement of teaching can be designed and implemented. It is well known that "scores averaged across an ill-defined assortment of items offer no basis for knowing what is being measured" (Marsh & Roche, 1997, p. 1187). Understanding how the-ories of effective teaching should or should not inform the selection, use, and improvement of teacher evaluation measures, such as student surveys, has important implications for practice given that in the present accountabil-ity context, measurement incentivizes how teachers teach. Underdeveloped measures may lead to ill-informed pedagogical choices.

As of publication, 45 U.S. states had developed statewide teacher evalua-tion systems. Common reform features include the use of multiple measures of teacher performance (e.g., observational instruments, students' standard-ized test scores, teacher portfolios) as well as teacher rating scales that denote a range of distinct performance levels. While variability exists in the details of what data are gathered and how those data are used to model student growth, a noteworthy and recent addition to the assessment of effective secondary teaching is the inclusion of student perception surveys.

In the present paper we use data from the large, U.S.-based Measures of Effective Teaching (MET) database to examine the underlying structure of the Tripod student perception survey (Ferguson, 2010). In part because of the publicity garnered by the MET project, the Tripod student perception survey has become among the most popular student perception surveys on the U.S. market. We estimate that during the 2015–2016 school year approx-imately 1,400 schools administered the Tripod. The 36-item Tripod survey is organized around seven distinct theoretical domains of classroom instruc-tion, or "the 7Cs." The components of effective teaching that the Tripod pur-ports to measure (e.g., care, challenge, confer) are central to many theoretical models of effective teaching and effective teachers, such as the concepts of warm demander (Kleinfeld, 1975; Ware, 2006) and culturally responsive teaching (Gay, 2010).

Two decades ago, Marsh and Roche (1997) argued that student evalua-tion of teaching instruments failed to provide an ample assessment of theoretically sound, multiple dimensions of teaching quality, in ways that undermined the use of such instruments to inform diagnostic feedback. As such, well-articulated theories of effective teaching, such as Ferguson's (2010) 7Cs, productively inform building an evidence base around the underlying explanatory mechanisms that link teacher action with adolescent outcomes. More specifically, attending to adolescent perceptions as a central aspect of theory-building acknowledges adolescents as active co-constructors of learning ecologies with the agency to, as Nakkula and Toshalis (2006) describe, rightfully resist educational experiences they perceive to be inauthentic or unsafe.

In 2014, Schweig took an atheoretical, exploratory approach to examining the multilevel factorial structure of the Tripod using results from an administration of the survey to California students ($N = 6,386$ students; $N = 349$ class sections) in one urban school district during the 2010 school year. Results from that exploratory analysis suggested "five factors at the within level, and two factors at the between level" (pp. 270–271). Our study extends this and other prior research on the Tripod instrument by empirically testing the underlying structure of the Tripod student perception survey through the lenses of predominant theories of effective teaching. This investigation is made possible due to the fact that despite Tripod items being developed in relation to a specific theory of effective teaching, the items cover a diverse range of classroom experiences described in rather general terms. Therefore, student endorsements of Tripod items can help us learn about student assessments of effective teaching more broadly. Our investigation brings to bear plausible and theoretically supported factor structures concerning the Tripod instrument by considering multiple theoretical factor structures and the extent to which there is comparative and absolute support for each structure across multiple school districts.

Student Perceptions of the Learning Environment

Prior research has demonstrated that student perceptions of the learning environment can be both reliable (e.g., Fauth, Decristan, Rieser, Klieme, & Büttner, 2014; Wagner, Göllner, Helmke, Trautwein, & Lüdtke, 2013) and predictive of learning (e.g., Kane & Cantrell, 2010; Kane & Staiger, 2012). Broadly speaking, student perceptions of the learning environment are likely indicative of the motivational aspects of classrooms (McCaslin, 2009; Spearman & Watt, 2013) for the fact that student perceptions of a classroom environment, constituted in youth-adult interactions, are the primary mechanism through which adolescents assent-to-learn in classrooms (Brophy & Good, 1974; Erickson, 1987; Erickson et al., 2007).

If students do not form a positive connection with their teacher, it is within their control to minimally learn core content or refuse to learn anything at all (Wallace & Chhuon, 2014). Thus, interactions between a student and his or her teacher are the source material for student-teacher connections, and these connections can strongly influence student learning (Davis, 2003). Given the importance of student perceptions of the learning environment, student reports of the quality of interactions and processes within a classroom are potentially an important measurement strategy for evaluating and developing teachers. Beyond providing firsthand impressions of the quality of student-teacher interactions and classroom processes, student reports offer a promising way to evaluate teaching because they can be used to measure theoretically informed and practically important dimensions of instruction; draw on the perspectives of multiple students, making survey measures potentially more reliable; and provide more efficient assessments of quality compared with alternative, resource-intensive assessments such as classroom observations (Turner & Meyer, 2000).

Students as Raters of Teaching Quality

Despite the advantages of student surveys, student raters are fundamentally different than the trained adult observers who use formal observational instruments to gather data relevant to teaching quality. Prior research has found low to moderate agreement between teacher ratings and student ratings of instruction (e.g., Desimone, Smith, & Frisvold, 2010; Kunter & Baumert, 2006). Unlike adult observers who undergo rigorous training and certification processes to establish their skill at consistently differentiating among complicated, theoretically proposed domains of instructional practice, students receive no training prior to data collection. As such, the implicit conceptualization of expertise is quite distinct between adult observers and student survey takers.

While adult observers gain expertise by mastering and applying the content of adult-created frameworks of effective teaching, student observers possess naturally acquired expertise through their lived, everyday experiences in classrooms. For example, students are often experts in "contingencies of their social environments" (McCaslin & Hickey, 2001, p. 137) and, therefore, likely attune to the nuances of peer interaction that are conditioned indirectly, but powerfully, by a teacher's instructional practice (Gest & Rodkin, 2011). Classrooms, by their very nature, are participatory, and it is probable that ongoing experiences of participation shape assessments of teaching quality in ways that are fundamentally distinct from a nonparticipant, outside observer.

Likewise, students' firsthand experiences of participation in instructional activities situate adolescents' assessments of teaching quality as originating primarily from the perspective of a learner versus that of the teacher. From a situative perspective, learning may best be characterized as the development of more effective participation in the practices of inquiry and discourse around collaborative sense-making and reasoning (Greeno,

1998). Thus, adolescents may be particularly sensitive to the affordances and constraints that support their effective participation, particularly interactions and experiences that are most salient to the continual renegotiation of resources for learning. These sensitivities to teachers' distribution of participation opportunities (i.e., framing of who gets to participate) and the meaningfulness of the work students are being asked to complete may influence how an adolescent rater interprets or makes sense of the significance of instructional interactions and subsequently endorses survey items.

Theories of Effective Teaching

Teaching is a complex and multidimensional practice with overlapping and simultaneous teacher actions occurring continuously over time (Carlisle, Kelcey, Berebitsky, & Phelps, 2011). Like practitioners in other clinical practices, such as counseling or medicine, teachers must enact specific competencies in real time under dynamic and evolving contexts. Teaching, however, is unique from other clinical practices in that it takes place publicly in front of up to 30 developing individuals. Moreover, teaching is a practice aimed at promoting positive development among a diverse set of persons entering at different starting points with unique histories both within school and out of school.

Within this context of complexity, theoretical models of teaching have emerged to summarize and advance particular conceptualizations of effective teaching. One aspect of teacher evaluation systems that often goes unchallenged is how particular theories of effective teaching are instantiated in the instruments used in such systems. At present, four alternative multidimensional models of effective teaching are prominent in the evaluation instruments used by many districts in the United States. As noted earlier, Tripod items were developed on the basis of one specific conceptualization of effective teaching. Yet, these items cover a diverse range of experiences in classrooms described in rather general terms. Thus, testing the underlying structure of the Tripod student perception survey instrument permits testing potential alternative conceptualizations of teaching from the student perspective. Below we review prominent conceptualizations of effective teaching informing our investigation of the underlying structure of the Tripod instrument.

One theoretically proposed model of effective teaching comprises a two-dimensional structure with factors representing academic press and social support for learning (Ferguson & Danielson, 2014; Lee & Smith, 1999; Lee, Smith, Perry, & Smylie, 1999). Academic press is defined as the "normative emphasis on academic success" (Lee et al., 1999, p. 10), which motivates a rigor and focus on fostering conditions so that children can learn what is expected of them by the standards of society (Ferguson & Danielson, 2014). Social support for learning is defined as the instructional supports that are both relational and social that provide students with a sense of trust, confidence, and psychological safety (Ferguson & Danielson, 2014; Lee et al., 1999).

An alternative, theoretically proposed model of effective teaching comprises a three-dimensional structure with dimensions corresponding to classroom organization, instructional support, and emotional support (Pianta & Hamre, 2009; see also Kunter & Baumert, 2006 for a similar, but differently worded formulation). Classroom organization is a teacher's ability to help students organize their attention and behavior toward academic activities and goals, and strong classroom organization is often materialized in the classroom through clear and consistent routines (Emmer & Strough, 2001). Instructional support distinguishes between the classroom activities and interactions that simply promote fact knowledge versus those that promote an understanding of how facts are organized, conditioned, and interconnected with one another (Mayer, 2002). The quality and nature of teacher-provided feedback are also critical components of instructional support (Kulik & Kulik, 1998). Emotional support has long been understood to be critical to child and adolescent development and motivation and is evidenced by teachers' dependability, their demonstration of genuine concern for and care about students, a desire to understand students' feelings and points of views, and respect for students (Patrick, Anderman, & Ryan, 2004).

Another theoretically proposed model of effective teaching is that which informs the Tripod (Ferguson, 2010) and comprises a seven-dimensional structure. These dimensions include the following: (a) care, (b) confer, (c) captivate, (d) clarify, (e) consolidate, (f) challenge, and (g) control. *Care* describes how a teacher creates interpersonal relationships that support perceptions of emotional closeness and belonging (Ferguson, 2010). Recent conceptualizations of care within the adolescent-adult relationship context have acknowledged the asymmetry of status that exists between a teacher and a student and the importance of understanding care in terms of the identities being ascribed to the student via experiencing the classroom environment in terms of coherency with deeply personal, evolving identities that students hold (Toshalis, 2015; Wallace & Chhuon, 2014). *Confer* describes how a teacher solicits students' points of view and invites students to express themselves (Ferguson, 2010). Support for the importance of student-centered approaches to instructional interactions comes from many sources but perhaps most centrally from autonomy support theory, which prescribes following student leads and incorporating student input into instruction (e.g., Reeve & Jang, 2006). Three dimensions—*captivate*, making material interesting and relevant to students; *clarify*, diagnosing students' particular gaps in knowledge and having multiple ways to explain ideas; and *consolidate*, helping students organize content knowledge in preparation for future learning (Ferguson, 2010)—all describe current conceptualizations of ambitious pedagogy. For example, Thompson, Windschitl, and Braaten (2013) identify the following four sets of practices: selecting big ideas/models, working with students' ideas, working with disciplinary ideas, and pressing for explanation. High-quality enactments of all of these would entail the features described by the former three Tripod dimensions. *Challenge*, pressing students to work and to think hard, attends to the role of high expectations in student learning (Ferguson, 2010). Investigations of the relation between teachers' expectancies and student academic outcomes have demonstrated weak to moderate associations, suggesting that teacher expectancy behavior is achievement relevant (Friedrich, Flunger, Nagengast, Jonkmann, & Trautwein, 2015; Good, 1987; Noguera, 2003). *Control* describes how a teacher manages her classroom and, in particular, maintains effective communication and focus (Ferguson, 2010). Recent conceptualizations of classroom management have emphasized relational factors such as prioritizing students' perceptions of trust, respect, and connectedness (e.g., Milner & Tenore, 2010), while keeping central a notion of minimizing disruptions so that teachers can teach and students can focus on academic work (e.g., Cartledge, Lo, Vincent, & Robinson-Ervin, 2015). In such a framework, evaluating a teacher's competence in managing a classroom has focused simultaneously on positive concepts like respect and negative concepts like disruptive behavior (Schweig, 2014).

The last proposed model conceptualizes teaching as comprising both general and specific dimensions. Recent research by Hamre, Hatfield, Pianta, and Jamil (2014) suggests that there are generic properties of interactive behavioral exchanges between students and teachers as well as properties that are specific to role, intent, and content of particular instructional interactions. This bifactor-like theory of effective teaching proposes a model wherein a general element of instructional quality related to responsivity influences all teacher-student interactions and, further, a set of domain-specific elements related to motivational supports, classroom management, and cognitive facilitation influence particular interactions dependent upon the specifics of the interaction (Hamre et al., 2014). The general element of instructional quality related to responsivity can also be understood as how successful a teacher is at establishing and maintaining a psychologically safe classroom for a diverse group of students (Wanless, 2016; Williams, Woodson, & Wallace, 2016). Lee's (1992, 2001) cultural modeling theory advances an implicit bifactor-like theory of effective teaching wherein teachers possess a general sensitivity to the importance of culturally based interaction styles but use specific kinds of scaffolding that prepare adolescents for future learning by using prior cultural knowledge as a foundation during instructional interactions. The bifactor-like theory of teaching is also supported by recent research on the importance of teachers' social and emotional competencies for effective enactment of more complex instructional practices (e.g., Jennings & Greenberg, 2009; Roeser, Skinner, Beers, &

Jennings, 2012), specifically mounting evidence that teachers interpret and respond differentially to similar types of classroom demands dependent upon the stress response, or an in-the-moment appraisal of whether the available resources are commensurate with the demand (McCarthy, Lineback, & Reiser, 2014).

The Current Study

In the present study, we address policy-relevant research questions related to supporting the measurement and improvement of teaching. We investigated the dimensionality of a popular U.S. secondary student percep-tions instrument, the Tripod student perception survey (Ferguson, 2010), using multilevel item factor analyses. Our aim was to examine whether dif-ferent conceptualizations of effective teaching were reflected in students' endorsements of Tripod items. To do so, we examined the structural validity of the Tripod using a novel sample and probing the extent to which there is empirical support for the underlying dimensions proposed by theory.

We considered five factor structures: (a) a baseline model comprising a unidimensional structure with one overall latent factor; (b) a two-dimensional structure with factors representing press and support (Ferguson & Danielson, 2014; Lee & Smith, 1999); (c) a three-dimensional structure with dimensions corresponding to classroom organization, instruc-tional support, and emotional support (Pianta & Hamre, 2009); (d) a seven-dimensional structure representing the conceptual organization used by the Tripod developers (Ferguson, 2010); and (e) a bifactor-like structure consist-ing principally of a general responsivity dimension that partially informs responses on all items and a classroom management dimension that governs responses on items surrounding classroom management issues (Hamre et al., 2014; Lee, 1992, 2001). Further, we examined correlations between our final Tripod measurement model and ratings using the Classroom Learning Assessment Scoring System-Secondary (CLASS-S; Pianta, La Paro, & Hamre, 2008), and we used multilevel structural equation modeling to examine the predictive validity of the Tripod as it relates to teacher value-added scores.

Methods

Supported by the Bill and Melinda Gates Foundation, the MET database is the largest dataset of classroom teaching ever collected in the United States. The MET database contains a variety of data sources related to teach-ing collected over a 2-year period (AY 2009–2010 and AY 2010–2011) in the classrooms of more than 2,500 fourth- through ninth-grade teachers working in 317 schools located in six large school districts in the United States (Charlotte-Mecklenburg Schools, North Carolina; Dallas Independent

School District, Texas; Denver Public Schools, Colorado; Hillsborough County Public Schools, Florida; Memphis City Schools, Tennessee; New York City Department of Education, New York).

Sample and Data Collection

Recruitment for study participation began at the district level with districts having prior connections to the Gates Foundation targeted for inclusion. Once a district agreed to participate, special education schools, alternative schools, community schools, autonomous dropout and pregnancy programs, returning education schools, vocational schools that did not teach academic courses, and any other schools that had team teaching or other structural features that made it impossible to assign responsibility for a student's learning to a single, specific teacher were excluded (White & Rowan, 2014). Of the eligible schools, principals decided whether to participate. Teachers in participating schools were then recruited. The participation of particular teachers and the specific class sections to be observed determined the student sample for the MET database. Once a teacher met all eligibility criteria and consented to be in the study, efforts were made to include all her students in the sampled class section. In all districts but one, a process of passive consent provided parents the opportunity to remove their child from the study. Given the sampling procedures, the students in the MET database were, as the MET User Guide describes, "included in the study simply as a result of all these prior opportunistic processes" (White & Rowan, 2014, p. 23).

Here, we limit our analyses to sixth (n = 388), seventh (n = 337), and eighth grade (n = 324) mathematics class sections. The students represented in these class sections were equally split among male and female students, with 40% of students self-identifying as Latinx, 31% self-identifying as African American, and 27% self-identifying as European American. The remaining 2% of students self-identified with other races and ethnicities. Our analysis focuses on mathematics classrooms because of the well-documented potential for threatening environments to exist for students of color in science, technology, engineering, and math classrooms (e.g., McGee and Martin, 2011) and, thus, the resulting need for greater understanding of effective teaching in these classrooms.

Measures

Student Perception Survey

Adolescents' perceptions of their mathematics teacher and adolescent self-report of personal experiences in their mathematics classrooms were measured using the Tripod scale items developed by Ferguson (2010) and other survey items authored by MET researchers. The 36-item Tripod scale includes questions as follows: "My teacher seems to know if something is bothering me" and "In this class, we learn to correct our mistakes." Each item was rated on a 5-point Likert scale ranging from *totally untrue* to *totally true*. Negatively worded items of the Tripod survey were reverse coded. See Table 1 for a listing of all 36 Tripod items. Despite the ordered nature of responses, prior analyses concerning the Tripod instrument and other student reports of teacher behavior that have used similar Likert items have largely treated student responses as if they are continuous. However, research has indicated that such approaches, which treat ordinal data as if they had metric properties, may lead to incorrect results and inferences (e.g., Jöreskog & Moustaki, 2006).

Classroom Assessment Scoring System-Secondary (CLASS-S)

This 10-dimension observational instrument (Pianta et al., 2008) assesses student-teacher interactions and is organized into three higher-level domains. The emotional support domain comprises positive climate, negative climate (in which a low score is desirable), teacher sensitivity, and regard for student perspectives. The classroom organization domain comprises behavior management, productivity, and instructional learning formats. The instructional support domain comprises content understanding, analysis and problem solving, instructional dialogue, and quality of feedback. Each dimension of the CLASS-S is scored on a 7-point scale, with 1–2 representing low scores, 3–5 representing moderate scores, and 6–7 representing high scores. Current or former teachers trained by MET researchers scored the videos. Working under a "scoring leader," each video coder participated in several practices, including joint review sessions and the double scoring of videos, to ensure reliable and valid coding (White & Rowan, 2014).

Teachers' Value-Added Scores in Mathematics

Because teachers in the dataset came from different states, MET researchers standardized test scores (mean of 0 and a standard deviation of 1) for each district, subject, year, and grade level. The value-added model predicts a student's end-of-year score on the state mathematics assessment accounting for that student's test score in that subject from the prior year, a set of student characteristics used as controls (which varied depending on what was available by school district but typically included student demographics, free or reduced-price lunch, English-language learner status, and special education status), and the mean prior test score and mean student characteristics in the specific course section or class that the student attended (for more details, see Kane & Cantrell, 2010).

Data Analysis

Different approaches are available to model student responses to survey items. One approach ignores existing theory and associated theoretically

Table 1

Alternative Factor Structures With Item Assignment at the Within Level

Survey Item	Tripod Original	Three-Factor			Two-Factor		Bifactor		
		Instructional Support	Emotional Support	Classroom Organization	Support	Press	General	Specific	Negative
My teacher in this class makes me feel that s/he really cares about me.	Care		□		□		□		
My teacher seems to know if something is bothering me.	Care		□		□		□		
My teacher really tries to understand how students feel about things.	Care		□		□		□		
Student behavior in this class is under control.	Control			□		□	□	□	
I hate the way that students behave in this class.	Control			□		□	□	□	□
Student behavior in this class makes the teacher angry.	Control			□		□	□	□	□
Student behavior in this class is a problem.	Control			□		□	□	□	□
My classmates behave the way my teacher wants them to.	Control			□		□	□	□	
Students in this class treat the teacher with respect.	Control			□		□	□	□	
Our class stays busy and does not waste time.	Control			□		□	□		
If you don't understand something, my teacher explains it another way.	Clarify	□			□		□		
My teacher knows when the class understands and when we do not.	Clarify	□			□		□		
When s/he is teaching us, my teacher thinks we understand even when we don't.	Clarify	□			□		□	□	□
My teacher has several good ways to explain each topic that we cover in this class.	Clarify	□			□		□		

(continued)

Table 1 (continued)

Survey Item	Tripod Original	Three-Factor			Two-Factor		General	Bifactor	
		Instructional Support	Emotional Support	Classroom Organization	Support	Press		Specific	Negative
My teacher explains difficult things clearly.	Clarify	■			■		■		
My teacher asks questions to be sure we are following along when s/he is teaching.	Challenge	■				■	■		
My teacher asks students to explain more about answers they give.	Challenge	■				■	■		
In this class, my teacher accepts nothing less than our full effort.	Challenge		■			■	■		
My teacher doesn't let people give up when the work gets hard.	Challenge		■			■	■		
My teacher wants us to use our thinking skills, not just memorize things.	Challenge	■				■	■		
My teacher wants me to explain my answers—why I think what I think.	Challenge	■				■	■		
In this class, we learn a lot almost every day.	Challenge			■		■	■		
In this class, we learn to correct our mistakes.	Challenge	■				■	■		
This class does not keep my attention—I get bored.	Captivate				■		■		■
My teacher makes learning enjoyable.	Captivate		■		■		■		
My teacher makes lessons interesting.	Captivate		■		■		■		
I like the ways we learn in this class.	Captivate				■		■		
My teacher wants us to share our thoughts.	Confer	■	■		■		■		
Students get to decide how activities are done in this class.	Confer		■		■		■		

(continued)

Table 1 (continued)

Survey Item	Tripod Original	Three-Factor			Two-Factor		Bifactor		
		Instructional Support	Emotional Support	Classroom Organization	Support	Press	General	Specific	Negative
My teacher gives us time to explain our ideas.	Confer			▪	▪		▪		
Students speak up and share their ideas about classwork.	Confer		▪		▪		▪		
My teacher respects my ideas and suggestions.	Confer	▪			▪		▪		
My teacher takes the time to summarize what we learn each day.	Consolidate	▪			▪		▪		
My teacher checks to make sure we understand what s/he is teaching us.	Consolidate	▪			▪		▪		
We get helpful comments to let us know what we did wrong on assignments.	Consolidate	▪			▪		▪		
The comments that I get on my work in this class help me understand how to improve.	Consolidate	▪			▪		▪		

proposed dimensions and summarizes the responses in a way that yields the best correlation with value-added scores or in a way that summarizes the observed variation (e.g., through averages or principal components). This data-driven approach prioritizes statistical associations as opposed to advancing theoretical explanation or supporting causal inference. If the goal is to predict the most variation in the value-added scores, then this approach is often reasonable.

An alternative approach is to try to understand the underlying factor structure that drives students' responses. Here the starting point is existing theory, and the statistical modeling of students' responses focuses on assessing theories using the data. In this approach, understanding the underlying core causal forces that drive student responses to survey items is the central priority. If the goal is to understand the factor structure and advance theory, then predictive value is important but is not the determining criterion for which model is better.

In this study, we take the latter approach. We investigate whether adolescents' responses to perception survey items support theoretically proposed models of teaching through multilevel item factor analyses within a structural equation modeling framework. We first examined the extent to which empirical evidence supported the multidimensional structures of effective teaching proposed in the literature. Fundamentally, we were interested in understanding what the Tripod items might be measuring in order to appreciate the extent to which student surveys might be useful not only in evaluating teaching but also in helping to improve teaching.

Within this context, our analyses considered five alternative factor structures. The first model we considered was a unidimensional structure in which each Tripod item loaded onto a single general latent factor. The second model was a two-dimensional structure with factors representing press and support. The third model was a three-dimensional structure with dimensions corresponding to classroom organization, instructional support, and emotional support. The fourth model was a seven-dimensional structure comprising the dimensions of care, confer, captivate, clarify, consolidate, challenge, and control. The final model was a type of multilevel double structure bifactor model (e.g., Rijmen, 2013) consisting of a general responsivity dimension driving all items with a secondary or specific dimension for classroom management–specific items. See Table 1 for item assignment in each model.

Our consideration of a fifth alternative factor structure (i.e., the bifactor) was motivated by the insufficient fit of each of the structures found in the literature to the current data. As we shall see, assessments of the first four structures persistently resulted in factors that were highly correlated and in the presence of a distinct and prominent classroom management factor. On the basis of these results, we reviewed existing theory and previous empirical investigations and identified an alternative bifactor-like structure that considers a general factor that informs student responses to all items along with a classroom management factor that additionally contributes to student responses on classroom management items.

Bifactor models have been rediscovered as a viable alternative structural representation of multiple types of higher order and multidimensional factor structures (Reise, 2012). Our implementation adopts a type of extended or double-structure bifactor model that extends the conventional bifactor model by drawing on a general factor and two types of secondary factors—a secondary factor governing classroom management items and a secondary factor tracking response style for negatively worded items (e.g., Cai, Yang, & Hansen, 2011; Gibbons & Hedeker, 1992; Rijmen, 2013). Although the classroom management factor constitutes a substantively meaningful construct, we introduced the negatively worded items nuisance factor, which we refer to as a "testlet" factor, across all of the aforementioned factor structures to accommodate the increased dependence among these items.[1] Such dependence does not generalize across contexts and thus is not of direct interest. However, ignoring these effects can lead to violations of the local item independence assumption (Sliter & Zickar, 2014). In this way, our proposed model imposes a type of double structure bifactor organization.

To empirically examine the fit of each factor structure to the data, we drew on multilevel (two-tier) item factor models (e.g., Cai, 2010). Inspection of the intraclass correlation coefficients suggested substantial classroom-level variance in the item responses (see Table 2).[2] We used a multilevel graded response model formulation, such that

$$P\left(Y_{isc}^f = k\right) = P\left(Y_{isc}^f \geq k\right) - P\left(Y_{isc}^f \geq k+1\right) P\left(Y_{isc}^f = k\right)$$

$$= \frac{1}{1+exp\left(-\left[a_i^{fc}\theta_c^f + a_i^{fS}\theta_{sc}^f - d_i^{k-1}\right]\right)} - \frac{1}{1+exp\left(-\left[a_i^{fc}\theta_c^f + a_i^{fS}\theta_{sc}^f - d_i^k\right]\right)} \quad (1)$$

Here, Y_{isc}^f is the rating given by student s in classroom c on Tripod item i belonging to factor f, and a_i^{fc} and a_i^{fS} represent the classroom and student-level loading parameters for item i on factor f with θ_c^f as the classroom-level factor and θ_{sc}^f as the student-level factor. Let K represent the number of categories on which items are graded (seven), with k as a specific category, and let $d_i^1, \ldots, d_i^{k-1}$ be a set of $K-1$ ordered item thresholds. To identify the scale, the distribution of each factor was set to be normally distributed with a mean of 0 and variance of 1.

Analogous to conventional multilevel regression, our multilevel factor analyses split students' observed judgments into two complementary components. The first component consisted of classroom-level factors (θ_c^f) that describe students' collective judgments of effective teaching in their classrooms. The second analytic component contained student-level factors (θ^f_{sc}) that captured student-specific deviations within classrooms. That is, these student-specific deviations describe how an individual student's judgments differ from the collective judgments of his or her classroom peers. Similar to scores based on value-added models and classroom observations, the focus of our study rests on the classroom-level factors that differentiate teachers in terms of their persistent effectiveness across all students rather than the residual discrepancies among students within classrooms.

For each model that included multiple dimensions at each level, we specified multidimensional versions of Equation 1 to capture the implied student and classroom structure. In these models, we specified $\theta^f \sim MVN(0, \Sigma)$ with Σ as covariance matrix and freely estimated the covariances among the dimensions within a level. For the bifactor-like model, the general teaching quality dimension was set to be orthogonal to the classroom management–specific dimension. This specification captured the unique influence of teachers' classroom management–specific practice (i.e., variance over and above the general responsivity factor). Similarly, in each instance, we designed the negatively worded testlet factor to be orthogonal to all remaining factors implied by a given structure.

To assess the relative or predictive fit among the models, we drew on full-information maximum marginal likelihood estimation (e.g., Cai, 2010). Using the resulting log-likelihoods, we compared the models through two information criteria: Akaike information criterion (AIC) and Bayesian information criterion (BIC). These predictive fit criteria assess the extent to which the observed model fit might replicate in future equivalent samples and are population based rather than sample based (Kline, 2010).

To supplement the relative comparisons among models, we further assessed their fit through multiple absolute, incremental, and relative fit statistics. To assess the absolute and incremental fit, we drew on fit statistics based on a limited information, mean- and variance-adjusted, weighted least squares estimator (e.g., Maydeu-Olivares & Joe, 2005). Using this estimator, we first assessed fit using the χ^2 test of model fit. The χ^2 test of model fit assesses how close the observed values are to the values expected under the fitted model. Second, we measured fit using the root mean square error of approximation (RMSEA). RMSEA is a parsimony-adjusted absolute fit index that estimates the amount of error of approximation per model degree of freedom while taking sample size into account. To measure incremental fit, we examined the comparative fit index (CFI). CFI assesses the relative improvement in fit in a model compared with the null model with no item associations.

Under the maximum likelihood estimator, we subsequently examined predictive validity. A guiding principle in theories of effective teaching is that instruments should measure quality as it relates to student achievement. As a result, a primary benchmark for the validity of student ratings is their

Table 2

Descriptive Statistics for Tripod Student Perception Survey Items

Item Number	Item Text	M	SD	ICC
1	My teacher in this class makes me feel that s/he really cares about me.	3.65	1.25	.19
2	My teacher respects my ideas and suggestions.	3.71	1.15	.14
3	If you don't understand something, my teacher explains it another way.	4.04	1.08	.15
4	Student behavior in this class is under control.	3.36	1.26	.20
5	I hate the way that students behave in this class.[a]	2.51	1.34	.17
6	Student behavior in this class makes the teacher angry.[a]	3.08	1.33	.22
7	My teacher asks questions to be sure we are following along when s/he is teaching.	4.39	0.93	.11
8	My teacher wants us to share our thoughts.	3.69	1.19	.16
9	My teacher knows when the class understands and when we do not.	3.83	1.11	.12
10	My teacher asks students to explain more about answers they give.	4.13	0.97	.11
11	Students get to decide how activities are done in this class.	2.31	1.07	.15
12	When s/he is teaching us, my teacher thinks we understand even when we don't.[a]	2.45	1.23	.11
13	Student behavior in this class is a problem.[a]	2.70	1.29	.24
14	This class does not keep my attention—I get bored.[a]	2.62	1.35	.12
15	My teacher takes the time to summarize what we learn each day.	3.50	1.23	.14
16	My teacher seems to know if something is bothering me.	3.06	1.32	.16
17	My teacher checks to make sure we understand what s/he is teaching us.	4.10	1.05	.16
18	My teacher gives us time to explain our ideas.	3.67	1.13	.16
19	Students speak up and share their ideas about classwork.	3.55	1.18	.12
20	My teacher has several good ways to explain each topic that we cover in this class.	3.92	1.09	.18
21	In this class, my teacher accepts nothing less than our full effort.	4.02	1.06	.11
22	My teacher makes learning enjoyable.	3.49	1.29	.26
23	My teacher really tries to understand how students feel about things.	3.48	1.22	.18
24	My teacher doesn't let people give up when the work gets hard.	4.04	1.09	.14
25	My teacher makes lessons interesting.	3.49	1.26	.24
26	My teacher wants us to use our thinking skills, not just memorize things.	4.10	1.02	.09

(continued)

Table 2 **(continued)**

Item Number	Item Text	M	SD	ICC
27	My classmates behave the way my teacher wants them to.	3.10	1.22	.25
28	Students in this class treat the teacher with respect.	3.56	1.17	.30
29	We get helpful comments to let us know what we did wrong on assignments.	3.69	1.19	.13
30	My teacher wants me to explain my answers—why I think what I think.	4.07	1.03	.11
31	Our class stays busy and does not waste time.	3.50	1.17	.20
32	In this class, we learn a lot almost every day.	4.00	1.04	.15
33	My teacher explains difficult things clearly.	3.86	1.13	.17
34	The comments that I get on my work in this class help me understand how to improve.	3.70	1.16	.13
35	I like the ways we learn in this class.	3.83	1.03	.21
36	In this class, we learn to correct our mistakes.	4.08	1.02	.14

Note. Item order matches order in administered survey. We report the intraclass correlation coefficients (ICC) of items only as a heuristic indicator of the multilevel structure of the items. Subsequent analyses treat the items as categorical because they were administered using Likert-style ordinal response.

[a]Reverse coded.

efficacy in predicting student achievement. For this reason, we assessed the correlation between Tripod and value-added scores in mathematics. To do so, we further extended the aforementioned equations to incorporate structural components using the latent factors as predictors of the average student achievement gains in each class:

$$Y_c = \pi_0 + \sum_{f=1}^{F} \pi_f \theta_c^f + \varepsilon_c \tag{2}$$

We continue with the preceding notation and introduce Y_c as the value-added score on state standardized achievement tests for classroom c, π_0 as the intercept, π_f as the regression coefficients capturing the relation between Tripod dimensions and value-added, and ε_c as the error term.

Results

The results are presented in two sections. In the first section, we report the results of factor analyses. In the second section, we outline results examining the validity of the factors by reporting associations of the two classroom-level dimensions from the bifactor model with other data sources—adolescent self-report of personal experiences in the classroom, an observational assessment of effective teaching, and student learning.

Investigating the Dimensionality of the Ratings

Our analysis of the null model (that assumed no item associations) suggested that the RMSEA for this null model was unusually low (<0.10). One consequence of such a low RMSEA for the null model is that incremental indices such as CFI/Tucker-Lewis Index (TLI) may not be particularly informative because even when a proposed model improves the RMSEA to levels that are typically considered to provide evidence of reasonable fit (e.g., 0.05; MacCallum, Browne, & Sugawara, 1996), such indices will often be practically limited to values less than common cutoff values (e.g., <0.95 for CFI/TLI).[3] As a result, we report the incremental fit index CFI but do not incorporate these indices into further assessments of the models. All results refer to the classroom-level unless otherwise noted.

Because the Tripod designers propose that the survey measures seven conceptual dimensions of classroom instruction, we first report the results pertaining to this structure. Despite probing multiple estimation and identification strategies, the seven-dimensional model did not reach a permissible solution (see Table 3). An assessment of the correlations among dimensions using simple classroom-level item averages for each dimension suggested that correlations were high (see Table 4). These results suggested that the

Table 3

Comparison of One-, Two-, and Three-Dimension Measurement Models

Model	χ^2	df	RMSEA	CFI[a]	SRMR (W/B)[b]	Log-Likelihood	AIC	BIC
Null	201126	1260	.10	—	.35/.71			
1D	103480	1188	.07	.49	.06/.12	−719067	1438576	1440289
2D	75329	1181	.06	.63	.05/.10	Did not converge		
3D	68720	1177	.06	.66	.05/.10	−729527[c]	1459508[c]	1461267[c]
7D	Did not converge					Did not converge		
Bifactor	31490	1169	.04	.85	.03/.06	−712138	1424746	1426567

Note. RMSEA = root mean square error of approximation; CFI = comparative fit index; SRMR = standardized root mean square residual; W/B = within/between; AIC = Akaike information criterion; BIC = Bayesian information criterion. χ^2, RMSEA, CFI, and TLI are based on the weighted least squares estimator adjusted for means, variance, and clustering; log-likelihood, AIC, and BIC are based on the maximum likelihood estimator. Information criteria are based on 30, 31, and 33 degrees of freedom for the one-, two-, and three-dimensional models, respectively.
[a]This criterion is not particularly informative because the null model RMSEA was so low.
[b]Indices presented as within/between.
[c]Model converged but to an unstable solution, suggesting the solution may not be unique, likely caused by the model being overly parametric (i.e., too many factors).

Table 4

Correlations Among Seven Factors Using Simple Item Averages

	Dimension						
	Care	Confer	Captivate	Clarify	Consolidate	Challenge	Control
Instructional							
Care	1						
Confer	.83	1					
Captivate	.85	.82	1				
Clarify	.82	.78	.84	1			
Consolidate	.85	.84	.84	.88	1		
Challenge	.78	.79	.80	.84	.85	1	
Control	.42	.50	.54	.44	.45	.59	1

indicators were unable to distinguish among classrooms along seven separate dimensions.

We next fit a three-factor model in which the three latent factors at the student- and classroom-levels comprised survey items that were reflective of the conceptual dimensions of instructional support, classroom organization, and emotional support (see Table 1 for the assignment of items into each of these domains). With the exception of the RMSEA, fit indices suggested that the fit of the three-dimensional model was marginal. Furthermore, assessment of the associations among latent factors indicated high correlations. The classroom organization factor was strongly associated with the instructional support factor ($r = .79$, $p < .05$) and the emotional support factor ($r = .77$, $p < .05$). The emotional support factor and the instructional support factor were even more strongly associated ($r = .97$, $p < .05$). These results suggested that a more parsimonious structure might better suit the observed data.

Given that the seven- and three-factor models have very high correlations between the latent factors, we estimated more parsimonious structures using a two-factor model representing academic press and support and the baseline, one-factor model (see Table 1 for the specific items assigned to each of these factors). Despite the reduction in the number of factors, the correlation between the two factors was exceptionally high ($r = .86$, $p < .05$). Results concerning fit for the one- and two-dimensional models also showed worse absolute, incremental, and relative fit as compared to the three-dimensional model.

Finally, we assessed the proposed bifactor model. Fit indices largely fell within acceptable ranges, and comparative assessments of relative fit indices demonstrated substantial improvements over the previous models (Table 3). With evidence supporting the plausibility of the proposed bifactor structure, we also evaluated the strength with which the Tripod items reflected each of the latent dimensions, using the loading parameters (as shown in Table 5). Loading parameters conceptually capture the strength of the correlation between responses on a particular item and underlying dimensions and, thus, describe how well an item can differentiate among classrooms in terms of their underlying quality. The results suggested that items were appreciably and significantly correlated with the underlying dimension(s). Collectively, the resulting estimates of the loading parameters indicated that most items were able to differentiate fairly well among different latent levels on each dimension.

General Responsivity and Classroom Management–Specific Associations With Adolescent Self-report of Personal Experiences in the Classroom

At the classroom level, adolescents' self-reports of the positivity of the classroom climate were strongly associated with the general responsivity factor. For example, "this class is a happy place for me to be" (.82), "for a new student, this class would be a good one to join" (.72), "being in this class makes me angry" (−.67), and "I feel stressed in this class" (−.61). Adolescents' self-reports of effort were weakly to moderately correlated with the general responsivity factor: for example, "I take it easy and do not try my best" (−.14), and "I stop trying when the work gets hard" (−.32). Across all items, self-reports of personal experiences in the classroom

Table 5
Loading Parameters of the Bifactor Model

	General Factor		Specific Factor		Negative Testlet	
	Within	Between	Within	Between	Within	Between
My teacher in this class makes me feel that s/he really cares about me.	1.9 (0.03)	1.11 (0.04)				
My teacher seems to know if something is bothering me.	1.34 (0.02)	0.78 (0.02)				
My teacher really tries to understand how students feel about things.	1.94 (0.03)	1.04 (0.03)				
If you don't understand something, my teacher explains it another way.	1.91 (0.03)	0.94 (0.03)				
My teacher knows when the class understands and when we do not.	1.52 (0.02)	0.07 (0.03)				
When s/he is teaching us, my teacher thinks we understand even when we don't.	0.82 (0.02)	0.53 (0.02)				
My teacher has several good ways to explain each topic that we cover in this class.	2.12 (0.03)	1.16 (0.04)				
My teacher explains difficult things clearly.	2.19 (0.03)	1.08 (0.04)				
This class does not keep my attention—I get bored.	1.15 (0.02)	0.8 (0.03)			0.68 (0.03)	—
My teacher makes learning enjoyable.	2.1 (0.03)	1.67 (0.05)				
My teacher makes lessons interesting.	2.17 (0.03)	1.57 (0.05)				
I like the ways we learn in this class.	1.57 (0.02)	1.21 (0.04)				
My teacher wants us to share our thoughts.	1.06 (0.02)	0.63 (0.02)				
Students get to decide how activities are done in this class.	0.68 (0.02)	0.67 (0.02)				
My teacher gives us time to explain our ideas.	1.99 (0.03)	0.90 (0.03)				
Students speak up and share their ideas about classwork.	1.37 (0.02)	0.69 (0.03)				
My teacher respects my ideas and suggestions.	2.13 (0.03)	0.95 (0.03)				

(continued)

Table 5 **(continued)**

	General Factor		Specific Factor		Negative Testlet	
	Within	Between	Within	Between	Within	Between
My teacher takes the time to summarize what we learn each day.	1.61 (0.02)	0.66 (0.03)				
My teacher checks to make sure we understand what s/he is teaching us.	2.36 (0.03)	1.00 (0.04)				
We get helpful comments to let us know what we did wrong on assignments.	1.82 (0.03)	0.78 (0.03)				
The comments that I get on my work in this class help me understand how to improve.	1.88 (0.03)	0.83 (0.03)				
My teacher asks questions to be sure we are following along when s/he is teaching.	1.33 (0.02)	0.53 (0.03)				
My teacher asks students to explain more about answers they give.	1.15 (0.02)	0.32 (0.02)				
In this class, my teacher accepts nothing less than our full effort.	1.37 (0.02)	0.48 (0.02)				
My teacher doesn't let people give up when the work gets hard.	1.61 (0.03)	0.74 (0.03)				
My teacher wants us to use our thinking skills, not just memorize things.	1.54 (0.02)	0.49 (0.03)				
My teacher wants me to explain my answers—why I think what I think.	1.42 (0.02)	0.42 (0.02)				
In this class, we learn a lot almost every day.	1.63 (0.03)	0.65 (0.03)				
In this class, we learn to correct our mistakes.	2.03 (0.03)	0.81 (0.03)				

(continued)

Table 5 (continued)

	General Factor		Specific Factor		Negative Testlet	
	Within	Between	Within	Between	Within	Between
Our class stays busy and does not waste time.	1.01 (0.02)	0.44 (0.04)	0.65 (0.02)	0.77 (0.03)		
Student behavior in this class is under control.	0.98 (0.02)	0.72 (0.05)	1.44 (0.03)	1.08 (0.03)		
I hate the way that students behave in this class.	0.14 (0.02)	0.28 (0.04)	1.13 (0.03)	1.00 (0.03)	1.06 (0.04)	—
Student behavior in this class makes the teacher angry.	0.4 (0.02)	0.61 (0.04)	1.03 (0.03)	0.96 (0.03)	0.98 (0.03)	—
Student behavior in this class is a problem.	0.5 (0.03)	0.63 (0.06)	1.55 (0.03)	1.37 (0.04)	1.15 (0.04)	—
My classmates behave the way my teacher wants them to.	1.26 (0.03)	0.99 (0.06)	1.84 (0.04)	1.29 (0.04)		
Students in this class treat the teacher with respect.	1.15 (0.03)	1.13 (0.06)	1.41 (0.03)	1.21 (0.04)		

Note. Maximum likelihood estimates of loadings were obtained using the typical logit link standard errors in parentheses.

were weakly correlated (.00–.31) with the classroom management–specific factor.

General Responsivity and Classroom Management–Specific Associations With Adult Assessments of Effective Teaching

A second set of correlational analyses were carried out to assess how the general responsivity and classroom management–specific factors related to the three domains (instructional support, emotional support, and classroom organization) of the CLASS-S (Pianta et al., 2008), an adult-scored observational measure of teachers' instruction based largely upon student-teacher interactions as the source material for effectiveness. Due to missing data, this correlational analysis could be conducted on slightly more than half of all classrooms in our initial sample. The classroom management–specific factor had the strongest relative association to the classroom organization domain of the CLASS-S (.19) but not to CLASS-S emotional support domain. In contrast, the general responsivity factor was unrelated to the classroom organization domain but had the strongest relative association with the emotional support domain of the observational instrument (.20). The general responsivity factor was weakly correlated with CLASS-S instructional support domain (.14), and the classroom management–specific factor was unrelated (–.01).

General Responsivity and Classroom Management–Specific Associations With Student Learning

Finally, we examined the predictive validity of the bifactor solution. The results, reported at the classroom level (i.e., standardized at the classroom level), suggested that both the general responsivity factor and classroom management–specific factor were positively and significantly associated with teachers' value-added measures based on the state mathematics test (standardized coefficients were .25 and .25, respectively). More specifically, a 1 standard deviation increase in either dimension was associated with a one-quarter standard deviation increase in teachers' value-added scores. Because these bifactor dimensions were orthogonal by design, a 1 standard deviation increase in both dimensions would be associated with an overall .50 standard deviation increase in teachers' value-added scores. Importantly, the correlation between teacher value-added and the classroom management–specific factor suggests that this factor is not a method effect due to differential wording of items.

Discussion

Adolescent students are unique reporters of classroom interactions. Without observing a teacher's instructional practice through the lens of an adult-developed theory of effective teaching, adolescents likely draw on their indigenous expertise of what makes them feel safe, respected, and competent. In other words, adult raters using observational instruments are trained (i.e., given descriptive or example anchors for the different scoring levels) in order to calibrate the assessment of effectiveness in relation to a particular theory of effective teaching. Adolescent raters using perception surveys, like the Tripod, however, are not subjected to a training process by which such explicit anchors are shared with raters in a systematic way.

Initial classroom-level analyses of Tripod data from the MET database indicated that student perceptions of a given teacher's strengths and weaknesses are fairly consistent across the different classrooms of students they teach (classroom-to-classroom correlations ranged from .58 to .68, depending on the dimension) and that aggregate student responses on a subset of Tripod items from one class section are significantly associated with student achievement gains in other class sections taught by the same teacher ($r = .219$ different section, $r = .235$ previous year; Kane & Cantrell, 2010). While these results are intriguing because of the sheer volume of classrooms from which the data were drawn, these studies did not explore the theory of teaching implied by the items comprising the Tripod instrument. We posit that the high correlations among the theoretical factors found in the literature on the Tripod measure (e.g., ranging from .65 to .95 in Raudenbush & Jean, 2014) and in our analyses as well as our evidence concerning the relative and absolute fit of the proposed factor structures suggest that those theoretical factors previously posed in the literature are largely implausible in the current sample and are fundamentally incomplete. That is, the theories found in the literature appear to be ill-defined and offer little basis for understanding how student surveys and theories of effective teaching intersect to inform teaching, teacher development, and assessments of teaching.

It is unclear whether the original 7Cs that describe the Tripod instrument were intended to capture seven distinct dimensions on which students can reliably discriminate among teachers or whether the 7Cs were merely intended to be more heuristic domains that map out important aspects of teaching. The initial investigations, both published and unpublished, of the Tripod have made important contributions, yet they are incomplete in many ways (e.g., Raudenbush & Jean, 2014; Schweig, 2014). Our study extends these investigations through a complementary but different perspective that endeavors to delineate the specific theoretical nature of the constructs being measured so as to inform teacher development and the appropriate use of student perception surveys.

Our results replicated the previous findings that student perceptions of teacher behavior and the learning environment measured in the Tripod track classroom features that relate to teachers' value-added scores. That said, what specific construct the general responsivity factor instantiates remains somewhat vague and indefinite. We produced preliminary evidence that the social and emotional experiences of students in a class section may be particularly salient source material influencing student endorsements when completing the Tripod survey. Evidence for this claim includes the moderate, but relatively strongest, association of the general responsivity factor with the emotional support domain of the CLASS-S as well as the strong association of the general responsivity factor with adolescents' self-reports of the positivity of the classroom climate.

On the basis of evidence generated across studies of the Tripod, including the one reported here, it seems reasonable to suggest that adolescents' interpretations of a teacher's enactment of particular classroom management actions contribute additional and unique information about the quality of a classroom experience above and beyond general responsivity. We contribute further evidence for this claim given that in this study, the classroom management–specific factor was moderately associated with the classroom organization domain of the CLASS-S but unrelated to the emotional support domain of the CLASS-S.

The level of cooperation among students and their teacher may provide student information on teacher effectiveness in the most unequivocal manner (Gregory & Ripski, 2008). For example, teachers can proactively support students' autonomous completion of tasks or seek compliance through controlling feedback (Wallace, Sung, & Williams, 2014). The role of appraisals and coping resources highlighted in a transactional model of teacher stress (e.g., McCarthy et al., 2014) may explain teachers' differential responses to specific events in classrooms. In turn, adolescents may well be sensitive to the resulting variation in cooperative interactions on the basis of the concrete particulars of the enactment of classroom management. For example, a student texting during the teacher's launching of a task may be experienced by a teacher as either (a) an energizing challenge to regain the student's attention or (b) a trigger for frustration and anger. This variability may be captured by the Tripod instrument through items such as "Student behavior in this class makes the teacher angry." This item may instantiate general teacher responsivity in terms of adolescents' broad perceptions of the teacher's disposition toward students and expression of negative emotions. This item may simultaneously instantiate adolescents' specific perceptions of the teacher's explicit public appraisals of student misbehavior as either a productive challenge that requires adapting instructional strategies or confirmatory evidence of deficit-based thinking about students. The critical role of such public appraisals to establishing and maintaining cooperative interactions is well documented in the culturally responsive classroom management literature (e.g., Weinstein, Tomlinson-Clarke, & Curran, 2004). Indeed, the work of culturally responsive teachers is a labor-intensive process that requires dedication and reflection of teachers to develop and refine such practices over time (Cholewa, Amatea, West-Olatunji, & Wright, 2012).

One unique feature of Tripod survey items comprising the classroom management–specific factor, relative to the rest of the survey items, is the extent to which they reference students rather than teachers. Indeed, four of the seven survey items ask students to reflect on other students in their classroom, not on the teacher. Particularly in adolescence, peer relationships become more salient in the classroom (Martin & Dowson, 2009; Wentzel, 2005). Adolescents' feelings of being connected to their classroom peers are associated with positive behavioral and motivational outcomes, including their self-efficacy (Ryan & Patrick, 2001), achievement motivation (Nelson & DeBacker, 2008; Ruzek, Hafen, Allen, Gregory, Mikami & Pianta, 2016), expectancies for success (Goodenow, 1993), engagement (Furrer & Skinner, 2003; Shernoff, Ruzek, & Sinha, 2016), and school interest (Wentzel, Battle, Russell, & Looney, 2010). To the extent that students answer these survey items thinking only about their peers, then these items may also reflect nuances in the peer context of the classroom and could provide unique assessments of peer effects as related to classroom management.

Without further research on the validity of the proposed bifactor model and theory-based augmentations of it, using this particular student survey measure as a basis for guiding teacher professional development efforts is limited. This is most especially true for the general factor, which is an amalgamation of all items on the survey instrument. If a teacher scores low on the Tripod's general responsivity factor, then what specific aspects of her instructional practice should an instructional coach or mentor attend to? Specificity is highly valuable in these professional development contexts because it provides guidance for improvement efforts. This is less of a concern with the classroom management–specific factor, which has specificity around the amount of respect students and teachers show each other, the extent to which the class remains productively focused on learning, and the degree to which peer behavior is perceived as psychologically safe. Low scores in the classroom management–specific factor are thus truly diagnostic and could likely be bolstered with focused efforts to improve the tenor of classroom discourse and the nature of peer interaction.

If surveys are to be used in efforts to evaluate and improve teachers' instructional practice, then it is critical to gain an understanding of what the surveys are, in fact, measuring about such practice. What unique information do survey results add to the other instruments or measures of teaching quality (e.g., value-added scores, observational protocols)? The results from this study suggest that the Tripod may provide unique information on classroom management. Interestingly, in prior research on the Tripod, the Control subscale (typically measured as a simple average of the individual items) has been among the best predictors of other measures of instructional quality (Ferguson & Danielson, 2014; Kane & Cantrell, 2010), so it is perhaps not surprising that our results suggest that these items provide valuable information about teaching. Similarly interesting is the fact that this information is provided by students, not adults, suggesting that students' views of classroom management are an important indicator of a high-functioning classroom.

While we have generated preliminary evidence for the plausibility of a bifactor-like theory of effective teaching that builds on recent research (e.g., Hamre et al., 2014; Lee 1992, 2001), a critical, but yet unknown, aspect of students' assessments of teacher quality gathered via surveys is whether adolescent reports of teaching quality may (a) detect substantive differences in teaching quality that have implications for our theories of effective teaching or (b) be influenced by rater effects (e.g., extreme response styles) due to the fact that adolescents are not trained to view and assess the classroom in any particular manner so by default draw on their naturally occurring interpretations to endorse items. Without an empirically based understanding of whether or how either of these two factors influence student perception survey results, it remains unclear how such data should be appropriately used in teacher evaluation and training efforts. Accordingly, the magnitude of the theoretical and practical implications of large-scale investigations of effective teaching necessitates thoughtful investigations of the construct validity of the data produced for the purposes of teacher evaluation.

Conclusion

To use student surveys in teacher evaluation systems (such as those being developed in the United States), policymakers and administrators must understand, at a minimum, the degree to which the survey items function as indicators of distinct aspects of instruction believed to be important—that is, we must amass evidence that indicators are linked to experienced aspects of teaching that drive effective teaching. In addition to exploring what Clausen (2002; as cited in Kunter & Baumert, 2006) calls "perspective-specific validities," we must examine additional questions such as whether student raters have the same interpretation of survey items across different contexts (allowing for the comparison of teacher instructional quality across classrooms, schools, districts, or even states) and why and how student characteristics influence interpretations of items. Only in the past decade have researchers begun to assess such aspects of student ratings of instruction (e.g., Fauth et al., 2014; Kunter, Tsai, Klusmann, Brunner, Krauss, & Baumert, 2008; Wagner et al., 2013), a necessity if these measures are to be used in high-stakes teacher evaluation systems. So while the general consensus among researchers is that student surveys are useful evaluation instruments—especially when used in combination with other evaluation tools—questions remain about what these surveys capture about teaching practice, and our results (e.g., the modest fit of several factorial structures we tested) suggest that this concern is particularly relevant to the Tripod.

Despite these unresolved issues, U.S. states and school districts increasingly rely upon student perception surveys in the mix of measures they use to evaluate teachers' instructional quality. In the United States, one of the most popular student surveys is the Tripod student self-perception survey (Ferguson, 2010), which was the focus of the present investigation. To our knowledge, this study is the first to systematically investigate the multidimensionality of the Tripod student perception survey using student-level data from the MET database.

Notes

[1]We conducted all of our analyses with and without the negative testlet factor; results were substantively the same in each instance, but fit was consistently better for models that included a negative testlet factor. For the bifactor model, items included in the negative testlet were part of both the general and specific factor.

[2]We report the intraclass correlation coefficients of items only as a heuristic indicator of the multilevel structure of the items. Subsequent analyses treat the items as categorical because they were administered using Likert-style ordinal response.

[3]For instance, if we rewrite the expression for TLI as a function of the RMSEA, we have

$$TLI = \frac{\chi^2_{null}/d_{null} - \chi^2_{my}/d_{my}}{\chi^2_{null}/d_{null} - 1} = \frac{\left(1 + R^2_{null}(n-1)\right) - \left(1 + R^2_{my}(n-1)\right)}{R^2_{null}(n-1)} = \frac{R^2_{null} - R^2_{my}}{R^2_{null}},$$

where $RMSEA = R = \sqrt{\frac{\chi^2 - d}{d(n-1)}}$, χ^2 is the model based chi-square, d represents the degrees of freedom, n is the sample size, *null* represents the null model, and *my* represents the proposed model. If the RMSEA from the null model is R_{null} = .10 (as is the case in our study) and a proposed model reduces the RMSEA from a null of .10 to levels typically described as very good, such as .05, the resulting TLI would be only $(.10^2 - .05^2)/.10^2$ = .75. In this way, CFI/TLI are not particularly informative when the null RMSEA is low (e.g., <.15).

References

Brophy, J. E., & Good, T. L. (1974). *Teacher-student relationships: Causes and consequences*. Oxford, England: Holt, Rinehart & Winston.

Cai, L. (2010). A two-tier full-information item factor analysis model with applications. *Psychometrika, 75*(4), 581–612. doi:10.1007/s11336-010-9178-0

Cai, L., Yang, J., & Hansen, M. (2011). Generalized full-information item bifactor analysis. *Psychological Methods, 16*, 221–248.

Carlisle, J., Kelcey, B., Berebitsky, D., & Phelps, G. (2011). Embracing the complexity of instruction: A study of the effects of teachers' instruction on students' reading comprehension. *Scientific Studies of Reading, 15*, 409–439. doi:10.1080/10888438.2010.497521

Cartledge, G., Lo, Y., Vincent, C. & Robinson-Ervin, P. (2015). Culturally responsive classroom management. In C. Evertson & C. Weinstein (Eds.), *Handbook of classroom management* (2nd Ed.). New York, New York: Routledge Publications.

Cholewa, B., Amatea, E., West-Olatunji, C. A., & Wright, A. (2012). Examining the relational processes of a highly successful teacher of African American children. *Urban Education, 47*(1), 250–279. doi:10.1177/0042085911429581

Davis, H. A. (2003). Conceptualizing the role and influence of student-teacher relationships on children's social and cognitive development. *Educational Psychologist, 38*(4), 207–234. doi:10.1207/S15326985EP3804_2

Desimone, L., Smith, T., & Frisvold, D. (2010). Survey measures of classroom instruction: Comparing student and teacher reports. *Educational Policy, 24*(2), 267–329. doi:10.1177/0895904808330173

Emmer, E. T., & Strough, L. (2001). Classroom management: A critical part of educational psychology, with implications for teacher education. *Educational Psychologist, 36*(2), 103–112. doi:10.1207/S15326985EP3602_5

Erickson, F. (1987). Transformation and school success: The politics and culture of educational achievement. *Anthropology and Education Quarterly, 18*(4), 335–356. doi:10.1525/aeq.1987.18.4.04x0023w

Erickson, F., Bagrodia, R., Cook-Sather, A., Espinoza, M., Jurow, S., Shultz, J. J., & Spencer, J. (2007). Students' experience of school curriculum: The everyday circumstances of granting and withholding assent to learn. In F. M. Connelly, M. F. He, & J. Phillion (Eds.), *The Sage Handbook of Curriculum and Instruction* (pp. 198–218). Thousand Oaks, CA: Sage.

Fauth, B., Decristan, J., Rieser, S., Klieme, E., & Büttner, G. (2014). Student ratings of teaching quality in primary school: Dimensions and prediction of student outcomes. *Learning and Instruction, 29*, 1–9. doi:10.1016/j.learninstruc.2013.07.001

Ferguson, R. (2010, October 14). Student perceptions of teaching effectiveness. Discussion brief from the National Center for Teacher Effectiveness and the Achievement Gap Initiative, Harvard University, Cambridge, MA.

Ferguson, R. F., & Danielson, C. (2014). How framework for teaching and Tripod 7Cs evidence distinguish key components of effective teaching. In T. Kane, K. Kerr, & R. Pianta (Eds.), *Designing teacher evaluation systems: New guidance from the Measures of Effective Teaching project* (pp. 98–143). San Francisco: Jossey-Bass.

Friedrich, A., Flunger, B., Nagengast, B., Jonkmann, K., & Trautwein, U. (2015). Pygmalion effects in the classroom: Teacher expectancy effects on students' math achievement. *Contemporary Educational Psychology, 41*, 1–12. doi:10.1016/j.cedpsych.2014.10.006

Furrer, C., & Skinner, E. (2003). Sense of relatedness as a factor in children's academic engagement and performance. *Journal of Educational Psychology, 95*(1), 148–162. doi:10.1037/0022-0663.95.1.148

Gay, G. (2010). *Culturally responsive teaching: Theory, research, and practice*. New York: Teachers College Press.

Gest, S. D., & Rodkin, P. C. (2011). Teaching practices and elementary classroom peer ecologies. *Journal of Applied Developmental Psychology, 32*(5), 288–296. doi:10.1016/j.appdev.2011.02.004

Gibbons, R. D., & Hedeker, D. R. (1992). Full-information item bi-factor analysis. *Psychometrika, 57*, 423–436.

Good, T. L. (1987). Two decades of research on teacher expectations: Findings and future directions. *Journal of Teacher Education, 38*(4), 32–47. doi:10.1177/002248718703800406

Goodenow, C. (1993). The psychological sense of school membership among adolescents: Scale development and educational correlates. *Psychology in the Schools, 30*(1), 79–90. doi:10.1002/1520–6807(199301)30:1<79::AID-PITS2310300113>3.0.CO;2-X

Greeno, J. (1998). The situativity of knowing, learning, and research. *American Psychologist, 53*(1), 5–26. doi:10.1037/0003-066X.53.1.5

Gregory, A., & Ripski, M. B. (2008). Adolescent trust in teachers: Implications for behavior in the high school classroom. *School Psychology Review, 37*(3), 337.

Hamre, B., Hatfield, B., Pianta, R., & Jamil, F. (2014). Evidence for general and domain-specific elements of teacher-child interactions: Associations with pre-school children's development. *Child Development, 85*(3), 1257–1274. doi:10.1111/cdev.12184

Jennings, P. A., & Greenberg, M. T. (2009). The prosocial classroom: Teacher social and emotional competence in relation to student and classroom outcomes. *Review of Educational Research, 79*(1), 491–525. doi:10.3102/0034654308325693

Jöreskog, K. G., & Moustaki, I. (2006). *Factor analysis of ordinal variables with full information maximum likelihood*. Unpublished manuscript.

Kane, T. J., & Cantrell, S. (2010). *Learning about teaching: Initial findings from the measures of effective teaching project*. Seattle: The Bill & Melinda Gates Foundation.

Kane, T. J., & Staiger, D. O. (2012). *Gathering feedback for teaching: Combining high-quality observations with student surveys and achievement gains*. Seattle: The Bill & Melinda Gates Foundation.

Kleinfeld, J. (1975). Effective teachers of Eskimo and Indian students. *The School Review, 83*, 301–344.

Kline, R. B. (2010). *Principles and practice of structural equation modeling* (3rd ed.). New York: Guilford Press.

Kulik, J. A., & Kulik, C. L. (1988). Timing of feedback and verbal learning. *Review of Educational Research, 58*(1), 79–97. doi:10.3102/00346543058001079

Kunter, M., & Baumert, J. (2006). Who is the expert? Construct and criteria validity of student and teacher ratings of instruction. *Learning Environments Research, 9*(3), 231–251. doi:10.1007/s10984-006-9015-7

Kunter, M., Tsai, Y.-M., Klusmann, U., Brunner, M., Krauss, S., & Baumert, J. (2008). Students' and mathematics teachers' perceptions of teacher enthusiasm and instruction. *Learning and Instruction, 18*(5), 468–482. doi:10.1016/j.learninstruc.2008.06.008

Lee, C. D. (1992). Literacy, cultural diversity, and instruction. *Education and Urban Society, 24*(2), 279–291. doi:10.1177/0013124592024002008

Lee, C. D. (2001). Is October Brown Chinese? A cultural modeling activity system for underachieving students. *American Educational Research Journal, 38*(1), 97–141. doi:10.3102/00028312038001097

Lee, V. E., & Smith, J. B. (1999). Social support and achievement for young adolescents in Chicago: The role of school academic press. *American Educational Research Journal, 36*(4), 907–945. doi:10.3102/00028312036004907

Lee, V. E., Smith, J. B., Perry, T. E., & Smylie, M. A. (1999). Social support, academic press, and student achievement: A view from the middle grades in Chicago. Improving Chicago's schools. Chicago: Chicago Annenberg Research Project.

MacCallum, R. C., Browne, M. W., & Sugawara, H. M. (1996). Power analysis and determination of sample size for covariance structure modeling. *Psychological Methods, 1*, 130–149.

Marsh, H. W., & Roche, L. A. (1997). Making students' evaluations of teaching effectiveness effective: The critical issues of validity, bias, and utility. *American Psychologist, 52*(11), 1187. doi:10.1037/0003-066X.52.11.1187

Martin, A. J., & Dowson, M. (2009). Interpersonal relationships, motivation, engagement, and achievement: Yields for theory, current issues, and educational practice. *Review of Educational Research*, *79*(1), 327–365. doi:10.3102/0034654308325583

Maydeu-Olivares, A., & Joe, H. (2005). Limited-and full-information estimation and goodness-of-fit testing in 2 n contingency tables: a unified framework. *Journal of the American Statistical Association*, *100*(471), 1009–1020. doi:10.2139/ssrn.1019782

Mayer, R. E. (2002). Rote versus meaningful learning. *Theory Into Practice*, *41*(4), 226–233. doi:10.1207/s15430421tip4104_4

McCarthy, C. J., Lineback, S., & Reiser, J. (2014). Teacher stress, emotion, and classroom management. In E. Emmer & E. J. Sabornie (Eds.), *Handbook of classroom management* (2nd ed.). New York: Routledge.

McCaslin, M. (2009). Co-regulation of student motivation and emergent identity. *Educational Psychologist*, *44*(2), 137–146. doi:10.1080/00461520902832384

McCaslin, M., & Hickey, D. T. (2001). Self-regulated learning and academic achievement: A Vygotskian view. In B. J. Zimmerman & D. Schunk (Eds.), *Self-regulated learning and academic achievement: Theory, research, and practice* (2nd ed., pp. 227–252). Mahwah, NJ: Erlbaum.

McGee, E. O., & Martin, D. B. (2011). "You would not believe what I have to go through to prove my intellectual value!" Stereotype management among academically successful black mathematics and engineering students. *American Educational Research Journal*, *48*(6), 1347–1389. 10.3102/0002831211423972

Milner, H. R., & Tenore, F. B. (2010). Classroom management in diverse classrooms. *Urban Education*, *45*(5), 560–603. doi: 10.1177/0042085910377290

Nakkula, M. J., & Toshalis, E. (2006). *Understanding youth: Adolescent development for educators*. Cambridge: Harvard Education Publishing Group.

Nelson, R. M., & DeBacker, T. K. (2008). Achievement motivation in adolescents: The role of peer climate and best friends. *Journal of Experimental Education*, *76*(2), 170–189. doi:10.3200/JEXE.76.2.170–190

Noguera, P. A. (2003). Schools, prisons, and social implications of punishment: Rethinking disciplinary practices. *Theory Into Practice*, *42*, 341–350. doi:10.1207/s15430421tip4204_12

Patrick, H., Anderman, L. H., & Ryan, A. M. (2004). Social motivation and the classroom environment. In C. Midgley (Ed.), *Goals, goal structures, and patterns of adaptive learning* (pp. 85–108). Mahwah, NJ: Lawrence Erlbaum Associates.

Pianta, R. C., & Hamre, B. K. (2009). Conceptualization, measurement, and improvement of classroom processes: Standardized observation can leverage capacity. *Educational Researcher*, *38*(2), 109–119. doi:10.3102/0013189X09332374

Pianta, R. C., La Paro, K., & Hamre, B. K. (2008). *Classroom assessment scoring system*. Baltimore: Brookes.

Raudenbush, S. W., & Jean, M. (2014). To what extent do student perceptions of classroom quality predict teacher value added? In T. Kane, K. Kerr, & R. Pianta (Eds.), *Designing teacher evaluation systems: New guidance from the Measures of Effective Teaching project* (pp. 170–202). San Francisco: Jossey-Bass.

Reeve, J., & Jang, H. (2006). What teachers say and do to support students' autonomy during a learning activity. *Journal of Educational Psychology*, *98*(1), 209–218. doi:10.1037/0022-0663.98.1.209

Reise, S. P. (2012). The rediscovery of bifactor measurement models. *Multivariate Behavioral Research*, *47*(5), 667–696. doi:10.1080/00273171.2012.715555

Rijmen, F. (2013). Hierarchical factor item response theory models for PIRLS: Capturing clustering effects at multiple levels. *IERI Monograph Series: Issues and Methodologies in Large-Scale Assessments*, *4*, 59–74.

Roeser, R. W., Skinner, E., Beers, J., & Jennings, P. A. (2012). Mindfulness training and teachers' professional development: An emerging area of research and practice. *Child Development Perspectives*, *6*(2), 167–173. doi:10.1111/j.1750-8606 .2012.00238.x

Ruzek, E. A., Hafen, C. A., Allen, J. P., Gregory, A., Mikami, A. Y., & Pianta, R. C. (2016). How teacher emotional support motivates students: The mediating roles of perceived peer relatedness, autonomy support, and competence. *Learning and Instruction*, *42*, 95–103. doi:10.1016/j.learninstruc.2016.01.004

Ryan, A. M., & Patrick, H. (2001). The classroom social environment and changes in adolescents' motivation and engagement during middle school. *American Educational Research Journal*, *38*(2), 437–460. doi:10.3102/00028312038002437

Schweig, J. (2014). Cross-level measurement invariance in school and classroom environment surveys: Implications for policy and practice. *Educational Evaluation and Policy Analysis*, *36*(3), 259–280. doi:10.3102/0162373713509880

Shernoff, D. J., Ruzek, E. A., & Sinha, S. (2016). The influence of the high school classroom environment on learning as mediated by student engagement. *School Psychology International*. doi:10.1177/0143034316666413

Sliter, K. A., & Zickar, M. J. (2014). An IRT examination of the psychometric functioning of negatively worded personality items. *Educational and Psychological Measurement*, *74*(2), 214–226. doi:10.1177/0013164413504584

Spearman, J., & Watt, H. M. G. (2013). Perception shapes experience: The influence of actual and perceived classroom environment dimensions on girls' motivations for science. *Learning Environments Research*, *16*(2), 217–238. doi:10.1007/s10984-013-9129-7

Thompson, J., Windschitl, M., & Braaten, M. (2013). Developing a theory of ambitious early-career teacher practice. *American Educational Research Journal*, *50*(3), 574–615. doi:10.3102/0002831213476334

Toshalis, E. (2015). *Make me: Understanding and engaging student resistance in school*. Cambridge: Harvard Education Publishing Group.

Turner, J. C., & Meyer, D. K. (2000). Studying and understanding the instructional contexts of classrooms: Using our past to forge our future. *Educational Psychologist*, *35*(2), 69–85. doi:10.1207/S15326985EP3502_2

Wagner, W., Göllner, R., Helmke, A., Trautwein, U., & Lüdtke, O. (2013). Construct validity of student perceptions of instructional quality is high, but not perfect: Dimensionality and generalizability of domain-independent assessments. *Learning and Instruction*, *28*, 1–11. doi:10.1016/j.learninstruc.2013.03.003

Wallace, T. L., & Chhuon, V. (2014). Proximal processes in urban classrooms: Engagement and disaffection in urban youth of color. *American Educational Research Journal*, *51*(5), 937–973. doi:10.3102/0002831214531324

Wallace, T. L., Sung, H. C., & Williams, J. D. (2014). The defining features of teacher talk within autonomy-supportive classroom management. *Teaching and Teacher Education*, (42), 34–46. doi:10.1016/j.tate.2014.04.005

Wanless, S.B. (2016). The role of psychological safety in human development. *Research in Human Development*, *13*(1), 6–14. doi: 10.1080/15427609.2016. 1141283

Ware, F. (2006). Warm demander pedagogy culturally responsive teaching that supports a culture of achievement for African American students. *Urban Education*, *41*(4), 427–456. doi:10.1177/0042085906289710

Weinstein, C. S., Tomlinson-Clarke, S., & Curran, M. (2004). Toward a conception of culturally responsive classroom management. *Journal of Teacher Education*, *55*(1), 25–38. doi:10.1177/0022487103259812

Wentzel, K. R. (2005). Peer relationships, motivation, and academic performance at school. In A. J. Elliot & C. S. Dweck (Eds.), *Handbook of competence and motivation* (pp. 279–295). New York: Guilford Press.

Wentzel, K. R., Battle, A., Russell, S. L., & Looney, L. B. (2010). Social supports from teachers and peers as predictors of academic and social motivation. *Contemporary Educational Psychology, 35*(3), 193–202. doi:10.1016/j.cedpsych .2010.03.002

Williams, J. D., Woodson, A. N., & Wallace, T. L. (2016). "Can we say the N-word?" Exploring psychological safety during race talk. *Research in Human Development, 13*(1), 15–31. doi:10.1080/15427609.2016.1141279

White, M., & Rowan, B. (2014). *User guide to the Measures of Effective Teaching Longitudinal Database (MET LDB)*. Ann Arbor: Inter-University Consortium for Political and Social Research, University of Michigan.

Manuscript received October 7, 2015
Final revision received July 1, 2016
Accepted September 1, 2016

Reviewer Acknowledgments

The editors of the *American Educational Research Journal* would like to thank the following people for reviewing manuscripts from July 2015 to November 2016.

Emma Adam, *Northwestern University*

Frank Adamson, *Stanford University*

Jill Adelson, *University of Louisville*

Tara Affolter, *Middlebury College*

Daisuke Akiba, *Queens College & The Graduate Center - CUNY*

Cynthia Alcantar, *University of California, Los Angeles*

Keisha Allen, *University of Maryland, Baltimore County*

Kristen Allen, *George Washington University*

Drew Allen, *Princeton University*

Elaine Allensworth, *University of Chicago*

Alicia Alonzo, *Michigan State University*

Rebecca Ambrose, *University of California, Davis*

Brian An, *University of Iowa*

Dorothea Anagnostopoulos, *University of Connecticut*

Lynley Anderman, *Ohio State University*

Celia Rousseau Anderson, *University of Memphis*

Daniel Anderson, *University of Oregon*

Paul Andrews, *Stockholm University*

Arya Ansari, *University of Texas, Austin*

Yuliya Ardasheva, *Washington State University, Tri-Cities*

Richard Arum, *University of California, Irvine*

Christa Asterhan, *The Hebrew University of Jerusalem*

Ron Astor, *University of Southern California*

Steven Athanases, *University of California, Davis*

Allison Atteberry, *University of Colorado, Boulder*

Catherine H. Augustine, *RAND*

Brianna Avenia-Tapper, *New York University*

Olena Aydarova, *Arizona State University*

Amy Azano, *Virginia Tech*

Roger Azevedo, *McGill University*

Drew Bailey, *University of California, Irvine*

Robert Bain, *University of Michigan*

Doris Baker, *Southern Methodist University*

Eva Baker, *University of California, Los Angeles*

Aydin Bal, *University of Wisconsin, Madison*

Maria Baltodano, *Loyola Marymount University*

Kiril Bankov, *University of Sofia*

Nicole Bannister, *Clemson University*

Holland Banse, *University of Virginia*

Stephanie Barclay McKeown, *University of British Columbia, Okanagan*

Nik Barkauskas, *Pennsylvania State University*

Johanna Barmore, *Harvard University*

Mariana Barragan Torres, *University of California, Los Angeles*

Kevin Bastian, *University of North Carolina, Chapel Hill*

Littisha Bates, *University of Cincinnati*

Michael Bates, *Michigan State University*

Dan Battey, *Rutgers University*

Erin Baumgartner, *Rice University*

Jos Beishuizen, *Vrije Universiteit, Amsterdam*

Clive Belfield, *Queens College*

Courtney Bell, *Educational Testing Service*

John Bell, *Alabama Department of Education*

Alain Bengochea, *University of Miami*

Peter Bergman, *Teachers College, Columbia University*

Theodorea Berry, *University of Texas, San Antonio*

Michael Besser, *University of Education, Freiburg*

Robert Bifulco, *Syracuse University*

Andrea Bingham, *University of Colorado, Colorado Springs*

Kendra Bischoff, *Cornell University*

Michael Bishop, *University of Chicago*

Russell Bishop, *University of Waikato*

Alieda Blandford, *Dalhousie University*

David Blazar, *Harvard University*

Mark Blitz, *University of Wisconsin, Madison*

Sigrid Blömeke, *University of Oslo*

Susan Blum, *University of Notre Dame*

Randy Bomer, *University of Texas, Austin*

Jill Bowdon, *University of Pennsylvania*

Alex Bowers, *Teachers College, Columbia University*

Elayne Bowman, *Oklahoma Christian University*

Nicholas Bowman, *University of Iowa*

Melissa Braaten, *University of Wisconsin*

Jameson Brewer, *University of Illinois, Urbana-Champaign*

Derek Briggs, *University of Colorado, Boulder*

Carol Brochin, *University of Arizona*

Karin Brodie, *University of the Witwatersrand*

Jeffrey Brooks, *Monash University*

Keffrelyn Brown, *University of Texas, Austin*

Katherine R. Bruna, *Iowa State University*

Andrea Bueschel, *Spencer Foundation*

Robert Bullough, *Brigham Young University*

George Bunch, *University of California, Santa Cruz*

Kri Burkander, *Educational Testing Service*

Soo-yong Byun, *Pennsylvania State University*

Jinfa Cai, *University of Delaware*

Jade Caines, *University of New Hampshire*

Brendan Calandra, *Georgia State University*

Rebecca Callahan, *University of Texas, Austin*

Shanyce Campbell, *University of Michigan*

Marisa Cannata, *Vanderbilt University*

Colleen Capper, *University of Wisconsin, Madison*

William Carbonaro, *University of Notre Dame*

Joanne Carlisle, *University of Michigan*

Deven Carlson, *University of Oklahoma*

Bradley Carpenter, *University of Louisville*

Martha Carr, *University of Georgia*

Deborah Carter, *Claremont Graduate University*

Dorinda Carter Andrews, *Michigan State University*

Reviewer Acknowledgments

Antonio Castro, *University of Missouri*
Hsun-Yu Chan, *Texas A&M University*
Madhur Chandra, *Michigan State University*
Aurora Chang, *Loyola University Chicago*
Thandeka Chapman, *University of Wisconsin, Milwaukee*
Charalambos Charalambous, *University of Cyprus*
Hua-Yu Cherng, *New York University*
Davinah Childs, *Temple University*
Matthew Chingos, *Brookings Institution*
Clark Chinn, *Rutgers University*
Gary Chinn, *Pennsylvania State University*
Adelino Chissale, *University of Johannesburg*
Sun-Joo Cho, *Vanderbilt University*
Vincent Cho, *Boston College*
Ikkyu Choi, *Educational Testing Service*
Amita Chudgar, *Michigan State University*
Joseph Cimpian, *New York University*
Christina Ciocca, *Columbia University*
Lawrence Clark, *University of Maryland*
Marilyn Cochran-Smith, *Boston College*
Leland Cogan, *Michigan State University*
Sarah Cohodes, *Teachers College, Columbia University*
Dennis Condron, *Emory University*
Dylan Conger, *George Washington University*
Liza Cope, *Delta State University*
Mimi Corcoran, *George Mason University*
Sean Corcoran, *New York University*
Lyn Corno, *Teachers College, Columbia University*
Mark Courtney, *University of Chicago*
Alejandro Covarrubias, *California State University, Los Angeles*
Jen Cowhy, *University of Chicago*
Bradley Cox, *Florida State University*
Cheryl Craig, *Texas A&M University*
Sandra Crespo, *Michigan State University*
Ulrike Cress, *Leibniz-Institut fur Wissensmedien*
Gloria Crisp, *University of Texas, San Antonio*
Jennifer Cromley, *University of Illinois, Urbana-Champaign*
Marnie Curry, *University of California, Santa Cruz*
Jerome Dagostino, *Ohio State University*
Julie Dallavis, *University of Notre Dame*
Julien Danhier, *Université libre de Bruxelles*
Linda Darling-Hammond, *Stanford University*
Amanda Datnow, *University of California, San Diego*
Miriam David, *University College London, Institute of Education*
Dennis Davis, *University of Texas, San Antonio*
Elizabeth Davis, *University of Michigan*
Larry Davis, *University of Pittsburgh*
Marcia Davis, *Johns Hopkins University*
Christopher Day, *University of Nottingham*
Noah De Lissovoy, *University of Texas, Austin*
Jasmin Decristan, *German Institute for International Educational Research*
Thomas Dee, *Stanford University*
Anne Deiglmayr, *ETH Zurich*
Shiv Desai, *University of New Mexico*
Laura Desimone, *University of Pennsylvania*
Leslie Dietiker, *Boston University*

Melanie DiLoreto, *University of West Florida*
Stephen Dinham, *University of Melbourne*
Adrienne Dixson, *University of Illinois, Urbana-Champaign*
Catherine Doherty, *Queensland University of Technology*
Thurston Domina, *University of North Carolina, Chapel Hill*
Morgaen Donaldson, *University of Connecticut*
Jamal Donnor, *William and Mary*
Alicia Dowd, *University of Southern California*
Doug Downey, *Ohio State University*
William Doyle, *Vanderbilt University*
Eleanor Drago-Severson, *Teachers College, Columbia University*
Corey Drake, *Michigan State University*
Timothy Drake, *Vanderbilt University*
Amy Dray, *Spencer Foundation*
Cheryl Duckworth, *Nova Southeastern University*
Nell Duke, *University of Michigan*
Xavier Dumay, *Université Catholique de Louvain*
Leah Durán, *University of Arizona*
Jacquelynne Eccles, *University of Michigan*
Jonathan Eckert, *Wheaton College*
Suzanne Eckes, *Indiana University*
Michael Edwards, *Ohio State University*
Susan Empson, *University of Missouri, Columbia*
Kathy Escamilla, *University of Colorado*
Dorothy Espelage, *University of Florida*
Michelle Espino, *University of Maryland*
Manuel Luis Espinoza, *University of Colorado, Denver*
Loris Fagioli, *Claremont Graduate University*
Beverly Faircloth, *University of North Carolina, Greensboro*
Benjamin Fauth, *University of Tuebingen*
Sharon Feiman-Nemser, *Brandeis University*
Li Feng, *Texas State University*
Erica Fernández, *University of Connecticut*
William Firestone, *Rutgers University*
Rachel Fish, *University of Notre Dame*
Anne Marie FitzGerald, *Duquesne University*
Terry Flennaugh, *Michigan State University*
Nelson Flores, *University of Pennsylvania*
Francesca Forzani, *University of Michigan*
Karly Ford, *Pennsylvania State University*
Kendra Freeman, *Hobart and William Smith Colleges*
Gavin Fulmer, *National Institute of Education, Singapore*
Fernandon Furquim, *University of Michigan*
Bonnie Fusarelli, *North Carolina State University*
Rachael Gabriel, *University of Connecticut*
Claudia Galindo, *University of Maryland, Baltimore County*
Sarah Gallo, *Ohio State University*
Jodie Galosy, *Knowles Science Teaching Foundation*
Adam Gamoran, *William T. Grant Foundation*
Patricia Gandara, *University of California, Los Angeles*
Liliana Garcés, *Pennsylvania State University*
David Garcia, *Arizona State University*

Georgia Garcia, *University of Illinois*
Jeremy Garcia, *University of Arizona*
Sandra Garcia, *University of Los Andes*
Lady Gaviria-Ochoa, *Universidad Pontificia Bolivariana*
James Gee, *Arizona State University*
Russell Gersten, *Instructional Research Group*
Matt Giani, *University of Texas, Austin*
Dan Gibton, *Tel-Aviv University*
Melissa Gilbert, *Santa Clara University*
Nicole Gillespie, *Knowles Science Teaching Foundation*
Robyn Gillies, *University of Queensland*
Karen Givvin, *University of California, Los Angeles*
Leah Gjertson, *University of Wisconsin, Madison*
Steven Glazerman, *Mathematica Policy Research*
Philip Gleason, *Mathematica Policy Research*
Kristen Goessling, *Pennsylvania State University, Brandywine*
Tsafrir Goldberg, *University of Haifa*
Claude Goldenberg, *Stanford University*
Sara Goldrick-Rab, *University of Wisconsin, Madison*
Pat Goldsmith, *Texas A&M University*
Ryan Goodwin, *University of Central Florida*
Evelyn Gordon, *Horizon Research, Inc.*
Rachel Gordon, *University of Illinois, Chicago*
Jennifer Gore, *University of Newcastle*
Paul Gorski, *George Mason University*
Michael Gottfried, *University of California, Santa Barbara*
Jessica Gottlieb, *University of Notre Dame*
Arthur Graesser, *University of Memphis*
Elizabeth Graue, *University of Wisconsin, Madison*
Colin Gray, *Purdue University*
Preston Green, *University of Connecticut*
Stuart Greene, *University of Notre Dame*
Christine Greenhow, *Michigan State University*
Cynthia Greenleaf, *WestEd*
Jacalyn Griffen, *University of the Pacific*
Jeffrey Grigg, *Johns Hopkins University*
Jason Grissom, *Vanderbilt University*
Eric Grodsky, *University of Wisconsin, Madison*
Alexander Groeschner, *Universitat Paderborn Fakultat fur Kulturwissenschaften*
Qing Gu, *University of Nottingham*
Doug Guiffrida, *University of Rochester*
Kathy Gullie, *University at Albany - SUNY*
David Gurr, *University of Melbourne*
Thomas Guskey, *University of Kentucky*
Eric Haas, *WestEd*
Carole Hahn, *Emory University*
Thomas Haladyna, *Arizona State University (Emeritus)*
Peter Halpin, *New York University*
Laura Hamilton, *RAND*
Karen Hammerness, *American Museum of Natural History*
Victoria Hand, *University of Colorado, Boulder*
Maria Hantzopoulos, *Vassar College*
Judith Harackiewicz, *University of Wisconsin, Madison*
Kristin Harbour, *University of Louisville*

James Harrington, *University of Texas, Dallas*
Elizabeth Hassrick, *Drexel University*
Tom Hatch, *Columbia University*
John Hattie, *University of Melbourne*
Jamie Hawkins, *University of Wisconsin, Madison*
Guro Helskog, *Buskerud and Vestfold University College*
Kevin Henry, *University of Wisconsin, Madison*
Joan Herman, *University of California, Los Angeles*
Leslie Herrenkohl, *University of Washington*
Daniel Hickey, *Indiana University*
Heather Hill, *Harvard University*
Nicholas Hillman, *University of Wisconsin*
Cindy Hmelo-Silver, *Rutgers University*
Andrew Ho, *Harvard University*
Michelle Hodara, *Education Northwest*
Tracey Hodges, *University of Southern Mississippi*
Flaviu Hodis, *Victoria University of Wellington*
Doris Holzberger, *Technical University Munich*
Ilana Horn, *Vanderbilt University*
Sonya Horsford, *George Mason University*
Elisabeth Hovdhaugen, *Nordisk institutt for studier av innovasjon forskning og utdanning*
Tyrone Howard, *University of California, Los Angeles*
Jessica Howell, *The College Board*
Lacey Huffling, *Georgia Southern University*
Charles Hughes, *Pennsylvania State University*
Seth Hunter, *Vanderbilt University*
Jenefer Husman, *University of Oregon*
Ethan Hutt, *University of Maryland, College Park*
Scott Imberman, *Michigan State University*
Ann Ishimaru, *University of Washington*
Zeynep Isik-Ercan, *Rowan University*
Felecia Jackson, *Florida State University*
Jacob Jackson, *University of California, Davis*
Margo Jackson, *Fordham University*
Anna Jacob, *University of Arkansas*
Robin Jacob, *University of Michigan*
Rebecca Jacobsen, *Michigan State University*
Stephen Jacobson, *University at Buffalo - SUNY*
Amanda Jansen, *University of Delaware*
Ozan Jaquette, *University of California, Los Angeles*
Jennifer Jennings, *New York University*
Bryant Jensen, *Arizona State University*
Jody Jessup-Anger, *Marquette University*
Rosa Jimenez, *University of San Francisco*
Oscar Jimenez-Castellanos, *Arizona State University*
Margarita Jimenez-Silva, *Arizona State University*
Jo Jimerson, *Texas Christian University*
Iryna Johnson, *Auburn University*
Matthew Johnson, *Teachers College, Columbia University*
Susan Johnson, *Harvard University*
Nate Jones, *Boston University*
Sosanya Jones, *Southern Illinois University, Carbondale*
Nicole Joseph, *Vanderbilt University*
Ute Kaden, *University of Alaska, Fairbanks*
Richard Kahlenberg, *The Century Foundation*
Joseph Kahne, *Mills College*

Reviewer Acknowledgments

Hosun Kang, *University of California, Irvine*
Seokmin Kang, *University of Wisconsin, Madison*
Avi Kaplan, *Temple University*
Elham Kazemi, *University of Washington*
Diana Kelly, *Southern University*
Sean Kelly, *University of Pittsburgh*
Sarah Kemp, *University of Wisconsin, Madison*
Kerry John Kennedy, *The Education University of Hong Kong*
Dorothe Kienhues, *Westfalische Wilhelms Universitat, Munster*
ChanMin Kim, *University of Georgia*
Daniel Kimmel, *Yeshiva University*
Barbara King, *Florida International University*
John Kirby, *Queen's University*
Zahid Kisa, *Florida State University*
Brian Kisida, *University of Missouri, Columbia*
Manja Klemencic, *Harvard University*
Matthew Kloser, *University of Notre Dame*
Michelle Knight, *Teachers College, Columbia University*
Julie Kochanek, *American Institutes for Research*
Cory Koedel, *University of Missouri, Columbia*
Alison Koenka, *Ohio State University*
Spyros Konstantopoulos, *Michigan State University*
Daniel Koretz, *Harvard University*
Matthew Kraft, *Brown University*
Catherine Kramarczuk Voulgarides, *New York University*
Beth Kubitskey, *Eastern Michigan University*
Linda Kucan, *University of Pittsburgh*
Stacy Kula, *Claremont Graduate University*
Dennis Kwek, *Nanyang Technological University, National Institute of Education*
Gloria Ladson-Billings, *University of Wisconsin, Madison*
Dragan Lambić, *University of Novi Sad*
Holly Lane, *University of Florida*
Amy Langenkamp, *University of Notre Dame*
Judith Langer, *University at Albany - SUNY*
Jennifer Langer-Osuna, *Stanford University*
Douglas Lauen, *University of North Carolina, Chapel Hill*
Fani Lauermann, *University of Bonn*
Judson Laughter, *University of Tennessee, Knoxville*
Seanna Leath, *University of Michigan*
Carol Lee, *Northwestern University*
Jaekyung Lee, *University at Buffalo - SUNY*
Okhee Lee, *New York University*
Jack Leonard, *University of Massachusetts, Boston*
Zeus Leonardo, *University of California, Berkeley*
Nonie Lesaux, *Harvard University*
Brett Levy, *University at Albany - SUNY*
Amanda Lewis, *Emory University*
Katherine Lewis, *University of Washington*
Tia Li, *Brooklyn College - CUNY*
Christian Liesen, *Interkantonale Hochschule fur Heilpadagogik*
Kuen-Yi Lin, *National Taiwan Normal University*
Terry Lin, *McGill University*
Lena Lindahl, *Swedish Institute for Social Research*
Guangming Ling, *Educational Testing Service*
Daniel Liou, *Arizona State University*

Allison Lombardi, *University of Connecticut*
Kofi Lomotey, *Western Carolina University*
Gerardo Lopez, *Loyola University New Orleans*
Dan Losen, *University of California, Los Angeles*
Lisa Loutzenheiser, *University of British Columbia*
Robert Lowe, *Marquette University*
Rebecca Lowenhaupt, *Boston College*
Zhenqiu Lu, *University of Georgia*
Sarah Lubienski, *University of Illinois, Urbana-Champaign*
Rosemary Luckin, *University College London, Institute of Education*
Sararose Lynch, *Westminster College*
Xin Ma, *University of Kentucky*
Katherine Magnuson, *University of Wisconsin, Madison*
Sachin Maharaj, *University of Toronto*
Fiona Maine, *University of Cambridge*
Joyline Makani, *Dalhousie University*
Betty Malen, *University of Maryland*
Ariana Mangual Figueroa, *Rutgers University*
Patricia Marin, *University of California, Santa Barbara*
Helen Marks, *Ohio State University*
Judy Marquez Kiyama, *University of Denver*
Herbert Marsh, *Australian Catholic University*
Julie Marsh, *University of Southern California*
Gary Martin, *Auburn University*
Matthew Martinez, *University of Texas, San Antonio*
Benjamin Master, *RAND*
Kavita Matsko, *National Louis University*
Jamaal Matthews, *Montclair State University*
Richard Mayer, *University of California, Santa Barbara*
D. Betsy McCoach, *University of Connecticut*
Alexander McCormick, *Indiana University*
Bo McCready, *University of Wisconsin, Madison*
Ebony McGee, *Vanderbilt University*
Liz Mckinley, *University of Melbourne*
Laura McMeeking, *Colorado State University*
Jon McNaughtan, *Texas Tech University*
Katherine McNeill, *Boston College*
Anna McPherson, *American Museum of Natural History*
Julia McWilliams, *University of Pennsylvania*
Julie Mead, *University of Wisconsin, Madison*
Judith Meece, *University of North Carolina, Chapel Hill*
Paul Melvin, *Southern Illinois University, Carbondale*
Debra Meyer, *Elmhurst College*
Coby Meyers, *University of Virginia*
Roslyn Mickelson, *University of North Carolina, Charlotte*
Ellen Middaugh, *Mills College*
Jamie Mikeska, *Educational Testing Service*
Jeffrey F. Milem, *University of Arizona*
Rich Milner, *University of Pittsburgh*
Elizabeth Minor, *National Louis University*
Gary Miron, *Western Michigan University*
Daniella Molle, *University of Wisconsin, Madison*
Chauncey Monte-Sano, *University of Michigan*

Bianca Montrosse-Moorhead, *University of Connecticut*
Nienke Moolenaar, *Utrecht University*
Cueponcaxochitl Dianna Moreno Sandoval, *Arizona State University*
Trish Morita Mullaney, *Purdue University*
Christopher Morphew, *University of Iowa*
Chandra Muller, *University of Texas, Austin*
Mark Murphy, *University of Glasgow*
P. Karen Murphy, *Pennsylvania State University*
Clara Muschkin, *Duke University*
Marielle Myers, *Kennesaw State University*
N. Hari Narayanan, *Auburn University*
Jennifer Nelson, *Emory University*
Erik Ness, *University of Georgia*
Veronica Newhart, *University of California, Irvine*
Wendy Newstetter, *Georgia Tech University*
Tuan Nguyen, *Vanderbilt University*
Sonia Nieto, *University of Massachusetts*
Kysa Nygreen, *University of Massachusetts, Amherst*
Brendan O'Connor, *Arizona State University*
Erin O'Connor, *New York University*
Sarah Oh, *University of Virginia*
Jason Okonofua, *University of California, Berkeley*
Michael O'Malley, *Texas State University, San Marcos*
Ann Owens, *University of Southern California*
Jayanti Owens, *Brown University*
Becky Packard, *Mount Holyoke College*
Natalia Palacios, *University of Virginia*
Anne-Marie Palincsar, *University of Michigan*
Deborah Palmer, *University of Colorado, Boulder*
John Papay, *Brown University*
Andrew Paquette, *NHTV*
Toby Parcel, *North Carolina State University*
Hyunjoon Park, *University of Pennsylvania*
Laurence Parker, *University of Utah*
Walter Parker, *University of Washington*
Leandra Parris, *Illinois State University*
Josh Pasek, *University of Michigan*
Donna Pasternak, *University of Wisconsin, Milwaukee*
Sarah Patten, *University of Toronto*
Reinhard Pekrun, *University of Munich*
James Pellegrino, *University of Illinois, Chicago*
Emily Penner, *Stanford University*
Daniel Perlstein, *University of California, Berkeley*
Laura Perry, *Murdoch University*
Ann Person, *Mathematica Policy Research*
Fabian Pfeffer, *University of Michigan*
Geoffrey Phelps, *Educational Testing Service*
Kate Phillippo, *Loyola University Chicago*
Michael Phillips, *Monash University*
Robert Pianta, *University of Virginia*
Diane Pimentel, *University of New Hampshire*
Jonathan Plucker, *University of Connecticut*
Michael Podgursky, *University of Missouri*
Joseph Polman, *University of Colorado, Boulder*
Sally Power, *Cardiff University*
Jeanne Powers, *Arizona State University*
Franzis Preckel, *University of Trier*
Courtney Preston, *Florida State University*

Heather Price, *Basis Policy Research, LLC*
Patrick Proctor, *Boston College*
Kevin Pugh, *University of Northern Colorado*
Jaymes Pyne, *University of Wisconsin, Madison*
Rand Quinn, *University of Pennsylvania*
Rosalind Raby, *California State University, Northridge*
Karen Rambo-Hernandez, *Colorado State University*
Jared Rawlings, *University of Michigan*
Shaun Rawolle, *Deakin University*
Douglas Ready, *Teachers College, Columbia University*
Mimi Recker, *Utah State University*
Sarah Reckhow, *Michigan State University*
Gabriel Reich, *Virginia Commonwealth University*
Abby Reisman, *University of Pennsylvania*
Janine Remillard, *University of Pennsylvania*
Carol Rentas, *George Washington University*
Linda Renzulli, *University of Georgia*
Jenny Reuf, *University of Oregon*
Arthur Reynolds, *University of Minnesota*
Anna Rhodes, *Johns Hopkins University*
Jennifer Rice, *University of Maryland*
Peter Rich, *Cornell University*
Paul Richardson, *Monash University*
Catherine Riegle-Crumb, *University of Texas, Austin*
Jessica Rigby, *University of Washington*
Sara Rimm-Kaufman, *University of Virginia*
Cecilia Rios-Aguilar, *University of California, Los Angeles*
Carly Roberts, *University of Washington*
Awilda Rodriguez, *University of Michigan*
Louie Rodriguez, *California State University, San Bernardino*
Alysia D. Roehrig, *Florida State University*
Gillian Roehrig, *University of Minnesota*
Craig Rogers, *Alabama State University*
Jane Rogers, *University of Connecticut*
Lisa Romero, *California State University, Sacramento*
Matthew Ronfeldt, *University of Michigan*
Andrea Rorrer, *University of Utah*
Cheryl Rosaen, *Michigan State University (Emerita)*
Rene Roselle, *University of Connecticut*
Emily Rosenzweig, *University of Maryland, College Park*
Dorene Ross, *University of Florida*
Emma Rowe, *Deakin University*
Kristie Rowley, *Brigham Young University*
Kathleen Rudasill, *University of Nebraska, Lincoln*
Robert Rueda, *University of Southern California*
Ning Rui, *Westat*
Nikol Rummel, *Ruhr-Universitat Bochum*
Jennifer Russell, *University of Pittsburgh*
Ehri Ryu, *Boston College*
Stephanie Sanders-Smith, *University of Illinois, Urbana-Champaign*
William Sandoval, *University of California, Los Angeles*
Rossella Santagata, *University of California, Irvine*

Reviewer Acknowledgments

Tim Sass, *Georgia State University*
Mistilina Sato, *University of Minnesota, Twin Cities*
Carolyn Sattin-Bajaj, *Seton Hall University*
Andrew Saultz, *Miami University*
Annie Savard, *McGill University*
R. Keith Sawyer, *University of North Carolina, Chapel Hill*
Katerina Schenke, *University of California, Los Angeles*
Alex Schmidt, *University of Wisconsin, Madison*
Sandra Schmidt, *Teachers College, Columbia University*
Barbara Schneider, *Michigan State University*
Jack Schneider, *College of the Holy Cross*
Paul Schutz, *University of Texas, San Antonio*
Janelle Scott, *University of California, Berkeley*
Judy Scott, *University of California, Santa Cruz*
Campbell Scribner, *Ohio Wesleyan University*
Nanette Seago, *WestEd*
Terri Seddon, *Australian Catholic University*
Avner Segall, *Michigan State University*
Tina Seidel, *Technische Universität München*
Elizabeth Setren, *Massachusetts Institute of Technology*
David Shaffer, *University of Wisconsin, Madison*
Niral Shah, *Michigan State University*
Charlotte Sharpe, *Vanderbilt University*
Emily Shaw, *The College Board*
Jianping Shen, *Western Michigan University*
David Sherer, *Harvard University*
Miriam Sherin, *Northwestern University*
Jeff Shih, *University of Nevada, Las Vegas*
Valerie Shirley, *University of Arizona*
Genevieve Siegel-Hawley, *Virginia Commonwealth University*
Klaas Sijtsma, *Tilburg University*
Iram Siraj, *University College London, Institute of Education*
Sinem Siyahhan, *California State University, San Marcos*
Russell Skiba, *Indiana University*
Christine Sleeter, *California State University, Monterey Bay (Emerita)*
Peter Smagorinsky, *University of Georgia*
Brigitte Smit, *University of South Africa*
BetsAnn Smith, *Michigan State University*
Carol Smith, *University of Massachusetts, Boston*
Mark Smith, *University of Northern Colorado*
Orin Smith, *University of Central Florida*
Thomas Smith, *University of California, Riverside*
Claire Smrekar, *Vanderbilt University*
James Soland, *Northwest Evaluation Association*
Susan Sonnenschein, *University of Maryland, Baltimore County*
Erica Southgate, *University of Newcastle*
James Spillane, *Northwestern University*
Jeffrey Sprague, *Institute on Violence & Destructive Behavior*
Megan Staples, *University of Connecticut*
Laura Stapleton, *University of Maryland*
Elizabeth Stearns, *University of North Carolina, Charlotte*
Marc Stein, *Johns Hopkins University*

Matthew Steinberg, *University of Pennsylvania*
Mitchell Stevens, *Stanford University*
Jamy Stillman, *University of Colorado, Boulder*
Clement Stone, *University of Pittsburgh*
Leslie Stratton, *Virginia Commonwealth University*
Jan-Willem Strijbos, *University of Groningen*
Katharine Strunk, *University of Southern California*
Moin Syed, *University of Minnesota*
Joan Talbert, *Stanford University*
Eran Tamir, *Tel Aviv University*
Edna Tan, *University of North Carolina, Greensboro*
Daniel Tannenbaum, *University of Chicago*
Stuart Tannock, *University College London, Institute of Education*
Maria Tatto, *Michigan State University*
Eric Taylor, *Harvard University*
Cathryn Teasley, *Universidade da Coruña*
Adai Tefera, *Virginia Commonwealth University*
Karen Thompson, *Oregon State University*
Kathleen Thorius, *Indiana University - IUPUI*
Robert Tierney, *University of British Columbia, University of Sydney, Beijing Normal University*
Marvin Titus, *University of Maryland*
Kerri Tobin, *Marywood University*
Sheila Trahar, *University of Bristol*
Ulrich Trautwein, *University of Tübingen*
Daniel Troehler, *University of Luxembourg*
Mary Truxaw, *University of Connecticut*
Sultan Turkan, *Educational Testing Service*
Erin Turner, *University of Arizona*
Ilana Umansky, *University of Oregon*
Tim Urdan, *Santa Clara University*
Ellen Usher, *University of Kentucky*
Jennifer Vadeboncoeur, *University of British Columbia*
Guadalupe Valdes, *Stanford University*
Veronica Valdez, *University of Utah*
Angela Valenzuela, *University of Texas*
Julian Vasquez Heilig, *California State University, Sacramento*
Vanessa Vega, *The George Lucas Education Foundation*
Terah Venzant, *Michigan State University*
Samantha Viano, *Vanderbilt University*
Adam Voight, *Cleveland State University*
Richard Waddington, *University of Notre Dame*
Jane Waldfogel, *Columbia University*
Bryce Walker, *George Washington University*
Michael Walker, *The College Board*
Tanner Wallace, *University of Pittsburgh*
Jordan Ware, *University of Oklahoma*
Paige Ware, *Southern Methodist University*
Chezare Warren, *Michigan State University*
Hersh Waxman, *Texas A&M University*
Rhona Weinstein, *University of California, Berkeley*
Amy Wells, *Teachers College, Columbia University*
Laura Wentworth, *California Education Partners*
Bruce Wexler, *Yale University*
Terrenda White, *University of Colorado, Boulder*
Thomas White, *University of Virginia*
Erin Whiting, *Brigham Young University*

Reviewer Acknowledgments

Meca Williams-Johnson, *Georgia Southern University*
Sweeny Windchief, *Montana State University*
Amanda Winkelsas, *CUNY Graduate Center*
Rachelle Winkle-Wagner, *University of Wisconsin*
Kathleen Winn, *University of Virginia*
Marcus Winters, *University of Colorado, Colorado Springs*
Alyssa Wise, *New York University*
Joseph Workman, *University of Oxford*
Tanya Wright, *Michigan State University*
Hsin-Kai Wu, *National Taiwan Normal University*
Lois Yamauchi, *University of Hawai'i*
Feifei Ye, *University of Pittsburgh*
David Yeager, *University of Texas, Austin*
April Yee, *James Irvine Foundation*
Rose Ylimaki, *University of Arizona*
Ee-Seul Yoon, *University of Manitoba*

Haeny Yoon, *Teachers College, Columbia University*
Irene Yoon, *University of Utah*
Kwang Suk Yoon, *American Institutes for Research*
Susan Yoon, *University of Pennsylvania*
Tara Yosso, *University of California, Santa Barbara*
Deborah Yost, *La Salle University*
Jamaal Young, *University of North Texas*
Peter Youngs, *University of Virginia*
Monica Yudron, *University of Massachusetts, Boston*
Michalinos Zembylas, *Open University of Cyprus*
Guanjian Zhang, *University of Notre Dame*
Qian Zhang, *Florida State University*
Shaoan Zhang, *University of Nevada, Las Vegas*
Zhiyong Zhang, *University of Notre Dame*
Ron Zimmer, *University of Kentucky*
William Zumeta, *University of Washington*

Reviewer Acknowledgments
AERJ Section on Social and Institutional Analysis

The editors of the *American Educational Research Journal's* Section on Social and Institutional Analysis would like to thank the following people for reviewing manuscripts from September 2015 to November 2016.

Arshad Ali, *George Washington University*
Sandra Alvear, *Rice University*
Daniel Anderson, *University of Oregon*
James Anderson, *University of Illinois, Urbana-Champaign*
Kathryn Anderson-Levitt, *University of California, Los Angeles*
Kathryn Asbury, *University of York*
Allison Atteberry, *University of Colorado, Boulder*
Aprile Benner, *University of Texas, Austin*
Sharon Bethea, *Northeastern Illinois University*
Angela Boatman, *Vanderbilt University*
Benjamin Boche, *Concordia University, Chicago*
Randy Bomer, *University of Texas, Austin*
Alex Bowers, *Teachers College, Columbia University*
Melissa Braaten, *University of Wisconsin*
Bryan Brayboy, *Arizona State University*
Nate Brown, *University of Washington, Bothell*
Rebecca Callahan, *University of Texas, Austin*
Brian Carolan, *Montclair State University*
Patricia Carroll, *University of California, Los Angeles*
Deborah Carter, *Claremont Graduate University*
Janet Cerda, *University of California, Los Angeles*
Jacob Clark-Blickenstaff, *Pacific Science Center*
Casey Cobb, *University of Connecticut*
Shana Cohen, *University of California, San Diego*
Wade Cole, *University of Utah*
Mary Carol Combs, *University of Arizona*
Kristy Cooper, *Michigan State University*
Sean Corcoran, *New York University*
Jen Cowhy, *University of Chicago*
Jennifer Cromley, *University of Illinois, Urbana-Champaign*
Marcela Cuellar, *University of California, Davis*
Kerry Dally, *University of Newcastle*
Alan Daly, *University of California, San Diego*
Erika Daniels, *California State University, San Marcos*
Miriam David, *University College London, Institute of Education*
Elizabeth DeBray, *University of Georgia*
John Diamond, *University of Wisconsin, Madison*
Sarah Diem, *University of Missouri*
Morgaen Donaldson, *University of Connecticut*
Sherman Dorn, *Arizona State University*
Alicia Dowd, *University of Southern California*
Kevin Eagan, *University of California, Los Angeles*
Stacy Ehrlich, *University of Chicago*
Catherine Emihovich, *University of Florida*
Susan Faircloth, *University of North Carolina, Wilmington*
Elizabeth Farley-Ripple, *University of Delaware*
Jeremy Finn, *University at Buffalo - SUNY*
Kenneth Frank, *Michigan State University*

Lance Fusarelli, *North Carolina State University*
Sarah Gallo, *Ohio State University*
Tray Geiger, *Arizona State University*
James Gentile, *Hope College*
David Gerwin, *Queens College*
Ameena Ghaffar-Kucher, *University of Pennsylvania*
Molly Gordon, *University of Chicago*
Elizabeth Graue, *University of Wisconsin, Madison*
Kathy Gullie, *University at Albany - SUNY*
Robert Haight, *Regis University*
Jon Hale, *College of Charleston*
Peter Halpin, *New York University*
R. Halsey, *Flinders University*
Laura Hamilton, *RAND*
Ian Handley, *Montana State University System*
Charles Henderson, *Western Michigan University*
Beth Herbel-Eisenmann, *Michigan State University*
Carolyn Herrington, *Florida State University*
Nicholas Hillman, *University of Wisconsin*
Megan Hopkins, *University of Illinois, Chicago*
Catherine Horn, *University of Houston*
Derek Houston, *University of Oklahoma*
Janise Hurtig, *University of Illinois, Chicago*
Jill Jeffery, *Brooklyn College - CUNY*
Jody Jessup-Anger, *Marquette University*
Michael Kieffer, *New York University*
Alana Kinarsky, *University of California, Los Angeles*
Daniel Klasik, *Stanford University*
Tatyana Kleyn, *City College of New York - CUNY*
Sabine Krolak-Schwerdt, *University of Luxembourg*
Dennis KWEK, *Nanyang Technological University, National Institute of Education*
Jaekyung Lee, *University at Buffalo - SUNY*
Hsiang Ann Liao, *Buffalo State College*
Kathryn Lindholm-Leary, *San Jose State University*
Robert Linquanti, *WestEd*
Lu Liu, *University of California, Los Angeles*
Gerardo Lopez, *Loyola University New Orleans*
Rebecca Lowenhaupt, *Boston College*
Allan Luke, *Queensland University of Technology*
Russ Marion, *Clemson University*
Judy Marquez Kiyama, *University of Denver*
Madeline Mavrogordato, *Michigan State University*
Craig McBride, *University of Washington*
Alyn McCarty, *University of Wisconsin, Madison*
Oren McClain, *Loyola University, Maryland*
Kathryn McDermott, *University of Massachusetts*
Andrew McEachin, *RAND*
Kent McIntosh, *University of Oregon*
Erika Mein, *University of Texas, El Paso*
Minas Michikyan, *California State University, Los Angeles*
Jeffrey F. Milem, *University of Arizona*
Peter Miller, *University of Wisconsin, Madison*

Julie Minikel-Lacocque, *University Wisconsin, Whitewater*

Elizabeth Minor, *National Louis University*

Paul Morgan, *Pennsylvania State University*

Chandra Muller, *University of Texas*

Clara Muschkin, *Duke University*

Milagros Nores, *Rutgers University*

Joseph Oluwole, *Montclair State University*

Sarah Ovink, *Virginia Polytechnic Institute and State University*

Deborah Palmer, *University of Colorado, Boulder*

Django Paris, *Michigan State University*

Morgan Polikoff, *University of Southern California*

Diana Porras, *University of California, Los Angeles*

Linn Posey-Maddox, *University of Wisconsin, Madison*

Jeanne Powers, *Arizona State University*

Douglas Reed, *Georgetown University*

Jennifer Reynolds, *University of South Carolina*

Jennifer Rice, *University of Maryland*

Cathy Ringstaff, *WestEd*

Cecilia Rios-Aguilar, *University of California, Los Angeles*

Steven Rivkin, *University of Illinois, Chicago*

John Roberts, *Pennsylvania State University*

Rosaline Rolon Dow, *University of Delaware*

Guillermo Ruiz, *University of Buenos Aires - CONICET*

Guadalupe San Miguel, *University of Houston*

Mavis Sanders, *University of Maryland, Baltimore County*

Jonathan Schweig, *RAND*

James Sebastian, *University of Missouri, Columbia*

Genevieve Siegel-Hawley, *Virginia Commonwealth University*

Susan Singer, *Carleton College*

David Slavit, *Washington State University, Vancouver*

Roger Slee, *University of South Australia*

Erica Southgate, *University of Newcastle*

Manuel Souto-Otero, *University of Bath*

Angeline Spain, *University of Chicago*

Kurt Squire, *University of Wisconsin, Madison*

Frances Stage, *New York University*

Laura Stapleton, *University of Maryland*

Candice Stefanou, *University of Florida*

Deborah Stipek, *Stanford University*

Adai Tefera, *Virginia Commonwealth University*

Karen Thompson, *Oregon State University*

Chris Thron, *Carnegie Foundation for the Advancement of Teaching*

Anne Traynor, *Purdue University*

Erica Turner, *University of Wisconsin, Madison*

Guadalupe Valdes, *Stanford University*

Linda Valli, *University of Maryland*

Christine Vega, *University of California, Los Angeles*

Kate Wegmann, *University of Illinois, Urbana-Champaign*

Sabine Weiss, *Ludwig Maximilians University, Munich*

Kristen Wilcox, *University at Albany - SUNY*

Daniel Willingham, *University of Virginia*

Mikyung Wolf, *Educational Testing Service*

Sarah Woulfin, *University of Connecticut*

Wayne Wright, *Purdue University*

Kajsa Yang Hansen, *Göteborgs Universitet*

Tarajean Yazzie-Mintz, *American Indian College Fund*

David Yeager, *University of Texas, Austin*

Irene Yoon, *University of Utah*

Juanjuan Zhao, *University of Cincinnati*

Reviewer Acknowledgments
AERJ Section on Teaching, Learning, and Human Development

The editors of the *American Educational Research Journal's* Section on Teaching, Learning, and Human Development would like to thank the following people for reviewing manuscripts from September 2015 to November 2016.

Dorothea Anagnostopoulos, *University of Connecticut*

Damian Betebenner, *NCIEA*

William Boerman-Cornell, *Trinity Christian College*

Christy Byrd, *University of California, Santa Cruz*

Hamish Coates, *University of Melbourne*

Julia Cohen, *University of Virginia*

Kai Cortina, *University of Michigan*

Rubén Fernández-Alonso, *Principality of Asturias Government*

Glenda Gunter, *University of Central Florida*

Megan Hopkins, *University of Illinois at Chicago*

Jung Wong Hur, *Auburn University*

Richard James, *University of Melbourne*

Sandra Kaplan, *University of Southern California*

ChanMin Kim, *University of Georgia*

Peter Kloosterman, *Indiana University*

Michael Krezmien, *University of Massachusetts*

Chad Lane, *University of Illinois, Urbana-Champaign*

Ariana Mangual Figueroa, *Rutgers University*

Gigliana Melzi, *New York University*

V Darleen Opfer, *University of Cambridge*

Pauline Slot, *Utrecht University*

Mark Smith, *Stanford University*

Carol Trivette, *East Tennessee State University*

Pedro Villarreal III, *University of Miami*

Thomas White, *University of Virginia*

Sam Wineburg, *Stanford University*

Ellen Winner, *Boston College*

Ji Seung Yang, *University of Maryland*

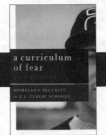

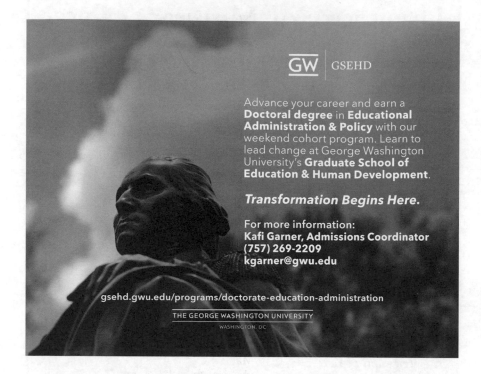